From Polis to Empire—
The Ancient World,
c. 800 B.C.–A.D. 500

Recent Titles in
The Great Cultural Eras of the Western World

Renaissance and Reformation, 1500–1620: A Biographical Dictionary
Jo Eldridge Carney, editor

The Late Medieval Age of Crisis and Renewal, 1300–1500: A Biographical Dictionary
Clayton J. Dress, editor

From Polis to Empire— The Ancient World, c. 800 B.C.–A.D. 500

A Biographical Dictionary

Edited by
ANDREW G. TRAVER

The Great Cultural Eras of the Western World
Ronald H. Fritze, Series Adviser

GREENWOOD PRESS
Westport, Connecticut • London

Library of Congress Cataloging-in-Publication Data

From polis to empire—the ancient world, c. 800 B.C.–A.D. 500 : a biographical dictionary / edited by Andrew G. Traver.
     p. cm.—(The great cultural eras of the Western world, ISSN 1534–9527)
     Includes bibliographical references and index.
     ISBN 0–313–30942–6 (alk. paper)
     1. History, Ancient—Dictionaries. I. Traver, Andrew G., 1967– II. Series.
D54F76 2002
930'.03—dc21   2001016056

British Library Cataloguing in Publication Data is available.

Library of Congress Catalog Card Number: 2001016056
ISBN: 0–313–30942–6
ISSN: 1534–9527

First published in 2002

Greenwood Press, 88 Post Road West, Westport, CT 06881
An imprint of Greenwood Publishing Group, Inc.
www.greenwood.com

Printed in the United States of America

The paper used in this book complies with the Permanent Paper Standard issued by the National Information Standards Organization (Z39.48–1984).

10 9 8 7 6 5 4 3 2 1

Contents

Introduction

This volume in Greenwood's series of biographical dictionaries on The Great Cultural Eras of the Western World covers the time period roughly spanning the years 800 B.C. to A.D. 500. The volume differs from other biographical dictionaries in that its focus is cultural rather than political. As such, this biographical dictionary is weighed heavily in favor of those individuals who made significant contributions to the arts, including—though not limited to—the fields of architecture, astronomy, history, literature, mathematics, philosophy, painting, sculpture, and theology. But as one cannot separate the arts from politics, one could not possibly have an understanding of the intellectual milieu of the ancient, classical, and late antique worlds without some knowledge of the policies and politics of figures such as Alexander the Great, Julius Caesar, and Constantine the Great. Therefore, while this volume considers the great political and military leaders of the period, it tries to emphasize their cultural contributions in addition to their political ones.

This volume covers such a large chronological period that only the briefest of introductions can be offered here. Its chronological scope begins with the archaic period of the eastern Mediterranean, advancing into the classical period of Greece, spanning the fifth century B.C. and the Persian and Peloponnesian Wars. It examines the period of the hegemons in Greece in the fourth century B.C., which ended with the victory of Philip II of Macedon at Chaeronea in 338 B.C. After Philip, Alexander ruled Macedon, conquering the Persian Empire and additional territory in India. After Alexander's death, the struggle of the Successors followed, thereby creating a social and geopolitical settlement commonly referred to as the Hellenistic world, consisting of three major empires: Antigonid (Macedon), Seleucid (Syria-Babylon), and Ptolemaic (Egypt). In the meantime, Rome had moved from a kingdom to a republic; after its victories in the three Punic Wars it rapidly became the master of the eastern Mediterranean. Rome defeated Macedon in 168 B.C. and again in 148 B.C., and in the following century, Pompey destroyed the Seleucid Empire. With Cleopatra's suicide in 30 B.C., the last independent Hellenistic state, Ptolemaic Egypt, fell to Rome.

While Roman troops were busy in the east, the government of Rome faced its own series of crises. These crises gradually weakened the republic, exposing it to dictatorship (Sulla), informal three-man rule (The "First Triumvirate"), civil war, and then dictatorship again under Julius Caesar. After Caesar's assassination in 44 B.C., three-man rule (The "Second Triumvirate") again briefly dominated Roman politics until the arrest of Marcus Lepidus and the defeat and death of Marc Antony left Octavian as the sole surviving triumvir. Octavian, renamed Augustus, transformed Rome into a principate, ruled by *principes* and characterized by one-man rule.

During the first century A.D., any belief that the republic would eventually be restored disappeared, and hereafter emperors ruled Rome. In this same century, a Jewish carpenter living on the periphery of the Roman world preached a message that would have radical implications for the Roman state. His followers spread his teachings throughout the empire, facing a series of state-sponsored persecutions in the early third century. In 313, Emperor Constantine made Christianity an official religion, while near the end of the same century Theodosius I made it mandatory. Nevertheless, the doctrinal conflicts of the fourth and fifth centuries prove that the fundamentals of belief were neither universal nor completely developed.

In the late fourth and fifth centuries, Germanic tribes seeking shelter from the nomadic Huns transformed the western Roman world. After receiving permission to settle on Roman land, a Gothic band revolted, sacked Rome, and eventually created a kingdom in southwestern Gaul. In 406, other Germanic tribes crossed the Rhine, raided Roman territory, and eventually created German successor states in formerly Roman territory including Britain, Gaul, Spain, Italy, and north Africa. By the year 500, the end of this volume, the Roman state had ceased to exist in the west, and the gradual fusion of the Christian, Roman, and Germanic elements of the early Middle Ages had begun.

The cultural focus of this volume is chiefly the Mediterranean basin and more specifically the Graeco-Roman world, but the volume is not confined solely to Greece and Rome. It also examines those people who influenced and impinged on them in some way. Thus the reader will occasionally encounter representatives of the Assyrian (e.g., Sargon II), Chaldean (e.g., Nebuchadnezzar II), Phrygian (e.g., Midas), Lydian (e.g., Gyges), Persian (e.g., Darius, Cyrus), and Carthaginian (e.g., Hannibal Barca) states in addition to the more familiar Greek and Roman ones. The book's goal is to introduce readers to the significant cultural contributors one would come across in an undergraduate Western Civilization survey course covering this period.

The only entry that strictly speaking falls outside of the chronological area in question is Zoroaster. The dating for Zoroaster has varied wildly since antiquity, with some offering a date as early as 6000 B.C., whereas others have placed him in the sixth century B.C. Although recent scholarship would seem to situate

Zoroaster in the thirteenth century B.C., he is nevertheless included in this volume due to his influence on the Persian Empire and on the development of the Hebrew, Christian, and Muslim faiths. Moreover, many scholarly works that are still current place him around 600 B.C.

The volume makes no attempt to be exhaustive. Its intention is to be a convenient reference manual to cultural contributors within the prescribed chronological era. It makes no attempt to supplant the standard reference manuals such as *The Cambridge Ancient History* and *The Oxford Classical Dictionary*. Due to page constraints, this volume considers the most influential individuals within this historical time frame—slightly less than 500 entries.

The *terminus ad quem* of this volume is the year 500. While the more important personalities of the fifth century A.D. are included in this volume, those whose accomplishments span into the next century—such as Boethius, Clotild, Clovis, and Theodoric—are considered in the volume on Medieval Europe.

Since this volume is a biographical dictionary, entries on battles, wars, literary works, and other topical events or subjects are not within the scope of the work. This volume tries, in most cases, to refrain from citing mythological figures. Nevertheless, as it is difficult to discuss the history of Rome and Athens without some reference to Romulus and Theseus, they have been included in this volume along with some of the dubious historical figures of the Roman kingdom (e.g., Tarquin the Proud) and early Roman republic (e.g., Gnaeus Marcius Coriolanus).

The system of cross-referencing used in this volume is the asterisk (*). The asterisk placed at the beginning of a name indicates that the individual has a separate entry within this work. Each entry has a suggestion for further reading, whereas a complete bibliography and a glossary can be found at the end of this work. The bibliography ranges from the general to the academic. With a few exceptions, most of the works are written in English and can be found in most libraries. The bibliography contains recently published works as well as the standards in the field. The glossary is intended to define the words and phrases that the reader may find obscure. A time line, following the introduction, puts this work within a proper chronological setting.

All names have been spelled in their Latinized or more common English form. Romans are listed under their familiar names; thus the entry for the Emperor Gaius (c. 12–41) is found under the entry "Caligula," whereas the one for Marcus Iunius Brutus (c. 85–42 B.C.) can be found under "Brutus." Also, as is standard in the field, when individuals have the same name, the more famous individual is always the default. The first line of the entry is intended to provide readers with a chronological referent and a short explanation of what the individual in question accomplished. If the author lived before A.D. 1, the abbreviation B.C. is used. If the individual spanned that century, both B.C. and A.D. are cited. If the individual lived after A.D. 1, no abbreviation is provided, as A.D. is the default for this volume.

In undertaking a work of this magnitude, I have incurred a great number of debts. I would especially like to thank all of the contributors to this volume. I would also like to thank my department head, Dr. William Robison, for suggesting this project to me. And I am very grateful to everyone involved in the project for their continuing patience and support.

Andrew G. Traver

Chronology

POLITICAL EVENTS B.C.

753 Traditional date for the founding of Rome

720 Sargon II of Assyria conquers Cilicia and Syria

700 Cimmerians destroy the Phrygian kingdom of Midas

687 Kingdom of Lydia founded by Gyges

675 Lycurgan reforms at Sparta

650–620 Sparta fights the second Messenian War

632 Attempted tyranny at Athens by Cylon

621 Draco promulgates Athenian law code

605–562 Reign of Nebuchadnezzar II

600–570 Cleisthenes of Sicyon flourishes

594 Solon, archon at Athens

587 Capture of Jerusalem by Nebuchadnezzar II

CULTURAL DEVELOPMENTS B.C.

750–700 Homer active

700 Hesiod's *Theogony* and *Works and Days*

675–640 Archilochus active as poet

650 Callinus of Ephesus, Tyrtaeus of Sparta active as poets

630 Mimnermus of Colophon and Alcman of Sparta active as poets

610 Alcaeus and Sappho active as poets in Lesbos

585 Thales of Miletus predicts an eclipse

579–534 Servius Tullius, king of Rome

570–550 Anaximander and Anaximenes active as philosophers

561–547 Croesus, king of Lydia

560–530 Reign of Cyrus I

560 Stesichorus active as poet

559 Cyrus conquers Media

546 Pisistratus establishes his tyranny at Athens

545 Persia captures Sardis; end of Lydian Empire

540 Theognis of Megara, Hipponax of Ephesus, and Ibycus of Rhegium active as poets

535 Polycrates, tyrant of Samos

535 Anacreon of Teos and Xenophones of Colophon active

534–509 Tarquin the Proud, king of Rome

530 Pythagoras active in south Italy

528 Death of Pisistratus; Athens ruled by Hippias

521 Darius I seizes power in Persia

520–490 Cleomenes I, king of Sparta

520 Simonides of Ceos active as poet

510 Expulsion of Hippias from Athens

509 Traditional date of the founding of the Roman Republic

508/507 Reforms of Cleisthenes at Athens

500 Alcmaeon of Croton (doctor), Hecataeus of Miletus (historian), and Heraclitus (philosopher) active

499–494 Ionian Revolt

498 Athenians help burn Sardis

498 Earliest surviving Pindar poem

496 Latins defeated at the Battle of Lake Regillus; treaty between Rome and the Latins

494 Sack of Miletus; end of the Ionian Revolt

493 Themistocles archon at Athens

490 Battle of Marathon

490 Parmenides of Elea active

489 Trial and death of Miltiades

486 Death of Darius I; accession of Xerxes

485 Gelon, tyrant of Syracuse

484 First victory of Aeschylus

482 Ostracism of Aristides the Just

480 Battles of Artemisium, Thermopylae, and Salamis; Athens sacked by the Persians

479 Battle of Plataea

478 Death of Gelon; succeeded by Hieron I

477–467 Naval campaigns of Cimon; foundation of Delian League

476 Victory of Hieron I in horse race at Olympia

476 Pindar's *First Olympic Ode* and Bacchylides' *Fifth Ode* for Hieron

472 Olympic victory of Hieron in horse race

472 *2nd and 3rd Olympians* of Pindar; *Persians* of Aeschylus

471 Ostracism of Themistocles

470 Pythian victory of Hieron I in a chariot race

470 Pindar's first *Pythian Ode*

470–430 Career of sculptor Myron

468 Olympian victory of Hieron I in chariot race

468 *3rd Ode* of Bacchylides; first victory of Sophocles over Aeschylus

467 *Seven against Thebes* by Aeschylus

466 Death of Hieron and end of tyranny in Syracuse

465 Revolt of Thasos from the Delian League

464 Death of Xerxes; succeeded by Artaxerxes I

462 Anaxagoras arrives in Athens

461 Cimon ostracized; radical reforms at Athens by Ephialtes; murder of Ephialtes; Pericles' supremacy begins

461–451 First Peloponnesian War between Athens and Sparta

460–420 Careers of sculptors Polyclitus and Phidias

458 *Oresteia* of Aeschylus

455 First production by Euripides

450 Zeno of Elea and Empedocles active as philosophers

447–438 Rebuilding of the Parthenon under Phidias

446 Pindar's last ode (*Pythian* 8)

445 Thirty Years Peace between Athens and Sparta

445–426 Herodotus active

441 *Antigone* of Sophocles

440 Revolt of Samos from Athenian Empire

440 Leucippus invents atomic theory

438 *Alcestis* of Euripides; Chryselephantine Athena set up in the Parthenon

431 Start of Peloponnesian War

431 Thucydides begins his history; *Medea* of Euripides

431/430 Pericles' *Funeral Oration*

430 Plague at Athens

430 Democritus (atomic theorist), Hippocrates (doctor), and Socrates and Protagoras (philosophers) active; Phidias' statue of Zeus at Olympia

429 Death of Pericles

428 *Hippolytus* of Euripides

427 Gorgias of Leontini at Athens

425 Cleon dominant at Athens

425 *Acharnians* of Aristophanes

424 *Knights* of Aristophanes; Thucydides exiled from Athens

423 *Clouds* of Aristophanes

422 Brasidas and Cleon killed in north Greece

422 *Wasps* of Aristophanes

421 Peace of Nicias between Athens and Sparta

421 *Peace* of Aristophanes

416 Athenians attack Melos and enslave its inhabitants

415 Athenian expedition to Sicily; Alcibiades exiled

415 *Trojan Women* of Euripides

414 *Birds* of Aristophanes

412 *Helen* of Euripides

411 Oligarchic revolution at Athens

411 *Lysistrata* and *Women at the Thesmophora* of Aristophanes

410 Democracy restored at Athens

410–398 Career of Lysias

409 *Philoctetes* of Sophocles

408 *Orestes* of Euripides

407–406 Alcibiades' return from exile

405 Dionysius becomes tyrant of Syracuse

405 *Frogs* of Aristophanes; *Bacchae* of Euripides performed

404 Capitulation of Athens; installation of the Thirty Tyrants

403 Fall of the Thirty; restoration of democracy at Athens

401 Expedition of Cyrus and 10,000 Greek mercenaries against the Persian king, recounted by Xenophon

401 *Oedipus* of Sophocles performed

400 Antisthenes active

399 Trial and execution of Socrates

398 Agesilaus succeeds as king of Sparta

397–338 Isocrates active

396 Capture of major Etruscan city of Veii by Romans

396–394 Campaigns of Agesilaus to free the Greeks of Asia Minor from Persia

396–347 Plato active

395–386 Corinthian War

395 Thucydides' *History* published

392 *Women at the Assembly* of Aristophanes performed

390–354 Xenophon active

388 *Wealth* of Aristophanes performed

387 Gauls sack Rome

387 Plato founds Academy

386 King's Peace ends war in Greece but gives Persia influence in Greek world

382 Sparta seizes Thebes

379 Liberation of Thebes

378 Alliance of Athens and Thebes; Foundation of Second Athenian Confederation

371 Thebes destroys Spartan power at Battle of Leuctra

371–362 Domination of Thebes under Pelopidas and Epaminondas

370–330 Praxiteles and Scopas active

367 Plato visits Syracuse to educate Dionysius II; Aristotle joins the Academy

362 Thebes defeats Sparta at the Battle of Mantinea; death of Epaminondas

360–315 Lysippus (sculptor) active

360–323 Diogenes of Sinope (philosopher) active

359 Philip II becomes king of Macedonia

357 War between Philip and Athens

357–355 Social War between Athens and members of its confederation

356 Dion, uncle of Dionysius II, controls Syracuse

356–352 Phocians seize Delphi and provoke Sacred War; Philip brought into central Greece against them.

355 Careers of Demosthenes and Aeschines begin

350–320 Apelles (painter) and Theopompus (historian) active

348 Philip seizes Olynthus

346 Philip and Athens make peace of Philocrates; second tyranny of Dionysius II

346–345 Demosthenes impeaches Aeschines

344 Timoleon arrives in Sicily

343–342 Aristotle is tutor to Alexander

341 end of *History* of Ephorus

338 Philip defeats Athens at Chaeronea; end of Greek independence

338 Suicide of Isocrates

337 Philip founds Corinthian League; League declares war on Persia

336 Accession of Alexander the Great

335 Accession of Darius III; Alexander sacks Thebes

335 Aristotle founds Lyceum; the Cynic Diogenes reputedly meets Alexander at Corinth

334 Alexander crosses into Persia; Battle of Granicus River

333 Defeat of Darius III at Battle of Issus

332 Sieges of Tyre and Gaza; Alexander enters Egypt

331 Alexander defeats Darius III at Gaugamela

330 Aeschines and Demosthenes defend their political careers in the speeches *Against Ctesiphon* and *On the Crown*

330–328 Alexander campaigns in Bactria and Sogdiana

327 Alexander enters India

326 Alexander crosses Indus and wins Battle of Hydaspes; begins trip home

325–300 Pytheas of Massilia circumnavigates Britain

324 Alexander at Susa

323 Death of Alexander

323–322 Athens tries to free itself from Macedonia in the Lamian War

323–320 Perdiccas struggles to maintain the unity of empire but is killed in Egypt

322 Death of Aristotle; Theophrastus becomes head of Lyceum

321–289 Career of Menander (New Comedy)

320–301 Antigonus I aims for a universal empire

320–305 Hecataeus (historian) active

317 Philip III Arrhidaeus murdered

317–289 Agathocles, tyrant of Syracuse

317–307 Demetrius of Phalerum at Athens

315 Olympias murdered

315–311 Coalition of satraps against Antigonus

311 Division of Alexander's Empire between Antigonus (Asia), Macedon-Greece (Cassander), Lysimachus (Thrace), Ptolemy (Egypt), and Seleucus (the eastern satrapies)

311–306 Wars between Agathocles and Carthage

310 Murder of Alexander IV, son of Alexander

310 Zeno of Citium establishes Stoic school at Athens

307 Demetrius I the Besieger "liberates" Athens

307 Epicurus establishes his school at Athens

306–304 Antigonus, Ptolemy, and Seleucus call themselves kings

305–304 Siege of Rhodes by Demetrius

302–290 Megasthenes at court of Chandragupta

301 Destruction of power of Antigonus and Demetrius at the Battle of Ipsus; Antigonus dies

300 Ptolemy I founds Library—Zenodotus royal tutor and first head; Euclid active

297 Death of Cassander, ruler of Macedon

297–272 Career of Pyrrhus of Epirus

290 Aetolian League captures Delphi and emerges as the main political unit in central Greece

285 Demetrius the Besieger captured by Seleucus; dies in 283

283 Ptolemy I dies; succeeded by Ptolemy II

281 Lysimachus killed; Seleucus assassinated and succeeded by son Antiochus I; Foundation of Achaean League

280 Pyrrhus of Epirus ships an army to Rome in support of Tarentum the city

279 Invasion of Macedonia and Greece by Gauls; sack of Delphi by Gauls

276 Antigonus II Gonatas, son of Demetrius, defeats Gauls and becomes king of Macedon

274–271 First Syrian War between Ptolemy II and Antiochus I

272–215 Hieron elected general, then king, of Syracuse

270 Callimachus, Theocritus, Lycophron, and Aratus active as poets; Manetho writes history of Egypt; Aristarchus of Samos proposes heliocentric theory of universe

270–242 Arcesilaus converts the Academy to Scepticism

267–262 Chremonidean War; Ptolemy II supports Greek independence; Antigonus II Gonatas enters Athens

264–241 First Punic War between Rome and Carthage

263–241 Eumenes founds independent kingdom of Pergamum

262 Cleanthes succeeds Zeno as head of Stoics

261 Antiochus II succeeds to Seleucid kingdom

260–253 Second Syrian War between Ptolemy II and Antiochus II

260 Historians Hieronymus of Cardia and Timaeus of Tauromenium die; Apollonius of Rhodes and Herodas (author of mimes) active; Erasistratus of Ceos and Herophilius of Chalcedon (doctors) active

260–212 Archimedes active

251–213 Career of Aratus of Sicyon

247 Hamilcar Barca begins Carthaginian offensive in Sicily

246 Ptolemy III, king of Egypt; Seleucus II, king of Seleucid Empire

246–241 Third Syrian War between Ptolemy III and Seleucus II

244–241 Agis IV attempts to reform Sparta and is executed

246 Eratosthenes head of Library at Alexandria

240 First Latin tragedy by Livius Andronicus

239 Demetrius II, king of Macedonia; war between Macedon and Aetolian and Achaean Leagues

238–227 War of Attalus of Pergamum against Galatians

237 Hamilcar begins Carthaginian expansion in Spain

236 Naevius' first play produced

235–222 Cleomenes III, king of Sparta; integration of helots into Spartan army

235 Apollonius of Perge (mathematician) active

232 Chrysippus succeeds Cleanthes as head of Stoics

226 Reforms of Cleomenes III at Sparta

225 Eratosthenes of Cyrene active

223 Antiochus III succeeds to Seleucid kingdom

222 Battle of Sellasia; capture of Sparta

221 Philip V succeeds to Macedon; Ptolemy IV succeeds to Egypt

219–217 Fourth Syrian War between Ptolemy IV and Antiochus III

218 Hannibal invades Italy

218–201 Second Punic War

217 Hannibal defeats Romans at Lake Trasimene; Battle of Raphia between Ptolemy IV and Antiochus III

216 Hannibal defeats Romans at Cannae

215 Philip V allies with Carthage

214–205 First Macedonian War between Philip V and Rome

213 Romans besiege Syracuse

212 Romans besiege Capua

211 Hannibal marches on Rome; Roman alliance with Aetolian League

211–206 Scipio Africanus defeats Carthaginians in Spain

204 Scipio invades Africa

204 Plautus' *Miles Gloriosus* performed

204–169 Ennius active at Rome

203 Hannibal recalled from Italy

203–200 Philip V and Antiochus III make a secret alliance against Egypt; Fifth Syrian War

202 Scipio defeats Hannibal at Battle of Zama

202 Fabius Pictor writes first prose history of Rome

200–197 Second Macedonian War between Philip V and Rome

200 Aristophanes of Byzantium becomes head of Library

197 Battle of Cynoscephalae

196 Declaration of the freedom of the Greeks by Roman commander T.Q. Flaminius

192–188 Syrian War between Rome and Antiochus III

191 Defeat of Antiochus III at Thermopylae

189 Defeat of Antiochus III at Magnesia

184 Censorship of Cato the Elder

179 Philip V succeeded by son Perseus

175 Antiochus IV succeeds to Seleucid Empire

171–167 Third Macedonian War

170–168 Sixth Syrian War

168 Defeat of Perseus at Battle of Pydna ends kingdom of Macedonia; Rome orders Antiochus IV out of Egypt; Maccabean Revolt

167 Polybius (historian) arrives in Rome

166 Terence's *Andria*

165 Terence's *Hecyra*

163 Terence's *Heautontimorumenos*

161 Terence's *Eunuchus* and *Phormio*

160 Terence's *Adelphi*

160 Cato the Elder's *On Agriculture* written

155 Carneades arrives in Rome

149–146 Third Punic War

148 Fourth Macedonian War and war against the Achaean League; Macedon becomes a Roman province

146 Corinth is sacked; Carthage is destroyed; Africa becomes a Roman province

133 Tribunate of Tiberius Gracchus; Attalus III of Pergamum bequeaths his kingdom to Rome; becomes the province of Asia

123–122 Tribunates of Gaius Gracchus

121 First use of *senatus consultum ultimum* to authorize massacre of Gracchan supporters

112–106 Wars against Jugurtha

107–100 C. Marius consul six times; he reforms the army

102–101 Marius defeats the Cimbri and Teutones

91–87 Attempted reforms of Marcus Livius Drusus lead to Social War between Rome and its Italian allies

88 Sulla marches on Rome

88–85 Mithridates VI of Pontus massacres Roman citizens in Asia; seeks to liberate Greece from Rome

87 Marius seizes Rome; dies following year

86 Sulla captures Athens and Greece

83–82 Sulla returns to Rome; civil wars; Second Mithridatic War

82–80 Sulla dictator of Rome

74–63 Third Mithridatic War

73–71 Slave Revolt of Spartacus

149 Publication of Cato's *Origines*, or *History of Rome*

144 Panaetius (Stoic) arrives in Rome

135 Nicander (medical poet) active

95 Meleager active

87–51 Posidonius active in Rhodes and in Rome

81 Cicero's earliest extant speech

75–35 Philodemus (philosopher) active at Rome

70 Cicero's *Verrine Orations* delivered

66–63 Pompey defeats Mithridates and re-organizes the east; end of Seleucid Empire

63 Consulate of Cicero; conspiracy of Catiline; Caesar elected *pontifex maximus*

63 Cicero's *Catilinarian Orations given*

62 Pompey returns to Italy and disbands army

61 Trial and acquittal of P. Clodius on religious charge

60 "First Triumvirate" formed between Pompey, Crassus, and Caesar

60–30 Diodorus of Sicily compiles his *Historical Library*

59 Consulate of Caesar

59–54 Catullus' poems to Lesbia

58–57 Cicero's exile and return

58–52 Caesar writes his account of the *Gallic Wars*

58–49 Caesar campaigns in Gaul

56 Agreement of the triumvirs renewed at Luca

55–54 Caesar's invasions of Britain

55 Death of Lucretius; his poems published posthumously

55–53 Crassus campaigns in east; killed by the Parthians at Carrhae (53)

54 Cicero's *Pro Caelio* delivered; death of Catullus

52 Clodius murdered by Milo in gang violence

52 Cicero's *Pro Milone* written

51 Cicero writes his *De republica*

50 Andronicus of Rhodes discovers and begins editing the lost works of Aristotle

49 Caesar crosses the Rubicon; Civil War

49–27 Varro (antiquarian) active

48 Caesar defeats Pompey at Pharsalus; Pompey murdered in Egypt

48–47 Caesar installs Cleopatra on the throne of Egypt

47–44 Dictatorship of Caesar

46 Cicero's *Pro Marcello* delivered

44 Caesar is murdered

44 Cicero's *De officiis* written; Cicero attacks Marc Anthony in his *Philippics*

44–21 Strabo (historian) active

43 Octavian (later called Augustus) seizes the consulate; Second Triumvirate of Antony, Lepidus, and Octavian formed

43 Murder of Cicero

42 Republicans defeated at Philippi; Brutus and Cassius commit suicide

40 Didymus (Alexandrian literary scholar) active; Sallust's *War with Jugurthine* written

38 *Eclogues* of Virgil published

37 Renewal of Triumvirate

37–30 Horace's *Satires* written

36–35 Campaigns against Sextus Pompeius

36 Varro's *On Agriculture*

31 Octavian defeats Antony at Actium

30 Antony and Cleopatra commit suicide

30 Horace's *Epodes* published

29 Virgil's *Georgics* and Propertius' *Elegies 1* completed

28–23 Vitruvius' *On Architecture* written

27 Octavian given the name Augustus

26–16 Propertius' *Elegies 2–4* written

25 Ovid begins writing *Amores*

24–23 Publication of Horace's *Odes 1–3*

23 End of Maecenas' patronage of poetry

20 Horace's *Epistles 1* published

19 Tibullus and Virgil die

18 Augustan marriage and social reforms

17 Horace's *Centennial Hymns* symbolizes his acceptance of the Augustan regime

12 Death of Marcus Agrippa; death of Lepidus; Augustus becomes *pontifex maximus*

12 Horace's *Epistles* to Augustus published

9 First edition of Ovid's *Art of Love* published

8 Death of Horace; end of Livy's history of Rome

2 Augustus declared *Pater Patriae*; second edition of Ovid's *Art of Love*

POLITICAL EVENTS A.D.

CULTURAL DEVELOPMENTS A.D.

1–4 Ovid's *Fasti* written

2–4 Lucius and Gaius Caesar die; Tiberius is given tribunician power and adopts nephew Germanicus

8 Ovid banished to Black Sea

9 Defeat of Varrus in Teutoburg Forest

14–37 Tiberius reigns

14–37 Manilius (poet) and Velleius Paterculus (historian) active

19 Death of Germanicus

26 Tiberius retires to Capri

29–31 Crucifixion of Jesus

31 Sejanus, praetorian prefect, executed

37–41 Gaius (Caligula) ruled

41–54 Claudius

45–58 Missionary journeys of Paul

43 Roman invasion of Britain

49 Seneca made tutor to Nero

54–68 Nero ruled

54 Seneca's *Apocolocyntosis* published; Lucan and Persius active

59 Murder of Agrippina the Younger

61 Revolt of the Iceni under Boudicca

64 Fire in Rome for nine days; persecution of Christians

65 Suicides of Seneca and Lucan

65–100 Composition of the Gospels and the Acts of the Apostles

66–73 Jewish Revolt

66 Suicide of Petronius

67 Josephus, rebel leader in Judaea, deserts to Romans

69 Year of the Four Emperors

69–79 Vespasian

70 Destruction of Temple at Jerusalem

74 Frontinus (technical writer) consul

78–85 Campaigns of Agricola in Britain

79–81 Titus ruled

79 Eruption of Vesuvius; death of Pliny the Elder

80 Colosseum dedicated

81–96 Domitian ruled

81–96 Silius Italicus, Martial, and Quintilian active

96–98 Nerva ruled

97 Tacitus consul

98–117 Trajan ruled

98–117 Dio Chrysostom, Epictetus, and Plutarch active in Greek literature

100–111 Pliny the Younger consul and governor of Bithynia; Tacitus writes *Histories* and *Annals*

101–106 Trajan conquers Dacia

114–117 Trajan's Parthian War

115–117 Jewish Revolt

117–138 Hadrian ruled

117–138 Appian, Lucian, and Claudius Ptolemy active in Greek literature; Suetonius and Juvenal in Latin

122 Hadrian's Wall in Britain

138–161 Antoninus Pius ruled

138–161 Pausanias writes his description of Greece

142 Antonine Wall in Britain

143 Herodes Atticus (Greek orator) and Fronto (Latin orator) consuls

144 Speech of Aelius Aristides in praise of Rome

c. 160 Gaius' *Institutes*

161–180 Marcus Aurelius ruled

161–180 Apuleius and Galen active

165 Justin Martyr killed

174–180 *Meditations* of Marcus Aurelius

180–92 Commodus ruled

193 After murder of Commodus, four emperors contend for power

193–211 Septimius Severus ruled

193–211 Philostratus, Herodian, Sextus Empiricus, Alexander of Aphrodisias, Tertullian, and Clement of Alexandria active

200–254 Origen active

203 Perpetua martyred in Carthage

208–211 Severus campaigns in Britain and dies in York

212–217 Caracella ruled

212 Death of jurist Papinian

218–222 Elagabalus ruled

222–235 Alexander Severus ruled

223 Death of jurist Ulpian

229–230 Cassius Dio's *Roman History*

241 Beginning of Mani's preaching

244 Plotinus settles in Rome

249–251 Decius' persecution of Christians

257 Valerian starts a new Christian persecution

258 Martyrdom of Cyprian

271–273 Aurelian fights Zenobia in Palmyra

284–306 Diocletian reestablishes central power and founds Tetrarchy

303–311 Great Persecution of the Christians

304–311 Lactantius' *Human and Divine Institutions* written

306–337 Career of Constantine the Great

312 Constantine wins Battle of Milvian Bridge

313 Edict of Milan in favor of Christians

324–330 Foundation of Constantinople

325 Council of Nicaea

333–379 Life of Basil of Caesarea

340 Death of Eusebius of Caesarea

c. 350 Preaching of Ulfila

356 Death of Saint Antony

360–363 Julian the Apostate Emperor

372 Saint Martin bishop of Tours

373 Death of Athanasius

374–394 Ambrose bishop of Milan

378 Goths defeat and kill Valens at the Battle of Adrianople

378–395 Theodosius I the Great, Emperor

378 Ammianus Marcellinus starts his history of the Empire

379 Consulship of Ausonius; Saint Jerome becomes a priest; death of Saint Basil

380s Jerome begins his Latin translation of the Old and New Testaments

381 Condemnation of Arianism by the Council of Constantinople

385 Augustine appointed professor of rhetoric at Milan

389 Jerome's foundation of a religious house in Bethlehem

394 Death of Saint Gregory of Nyssa and Saint Martin

394–404 Claudian, propagandist for Stilicho

395 Division of the Empire between the sons of Theodosius

395–408 Stilicho commander in chief in west

395–430 Augustine bishop of Hippo Regius

397–400 *Confessions* of Augustine

398 John Chrysostom appointed archbishop of Constantinople

408–450 Theodosius II emperor in the east

410 Sack of Rome by Alaric; Rome formally renounces Britain

413–426 *City of God* by Augustine

415 Murder of Hypatia

430 Death of Saint Augustine

431 Council of Ephesus proclaims Mary to be *Theotokos* (mother of God)

432–454 Aetius commander in chief in west

438 The Theodosian Code

439 Vandals conquer Carthage and Africa

451 Battle between Aetius and Huns at Catalaunian Plains

451 Council of Chalcedon

455 Sack of Rome by Vandals

456–472 Ricimer commander in chief in west; makes and unmakes emperors

457–474 Reign of Pope Leo I

464–491 Zeno emperor in east

472 Sidonius Apollinaris bishop of Clermont-Ferrand

476 Last Roman emperor, Romulus Augustulus, deposed in west

476–493 Odoacer king of Italy

From Polis to Empire—
The Ancient World,
c. 800 B.C.–A.D. 500

A

AENESIDEMUS (first century B.C.)

Aenesidemus was a Sceptic philosopher of the first century B.C. who revived Pyrrhonnian Scepticism (cf. *Pyrrhon).

Little is known of Aenesidemus' early life, apart from that fact that he was born at Cnossos in Crete and taught in Alexandria. In his writings, he attempted to restore the Sceptic character of the Academy. He argued that the Academic Scepticism had abandoned its original uncompromising attitude toward knowledge. Aenesidemus' works included *Against Wisdom*, *On Inquiry*, and *First Introduction*. Yet all of these works were lost.

The fundamental arguments of the ten modes of Scepticism are attributed to Aenesidemus and first appear in his eight-volume *Pyrrhonian Discourses*. These arguments were all directed against the unreliability of sense perceptions and the need to withhold judgment. The *Pyrrhonian Discourses* only survives in a summary in the ninth-century patriarch Photius' library catalog.

Although his works have not survived, Aenesidemus' influence on later Scepticism was great, and his teachings are preserved in the works of *Diogenes Laertius and *Sextus Empiricus.

Bibliography: R.J. Hankinson, *The Sceptics*, 1998.

Andrew G. Traver

AESCHINES (c. 390–c. 320 B.C.)

Aeschines was an Athenian politician who is best known for his rivalry with *Demosthenes about Athens' relationship with *Philip II of Macedonia.

Aeschines was born in the early fourth century to a family that boasted no particular connections to Athenian politics. When he was young, Aeschines served in the army and then became a tragic actor. In the middle of the fourth century, Aeschines began to participate in Athenian political life, and in 347 he served on the boule at the same time as Demosthenes. These two clashed over the question of how Athens should respond to Philip's incursions into Greece.

Although Aeschines probably had no formal rhetorical training, three speeches from his political career survive. They are all connected somehow to his rivalry with Demosthenes. The first two are related to Demosthenes' charge of treason against Aeschines for his dealings with Philip. Demosthenes brought his charges with a certain Timarchus, a man with a reputation for sexual excesses. Aeschines responded with a suit claiming that Timarchus' alleged actions rendered him ineligible to participate in this case. Aeschines' suit, designed to delay his trial, was successful. His defense in 343 against the actual charges is contained in the speech *On the Embassy*, and it was also successful.

Aeschines' other surviving speech is also a product of his rivalry with Demosthenes. After the Battle of Chaeronea (338), Demosthenes' ally Ctesiphon proposed that Demosthenes should be awarded an honorary gold crown to celebrate his service to the Athenians. Aeschines tried to block this move by prosecuting Ctesiphon under the procedure of the *graphe paranomon* for proposing an illegal decree. This case led to a showdown between these two political figures; Aeschines' prosecution is preserved in his *Against Ctesiphon*, whereas Demosthenes' defense is preserved in his *On the Crown*. Aeschines failed to receive one-fifth of the votes at this trial, and because of this, he was subject to a large fine. Rather than paying this fine, Aeschines elected to go into permanent exile at Rhodes.

Bibliography: E.M. Harris, *Aeschines and Athenian Politics*, 1995.

Jeff Rydberg-Cox

AESCHYLUS OF ELEUSIS (c. 525–456 B.C.)

Aeschylus was the oldest of the three great Athenian tragedians who, according to *Aristotle, was the founder of tragedy.

Aeschylus was born at Eleusis of a noble family. He fought against the Persians at Marathon (490) and may have been with the Athenian troops at Salamis (480). His involvement in politics can be seen in many of his plays, where he addresses and critiques many of the political and social issues of importance to Athens: the nature of democracy, tyrants, rulers and their relationship with their subjects, and relationships between men and women, among others.

Although Aeschylus wrote more than ninety plays, only seven survive: the *Persians* (472); the *Suppliant Maidens* (460s); *Seven against Thebes* (467); *Prometheus* (before 458); and the *Oresteia*, the only surviving trilogy of Greek tragedy (458). He won the prize for the annual contest in tragedy at the Great Dionysia at least twelve times, and three plays—the *Persians, Seven against Thebes*, and the *Oresteia*—took first prize.

Aristotle called Aeschylus the founder of tragedy because he introduced a second actor that allowed for real dialogue (as opposed to one actor and the chorus), thereby emphasizing the dialogue and reducing the importance of the chorus. He may also have introduced the third actor; the *Oresteia* requires at least three actors. In addition, Aeschylus refined the use of costumes, creating a tragic grandeur by means of masks and appropriate dress. His poetic style became the standard structure for tragedies; later tragedians followed his example, beginning each play with a prologue, followed by an opening chorus, and then the entrance of the actors who talk to their antagonists, to their sympathetic friends, or to the chorus. Choral odes bridge each of these episodes or parts.

Aeschylus traveled to Sicily at least three times, at least once at the invitation of King *Hieron I of Syracuse, who became his patron, and then emigrated or was exiled there. He died and was buried at Gela in 456. Legend has it that he was killed when an eagle let a tortoise fall on his bald head, mistaking it for a stone. The Athenians' respect for him was such that his plays were exhibited at public expense (as opposed to the poet's own expense); in the middle of the fourth century, a statue of Aeschylus was placed in the theater of Dionysus at Athens.

Bibliography: D. Slavitt, ed. and trans., *Aeschylus: The Oresteia*, 1998.

Jana K. Schulman

AESOP (early sixth century B.C.–564 B.C.?)

Aesop was a supposed author of a collection of Greek fables and quite possibly a legendary figure.

Very little is known about Aesop's life: He came from Thrace and was taken to Samos, where he was made a slave. He seems to have been a storyteller renowned for his wit, and his fables were mentioned by *Herodotus, *Aristophanes, *Plato, and *Plutarch. He may also have been a lawyer before his enslavement; Plutarch's story that he was an adviser to King *Croesus is without foundation.

Aesop used his fables much in the way they are still used today: as illustrations and analogies. Animal fables were of eastern (probably Babylonian) origin, but Aesop's influenced writers well into the fifteenth century.

The stories associated with him are still current, and the oldest collection was made by *Demetrius of Phalerum in the fourth century B.C. The morals we currently assign to the stories are of very recent addition, but the fables' uses as analogies prompted many collectors to affix tags or maxims for ease of reference or as mnemonic devices.

Bibliography: O. Temple and R. Temple, trans., *Aesop, the Complete Fables*, 1998.

Andrea Schutz

AETIUS, FLAVIUS (c. 390–454)

Aetius was the leading general of the western half of the Roman Empire from 432 to his death.

The son of a general, Aetius spent stretches of his youth as a voluntary hostage with the Gothic army of *Alaric in the Balkans (405–408) and later with the Huns, outside Roman territory. He established long-lasting ties with the latter; Hunnic auxiliaries later supported Aetius' rise to power. In 425, the young Valentinian III (419–455) became emperor of the western half of the empire, ruling from Ravenna and Rome, with his mother *Galla Placidia (d. 450) as regent. Aetius defeated rival generals to succeed to the informal position created by *Stilicho ("generalissimo"), dominating the court (cf. *Ricimer). Aetius held the office of *magister utriusque militiae* (master of military forces, from c. 425) and the highest honorary positions, consul (432, 437, 446) and *patricius* (from 435). He was much involved with barbarian and frontier matters: He contained the Goths (settled in southwestern Gaul since 418); he settled quiescent Burgundians in eastern Gaul in 443; he repressed rebellious Roman provincials on the Danube and in northern Gaul; he assisted provincials living in now-independent kingdoms in Spain and Britain. Aetius married a noble barbarian woman and adopted a Frankish prince in barbarian fashion as means to maintain alliances. His Hunnic support became a liability when *Attila launched major raids on Gaul in 451 and Italy in 452. Aetius retained power until 454 when, planning to marry his son to a daughter of Valentinian III, he was assassinated at Rome by the emperor. The following year, two of Aetius' followers killed Valentinian in revenge.

Sixth-century Byzantine historians regarded Aetius as the last effective western general, dominating a puppet emperor, and saw his death as prefiguring the collapse of the West two decades later. Modern scholars have largely concurred.

Bibliography: J.M. O'Flynn, *Generalissimos of the Later Roman Empire*, 1983.

Andrew Gillett

AGATHOCLES (361–289 B.C.)

Agathocles was tyrant of Syracuse from 317 to 304 and the king of Sicily after 304.

Born at Thermae Himeraeae, Sicily, Agathocles was the son of a potter. He moved from his native town to Syracuse during the reign of *Timeoleon (c. 343) and served in the army. As an opponent of the oligarchic party, he was twice banished from that city for attempting to overthrow the government. He returned in 317 with his own army. He banished and murdered his opponents and set himself up as tyrant.

Agathocles then fought against the other Sicilian Greek states, bringing much of eastern Sicily under his control. Carthage, however, feared losing its influence and possessions in Sicily, so it sent over a force against him. In 311, under siege by the Carthaginians in Syracuse, Agathocles broke through the blockade and opened up a front in Africa (310–306). Although he almost succeeded in capturing Carthage, he was finally defeated in 307. The subsequent peace agreement of 306 limited Carthage to the portions of Sicily west of the Halycus River. Agathocles returned home and had himself crowned king. He thereafter took interest in the Adriatic and southern Italy, invading the latter territory. He died at Syracuse in 289, possibly poisoned by his grandson. His son-in-law, King *Pyrrhus of Epirus, inherited his influence in Sicily and southern Italy.

Although known for his cruelty, he had the support of the Syracusan lower classes. Our main source for his reign, the historian *Timaeus, has judged him harshly.

Bibliography: P. Green, *Alexander to Actium: The Historical Evolution of the Hellenistic Age*, 1990; K. Lomas, *Rome and the Western Greeks 350* B.C.–A.D. *200: Conquest and Acculturation in Southern Italy*, 1993.

Andrew G. Traver

AGESILAUS II (c. 443–358 b.c.)

Agesilaus II was a Spartan king of the Eurypontid line who stewarded the Spartan state during its period of greatest success and ultimate failure.

Although the son of a Spartan king (Archidamus II), Agesilaus was never expected to gain the throne at Sparta because of the presence of an elder half brother, Agis II. As a result, he was given the education of an ordinary Spartan citizen, despite a birth defect that caused him to limp permanently; Spartan law ordinarily proscribed against the rearing of children born with deformities. However, in 398, after the death of Agis, and in his mid-forties, Agesilaus gained the throne with the help of his patron *Lysander. Agesilaus claimed that Leotychidas, the son of Agis and heir apparent, was illegitimate. His arguments, and Lysander's spin on an apparently inauspicious prophecy, convinced the ephors to award the kingship to Agesilaus.

In 396, Agesilaus set out for Asia Minor in order to liberate the Greek cities that were being terrorized by Persian satraps there. But in 394, he was forced to return to Greece where an anti-Spartan coalition had formed (Corinthian War, 395–387). The confederacy was composed of two of Sparta's former allies, Corinth and Thebes, its ancestral enemy Argos, and the city it had defeated in the Peloponnesian War, Athens. Eventually, Agesilaus was able to suppress the revolt. During the 380s, Sparta reigned supreme throughout the Greek mainland. But its strong-arm tactics made it unpopular, and by 378, both Athens and Thebes had liberated themselves from Spartan control. In 371, the Spartans, Thebans, and Athenians attempted to negotiate peace. However, when Agesilaus demanded that the Thebans, against whom he had a personal vendetta, sign only for themselves and not for the Boeotian League, they refused. Agesilaus declared war but was soundly defeated by *Epaminondas in the Battle of Leuctra later that year. Sparta never recovered from this blow.

In 370, the Thebans invaded Spartan territory, and Agesilaus led a heroic defense at the city's walls. While the city itself was spared, Sparta was stripped of most of its surrounding countryside, and its subject population, the helots, was freed. Although Sparta tried to reassert its hegemony throughout the rest of Agesilaus' life, it failed. Agesilaus died in 359/358 while on mercenary service with the king of Egypt.

Although historians praised Agesilaus as the greatest and most important man of his day, we must ultimately ask whether the collapse of Spartan hegemony was due to his policies or larger sociological factors such as loss of manpower.

Bibliography: C.D. Hamilton, *Agesilaus and the Failure of Spartan Hegemony*, 1991.

Luis Molina

AGIS IV (263–241 B.C.)

Agis IV was a Spartan king who attempted to restore the Lycurgan constitution known as "The Discipline."

Agis succeeded his father Eudamidas II as king of Sparta in 244 at age nineteen. As king, Agis attempted to arrest a century-long decline in Sparta's power that saw the ranks of its citizens dwindle to under a thousand and the tensions between rich and poor become acute. Basing his model upon that of the tradition of the famous lawgiver *Lycurgus, Agis strove to redistribute Spartan land and proposed a complete abolition of debt. In the spirit of Lycurgus, Agis sought to repartition the division of the Spartan homeland into 4,500 lots for citizens. He hoped to increase a depleted citizenry by extending full citizenship to many *perioeci* (voteless freemen) and foreigners. Agis also attempted to restore the Lycurgan system of military training.

Supported in these reforms by his mother, grandmother, his uncle Agesilaus, and an ephor named Lysander, Agis found stalwart opposition from the wealthy. The rich soon allied with the other Spartan king, Leonidas II, and rebelled against these reforms. Agis then had Leonidas deposed. When the ephors tried to have Leonidas reinstated, Agis replaced them by a commission headed by Agesilaus.

Supported by Agesilaus, Agis then began implementing the cancellation of debts. He was called away from Sparta (241) when *Aratus of Sicyon requested Sparta's aid. Upon his return, Agis discovered that Leonidas II had returned and taken control of the state. Agis took sanctuary but was eventually enticed out. He was summarily tried and executed along with his mother and grandmother.

Although *Plutarch presents a highly favorable account of Agis, the king's attempts to reform Sparta's economic and political structure ultimately failed.

Bibliography: A.H.M. Jones, *Sparta*, 1967.

Andrew G. Traver

AGRICOLA, GNAEUS JULIUS (40–93)

Agricola was the longest-serving governor of Roman Britain (almost seven years, 78–84) and the best known, thanks to the biography written by his son-in-law *Tacitus.

Agricola was born on 13 June 40 in Galla Narbonensis (southern Gaul) to Julius Graecinus, a former senator and praetor, and his wife Julia Procilla. His father ran afoul of Emperor Gaius (*Caligula) and was executed in 40; his mother obtained a traditional Roman education for him in Massilia (Marseilles).

Agricola served as military tribune in Britain under Suetonius Paulinus (58–61), quaestor in Asia (64), tribune (66) and praetor (68) in Rome, legate of the Twentieth Legion in Britain under Petillius Cerialis (70–74), governor in Aquitaine (74–77), consul in Rome (77 or 78), and governor in Britain (78–84). In 84 Emperor *Domitian recalled him to Rome, where he lived in retirement until his death on 23 August 93. Tacitus' hint that Domitian had him poisoned is without foundation.

Agricola conducted annual campaigns in Britain. In 78 he defeated the Ordovices in northern Wales and completed the conquest of Anglesey abandoned by Suetonius Paulinus at the time of *Boudicca's rebellion in 60. He then secured northwestern England in 79, advanced into eastern Scotland as far as the Tay River in 80, built a line of forts between the Firths of Forth and Clyde in 81, moved up the west coast of Scotland to the Galloway peninsula in 82, and advanced north of the Tay in 83. He won his most famous victory in 84, defeating the Caledonians at Mons Graupius, the location of which remains uncertain. However, he allowed much of the defeated army to escape, and thus his conquest of Britain remained less complete than Tacitus suggests when blaming Domitian for letting it go (though, in fact, the Romans continued to hold some of his fortresses in the subsequent reign of *Trajan). Agricola also contemplated invading Ireland; but he never attempted it, and there was little real chance of success if he had.

Agricola's cultural significance lies partly in his attempt to establish Roman civilization in the wake of conquest. Thus, he carried on a program of public works in addition to constructing fortresses, and he helped bring Roman education to Rome's British subjects. Otherwise, in Tacitus' biography he serves as the exemplary Roman statesman to whom his son-in-law compares the tyrant Domitian. In this guise Agricola remains one of the best-known figures in the history of Roman Britain. Every generation that has deemed a classical education essential, particularly from the Renaissance through the early twentieth century, has read the Roman historians, including Tacitus, and thus has been familiar with Agricola. Naturally, in Britain his appeal has been especially strong. If not for Tacitus, however, he would be virtually forgotten, as the only other Roman historian to even mention him is *Cassius Dio. Given Tacitus' inevitable bias, this renders modern perceptions of Agricola somewhat problematic.

Bibliography: W.S. Hanson, *Agricola and the Conquest of the North*, new ed., 1991.

William B. Robison

AGRIPPA, MARCUS VIPSANIUS (64/63–12 B.C.)

Italian statesman, general and grand builder, Agrippa played a large role in the consolidation of *Augustus' principate.

Agrippa was born feet first (hence, according to *Pliny the Elder, the name). In 44 he was at Apollonia with Octavius (later Octavian/Augustus) when news arrived of *Caesar's assassination and Octavius' inheritance. They returned to

Italy, Agrippa taking a leading role in recruiting troops and, subsequently, fighting the enemies of Octavian (*Brutus and Cassius, L. Antonius, *Sextus Pompey and, finally, *Marc Antony). In 37, at only twenty-five years of age, he held his first consulship, during which he trained a new fleet and converted Lake Avernus into a harbor (Portus Iulius); and in 36 his victory at Naulochus (3 September) ended Sextus Pompeius' domination of the sea. After campaigning in Illyria and Dalmatia (35–34) he returned to Rome, taking the unusual step of holding, four years after his consulship, an aedileship. In this office, at his own expense, he undertook a vast public building program (utilitarian and ornamental), public games, and distributions. In the war against Antony and *Cleopatra, Agrippa was commander in chief of the navy and mainly responsible for the victory at Actium (2 September 31). In 28, as consul for the second time, Agrippa shared censorial power with Octavian. In 27, consul for the third time, he again shared office with Octavian (now Augustus). From 29 to 23, he embellished the Field of Mars with buildings that included the Pantheon and the first stage of his bath complex. Beginning in 23 he undertook a tour of the East—it is thought to have eased the political tensions between himself and his brother-in-law, Augustus' nephew Marcellus, Augustus' most likely heir. In 21, he married Marcellus' widow, Augustus' daughter Julia, who bore him two sons, Lucius (20) and Gaius (17), thus providing Augustus with direct male heirs. From 20 to 18, Agrippa toured the West, in Gaul undertaking further building programs, and in 19 campaigning against the Cantabrians. Offered a triumph, he refused. In 18, Agrippa received proconsular imperium and tribunician power for five years (renewed for another five in 13), becoming a virtual partner with Augustus in government. From 17 to 13 he conducted another tour of the East (Greece, Asia, Syria, and Judaea), founding Berytus (Beirut) in 15, and campaigning on the Bosporus (14). In 13–12 he campaigned in Pannonia, after which he died unexpectedly in Campania and was buried in the mausoleum of Augustus.

He left memoirs and commentaries (now lost). His image is one of immense but modest energy and willingness to serve the interests of Augustus and the Roman Empire.

Bibliography: M. Reinhold, *Marcus Agrippa*, 1965.

Tom Hillard

AGRIPPINA THE ELDER (Vipsania Agrippina, c. 14 B.C.– A.D. 33)

Agrippina the Elder was a woman of the Julio-Claudian family who was instrumental in setting the formal public role of women in the imperial court.

Agrippina the Elder, the daughter of *Marcus Vipsanius Agrippa and Julia, the daughter of *Augustus, was the wife of *Germanicus and the mother of the emperor Gaius (*Caligula), *Agrippina the Younger, and as many as seven other children. She also was the grandmother of *Nero. She traveled with the imperial court and seems to have served as a model for female virtue during her floruit.

She accompanied her husband to Germany and the East, where he died at Antioch in 19. The death of *Tiberius' son Drusus in 23 brought her sons in direct line for the succession. However, Tiberius' adviser Sejanus sought to use this affair for his own ends. Sejanus roused the emperor's suspicions against Agrippina and her family and encouraged the emperor to detect seditious intentions in all of their activities. In 30, Tiberius, fearful of her persuasive powers, banished her to Pandataria, where she died.

Agrippina seems to have been the first member of the imperial family to be individually recognized in Roman coinage without association with the emperor. Her public image was modified after her death from martyr to role model. She was well respected by later historians.

Bibliography: R.A. Bauman, *Women and Politics in Ancient Rome*, 1992; S. Wood, "Memoriae Agrippinae. Agrippina the Elder in Julio-Claudian Art and Propaganda," *American Journal of Archaeology* 92 (1988): 409–426.

Lisa Auanger

AGRIPPINA THE YOUNGER (Julia Agrippina, 15-59)

Julia Agrippina was the sister of Emperor *Caligula, the wife of her uncle Emperor *Claudius, and the mother of Emperor *Nero.

Born on 6 November 15, at the colony of Ara Ubiorum, Agrippina Minor was the eldest of six children. Defying tradition, Agrippina was named after her mother Vipsania Agrippina (*Agrippina the Elder) rather than her father, the distinguished General *Germanicus. Agrippina's first marriage to Gnaeus Domitius Ahenobarbus in 28 resulted in her only child, Lucius Domitius Ahenobarbus, who later became known as Nero.

During Caligula's reign, both her image and her name were used widely in propaganda advertising the foundation of a new imperial dynasty. The prominence of Agrippina and her sisters led to unsubstantiated accusations of incest with their brother by later authors such as *Tacitus and *Suetonius. In 39, Agrippina and her sister Livilla were implicated in a plot against Caligula and exiled to the island of Pontia. Caligula's assassination in January 41 saw their prompt recall to Rome by the new emperor, their uncle Claudius, and Agrippina's marriage to her second husband, Gaius Sallustius Passienus Crispus.

Roman law prohibited marriages between uncles and nieces, so when Crispus died, Claudius had the law changed and married Agrippina on 1 January 49. Agrippina engineered Nero's adoption by Claudius in 50 and his subsequent designation as imperial heir over Claudius' own son Britannicus. When Nero ascended to the principate in 54, Agrippina was at the height of her power, as is reflected in the visual record, especially on coins. However, Nero quickly grew tired of his mother's influence, and Agrippina retired to her villa at Baiae for the last years of her life, where she was murdered on Nero's orders in March 59.

Bibliography: A. Barrett, *Agrippina. Sex, Power, and Politics in the Early Empire*, 1996.

Katrina M. Dickson

ALARIC (c. 360–410)

Alaric was the leader of a Gothic war band that sacked Rome in 410.

The core of Alaric's following probably came from the Goths who had fought *Valens at Adrianople (378) and had been settled as semiautonomous military auxiliaries by *Theodosius I (382); later immigrants and mercenaries also joined. Alaric served Theodosius in the early 390s. Later, he alternated between serving the empire and raiding its territories to extort supplies and land; he also sought permanent Roman military office. This erratic relationship arose from the unwillingness of the eastern court after Theodosius' death (395) to continue his policies. Moving from the East to Italy in 401, Alaric was defeated by *Stilicho (402) but later (c. 405) became his auxiliary. The expense of Alaric's mercenaries was unpopular with the Roman aristocracy, and Stilicho's execution under the emperor Honorius (408) left Alaric's army unpaid and without rations. This led, after several sieges of Rome and the brief elevation of a rival emperor, to Alaric's capture and sack of Rome for three days (24–26 August 410) to extract payment forcibly. Christian apologists claimed that Alaric, an Arian Christian (cf. *Arius), respected Church property and allowed sanctuary in churches. Expressions of horror at the violation of "the eternal city" came from around the Mediterranean. Later in 410 Alaric died. His followers, defeated by an imperial army in Gaul (414), were settled in a semiautonomous kingdom in southwestern Gaul, centered on Toulouse (418; cf. *Euric), the first major "barbarian kingdom" of early medieval Europe.

The sack of Rome, a symbolic shock to contemporaries, was deeply embedded as a crucial event in medieval historiography because it prompted the publication of both *Augustine's *City of God* and *Orosius' *Seven Books of History against the Pagans*, respectively, the most influential theological work and history of antiquity in the Middle Ages.

Bibliography: P. Heather, *Goths and Romans 332–489*, 1991.

Andrew Gillett

ALCAEUS (c. 620–c. 580 B.C.)

Alcaeus was a Greek lyric poet who is said to have invented the alcaic meter.

He was born of an aristocratic family in Mytilene in Lesbos. He was extensively involved in the political factions within his city; when he was a child, his brothers overthrew the tyrant Melanchros, who was succeeded by Myrsilus and Pittacus. Alcaeus apparently fought against all three of them and as a result was exiled to Pyrrha. He also took part in the war of Lesbos against Athens in Sigeum. Here he lost his shield in battle, which the Athenians triumphantly hung in a temple. When Pittacus came to power in Mytilene, Alcaeus turned violently against him. He left for Egypt and also traveled to Thrace and Lydia. The two were eventually reconciled, and Alcaeus returned home. It is unknown exactly when he died.

An elder contemporary to *Sappho, Alcaeus wrote lyrical songs, many of which treat contemporary politics. His best-known works are his invectives against Pittacus. He also wrote about themes of the symposium, such as love and wine, in addition to religious hymns and mythological verse. His works were originally edited in ten volumes by *Aristophanes of Byzantium and *Aristarchus of Samothrace; today they only survive in fragments. He wrote in a simple direct style, using two-to four-line stanzas in a variety of meters, one of which was called the alcaic. *Horace later tried to imitate him. As a lyric poet, Alcaeus is best remembered for his political lyrics.

Bibliography: C.A. Trypanis, *Greek Poetry: From Homer to Seferis*, 1981.

Andrew G. Traver

ALCIBIADES (c. 450–404 b.c.)

Alcibiades was a charismatic Athenian of noble birth who promoted the Peloponnesian War against Sparta, inspired the disastrous Sicilian Expedition (415), and later allied himself with his city's greatest enemies, Sparta and Persia. His actions both for and against Athens ultimately contributed to the downfall of the city.

Raised by his relative and guardian *Pericles, and befriended early by *Socrates, who allegedly saved his life in the Battle of Potidaea (432–430), Alcibiades was known for his physical beauty, engaging speech, brilliant mind, and chameleonlike character. A rebellious youth, he frequently challenged Pericles' authority, publicly assaulted his prospective father-in-law, and mocked the Assembly, yet he still attracted the admiration of the Athenian crowds through stunts such as entering seven chariots in the Olympic games and winning first, second, and fourth place (424). Elected at perhaps the youngest legal age to the office of *strategos* (420), he became a leader of the extreme democrats and outmaneuvered *Nicias, an elderly adversary who advocated peace, convincing the Assembly to appoint him as a leader of a gigantic naval expedition against the Spartan stronghold of Sicily. Suspected of having desecrated sacred phallic statues ("Hermae") during orgiastic celebrations the night before departure and of having profaned the Eleusinian mysteries, Alcibiades was recalled from Sicily upon his arrival in order to face trial. One step ahead of his opponents, he fled to Sparta instead of returning home, causing Athens to condemn him to death in absentia and to confiscate his property. In Sparta, he forfeited his effete Athenian mannerisms, charmed his hosts with his ability to adapt to their rough culture, and successfully directed Spartan war efforts against his own homeland. He advised Sparta to send one of their generals to help Syracuse and recommended that Sparta fortify Decelea, a town near Athens. Later, as a Spartan naval commander, he sparked revolt against Athens along the Ionian coast. However, when his adulterous affair with the queen of Sparta and his suspicious dealings with the Persian satrap Tissaphernes were discovered by Sparta's King Agis, Alcibiades fled to Persia, the common enemy of all Greece. Here again he charmed his hosts, turned against his homeland, and counseled his enemy successfully in maneuvers against his former allies. Never having lost his love for Athens, however, Alcibiades eventually betrayed the Persians, persuaded the Athenian fleet at Samos to make him a general (411), and for several years waged brilliant naval battles against Sparta on behalf of Athens. He became reconciled with a new democratic government in Athens (407) and was held in high favor as an Athenian naval commander until the Battle of Notium, where commanders who disobeyed his orders were defeated. Still, he continued to advise the Athenian navy until commanders ignoring his advice were defeated in the Battle of Aegospotami (405). He was murdered at his home in Phrygia by assassins who, according to various accounts, could have represented Athens, Sparta, or Persia.

Alcibiades' life has come to represent the best and worst of Athenian culture. His power, charm, and resilience recall the city that built the Parthenon and produced *Aristophanes' comedies, whereas his arrogance, ambition, and unscrupulousness recall the city that razed Melos and executed Socrates. The Sicilian Expedition, Alcibiades' most ambitious achievement as an Athenian, ended without him in a defeat that robbed his city of about 45,000 of its finest young men and signaled the beginning of its end.

A Platonic dialogue is named after Alcibiades, and he also figures in *Plato's *Symposium*, where the drunken youth interrupts a philosophical discussion on love to sing the praises of Socrates. He is also referred to as a character of questionable value in Aristophanes' *Frogs*, is discussed by *Thucydides, and is the subject of one of *Plutarch's *Lives*.

Bibliography: E.F. Benson, *The Life of Alcibiades*, 1928; W.M. Ellis, *Alcibiades*, 1989.

Richard Louth

ALCMAEON OF CROTON (or Alcmeon, c. 500–450 B.C.)

Alcmaeon was a Greek natural philosopher and physician significant for his theory of health and disease and for his investigations into the nature of the sense organs.

Alcmaeon is the only pre-Hippocratic writer whose medical theories have survived. He formulated one of the earliest rational explanations for health and illness. He originated the notion that health is dependent upon a balance within the body between opposite qualities such as wet/dry, cold/warm, and sweet/bitter. Alcmaeon rejected earlier conceptions of disease as something possessing a separate existence of its own. He maintained that disease is due to the disturbance of the body's natural equilibrium. This theory became influential in the development of Hippocratic humoral medicine. Alcmaeon's investigations of the sense organs led to several advances in anatomical knowledge. In his study of the eye (most likely through surgical excision, not dissection), he identified the optic nerve. The discovery of such "passages," which he believed carried *pneuma* from the sense organs to the brain, provided evidence for the theory of the brain (rather than the heart) as the center of sense perception and intelligence.

Alcmaeon's contributions in natural philosophy were also significant. He reportedly wrote the earliest treatise *On Nature*. *Aristotle devoted an entire work, *Against Alcmaeon*, to his philosophy. The physiological inquiries of Alcmaeon concerning sleep, reproduction, and embryonic development became standard topics for subsequent natural philosophers.

Bibliography: J. Longrigg, *Greek Rational Medicine: Philosophy and Medicine from Alcmaeon to the Alexandrians*, 1993.

Michael Anderson

ALCMAN (fl. 651–611 B.C.)

Alcman was a lyric poet active in Sparta perhaps in the late seventh or early sixth century B.C. His poetry is representative of a rich cultural and artistic tradition at Sparta before the military reforms of the legendary *Lycurgus.

Tradition records that Alcman was born in Lydia (Asia Minor) and brought to Sparta as a slave, but this probably stems from a belief that Sparta, noted for its austerity in later times, could not have produced a poet of Alcman's talent. Whatever the truth, Alcman composed his works in the local Spartan dialect. His poems were collected into six books, of which only fragments exist today. He was known for his love poetry, and traces of eroticism are indeed evident in some of the fragments. He also wrote *parthenia*, or maiden songs, hymns, and wedding songs (*hymenaioi*), most of which were designed to be performed in chorus. The most extensive fragment, known as the Louvre Parthenion, seems to have been composed for competing female choruses at a festival commemorating a Spartan goddess. The poem is important in allowing us to reconstruct features of Spartan religious ceremony, for which little literary or physical evidence exists otherwise. In other fragments, Alcman discusses Spartan gods, heroes and kings, the Laconian countryside, and Spartan customs.

Besides the obvious devotion to the community around him, Alcman's poetry also expressed personal feelings such as desire, nostalgia, and pride. This turn to self-reflection, which Alcman shared with other lyric poets of the archaic period (e.g., *Sappho, *Archilochus) represents a shift from the less personal poetry of the earlier epic poets, such as *Homer. Alcman was buried near the shrine of Helen in Sparta.

Bibliography: M.L. West, trans., *Greek Lyric Poetry*, 1993.

Luis Molina

ALEXANDER OF APHRODISIAS (fl. 200)

Alexander of Aphrodisias was the most important and influential ancient interpreter of *Aristotle's works.

Very little is known about Alexander's life. Often called "the second Aristotle," he was born in Caria, Asia Minor, and occupied the Peripatetic chair under *Septimius Severus in Athens from 198 to 211. His commentaries on Aristotle's works were very decisive for their later reception and determined in great part the formulation of some central problems in the history of philosophy. Alexander tried to explain and systematize Aristotelian doctrines, defending them against concurrent philosophic schools, particularly against the Stoa. Many of his commentaries have been lost; those on the first book of the *Prior Analytics*, the *Topics*, *Meteorology*, and *On Sense and the Sensible*, as well as his exposition on some books of the *Metaphysics* all survive. Apart from these, there exist two other original works by him: *On the Soul* and *On Fate*.

Although he was primarily a commentator, he diverges from Aristotle on some points. Alexander came close to a nominalist position by maintaining that the universal concepts exist only in the mind, being the result of abstraction from things and having no type of priority over them. He defended individual freedom against determinism. His distinction between the material, the habitual, and the agent intellect was very influential. Affirming the supraindividual nature of the agent intellect and identifying it with God, he can be seen as the precursor of the important medieval doctrine of the unity of the intellect.

Bibliography: R.W. Sharples, "Alexander of Aphrodisias: Scholasticism and Innovation," *Aufstieg und Niedergang der römischen Welt* 2.36 (1988): 1176–1243.

Fernando Oreja

ALEXANDER THE GREAT (Alexander III of Macedon, 356– 323 B.C.)

Alexander was king of Macedonia from 336 to 323 and conqueror of the Persian Empire.

He was the son and heir apparent of King *Philip II and his queen, *Olympias, who was the daughter of the neighboring king of Epirus. Alexander was apparently a very precocious child; stories are told of his questioning visiting Persian ambassadors about road systems and imperial finances when he was but a small boy and that he alone could determine how to train a spirited horse his father had purchased. Philip gave the horse, named Bucephalus, to Alexander, and the horse served him well in battle for over twenty years. The often sentimental Alexander built a city, Bucephala, in India where the horse was buried. Philip made certain that his exceptional son had a good education; when Alexander was thirteen, the noted philosopher *Aristotle was summoned to be his private tutor. This relationship lasted for about three years and had a profound effect on both of them. Alexander kept in touch with Aristotle and sent him information and specimens from his travels; he said he considered Aristotle his "second father."

Alexander was placed in independent command of armies by Philip at the young age of sixteen and was an experienced military commander not yet twenty years old when Philip was assassinated in 336. Alexander succeeded his father without opposition.

Philip had extended Macedonian territory, subdued neighboring Celtic tribes, and brought all of Greece under his power as leader of an enforced alliance that had the invasion of Persia as its primary mission. On the news of his death, several of the northern chieftains decided to "revolt," that is, to declare their obligations to Philip null and void, thinking that the young Alexander could not be as forceful as Philip. They were wrong. While Alexander was with an army subduing northern tribes, word reached him that the Greek city of Thebes was also in revolt. He quickly marched southward and placed the city under siege. It was eventually destroyed as an object lesson to other Greeks. The ability to move a large army quickly and fight effectively would be typical of Alexander for the rest of his life.

In the spring of 334, Alexander crossed the Hellespont into Asia with an army of about 30,000 infantry (the famed Macedonian phalanx developed by his father) and 15,000 cavalry and enough supplies and money for less than thirty days. He was confident that he would find more resources in conquered territory soon enough. He also had a large contingent of geographers, surveyors, and secretaries. Aristotle's student was genuinely curious to learn about the world, and he intended to keep good records and, indeed, to create his own legend.

His plan was to march along the coast and gain control of all seaports, thus depriving the Persian navy of their bases and forcing their surrender. The fleet of Athens would sail along the coast to intercept any Persian ships. This fleet in Alexander's service also served as hostage for the good behavior of Athens and other Greek states now in his rear. Alexander was aware that much of the Persian naval and military force was composed of Greek mercenaries. Military success on his part would not only bring them over to his side but deprive the Persians of their services.

There were many battles over the next decade as Alexander pushed on relentlessly. They were characterized by boldness, as at the first battle at the Granicus River (334), when Alexander led a cavalry charge up the muddy banks of the river against the opposing forces on higher ground, and especially by good tactical use of combined infantry and cavalry forces, as at Issus in Syria in 333 and Gaugamela in northern Iraq in 331. He was almost always outnumbered, but his exquisite sense of timing, topography, and tactical good sense carried the day. King *Darius III of Persia was personally present at two battles (Issus and Gaugamela) and fled the field in both instances. Alexander's boldness and sense of topography were evident in his siege of Tyre, a city on the Phoenician coast. The city refused to surrender, confidant in its invulnerability as an island. The island was less than a mile offshore; Alexander ordered an earthen causeway to be built, on which he moved up wheeled siege engines to take the city by storm. Normal silting over the millennia since has resulted in the city of Tyre, which still exists (in Lebanon), becoming a part of the mainland.

Most of the cities along the coast surrendered to Alexander without a fight, especially after the siege of Tyre. He advanced into Egypt, where he was hailed as Pharaoh and a god. The Egyptians had been unhappily under Persian rule for a few centuries and were willing enough to try a new overlord. At the westernmost mouth of the Nile River along the Mediterranean coast, Alexander ordered a new city to be built. It would be called "Alexandria" and would become one of the largest and most important cities of the world after his death.

Alexander then proceeded into Asia to do final battle with Darius near Gaugamela (331). Darius fled the scene, and Alexander chased him into what is now northern Afghanistan, where he found him murdered by one of his companions (who was executed by Alexander). There was now no barrier to Alexander claiming all of the Persian Empire as his own. He entered Persepolis, the capital city, and found a huge hoard of treasure that was distributed among his troops (with significant economic consequences). Either by design or by accident (the sources are ambiguous), the palace and much of the city were burned to the ground.

He continued his conquests, partly out of curiosity and ambition but also because there were local governors who had not yet been convinced that they should change their loyalty. He campaigned in all seasons of the year, in all kinds of terrain, into what is now Afghanistan and Kazakhstan, Pakistan, and northern India. He founded cities along the way, perhaps as many as eighty in all. Most were small settlements, some did not last, and many survive to this day, such as Samarkand and Tashkent. In Afghanistan he took as his wife Roxane, daughter of a powerful local chieftain. Finally, at the Hyphasis River in northern India, his troops refused to go any farther. Alexander was angry and sulked in his tent for three days but eventually agreed to lead them home. He chose the most difficult route, down the Indus River and through the Iranian desert back to Babylon. A fleet would sail nearby and explore the lands, waterways, and people en route.

He returned to Babylon in 324 to address many administrative problems. A treasurer had absconded with money, and some who had been appointed to high office in various parts of the large empire had proved either incompetent or disloyal. He also faced increasing displeasure among his own officers and men, because they accused him of adopting Persian dress and manners and forgetting his Macedonian heritage. Alexander personally murdered one of his best friends in just such a dispute. His increasing arrogance also alienated Greek allies; he demanded to be worshipped as a god and presumed to give orders to Greek cities on a variety of internal matters. While in Babylon, he took a second wife, the daughter of the late Persian king, and at the same time ordered eighty of his officers to take local Persian noblewomen as wives, and several thousand of the troops also married local women. This was part of his announced plan of *Homonoia*—harmony or brotherhood: He wanted to unite Greeks and barbarians in one empire of universal brotherhood.

In early summer of 323, Alexander became ill after a banquet. It was a usual Macedonian banquet, including heavy consumption of wine. He developed a high fever, which did not diminish, and he became intermittently comatose. He died on 11 June 323. The cause of death cannot be determined with certainty, but it is worth noting that he had suffered several bouts of malaria, had been wounded at least twenty-two times, and was generally physically exhausted. He was not yet thirty-three years of age.

His generals fought over his empire for the next forty years. They named Alexander's feebleminded half brother, Philip III Arrhidaeus, and his infant son by Roxane, Alexander IV, as joint kings, but these two did not survive the initial struggle of the Successors of Alexander. Eventually three major kingdoms were carved out of Alexander's territory: Egypt, ruled by the general *Ptolemy and his successors; Macedonia, ruled by *Antigonus and his successors; and "Asia" (not much more than modern Syria/Jordan/Iraq), ruled by *Seleucus and his successors. These kingdoms lasted for several hundred years.

Throughout the territory conquered by Alexander, Greek language and culture were introduced and remained important for many centuries (until the Islamic conquest in the seventh and eighth centuries A.D.). The city of Alexandria in Egypt became the seat of learning in literature, language, science, and mathematics.

Alexander accomplished so much, traveling more than 25,000 miles in eleven years, bringing most of the civilized world under his power, that he became the model for ambitious men ever since. Few have dared to consider themselves equal to Alexander.

The official histories were well known in antiquity, but none have survived. Fantastic legends began to be circulated almost immediately after his death, so that after a few centuries it was already difficult to determine truth from legend. The *Anabasis of Alexander*, written by *Arrian in the second century A.D., is the best single source of information, and *Plutarch's *Life* of Alexander (late first century A.D.) is also useful.

Bibliography: A.B. Bosworth, *Conquest and Empire. The Reign of Alexander the Great*, 1989; N.G.L. Hammond, *The Genius of Alexander the Great*, 1998.

Janice J. Gabbert

AMBROSE OF MILAN, SAINT (339–397)

Ambrose was a bishop of Milan, an expositor of scripture, and along with *Augustine, *Jerome, and Gregory the Great, one of the four traditional doctors of the Church.

Ambrose was born the second son of the praetorian prefect of Gaul in Augusta Treverorum (Trier). His father died soon afterward, and Ambrose was raised in Rome. He studied Greek and later law, and around 365, he was appointed an advocate to the court of Probus, the praetorian prefect for Italy. He practiced law until he was appointed governor of Aemilia-Liguria c. 370 and lived in its principal city, Milan. In 374, upon the death of its bishop, serious frictions developed in Milan between Arians and Catholics over the election of a successor. When Ambrose entered the cathedral to calm the factions, he was elected bishop against his wishes by popular acclamation. He was a Christian, although a catechumen and unbaptized; however, he was baptized, passed through the successive orders, and elevated to the episcopal see within eight days.

As a bishop, Ambrose rapidly became famous as a diplomat, preacher, teacher, scriptural interpreter, and defender of orthodoxy. As the imperial court frequently resided in Milan, Ambrose could use his influence as both bishop and senator to help sway imperial position. In 390, he imposed public penance on the Emperor *Theodosius I for having punished a riot in Thessalonica by a massacre of its citizens. Events throughout his reign brought him in close contact with several western emperors, including Gratian (375–383) and Valentinian II (375–392). Ambrose defended the autonomy of the Church from secular control and argued that the emperor was a dutiful son subject to the strictures of his bishop. In this manner, Ambrose helped anticipate the medieval understanding of the relationship between Church and state.

In his letters, Ambrose combated both paganism and Arianism and championed Christian morality. Ambrose was perhaps most famous for his sermons, which helped him to win his most notable convert, Augustine of Hippo. Ambrose's classic work *De officiis ministrorum*, based on *Cicero's *De officiis*, is a treatise on Christian ethics, referring specifically to the clergy. His *Commentary on the Gospel of *Luke* was his largest work and was widely disseminated.

Ambrose's knowledge of Greek enabled him to play a large role in transmitting much of Greek theological and philosophical (both pagan and Christian) learning to the West, especially with respect to the works of *Origen, *Philo, *Saint Basil of Caesarea, and the pagan Neoplatonist *Plotinus. Ambrose's *Hexaemeron* (On the Six Days of Creation) is heavily indebted to Saint Basil. Ambrose introduced the West to eastern melodies; he composed hymns himself and can be seen as the father of western hymnology. Ambrose also wrote many ascetic works and helped to encourage the development of monasticism in Italy. Augustine and others perceived Ambrose as the model bishop.

Bibliography: J. Moorhead, *Ambrose: Church and Society in the Late Roman World*, 1999.

Andrew G. Traver

AMMIANUS MARCELLINUS (c. 325–c. 395)

Ammianus Marcellinus was a military officer from Antioch who wrote a history of the Roman Empire in the fourth century.

Ammianus was born in Antioch of a Greek family of comfortable means. He joined the army and by 354 had become a member of the elite corps of officer cadets on the staff of the general Ursicinus. Under his command, Ammianus served at Nisibis, Milan, Samosata, and Amida. He was also present in Amida when the city was besieged and captured by the Persians in 359. Although Urscinus was blamed for the fall of Amida, Ammianus refused to hold him responsible, and his respect for his old commander is a constant theme in his historical narrative of the period. In later years, Ammianus also served under Emperor *Julian in Persia but then seems to have left military service.

He traveled to Rome, where he wrote his history, and seems to have lived there for most of the remainder of his life. He may have been briefly expelled from the city in 384, along with other nonresidents, during a period of food shortage. This would certainly explain his antipathy to many of Rome's noble families, many of whom were regarded by Ammianus as unworthy bearers of their heritage.

Ammianus' history is the last great narrative history of the Roman Empire written in Latin. His account began with the accession of the emperor Nerva (96) and continued until his own time. Unfortunately the first thirteen books of Ammianus' history, down to the year 353, are lost. The extant portions of Ammianus' work give a very full account of the latter part of the reign of Constantius II including the fall of Gallus, the rule of Julian in Gaul, his usurpation and sole rule after the death of Constantius, as well as the reigns of Jovian, Valentinian, *Valens, and Gratian.

His history was published in installments, between the early 380s and the early 390s in Rome. Although a very discursive writer, Ammianus only rarely discusses the emerging influence of the Christian church. A pagan himself, his silence has been taken either as an explicit criticism of the Church or as an implicit rejection of its affairs as not being a fit subject for historical narrative. Ammianus' admiration for Julian certainly emerges from his narrative, as does a guarded and qualified approval for the Emperors Valentinian and Valens. He reserves his most savage censure for the frivolous aristocrats of Rome and the self-seeking courtiers who ruined Ursicinus, his first commander and patron.

Bibliography: J.F. Matthews, *The Roman Empire of Ammianus Marcellinus*, 1995.

William Leadbetter

AMMONIUS (Ammonius Saccas, fl. c. 200–243)

Ammonius was a philosopher who was instrumental in the beginnings of Neoplatonism.

Very little is known of Ammonius, sometimes called Ammonius Saccas. He was a philosopher in Alexandria who left behind no writings and who is known only from secondary accounts of his activities. Among the primary sources that give evidence of him are *Porphyry's *Life of Plotinus* and *Eusebius' *Ecclesiastical History*.

Ammonius is best known as the teacher of *Plotinus, and the two are usually credited as the originators of Neoplatonic philosophy. Plotinus' teachings are known because his student Porphyry collected his master's notes and published them, along with a short biography. But the philosophy of Ammonius survives only in Plotinus' teachings. Thus we cannot be certain what of Neoplatonism was original to Ammonius or what was added by his student.

Ammonius apparently was originally a Christian, but he forsook Christianity in favor of Greek philosophy. His other famous student was the Christian theologian *Origen.

Ammonius' legacy is in the formation of Neoplatonism—the final major development of Greek philosophy in antiquity—and in its establishment as an important school of thought through the writings of Plotinus. But an even more lasting legacy is that as Neoplatonism was adopted by Christian philosophers and theologians, it became the philosophical base of Christianity through the medieval period and in some respects to the present time.

Bibliography: A.H. Armstrong, "Plotinus and the Religion and Superstition of His Time," in *Cambridge History of Late Greek and Early Medieval Philosophy*, 1967, 195–210.

Kent P. Jackson

ANACREON OF TEOS (c. 570–485 b.c.)

Anacreon was a Greek lyric poet from the Ionian city of Teos whose poetry gave rise to the anacreontic tradition.

Only a little is known of Anacreon's life. He and other Teians founded Abdera in Thrace after fleeing from the attacks of King *Cyrus' lieutenant Harpagus on the Greek coast c. 540. Soon after, Anacreon's poetry won him an invitation to Samos by the tyrant *Polycrates. In 522 Polycrates was murdered, and Anacreon found himself in Athens at the request of Hipparchus, son of *Pisistratus. Anacreon quickly gained popularity for his witty poetry on the pleasures of love and wine. Events are less clear after Hipparchus' murder in 514. Anacreon may have remained in Athens. He is reputed to have died by choking on a grape pip.

After his death, Anacreon continued to be celebrated as a poet and as a lover of boys, women, and wine. Anacreon's surviving works are fragments on erotic and "symposiastic" themes. He is credited with the writing of elegiacs, iambics, hymns, drinking songs, and maiden songs. Anacreon is best known for the form that bears his name: a lesser ionic with anaclasis. Both the form and content of Anacreon's poetry were imitated in the *Anacreontea*, a collection of about sixty short poems composed by postclassical Greek writers. From here his influence was felt in Latin writers including *Seneca and Boethius and had considerable impact on European literature from the Renaissance to the nineteenth century.

Bibliography: P.A. Rosenmeyer, *The Poetics of Imitation: Anacreon and the Anacreontic Tradition*, 1992.

Christine Cornell

ANAXAGORAS OF CLATOMENAE (c. 500–428 b.c.)

Anaxagoras is credited with having been an important influence in the intellectual development of *Socrates. Anaxagoras also extends the pluralistic philosophy of *Empedocles and anticipates the atomistic philosophy of *Democritus.

Anaxagoras was born in the Ionic town of Clatomenae, though he did not begin his philosophical activities until after he moved to Athens. In Athens, Anaxagoras acquired the support of *Pericles, who began as Anaxagoras' student. Anaxagoras was later accused in Athens with being an atheist. This charge was lodged at the same time as *Aspasia's (Pericles' *hetaira*) trial for impiety and was clearly politically motivated. According to *Plutarch, the Athenians issued a decree against atheists (c. 433). As a result of the charges against Anaxagoras, he left Athens and settled in the town of Lampascus, though no one knows whether he ever stood trial. Anaxagoras remained in Lampascus until his death in 428, the first year of the eighty-eighth Olympiad.

Anaxagoras' writings are only available in fragments, and these only thanks to the writings of Simplicius, who cites from the one and only book *Plato and others claimed Anaxagoras wrote. Despite the lack of a complete work, enough of the fragments survived to get a sense of his philosophy as a whole; and the key notion in his philosophy is the "seeds," or what is also referred to as the *homoiomeries*. What Anaxagoras attempted to do with this concept was to explain the phenomena of everyday perception while simultaneously maintaining the Parmenidean view that the fundamental elements—Being—are eternal and unchanging. To this extent, Anaxagoras was extending the efforts of Empedocles; however, whereas Empedocles attempted to account for the variety of changing phenomena in terms of four fundamental elements (earth, air, fire, water), Anaxagoras found this approach inadequate. For Anaxagoras, there are an infinite number of "seeds," and in each thing there are all seeds (e.g., hair is hair because it has more seeds than anything else, even though it has traces of all seeds). The process whereby these seeds are ordered and constituted into the various phenomena of nature is carried out by an infinite mind, or *Nous* in Greek. It is this emphasis on mind that would most interest Socrates and eventually Plato, and it is this influence that continues to be one of Anaxagoras' continuing legacies.

Bibliography: G.S. Kirk, J.E. Raven, and M. Schofield, *The Presocratic Philosophers*, 2nd ed., 1983.

Jeffrey A. Bell

ANAXIMANDER OF MILETUS (c. 611–546 B.C.)

Anaximander was the successor and pupil of *Thales. Anaximander is considered to be the first philosopher for whom we have concrete evidence that he attempted to account for the entirety of the cosmos, and the human experience of it, in terms of a principle, or what in Greek was referred to by the term *arche*.

Little is known about the life of Anaximander. We do know that he was from Miletus, that he was a student and successor to Thales; and we know, at least according to the account of *Apollodorus of Athens in his *Chronicle*, that he died shortly after the conclusion of the second year of the fifty-eighth Olympiad (547/546). As was the case generally with the pre-Socratic philosophers, Anaximander was acutely interested in explaining natural phenomena such as eclipses (he is reputed to have predicted a solar eclipse), the making of maps, along with the more abstract speculations more commonly associated with philosophy. As a resident of Miletus, an active trading port in the sixth century, Anaximander likely used the observations of sea travelers to draw what *Diogenes Laertius claimed was the first map.

Anaximander's most significant break with his teacher and mentor, Thales, concerns what each considered to be the fundamental element or principle of the cosmos. For Thales this fundamental element is water, but for Anaximander he raises this first principle to a higher plane of abstraction by referring to it as "the Indefinite." The book in which Anaximander is reputed to have explained this concept is largely lost, and only fragments exist. As a result, we are left relying upon the commentaries of much later writers to determine more specifically what Anaximander argued, and on this there is no consensus. Thus, some argue that "the Indefinite" becomes the ordered cosmos through the play and development of opposites (e.g., hot and cold, light and dark, heavy and light). Hegel would later claim that this key idea in Anaximander's thought anticipates his own development of the notion of dialectical development.

Despite a lack of consensus regarding how the scant fragments of Anaximander's book should be translated, it is nonetheless clear that with Thales and Anaximander the foundations for a new nonmythological tradition of philosophical thought had been laid.

Bibliography: G.S. Kirk, J.E. Raven, and M. Schofield, *The Presocratic Philosophers*, 2nd ed., 1983.

Jeffrey A. Bell

ANAXIMENES OF MILETUS (c. 587–527 B.C.)

Anaximenes was a pupil and a follower of *Anaximander. Anaximenes argued that the basic substance of nature is Infinite Air.

Little is known about Anaximenes. We do know that he wrote at least one book, for *Theophrastus (student of, and successor to, *Aristotle) refers to this book in criticizing Anaximenes. Anaximenes agrees with Anaximander's claim that the underlying principle of nature is one and infinite, but Anaximenes breaks with Anaximander's claim that this infinite one is undefined (i.e., "the Indefinite") and defines it as infinite air. As for how this infinite air gives rise to the changing phenomena of nature, Anaximenes argues that condensation and rarefaction are the two processes whereby infinite air gives rise to distinct, identifiable matter and to the dissolution and decay of this matter. There is some debate as to whether or not Anaximenes later qualified his understanding of infinite air by claiming that there are distinct types of air (e.g., clouds, fire, earth, water). Theophrastus argues that Anaximenes does make this shift, but the evidence to support this claim is based solely upon Theophrastus' claim, which he does not document with citations from Anaximenes' text. Whether Anaximenes does argue what Theophrastus says he does, Anaximenes began to work through problems in a way that would become standard and routine by later philosophers (e.g., the pluralistic philosophies of *Empedocles, *Anaxagoras, and *Democritus). As Anaximenes thus inherits the philosophical problems and approaches of his predecessors (Anaximander and *Thales), so, too, might Anaximenes' successors have inherited his approach.

Bibliography: G.S. Kirk, J.E. Raven, and M. Schofield, *The Presocratic Philosophers*, 2nd ed., 1983.

Jeffrey A. Bell

ANDRISCUS ("Pseudo-Philip," ?–146 B.C.)

Andriscus led a rebellion against the Roman subjugation of Macedonia.

Andriscus is said by the ancient sources to have been of low birth and low station (possibly a fuller and subsequently a mercenary in the army of the Seleucid Demetrius Soter) and to have been a native of Adramyttium in Mysia. In 150–149, claiming to be a son of *Perseus, the last king of Macedonia (defeated 168), receiving enthusiastic popular support in Seleucid Syria and escaping consequent detention in Italy, Andriscus, as "Philip," raised the standard of revolt and sought to reestablish the Macedonian monarchy. He raised support both in Macedonia and Thrace, occupying the former and a section of Thessaly. He defeated and killed the Roman praetor P. Iuventius, a victory that temporarily challenged the notion of Roman invincibility in the eastern Mediterranean and that brought recognition and encouragement from Carthage but was vanquished in 148 by Q. Caecilius Metellus (Macedonicus). Andriscus was taken in chains to Rome and paraded in the triumph of Metellus. His defeat led to the direct Roman administration of Macedonia, if not its annexation as a province.

The accounts of *Polybius and *Livy that might have provided the chief sources of information are mostly lost. The narrative, which may be pieced together from late sources, presents contradictory details.

Bibliography: E.S. Gruen, *The Hellenistic World and the Coming of Rome*, 1984.

Tom Hillard

ANDRONICUS, LUCIUS LIVIUS

See **Livius Andronicus, Lucius**.

ANDRONICUS OF RHODES (fl. first century B.C.)

Greek philosopher and scholar, he directed the Peripatetic school in Athens and prepared the definitive edition of the critical works of *Aristotle.

Between 78 and 47 Andronicus presided over the Peripatetic school in Athens; he also helped edit the scholarly texts of Aristotle, which in turn allowed the Stagrite's teaching to be safely handed down to posterity.

Aristotle's texts, known as "acroamatic" or "esoteric" (i.e., school-lecture treatises), were not intended for a large audience and were circulated little—if at all—after his death; they had been brought to Rome after the conquest of Athens (86) and studied by the Roman grammarian Tyrannion, who supplied Andronicus with accurate copies of them. Andronicus' edition, which also was composed of some works by *Theophrastus, was based on these copies, or perhaps even on some of Aristotle's own manuscripts; it was therefore close to a modern "critical" edition, that is, prepared with philological methodology.

Andronicus' work was instrumental in renewing interest in Aristotle's thought toward the end of the first century B.C. and in its later fortune. However, he probably left out Aristotle's works that were intended for the general public, the "exoteric" works, written mostly at the time of Aristotle's tenure at the Academy and rather well known in the Greek and Roman world, thus contributing to their gradual disappearance. His intention was to provide a complete edition of all of Aristotle's school treatises in order to avoid inconsistencies, gaps, and misattributions and to stress the connections between them. He appears to have grouped certain short treatises on related subjects into larger units, giving these units titles and arranging them first by logical treatises, followed by works on natural philosophy, metaphysics, ethics, politics, and literary theory. In particular, the title *Metaphysics* referred to the collected group of treatises that were positioned "after" (Gr. *meta*) natural philosophy, which included *Physics*; however, the term may also indicate that the search for the first and "highest" principles and causes, the object of primary philosophy, must come "after" the less abstract investigations concerning the physical world and its "lower" causes.

Also relevant to the history of Western civilization is the order of subjects in his edition, because it became the basic arrangement of higher education for eighteen centuries. The edition was followed by an important catalog of Aristotle's writings, in which he listed about a thousand titles, and by an explanation of his editorial method. Andronicus also commented on some Aristotelian works of logic, thus beginning the tradition of Aristotle's commentators.

Bibliography: A.H. Armstrong, "The Peripatos," in *Cambridge History of Later Greek and Early Medieval Philosophy*, 1967, 107–123; H.B. Gottschalk, "Aristotelian Philosophy in the Roman World from the Time of Cicero to the End of the Second Century A.D.," *Aufstieg und Niedergang der römischen Welt* 2 (1987): 1079–1139.

Roberto Plevano

ANTHONY
See **Antony of Egypt, Saint**.

ANTIGONUS I MONOPHTHALMUS (c. 382–310 B.C.)

Antigonus Monophthalmus was a Macedonian general who served in the armies of both *Philip II and *Alexander the Great, and played a prominent role in the wars of the Successors.

Antigonus, who is said to have lost his eye in the service of Philip II at the siege of Perinthos, was left behind by Alexander as satrap of Greater Phrygia in 334 when Alexander advanced into Asia. Antigonus established his authority there by defeating the Persian remnants that had fought at Issus in 333. After the death of Alexander, Antigonus was given all western Asia Minor as the empire was carved up. Almost at once trouble flared up, and Antigonus found himself in a coalition with *Antipater, *Lysimachus, Craterus, and *Ptolemy against *Perdiccas, who had gained control of the two legitimate heirs to the empire. War was avoided when Perdiccas was murdered in 320 when attempting to take control of Egypt.

New arrangements were made at Triparadisus in 320 where Antigonus was given the task of eliminating *Eumenes of Cardia, erstwhile ally of Perdiccas, and the remnants of Perdiccas' army. He inflicted defeats on both camps in 319. The death soon after of Antipater gave Antigonus the same aspiration that had led to Perdiccas' downfall, namely, sole control of the empire. But first he came to terms with Eumenes and joined a coalition against Polyperchon, who had been appointed regent by Antipater over the head of Antipater's son *Cassander. Soon, however, he was back on the trail of Eumenes again, and a final defeat of Eumenes at Gabiene in 316 gave Antigonus control of all the territory between Asia Minor and Iran. Now he was a serious threat to the other contenders. He drove the future *Seleucus I out of Babylon and forced him to take refuge with Ptolemy in Egypt. Although the others opposed him, the die was cast, and Antigonus made his bid to secure control of the entire empire. Like Perdiccas before him, Antigonus struggled to confront the coalition against him. While Antigonus was attacking Lysimachus, his son, the future *Demetrius I of Macedonia was defeated by Ptolemy at Gaza, and Seleucus was making an attempt to recover Babylon. A peace treaty was agreed in the summer of 311 but never implemented. In the same year Seleucus invaded Babylon, and full-scale hostilities resumed.

Throughout the next ten years the general alignment was against Antigonus, but alliances also shifted from time to time. The old Greek world now became the focus of attention as each of the surviving generals tried to present himself as a champion of its liberty. Antigonus and his son Demetrius were welcomed ostentatiously at Athens. In 306 both proclaimed themselves "kings" and were quickly followed in this by Ptolemy and Lysimachus. Finally another coalition formed against Antigonus consisting of Seleucus, Lysimachus, and Cassander. All sides came together at the Battle of Ipsus in 301, in which the Antigonids were soundly defeated, and Antigonus, now in his eighties, was killed.

Antigonus was one of a number of the successors who effectively sealed the division of the empire Alexander left behind. From 320 his attempt to gain total control increased the divisions that emerged as the Hellenistic monarchies. In the end, the weakened Hellenistic world made it easy prey for the emerging Roman Empire.

Bibliography: R.A. Billows, *Antigonus the One-Eyed and the Creation of the Hellenistic State*, 1990.

Karen McGroarty

ANTIGONUS II GONATAS (c. 320–239 b.c.)

He was the son of *Demetrius I Poliorcetes and grandson of *Antigonus I Monophthalmos, one of the generals serving *Alexander the Great. He is aptly called the "second founder" of the Antigonid dynasty of Macedonia that, due largely to his efforts, would rule Macedonia until 167 b.c.

Demetrius Poliorcetes was king of Macedonia from 294 to 287, when he was expelled by a joint invasion of *Lysimachus and *Pyrrhus and died a few years later, in 283. Antigonus II, his thirty-five-year-old son, immediately claimed the title but did not enter Macedonia until 276. These were chaotic years; Antigonus defeated an invasion of Gauls, another incursion by Pyrrhus of Epirus, and then a "revolt" of Athens, the so-called Chremonidean War in the 260s. In this war, Athens was joined by Sparta and several other smaller Greek cities and supported by *Ptolemy II of Egypt. Antigonus was successful in defeating a Spartan army in battle twice, besieging Athens, and after the war was essentially over, he defeated a Ptolemaic fleet near the island of Cos.

He maintained a strong fleet and controlled much of Greece through a system of garrisons in some cities (Athens and its seaport Piraeus, Corinth, Chalcis among them, as well as the fortress Demetrias in Thessaly established by his father) and through friendly relations with local politicians in many other cities. The democracy in Athens continued to function with little hindrance through most of his long reign, except for the period immediately following the Chremonidean War. He was known for his personal friendships not only with political figures but also with leading philosophers in Athens, such as *Zeno of Citium. The largely personal and political nature of his control seems evident in the fact that the loss of the garrison and naval base at Corinth late in his reign had no discernible effect.

He died quietly in 239 at about eighty years of age and was succeeded by his already well-experienced son *Demetrius II.

Bibliography: J.J. Gabbert, *Antigonus II Gonatas: A Political Biography*, 1997.

Janice J. Gabbert

ANTIGONUS III DOSON (c. 263–221 b.c.)

He was the cousin of the previous king, *Demetrius II, who died, leaving a nine-year-old son, *Philip (V), as his heir. Doson was initially regent but soon assumed the kingship in his own name, presumably pending the majority of Philip, who was only seventeen when Doson died suddenly in 221.

He inherited a war between Macedonia and both the Aetolian and Achaean Leagues of Greek cities, both supported by King *Ptolemy II of Egypt. *Aratus of Sicyon, the head of the Achaean League, persuaded Athens (not a member) to pay the Macedonian soldiers in the Piraeus garrison to turn over the fortress to Athens. Piraeus had been in Macedonian control for over sixty years and was a crucial strongpoint for control of Greece. The equally important garrison at Corinth had been lost to Aratus in 243. Despite the loss of the Piraeus, Doson seems to have had considerable success against both leagues. In 224, Aratus and the Achaean League were desperate for help against King *Cleomenes III of Sparta and made an alliance with Macedonia, their previous enemy. Doson's price for his help was that Corinth should be returned to his control. He prosecuted the war against Sparta vigorously and defeated Cleomenes at Sellasia in 222. Cleomenes fled to Egypt, ending any threat from Sparta.

Perhaps the greatest challenge to Antigonus Doson was to maintain and strengthen the Antigonid dynasty of Macedonia. For the first time in almost a century, there was no adult male relative available to assist a young king if the present king should die too soon. He appointed competent advisers and established a more complex hierarchy of officials so that the kingdom could function without the strong personal leadership of an older, more experienced king. The details are unfortunately not known, but there are hints of administrative and bureaucratic arrangements similar to those that had long existed in the Seleucid and Ptolemaic kingdoms.

Antigonus Doson was a caretaker king, an interval between Demetrius II and Philip V of the Antigonid dynasty of Macedonia.

Bibliography: P. Green, *Alexander to Actium: The Historical Evolution of the Hellenistic Age*, 1990; N.G.L. Hammond and F.W. Walbank, *A History of Macedonia*, vol. 3, 336–167 B.C., 1988.

Janice J. Gabbert

ANTIOCHUS I SOTER (324–261 B.C.)

Antiochus was the second king of the Seleucid kingdom and the defender of his realm against the Gauls.

Antiochus was the son of *Seleucus I, the founder of the Seleucid kingdom, and his Bactrian queen Apama. When a nomadic invasion threatened the eastern possessions of the realm, Seleucus appointed Antiochus king in the East (292). In this capacity, he restored some of the damage caused by the invaders and rebuilt several cities.

After his father's assassination in 281, Antiochus succeeded to the entire realm and took his father's young Macedonian widow Stratonice as his own wife. Antiochus, however, was troubled by revolts in Syria and northern Anatolia and a war in the West led by *Antigonus II Gonatas. *Antiochus renounced his father's ambitions in the West and in 278 signed a pact with Antigonus promising not to interfere in each other's territories. That same year 20,000 Gauls invaded Greece and crossed over to Asia Minor. Preoccupied with the pacification of Syria until 275, Antiochus, relying upon the use of Indian elephants, finally defeated the Gauls. As a result of this victory (The Elephantine Victory), the Ionian Greek states praised Antiochus for saving them from the Gauls and hailed him as Soter (Savior).

Antiochus was less successful in his dealings with *Ptolemy II Philadelphus, losing to him in two wars (First Syrian War, 274–271; and the war of 263–261)

Phoenicia and the coasts of Anatolia. These disturbances in the western parts of his kingdom caused the eastern portion to weaken. In 280 Antiochus made his eldest son Seleucus king in the East, but he proved to be a failure. Between 266 and 261 Antiochus became involved in a war with Pergamum that resulted in his defeat and loss of yet more territory. He died soon afterward, leaving his son *Antiochus II as successor.

Antiochus was known as a great city-builder, founding around twenty new settlements within his kingdom. He encouraged Greek immigration into his realm and used many of these new cities as counterweights against the Gauls. He also built cities in Persia to prevent the Parthian threat to his frontier. It also seems that he fostered a revival of Babylonian culture, perhaps as an attempt to diminish Parthian influence. He rebuilt the Esagila shrine at Babylon, and the priest of Bel at Babylon, Berossus, dedicated a three-volume history of Babylon (*Babyloniaca*) to him.

Bibliography: P. Green, *Alexander to Actium: The Historical Evolution of the Hellenistic Age*, 1990.

Andrew G. Traver

ANTIOCHUS II THEOS (287–246 B.C.)

Antiochus recaptured many of the portions of the Seleucid kingdom his father had lost to Egypt.

Antiochus was the second son of his father *Antiochus I and his wife Stratonice. Antiochus succeeded as king upon his father's death (261) and soon followed a policy to reconquer all the Seleucid territory lost to *Ptolemy II Philadelphus. Allied with *Antigonus II Gonatas, Antiochus waged the Second Syrian War (260–252) against Egypt, regaining Phoenicia, and coastal regions of Asia Minor (except Pergamum, Caria, and Lycia). In the city of Miletus, Antiochus overthrew a tyrant and received in return the cult name Theos (God).

In 252, Antiochus reputiated his first wife Laodice and married Ptolemy II's daughter Berenice. When Antiochus died in 246, a civil war erupted between the two queens. He was succeeded by his son *Seleucus II, although another son, Antiochus Hierax, set up a rival kingdom in Asia Minor.

Although Antiochus' reign marks an obscure period in Seleucid history, it appears that he followed in his father's policies of founding cities.

Bibliography: P. Green, *Alexander to Actium: The Historical Evolution of the Hellenistic Age*, 1990.

Andrew G. Traver

ANTIOCHUS III MEGAS (241–187 B.C.)

Antiochus III was the great conqueror of the East who failed in his attempt to challenge growing Roman power in Greece.

Antiochus was the grandson of *Antiochus II, son of *Seleucus II, and succeeded his brother Seleucus III as king. When he became king in 223, separatist movements threatened to tear his kingdom apart. Antiochus first had to establish his position, and once this was accomplished, he sought to expand it. Although he initially had much success in the Fourth Syrian War (219–216), conquering much of Phoenicia and Palestine from Ptolemaic Egypt, after his defeat at Raphia (217), he was forced to cede much of this territory to *Ptolemy IV.

Undeterred, between 212 and 205 Antiochus began his famous eastward campaign, pressing as far east as India. In the process he acquired Armenia and reduced Bactria and Parthia to vassal states. Having acquired a vast system of client states throughout Asia, the Greeks, in imitation of *Alexander the Great, gave him the title of "Great" (Megas).

After the death of Ptolemy IV, *Philip V of Macedon and Antiochus concluded a secret alliance that sought to partition the overseas possessions of Egypt (202). Antiochus then invaded and took possession of Syria and Palestine (202–198). Philip, however, became involved in a war with Rhodes and Pergamum, both of which appealed to Rome for aid. The Romans defeated Philip in the Second Macedonian War (200–196), and Antiochus refused to help him. Rather, Antiochus took this opportunity to march on Egypt proper, turning it into a virtual protectorate.

In 196 Antiochus crossed the Hellespont and occupied Thrace, arguing that his sovereignty over that territory had previously been obtained by *Seleucus I. After lengthy diplomatic negotiations with Rome, Antiochus ignored the demand that he remove his forces from Europe. His position deteriorated in Rome after 195, when he accepted the great Carthaginian general *Hannibal as an adviser.

Antiochus again sought an alliance with Philip V, yet was this time rebuffed. Philip, along with Rhodes, Pergamum, and the Achaean League, allied with Rome. Only the Aetolian League, discontent with Rome's growing influence in Greece, sided with Antiochus and appointed him commander of the League. Antiochus landed in Demetrias and marched into Greece in fall 191. The Romans cut him off from his reinforcements and defeated him at the pass at Thermopylae in the following year. While Antiochus' forces retreated into Asia Minor, the Romans won a naval battle against them and in 190 crossed the Hellespont into Asia.

The Romans now demanded that Antiochus evacuate the portion of Asia Minor west of the Taurus Mountains; when he refused, the Romans met him in battle again at Magnesia (ad Sipylum). Defeated by Lucius Cornelius Scipio (brother of *Scipio Africanus), Antiochus accepted the Peace of Apamea (188). In this agreement, Antiochus surrendered Asia Minor west of the Taurus, gave the Romans an indemnity of 15,000 talents over twelve years, relinquished his elephants and his fleet, and provided the Romans with hostages, including his son *Antiochus IV. The following year, Antiochus was assassinated while trying to obtain tribute in Susa.

Despite his errors of judgment concerning Rome, Antiochus was a very competent military leader.

Bibliography: Green, P. *Alexander to Actium: The Historical Evolution of the Hellenistic Age*, 1990; J. Ma, *Antiochos III and the Cities of Western Asia Minor*, 1999.

Andrew G. Traver

ANTIOCHUS IV EPIPHANES (215–164 B.C.)

Antiochus was a Seleucid Hellenizer whose external policies brought him into conflict with Rome. His internal policies sparked the Maccabean Revolt.

Antiochus was the third son of *Antiochus III. After his father's defeat at Magnesia (ad Sipylum), Antiochus served as a hostage in Rome, where he learned to admire Roman institutions. He became king in 175 and initially faced internal turmoil, rival claimants, and an Egyptian claim to Syria, Phoenicia, and Palestine, all areas conquered by his grandfather. Antiochus repaid the indemnity imposed on the Seleucids by Rome in the Treaty of Apamea (188) and then invaded Egypt to prevent a possible incursion into Palestine by Ptolemy VI. In 169 Antiochus occupied Egypt, with the exception of Alexandria, yet turmoil in Palestine forced him to retreat.

In that same year, *Perseus of Macedon requested aid from Antiochus against Rome, while Ptolemy VI in Egypt sought assistance from Rome against Antiochus. Antiochus invaded Egypt again in 168, while the Romans, led by *Lucius Aemilius Paullus, defeated Perseus at Pydna in June of that year. Outside of Alexandria, the Roman ambassador Gaius Popillius Laenas demanded that Antiochus evacuate Egypt immediately. When Antiochus requested time to consider, Popillius drew a circle around the king with a walking stick and demanded an unequivocal answer before Antiochus left the circle. Antiochus agreed to comply and quit Egypt.

Antiochus was also known as a prominent Hellenizer who founded and fostered cities throughout his realm. His Hellenizing policies, however, brought him into conflict with the Jews. While the Reform party of the Jews favored Hellenization, the Hasideans (Pious Ones) detested it. Antiochus aided the Reform party and urged Hellenization by the construction of a gymnasium in Jerusalem and by introducing the Jews to Greek methods of education. Disturbances in Jerusalem forced Antiochus to take that city by force in 167. He then began a policy of forced Hellenization. He stationed Syrian soldiers in the city, forbade the worship of Yahweh and all Jewish rites, and had an altar to Zeus erected in the Temple. In reaction to this desecration, the leader of the anti-Greek Jews, *Judas Maccabeus, coalesced the Hasideans into a guerrilla-style fighting force and broke into open revolt. Surprisingly, the Hasideans met with much success, defeating several of Antiochus' generals and recapturing most of Judaea by 164. Antiochus had unknowingly helped galvanize the Hasideans into a nationalistic force, and as a result, Judaea would remain an independent state for about a century. Antiochus then launched an expedition out east against the Parthians but died soon after in Iran.

The source tradition remains hostile to Antiochus, largely due to his policies toward the Jews. Nevertheless, he was an able leader and probably could have annexed Egypt if Rome had not interfered.

Bibliography: P. Green, *Alexander to Actium: The Historical Evolution of the Hellenistic Age*, 1990.

Andrew G. Traver

ANTIPATER (c. 400–319 b.c.)

Antipater was a Macedonian nobleman who served Kings *Philip II and *Alexander the Great.

Antipater was already an elder statesman when Philip II defeated the Greeks at Chaeronea in 338. He remained true to Alexander after Philip was murdered in 336. Trustworthy and experienced, he was a wise choice for the position of viceroy when Alexander left for Asia in 334.

In Alexander's absence, Antipater ran the kingdom competently. His biggest challenges were revolts in the Peloponnese and in Thrace. In 324, despite Antipater's commendable handling against these threats, Alexander sent one of his generals, Craterus, back from Asia to replace Antipater. Opposition to Antipater by Alexander's mother *Olympias may explain this move. Alexander died before Craterus could take over, and when a rebellion arose among the Greek cities at the news of the king's death, Antipater and Craterus joined forces to defeat them.

In the aftermath of Alexander's death, Antipater maintained his position in Macedonia. When Alexander's generals began to show signs of aspiring to the kingship, Antipater steadfastly opposed them. But he added to the chaos of this period himself by naming his own lieutenant Polyperchon, rather than his son *Cassander, as his successor. When Antipater reached the end of his long life in 319, Cassander joined forces with other leaders against Polyperchon, and the series of wars between Alexander's successors was perpetuated.

As elder statesman among the Macedonian elite, Antipater was the last link to the old days of the Macedonian monarchy. His death was one of the final blows to whatever slim hopes there might have been of keeping Alexander's empire unified.

Bibliography: W. Heckel, *The Marshals of Alexander's Empire*, 1992.

William Hutton

ANTIPHON (c. 480–411 b.c.)

Antiphon was an Athenian orator, politician, and probably also a sophist. His rhetorical works are among the oldest to survive in any significant quantity.

Antiphon was born in the deme of Rhamnus, located on the coast of Attica. *Thucydides praises him for having the skill both to form good plans and to convince others to follow them. He also claims Antiphon was one of the best advisers about conduct in the law courts and the assembly. He is one of the first people known to have composed speeches for delivery by others, and he probably was also a teacher of rhetoric. In politics, Antiphon participated in the planning of the oligarchic coup of the Four Hundred against the Athenian democracy in 411. After the restoration of the democracy, Antiphon was convicted of treason and executed.

Antiphon's writings can be grouped into three categories: forensic speeches, model speeches called the *Tetralogies*, and sophistic works. The three surviving forensic speeches all deal with charges of murder. The three *Tetralogies* each contain four speeches—two for the prosecution and two for the defense—in hypothetical murder cases that illustrate the different legal arguments that can be used in homicide cases. The sophistic works survive as fragments, and there is some disagreement about whether these works should be attributed to the orator Antiphon or another fifth-century Athenian with the same name.

These writings are important for several reasons. They provide an illustration of two important stylistic devices in Greek rhetoric: the use of antithesis and arguments based on probability. The *Tetralogies* also provide some of the only illustrations of the ways that opposing arguments would be constructed in a case. Finally, they provide valuable information about Athenian beliefs about murder and Athenian homicide law.

Bibliography: M. Gagarin and D.M. MacDowell, trans., *Antiphon & Andocides*, 1998.

Jeff Rydberg-Cox

ANTISTHENES OF ATHENS (c. 445–370 b.c.)

Antisthenes was a Socratic philosopher whose works influenced *Xenophon, the Cynics, and Stoics of the Hellenistic period.

Antisthenes first studied rhetoric under the Sophists, composing two show-speeches in the style of *Gorgias (*Odysseus* and *Ajax*). He later became attached to *Socrates, absorbing his philosophy of virtue. He first met Socrates when *Plato was young but was still with his teacher at his execution. Antisthenes was perhaps the first of the Socratic writers to compose dialogues. His are quite different from those of Plato. Antisthenes often composed short imaginary conversations between figures of mythology (e.g., Hercules, Prometheus, Achilles) or of remote history (*Cyrus the Great), expressing their views in a rhetorical style rather than in Socrates' dialectic.

Antisthenes' interpretation of Socrates' philosophy was also different from that of Plato. In his *Hercules* dialogues, he states that virtue (*arete*) was teachable when a pupil had a teacher with "a Socratic strength." Once truly acquired, this virtue could not be lost and was like a wall that would fortify us against the assaults of life. As with Socrates, an examination of the meaning of words is an important preliminary in learning (*On Education*). However, human learning is useful only in a basic form and would confuse a hero, who must study the divine (*Hercules*). He developed *Xenophanes' concept of the divine: There are many gods by convention but only one by nature (*Physikos*). Unlike Plato, he was poor, unaristocratic, and perhaps illegitimate. Antisthenes thus developed an ethics that placed true wealth in the soul, claiming that he learned from Socrates to espouse the simple life. In logic, he believed that the only method of definition (*logos*) was to say that a concept was itself. To define gold as a yellow metal is mere metaphor. Consequently, it was impossible to refute and deny (*antilegein*) a statement since any negation refers not to the original but to another statement.

Antisthenes' works survive only in brief fragments and summaries. He features in Xenophon's *Symposium and Memorabilia*, where he explains his ethics and love of Socrates. *Diogenes of Sinope knew his works, absorbing part of his ethics. However, unlike the Cynics, Antisthenes did not consider self-sufficiency to mean a renunciation of property on principle.

Bibliography: M. Luz, "Antisthenes' Prometheus Myth," *Cahiers de Philologie* 16 (1996): 89–103; L.E. Navia, *Classical Cynicism*, 1996; H.D. Rankin, *Antisthenes Sockratikos*, 1986.

Menahem Luz

ANTONINUS PIUS (86–161)

Antoninus Pius was the fourth of the "five good emperors" of Rome and reigned from 138 to 161.

Titus Aurelius Fulvus Boionius Antoninus was born in Lanuvium near Rome in 86. His family originated in Gaul (Nîmes), and both his father and grandfather had attained the rank of consul. Antoninus served as quaestor and praetor before attaining the consulship himself in 120. He married Faustina and served in various legal capacities in Etruria and Umbria. He held the office of proconsul in Asia from 133 to 136. Due to his reputation for integrity, Antoninus became a member of the Emperor *Hadrian's *consilium*, his chief advisory body. Upon the death of his assumed successor Lucius Aelius, Hadrian adopted Antoninus and had him adopt both Lucius Verrus and Faustina's nephew, later known as *Marcus Aurelius. After Hadrian's death, Antoninus urged the Senate to consecrate the late emperor. This act, in addition to his own religious devotion, earned him the title Pius (devout).

The twenty-three-year reign of Antoninus was a prosperous and peaceful period for Rome. Revolts in Numidia and Mauretania were quelled, as were uprisings in Egypt and Judaea. Antoninus advanced the British frontier and built an earthen wall as a boundary extending from the Firth of Forth to the Firth of Clyde. Unlike his predecessor, Antoninus did not tour the empire.

Antoninus maintained good relations with the Senate and consulted the *consilium* on all matters of public interest. Upon the death of Faustina (140), Antoninus established the Puellae Faustinianae, a charitable institution for the daughters of the poor.

Antoninus' reign has generally been characterized as a period of well-being. The orator *Aelius Aristides reflects this sentiment in his famous pangyric to

Antoninus (143–144). In his *Meditations*, Marcus Aurelius described Antoninus
as mild, even-tempered, and just.

Bibliography: M. Grant, *The Antonines: The Roman Empire in Transition*, 1994.

Andrew G. Traver

ANTONY, MARC (Marcus Antonius, c. 83–30 B.C.)

Marc Antony was a Roman politician and general remembered primarily as
the lieutenant of *Caesar, lover of *Cleopatra, and rival of Octavian (*Augustus).

Antony was born into a family active in Roman politics. His grandfather had
served as consul and was widely regarded as one of the leading orators of his
age; his father had been commissioned by the Senate in 74 to clear the Mediterranean of pirates. Antony himself pursued the life of a soldier, serving first
in the eastern Mediterranean (57–54) and later joining Caesar's legions in Gaul
(54). Caesar treated him as a valuable lieutenant, depending upon him first while
campaigning against the Gauls and later as his spokesman in Rome. After the
Senate refused to grant Caesar's demand for an extension of his Gallic command, Antony traveled north to support his superior's invasion of Italy (49).
Caesar drew upon Antony's services throughout the ensuing civil war, entrusting
him with a command at the Battle of Pharsalus (48) and afterward appointing
him to govern Rome during his absence. Antony was serving as consul when
Caesar, then dictator, was assassinated in 44; the majority of conspirators wanted
to kill him as well, but *Brutus prevented them from doing so. Antony's attempts to promote himself as Caesar's successor were complicated by the rise
of Octavian, the dictator's eighteen-year-old grandnephew and adopted son. He
spent the remainder of the year trying to identify himself as the champion of
the "Caesarian" party, while Octavian was courted by the opposing Republican
faction. Antony left Rome with several legions at the end of the year to serve
as a governor of a Roman province in southern Gaul.

The Senate, urged by the orator *Cicero, soon declared Antony a public enemy and dispatched several Republican armies to confront him. Suffering serious losses at the Battle of Mutina (43) in northern Italy, Antony withdrew in
apparent defeat. But to the dismay of the senators, Octavian abandoned the cause
of the Republicans and reconciled with Antony. Soon the two generals joined
with *Marcus Lepidus to form a political coalition normally termed the Second
Triumvirate (43). To rid themselves of political opposition and to finance their
armies, they called for the assassination of some 2,300 rivals and confiscated
their property; Cicero was murdered on the special instruction of Antony. While
Lepidus was charged with maintaining order in Italy, Antony and Octavian traveled to Greece, pursuing the Republican forces. In the two Battles of Philippi
(42), Antony defeated the armies of Cassius and then Brutus, effectively ending
the Republican cause. He and Octavian divided the Roman legions and provinces between themselves, greatly diminishing the role of Lepidus in the coa-

lition. From the outset of his agreement with Octavian, Antony clearly was in a stronger position than his young rival, an imbalance that would persist for several years. Antony's power lay primarily in his control of the rich eastern provinces, and there he traveled in 41 to strengthen his position. On this trip he met Cleopatra, queen of Egypt, and soon fathered twins by her (a third child would follow).

Although he solidified his alliance with Octavian the following year by marrying Octavia, his sister, he did not end his relationship with the Egyptian monarch. After renewing the triumvirate in 37, he removed Octavia and their two daughters from his home and then married Cleopatra in an Egyptian ceremony. In order to strengthen his support among the eastern peoples he permitted himself to be deified, and a cult of Antony was initiated. He invaded Parthia in 36, hoping to avenge the failed campaign of *Crassus eighteen years earlier, but the campaign was a complete failure. In the meanwhile, Octavian had taken advantage of Antony's neglect of events in Rome to strengthen his position, and by 33 his supporters were openly criticizing his rival's unpatriotic behavior. Following Antony's divorce of Octavia and the publication of his will (in which he requested a burial in Egypt and recognized his children by Cleopatra as his legitimate heirs), Octavian won a declaration of war against the Egyptian queen; refusing to abandon his lover, Antony supported Cleopatra, thus appearing as a traitor in the eyes of many Romans. He and Cleopatra brought forces to western Greece, but they were besieged by Octavian's army, and at the Battle of Actium they lost most of their force in a desperate attempt to escape to Egypt (31). When Octavian took Alexandria in August of the following year, Antonius committed suicide; Cleopatra followed his example nine days later.

The historical representation of Antony has been subject to great attention and distortion throughout the ages. His enemies accused him of succumbing to many temptations, especially alcohol and adultery, but his apologists faulted a seductive Cleopatra for compelling an honest yet naive man to forget his duties as a Roman citizen and husband. A romanticized relationship between the two lovers has been the subject of many plays (e.g., Shakespeare's *Antony and Cleopatra*, 1606) and movies. The final assessment of Antony is more complicated: He was a talented general and politician, despite personal failings; his greatest mistake was underestimating Octavian, and in this respect he was not alone.

Bibliography: E.G. Huzar, *Mark Antony: A Biography*, 1978; R. Syme, *The Roman Revolution*, 1960.

David Christiansen

ANTONY OF EGYPT, SAINT (c. 251–355)

Antony is regarded in the Christian tradition as the founder of the solitary monastic life; the story of Antony's life had a major impact on the development of Christian monasticism.

Antony was an Egyptian raised in a Christian family who was orphaned at a relatively early age. In his late teens Antony was inspired to sell all his property and live a Christian ascetic life. Placing his younger sister in the care of virgins, Antony lived a life of poverty, charity, and prayer in his own town and traveled to learn the wisdom and virtues of other ascetics. As he began to exceed the abilities of his teachers, Antony yearned for a new challenge and began to live in an isolated tomb where he could dedicate himself entirely to prayer. His decision to remove himself entirely from the larger population inaugurated a new form of Christian ascetic life, called *anchorism* after the Greek word for "withdraw." Ironically, the more Antony sought a life of isolation, the more famous he became. In a series of relocations, Antony traveled further into the Egyptian desert, only to followed by fellow monks and sought by many as both a miracle-worker and a man of wisdom. At a crucial time in the Arian controversy, Antony lent his support to *Athanasius, the archbishop of Alexandria. Athanasius would later compose a *Life of Antony* that would have enormous impact on the development of Christian monasticism. From Antony's own hand we have little other than a collection of seven letters generally regarded as genuine.

The Life of Antony was extremely popular and was quickly translated into Latin. It provided an inspiration for individual conversions to the ascetic life, the most famous being that of Saint *Augustine of Hippo. It also provided a basis for a conceptual (if not actual) division of Christian monastic life into two separate vocations: the solitary and the communal. It is somewhat of a mystery, however, why the story of such a singular person following such a rigorous vocation would be so popular among the Christian population more generally. Perhaps his appeal rested in the fact that Antony could not fully escape the world. He thus remained in service to the needs of others and taught a form of Christian wisdom based on prayer, purity of heart, and equanimity of the soul that could be adopted at least partially by those not inclined to the solitary life.

Bibliography: S. Rubenson, *The Letters of St. Antony. Origenist Theology, Monastic Tradition and the Making of a Saint*, 1990.

Steven D. Driver

APELLES OF COLOPHON (fourth century B.C.)

Apelles was a painter in the court of *Philip II of Macedonia and *Alexander the Great.

Little is known of Apelles' early life. *Pliny the Elder dates him to 332, because of his portrait of Alexander. He was Ionian by birth but studied at Sicyon in southern Greece under the painter Pamphilius.

He became a court painter of Philip II and painted portraits of Philip, Alexander, the various members within their circle, and a self-portrait. He also painted Aphrodite rising from the sea, Calumny, and Alexander with a thunderbolt. He was known for the simplicity of his designs and his sparing use of color; he used a secret varnish to preserve his paintings and soften the colors. He also wrote a book on painting, but this no longer survives.

While none of Apelles' paintings survive today, at least three of his master-pieces were placed on public display at Rome, and many copies of them were made. The descriptions that we have of them today come largely from literary sources such as Pliny.

Bibliography: M. Robertson, *A History of Greek Art*, 2 vols., 1975.

Andrew G. Traver

APOLLINARIS OF LAODICAEA (c. 310–390)

Apollinaris was a bishop and teacher who formulated the heretical Christo-logical doctrine known as Apollinarianism.

Apollinaris was born in Laodicaea of Syria, the son of Apollinaris the Elder, a respected priest and grammarian. He was elected bishop of Laodicaea c. 361. Apollinaris gained early renown for his defense of the Trinitarian doctrines that emerged from Nicaea (325), his staunch opposition to *Julian the Apostate, and his tutelage of *Jerome (later of Vulgate fame). He had a thorough knowledge of Hebrew and wrote biblical commentaries.

In this century of undefined Christology, it was not difficult to fall into heresy, and Apollinaris soon found himself embroiled in controversy. For the bishop, human beings consisted of body, soul, and spirit. The spirit was the rational element that set humans apart from animals. Apollinaris argued that Christ could not have had a human spirit, for human intelligence was limited and could fall into sin. Rather, he asserted that the divine *logos* replaced the human spirit in Jesus. In 374 *Basil of Caesarea opposed this doctrine and brought it before Pope Damasus I. In 377 Apollinaris' formulation was condemned in the Council of Constantinople I. *Gregory of Nyssa wrote a refutation in 385. However, the heresy continued to emerge in various forms through the sixth century.

Bibliography: D. Christie-Murray, A *History of Heresy*, 1989.

Jennifer L. Koosed

APOLLODORUS (fl. 408 B.C.; active 425–400 B.C.)

Apollodorus was an Athenian painter who is attributed with the invention of shadowing, *skiagraphia*.

Few details about Apollodorus of Athens were transmitted through antiquity. He was a native of Athens, but some of his work was preserved in Pergamum during the Roman Empire. Apollodorus was called the *skiagraphos* in reference to his painting, recognized from his time onward for his work with the shadow, his ability to show depth through shading. The technique that he pioneered is now referred to as *chiaroscuro*. *Plato believed that this technique led humans astray in their ability to perceive.

Apollodorus is also said to have been the first to have painted in a manner that could hold the viewer's eyes. It thus appears to some that he had a greater understanding of how humans see and perceive than his predecessors and con-temporaries. He also made advances in representing objects as both individuals and as a class or group. Paintings that ancient writers claim to be his works include both mythical subjects and everyday life: the *Herakledei* and *Alcmene*, Odysseus wearing a cap, Ajax struck by lightning, and a priest praying.

Bibliography: V.J. Bruno, *Form and Colour in Greek Painting*, 1977; J.J. Pollitt, *The Art of Ancient Greece: Sources and Documents*, 1990.

Lisa Auanger

APOLLODORUS OF ATHENS (c. 180–140 b.c.)

Apollodorus was a Greek scholar whose most influential work, the *Chronicle*, provided a systematic chronology for Greek history.

Born in Athens c. 180, Apollodorus was first a pupil of the Stoic philosopher Diogenes of Babylon, later a prominent student of *Aristarchus of Samothrace in Alexandria. Under persecution by Ptolemy VIII in 144, Apollodorus fled to Pergamum, where he dedicated his *Chronicle* to King Attalus II Philadelphus. This work, written in verse form for easy memorization, popularized the chronographic researches of *Eratosthenes and provided a system of dating for the events of Greek history from the fall of Troy (1184) to the time of composition (c. 145).

Two innovations are evident in Apollodorus's *Chronicle*: (1) more accurate dates based on lists of the Athenian magistrates and (2) a system for deriving previously unknown dates of birth and death from the assumption that the most important events and deeds occur at the *acme* of an individual's life—that is, around forty. Other important works of Apollodorus included a twelve-volume commentary on the geographical names included in the Catalogue of Ships in the second book of *Homer's *Iliad* and a twenty-four-volume treatment of Homeric religion called *On the Gods*.

Bibliography: R. Pfeiffer, *History of Classical Scholarship: From the Beginnings to the End of the Hellenistic Age*, 1968.

Michael Anderson

APOLLONIUS OF PERGE (c. 262–c. 190 b.c.)

Apollonius of Perge was a Greek mathematician and astronomer who wrote the definitive work on the conic sections.

Apollonius was born in Perge in Pamphylia but emigrated to Alexandria, where he remained there for most of his life, studying and writing in mathematics and astronomy. Early in his career, Apollonius worked in pure mathematics, authoring *Conics* and at least thirteen other treatises in plane and solid geometry. Later in his life he was better known as an astronomer. He estimated the diameter of the lunar orbit and postulated a system to explain the movements of Mars, Jupiter, and Saturn, which in combination with the established system used for the motion of the inferior planets, Mercury and Venus, resulted in a comprehensive model for the motion of the solar system.

Among the mathematical papers of Apollonius, the most significant is the

Conics, which introduces the terms *ellipse*, *parabola*, and *hyperbola*. The first four books are an introduction to the subject, and the second four expound fully on various aspects and application of the conic sections. The *Conics* is a work so comprehensive and foundational that it served as a primary reference and basis for theoretical developments for centuries.

Bibliography: T.L. Heath, *A History of Greek Mathematics*, 1921.

Michael Labranche

APOLLONIUS OF RHODES (c. 296–c. 215 b.c.)

Apollonius of Rhodes was the author of the *Argonautica*, an epic treatment of the stories surrounding Jason and Medea.

Not much is known about Apollonius' life. He was born either in Alexandria or Naucratis and lived in Ptolemaic Egypt. He was a pupil of *Callimachus of Cyrene, with whom he later quarreled. As a young man, he composed the *Argonautica* and recited it in public, to a less-than-favorable review. For this reason, possibly, he may have retired to Rhodes. While there, he revised his poem and recited it to great acclaim. At some point, he returned to Alexandria, where he may have been the head librarian.

His quarrel with Callimachus, if it in fact occurred, arose from differences of opinion about literature. Apollonius continued in the Homeric tradition of epic, which Callimachus believed needed to be changed to meet the requirements of a new literary sensibility. While the two do exchange some personal barbs in their respective writings, more recent scholarship has indicated that Apollonius quoted Callimachus frequently. One does not, presumably, quote one's enemy.

Because of the importance of the *Argonautica* for later writers, it is worth mentioning the work's structure and content. The epic, unlike *Homer's works, is not unified; instead, it contains a series of episodes. The first and second books tell the history of the voyage to Colchis. The third book is, primarily, about the love of Jason and Medea. The fourth book describes the return voyage. Regardless of Callimachus' opinion regarding the *Argonautica*, later poets enjoyed and borrowed from it. Varro Atacinus translated the *Argonautica* into Latin; it was copied by *Ovid and *Virgil, and in the first century A.D., Valerius Flaccus based his poem of the same name on it.

Bibliography: C. Beye, *Ancient Epic Poetry. Homer, Apollonius, Virgil*, 1993.

Jana K. Schulman

APPIAN (c. 95–c. 160)

Appian, called Appianos in his native Greek, was born at Alexandria and is known primarily for his history of Rome.

Having obtained Roman citizenship, he went to Rome in 116 to commence a legal career. His friendship with *Fronto, the tutor of the future emperor *Marcus Aurelius, brought him to the attention of the emperor *Antoninus Pius, who subsequently made Appian a procurator.

Appian wrote, in Greek, the *Romaica*, a history of Rome in twenty-four books. This history he arranged ethnographically, that is, with books on the various peoples or lands (Celts, Sicily, Hannibal, northern Africa) introduced in order of their conquest by the Romans. This ethnographical organization and treatment of the individual areas of the Empire in isolation from each other, however, prevented him from showing how the Roman Empire grew organically and from paying attention to the chronology of events. Appian's uncritical use of earlier Greek and Roman historians also diminishes the value of his work. Books 13–17 on the Civil Wars, however, are particularly important because he used many sources no longer extant. Appian wrote fairly impartially about the political leaders of these times, particularly the Gracchi.

Appian intended to give his fellow Greeks what he considered important information about Rome. His interest in imperial finance and administration, which is unusual for a historian, led him to insert much social and economic information. Loyal to his native Alexandria, Appian presents the Roman acquisition of Egypt as the climax of her history.

An admirer of Rome, Appian argues that the Romans' fortitude, bravery, and virtue led them to world domination.

Bibliography: A.M. Gowing, *The Triumviral Narratives of Appian and Cassius Dio*, 1992; M. Grant, *Greek and Latin Authors, 800* B.C.–A.D. *1000*, 1980.

Judith Sebesta

APULEIUS, LUCIUS (c. 125–171)

Apuleius authored the *Metamorphoses*, also known as *The Golden Ass*, considered to be the first complete Roman novel extant. The *Metamorphoses* concerns the bawdy misadventures of Lucius, a young man turned into an ass when he experiments with sorcery and restored to human form when he becomes a disciple of the goddess Isis.

Apuleius was born into a prominent family in Madaurus, a Roman colony in northern Africa. He traveled extensively, studying philosophy and language in Carthage, Athens, and Rome, as well as becoming acquainted with religious cults, magical practices, and supernatural tales throughout Asia Minor. After he married a friend's mother, the death of both friend and mother caused Apuleius to be accused of sorcery, a charge he refuted in his *Apologia*. He eventually settled in Carthage, where he was a Platonic philosopher, lecturer, lawyer, and priest of Asclepius.

Apuleius' interest in sorcery is most evident in the *Metamorphoses*, a first-person narrative preoccupied with macabre deeds and stories of witchcraft. However, elements of philosophy, allegory, and religion balance the work despite its seeming preoccupation with dark mysteries. What first appears to be a loose, episodic tale about earthy misadventures can also be viewed as a tightly structured work of art about religious pilgrimage. Although some of the book seems derivative, based on Milesian tales and previous Greek "ass narratives," the central tale of Cupid and Psyche and concluding account of religious conversion seem original. While the *Metamorphoses* was disturbing to St. *Augustine, who was born nearby and who battled competing religions and sorcery during the infancy of Christianity, other readers have delighted in the work's playful prose style and entertaining stories. In addition, writers have been influenced by its treatment of man's physical and religious conversions, and artists have rendered many versions of the Cupid and Psyche tale.

Bibliography: E.H. Haight, *Apuleius and His Influence*, 1963.

Richard Louth

ARATUS OF SICYON (271–213 B.C.)

Araratus was a political and military leader of the Achaean League and his native city of Sicyon for about forty years.

The political life of the Greek world in the third century B.C. was dominated by the great kingdoms established by the successors of *Alexander the Great, leaving little room for action by the nominally independent Greek cities. The establishment of leagues, both the Aetolian League and the Achaean League of cities, was an attempt to gain some influence by the cities and is the first instance of any kind of federalism in Greece. Each league had an organized structure of elected council and executive. Aratus held the chief executive and military office of the Achaean League in alternate years (since the executive was not allowed to be reelected immediately) for several decades.

Since none of the leagues or cities was equal in power to the major kingdoms, it was necessary to maintain alliances; Aratus generally sought to ally the Achaean League with *Ptolemy II of Egypt (who was distant) against the Antigonids of Macedonia (who were the nearer threat). Ptolemy's support was mostly in the form of money.

Aratus succeeded in expelling the Macedonian garrison from Corinth by a stealthy night attack in 243 and added that major city to the Achaean League. He joined forces with the Aetolian League against *Demetrius II of Macedonia and Athens for most of the decade from 239 to 229 when, on the death of Demetrius, he arranged for Athens to pay the Macedonian soldiers to abandon the Piraeus garrison to them. Aratus even supplied some of the money, no doubt with Ptolemy's help, but Athens refused to join the League.

He was at war with King *Cleomenes III of Sparta from 227 to 222 and was forced to seek alliance with Macedonia and hand over Corinth to Macedonia in 224 in order to end the war with Cleomenes. Aratus' last years were consumed with war against the Aetolian League, during which he continued his alliance with Macedonia.

Aratus wrote his memoirs, which have not survived but were known to the historian *Polybius and the biographer *Plutarch, who wrote a short biography.

Bibliography: F.W. Walbank, *Aratos of Sicyon*, 1933.

Janice J. Gabbert

ARATUS OF SOLI (c. 310–240 B.C.)

Aratus is famous for his poem on constellations and weather signs, *Phaeno-mena*.

Aratus' biography is uncertain. He came from Soli (Cilicia) and spent several years in Athens associating with other poets and philosophers, especially Stoics. In 276 he was summoned by *Antigonus II Gonatas, who was a patron of the arts, to his court at Pella (Macedonia), along with other writers. Antigonus had finally claimed his kingdom, strengthened by his defeat of the Gauls at Lysimachia in 277. His invitation to Aratus was probably linked with the king's marriage to Phila, half sister of *Antiochus II of Syria. Aratus possibly later went to the court of Antiochus in Syria to work on a recension of the *Iliad*. It is reported that Aratus died in Macedonia; after his death, a monument was erected to him at Soli, and his portrait appears on coins of that town.

Although a critical edition of the *Odyssey* and a dissertation *On *Homer and the Iliad* are both ascribed to Aratus, he was essentially a poet. Aratus wrote a *Hymn to Pan* (probably celebrating Antigonus' victory in 277), funeral laments, elegies, and epigrams. Smaller works were possibly collected under the title *Catalepton* (a title used later for the collection of miscellaneous poems ascribed to *Virgil). His didactic poems include the *Table*, which dealt with the harmony of the spheres, *On Stars*, and *Medicinal Virtues*, presumably those of herbs or minerals. The most famous of Aratus' works, and the only one still extant, was the *Phaenomena*, which deals with astronomy and meteorology. Aratus derived his astronomical material from *Eudoxus of Cnidos. Aratus' reputation was so enormous as to place him among the great names of this period.

Apart from his influence on *Lucretius and Virgil, we possess Latin translations of his works by *Cicero and *Germanicus.

Bibliography: D. Kidd, int. and trans., *Aratus Phaenomena*, 1997.

Cecilia Saerens

ARCESILAUS (or Arcesilas, c. 316/315–241/240 B.C.)

Arcesilaus was founder of the Second or Middle Academy at Athens. Succeeding as its head in c. 268, he transformed the Old Academy from a Platonist "dogmatic" school into a Socratic sceptical one.

A native of Pitane in Aeolis, he marked a return to *Socrates' dialectic of question and answer, developing a counterbalanced discussion with arguments presented on both sides of every issue but ending in no final judgment. Up to his time, the Old Academy had interpreted *Plato's dialogues as indicating a dogmatic (positivist) theory. He initiated the epistemological debate between the Academic Sceptics and the positivist Stoa under *Zeno of Citium. Arcesilaus argued against the possibility of attaining certain knowledge, even the Socratic one (that one knows that one does not know). He also proposed a criterion of reasonableness (*eulogon*), for choosing between equal possibilities but opting for the apparently most reasonable. On a metaphysical level, his scepticism is derived from Plato's belief in the unreality of the physical world and the impossibility of attaining true knowledge from it. His scepticism may also have been influenced by *Pyrrhon.

Like Socrates, Arcesilaus did not set his philosophy down in writing but placed the Academy at the forefront of sceptical dialectic for the next 200 years. Pyrrhonist Sceptics, from *Sextus Empiricus to David Hume, reused his arguments and methodology.

Bibliography: R.J. Hankinson, *The Sceptics*, 1998; A.A. Long, *Hellenistic Philosophy*, 1974; A.A. Long and D.N. Sedley, *The Hellenistic Philosophers*, 2 vols., 1987.

Menahem Luz

ARCHILOCHUS (fl. c. 650 b.c.)

Archilochus was a Greek elegiac and iambic poet from the Aegean island of Paros. His surviving poems are mostly fragmentary.

Archilochus' biography is derived largely from details in the poems, but this information is not very reliable. There are, however, references in the poems to historical figures and events. For example, a total solar eclipse, probably that of 6 April 648, places Archilochus in the mid-seventh century. In addition, he mentions *Gyges, king of Lydia, who died c. 652, and a friend Glaucus, son of Leptines, who is commemorated in a late seventh-century inscription found on the Aegean island of Thasos.

Many of Archilochus' poems employ first-person narratives and would seem to reflect the poet's personal feelings. He was famous in antiquity for biting verbal attacks on enemies and sometimes friends, an irreverent attitude toward military prowess, as in his poem about abandoning his shield and fleeing the enemy in order to save himself, and seductions of young women. In all likelihood such attacks and attitudes reflect the conventions of Ionic iambic poetry, a genre associated with ribald jesting. Hence, it is probably impossible to construct a historically reliable account of Archilochus' life based on material derived from the poems themselves.

In addition to iambic and elegiac poetry, Archilochus wrote poems in a variety of other meters, including trochaic trimeters and terameters. His most famous poem is the "Cologne Epode," preserved largely intact on a papyrus and first published in 1974. The poem deals with the theme of seduction. His poetry influenced the poets of Athenian Old Comedy and the Roman poets, especially *Catullus and *Horace.

Bibliography: A.P. Burnett, *Three Archaic Poets*, 1983; M.L. West, trans., *Greek Lyric Poetry*, 1993.

Carl A. Anderson

ARCHIMEDES OF SYRACUSE (278–212 B.C.)

Archimedes of Syracuse, one of the great minds of antiquity, was a Greek mathematician and inventor known for his advanced methodologies and heroic role in the defense of his homeland.

Archimedes was born the son of the astronomer Phidias in Syracuse. There are many traditional legends associating him with King *Hieron II and ascribing to him the invention of many machines, and there are several well-documented facts. It is known that he traveled to Egypt, carried on fruitful correspondences with *Eratosthenes of Cyrene and other Alexandrian scholars, managed the defenses of Syracuse, and wrote many books of original mathematics.

Though Archimedes did not consider his mechanical inventions of great importance, he is credited with the discovery and application of some important physical principles. His understanding of leverage enabled him to develop devices for moving heavy weights given only a slight force. It is said that Archimedes used one of his machines to launch a ship singlehandedly. The theory of the lever is discussed in his work *On the Equilibrium of Planes*. The well-known story of Archimedes' naked dash through the streets of Syracuse yelling "Eureka!" is often associated with his discovery of the law of hydrostatics. The *cochias*, or Archimedean screw, is a pumping device that is usually attributed to him. He also made mechanical planetaria, showing the relative motion of the heavenly bodies.

Although Archimedes considered his mechanical applications inferior to his pure mathematics, his facility with devising machines played an important role in the military defense of Syracuse. In 214, the city was besieged by Roman troops under the command of the general *Marcus Claudius Marcellus. On the seaward side of the city, Archimedes deployed engines that dropped stone blocks and lead weight onto the Roman ships and cranes to lift ships from the water. On the landward side of Syracuse the Romans were repelled by powerful, long-range ballistic machines and by the short-range scorpion that discharged missiles through protected apertures in the walls.

Though long frustrated in his attempts to take the city, Marcellus developed an admiration for Archimedes, his adversary. When the Roman attack finally succeeded in 212, Archimedes was killed by an overzealous soldier, contrary to the orders of Marcellus. He was so greatly distressed by the death of his foe that he made arrangements for the care of Archimedes' family and attended to the funerary plans, erecting a tomb inscribed with one of Archimedes' favorite mathematical results.

The scholarly works of Archimedes have had a lasting and profound effect on mathematics. Though many of his works are lost, there are complete texts of ten of his volumes of highly original mathematics. Some of these are *On the Sphere and Cylinder, On Spirals, On Plane Equilibrium, Quadrature of the Parabola*, and *The Method*. The last of these is a communication to Erathosthenes in which Archimedes divulges the procedure he used to generate many of his results. That method is closely related to the ideas central to the development of integral calculus but was not recognized and elaborated upon until the seventeenth century.

Bibliography: E.J. Dijksterhuis, *Archimedes*, 1987; T.L. Heath, *A History of Greek Mathematics*, 1921.

Michael Labranche

ARISTAGORAS (fl. 499 B.C.)

Aristagoras, political leader of Miletus, instigated the revolt of Ionian Greek city–states that precipitated war between Greece and the Persian Empire.

In 499, Aristagoras was tyrant of the important city of Miletus in Asia Minor. While his co-ruler, Histiaeus, was under house arrest in the Persian capital, Susa, Aristagoras fomented a rebellion against Persian overlordship, first in Ionia, along the central portion of the west coast of Asia Minor, then as far afield as the Black Sea and the island of Cyprus. *Herodotus, our chief source for his career, says Aristagoras intended to make up for the Bay of Pigs–like fiasco of a failed attack on government forces on the island of Naxos. He was also likely seeking to exploit the Ionian Greek city-states' ripeness for insurrection to further plans for Milesian dominance in the Aegean region. Aristagoras seized the Persian ships stationed in Ionia, abjured his own autocratic powers as tyrant, and sought assistance in mainland Greece, winning help from the Athenians and the Eretrians (but not, significantly, from the Spartans). After initial successes, including the seizure and burning of the Persian provincial capital of Sardis, the Ionian alliance suffered from internal disputes, lack of financial resources, and the withdrawal of mainland support. In 496, Aristagoras was killed by Thracians during an attempt to consolidate his power in Myrcinus.

The Ionian revolt he had initiated was crushed at the Battle of Lade and the subsequent siege and fall of Miletus in 494.

Bibliography: A.R. Bum, *Persia and the Greeks: The Defense of the West, 546–478 B.C.*, 2nd ed., 1984.

James Holoka

ARISTARCHUS OF SAMOS (c. 310–230 B.C.)

Aristarchus was a Hellenistic astronomer and a proponent of the heliocentric theory.

Two facts enable us to establish Aristarchus' dates approximately. First, in 281–280 he made an observation of the summer solstice. Second, his work *On the Sizes and the Distances of the Sun and the Moon* was published prior to *Archimedes' Sand-reckoner* (c. 216). Aristarchus therefore probably lived in the generation before Archimedes.

All of Aristrachus' works are lost, save for the short treatise *On the Sizes and the Distances of the Sun and the Moon*. This essay is one of the most complex extant Greek texts, as in it Aristarchus uses the principles of geometry and trigonometry in the service of astronomy to determine the dimensions of heavenly bodies. Aristarchus also helped to refine time keeping and the calendar.

Aristarchus is most famous for his hypothesis that the earth rotates on its own axis in an oblique circle around the sun within a spherical cosmos. This cosmos, he postulated, was far greater than anyone had yet imagined. *Cleanthes the Stoic immediately challenged this hypothesis on the grounds that it reduced the earth to a minor satellite of the sun. Aristarchus' heliocentric theory was largely dismissed and followed only in Babylonia but was then abandoned again until Nicholaus Copernicus revived it in the sixteenth century.

The original text of Aristarchus' heliocentric theory is no longer extant, but the fundamental hypotheses can be found in the beginning of Archimedes' work *Sand-reckoner*.

Bibliography: M.R. Wright, *Cosmology in Antiquity*, 1995.

Cecilia Saerens

ARISTARCHUS OF SAMOTHRACE (c. 216–144 B.C.)

Aristarchus, as head of the library at Alexandria, represents the epitome of the tradition of Hellenistic literary and linguistic scholarship.

Aristarchus, a native of Samothrace, after attending the school of *Aristophanes of Byzantium at Alexandria, became tutor of Ptolemy VII and then served as superintendent of the great Library (c. 153–145). His career marks the pinnacle of the Alexandrian scholarly tradition that included *Zenodotus, *Callimachus, and Aristophanes of Byzantium, among others.

Like his predecessors, Aristarchus produced critical recensions of major authors (especially epic and lyric poets). These—as we know of them from references in later scholars, especially the scholiasts—show remarkable learning and bold emendation. Aristarchus' exceptional interest in epic led to specialized treatises on Homeric topics as well as attacks on theories of authorship espoused by other scholars, in particular, those who ascribed composition of the *Iliad* and the *Odyssey* to different authors. As a stated guiding principle, Aristarchus strove "to elucidate *Homer from Homer," to adopt or emend a given reading based on its compatibility with the ethical and linguistic character of Homer's work. Besides producing critical texts, Aristarchus was the first to write extensive commentaries on Homer, *Hesiod, lyric and dramatic poets, and the historian *Herodotus.

Bibliography: R. Pfeiffer, *History of Classical Scholarship: From the Beginnings to the End of the Hellenistic Age*, 1968.

James Holoka

ARISTIDES, MARCIANUS (fl. 125?)

Marcianus Aristides wrote one of the first defenses of Christianity.

A philosopher in Athens before his conversion, Aristides found his training useful when he wrote a treatise to the emperor (probably *Hadrian) on behalf of the new religion. Stoic conceptions of the cosmos color his account of how the world itself bears intimations of the Divine Creator. He also followed a venerable philosophical tradition in rejecting Greek mythology, which attributes such crimes as adultery to Zeus and the other gods. Conversely, Aristides praised his fellow-Christians for their ethical behavior and charitable practices. He concluded with an appeal to the emperor to read the Christian Scriptures for himself.

Although Aristides' treatise was held in respect as late as the end of the fourth century, it was thought to have been subsequently lost. But in the nineteenth century, two translations, differing somewhat from each other, were discovered in Armenian and Syriac manuscripts. These led to the recognition that a Greek version had been known all along, incorporated into *Barlaam and Josaphat*, a medieval Christian novelization of the life of the Buddha. A scrap from a copy of Aristides' original Greek text has since been recovered from an Egyptian papyrus.

Bibliography: J. Lieu, *Image and Reality. The Jews in the World of the Christians in the Second Century*, 1996.

John Quinn

ARISTIDES, PUBLIUS AELIUS (117–c. 180)

Aristides was the most famous of the Greek orators who flourished in the period known as the Second Sophistic (c. 60–230).

Aristides was born in Hadrianotherae in Mysia (Asia Minor). After his education in Athens and Pergamum, he entered on a career as a writer and a "concert-orator." He traveled widely during lecture tours, mainly in the Greek-speaking world, including Egypt. He visited Rome, whose civilization he admired and celebrated in his oration *To Rome*. Chronic ill health precluded a fully active public career. He resided most of his life in Smyrna, with frequent stays at the shrine of the healing god Asclepius in Pergamum.

Aristides' literary output was varied and voluminous, embracing both public and private orations, addresses on historical topics, argumentative essays, and hymns in prose to various gods. Six speeches on *The Sacred* attest to a fervent conviction of his special relationship with Asclepius, who he believed not only restored his physical health but also secured him fame in his chosen field.

Aristides' work, like that of other figures in the Second Sophistic, is an early example of the close and largely successful emulation, in both style and content, of revered classical Attic models, especially *Isocrates.

Bibliography: D.A. Russell, ed., *Antonine Literature*, 1990.

James Holoka

ARISTIDES QUINTILIANUS (third–fourth century A.D.?)

Aristides Quintilianus wrote one of the most complete philosophical and technical treatises in Greek on music.

Nothing is known of his life outside his three books, *On Music*; even his date must be inferred. He mentions a treatise on poetics, which is not extant. His *On Music* begins with the structures of harmony, rhythm, and meter, noteworthy for the detail and comprehensiveness, including matters not extant from or covered by *Aristoxenus. In Book 2, Aristides argues for music as the means of education and therapy for the irrational part of the soul, as philosophy is for the rational part. He associates various kinds of harmonies, rhythms, instruments, and musical syllables with different genders (male, female, and degrees of combinations of both), and he discusses the use of emotional responses to music as a means of creating social harmony as well as healthy individuals. He also compares different societies, characterizing them in relation to their music. His unifying philosophy is based on his belief in corresponding structures in music, the soul, and the universe, using Pythagorean and Neoplatonic principles, mathematical ratio, astrology, numerology, and gender associations.

*Martianus Capella, one of the most popular authors of the Latin Middle Ages, borrowed heavily from Aristides. Aristides' work was also used in the Byzantine east and was probably translated into Arabic. His work has been a basis for the study of ancient Greek music since the Renaissance.

Bibliography: A. Barker, ed., *Greek Musical Writings*, vol. 2, 1989.

Rebecca Harrison

ARISTIDES THE JUST (c. 520–467 b.c.)

Aristides the Just was an Athenian politician during the city's early rise to prominence.

Although he was born of a well-to-do family, Aristides was known for his frugal lifestyle. He came to assembly meetings in little more than a tattered cloak, and when he died, he could not bequeath enough money to pay for his funeral or support his children. He endorsed an aristocratic form of government and found himself in opposition to the more democratically minded politician *Themistocles. In his early career, Aristides gained a reputation as a man of justice. For instance, when a jury was prepared to decide the case of a man Aristides was prosecuting without hearing the defense, Aristides interceded and argued that his opponent should be heard and his rights not violated. For these reasons, he earned the nickname "the Just."

In 490, when the Athenians prepared to resist an invasion of Greece by Persia, Aristides was selected as one of the ten Athenian generals. However, on the day on which he was to assume supreme command, Aristides surrendered it to his colleague *Miltiades, recognizing his superiority in military tactics. The remaining generals followed Aristides' example. Under the generalship of Miltiades, the Athenians defeated the Persians at the Battle of Marathon (490) and saved Greece. Aristides' unit played an important part in the enveloping movement employed by Miltiades. The following year, Aristides was elected archon, the supreme magistracy in Athens at the time. As Aristides continued to gain popularity, Themistocles, his chief political opponent, sought to diminish his influence. He convinced the Athenian people that Aristides wished to become tyrant.

In 483, Aristides was ostracized from Athens for ten years. Three years later, however, as Greece faced another invasion by Persia, Aristides was recalled. Aristides rendered useful service in the Panhellenic defense against the invaders and commanded the Athenian forces at the Battle of Plataea (479). After the battle, Aristides played an important role in mending a quarrel between the Spartans and Athenians and in establishing commemorative ceremonies for the battle. As the Greeks pursued the Persians back toward Asia, they became disaffected with the heavy-handed leadership of the Spartans. Impressed with the tact and diplomacy of Aristides and by the Athenians' recent successes, the allies approached the Athenians and asked them to assume supreme command. In 478, the Delian League was established, a confederacy consisting of Athens and most of the Greek islands of the Aegean Sea, whose primary goal was to prevent future aggression by Persia. Aristides was asked to assess the contribution that was to be made by each state. For his equitable assessment and honest administration, Aristides became internationally recognized as a man of integrity.

Aristides died approximately ten years later. Over the next several decades, the Delian League was transformed from a loose confederation of independent states to a sham for Athenian imperialism. The separation of Athens and Sparta into distinct spheres of influence eventually led to the Peloponnesian War. In subsequent years, writers would hearken back to the days of Greek cooperation during the Persian Wars, recall the gentlemanly politics of the aristocratic Aristides and the democratic Themistocles, and idealize the simple justice of a politician like Aristides.

Bibliography: P. Green, *The Greco-Persian Wars*, 1996.

Luis Molina

ARISTOMENES (c. 650 b.c.?)

Aristomenes was the first recorded freedom fighter in Greek history. He led his people, the Messenians, in a daring but unsuccessful revolt against their Spartan overlords.

Messenia had been conquered by the neighboring Spartans sometime before 700 b.c. In the second generation after this conquest, perhaps around 668, Aristomenes arose as the leader of a Messenian rebellion. His army was defeated by the Spartans at the Battle of the Great Trench, but following this defeat the rebels took refuge in the mountain fortress of Eira and continued a campaign of guerrilla warfare for several years. Eventually, the Spartans succeeded in capturing the fortress and the rebellion ended, whereupon Aristomenes escaped with his life and made his way into exile. He died on the island of Rhodes, in the course of gathering support for another rebellion.

The accounts we have of Aristomenes possess a number of fabulous and miraculous elements, and it is possible that many parts of his story (including some of the basic facts recounted above) were invented as propaganda after the Messenians were finally liberated from Sparta in 369. Still, it is unlikely that Aristomenes was wholly fictional.

Bibliography: P.A. Cartledge, *Sparta and Lakonia: A Regional History, 1300–362* B.C., 1979.

William Hutton

ARISTOPHANES OF ATHENS (c. 445–385 B.C.)

Aristophanes was a comic poet whose plays provide the earliest record of comic drama in Western culture.

The comedies that Aristophanes wrote define "Old Comedy." The spirit of this comedy involved political awareness and criticism of issues and personalities before the public. His plays tend to the exuberant, the satirical, and the obscene—all attributes that identify the drama performed at the Great Dionysia in the fifth century. His topics generated controversy; he clearly felt that the Athenian presence in the Peloponnesian Wars was questionable, and several of his plays are antiwar in nature. In addition, he satirized and, to some extent, censored famous people and their scandals, popular entertainment, and methods of education. In the first five of his extant plays, he focuses on *Cleon, a politician. In addition, in the *Clouds*, he satirizes *Socrates; in the *Frogs*, he pokes fun at the tragic poet *Euripides.

Unlike the tragic poets, Aristophanes did not have to use historical or mythical tales as the basis of his dramas; he could invent his plots, and in fact, he often tended to the fantastic. In addition, the tone of the comedies is far less formal than that of the tragedies, allowing allusions to famous people and expressions of the poet's own personal authority. He first won the prize for comedy in 427, but this play is no longer extant. However, eleven of his forty to sixty plays are extant: *Acharnians* (425), *Knights* (424), *Clouds* (423), *Wasps* (422), *Peace* (421), *Birds* (414), *Lysistrata* (411), *Women at the Thesmophora* (411), *Frogs* (405), *Women at the Assembly* (392), and *Wealth* (388). He won first or second prizes for all of the above-mentioned plays with the exception of the *Clouds*, *Lysistrata*, and *Women at the Thesmophora*.

Aristophanes' earlier plays make copious use of the chorus; in fact, the titles of eight of the extant plays come from their respective choruses. He also uses a structural device called *parabasis* that allowed him to insert himself into the drama by means of the chorus. This digression allowed the poet to voice his concerns, to ridicule his enemies, and to generate controversy. His last two plays, however, do not belong in the category of Old Comedy. The role of the chorus has diminished; Aristophanes has eliminated most, if not all, of the *parabasis*; and the humor is no longer found in biting satire but in what might be called situational comedy.

Bibliography: D. Slavitt and P. Bovie, eds., *Aristophanes*, vol. 1, 1998; L. Spatz, *Aristophanes*, 1978.

Jana K. Schulman

ARISTOPHANES OF BYZANTIUM (c. 257–180 b.c.)

Aristophanes was head of the Alexandrian Library and a very learned scholar in the fields of textual criticism, linguistics, and science.

Aristophanes of Byzantium was the immediate successor of *Eratosthenes as the superintendent of the great research library at Alexandria. As a textual critic, he made distinct improvements on the work of his predecessor *Zenodotus in his editions of the *Iliad* and the *Odyssey*. He also produced the first proper critical editions of *Pindar, *Aristophanes, and *Menander. In the area of evaluating and classifying ancient poets, his tabulations (with those of his student and successor *Aristarchus of Samothrace) were instrumental in the evolution of the Alexandrian canon of writers. Shortened versions of his introductions to several tragedies by *Sophocles and *Euripides survive the "hypotheses" prefixed to later editions of these works.

In addition to his textual criticism, Aristophanes also compiled a lexicon canvassing vocabulary in both prose and verse works, drawing on and advancing earlier work in Zenodotus' *Glossai* and *Callimachus' *Onomastikon*. Finally, he was the author of a scientific treatise, "On Animals," influenced by *Aristotle and *Theophrastus.

Bibliography: R. Pfeiffer, *History of Classical Scholarship: From the Beginnings to the End of the Hellenistic Age*, 1968.

James Holoka

ARISTOTLE OF STAGIRA (c. 384–322 b.c.)

Aristotle was a Greek scientist and philosopher whose philosophical acumen and rational research into the natural world originated fundamental doctrines in the fields of logic, biology, physics, psychology, metaphysics, theology, literature, aesthetics, ethics, and politics.

Born on the island of Stagira in 384/383, he was the son of Nicomachus, physician to the Macedonian king Amyntas II. In 368/367 he went to Athens and enrolled in *Plato's Academy, where he studied and lectured for twenty years until Plato's death (348/347). From Athens he moved to Assos in the Troad and married Pythias, daughter of the local ruler Hermias, who was later executed by the Persians. In 345 Aristotle went to Mitylene in Lesbos, where he met *Theophrastus, who was to become his most famous disciple. In 343/342 Aristotle was put in charge of the education of the thirteen-year-old prince of Macedonia, Alexander, who was to become known to posterity as *Alexander the Great. When Alexander became king (336/335), Aristotle returned to Athens, where he founded his own school, called either the Lyceum, after the name of a garden consecrated to Apollo Lyceus where the school was located, or Peripatos, because of the custom of its members of conversing while walking up and down the covered ambulatory. The school had a structured organization, offered regular lectures, and possessed a rich library. When Alexander the Great died (323), Aristotle left Athens and went to Chalcis to spend his last days. He died in 322/321 at the age of sixty-three.

In the classical world, Aristotle was better known for dialogues and works that he wrote while still at the Academy. These writings, called "exoteric," were intended for a large public and were written in a highly polished literary form. However, only a few fragments of them survived. Aristotle's enduring influence on many areas of knowledge is mainly due to the "acroamatic" or "esoteric" works he composed for the instruction of the Peripatetic students. These treatises were written in difficult technical language and were not intended for public circulation; Aristotle never organized them as finished projects. The classification, edition, and commenting on these writings was later undertaken by *Andronicus of Rhodes in the first century B.C.

Aristotle's great contribution to logic, which for him is preliminary to every science, is the analysis of the reasoning of human thought and the definition of the rules of correct demonstration, that is to say, the inference of a conclusion—conveying some truth—from a set of premises. Of his six logical treatises, grouped in later times into a collection called *Organon* (i.e., "instrument"), the *Categories* deals with the classification of terms denoting (i.e., "predicating upon," according to the meaning of the verb "categorize" in Greek) the main kinds of realities, which can be either substances—the first of the categories—or accidents, such as quality, quantity, place, and so on; the material covered here would today pertain to semantics. The *De Interpretatione* considers the combination and separation of these terms into propositions: *Truth* and *falsity* refer not to simple terms but only to propositions, which can be either universal or particular, positive or negative, necessary or impossible. The *Prior Analytics* illustrates the principles of demonstration: Three propositions form a proper reasoning, which is called a syllogism, whereby the first two act as premises, whereas the third follows as the rational conclusion. The *Posterior Analytics* considers the conditions under which the syllogism gives true knowledge, which has its beginning in procedures of induction from sensible things. The *Topics* deals with dialectical reasoning, which originates from premises that are merely probable and not scientifically defined as true or false. The *Sophistical Refutations* illustrates many examples of fallacious arguments, which have the same structures of valid demonstrations or dialectical procedures but represent analytical errors.

Aristotle's vision of the unity of all knowledge is at the core of his all-encompassing division of the sciences into those that consider natural realities and those that treat human actions and productions. The first group, the speculative—or theoretical—sciences (Physics, Psychology and Biology, Mathematics-Astronomy, Metaphysics), have their foundation in the known things and view knowledge as such as their ultimate end, while the second group, the practical (Economy, Ethics, and Politics) and productive (Aesthetics and Theory of Literature) sciences, has their foundation in the agent and aims at courses of action and productions.

The science of Physics—mainly exposed in the *Physics*—has its beginning in objects perceived by the senses and, according to the principles expounded in the *Categories*, determines the existence in the universe of a plurality of substances and accidents inhering in the substances. Contrary to the Eleatic claim, change for Aristotle is real and is firstly explained as the succession in time of contrary accidents within an underlying substance. The example is of a man acquiring knowledge of music from a previous state of ignorance; the man (substance) is the subject of a change, which is the acquisition of musical knowledge from a previous state of privation of that knowledge. Furthermore, changes can be substantial, that is, from one substance into another, and in this case the underlying subject is matter itself, and what is acquired is the form, by which a substance is such as it is: Every physical substance is a composite of matter and form; examples of substantial changes are generation (a substance's coming to be) and corruption (a substance's ceasing to be). Matter and form are also said to be the intrinsic causes of any given physical substance, while the extrinsic acting principle of change is called the efficient cause, just as a father is the efficient cause of his child's generation, and the final end of a change is called the final cause, as a person's well-being is the final cause of medication; these four causes account for everything that happens in the universe. Change is found in all the categories of reality: It is a movement from an anterior to a posterior state; it is therefore properly defined as the motion from potentiality to actuality. In the category of quality this motion is alteration; in the category of quantity, increase or decrease; in the category of place, locomotion; and so on. Change/ motion can be measured according to the "before" and "after": This measurement is time. Space is continuous and infinitely divisible, and so is time, though it is only through the indivisible "now"—which has no duration—that the different parts of time can exist. Motion and time are eternal but cannot be infinite: Aristotle does not admit the existence of any infinite other than the potential one of a magnitude infinitely divisible. Every motion comes from another motion and causes further motion; this process is not, however, infinite but originates from one eternal moving agent, which is the first and necessary cause of the circular movements of the celestial objects. Drawing on earlier astronomical observations, and arguing that circular regular movements have no contrary, Aristotle conceives of the heavenly bodies as unchangeable and imperishable.

In the treatise *On the Soul*, which gives the main outlines of Aristotle's psychology, the soul is defined as the form of any natural body capable of life. It is therefore one of the two inseparable constituents of any composite living substance, matter, to which it gives actuality. The soul governs all the faculties of living beings: nutrition and growth (vegetative powers), senses and movement (animal powers), and thought, which is, or should be, peculiar to humans. Knowledge—a change—is the actualization of this human power, in the sense that the part of the soul that knows, the mind, becomes in some way identical with the known object, which can be a material substance, or else a form abstracted from matter: In the latter case the mind achieves perfect knowledge and reveals itself to be separated from matter and is therefore eternal, attributes that seem to contradict the earlier definition and are close to Plato's view of the soul.

The *Metaphysics*, a collection of material on the highest theoretical science, which Aristotle calls either primary philosophy or theology, opens with the famous remark that all men by nature desire to know; knowledge, however, although it has its starting point in individual material substances, must deal primarily with their first principles, namely, the forms in their actuality. The metaphysical science, as it is concerned with being as such, taken in its widest meaning, reaches perfection when examining the separate substances. These are pure, immaterial forms, immovable, unchangeable, and without potentiality, whose very essence, unlike the Platonic Ideas, is actuality. The immaterial forms are the first causes, which, unlike the universals, are capable of knowing themselves as the only possible objects of knowledge: They are thinking of thinking. Since they possess the life that consists of self-contemplation, the separate substances move the universe as objects of love, thus acting as final causes.

In his works on Ethics, the *Nicomachean* and the *Eudemian Ethics*, Aristotle begins with the fact that men usually act in view of some good. This observation introduces the necessity of a science having as its object the many benefits of human actions and their coordination. Political science, also treated in the *Politics*, determines that the good of the individual is the good of the city, since man is by nature social. The political implication of this statement is that the state exists for the good of the citizens. Thus, a moral person is first of all a good, law-abiding citizen. When man's activity is ruled consistently by reason, he lives in accordance with virtue and can enjoy the pleasure and happiness (Gr. *eudaimonia*) found in the correct activity of the soul. Aristotle also wrote an influential treatise on poetry and art, the *Poetics*, most of which has survived, in which he analyzed the main characteristics of the Greek tragedy and examined its psychological effects on the audience, namely, the arousing of pity and fear and the purification (Gr. *katharsis*) of these emotions through dramatic representation.

Aristotle is one of the most enduring authoritative influences in Arabic and Western civilization.

Bibliography: J.L. Ackrill, *Aristotle the Philosopher*, 1981; J. Barnes, M. Schofield, and R. Sorabji, eds., *Articles on Aristotle*, 4 vols., 1975–1979, W.D. Ross, *Aristotle*, 5th ed., 1964.

Roberto Plevano

ARISTOXENUS (c. 370 b.c.–?)

From Tartentum in Italy, Aristoxenus is best known for his theoretical musical writings. However, he also was a philosopher, biographer, and historian credited with writing at least 453 works. The main source for his life and works is the tenth-century historical and literary encyclopedia the *Suda*.

Aristoxenus studied music with his father Spintharus and Lampon of Erythrae before traveling from Italy to Greece, where he studied under the Pythagorian school prior to joining *Aristotle's Lyceum. Although he expected to be the successor of Aristotle, Aristotle chose *Theophrastus. This decision apparently caused a rift between Aristoxenus and Aristotle. Nothing is known about his activities nor his death after 322.

Extant writings credited to Aristoxenus include incomplete works on music, *Harmonics* and *Rhythmics*, and fragments of ethics and biographies. Titles of additional works and brief quotations from them are found in the works of later writers, such as *Plutarch and *Aristides Quintilianus.

Aristoxenus' theoretical writings on harmony and rhythm have been influential in understanding music theory. His reduction of musical principles to mathematical and philosophical terms provides the basis for understanding Greek music. His description of rhythm expressed in ratios abstracted from the words, melodies, and dance movements appears to be the first statement of this relationship.

Bibliography: L. Pearson, *Aristoxenus: Elementa Rhythmica*, 1990.

Roger W. Anderson

ARIUS (c. 256–336)

Arius was a Christian priest of Alexandria who formulated the heretical doctrine known as Arianism.

Many discrepancies exist about the details of Arius' early life. He was probably born in Libya and educated at Antioch. He was ordained a deacon in Alexandria but later excommunicated for his schismatic views in 311. He was reinstated in 313 and made priest in Alexandria in charge of a church named Baucalis. Here he was renowned both for his preaching and his ascetic lifestyle. Arius, however, disagreed with Alexander, the bishop of Alexandria, on the nature of Christ. Arius emphasized the created, finite nature of Christ and reportedly taught that since Christ was created by God the Father, he was therefore less than God, although higher in creation than man. Alexander censured Arius in 318 and then convened a synod of bishops that excommunicated and banished him in 321.

Arius succeeded in popularizing his opinions by publishing the *Thalia* (Banquet), a theological treatise that explained his position both in poetry and prose. Arius also gained some episcopal support, most notably in the person of *Eusebius of Caesarea. When the issue of Arianism began to divide the Church, the Emperor *Constantine convened the first ecumenical council of the Church, the Council of Nicaea, in 325. This Council decreed that Christ was begotten, not made, and stipulated that Christ was of one essence with the Father. When Arius refused to sign the conciliar decrees, he was anathematized and banished.

Due to the influence of Eusebius and Constantine's daughter Constantia, Arius was recalled from exile in 334. He presented a compromise formula, and Constantine ordered the current bishop of Alexandria and the champion of orthodoxy at Nicaea, *Athanasius, to receive Arius back into communion. When Athanasius refused to comply, Constantine exiled him to Gaul for insubordination. Arius returned to Constantinople, where he collapsed and died on the streets shortly before his reconciliation.

Apart from the *Thalia*, Arius seems to have written very little. The *Thalia* only survives in fragments, and most of what is known about Arius' life was written by critics. However, Arianism persisted and spread to many of the Germanic tribes by *Ulfila, an Arian missionary and apostle to the Germans.

Bibliography: W. Sumruld, *Augustine and the Arians*, 1994.

Andrew G. Traver

ARRIAN (Lucius Flavius Arrianus, c. 95–c. 175)

Arrian was a Roman military and administrative leader and a historian.

Arrian was born in Nicomedia in Bithynia. His early life and career were as a Roman military officer whose success brought him to the attention of *Hadrian, who elevated him to senatorial rank and then legate of Cappodocia. He successfully directed the defense of his province from the invasion of the Alans.

Early in Arrian's life he studied with *Epictetus and published notes he had taken of Epictetus' lectures (*Discourses* and *Manual* [*Encheiridion*]). However, Arrian preferred to think of himself as a historian using *Xenophon as his primary model. He apparently thought himself as being in the company of other historians such as *Herodotus and *Thucydides. His *Anabasis *Alexander* and *Indica* are based on writings from some involved in the campaigns such as *Ptolemy I and Aristobulus, since the events occurred 500 years before his time. As governor of Cappodocia, he wrote military tactics books, *Tactical Manual* and *Order of Battle against the Alans*, and a navigational work, *Periplus Ponti Euxini*. Arrian also wrote two lost local histories, *Bithynica* and *Parthica*.

Arrian used various firsthand sources for his works with additional stories to make the narratives more exciting. His writings exhibit a tendency to be more concerned about presenting a readable style than accuracy in his presentations. Thus, while his presentations are interesting and provide insight, especially into military maneuvers and tactics of the day, the material should be read with caution.

Bibliography: A.B. Bosworth, *A Historical Commentary on Arrian's History of Alexander*, 1980–.

Roger W. Anderson

ARSACES I (c. 247–? B.C.)

Arsaces was chief of the Parni and founder of the Parthian kingdom in eastern Iran.

The origin and rise of the Parthians under Arsaces have been obscured by fragmentary and uncertain evidence. The Arsacid dynasty traced its genealogy to the Achaemenid *Artaxerxes II, but this is a traditional way by which a new dynasty legitimates itself. Arsaces was once regarded as a legendary figure, but a recently discovered inscription from Nisa mentions a descendant of the nephew of Arsaces, confirming his historicity.

Some traditions claim that Arsaces was a governor in Bactria, though this is uncertain. In any case, Diodotus, the satrap of Bactria, rebelled against the Seleucid kingdom in 239 and founded the Bactrian kingdom. A year later, in 238, Arsaces led a revolt against Andragoras, the Seleucid satrap of Parthia and Hyrcania who appears to have already asserted his independence from the Seleucid kingdom, perhaps by 247, the traditional founding of the Parthian kingdom. Nisa possibly served as the capital of Arsaces; under later kings the capital was moved to Hecatompylos. Arsaces expanded his domain to include Hyrcania. He repelled a campaign by *Seleucus II in 228. The end of Arsaces' reign is uncertain. He was succeeded by his brother Tiridates, who reigned until 211. Each of the succeeding Parthian kings took Arsaces as a throne name, further complicating the chronology of the dynasty.

Bibliography: M. Colledge, *The Parthians*, 1967.

Ronald A. Simkins

ARTAXERXES I MACROCHEIR (r. 464–424 B.C.)

Artaxerxes helped stabilize the Persian Empire internally and finally negotiated an end to hostility with Athens in the Peace of Callias (449).

The Persian emperor *Xerxes was murdered in 465. According to *Ctesias, although not the most reliable source, there was a battle between brothers before Artaxerxes emerged victorious to assume the throne. *Plutarch, one late source for the reign of Artaxerxes I, reports him to be an honorable and fair emperor. It is widely held that Artaxerxes I began a policy of encouraging more authority for court eunuchs and advisers—a tradition perhaps behind the tales of the biblical Nehemiah. The most important events under the reign of Artaxerxes I for which we have information are the revolts in Egypt—the first under "Inaros" (put down by the general Megabyxos) and the second initiated by the Persian warrior Megabyxos himself before reconciling with Artaxerxes. Artaxerxes I is most likely the monarch in the famous biblical accounts of Ezra the Priest and Nehemiah the wall-builder of Jerusalem, although some scholars dispute this in favor of one of the latter monarchs who carried the same name. It is now considered likely that the wall building of Nehemiah (c. 445–440?) was part of a Persian campaign to reinforce loyal military outposts on the western front facing both Egypt and the Mediterranean, especially following the Inaros Revolt.

In 449, Athens sent representatives to Susa to negotiate an end to the long conflict between the Greeks and Persia. Although Artaxerxes had earlier attempted to instigate conflict between Sparta and Athens, recent Athenian victories in Cyprus by *Cimon made the negotiated settlement acceptable to both parties. There are no major notices in the sources on further conflict until the very end of the reign of Artaxerxes, when there is some suggestion that he was once again in contact with Sparta.

Bibliography: J.M. Cook, *The Persian Empire*, 1983.

Daniel Smith-Christopher

ARTAXERXES II MNEMOM (c. 436–358 B.C.)

Although Artaxerxes succeeded both in thwarting his brother Cyrus II's rebellion and repelling Spartan forces in Persia, his reign led to a period of decline within the Persian Empire.

Darius II's second son, Cyrus, assumed command in the West in 408 and built up an army of Greek mercenaries to march against his brother, Artaxerxes II. Part of this campaign was recorded by *Xenophon in his famous *Anabasis*. Having assumed the throne already in 405/404, these later battles were to determine the sole rule of the Persian Empire. Despite the apparent success of the mercenary armies, Cyrus was killed c. 401, and Artaxerxes II ruled without rivals from that time on. The drama leading up to this quiet time, however, is complex, although our lack of information about the eastern sections of the empire suggests that Artaxerxes II's attention was justifiably always directed west.

Pissouthnes, sometime satrap of Sardis, had himself revolted against Persian rule and engaged in dealings with the Greeks under Darius II. The son of Pissouthnes, Amorges, also revolted in 414, forcing Darius II to send the ill-fated Tissaphernes to deal with Amorges. What resulted was a series of internal struggles between rival Persian satraps and their Athenian and Spartan partners— alliances that changed easily and quickly when the occasion demanded flexibility. It was as late as 387/386 that Artaxerxes II was able to secure peace with the Spartans, which returned Cyprus, and much of the lucrative Asian Greek cities, to Persian control. Artaxerxes II, however, was never able to regain a restive and independence-minded Egypt, despite numerous campaigns and attempts. In the last years of his reign, Artaxerxes II faced a massive revolt among most of his western satrapies, but the revolt was betrayed by Orontes, who was placed at the head of the revolt only to turn to Artaxerxes II in hopes of securing leadership in the West.

The reign of Artaxerxes II was one in which bribery, betrayal, and shifting loyalties were the order of the day, and Persian power was never so important as the well-placed Persian bribe.

Bibliography: J.M. Cook, *The Persian Empire*, 1983.

Daniel Smith-Christopher

ARTAXERXES III OCHOS (c. 359/358–338/337 B.C.)

Through the execution of his brothers and the reconquest of Egypt, Artaxerxes III was able to restore the power of the Persian Empire.

Artaxerxes III was commander of the King's armies for some years before the death of *Artaxerxes II and his own rise to the throne. Artaxerxes III is generally held to be a ruthless ruler who carefully eliminated all threats to his power. He demanded that the restive western satrapies disband their private armies, but occasional revolts took place in the West nonetheless.

By 352, Artaxerxes felt free enough from internal disputes to launch a new western offensive apparently aimed at restoring full Persian rule over Egypt. However, the western Mediterranean revolted, prominent among them the city of Sidon, led by King Tennes. Thus some scholars refer to the "Tennes Revolt." Although Tennes tried to surrender, he was executed, and many citizens of the city of Sidon committed suicide rather than submit to the Persian rule. After putting down a revolt in Cyprus, Artaxerxes III then moved on Egypt. His military advisers Mentor and Bagoas are credited with the great victories in Egypt by 343, but it was Bagoas himself who later murdered Artaxerxes III and all his sons save one, Arses, who also failed in his attempt to remove Bagoas. In the end, Bagoas was killed by a certain Kodomannos, who claimed descent from Darius II.

Bibliography: J.M. Cook, *The Persian Empire*, 1983.

Daniel Smith-Christopher

ARTHUR
See **Riothamus**.

ASPASIA (fl. fifth century B.C.)

Aspasia was the *hetaira* (mistress) of the statesman *Pericles and a woman of renowned intellectual ability.

Aspasia came from the Greek Anatolian city of Miletus; she came to Athens in the 440s and lived with Pericles from about 445 until her death in 429. She quickly became famous for her intellectual bearing. She conversed with *Socrates, and *Plato once jokingly gave her credit for writing Pericles' speeches.

Around 440, Aspasia bore Pericles a son, also named Pericles. Because the elder Pericles had sponsored a law in 451 that limited citizenship to only the offspring of Athenian citizens, his son was excluded from civic participation. After the death of his two other sons in the Plague of 430, Pericles requested and received the enfranchisement of the younger Pericles.

The scandal involving Pericles' relationship with Aspasia was enormous. She was frequently the object of attacks, especially by the comedic stage, which were often politically inspired. *Plutarch reports many of these assaults; Aspasia was accused of inciting Pericles to start the Samian War (444–439), which arose due to a conflict between Samos and her native Miletus. *Aristophanes later charged her for provoking the Peloponnesian War as well. Aspasia was also once charged with impiety; however, Pericles defended her successfully.

While some contemporaries criticized her private life and public influence,

Aspasia's friendship with Socrates allowed her to be remembered and immortalized by *Aeschines, *Antisthenes, and Plato.

Bibliography: D. Kagan, *Pericles of Athens and the Birth of Democracy*, 1991.

Andrew G. Traver

ATHANASIUS OF ALEXANDRIA, SAINT (c. 295–373)

Athanasius, the bishop of the powerful see of Alexandria in Egypt, was one of the main architects of the Nicene Creed.

Born sometime near 296, he was educated in Alexandria and attached himself to the service of the bishop, Alexander, becoming his deacon and secretary. He attended the Council of Nicaea in 325 at which the Emperor *Constantine addressed the controversial doctrine of the Alexandrian priest *Arius. In 328, Athanasius succeeded Alexander as bishop; he increasingly saw how the dynasty of Constantine and his successor Constantius was veering away from the complete condemnation of Arius. He soon became a prominent symbol of opposition to this imperially sponsored theology and was deposed by ecclesiastical enemies at the Council of Tyre in 335, on the grounds of unbecomingly violent suppression of opposition factions in Alexandria.

He returned from exile on the death of Constantine in 337 but was soon forced to flee from Alexandria and took refuge in Rome, where he was received as a champion of orthodoxy. From this time onward he gained the constant support of the western churches, who protected him and followed his career with interest.

In 346 the western emperor Constans pressed upon his unwilling colleague Constantius the case for Athanasius' return and rehabilitation, but though he came back to Alexandria in 346, he was soon exiled again by the eastern emperor. This time he stayed in the Egyptian desert in hiding, where he fostered his relations with the growing monastic movement whose early hero, *Antony, he publicized in a widely influential "*Life*."

On the death of Constantius in 362 he returned once more to the city but was exiled soon afterward by *Julian. On that emperor's unexpected death in 363, he was able to return to his followers in Alexandria in the following year, and with the exception of another short exile in 365–366, he retained his political and ecclesiastical hold on the city. There he worked in his later years to assemble a coherent international group of eastern "Nicene" theologians, bringing in finally those who had regarded the main trend of the Nicene faith as correct but had balked at the precise terms used. In a synod in Alexandria in 362, Athanasius made a striking move to harmonize the different parties of the anti-Arian alliance by agreeing that the precise vocabulary was not as important as the reality of consensus in a Christology that was organized around the idea of the full deity of the Logos incarnate. Even so, he managed to secure his own vocabulary. His work in creating a more widely based "Nicene party" was taken to its pitch by the generation of Cappadocian theologians that came after him, especially *Gregory of Nazianzus, *Basil of Caesarea, and *Gregory Nyssa. The policy came to fruition with the accession of *Theodosius I as emperor in the East who, after entering his capital and summoning the Council of Constantinople in 381, established Nicene orthodoxy as the subsequent standard for the churches. Athanasius had spent his life in this cause but did not live to see the effects of his labors. He died in Alexandria on 3 May 373.

Bibliography: T.D. Barnes, *Athanasius and Constantius*, 1993; F. Young, *From Nicaea to Chalcedon*, 1983.

John A. McGuckin

ATHENAEUS (fl. 200)

Athenaeus was a Greek writer who compiled a polymathic imaginary dialogue among some of historical educated men including the physician *Galen and the jurist *Ulpian.

Other than the fact that he was from Naucratis and worked in Alexandria after the death of *Commodus, probably during the reign of Alexander Severus (222–235), little is known of the life of Athenaeus. Athenaeus' *Deipnosophistae* (Banquet of the Learned) survives in just one manuscript, the *Codex Veneto Parsiensis* (probably tenth century). The dialogue is written with influences of the style of several writers, beginning apparently with an imitation of *Plato's *Phaedo*. Replete with information and trivia that would otherwise be lost to the modern reader, Athenaeus' work probably originally comprised thirty books; these have survived as fifteen. Athenaeus provides us with information about as many as 700 writers who would be otherwise unknown and is one of the most important sources for Middle and New Attic Comedy. In addition, since an enormous amount of gastronomic trivia is preserved through the writings of Athenaeus, it is fair to consider him the author of the oldest cookbook. In addition to the famous *Deipnosophistae*, Athenaeus wrote a history of the Syrian kings and an essay on a fish, the *thratta*. Athenaeus seems to have influenced later writers such as *Macrobius.

Bibliography: C.B. Gulick, int. and trans., *Athenaeus, The Deipnosophists*, 1961.

Lisa Auanger

ATTALUS I SOTER (269–197 B.C.)

Attalus I established the Attalid dynasty in Pergamum, while his foreign policy played a central role in drawing Rome into Asia Minor.

Attalus was the third ruler of the independent principality of Pergamum, assuming authority in 241 upon the death of his cousin Eumenes I. After his defeat of the Tolistoagii Galatians in 238, Attalus took the title of king and transformed Pergamum into a monarchy and the protector of Hellenism in Anatolia. To maintain and expand his kingdom, Attalus pursued a very active foreign policy aimed at undermining the power of both the Seleucids and Antigonids. Although he married a Seleucid princess, Attalus tried to cultivate an entente cordiale with Ptolemaic Egypt. He intervened in Seleucid affairs during the War of the Two

Brothers (239–236) and expanded his frontiers at their expense. Attalus also always held Antigonid motives and maneuvers in the deepest suspicion, and he allied with the Aetolian League against *Philip V in both the Social War (221–217) and the First Macedonian War (215–205). Along with the island of Rhodes, Attalus worked to thwart Philip's designs on the Aegean Sea and eventually convinced Rome to intervene forcefully in Greece. He collaborated closely with Rome to achieve final victory, but he died shortly before the war's end.

Beyond raising Pergamum to a regional power, Attalus made his city a center of the Hellenistic world. With 200,000 volumes, Pergamum's library was second only to Alexandria's and owed, in part, its creation to the efforts of the Platonic Academy and the Aristotelian Lyceum at Athens. The city also boasted numerous temples, gymnasia, and a theater. Attalus encouraged competition between royal factories and private enterprise that promoted efficiency. Pergamene parchment and textiles represented standards of excellence. Attalus personally sponsored many artistic endeavors such as the famous sculpture, *The Dying Gaul*, which commemorated his victory over the Galatians. The mathematician *Apollonius of Perge dedicated his *Conics* to Attalus.

While Attalus made Pergamum a power with which to be reckoned, he accomplished this only by encouraging Roman intervention in his sphere of influence. The immediate benefits of a Roman alliance were eventually canceled in 133 when Rome annexed the Attalid kingdom.

Bibliography: R.E. Allen, *The Attalid Kingdom: A Constitutional History*, 1983.

Cyril M. Lagvanec

ATTICUS, TITUS POMPONIUS (110–32 B.C.)

A wealthy Roman equestrian banker with extensive property in Epirus, *Cicero's brother-in-law and closest friend, Atticus was an Epicurean and rejected politics.

Atticus lived in Athens from 85 to the mid-60s. He was a friend and financial supporter of many prominent politicians, including *Lucullus, *Brutus, *Clodius, *Marc Antony, and *Octavian/Augustus. *Nepos in his *Life* testifies that he was universally loved for his friendly, circumspect character. His daughter married *Agrippa and was the mother of Vipsania Agrippina, wife of *Tiberius. As a good Epicurean, he remained friends with Cicero's worst enemies, Clodius and Marc Antony, even at the most vicious moments of those relationships, such as the proscription of Cicero by Antony. Cicero's letters to him were published in A.D. 55 and survive, but his own letters and other writings, including a short *Annals* of Rome, long used as a textbook, and a commentary on Cicero's consulship, are lost.

His library and its copyists functioned as the first known Roman publishing house and published Cicero's works. His freedman Q. Caecilius Epirota was *Gallus' friend and later gave lectures on *Virgil's *Aeneid*.

Bibliography: D.R. Shackleton-Bailey, ed., *Cicero, Letters to Atticus*, vol. 1, 1999.

Robert Dyer

ATTILA (r. c. 435?–453)

Attila, king of the Huns and ruler over a vast but temporary empire across central Europe, destabilized Roman power.

The Huns were unknown in Europe before 376, when, arriving in central Europe, they forced many Goths to enter east Roman territory, precipitating the Emperor *Valens' defeat at the Battle of Adrianople (378). Several Hunnic kings, perhaps ruling individual bands, are attested during the next few decades. They occupied central Europe north of the Danube, subjugating many tribes, including the Gothic ancestors of Theodoric, and according to legend ruled a vast area of northern Europe. Attila and his brother Bleda succeeded their uncle Rua as rulers. In 444 Attila murdered his brother. He provided military aid to the western half of the Roman Empire (cf. *Aetius) but waged war and negotiated extortionate treaties with the East. In 451 he turned against the West, under the pretext of internal conflicts at the western imperial court of Valentinian III and among the Frankish tribes on the Rhineland. He undertook a devastating raid of cities in Gaul but was defeated by Aetius with the assistance of the Goths of Toulouse (cf. *Alaric, *Euric). In 452 Attila raided northern Italy but withdrew before advancing south, because of disease among his troops and an eastern imperial assault on Attila's base north of the Danube. While in Italy, Attila had received a Roman embassy that included Pope *Leo I; later Western writers attributed Attila's departure to the pope's intervention. In 453, Attila died suddenly, either of a hemorrhage or murdered by a newly wed wife. His empire collapsed almost immediately, split by his quarreling sons and rebelling subject tribes.

Attila's was the first of several central European empires, founded by nomads, that threatened the medieval West. He was remembered chiefly in saints' legends, for the role of saints (including Geneviève of Paris) and of Pope Leo in repelling his attacks on Gaul and Italy.

Bibliography: E.A. Thompson, *The Huns*, 1996.

Andrew Gillett

AUGUSTINE OF THAGASTE, SAINT (Aurelius Augustinus, 354–430)

Augustine was a bishop of Hippo, autobiographer, and theologian.

Augustine was born in 354 in Thagaste, a small city in the Roman province of Numidia in north Africa. His father, Patrick, was a town councilor of modest means; his mother Monica, a Christian who served as a constant reminder of Christianity for her son. Augustine's prospects as a boy would have been poor if a local dignitary named Romanianus had not provided him with the classical education essential for political and social advancement in the late Roman Empire. Educated at Thagaste, Madouros, and Carthage, Augustine taught rhetoric at Thagaste, Carthage, and Rome (383); in 384 he obtained a post as professor of rhetoric in Milan with the help of Symmachus. Hoping to obtain the

governorship of a Roman province by an advantageous marriage, he sent away
his concubine of several years and the mother of his son, Adeodatus (d. 390).

At war with his professional ambitions, however, was Augustine's desire for
wisdom, which he encountered through a series of "conversions." These began
with his introduction to *Cicero's *Hortensius* and continued with his exposure
to Manicheism (cf. *Mani) in Carthage. Considered a heretical sect by the
Church, Manicheism was a dualistic religion that explained the origin of evil as
resulting from a primeval battle between Light and Dark. For about nine years,
the Manichee explanation of evil in the world satisfied Augustine, but he eventually became disillusioned with the sect and left their circle. Soon after, Augustine stumbled across the Neoplatonic works of *Plotinus and *Porphyry,
translated into Latin by Marius Victorinus. These provided a view of the universe that he never entirely rejected, even after his conversion to Christianity.
His move to Milan introduced him to *Ambrose, the bishop of Milan, the first
Christian whom he could respect intellectually and whose sermons opened up
the spiritual interpretation of the Bible for him. In 386 Augustine finally converted to Christianity, and he was baptized on Easter Day of 387.

Augustine then retired from professional life, and he and friends returned to
north Africa to establish a monastic community. While traveling through the
town of Hippo, Augustine was acclaimed priest. He remained there for the rest
of his life, first as priest and then as bishop of Hippo (395), taking part in the
doctrinal controversies of the day. Toward the end of his life, Augustine experienced the stresses shaking the Roman world in the fifth century. In 410 Rome
was sacked by the Goths, a traumatic event to most Romans. Augustine wrote
his *City of God* partly to counter accusations that Christians were somehow
responsible for the disaster. In 430 the Vandals ravaged Hippo, and Augustine
died of a sudden fever in the same year.

Augustine was the most influential theologian on medieval Christianity. He
achieved this influence by the sheer volume of his writings (Isidore of Seville
once said that anyone who claimed to have read all of Augustine's works was
a liar) and the profundity of his thought. His *Confessions* (c. 397–400) was a
moving and dramatic autobiography, making Augustine one of the best-known
figures in late antiquity. *On Christian Doctrine* provided Christians with a
method of employing classical learning in the interpretation of the Bible. Many
of his theological opinions were developed through his participation in a series
of doctrinal disputes over the nature of Christianity and the Church. He criticized
the Manichee explanation of the origin of evil in the world, coming to see it as
a result of Original Sin. He also battled the Donatists, who outnumbered Catholics in North Africa. The Donatists contested the purity of bishops who had
handed over holy books to Roman authorities during the Great Persecution under
*Diocletian (303–305). In their view, the sacraments dispensed by these bishops
and any priests ordained by them were invalid and indeed harmful. Augustine's
answer was to work out a theory of sacraments that defined them as belonging
to Christ and as unaffected by the purity of the priest. He also supported the

group's suppression by force. The final major debate in his lifetime was over the views of *Pelagius, a lay ascetic from Britain who taught that it was possible and necessary for human beings to strive toward perfection in the Christian life. Augustine tried to refute Pelagius by further developing the doctrine of Original Sin. Because of the dead weight of sin inherited from the first human parents, humans were unable to achieve perfection in this life. In fact, they could not even begin the search for God and salvation without the gift of grace from God, which was distributed according to a divine plan. Augustine's teachings on grace and free will were to have great influence during both the Middle Ages and the Reformation.

Bibliography: P. Brown, *Augustine of Hippo*, 1967; H. Chadwick, *Augustine*, 1986.

Kimberly Rivers

AUGUSTUS (63 B.C.–A.D. 14)

Augustus, first emperor of Rome, was responsible for the establishment of the principate.

Gaius Octavius, known as Octavian, was born on 23 September 63 to Gaius Octavius and Atia, *Julius Caesar's niece. Involved in public life from an early age, he gave his grandmother Julia's funeral oration at age twelve and accompanied Caesar in his triumphal procession in 46. In 44 Caesar died, naming Octavian his heir. Renamed Gaius Julius Caesar Octavianus, Octavian formed a triumvirate with *Marc Antony and *Marcus Lepidus. On 1 January 42 Caesar was officially deified, and Octavian and Antony set out to avenge his murder. That same year, Octavian vowed to construct a temple to Mars Ultor (Mars the Avenger) if he and Antony defeated Caesar's murderers *Brutus and Cassius at the Battle of Philippi (42) in Macedonia, which they did.

To cement their alliance further, in 40 Antony married Octavian's sister Octavia. Octavian also tried to accommodate *Sextus Pompey by marrying his relative Scribonia. However, the very day his only daughter Julia was born, he divorced Scribonia in order marry *Livia Drusilla. Already mother of the future Emperor *Tiberius and pregnant with a second child, Livia divorced her husband and married Augustus in January 38. This year Octavian officially changed his *praenomen* (personal name) from *Gaius* to *Imperator* and used the name Imperator Caesar Divi Filius (Emperor Caesar son of the God).

Octavian represented himself on coins as an army leader who espoused basic Roman values and chose Apollo, a god who stood for discipline and morality, as his patron deity. Antony sent a letter to Rome in 32 divorcing Octavia. Exasperated, Octavian had Antony's will, which provided for his lover *Cleopatra and their two children, read aloud. In response, the inhabitants of Italy and the provinces swore an oath of individual allegiance to Octavian, who declared war on Cleopatra alone, allowing him to avoid the appearance of initiating a civil war. In 31 Octavian was voted consul for the third time, a position that he held continually through 23, and in September 31 defeated the combined forces of Antony and Cleopatra in a naval battle at Actium, following which they committed suicide in Alexandria early in 30. Octavian promptly celebrated a triple triumph in 29 for his conquest of Illyricum, his victory at Actium, and the annexation of Egypt.

On 13 January 27 Octavian went before the Senate and renounced all his powers and provincial authorities. The Senate convinced him to remain consul and to take over the proconsulship of Spain, Gaul, and Syria for a period of ten years. This placed him in charge of the bulk of Rome's armies, further solidifying his position. On 16 January 27 he was given the name Augustus and declared the Republic had been restored and began referring to himself as Princeps, which he translated as "first among equals." In 23 Augustus abdicated the consulship but was granted tribunician power for life.

In the late 20s Augustus became increasingly concerned with establishing a dynasty. In 25 Augustus married Julia to his first intended heir, Marcellus, who died in 23. In 21 he married her to *Agrippa, who died in 12. Augustus adopted his grandsons Gaius and Lucius as heirs in 17, but they died in 4 B.C. and A.D. 2, respectively, leaving only Tiberius, whom he officially adopted in A.D. 4.

Between 18 B.C. and 12 B.C. Augustus passed several important laws. In 18 the *Lex Julia de adulteriis* made women criminally liable for adultery, and the *Lex Julia de maritandis ordinibus*, affirmed by the *Lex Papia Poppaea* in A.D. 9, provided incentives for procreation. In 12 B.C. Augustus became the head of the state religion when he was named *pontifex maximus*, or chief priest of Rome, and in 2 B.C. he was given the title *pater patriae*, father of his country.

These accomplishments were reinforced by visual propaganda that proudly proclaimed the role that Augustus had played in leading Rome to the Pax Augusta, or Augustan Peace. He also reinforced his moral legislation by portraying families together on prominent public monuments such as the *Ara Pacis Augustae*. He placed portraits of Rome's famous ancestors in the forum bearing his name surrounding the Temple of Mars Ultor. Augustus died on 9 August 14 at Nola, leaving behind an account of his accomplishments known as the *Res Gestae Divi Augustae*. In this work Augustus explains how he found Rome a city of brick and left her a city of marble, laying the foundations of the Roman Empire.

Bibliography: K. Raaflaub and M. Toher, eds., *Between Republic and Empire: Interpretations of Augustus and His Principate*, 1990; P. Zanker, *The Power of Images in the Age of Augustus*, 1988.

Katrina M. Dickson

AURELIAN (Lucius Domitius Aurelianus, c. 215–275)

Aurelian was the Roman emperor from 270 to 275.

Aurelian was probably a native of the Balkan peninsula. He had established himself as an army officer under Emperor Gallienus (253–268), and by 260, Aurelian and his friend Claudius had become his chief officers. When Gallienus was assassinated (268), Claudius succeeded him as Emperor Claudius II Gothicus (268–270). Claudius died of the plague soon afterward, and the troops elected Aurelian emperor. Aurelian defeated Claudius' brother in battle (270) and then tried to restore Roman authority to Europe.

Aurelian first turned back Vandal invaders of Pannonia and then expelled the Juthungi from northern Italy, forcing them across the Danube. He returned to Rome and ordered the construction of a new wall around the city (Aurelian Wall) to protect it from tribal incursions.

In 271 Aurelian marched to the east and defeated the Goths. Due to security concerns, he evacuated the old Roman province of Dacia and resettled its populace south of the Danube. He then set his sights on Queen *Zenobia. For the past few years, she had ruled over an eastern kingdom consisting of much of Asia Minor and Egypt with its capital at Palmyra. He defeated the Palmyrene forces, captured Zenobia, and Palmyra surrendered. When Palmyra revolted again in 273, Aurelian destroyed it.

In the following year, Aurelian turned westward to confront the rival emperor Tetricus who governed areas of Spain, Gaul, and Britain. Aurelian defeated his forces at Châlons, and Tetricus was later captured. Having seemingly reunited the Roman Empire, Aurelian received the title *Restitutor Orbis* (Restorer of the World). Aurelian marched east again in 275 against Persia but was murdered by his soldiers in a military coup.

In his short reign, not only did Aurelian restore the empire, but he also instituted a reform of coinage and increased the distribution of free food to the poor. He was an adherent of the cult on the Unconquered Sun (*Sol invictus*) and was said to have wanted to make it the universal religion of the empire.

Bibliography: R.L. Fox, *Pagans and Christians*, 1987.

Andrew G. Traver

AURELIUS, MARCUS (121–180)

Marcus Aurelius was a popular emperor of the second century most remembered for embracing Stoic philosophy as expressed in his personal notebooks called the *Meditations*.

Emperor from 161 to 180, Marcus Aurelius was born to the wealthy Domitia Lucilla and given the name Marcus Annius Verus, the same as that of his grandfather from Baetica, who raised him after his father's early death. A favorite of his paternal relative *Hadrian from an early age, at fifteen Marcus was engaged to Ceionia Fabia, the daughter of Hadrian's adoptive heir Lucius Aelius Caesar. Marcus became an imperial heir in 138 when Hadrian ordered his second adoptive heir, *Antoninus Pius, to adopt both Marcus and Aelius' natural son Lucius, which resulted in a new name for Marcus: Marcus (Aelius) Aurelius Verus Caesar. That same year Hadrian died, and Marcus' first engagement to Ceionia was canceled in favor of a new betrothal to Antoninus' daughter, Annia Galeria Faustina, also known as Faustina Minor.

Marcus received the best education available as a youth and was especially influenced by *Fronto and by *Epictetus. Though he is usually labeled a Stoic, Marcus' *Meditations*, a modern name given to his personal journals, also reflect the influences of both Platonism and Epicureanism. Faustina bore several children, some dying in infancy, and when Marcus succeeded to the throne on 7 March 161 they had a family of four children and Faustina was pregnant again. Marcus immediately requested that the Senate elevate his adoptive brother Lucius to the status of co-emperor. Marcus took the name of Antoninus, and Lucius assumed Marcus' previous name of Verus. Two Augusti reigned for the first time in Roman history, but Marcus, as *pontifex maximus*, was considered the senior.

All was well in Rome with Lucius Verus betrothed to Marcus' eldest daughter Annia Aurelia Galeria Lucilla and twin sons born to Faustina, but trouble brewed on the frontiers. During the winter of 168 when the emperors were at Aquileia dealing with the Danube problems, plague broke out, causing their departure in January 169. On this journey, Verus had a stroke and died, leaving Marcus to spend the rest of his reign dealing with border problems alone. His victories in Germany and Sarmatia are celebrated on a huge sculpted column built by *Commodus after his father's death abroad in 180. Marcus' long association with the imperial family from an early age was commemorated in numerous portraits, including several as a youth and the famous equestrian portrait that now stands at the center of the *Campidoglio* in Rome on a base designed by Michelangelo. Marcus is most famous for being a militarily powerful yet merciful philosopher–emperor.

Bibliography: A.R. Birley, *Marcus Aurelius*, 2nd ed., 1987.

Katrina M. Dickson

AUSONIUS, DECIMUS MAGNUS (c. 310–393)

Ausonius was a writer, politician, and teacher in the school of Bordeaux.

Ausonius was born in Bordeaux, the son of a doctor. His career teaching grammar and rhetoric in a local school lasted for three decades, until he was summoned to the imperial court (in Trier) in the mid-360s. He served as tutor to the emperor Valentinian I's young son and heir Gratian. When Valentinian died, in 375, Gratian ascended the throne, and Ausonius' fortunes rose correspondingly. As courtier, praetorian prefect, and then consul, he played a significant role in the imperial administration. In 379 he returned home in retirement.

Most of the biographical details are known from Ausonius' own writings, which span much of his life. They consist of: letters (to such luminaries as Symmachus, Petronius Probus, and *Paulinus), a prose panegyric of Gratian, and much and various poetry (including verse epistles, epigrams, catalogs, obituaries, a wedding ode, and most well-known, the *Mosella*, about his experiences on the river on which Trier stood). His works provide much important information for contemporary social history, and they attest to Ausonius' Christianity as well as his interest in and attention to the long-standing pagan traditions.

Bibliography: H. Sivan, *Ausonius of Bordeaux*, 1993.

Mark Gustafson

B

BACCHYLIDES OF CEOS (early fifth century B.C.)

Bacchylides was a Greek lyric poet and a rival of *Pindar.

Little is known about his early life. He was born on the island of Ceos and was the nephew of *Simonides, the poet to *Hieron I, tyrant of Syracuse. Bacchylides lived for some time at Hieron's court and may also have lived in Macedonia and the Peloponnese. He probably died around the time of the outbreak of the Peloponnesian War.

Apart from fragments of verse, Bacchylides' work was little known until 1896. In that year, Sir Frederic Kenyon discovered a well-preserved papyrus in Egypt that restored a considerable portion of Bacchylides' poetry. Of his twenty-one partial or complete poems, fourteen are epinician (odes commisioned by victors at the major athletic festivals), and seven are dithyrambs (originally choric songs in honor of Dionysius). Other fragments include portions of paeans, hymns, and encomia.

Ode 5 can be dated with certainty, as it is an epicinian ode to celebrate the victory of Hieron in the horse race at the Olympian games of 476. Bacchylides celebrated Hieron's victories in the Pythian horse race in 470 and the Olympian chariot race of 468 in Odes 4 and 3, respectively. Bacchylides' penchant for epinician odes apparently brought him into conflict with Pindar, who is thought to have made disparaging remarks about him.

Bacchylides' style is simpler than that of Pindar, and he often uses narrative. Many of his poems deal with subject matter familiar to people living in the various parts of the Greek world. One fragment deals with the rescue of *Croesus in Lydia. Two Odes (18 and 19) treat the civic hero of Athens, *Theseus. Ode 18 is unique in the history of Greek poetry as it is the only known dithyramb taking the form of a dialogue between the chorus and their leader.

Bacchylides was among the last important lyric poets of fifth-century Greece.

Bibliography: A. Burnett, *The Art of Bacchylides*, 1985.

Andrew G. Traver

BASIL OF CAESAREA, SAINT (329/330–379)

Basil, bishop of Caesarea in Cappadocia, played pivotal roles in resisting Arianism and in shaping Byzantine asceticism.

Basil was born into an aristocratic family that traced its Christian heritage to Gregory the Wonderworker (mid-third century). Following an extensive education at Constantinople and Athens (348/349–355), Basil taught rhetoric briefly before dedicating himself to Christian philosophy (i.e., asceticism). This shift toward a contemplative, ascetic practice of Christianity was influenced by Basil's older sister Macrina and Eustathius of Sebaste. In 356 he accompanied Eustathius on a tour of ascetic groups from Egypt to Syria. He withdrew to Annisa on the family estate in Pontus and was joined by *Gregory of Nazianzus, his close friend and fellow student in Athens. In 362 Basil was ordained a priest. Despite a tense relationship with the bishop of Caesarea, Basil eventually played a central role in the Cappadocian church and succeeded to the episcopal office in 370.

Ascetics directed many questions to Basil, who later organized his responses into the so-called *Rules*, which together with several treatises formed the *Asceticon*. Basil believed that ascetics should be at the center of the church both as mentors to fellow Christians and as witnesses to Christian practice in the world. The episcopal complex, known as the Basileia, was a masterpiece of applied belief and derived from similar programs organized by Eustathius. It included a hostel, hospital, alms distribution, and job-training facilities run primarily by ascetics. Basil's activities resulted in the foundation of hospitals throughout the Byzantine Empire as well as earned him the anachronistic title "Father" of eastern monasticism.

Basil also participated in the controversies of his day. His three books, together entitled *Against Eunomius*, written before 364, became the standard position against attempts to identify the essence of God with a precise verbal formulation. He waged a campaign to preserve Nicene Christianity from imperial attempts to establish Arian Christianity in the eastern empire. This entailed dialogue with western Christians as well as local resistance to imperial policy, including a personal confrontation with Emperor *Valens in 372. Basil sought to multiply his episcopal support by appointing his brother *Gregory of Nyssa and Gregory of Nazianzus as bishops in obscure villages. This event permanently soured the relationship between Basil and Gregory of Nazianzus. Furthermore, Basil led the way for formal equality of veneration for the Holy Spirit within the Trinity through the treatise *On the Holy Spirit* (375). Many homilies, treatises, and letters are extant, illustrating the multiple roles he molded into the episcopal office.

Bibliography: P. Rousseau, *Basil of Caesarea*, 1994.

Lisa D. Maugans Driver

BOUDICCA (?–61 A.D.)

Boudicca was queen of the Iceni tribe in East Anglia and led a rebellion in 60 or 61 that threatened Roman control of southeast Britain.

The Roman reconquest of Britain that began in 43 under the emperor *Claudius encountered serious resistance from indigenous Celtic tribes. Initially cooperative, the Iceni rebelled unsuccessfully in 47 against Roman governor Publius Ostorius Scapula when he attempted to disarm them, though thereafter relations were peaceful until Boudicca's husband Prasutagus died in 59. The Iceni king made *Nero co-heir with his two daughters (whose names are unknown), apparently to guarantee their inheritance by granting the emperor part of his lands and possessions. However, officials of the governor Suetonius Paulinus and provincial procurator Decianus Catus looted the kingdom, seized lands, and responded to the royal family's resistance by flogging Boudicca and raping her daughters.

Boudicca and the Iceni retaliated, joined by the Trinovantes of Essex, who despised Roman settlers there, and other tribes who were as yet unconquered. Boudicca quickly captured Camulodunum (Colchester) and made for Londinium (London). En route she encountered part of the Ninth Legion from Lindum (Lincoln) under Pettilius Cerialis and destroyed his infantry, though he escaped with his cavalry. Decianus fled to Gaul. Suetonius, who was attempting to subdue Anglesey when news reached him, hastened toward Londinium with his cavalry. Finding no reinforcements, he abandoned the city to Boudicca's forces, who brutally sacked it. Shortly afterward they did likewise at Verulamium (St. Albans). Thus Boudicca destroyed the three main Roman cities in Britain, reportedly killing some 70,000 Romans and pro-Roman natives, though she captured no Roman military positions. Suetonius ultimately brought Boudicca to battle in the Midlands, probably between Lactadorum (Towcester) and Wall. His Fourteenth Legion, part of the Twentieth, and various auxiliaries (Poenius Postumus' Second Legion failed to show) smashed the larger opposing army, drove them back onto wagonloads of women and children behind the Britons' lines, and killed some 80,000 while losing only 400. Boudicca escaped but soon poisoned herself. Thus ended the greatest revolt the Romans had faced in half a century. Subsequently Romanization proceeded along more peaceful lines.

Boudicca's rebellion was long forgotten in the Middle Ages. *Tacitus, the primary source, was rediscovered in the fourteenth century, and in the sixteenth, Polydore Vergil restored Boudicca to British history. The Tudors, with their Celtic origins, found Boudicca attractive, especially Elizabeth, a courageous queen facing invasion by a hostile empire. Early in the Stuart era, about the time that Shakespeare produced *King Lear* and *Cymbeline*, both drawn from British antiquity, John Fletcher authored a play titled *Bonduca* [sic], performed by Richard Burbage and the King's Men in 1610. Others who have retold Boudicca's story include Petruccio Ubaldini, William Camden, John Leland, John Milton, Thomas Cowper, David Hume, Alfred Lord Tennyson, and Winston Churchill. Accounts have often been garbled (e.g., one placed her in Scotland;

another suggested that Stonehenge was constructed as her tomb!) and frequently reveal more about the author than the actual event (e.g., recent feminist literary critics). However, as modern historians and archeologists have revealed more of the truth, the story has only become more fascinating.

Bibliography: G.A. Webster, *Boudica: The British Revolt against Rome*, 1978.

William B. Robison

BRUTUS (Marcus Iunius Brutus, c. 85–42 B.C.)

Brutus was a Roman statesman who led the conspiracy that assassinated *Caesar in 44.

While Brutus was still a child, *Pompey executed his father for involvement in a military coup. Under the tutelage of his uncle *Cato the Younger, Brutus devoted himself to philosophy, especially the dialogues of *Plato. His scholarship won him a reputation as an honorable man among his contemporaries, but he was capable of unprincipled activities, as when he ignored Roman law to lend money at a usurious 48 percent interest. *Cicero, as governor of Cilicia, was obliged to deal with Brutus' intrigues in an elaborate moneylending scheme to an eastern monarch. Nevertheless, blessed with a well-known name and ample finances, Brutus' political career proceeded successfully. In 49 he opposed Caesar's invasion of Italy and even reconciled with his father's murderer, Pompey, in order to support the loyal Republican forces. He was present at Pompey's defeat in Pharsalus (48), but he received a pardon from a gracious Caesar and became his ally.

Brutus was richly rewarded under Caesar's dictatorship, receiving political appointments and public honors. Yet senators opposed to Caesar sensed that Brutus sympathized with their views, and after some hesitation he joined forces with Cassius and led the plot to assassinate the dictator on the Ides of March in 44. The assassins were unable to convince the public of the appropriateness of their actions, and so Brutus left for Crete, ostensibly to serve as governor but in actuality to gather an army to await the avengers of Caesar. His resistance to Caesar's tyranny attracted the support of many young Romans studying in Athens, including Cicero's son and the future poet *Horace. He coordinated his movements with Cassius, and together they seized Roman provinces in the eastern Mediterranean throughout 43 and 42. They crossed over to Greece and met the armies of *Antony and Octavian (the future *Augustus) in October 42. Brutus was victorious in the first Battle of Philippi, but his colleague was defeated and died at his own hand. Brutus committed suicide three weeks later after Antony routed his forces in a second battle.

Brutus' character is especially problematic in assessing his career. He acted unethically in his moneylending operations, yet he chose to set aside his hatred of Pompey to resist Caesar's invasion of Italy. His initial willingness to participate in Caesar's dictatorship is also inconsistent with his participation in the events of the Ides of March. The judgment of posterity has likewise been ambiguous. Many have celebrated him as a tyrannicide, yet Dante places Brutus alongside Cassius and Judas in the innermost circle of Hades, guilty of betraying their masters (*Inferno*, c. 1317). Perhaps the most sympathetic literary assessment is Shakespeare's "noblest Roman of them all" (*Julius Caesar*, 1599).

Bibliography: M.L. Clarke, *The Noblest Roman Marcus Brutus and His Reputation*, 1981.

David Christiansen

C

CAESAR, GAIUS JULIUS (100?–44 B.C.)

Caesar was a skillful politician who used his military successes and political acumen to establish himself as dictator of Rome. His subversion of the traditional senatorial control of the government prepared the way for imperial rule.

Caesar was born to a noble family that claimed descent from the goddess Venus, but his ancestors had not been prominent in political affairs in recent years. His aristocratic heritage won for him a nomination as priest of Jupiter while he was only in his teens, but it is uncertain whether he ever held the office. Once the aristocrat *Sulla emerged as the winner of a long civil war, Caesar withdrew to Asia Minor because of his family's involvement with the losing side (81 or 80). While abroad he served in the army and was recognized for his bravery, but after Sulla's death he returned to Rome and accused two prominent allies of Sulla of extortion. Although his prosecutions failed, his talented courtroom orations captured the attention of the general public (77–76). He traveled to Rhodes to study rhetoric, but while abroad he was abducted and ransomed by pirates, whom he later captured and crucified. He returned to Rome in 73 and resumed his political career, borrowing substantial funds from creditors to win a series of public honors.

Throughout his career Caesar depended heavily on the support of the masses, whom he courted with gladiatorial contests and lavish entertainment. Although he belonged to an aristocratic family, he associated himself with the deceased champion of the lower classes, his uncle *Marius. At the funeral of his aunt Julia (69), he displayed Marius' funeral mask, and he afterward replaced public trophies honoring Marius that Sulla had destroyed years earlier. Caesar calculated that these measures would ensure his status as leader of the "Popular" party, but they infuriated the aristocratic Senate, which did not approve of his maverick behavior. In 63 Caesar, relying on his heritage and extravagant bribery, was chosen chief priest of Rome over two aristocratic opponents, and so he was clearly a major political figure at the time of *Catiline's conspiracy. Some of Caesar's political rivals accused him of involvement in Catiline's attempt to overthrow the government, but the truthfulness of this charge cannot be determined. After serving as Spain's governor in 61, Caesar returned to Rome to campaign for the consulship of 59, but he determined that he needed to take extraordinary measures to overcome aristocratic resistance to his candidacy. He arranged for the politically advantageous marriage of his daughter Julia to *Pompey, and soon afterward the two men joined with *Crassus to form a political coalition to challenge the aristocratic dominance of the Senate. Through the support of this informal alliance, normally termed the "First Triumvirate," he was easily elected as one of the two consuls, but he spent much of the year feuding with his aristocratic colleague. Nevertheless, Caesar, relying upon mobs of armed men to intimidate his political opponents, managed to pass legislation pleasing Pompey and Crassus.

In 58 he began a military command in Gaul that occupied his activities for the remainder of the decade. Population movements in Europe threatened Gallic allies of Rome, and Caesar moved north to challenge the invading tribes. Yet even in the initial stages of his campaigning he was involved in the internal feuds of Gallic tribes, and his attention soon shifted from repelling invaders to conquering all the peoples opposed to a Roman presence in Gaul. By 50 he had subdued the entire region, killing or enslaving as many as 2 million people and incorporating Gaul into the Roman Empire. He invaded Britain and Germany, disobeying the law that restricted his activities to Gaul, and although he failed to establish a permanent Roman presence in either location, his actions delighted the masses in Rome. His activities further alienated the aristocrats, and by the end of the 50s they moved against him. The personal bond between Pompey and Caesar had been weakened by the death of Julia in 54, and the death of Crassus in the following year ended the triumvirate. The aristocrats courted Pompey, who supported their demand that Caesar disband his army and return to Rome to face criminal prosecution. Caesar gambled his political future on an invasion of Italy ("The die is cast," he reportedly said), and so he led his veteran legions across the Rubicon River to march on Rome (49). Pompey and his allies withdrew to Greece to train an army.

Caesar quickly overcame opposition in Italy and Spain, and he crossed over to Greece in 48 to confront Pompey. After several months of maneuvering, the two met at Pharsalus, and Caesar, despite being greatly outnumbered, won a decisive victory. He pursued Pompey to Egypt, but upon his arrival in Alexandria, he discovered that his rival had been murdered. Once he established *Cleopatra as the Egyptian monarch (who bore him a son in the following year), he traveled to Asia Minor to defeat a Pontic king in a rapid campaign, which he later summarized with the phrase "veni, vidi, vici" (I came, I saw, I conquered). After he routed aristocratic armies in Africa and Spain, he returned to Rome and focused on domestic affairs. Nevertheless, many senators resenting his autocratic behavior feared that he would establish himself as a monarch, and so by the time Caesar compelled the Senate to declare him "dictator for life" in

February 44, political enemies were contemplating his assassination. A conspiracy initiated by Cassius was solidified with the support of *Brutus, one of Caesar's allies, and on 15 March (the "Ides of March") the conspirators assassinated Caesar at the Theater of Pompey, striking him twenty-three times. According to legend, only the wound inflicted by Brutus was fatal.

The legacy of Caesar to Western culture is scarcely calculable. He is regarded as one of the ancient world's most skilled generals, whose martial accomplishments on three continents rank him with *Alexander the Great and *Hannibal. The desire of Roman emperors to associate themselves with his legend is seen in their adoption of the title "Caesar," and his identification with leadership persisted into the modern world in two political offices derived from his name, the German *kaiser* and the Russian *czar*. Our modern calendar is based on Caesar's "Julian" calendar, the seventh month of which was renamed "July" to immortalize its creator. Caesar brought Western culture into many conquered areas by founding colonies that gradually Romanized the native inhabitants.

Our knowledge of Caesar's life is based primarily on ancient literature, including his own writings. His accounts of the Gallic campaigns and the civil war have survived, providing a model of Latin prose with their simple but eloquent writing style. His *Gallic Wars* is marked by a clear description of military activities, but it also includes valuable ethnographical accounts of the ancient Celtic and Germanic cultures. His other writings, including speeches, a political tract, and an essay on rhetoric, have all been lost. Caesar's career has been preserved in the literature of his contemporaries (e.g., *Cicero and *Sallust), historians (e.g., *Velleius Paterculus, *Appian, and *Cassius Dio), and ancient biographers (e.g., *Plutarch and *Suetonius). Many people in the modern world view Caesar in positive or even romanticized terms, influenced by sympathetic portraits such as Shakespeare's *Julius Caesar* (1599), but modern historians are divided on their assessment of the man and his motives. Nineteenth-century scholars tended to view him as a populist leader intent on breaking aristocratic domination of the government, but today historians are more willing to address his faults, including his brutal behavior in the Gallic Wars (e.g., Caesar claimed to have massacred virtually all 430,000 members of two German tribes). Despite disagreeing over Caesar's motives, all scholars concur that this remarkable man greatly influenced the character of Western culture.

Bibliography: C. Meier, *Caesar*, 1995; T.P. Wiseman, "From the Conference of Luca to the Rubicon," in *The Cambridge Ancient History*, 1985, IX: 614–637; Z. Yavetz, *Julius Caesar and His Public Image*, 1983.

David Christiansen

CALCIDIUS (fourth century A.D.)

Calcidius was a Christian scholar who composed a Latin translation and commentary of part of *Plato's *Timaeus*. The scant, indirect biographical details recorded in the prologues of his work are our only historical data on his life.

Calcidius' original source of *Timaeus* was probably a single text based on a combination of Platonic philosophy, perhaps compiled by *Porphyry. Calcidius translated in Latin the Greek original and added a commentary in which he tried to combine Plato's two concepts of matter (identified, in the Greek philosopher's work, with the terms *chaos* and *chora*). In *Timaeus* Plato clearly expresses his own opinion on the origin of things. The great philosopher thought of matter as empty "space" (*chora*). Most philosophers before him had attempted to detect the material from which the world was made by pointing to one or more elements. From the constant change of the so-called elements Plato deduced their dependence upon a single, all-comprising reality, that "inside which everything is." To Plato's understanding, this reality was "space."

For Calcidius "space" and "chaos" are two different stages in the evolution of the matter: The former is matter as such; "chaos" is matter put in disorderly motion by "vestiges of bodies dropped" into it. *Timaeus* quickly became one of the most popular Platonic treatises; it occupied a central place in the tradition of Platonism, both in the late antiquity and the Middle Ages; and it became the Platonic dialogue with the greatest impact upon Western thought. Calcidius' translation and commentary on its most important chapters stand at the end of Western antiquity. For centuries afterward the West drew its knowledge about Plato mostly from this work.

Bibliography: J.C.M. van Winden, *Calcidius on Matter. His Doctrine and Sources*, 1965.

Sophia Papaioannou

CALIGULA (Gaius Julius Caesar Germanicus, 12–41)

Caligula was the erratic and ill-famed emperor of Rome.

Son of *Germanicus and *Agrippina the Elder, he received his nickname Caligula ("little boots") from the soldiers while his father campaigned on the Rhine in 14–16. Along with his older siblings, he accompanied his parents to the East, where in 19 his father died. After his mother's arrest in Rome in 29, he lived with various female relatives until he joined his uncle *Tiberius on Capri. Tiberius made Caligula and Tiberius Julius Caesar Nero Gemellus his heirs. Caligula became pontifex in 31 and quaestor in 33.

Upon Tiberius' death on 16 March 37, Caligula was proclaimed emperor by Macro, prefect of the praetorian guard, and acclaimed by the populace with great joy and hope. Within six months the character of his reign changed, due first to the death of his grandmother, Antonia Minor, who had had a restraining influence on him. Second, his serious illness in October 37 raised the question of succession, and Caligula executed his likeliest successors Gemellus and Macro before May 38.

In 39 matters became worse. The Senate quarreled with him over his incest with his sister, his disgraceful performances as a singer and charioteer, and his claim to be divine. Late in the year, he executed for treason his sister, Julia

Livilla, along with his brother-in-law, Marcus Aemilius Lepidus, and some senators. He became increasingly brutal, executing many senators for conspiracy and using their confiscated estates to fill the depleted imperial treasury. Finally on 22 or 24 January 41, he was murdered in his palace.

Caligula, however, was keenly interested in Italy's roads and Rome's water supply. He began to improve the harbor of Rhegium to facilitate the importation of grain for the people. He laid out a circus in the Vatican (over which St. Peter's more or less lies) and reconstructed the Theater of Pompey. His eccentric conduct provoked strife in Alexandria between Greeks and Jews and rebellion in Mauretania and nearly caused religious revolt in Judaea.

Bibliography: *J.P.V.D.* Balsdon, *The Emperor Gaius*, 1934; A. Ferrill, *Caligula: Emperor of Rome*, 1991; R. Mellor, ed., *From Augustus to Nero: The First Dynasty of Imperial Rome*, 1990.

Judith Sebesta

CALLICRATES (c. 440 b.c.)

Callicrates was a fifth-century Athenian architect associated with the Parthenon, the Temple of Athena Nike, and the Middle Long Wall.

Little is known of Callicrates' life or his specific contributions to architectural works associated with his name. While *Plutarch cites him along with *Ictinus as an architect of the Parthenon (447–438), it is likely that his role was subordinate and that he was more a master builder than designer. Plutarch also notes him as the builder of a defensive wall linking Athens to Piraeus (445–443), which suggests that as an official city architect he was more involved with technical, managerial, and contractual matters than with aesthetics. An inscription calls for him to design the Temple of Athena Nike (c. 450), but as this structure was not built until much later (c. 425), Callicrates' role is uncertain. The Temple of Athena Nike, with its Ionic columns, unusual internal design, and innovative adaptation to terrain, was a significant influential architectural achievement. If Callicrates were the architect of this building, he deserves credit for influencing later architects, and he also might be credited for building or influencing similar Athenian structures such as the Erechtheion and temples located at Ilissos and Delos.

Bibliography: A.W. Lawrence, *Greek Architecture*, 5th ed., 1996.

Richard Louth

CALLIMACHUS OF CYRENE (c. 310–c. 235 b.c.)

Callimachus was a critic, poet, bibliographer, and possibly head librarian at the Library in Alexandria.

Callimachus was born in Cyrene in North Africa. His family was well known; he himself claims that one of his ancestors was Battos, the reputed founder of Cyrene. He studied with Praxiphanes, a philosopher, in Athens c. 287–281. Later, he taught grammar in Eleusis, a suburb of Alexandria; his most famous pupils were *Eratosthenes of Cyrene, *Aristophanes of Byzantium, and *Apollonius of Rhodes. Still later, he joined the court of *Ptolemy II Philadelphus and worked there until he died.

His list of works is extensive; he is rumored to have written poems in every meter in addition to prose works, some 800 volumes in all. Whether he actually held the position of head librarian at Alexandria is debatable, but his contributions, in the form of prose catalogs, to the library are phenomenal. Callimachus' poetic aesthetic reveals itself in his desire for shorter, more polished poems. Six of his hymns to the gods survive, as do sixty-four of his epigrams. His hymns and epigrams are elegant, brief, and refined; he felt that epic works in the Homeric tradition no longer belonged in the Alexandria in which he lived and wrote—hence, his reported feud with his pupil Apollonius of Rhodes. One of his proverbial sayings, which appears to characterize all his works, is "Big book, big bother."

Bibliography: S. Lombardo, int. and trans., *Callimachus*, 1988.

Jana K. Schulman

CALLINUS (fl. c. 650 B.C.)

Callinus was a Greek elegiac poet from Ephesus in Asia Minor.

Callinus' few surviving poems, which are fragmentary, deal with military themes. His most extended fragment reflects a concern with public ethics, especially in wartime.

The biography of Callinus is largely unknown. There are, however, references in the poems themselves to historical events. For example, the war of Ephesus with Magnesia and the invasions of the Cimmerians and Treres, c. 652, situate the poet in the mid-seventh century. Callinus was contemporary with the Spartan elegiac poet *Tyrtaeus, who likewise wrote about military subjects.

Bibliography: H. Fränkel, *Early Greek Poetry and Philosophy*, 1973; M.L. West, trans., *Greek Lyric Poetry*, 1993.

Carl A. Anderson

CAMILLUS, MARCUS FURIUS (?–365 B.C.)

According to Roman tradition, Camillus was one of the greatest of Roman Republican heroes, having served as consular tribune six times, censor once, and dictator five times. He celebrated four triumphs.

Camillus served with great distinction in the war against the Aequians and Volscians in 429. An incident of this war reveals his strength of mind and body: Wounded in the thigh by a javelin, he pulled it out and continued to fight. His political and military career brought him both praise and censure. In 403, as censor, he compelled Roman men to marry because the frequent wars with their enemies had made many women widows. In 396, he was made dictator to bring to an end the seven-year siege of Veii. After sacking Veii, he placed that city's statue of Juno in the temple of Juno Regina that he built on the Aventine. During his triumph, however, he outraged Romans by riding in a chariot drawn by white horses that heretofore had only been used to convey the sacred images of Jupiter.

In 394, he is said to have won the capitulation of Falerii when he returned to the city some Falerian schoolboys whose teacher had kidnapped them and offered them as hostages to Camillus. Three years later (391), accused of not dedicating one-tenth of the plunder of Veii to Apollo, he went voluntarily into exile at Ardea.

The next year, however, the Gauls under the leadership of Brennus plundered and burned Rome except for the Capitoline Hill that a Roman garrison still occupied. Pretending to capitulate, the Romans sent for Camillus, offering him the dictatorship. Just as the Romans were paying out the ransom for the city, Camillus arrived and routed the Gauls. He was honored with another triumph. Though many Romans wished to abandon the ruined city and go to Veii, Camillus purified Rome and it was rebuilt within a year. This feat earned Camillus the title "The Second Founder of Rome." He died in 365 due to a plague.

Modern historians, however, think that some of traditional narrative of Camillus' career is suspect, being, for example, patriotic stories invented to compensate for Roman humiliation (e.g., the Gallic sack of Rome) or dramatic episodes that make him similar to later Roman leaders such as *Scipio Africanus or *Sulla.

Bibliography: T.J. Cornell, *The Beginnings of Rome: Italy and Rome from the Bronze Age to the Punic Wars (c. 1000–264 B.C.)*, 1995; R.M. Ogilvie, *A Commentary on Livy Books 1–5*, 1965.

Judith Sebesta

CAPITOLINUS
See **Manlius Capitolinus, Marcus**.

CARNEADES (c. 214/213 or 219/218–129/128 B.C.)

Carneades was the founder of the Third, or New, Academy at Athens (c. 164/160–137/136), developing sceptical arguments and methodology to attack epistemological positivism.

A native of Cyrene in North Africa, he studied under *Arcesilaus' successors. Carneades created a form of antithetical speech in which he himself debated the pros and cons of an issue, suspending final judgment (*epoche*). Carneades lectured on justice at Rome (156/155), propounding all the arguments on behalf of law and justice on the first day—and the arguments against them on the second. He further refined Arcesilaus' philosophy of reasonableness: The truth may not be known absolutely, but we should adopt the most logically probable (*pithanon*) course for everyday life. He refuted *Chrysippus' attempts to use logic to prove that there is certainty of knowledge, that events are determined, and that the gods exist. Since his aim was also to oppose the Stoa for the sake of argument, it was said that had Chrysippus not existed, Carneades would not have either! He also invented the Carneadean classification (*Carneadia divisio*) to oppose not only the arguments of the schools but all possible arguments on an issue.

Like *Socrates and Arcesilaus, Carneades did not publish in his lifetime. His pupil and successor, Clitomachus of Carthage, later wrote and systematized his philosophy. *Cicero was much influenced by his thought and method of argumentation.

Bibliography: R.J. Hankinson, *The Sceptics*, 1998; A.A. Long, *Hellenistic Philosophy*, 1974; A.A. Long and D.N. Sedley, *The Hellenistic Philosophers*, 2 vols., 1987.

Menahem Luz

CASSANDER (c. 358–297 b.c.)

Cassander was the regent (319) and king (305) of Macedonia until his death in 297.

Cassander was the only son of *Antipater, who had served as general for *Philip II and *Alexander the Great and was regent for the joint kings Philip III Arrhidaeus and Alexander IV who succeeded Alexander. When Antipater died in 319, he named as his successor an old friend named Polyperchon, bypassing his son Cassander.

Cassander contested that decision, seeking various generals of Alexander as allies against Polyperchon, with whom he was at war for the next decade. He gained control of Athens and its port at Piraeus in 317 and held it until 307, liberalizing the oligarchic constitution imposed on it by Antipater. The city was supervised by *Demetrius of Phalerum, an Athenian who had long been a student of *Aristotle. In 307, *Demetrius Poliorcetes arrived in Athens with a strong fleet and expelled Demetrius of Phalerum, who joined Cassander in Macedonia for a time before ending his life in Egypt, where he was instrumental in establishing the Library at Alexandria.

The complex struggles of the Successors found the queen mother *Olympias allied with Polyperchon against Cassander. After she had murdered one of the nominal kings, Philip Arrhidaeus, and his wife Eurydice, she was captured by Cassander and executed after a brief show trial in 316. A few years later, in 311, a general peace confirmed Cassander as regent for the young Alexander IV, who was in his custody along with his mother, Roxane. Within a year, Cassander had murdered Alexander and Roxane, thus ending the direct line of Alexander the Great. Cassander did not formally take the title of "king" until other dynasts did, in 305.

He continually attempted to regain control of Athens (Four Years War, 307–304) and joined almost all of the other "kings" in a coalition against *Antigonus I and Demetrius Poliorcetes, which ended with the death of Antigonus at the Battle of Ipsus in 301.

He married Thessaloniki, an illegitimate daughter of Philip II (and half sister of Alexander) in 315 and founded a city in Macedonia named for her, which became and remains an important city in the eastern Mediterranean; he also founded the city of Cassandreia nearby. They had three sons, none of whom long survived their father.

Cassander died of an illness (possibly tuberculosis) in 297 and was succeeded by his eldest son Philip (IV), who died of the same disease only four months later. Thessaloniki preferred her youngest son as successor, which led to her murder by the second son, Antipater. Antipater's matricide cost him support; he disappears from the historical record (but may be the same "Antipater Etesias" who was killed in battle with invading Gauls in 280 after being king for a few months). The younger Alexander was murdered by Demetrius Poliorcetes, who then became king in 295.

Bibliography: N.G.L. Hammond and F.W. Walbank, *A History of Macedonia*, vol. 3, 336–167 B.C., 1988.

Janice J. Gabbert

CASSIAN, JOHN (c. 360–435)

Cassian was a Christian monk of Egypt and later southern Gaul who was instrumental in articulating the nature of the monastic life.

Born of wealthy Christian parents, Cassian decided early in his life to take up the monastic life with his friend Germanus. The pair traveled to Palestine and entered a monastic community near the cave of the Nativity. They later left Palestine in search of a more fruitful monastic life in Egypt. They left Egypt in 400 when a theological dispute became increasingly acrimonious and resulted in riots between the competing parties. While many suggestions have been made, we cannot be certain when Cassian traveled to Palestine, how long he remained there, or when he arrived in Egypt. Cassian is next seen in Constantinople, where he was ordained deacon by *John Chrysostom and served as Chrysostom's emissary to Pope Innocent. Cassian eventually arrived at Marseille and established two monasteries, one each for women and for men. There he wrote the *Institutes*, the *Conferences*, and *On the Incarnation*. The *Institutes* were dedicated to Castor, for whom the only date is a mention in a papal letter from 419. The *Conferences* were published in three sets, the last two likely being composed around 427–428. *On the Incarnation*, commissioned by Pope *Leo I, was written against *Nestorius and would have been superfluous after the Council of Ephesus in 431. Cassian was prominent in Gallic monastic and ecclesiastical circles, and he received the singular honor of being translated quickly into Greek for the benefit of eastern monks.

The *Institutes* consist of twelve books. The first four describe proper conduct for a monastic novice, while the remaining eight offer an extensive discussion of the eight vices. These vices became a popular motif in later monastic literature and were received into medieval preaching traditions as the seven deadly sins. For Cassian, however, they were not sins so much as disturbances of the mind and soul that prevent the monk from gaining the tranquility necessary to advance in prayer and to achieve a closer union with God. The *Conferences* consist of twenty-four dialogues that were supposed to have occurred between Cassian and Germanus, on the one hand, and various Egyptian monastic elders on the other. The topics of these dialogues range from the physical practices of monastic life to an exploration of the unmediated contemplation of God that is the monk's ultimate goal. The *Benedictine Rule* would later recommend the daily reading of the *Conferences*. While Cassian's monastic writings were enormously influential in the Middle Ages, his fourfold method of interpreting scripture is also of importance.

Bibliography: C. Stewart, *Cassian the Monk*, 1998.

Steven D. Driver

CASSIUS DIO (Cassius Dio Cocceianus, c. 164–235)

Cassius Dio was a Roman author and administrator of Greek birth who wrote *The Roman History*.

Born into a Roman senatorial family of some prominence at Nicaea in about 164, Cassius Dio quickly was promoted due to his father's influence. By 180, he had traveled to Rome, taken a seat in the Senate, and about a year later had taken up a position as his father's assistant in Cilicia. Returning to Rome in 194, he served as aedile and quaestor in the city. With the ascension of *Septimius Severus as emperor, he served as praetor and later as consul before traveling with Severus' son Caracalla on a tour of the Eastern empire. Although Cassius Dio personally disliked Caracalla, he remained in high favor and probably began to work on *The Roman History* during his reign. During the reign of Macrinus (217–218) he again served in the East as curator of Pergamum and went on to rule in Africa as proconsul. Returning to Rome in 229, he served as Roman consul for a second time and retired to his home in Bithynia shortly thereafter. During his retirement he continued to write and died in Nicaea around 235.

The Roman History, a work monumental in scope, begins with Aeneas in Italy and continues through the reign of Alexander Severus (222–235). The complete work, unfortunately, does not survive intact. What does survive are a number of books that correspond roughly to the years of 68 B.C. to A.D. 47. The style of the work is clearly Greek in origin, with the main personages in the work given to long speeches that could not possibly have been verbatim. His position in the government obviously gave him access to imperial archives to which others may not have been privy. *The Roman History* is an important work because of the insights and information that Cassius Dio provides on the period that is extant, especially that of *Augustus.

Bibliography: F.G.B. Millar, *A Study of Cassius Dio*, 1964.

Charles S. Paine III

CASSIUS VECELLINUS, SPURIUS (late sixth–early fifth century B.C.)

Sp. Cassius was a Roman political and military leader whose championship of the plebeians resulted in the foundation of the office of the tribune of the people (*tribunus plebis*), an office exclusively associated with the plebeians until the last century of the Republic.

According to the old sacred Roman calendar, which annually recorded the names of the eponymous magistrates, Sp. Cassius was consul three times (502, 493, and 486). During his second consulate the Roman plebs seceded, and the riot ended only after the patricians conceded to found an office, the tribunate, for the championship of the plebeian rights. Also in the same year, Cassius dedicated the temple of Ceres and instituted in the goddess' honor a cult that, in later years, became a major plebeian cult.

In the sphere of foreign policy, the years of Cassius' second and third consulate coincide with two important peace treaties for Rome, with the Latins and the Hernicii, respectively. This event suggests to see Cassius, probably the officiating magistrate, as a keen politician who strengthened Rome's defense against her Italian enemies by compacting alliances with the neighboring Latin tribes.

Sp. Cassius was condemned to death in 485, the year following his third consulate, after being accused of conspiring to become a tyrant, largely leaning on the plebeian support he won with the initiation of an agrarian law. One might consider this piece of tradition to be anachronistic, however, since all the sources recording it date from the last century of the Republic, a time that witnesses a series of agrarian laws followed by major political turmoil.

Bibliography: R.M. Ogilvie, *A Commentary on Livy Books 1–5*, 1965.

Sophia Papaioannou

CATILINE (Lucius Sergius Catalina, c. 108–62 B.C.)

Catiline was a Roman aristocrat who attempted to overthrow the government in 63.

Catiline was born to a patrician family once actively involved in Roman politics but recently fallen into poverty. Despite these unfavorable circumstances he resolved to become a prominent politician, first serving in the army of *Pompey during the Social War (91–87) and later as quaestor under *Sulla. Yet his career was hounded by private and public scandal, including accusations of murdering several family members, violating a Vestal Virgin, and extortion. Whatever the truthfulness of these charges, his attempts to be elected consul repeatedly failed, and by the summer of 63 he covertly prepared to overthrow the government. He gathered an army of impoverished ex-soldiers outside of Rome, and in the city he enlisted the urban poor to take up arms against the government. Before he was prepared to strike, however, the consul *Cicero learned of Catiline's machinations and took precautionary measures; Catiline was denounced at a dramatic meeting of the Senate, and he fled the city. Cicero oversaw the arrest and execution of the leading conspirators remaining in Rome, while Catiline tried to flee to Gaul with the army of rebels. In January 62 he was killed in battle near Pistoria after a Roman army overtook and defeated his troops.

Later observers have been fascinated with the audacity of Catiline's activities as recounted by Cicero and the historian *Sallust, who presented him as a villain corrupted by Rome's declining moral standards. His career even interested Ben Jonson, who wrote the play *Catiline's Conspiracy* in 1611.

Bibliography: L. Hutchinson, *The Conspiracy of Catiline*, 1967.

David Christiansen

CATO THE ELDER (Marcus Porcius Cato, Cato the Censor, 234–149 B.C.)

Cato became an icon of conservative Roman tradition.

Cato was born in Tusculum into an equestrian family. Physically distinctive with red hair and gray eyes, Cato brought himself to public attention through bravery on the battlefield (during the war against *Hannibal, in which he first served at the age of seventeen), forensic activity in the districts around Rome, and a reputation for rustic sobriety, frugality, and discipline. With the political patronage of the patricians *Q. Fabius Maximus and L. Valerius Flaccus, he became the first member of his family elected to public office at Rome (a "new man"). Quaestor in 204, he served under *Scipio Africanus in Sicily and Africa. In 199 he was plebeian aedile; and in 198, as praetor, he governed Sardinia where he was able to put into practice his ideology of austerity, reducing official expenditure and expelling moneylenders. In 195 he held the consulship with his friend and patron Flaccus.

During this year he spoke unsuccessfully against the repeal of the Oppian law (passed in 215), legislation that had restricted the display of wealth by women. He then proceeded to Spain, where a serious rebellion against Roman rule had erupted in 197. There he displayed military expertise, reconquering much of the east coast and lower Ebro valley, then campaigning in both Turdetania and Celtiberia before repacifying tribes in the northeast. The ruthless determination with which he suppressed rebellious elements signaled that Rome was now in Spain to stay. He boasted that the cities he had destroyed numbered more than the days he had spent in the country. Back in Rome (194), he celebrated a triumph, exhibiting a vast amount of booty and richly rewarding his troops.

In 191 he served as a subordinate officer in the Second Macedonian War against the Seleucid ruler *Antiochus III, winning further military distinction in a decisive battle at Thermopylae (191). In the following years he entered with great energy into the bitter squabbles of Rome's internal politics, in particular manifesting hostility to Scipio Africanus and his brother. After an unsuccessful bid for the censorhip of 189, he and his ally Flaccus were successful for that censorship of 184, after a hotly contested campaign in which Cato advocated a drastic purification of the city by way of an assault on luxury. In office, Cato did not disappoint expectations. Although it featured a considerable building program and much else for which it might have been remembered, Cato's censorhip became synonymous with stern severity.

In the following thirty-four years of his life, Cato remained active, exercising his influence in public debates and embroiled as ever in personal disputes. Litigation marked his life. He was remembered as one sued more frequently than any other; he participated in forty-four legal actions. In his later life prosperity brought a more comfortable lifestyle. He invested in resource-rich lands and underwrote shipping ventures but remained an outspoken champion of the virtues of Rome's simpler past and a critic of Rome's embrace, for example, of the attractions of Greek culture. In his later years, Cato became the outstanding advocate of the destruction of Carthage. He lived to see war declared but not its conclusion.

Cato was a prolific writer, his works including a treatise on agriculture, a military handbook (the first in Latin), a work on civil law, a collection of sayings, and a history (the *Origines*), probably the first in Latin, which dealt with Rome and Italy up until his own time. Cato's literary endeavors expanded the horizons of Latin. His reputation as an orator (the "Roman *Demosthenes") was considerable in antiquity. Over 150 speeches were preserved (only fragments remain).

Cato was remembered chiefly for his advocacy, in a time of fundamental changes, of Rome's traditional values (austerity, discipline, and frugality). It was an image of early Rome that he did much to foster if not create.

Bibliography: A.E. Astin, *Cato the Censor*, 1978.

Tom Hillard

CATO THE YOUNGER (Marcus Porcius Cato, 95–46 B.C.)

Cato was a Roman senator who epitomized traditional Roman austerity and solemnity.

From an early age Cato, the great-grandson of *Cato the Elder, displayed the integrity of character for which he was celebrated as an adult. In 72 he served in the war against the rebellious gladiator *Spartacus, and five years later he held his first public office. His diligence in the Senate beginning in 64 earned the admiration of his fellow senators, among whom he exercised an influence that belied his youth. His demand for the execution of *Catiline's conspirators in 63 identified him as an uncompromising supporter of ancestral Roman dignity, and this perception was enhanced by his opposition to ambitious men such as *Caesar, *Pompey, and *Crassus, who were willing to subvert the traditional dominance of the Senate for their own self-interest. Cato's obstructionistic tactics drove the three men into a coalition commonly called the "First Triumvirate" in 60, and he was even briefly imprisoned for his vigorous opposition to Caesar's consulship in the following year. Supporters of the triumvirs succeeded in removing Cato from Rome for two years, but upon his return in 56, he resumed his role as leader of the conservative faction. At the end of the decade he began supporting Pompey, viewing him as the only man who could prevent an absolutist government under Caesar. After Caesar invaded Italy in 49, Cato served with the loyal Republican forces in Sicily and Greece, and after Pompey's death he organized resistance in Africa. He committed suicide in Utica in April 46 after he realized that Caesar's victory was inevitable.

Cato's reputation for honor and integrity continued to grow after his death, spurred especially by debate surrounding the publication of *Cicero's laudatory *Cato* and Caesar's response, the virulent *Anticato*. He and his enemy Caesar became linked in the minds of many as symbols of contradictory government forms (republic versus dictatorship) and moral character (Cato's uncompromising standards versus Caesar's affability). He has often been linked to libertarianism in Western culture, as exemplified by the *Cato Letters* (John Trenchard and Thomas Gordon, 1720–1723), which influenced American revolutionaries, and by the Cato Institute, an American political foundation.

Bibliography: E.S. Gruen, *The Last Generation of the Roman Republic*, 1974.

David Christiansen

CATULLUS, GAIUS VALERIUS (c. 84–c. 54 B.C.)

Catullus was a composer of 116 lyric and elegiac poems.

Catullus was born in Verona of a wealthy family that was on personal terms with *Julius Caesar. Chance alone has allowed Catullus' poems to survive: The three existing manuscripts are descended from one that was discovered in the early fourteenth century. It is for his poems to and about his mistress Lesbia, who is presumed to be *Clodia, the sister of *P. Clodius Pulcher, that Catullus is most famous.

He came to Rome, and attracted by a movement among the youth there that embraced the ideals of Hellenistic Greece, he became one of the neoteric poets who sought new forms and content for their poetry.

The collection of Catullus' work falls into three sections of which only the first can be said with any certainty to be in the order set by the author. Poems 1–60, covering love, politics, and friendship, are composed predominantly in hexameters; 61–64 are *epylls*, longer poems, among which are stories of the legend of Attis and of the marriage of Peleus and Thetis; 65–116 comprise longer elegiacs and short epigrams, many of which are either personal invective or political satire.

The poems are innovative in their use and invention of words; clever in their manipulation of purely Greek meters; racy, at times to the point of extreme crudity; and deceptive in their simplicity of form, showing Catullus to be a master of the poetic arts. His contemporary impact was felt by people such as *Cornelius Nepos, *Cicero, and Julius Caesar. His style had influence in the subsequent ages on writers such as *Virgil, *Horace, *Tibullus, *Propertius, and especially *Martial.

Bibliography: T.P. Wiseman, *Catullus and His World: A Reappraisal*, 1985.

Deborah Eaton

CELSUS (fl. mid-second century)

Celsus was a Middle Platonic philosopher who wrote the first known systematic critique of Christianity, *True Doctrine*, during the reign of *Marcus Aurelius.

This work, known only through excerpts in *Origen's *Against Celsus*, employs Jewish criticisms of Christianity and then proceeds to attack Judaism as the origin of Christianity. Celsus belittled Christians as vulgar, illiterate barbarians whose "god" was a bastard and an amateur magician. The newness of Christianity raised suspicions in contrast to the ancient and honorable traditions of Greece and Rome. Celsus was concerned that Christianity could only weaken the empire through an exclusive belief in one God that manifested itself as an affront to the empire's gods and resulted in a withdrawal from the responsibilities of civil society. Celsus found some merit in the *logos* doctrine of Christ; however, he shared the Greco-Roman repugnance for Christianity's claim that God became man in Christ, believing that such an event would corrupt and destroy that which makes God divine. Celsus was somewhat familiar with Christian scripture and the general arguments made by Christian apologists. Nearly a century later Origen specifically addressed Celsus' challenges to Christian belief and practice. Close to 90 percent of Celsus' original work is quoted within the eight books *Against Celsus*.

Bibliography: R. Wilken, *Christians as the Romans Saw Them*, 1984.

Lisa D. Maugans Driver

CHRYSIPPUS (c. 280–207 b.c.)

Chrysippus was a Greek philosopher who is known as the second founder of Stoicism, after *Zeno of Citium because of his systematization of Stoic doctrine.

Chrysippus was born in Soli in Cilicia. Around 260 he went to Athens to study philosophy; he initially attended the lectures of the Academic Sceptic *Arcesilaus. He subsequently became the disciple of *Cleanthes, the successor of Zeno. In 232 he succeeded Cleanthes as the head of the Stoic school.

Chrysippus was famed for his dialectical skill and for his defense of Stoicism against the Academy. He spent a good portion of his life in disputation and frequently took the opposite sides of the same question. This practice provided his opponent *Carneades with ammunition against him.

Though he is reputed to have written over 700 works, covering the fields of logic, physics, and ethics, only fragments remain today. His importance for the development of Stoic philosophy was immense though, and the ancient phrase "Had there been no Chrysippus, there would be no Stoa" attests to his own role in the formulation of Stoicism.

Fragments of his work are preserved in the works of *Cicero, *Aulus Gellius, *Plutarch, and *Seneca.

Bibliography: J.B. Gould, *The Philosophy of Chrysippus*, 1970.

Andrew G. Traver

CHRYSOSTOM, JOHN, SAINT (c. 347–407)

John was an ascetic, an orator, and an archbishop of Constantinople.

John was born to a pagan father, Secundus, and a Christian mother, Anthusa. His father carried the title *Magister militum Orientis* (master of the eastern armies), yet we know little about him and he died shortly after John's birth. Raised by his mother, at about the age of fourteen he began school under the pagan orator Libanius at Antioch. John also started his religious studies under the monk Diodore of Tarsus who had founded the exegetical school at Antioch. In 369, he was baptized and became determined to live as an anchorite. He first lived as a member of a Pachomian community outside of Antioch and then for two years as a hermit, but his asceticism and self-mortification seriously imperiled his health, and he had to return to the city.

In 381 he was made a deacon and ordained a priest in 386. Archbishop Flavian of Antioch had appointed John as a preacher, a role that he performed so well that he earned the name Chrysostom (the golden mouthed). In 387 the citizens of Antioch rebelled against the taxation policies of *Theodosius I by smashing imperial statues throughout the city. John delivered a series of sermons (*On the Statutes*) that emphasized God's mercy and focused on the moral reform of the citizens. John's powers of oratory were able to bring a measure of calm to the city. In 390, he preached a series of homilies on the Gospels of *John and continued to preach on Genesis, Psalms, Isaiah, *Matthew, Acts, and the Pauline epistles.

In 398 he was appointed archbishop of Constantinople against his will and largely due to his oratorical abilities. When John tried to clean up the corrupt and vice-ridden city, he quickly fell afoul of the Empress Eudoxia, who took many of his criticisms of the city and its inhabitants as personal slanders. Working in conjunction with the archbishop of Alexandria, Eudoxia was able to have Chrysostom deposed in 403 at the Synod of the Oak, yet he was later recalled by the court. He again earned Eudoxia's displeasure and was banished in 404 to Armenia despite the protestation of the West and the citizens of Constantinople. In exile, Chrysostom continued to write and remain in contact with those in Constantinople. He died in 407 while en route for an even more remote exile.

Chrysostom was a prolific writer. In addition to his hundreds of homilies and letters, he also wrote didactic and institutional (e.g., *On the Priesthood*) works. His relics were returned to Constantinople in 438, and he later became a doctor of the Church.

Bibliography: J.N.D. Kelly, *Golden Mouth: The Story of John Chrysostom, Ascetic, Preacher, Bishop*, 1995; W. Mayer and P. Allen, *John Chrysostom*, 2000.

Andrew G. Traver

CICERO, MARCUS TULLIUS (106–43 B.C.)

Cicero, also known as Tully, was Rome's greatest orator and philosopher.

The elder son of a wealthy Italian farmer from the Volscian town Arpinum and a mother from the minor Roman nobility, Cicero was educated in rhetoric and philosophy in Rome and Athens and studied law with the leading Roman jurists, the Scaevolae. His defense in 81 of the farmer Roscius of Ameria against the abuse of power by the dictator *Sulla and his henchman won him political recognition. Perhaps wisely, he left Rome from 79 to 77 to study philosophy in Rhodes and Athens. He was elected quaestor for 75 and served in western Sicily. In 70, speaking for the Sicilians against the corrupt governor Verres, he assembled so much evidence and placed Verres' patrons, the Metelli, in such a bind that Verres fled into exile after Cicero's opening speech. He later published all his prepared *Verrine orations*. In 66 as praetor he won public support with a speech in the Roman Forum (*de imperio Gn. Pompei*) for *Pompey's special command against *Mithridates VI in Asia. Although defending the wealthy class (the *equites*), whose income from tax collection had been greatly reduced by the incursions of Mithridates, he appealed adroitly to the self-interest of the Roman people, exempt from taxes because of those collected abroad. Pompey's swift success brought a windfall to the *equites*, which led to Cicero's election as one of the two consuls for 63. Agitation for a wider distribution of the profits of empire and for *res novae*, a cancellation of all private debt, also grew. Cicero as consul drove an extreme faction of these populares into a premature rebellion, which he quelled with four *Catilinarian orations* (cf. *Catiline) and with military action before it won wider support. He saw himself as the savior of the traditional republic and upper classes, but under an extreme decree of the Senate, he had executed a Roman praetor and four other leading citizens, with dubious legal authority. The *populares* and his personal enemies forced him into exile in 58 and confiscated his house in Rome. He was restored to Rome the next year and had his house rebuilt.

He was now at the height of his oratorical powers, as we see from three of his greatest courtroom speeches (*pro Sestio*, 57; *pro Caelio*, 56; *pro Milone*, 52), but in the competition for political power between *Caesar and Pompey that led to the First Triumvirate (with *Crassus) and the Civil War, he was sidelined by his inability to organize a political base. He was identified with the wealthy, whose causes he had promoted, but not accepted by them. Handicapped by a tongue often too fast and sharp, he was never widely liked outside a circle of intimate friends and aspiring young lawyer/politicians. His character, revealed in unvarnished clarity in his *Epistles to Atticus* (cf. *Atticus) and *To Friends*, is often repellent. His self-aggrandizement can only partially be justified by the need of an outsider to promote his own achievements and dignity. His choice of a house on a hillside of the Palatine near those of revered old families such as Claudii and Livii, ostentatiously overlooking the Roman Forum and Senate house, reveals a lack of social discretion that branded him in the code of polite society as inurbane. When he had attempted to mingle in fashionable society at the bathing resort Baiae, he was met with the quip, "What does a man from Arpinum know about baths?" In these years he wrote two major dialogues, *On* (the education of) *the Orator* (55) and *On the Republic* (or *Commonwealth*, 54–51, including the important *Dream of Scipio*, with its vision of the reincarnation of the servants of the Republic), and began his *On Laws*. He also governed the province Cilicia from 51 to 50, without distinction.

Despite overtures from Caesar he belatedly joined Pompey in the Civil War, quipping that a dinner guest is never late who arrives before dinner is ready. He was afterward left in peace by Caesar in Rome, where he wrote works on duty, death, fate, the nature of the gods, divination, old age, friendship, the history of oratory, and techniques of rhetoric and practiced public speaking with his friends, always in nostalgia for the republic. His intentions in these writings, to defend the liberties impossible under a dictator and to arouse indignation against Caesar, are clearer in three *Caesarian orations*, where he begs clemency for Caesar's enemies. Crushed by the death of his daughter Tullia in 45, his opposition became less veiled. Excluded from the conspiracy, he rejoiced at Caesar's assassination, and in the *Philippics*, probably his greatest speeches, he attacked *Marc Antony mercilessly for his irrationality. He tried to guide Caesar's heir Octavian (*Augustus), but proscribed under the Second Triumvirate, he was executed at Caieta by a former client, of whom he had quipped that only a great lawyer could have saved a man so clearly guilty. His head and writing hand were displayed first in Antony's dining room, later in the Roman Forum.

His speeches have lasted as models of aggressive legal and political argument and the forceful rhetorical style. His greatest influence has lain in the casting of binds or dilemmas on opponents (the Metelli in the *Verrines*, the popular supporters of Catiline, *Clodia in *pro Caelio*) and on authoritarian leaders (Sulla in *pro Roscio Amerino*, Caesar in the *Caesarians*). Where *Aristotle discussed how to arouse various emotions in persuasion, Cicero concentrated in theory (*On Invention*) and practice on indignation and the human desire for independence and self-respect. He also developed an allusive, allegorical style of playing on these emotions under tyrants, derived from *Demetrius of Phalerum and widely copied in the empire and the Renaissance.

His philosophical dialogues introduced a new form of discourse based on the adversary principle of the law courts, where, although Cicero often makes himself spokesman for one case, judgment is left to the reader. He advances Academic and Stoic views, even when opposed to his own, with eloquence and sympathy, but castigates the Epicureans as too dogmatic. His dialogues privilege individual judgment against the tyranny of moral, political, or religious codes.

Cicero's chief legacy remains his formulation of the republic as the political institution best adapted to promote the rule of reason and the rights of the individual citizen to dignity and protection under the law. This concept owes much to *Plato's *Republic* and to the formulation of the mixed constitution (monarchy, oligarchy, democracy) by *Polybius and the circle around *Scipio Aemilianus. Cicero's republic requires for its leaders three sorts of education: a moral education in the performance of duty and how to reconcile the conflict of duties and of duty and self-interest (provided in his *On Duties*, or *Moral Obligations*, his most widely read textbook); a rhetorical education in how to present proposals and policies in the clearest and most persuasive manner; and a humane or liberal education in history, literature, and philosophy from which to understand the principles, norms, and limits of human behavior and freedom (both provided in his *On the Orator*). Cicero subscribes to a view first advanced by Plato of reason (or the mind) as the controlling force or charioteer within the human *animus* (psyche, spirit), housed within the body. Reason is that which appeals to the laws and norms of social behavior, acquired during education, to control both the responses of the body such as grief, anger, hatred, and sexual lust and the appetitive desires of the human spirit such as ambition and love. He thus provides the chief textbooks of classical education for Western elites. It has been the naive assumption of the Ciceronian view that the electorate of a republic will choose as its leaders those who have learned and demonstrated the pursuit of duty to the state and to humanity and the ability to control by reason desires and responses in themselves and in society. Moreover, those educated in duty to these values and in the supremacy of reason over desire and emotion have tended to dismiss as "irrational" those not so educated, whether women, the lower classes, or "native" populations. Twentieth-century philosophies, defending the relativism of values and the rights of women, the masses, and minorities, usually rejected Cicero, republican values, and classical education.

Bibliography: T.N. Mitchell, *Cicero the Senior Statesman*, 1991; N. Wood, *Cicero's Social and Political Thought*, 1988.

Robert Dyer

CIMON (early fifth century B.C.)

Cimon was an Athenian politician and military leader who was active in the fifth century.

Cimon was born to a wealthy and well-known family; his father was *Miltiades, a successful Athenian military commander, and his mother was Hegesipyle, the daughter of the Thracian king Olorus. Cimon came to prominence as a supporter of *Themistocles at the end of the Persian Wars.

Cimon's principal accomplishments involve the consolidation of the Delian League as a naval power and the command of Athenian military operations in the Aegean. During these campaigns, Cimon also restored *Theseus' body to Athens. According to *Plutarch, when Cimon took the island of Scyros, he discovered Theseus' tomb. In response to an oracle that urged the Athenians to find Theseus' bones and to set them up in a position of honor in Athens, Cimon returned the body to Athens with much celebration and ceremony.

During his consolidation of the Delian League as a naval power, Cimon seems to have favored a policy of peace with Sparta. In 462–461, *Thucydides reports that Sparta found itself in a civil war against the helots and asked its allies, including Athens, to come to their aid. According to Thucydides, Cimon brought a large force to Sparta, but the Spartans refused their help and sent them home because of their size and "enterprising and revolutionary character." The Athenians did not endure this humiliation well; they broke off their alliance with Sparta, and a short time later—in 461—Cimon was ostracized.

When Cimon returned to Athens at the conclusion of his ostracism, he once again led Athenian naval operations, this time against the Persians at Cyprus. Cimon died during this action in 451.

Bibliography: C.W. Fornara and L.J. Samons, *Athens from Cleisthenes to Pericles*, 1991.

Jeff Rydberg-Cox

CINCINNATUS, L. QUINTIUS (fifth century B.C.)

Cincinnatus was a Roman patrician who participated in freeing the consul Minucius from the Aequi, though the tradition of Cincinnatus' involvement seems to derive from Roman folklore.

There is a divergence of opinion as to the life of Cincinnatus, but it is popularly suggested that Cincinnatus served as a valiant dictator who saved Minucius from the Aequian siege on Mt. Algidus. Due to the military successes of the Aequi, the Romans found it necessary to employ a dictator to pull all the city's resources together and present a strong resistance to a determined enemy. Legend has it that among a group of candidates the Romans chose Cincinnatus because his character was of the highest caliber. Tradition stresses the idea declaring that the delegates who carried the news of his election found the Roman patrician humbly plowing his own fields.

When called upon to assist Rome, Cincinnatus put down his farming tools and accepted the magistracy of dictator, assuming absolute power over the state. As soon as he took his place, he quickly assembled an army of new troops to fight against the enemy forces of Aequi. He marched his army all night in an attempt to catch the unwary enemy. Successful, he continued to battle for the next fourteen to sixteen days and succeeded in totally vanquishing the field army of the Aequi. After observing the swift and powerful counterattack, the Aequi besiegers released Minucius.

Upon returning to Rome, Cincinnatus relinquished his authority and went back to work on his farm beyond the Tiber. The people were so impressed by Cincinnatus' noble behavior that they proclaimed him a national hero. Many years later, so tradition goes, Rome was having problems with the powers of *Spurius Maelius. Once again she reached out to her respected general. Though Cincinnatus was older, he provided the leadership that triumphed over Spurius Maelius.

Although it is speculated that the events of Cincinnatus' life are only folklore, the stories were very popular among the Romans. There is no evidence either to prove or disprove Cincinnatus' reigns as dictator. The only thing that can be established is the success of the Romans against their enemies from a very early period. Whether or not Cincinnatus is responsible for Rome's triumph over the Aequi remains in question.

Bibliography: R.M. Ogilvie, *Commentary on Livy Books 1–5*, 1965.

Richard Draper

CINNA, LUCIUS CORNELIUS (c. 128–84 b.c.)

Cinna was a Roman patrician who eventually became the absolute ruler of Rome after becoming exiled by his colleague Octavius. Cinna also played a significant role in the civil war between the socialists and *Sulla.

As consul in 87, Cinna was illegally driven out of Rome after promoting the law of *Sulpicius, which allowed Italians into all thirty-five tribes, regardless of their background. Because the surrounding populace found Cinna's plight to be their own, they rallied against Sulla in order to help reinstate Cinna's Roman citizenship as well as effect the law of Sulpicius. After gathering together thirty legions of men and the support of Carbo, Sertorius, and *Marius, Cinna marched against Rome and overthrew the government, appointing himself as joint consul with Marius in 86. Ironically, though Cinna and Marius massacred Sulla's troops in order to achieve the status of consul in Rome, after the death of Marius, Cinna effected a well-organized government that eliminated the use of force to control its citizens. In addition to dismissing violence to establish order in Rome, Cinna conducted financial reforms. Since Cinna held absolute power over the Republic, he was enabled to make his government reformations without much opposition.

In an attempt to regain Rome, Sulla decided to prepare his eastern forces for an attack on the capital once they had finished their war with *Mithridates VI. Cinna suspected Sulla's plans and, in an attempt to frustrate Sulla's designs, with Carbo, his fellow consul in 85 and 84, decided to attain an army, cross the Adriatic sea, and make a preemptive strike against Sulla in Greece. His plans led to his downfall and death in 84. While making the journey, his army mutinied and killed him. Soon after Cinna's death, Sulla invaded Rome and disintegrated Cinna's new governmental reforms.

Though Cinna's powers in Rome were as absolute as those of Sulla or of *Caesar, there is little about him on record. As a controversial figure, what little information that has survived in the historical record has been greatly colored, and a clear evaluation of his life and motives is difficult to make.

Bibliography: H. Bennett, *Cinna and His Times*, 1923; H.H. Scullard, *From the Gracchi to Nero: A History of Rome from 133 b.c. to a.d. 68*, 5th ed., 1982.

Richard Draper

CLAUDIAN, CLAUDIUS (c. 370s?–404?)

Claudian was a poet whose innovative use of Latin epic verse in panegyric was influential to modern times.

Claudian was born in Egypt, perhaps Alexandria, where many youths received rhetorical training as preparation for civil careers. His early poetry was in Greek, but he adopted Latin when seeking patronage in Italy in the mid-390s. He produced verse panegyric in epic form with strongly classicizing motifs at a time when panegyric was usually in prose, structured according to nonnarrative, thematic topics. His new style was popular with the Roman aristocracy. From 395, he was employed by the imperial court of Honorius (394–423) and specifically by *Stilicho, who used him, unusually, as a regular mouthpiece. Hitherto, panegyric was usually produced for individual occasions, without an ongoing relation between poet and honorand, and though its purpose was praise, this did not commonly entail systematic propaganda advocating specific policies and claims. Active propaganda, however, is evident in Claudian's extant panegyrics, invectives, and epic poems. Claudian also produced over fifty minor poems and one major mythological epic, the unfinished "Rape of Proserpine." Claudian's work halted in 404; possibly he died then. Stilicho published a deluxe omnibus version of his major works.

Stilicho's patronage of Claudian set a vogue for epic panegyricists as the propagandists of leading generals and emperors in the fifth-century West. Claudian was used as a model for panegyric and invective by poets from *Sidonius Apollinaris through the Middle Ages (e.g., Alan of Lille) to early modern French rhetoric.

Bibliography: A. Cameron, *Claudian: Poetry and Propaganda at the Court of Honorius*, 1970.

Andrew Gillett

CLAUDIUS (Tiberius Claudius Nero Germanicus, 10 B.C.– A.D. 54)

Claudius was a Roman emperor and scholar whose usurpation of the throne in 41 marked a significant change in the acquisition and maintenance of imperial power in Rome.

An heir of third degree to the Roman imperial throne, Claudius was given short shrift in his childhood and youth due to a number of physical deformities; his slurred speech and wild gesticulations repelled even his own family. Given no official role despite his familial connections, Claudius devoted himself to his studies and began writing history.

In 37, Gaius Caesar (*Caligula) became *princeps* and named his uncle Claudius as a consul but made him the object of ridicule. Claudius thus remained isolated from the affairs of state. Caligula, hated and feared by almost everyone, was assassinated by officers of the Praetorian Guard in 41. Claudius was pressed to take the throne by the Guard, a move to which the Senate acceded, conferring the powers of the principate upon Claudius.

Claudius owed his elevation to the Guard, a fact he could not forget. He moved to consolidate power into a single family—his own—and got the loyalty of the military and subordinates through awards and improvements in status. Under Claudius, the informal court became more defined, with one of the central figures being his third wife, Messalina. She bore Claudius a son, Britannicus, but began to indulge in adulterous affairs, a practice that ultimately resulted in her execution for treason.

Claudius was able to achieve his dream of invading Britain, which he planned for a year before executing it in 43. He completed a road over the Alps toward the Danube, and though he spent only sixteen days in Britain, he considered this adventure the high point of his life.

Claudius was concerned with the smooth transition of power after his death and made a will naming Britannicus and *Nero, the son of Claudius' fourth wife *Agrippina the Younger, joint rulers. After Claudius' death in October 54, Britannicus subsequently died under suspicious circumstances two months after his father. Nero assumed sole power immediately and set about denigrating the reputation of Claudius, who, in many ways, was the first "true" emperor of Rome.

Bibliography: B. Levick, *Claudius*, 1990.

Connie Evans

CLAUDIUS CAECUS, APPiUS (c. 350–after 280 b.c.)

Appius Claudius Caecus was a Roman aristocrat especially remembered for building the first major road to connect Rome with other Italian cities.

A lack of ancient sources hampers our knowledge of Appius Claudius' early career. He was born to the aristocratic Claudian family in the mid-fourth century B.C. and held a series of political offices, but only through his dramatic activities as censor for 312–308 did he come to the forefront of Roman politics. In this office he built the first aqueduct to bring water into Rome and constructed the first stage of the Appian Way, connecting Rome to Capua (132 miles). His actions proved to be controversial, however, for he did not consult the Senate, and eventually these projects drained the treasury of its resources. He also tried as censor to democratize Roman politics, but he met with strong senatorial opposition. His plan to enroll sons of ex-slaves as senators and his restructuring of voting procedures to increase the value of the lower-class vote, though progressive, were certainly attempts to bolster his own political position. Appius served as consul in 307 and 296, commanding the army in the Third Samnite War and commemorating his achievements by building a temple to Bellona, the Roman goddess of war.

In his later years Appius solidified his legacy as an archetypical Roman patriot: Though blind (*caecus*), he entered the Senate in 280 to argue against making peace with *Pyrrhus of Epirus. Among later Romans his published speeches, legal treatises, and moral sayings served as a model for Latin prose.

Bibliography: T.J. Cornell, *The Beginnings of Rome*, 1995.

David Christiansen

CLEANTHES (331/330–230/229 B.C.)

Born in Assos in Asia Minor, Cleanthes succeeded *Zeno of Citium as second head of the Stoa. He developed the cosmological and theological elements in Zeno's system.

Cleanthes was a boxer in youth but was converted to Stoicism on meeting Zeno in Athens in 281/280. Impoverished, Cleanthes labored by night in order to attend Zeno's lectures by day. He was critical of *Arcesilaus' theory of the reasonable, which he considered inconsistent with the Sceptic's theory of suspension of judgment. Cleanthes' works also attacked the atomists and astronomers. Although little survives from Cleanthes' writings, we do possess his *Hymn to Zeus*, in which he lays the basis for the Stoic cosmology of God as the vital and material principle (*logos*) of the universe, predetermining its course and reconciling its contradictions. The wise are in harmony with the nature of the cosmos, while the wicked suffer because of disharmony in their souls. Developing *Heraclitus' philosophy, Cleanthes describes the cyclic death and rebirth of the cosmos out of chaos and fire. At the end of every cycle, there is a cosmic conflagration (*ekpyrosis*) when all returns to a singularity. These ideas were developed even further by later Stoics, who worked out a logical formula for Cleanthes' theory of determinism. On a cognitive level, he upheld Zeno's theory of a material, mortal soul but explained our arrival at a notion of God by means of the intellect. While the soul dies in this life, it will be recreated along with the rest of the cosmic material at the next world cycle.

Cleanthes' successor, *Chrysippus, was critical of his master but developed his theories more methodically. Cleanthes' theology left its mark on later Stoicism and was thus passed down to Christian writers as Boethius. Later philosophers, like Spinoza and his Neo-Stoic companions, reused Cleanthes' notion of God, the soul, and the universe.

Bibliography: A.A. Long and D.N. Sedley, *The Hellenistic Philosophers*, 2 vols., 1987; M.R. Wright, *Cosmology in Antiquity*, 1995.

Menahem Luz

CLEISTHENES (sixth century B.C.)

Cleisthenes is the Athenian statesman who is generally considered to be the founder of Athenian democracy.

Cleisthenes was the son of Megacles and Agariste, a daughter of *Cleisthenes of Sicyon. He was from the aristocratic Alcmaeonid family. He had been archon under the tyrant *Hippias in 525/524, yet Hippias later expelled the Alcmaeonids, as well as other Athenian families, probably after an assassination attempt in 514. After the expulsion, Cleisthenes helped rebuild the temple of Delphi, on the condition that the prophetess there continually recommend to the Spartans that they overthrow the Athenian tyranny. After King *Cleomenes I of Sparta deposed Hippias in 510, Cleisthenes reentered the city to compete for leadership in the new government. When his rival Isagoras was elected archon in 508, Cleisthenes made an alliance with the people and promised to pass wide-ranging democratic reforms. Isagoras appealed to Cleomenes for assistance, citing the ancient curse against the Alcmaeonids (cf. *Cylon). Cleisthenes then withdrew from Athens while Spartan forces advanced. The Spartan forces, however, met with strong popular resistance, and both Cleomenes and Isagoras were forced to leave. Cleisthenes and his partisans returned to Athens, setting up a new democratic constitution.

Cleisthenes began his reform program by changing the basis of Athenian citizenship and the nature of the four tribes, which were the previous political and military divisions of the people. Athenian citizenship had formerly depended on birth into one of the phratries (brotherhoods), a subdivision of the four tribes. To break the old tribal orientation of Attica, Cleisthenes now made the basis for citizenship geographical by dividing Attica into more than 150 demes. Those living within a specific deme were placed on a roll, and hereafter deme rolls were basic citizenship lists.

Next Cleisthenes formed ten new tribes, each composed of groups of demes from the three geographical areas of Attica: plain, coast, and city. Cleisthenes hoped that these new tribes would destroy the old regional loyalties and place city residents within all the tribes.

The new base of ten tribes led to the creation of a new body, the Council of Five Hundred (boule). In this Council, fifty members were chosen annually by lot from each of the ten tribes. The boule replaced *Solon's Council of Four Hundred, taking over its function of preparing business for the Assembly (*ec-clesia*) and also managing financial and foreign affairs in the city. Each group of fifty men served in turn for one-tenth of the year as a standing committee of the Council. During their period of service, the presiding fifty members of the Council were called *prytaneis*; the chair and the secretary of the *prytaneis* changed every day.

Cleisthenes' system led to a much wider and active participation in politics by all Athenian men. This system prevailed in Athens for centuries with only a few interruptions.

Bibliography: J. Ober, "The Athenian Revolution of 508/7 B.C.E. Violence, Authority, and the Origins of Democracy," in *Cultural Poetics in Archaic Greece: Cult, Perform-ance, Politics*, 1993, 215–232, D. Stockton, *The Classical Athenian Democracy*, 1990.

Andrew G. Traver

CLEISTHENES OF SICYON (r. c. 600–570 B.c.)

Cleisthenes was a tyrant of the Peloponnesian city Sicyon who was an ancestor of the great Athenian statesmen *Cleisthenes and *Pericles.

Cleisthenes belonged to the family of Orthagoras, which ruled for a record

100 years (c. 665–565). He deposed his predecessor, the Argive Adrastus, by driving public opinion against him. First he invited Adrastus' personal enemy, Melanippus, to Sicyon and transferred to him all the personal honors that had been previously due Adrastus. He then changed the names of the city tribes to create a distinction between the Argives and Sicyonians. The Sicyonians were given derogatory names, such as "pig-men" and "donkey-men," whereas the Argives received the presumptuous title "rulers of the people." He also expelled the Homeric rhapsodes because of their praise of Argos. After attaining power in this way, he decided to betroth his daughter, Agarista, to the best Greek man. In order to identify him, he sent out a general invitation for a yearlong contest at Sicyon. Men from as far away as Italy competed in games of wrestling, racing, and conversation. Cleisthenes chose an Athenian, Megacles of the famous Alcmaeonid clan. The marriage produced another Cleisthenes, who became an important democratic reformer for Athens, and a grandson, Pericles. Cleisthenes, the Sicyonian tyrant, is also credited with having won the chariot race at the Olympics.

Bibliography: A. Griffin, *Sicyon*, 1982.

Luis Molina

CLEMENT OF ALEXANDRIA, SAINT (Titus Flavius, Clemens, c. 150–c. 215)

Clement was a Christian writer and head of a school at Alexandria.

As tradition holds, Clement was born a pagan in Athens. Very little is known of his life, due to his own reticence about himself and a dearth of contemporary evidence. Our principal informant is *Eusebius of Caesarea, though he does not tell us much more than Clement himself does. Clement indicates that, avid for Christian instruction, he traveled to Greece, Italy, Syria, and Egypt. Eventually he arrived in Alexandria, where he found the right teacher for him (probably Pantaenus, who may have headed a catechetical school there). His education there must have consisted of much Greek philosophy and Gnostic ideas. It seems that he succeeded his teacher as head of a school that taught Christianity as the one true philosophy. That Clement became *Origen's teacher, as Eusebius indicates, is open to question. He left Alexandria at some point and reappeared in 211 as the bearer of a letter from Alexander (in Cappadocia), a possible former pupil with whom he may have been staying, to the church at Antioch. Clement's death may be presumed from another letter from Alexander that speaks about him in the past tense.

Much of Clement's writing remains, and it provides a clear view of the remarkable nature of his ideas. *Exhortation to the Greeks* comprises an introduction to Christian philosophy, showing how Greek philosophy prefigured Christianity. It also attacks Greek religion and "reveals" the secrets of the mysteries. The *Tutor* examines Christian ethics. The *Miscellanies*, in eight books, gathers more advanced and esoteric philosophical ideas, both Greek and Chris-

tian. Other, lesser works are also extant. Clement is significant for his furthering
the development of Christian theology and ethics. Although he was very interested (and largely successful) in reconciling classical Greek culture and Christianity, it is clear that much of his knowledge of Greek literature came from
florilegia rather than from deep familiarity with the sources.

Bibliography: S.R.C. Lilla, *Clement of Alexandria: A Study in Christian Platonism and
Gnosticism*, 1971.

Mark Gustafson

CLEOMENES I (r. c. 520–490 b.c.)

Cleomenes I was a king of Sparta in the generation preceding the Persian
Wars. He played an important role in the city's relations with other Greek states
and was famed for his madness.

Although he had already shown signs of mental illness by the time of his
father's death, Cleomenes was allowed to succeed to the throne because he was
the eldest of four sons. In 510, after learning from the Delphic Oracle that the
Spartans must free Athens, Cleomenes marched to Attica and expelled the tyrant
*Hippias, son of *Pisitratus, whose family had ruled Athens for thirty-six years.
It was later learned, however, that the Alcmaeonids, a family who wished to
regain power in Athens, had bribed the Delphic priestess. Cleomenes subsequently attempted to reinstall Hippias but failed. Around this time, the Greek
cities of Asia Minor were in a state of rebellion against the Persian king. *Aristagoras, one of the leaders of the revolt, attempted to gain the support of
Sparta. However, when he attempted to bribe Cleomenes, the king's daughter,
Gorgo, warned her father that this would be improper, and the mission failed.
(Aristagoras was later able to obtain the support of Athens, which subsequently
earned the glory for the defeat of the Persians at the Battle of Marathon.) In
491, Cleomenes bribed the Delphic priestess in order to depose his political
opponent, Demaratus. Although he was acquitted of criminal wrongdoing, he
subsequently went mad and was imprisoned. There he committed suicide by
slashing himself to pieces.

Bibliography: P. Cartledge, *Sparta and Lakonia*, 1979.

Luis Molina

CLEOMENES III (c. 260–222 b.c.)

Cleomenes was the Spartan king who reorganized Sparta's political structure
and struggled unsuccessfully against the Achaean League.

The son of King Leonidas II, Cleomenes married Agiatis, the widow of the
murdered reformer *Agis IV. Perhaps influenced by her, Cleomenes later began
a program of radical social change similar to that of Agis. In the spirit of the
constitution of *Lycurgus, Cleomenes canceled debt, redivided the land, and
restored the old Spartan training of the youth.

In 229, he began an expansionistic program and annexed the Acadian cities of Tegea, Mantinea, and Orchomenus. Because of Sparta's aggressive military actions, Cleomenes soon found himself involved in a war with the Achaean League led by *Aratus of Sicyon. In 227, Cleomenes established himself as absolute ruler in Sparta by staging an almost bloodless coup. He ejected the ephors and abolished their office. Having increased his power at home, Cleomenes first sought to implement his Lycurgan reforms, then strove to expand his boundaries at the expense of the Achaean League. By 224 he had captured Argos, placed Corinth under siege, and seriously threatened the League's survival.

In desperation, the Achaean League appealed to its former enemy King *Antigonus III for assistance. Although Antigonus initially failed to break Spartan lines, a revolt in Argos (224) thwarted Sparta's expansionary program. The rebellion of Argos stimulated a chain of events that finally ended with Antigonus' defeat of Cleomenes at Sellasia (222). Sparta fell to Antigonus, and Cleomenes escaped to Egypt to live with his patron *Ptolemy III. His plan worked for only a short time, for Ptolemy's successor imprisoned him. His intrigue to start a revolution in Alexandria having failed, Cleomenes committed suicide.

Though Cleomenes was successful in conquering a number of Greek lands during his lifetime, he did not organize his government in an enduring fashion. Soon after Cleomenes' death, most of Sparta's annexed victories were lost.

Bibliography: P. Cartledge, *Sparta and Lakonia*, 1979.

Richard Draper

CLEON (c. 465–422 B.C.)

Cleon, son of Cleaenetus, was a leading Athenian politician and one of the so-called demagogues who dominated the assemblies and law courts after the death of *Pericles in 429.

Although little is known of Cleon's early career, there is abundant evidence for his activities in the 420s. In 427 he persuaded the assembly to vote for the execution of all the men of Mytilene for revolting against Athens (the decision was reversed the next day). The following year he charged the poet *Aristophanes, who had portrayed him in an unflattering light in a comedy, with slander against the state. In 425 Cleon oversaw an increase both in the tribute levied on Athens' subject-allies and in the amount the city paid citizens for jury service. This was the same year in which he achieved military victory over the Spartans at Pylos. In 423 Cleon successfully argued for the execution of all the citizens of Scione, and in the following year he led an expedition to Thrace against the Spartan general Brasidas. Cleon was killed in a battle outside of the city of Amphipolis in 422.

Cleon was the first of a new breed of Athenian politicians whose power depended on gaining and keeping the support of the assemblies and law courts rather than on regular officeholding, the traditional avenue to political power. The biographical tradition, which is aristocratic in perspective, is hostile to the new politicians and in particular to Cleon. On balance, Cleon's career included successes and failures.

Bibliography: W.R. Connor, *The New Politicians of Fifth-Century Athens*, 1971; M. Ostwald, *From Popular Sovereignty to the Sovereignty of Law*, 1986.

Carl A. Anderson

CLEOPATRA VII (69–31 B.C.)

Cleopatra was the last of the Ptolemaic rulers of Egypt whose political and romantic liaisons with *Julius Caesar and *Marc Antony ultimately failed to preserve Egypt's independence from the Roman Empire.

Cleopatra, whose ancestry was Macedonian Greek, was, in accordance with ancient Egyptian practice, almost certainly the result of an incestuous relationship between her father, Ptolemy XII, and one of his sisters. Inbreeding weakened the Ptolemaic rulers—though Cleopatra seems to have been an exception—and the kingdom suffered a concomitant decline, despite its great natural resources and its support of intellectual activities.

By the time of Cleopatra's birth, Egypt was almost entirely in the thrall of the Roman Empire. On one of Ptolemy's trips to Rome, his two eldest daughters, in turn, tried to seize power, but with the help of the Romans, Ptolemy was restored to the throne in 57 and had his rebellious daughters executed. On his death in 51, therefore, he left the throne to Cleopatra VII and her younger brother, Ptolemy XIII, whose advisers wanted to get rid of his sister.

Cleopatra showed early skill in her handling of a revolt in Syria and deftly handled the court intrigue that swirled around her at home. She also observed events unfolding in the Roman republic, where Julius Caesar, having disposed of his rivals for control of Rome, was now the effective ruler of the ancient world. With civil war imminent in Egypt between Cleopatra and her brother, Caesar traveled there in 48, intending to resolve the crisis. Cleopatra managed to meet Caesar shortly after his arrival, and they very quickly became lovers, ensuring that Caesar would take her side in the dispute. Caesar ordered that Cleopatra and Ptolemy should rule jointly and, in accordance with custom, marry, but a subsequent rebellion led by their younger sister, Arsinoe, in which she enlisted the support of Ptolemy, put an end to hope for a peaceful joint rule. In the subsequent conflict, Ptolemy was killed and Arsinoe taken prisoner; Cleopatra henceforth became the *de facto* ruler, though Caesar insisted that she marry her youngest brother, Ptolemy XIV, and rule jointly with him.

Caesar left a pregnant Cleopatra behind in 47 and, after pursuing some foreign campaigns, returned to Rome in triumph the following year. Cleopatra, having given birth to their son, Ptolemy Caesar (Caesarion), soon traveled to Rome. The Romans branded Cleopatra as Caesar's whore, and Caesar refused to acknowledge their son publicly. Caesar's increasing power and perceived aspirations for an imperial crown led to his assassination by a group of conspirators in 44. Fearing for her and her son's safety, Cleopatra fled back to Egypt that summer; soon after her return, her coruler and husband Ptolemy XIV died, probably murdered on her orders. Cleopatra made her son coruler as Ptolemy XV Caesar in the hope that he might one day be recognized as Caesar's heir.

Cleopatra began to focus her energies on the renewal of her country and was able to maintain stability even in the face of a series of natural disasters. In Rome, Caesar's assassins, *Brutus and Cassius, left for the East to gather support, leaving Caesar's nephew and acknowledged heir, Octavian (*Augustus) in control of Rome, though Caesar's close ally Marc Antony challenged his dominance there. Civil war was averted in Rome by the creation of the Second Triumvirate, in which Octavian, Antony, and *Lepidus ruled Rome jointly.

All of the triumvirs, as well as Caesar's assassins, courted Cleopatra for her support, but she wisely prevaricated until the Battle of Philippi in 42 eliminated all the challengers for Roman control except Octavian and Antony. The two men agreed to split the empire between them, with Octavian taking the west and Antony the east. A skilled military leader and a shrewd politician, Antony sought Cleopatra's financial support for a plan to conquer Parthia. Meeting at Tarsus, Antony and Cleopatra became lovers, and she agreed to support his venture in return for protection. Antony departed for Italy to reach an understanding with Octavian, and to seal the bargain, he agreed to marry Octavian's sister, Octavia, in 40; Cleopatra meanwhile had given birth to twins by Antony.

With Antony absent for most of the next four years, Cleopatra once again concentrated her energies on reviving her country's economy and infrastructure. She learned Egyptian—the only one of her line to do so—and immersed herself in her country's religion, taking on the persona of the goddess Isis. The economy recovered quite well under her guidance, and she was able to build an exceptional military force as well.

In 37, Antony returned to pursue the Parthian campaign and asked Cleopatra to join him in Syria. His position in Rome declining, he made a political decision to renew his relationship with Cleopatra in order to reassert himself. Cleopatra, however, insisted on being given title to several territories within the Roman Empire in exchange for underwriting his army and constructing a large fleet to support it, a proposal to which Antony readily agreed.

Living together again, Cleopatra became pregnant and gave birth to their second son before meeting Antony in Syria in 35 in the aftermath of his failed campaign to conquer Parthia. Spurning a request from Octavia to join him, Antony made a final decision to remain with Cleopatra, whom he regarded as his ally in the inevitable confrontation with Octavian, who had branded Antony as a traitor. Antony responded with a ceremony that named Caesarion as Caesar's legitimate heir, a patently untrue claim meant as a direct challenge to Octavian.

Antony and Cleopatra began to concentrate their forces in Ephesus in 33 in anticipation of the conflict with Octavian, but their failure to attack him in Italy allowed Octavian time to gather his forces. Meeting at Actium in 31, Antony and Cleopatra's forces were trapped, and they moved the battle to sea rather than face Octavian on the field. The confrontation was a disaster, and Antony and Cleopatra just managed to escape, with Octavian capturing much of their fleet; Antony's army also was forced to surrender.

On 1 August 30, with Octavian entering Alexandria, Cleopatra hid herself in her mausoleum. Antony, believing her dead, attempted suicide; mortally wounded, he was informed of her survival and had himself carried to her tomb, where he died in her arms. Octavian and his troops arrived before Cleopatra could kill herself and placed her under strict guard. Probably with the complicity of Octavian, Cleopatra managed to have the guard leave her alone briefly and proceeded to complete her suicide attempt. When Octavian and his men returned to the tomb, they found her dead and her attendants dying, either of poison or snakebite. Shortly after Octavian's victory, Egypt was annexed to the Roman Empire, and Octavian himself became *princeps* of the empire under the name Augustus Caesar.

Most historians agree that very little is known of Cleopatra apart from the accounts written by the Romans, her avowed enemies, whose opinions of the Egyptian queen are colored by their bias. Her abilities as a ruler and a politician were thus subsumed by representations of her as a temptress who had seduced the two most powerful men in the ancient world and led them to ruin. The real Cleopatra was a woman ahead of her time whose skills as a monarch not only compared favorably with those of her male counterparts but, in several ways, exceeded them.

Bibliography: M. Grant, *Cleopatra*, 1972; L. Hughes-Hallett, *Cleopatra: Histories, Dreams and Distortions*, 1990.

Connie Evans

CLODIA (c. 95–45 b.c.)

Clodia, a member of the powerful Claudian family, was made notorious in *Cicero's *Pro Caelio*.

Clodia was the sister of *Publius Clodius Pulcher and was married to her first cousin Quintus Caecilius Metellus Celer, who died in 59. Clodia is frequently identified with the beautiful, cultured, and fickle Lesbia of *Catullus' poetry, although hard evidence is lacking. For a picture of Clodia, we rely primarily on the evidence of her enemy Cicero. Marcus Caelius Rufus was Clodia's lover from 59 to 57 when he apparently broke off the relationship. In 56, Lucius Sempronius Atratinus charged Caelius with a series of offenses including an attempt to poison Clodia. In *Pro Caelio*, Cicero's defense of Caelius clearly depends on a subtle attack on Clodia's morals, while defending the questionable behavior of Caelius. Caelius was acquitted, and at this point Clodia passes from the public record.

Bibliography: A. Vasaly, *Representations: Images of the World in Ciceronian Oratory*, 1993.

Christine Cornell

CLODIUS PULCHER, PUBLIUS (92–52 B.C.)

Clodius was a populist Roman statesman who championed the interests of the urban plebs and whose willingness to utilize violence characterized the disintegration of the republican political process in the 50s.

Born the youngest son into a noble patrician house but left in relatively strained circumstances after his father's death in 76, Clodius, of fine appearance, eloquent, and noted for bold behavior, amassed, during his foreshortened career, considerable wealth and equal notoriety. His early military career included the incitement of discontent among the troops of his brother-in-law *Lucullus (68/67) and capture by pirates in 67. In 62 he was accused of intrusion into the exclusively female ceremonies in honor of the Bona Dea. In the lead-up to his trial in 61, his supporters resorted to violence in the voting assembly. At the trial, *Cicero gave evidence that contradicted Clodius' alibi, sparking a vendetta that would become one of the defining aspects of Clodius' subsequent career. When Clodius was acquitted, his opponents cried bribery and intimidation. In 59, while remaining politically independent, Clodius aligned with the powerful coalition of *Pompey, *Crassus, and *Caesar. This alliance smoothed the way to his unusual adoption by a plebeian, allowing his election to the tribunate of 58. He quickly passed popular legislation that included the unprecedented distribution of free grain to the Roman populace and the restoration of the *collegia* (trade guilds, religious associations, and local clubs). His systematic registration of college membership seems to have allowed Clodius to exploit these clubs for political purposes, both electorally and in the environment of escalating violence. In the cause of popular sovereignty, he promulgated a law prescribing the execution of citizens without trial. Cicero, the target, fled Rome, and Clodius had a law passed formalizing his exile. Clodius then fell into political conflict with Pompey, effecting for the rest of that year Pompey's withdrawal from public life.

In 57, two of Clodius' rivals (Milo and Sestius) gained the tribunate, their followers meeting Clodius' followers with similar violence; and those who wished to see Clodius' influence curbed joined with Cicero's supporters, gaining Pompey's backing for Cicero's recall. Cicero, upon his return to Rome, advocated a special commission for Pompey that cut across Clodius' interest in the corn supply. Violence continued to mark this, and the following year, though, during 56, while aedile, Clodius eventually reconciled with Pompey. In early 52 (a year that, owing to political disruption, had opened without elected magistrates), Clodius was canvassing for the praetorship, Milo for the consulship, when their retinues met on the Appian Way (18 January 52), and a brawl resulted in Clodius' death. The following day, an urban crowd cremated his body, the Roman Senate House being consumed in the conflagration.

Clodius was demonized by a historical tradition that took its cue from hostile

Ciceronian rhetoric and an instinctive aversion to popular reform. It is clear that Clodius retained the deep affection of the urban plebs. The rioting after his death, with houses looted and assaults made on individuals displaying signs of wealth, offers a rare but telling example of class hatred being given public expression.

Bibliography: J. Tatum, *The Patrician Tribune. Publius Clodius Pulcher*, 1999.

Tom Hillard

COMMODUS, LUCIUS AELIUS AURELIUS (161–192)

Commodus was the last of the Antonine dynasty of Roman emperors.

Commodus, the son of *Marcus Aurelius, was born in Lanuvium, one of twins. His brother died as a child. Commodus was educated both by Marcus Aurelius himself and by several teachers. He was a Caesar from 166, Augustus from 177 onward with his marriage to Crispina, and emperor from 180 to 192. His main political action may have been reversing his father's policy of expansion into Germany and declaring peace with the Germans, an action that some analysts believe led to the eventual decline of Rome at the hands of northern Europeans.

By most ancient accounts and modern analyses, Commodus made no contributions to the history of culture and is remembered mainly for his depravity. Yet his reign left its physical mark on the city of Rome: the Temple of Divus Marcus Aurelius was constructed, the Colossus of Sol was changed to represent Commodus as Hercules, and the Thermae Commodianae were built in Rome. His own role in these varied. His propaganda on coins was fairly traditional, following the norms set by his predecessors.

Commodus was the object of dislike, both modern and ancient. He is most frequently renowned for presenting himself in the guise of Hercules, a conflation that was not innovative in itself, since from at least the time of *Augustus rulers presented themselves as descendants of gods and conflated mortal and divine iconography in programs of public propaganda. Commodus' fault may have been in the monumental scale of his propaganda.

Bibliography: M. Grant, *The Antonines: The Roman Empire in Transition*, 1994.

Lisa Auanger

CONSTANTINE (Flavius Valerius Constantinus, c. 270–337)

Constantine was the first Roman emperor to profess Christianity publicly.

Born in about 270, in the Pannonian city of Naissus (modern Nis), Constantine was the son of an officer named Constantius and his concubine *Helena. In 289, Constantine's father put his mother aside in order to marry Theodora, the daughter of Maximian, and four years later became Caesar.

Like his father, Constantine followed a military career, no doubt assisted by his father's exalted rank. He fought in the army of Galerius during a successful invasion of Persia and was serving in the bodyguard of *Diocletian when that emperor abdicated. Although Constantius became senior emperor at that point, Constantine himself was passed over for promotion to imperial rank in favor of connections of Galerius. Although Galerius tried to keep Constantine close to him in the east, he managed to escape and join his father in Gaul.

When Constantius died at York in 306, his army declared Constantine to be his lawful successor. Galerius extended limited recognition to Constantine, awarding him the rank of Caesar in the west. Never a loyal member of Galerius' tetrarchy, Constantine sought dynastic legitimacy through a marriage with Fausta, Maximian's second daughter. This placed him at odds with both Galerius and Maximian's son Maxentius, who had seized control of Italy. After the death of Galerius, Constantine allied himself with Licinius, Galerius' successor, and marched against Maxentius.

Before his final confrontation with Maxentius, he claimed to have had a vision that he interpreted as a sign from the Christian God. He instructed his soldiers to say a prayer and instructed them to affix a Christian symbol (the *labarum*—a version of the Chi-Rho) to their shields. When they were victorious, Constantine ascribed his victory to divine favor and immediately embarked on a policy of favoring and promoting the Christian church.

Although he had already indicated that he tolerated Christianity within the lands that he ruled, and had bishops at his court, he now actively patronized the Church. In Rome, the first great city of the empire that came under his control, he founded a great cathedral, now St. John Lateran, and embellished the shrines of many saints, especially that of St. Peter, where a great basilica was founded after 324.

Constantine also became involved in the internal disputes within the Church. Soon after he had captured Rome a letter reached him from some dissident Christians in Africa who sought his intervention to determine which group of African Christians was correct in a dispute over behavior during the persecution under Diocletian. Constantine sought to refer to matter to councils of bishops in Rome and in the city of Arles, but the dissident group (the Donatists, cf. *Donatus of Casae Nigrae) refused to accept judgment against them, and so Constantine was obliged to legislate against them.

Constantine's victory over Maxentius had brought him control only of the western provinces, but in 324, Constantine finally defeated Licinius at Byzantium and unified the entire empire under his sole rule. That brought him into direct contact with the Arian (cf. *Arius) dispute that had been brewing in Egypt for some years. Constantine sought to intervene directly. He sent his own emissary, Ossius of Cordova, to Alexandria and, when he failed to find a solution, diverted a church council from Ankara to the town of Nicaea so that he could attend himself.

He also ensured that a large number of bishops could attend, so that the Council of Nicaea became the first general synod of the entire church. The Council determined many contentious matters, but Constantine's own intervention was required to settle the wording of the Creed composed by the Council as the definition of orthodox Christian belief.

In 326, Constantine horrified many of his subjects, both Christian and non-Christian alike, by his execution of his wife, Fausta, and his eldest son Crispus. Crispus was Constantine's son by a concubine and had enjoyed the rank of Caesar for nearly ten years and had distinguished himself in the war against Licinius. The reason for the executions remains unclear, although some maintain that Fausta, anxious to promote her own sons, tricked Constantine into executing Crispus. When he discovered the ruse, he had her murdered in revenge.

One of Constantine's most enduring achievements was the foundation of the city that for many years bore his name—Constantinople (now Istanbul). He founded this city on the site of his victory over Licinius, embellished it, and lived there for his final years. He also continued to found churches over the breadth of the empire, most notably the Church of the Holy Sepulchre in Jerusalem, and the Church of the Twelve Apostles in his own city, which he furnished with relics of the apostles and in which he was later entombed.

Constantine also gave attention to matters other than religion and construction. He continued Diocletian's work of reform, abandoning the old silver standard that Diocletian had retained and, instead, striking a new gold coin, the *solidus*, tariffed at seventy-two to the pound. His openhandedness toward the Christians resulted in heavy expenditure, which was only partly financed by the confiscations of temple treasuries. Otherwise Constantine raised taxation, both in cash and in kind, and, within his legislation, continued the process of regulating the economic life of the empire to the benefit both of the central government and of the landowning aristocracy.

He also sought to regulate his own succession, raising his sons Constantine II, Constans, and Constantius II to the rank of Caesar, along with his nephew Julius Dalmatius. Another nephew, Hannibalianus, was appointed as "King of the Pontic peoples." Both of these nephews, however, along with Constantine's half brothers, were murdered after his death.

In his later years, Constantine became more aggressive in his promotion of Christianity, even going so far as to trigger a war with the Persians over their alleged treatment of Christians under their rule. He also grew closer to the Arians, particularly as a consequence of the proximity and skill of Eusebius, bishop of Nicomedia. When Constantine felt his last illness upon him, in May 337, it was Eusebius whom he summoned to baptize him so that he might die a full and blameless member of the Church.

Bibliography: T.D. Barnes, *Constantine and Eusebius*, 1981.

William Leadbetter

CORIOLANUS, GNAEUS MARCIUS (fifth century B.C.)

Coriolanus was a legendary Roman aristocrat.

He received his name in recognition of his capture of the city of Corioli from the Volsci in 493. Though an excellent military leader, he was an abysmal politician, alienating both friends and foes with his strongly held positions. His political opinions brought charges of tyrannical conduct and exile when, during a famine, he opposed the distribution of food to the starving plebeians unless they agreed to forfeit recently won political rights. Exiled, he moved to the Volscian city of Antium, where he soon became a military leader in their wars against his native Rome. He led the Volscians in a series of campaigns, reaching the gates of Rome. There, his mother Veturia and his wife Volumnia confronted him and persuaded him not to sack the city. In consequence of his retreat, the Volscians killed him.

This legend addresses two issues of importance to the study of early Rome: "horizontal social mobility," evident in his ability to move effortlessly from Roman to Volscian aristocracy, and the influence and importance of Roman mothers and wives, a challenge to the ideal of the Roman patriarchy.

Bibliography: R.M. Ogilvie, *Commentary on Livy Books 1–5*, 1965.

Ron Harris

CORNELIA (c.195–after 121 b.c.)

Cornelia, mother of *Tiberius and *Gaius Gracchus, was remembered in antiquity as a paragon of womanly virtue.

The second daughter of Aemilia, one of the most conspicuous women of her day, and of *Scipio Africanus, the conqueror of *Hannibal, Cornelia married Ti. Sempronius Gracchus (cos. 177, 163, cens. 169), by whom she had twelve children, only three of whom survived to maturity. Widowed early (and rejecting an offer of marriage from Ptolemy VII), she devoted herself to household management and attended to the education of her sons Tiberius and Gaius, later taking an active, sometime interventionist, interest in their political careers and expressing only pride after their controversial deaths. Her daughter married *Scipio Aemilianus. At her villa at Misenum, Cornelia was celebrated as a learned hostess and philhellene, applauded for the elegant style of her speech and writing, her letters being circulated, if not published. Two fragments, said to be from letters to her son Gaius, may represent, if genuine, the earliest surviving Latin prose by a woman. (Their authenticity is debated.) She was honored (probably posthumously) with a statue, which will have been an early example of its kind. Her pride in her children became a popular theme of late eighteenth-century painting.

Bibliography: R.A. Bauman, *Women and Politics in Ancient Rome*, 1992.

Tom Hillard

CRASSUS, MARCUS LICINIUS (c. 112–53 b.c.)

Crassus was an exceptionally wealthy Roman politician and general who was a member of the First Triumvirate.

Born to a father active in Roman politics, Crassus aspired to an equally important role. After his father and brother both perished during the civil war of the mid-80s B.C., Crassus fled to Spain, fearing for his life. He hid in a cave for eight months, emerging to support *Sulla's invasion of Italy in 83. He proved to be a worthy general for the future dictator, and he profited immensely from the war plunder. The turmoil of the war enabled him to acquire the property of several of Sulla's murdered opponents, and henceforth Crassus was surnamed *dives* ("wealthy"). At this time he became a rival of another of Sulla's commanders, the young *Pompey, and their contentious relationship worsened when Crassus put down the slave rebellion of *Spartacus (72–71), but Pompey boasted that his own minor role had been instrumental in ending the insurrection. The two served as consuls in 70, passing popular legislation that undermined many of the measures instituted by Sulla during his dictatorship a decade earlier.

As Pompey went on to military glory in the next decade, Crassus solidified his political support by acting as a generous moneylender to fellow senators and other men of influence. Chief among these was *Caesar, who relied upon Crassus' financing to run for a series of public offices. Many suspected Crassus of complicity in *Catiline's attempt to overthrow the government in 63, but the Senate refused to move against him. By the end of the decade he realized that a bloc of conservative senators led by *Cato the Younger and *Cicero was preventing him from increasing his wealth and power, and so he was receptive to Caesar's suggestion that the two of them form a political alliance with his rival Pompey (60). Crassus benefited immensely from this informal coalition, normally termed the "First Triumvirate," for it allowed him to obtain legislation profitable for his business interests, a second consulship (55), and a five-year command in Syria. Many senators protested when Crassus departed Rome, claiming that he was proceeding with a war of aggression for his own self-aggrandizement, but they could not prevent him from invading a peaceful Parthia in 54. He failed to follow up on initial successes against the unprepared natives, and in the following year, he was ambushed and died at Carrhae. According to some sources, a Parthian commander captured Crassus and killed him by pouring molten gold down his throat.

Crassus is not as well remembered as Caesar or Pompey, for he did not achieve the same dramatic military successes as his colleagues. Nevertheless, his career has interested scholars, who view him as emblematic of ambitious politicians who hastened the end of the Roman Republic.

Bibliography: A.M. Ward, *Marcus Crassus and the Late Roman Republic*, 1977.

David Christiansen

CRATES OF ATHENS (fifth century B.C.)

Crates was an Athenian comic poet.

According to ancient testimonies, he first started his career in the ancient theater as actor performing in the comedies of the poet Catinus. Later, a comic poet himself, he produced six (or seven) comedies, only the titles of which and a total of sixty fragments have reached our times, and won three victories in the Great Dionysia. According to *Aristotle, Crates was the first to produce comedies with plots that advance beyond the ridiculing of contemporary individuals and particularly politicians. In this way he may be rightly considered among those comic dramatists that facilitated the transition from Old to Middle Comedy.

A study of two of the most extant of his surviving fragments, both coming from the play *Animals* (*Theria*), leads us to deduce that the imaginary stage of the play must have been a land of utopia (perhaps a place similar to *Aristophanes' "Cloudokooland"). In this imaginary setting, one of the speakers argues that he may invent household items able to move automatically at their master's will; and we also read of a bath that may be prepared at the invitation of the water, of food that may be cooked without human intervention, and of animals that may speak in human voice and object to being eaten.

Bibliography: C. Austin and R. Kassel, eds., *Poetae Comici Graeci*, vol. 4, 1983.

Sophia Papaioannou

CRATES OF MALLOS (second century B.C.)

Crates was a Stoic philosopher, grammarian, and literary critic who introduced the serious study of poetry to Rome in 168 B.C.; he was also the major scholar of the Library of Pergamum built by *Eumenes II.

We have no list of his works or idea of his role in Eumenes' Library. Of his life we know only that on the embassy of the future Attalus II to Rome in 168 he broke his leg in an opening of the sewer on the Palatine hill and, forced to stay longer in Rome, began successfully to lecture on poetry. He was a serious critic (as he called himself) of Greek literature, best known for his account of the shield of Achilles in the *Iliad*, although his commitment to Stoic cosmology makes some of his allegorical commentary bizarre. In grammar he followed *Chrysippus' Stoic doctrine of "anomaly," which accepted anomalous forms from everyday usage, and opposed the more prescriptive grammatical rules of "analogy" at the rival Alexandrian Library. He taught *Panaetius, who influenced Roman thought from the circle around *Scipio Aemilianus, and his school later produced Apollodorus, the rhetorician who taught Octavian (*Augustus). He had a practical side. He developed a new method of treating sheepskin as a writing material; this "Pergamena" became fashionable in Rome and gives us the word *parchment* for "vellum." The notion that he constructed a spherical globe of the world rests on a misinterpretation of the term *sphaeropoeia*, used for maps of the revolutions of the planets in the sky "around the earth."

Bibliography: R. Pfeiffer, *History of Classical Scholarship: From the Beginnings to the End of the Hellenistic Age*, 1968.

Robert Dyer

CRATINUS (c. 480–420 B.C.)

Cratinus, son of Callimedes, was one of the earliest and greatest poets of Athenian Old Comedy.

Cratinus' biography is derived from details in the plays and remarks of later commentaries, but this information is not very reliable. However, precise dates for three of his plays, and approximate dates for three others, firmly establish that Cratinus was professionally active from the 450s through the 420s and at the height of his career in the 440s. He won first prize on nine occasions at the dramatic festivals of Dionysus. In all, twenty-nine titles and over 500 citations of his comedies survive. The date of Cratinus' death is uncertain, but his poetic activity ceases by 421/420.

Cratinus' comedies were famous for their abusive language and virulent *ad hominem* attacks against contemporaries. According to the biographical tradition, he was a pederast and a heavy drinker so enamored of wine that he once fainted at the sight of broken wine jars. This tradition, however, is based primarily on comments and allegations of rival comic poets whose motives were professionally self-serving. Hence, it is probably impossible to construct a historically reliable account of Cratinus' life based on material derived from the ancient sources.

Cratinus' work greatly influenced *Aristophanes, his younger contemporary, and to a lesser degree the Roman satirist *Horace. Ancient sources report that Cratinus was the subject of commentaries in Hellenistic times.

Bibliography: C. Austin and R. Kassel, eds., *Poetae Comici Graeci*, vol. 4, 1983; M.R. Lefkowitz, *The Lives of the Greek Poets*, 1981; R.M. Rosen, *Old Comedy and the Iambographic Tradition*, 1988.

Carl A. Anderson

CRESILAS (fl. 450–430 B.C.)

Cresilas, a native Cretan, was a sculptor in Athens during the Periclean period who integrated passionate representation of pain and pathos into art.

The sources show some confusion about the sculptor identified as Cresilas, and little is known of his life. He may have been the same artist as the person identified as Ctesilaus. He appears to have been a native of Cydonia and to have worked in Athens during the age of *Pericles when he was a competitor of *Phidias. Signatures on statue bases show that his work was displayed at various sites throughout Greece and even in Asia Minor. His interest in representing the wounded follows in the regional tradition and seems to have influenced later artists. His works include a portrait of Pericles, a wounded man, a wounded Amazon, a *Doryphorus* (youth with a spear), and votives to various goddesses. His image of an Amazon for the temple at Ephesus was ranked third place in a sculptor's competition in the fifth century, following those of *Polyclitus and Phidias.

Bibliography: A.F. Stewart, *Greek Sculpture: An Exploration*, 2 vols., 1990.

Lisa Auanger

CRITIAS (c. 460–403 b.c.)

Critias was an Athenian philosopher and politician active near the end of the Peloponnesian War. He became infamous for his bloodthirstiness as a member of the oligarchic regime known as the Thirty Tyrants.

As a young man, Critias associated with the philosopher *Socrates. Critias was gifted with a keen mind, and a healthy intellectual rivalry seems to have developed between him and Socrates. This rivalry later flared into an open rift when in 403, as head of the Athenian government, Critias attempted to diminish Socrates' influence by banning philosophy. Critias' writings, which span several genres such as tragedy, political theory, and cosmogony, are infused with original philosophical ideas. For instance, in a famous passage, Critias suggests that man invented religion in order to instill fear in, and thus control, those around him.

As both a writer and a politician, Critias admired the Spartan system of government, and in 415, when Athens was at war with Sparta, Critias may have been involved in a plot to overthrow the Athenian government. In 411, he not only participated in an oligarchic coup against Athens but also headed the party's pro-Spartan wing. Although democracy was reestablished within a year, it was not until four years later that Critias was finally banished. In 404, after the Spartans defeated the Athenians, Critias was recalled and appointed as one of a board of thirty men responsible for rewriting Athens' constitution to resemble Sparta's. The Thirty assumed *de facto* power and initiated a reign of terror against all supporters of democracy. Within the Thirty, a power struggle soon developed between the extremist Critias and the more moderately minded Theramenes. Critias succeeded in condemning Theramenes and had him executed. Less than one year later, Critias met his death in a battle against a democratic opposition group near Athens. The democrats successfully reaffirmed power, and Critias became one of the most detested names in Athenian history.

Critias' writings were almost completely forgotten but were later appreciated for their contributions to philosophical inquiry.

Bibliography: D. Kagan, *The Fall of the Athenian Empire*, 1987.

Luis Molina

CROESUS (fl. 561–547 b.c.)

Croesus was the last king of Lydia.

We are dependent on *Herodotus for most of what we know about Croesus. He assumed the Lydian throne in 560/561. He began a military campaign of conquest of the Ionian Greek communities, even while maintaining peaceful relations with Delphi, where he patronized Apollo's Shrine, and Sparta. At its height, his empire extended throughout Asia Minor, to the Halys River on the east, to the Taurus River in the south.

Croesus was defeated by *Cyrus the Great when the latter led his Persian forces in an unexpected attack on Sardis. Croesus was taken prisoner by Cyrus, and Herodotus reports that Cyrus defeated the Lydian cavalry by the interesting tactic of placing camels at the head of his forces, throwing the Lydian horses into disarray at the strange odor of the exotic animals.

There are a number of interesting legends surrounding Croesus recounted by Herodotus. Among the intellectuals that sought refuge in Croesus' kingdom was *Solon, the great Athenian reformer. Herodotus reports that the two matched wits in numerous conversations. Later, when Cyrus prepared an execution of the Lydian king by burning, Croesus is said to have been reminded of Solon's often troubling advice even in the midst of the flames. When Croesus called out the name of Solon, Cyrus was curious about what Croesus was saying and stopped the execution to question the prisoner. So impressed was Cyrus with Croesus' responses to his questions, Herodotus tells us, that he is said to have changed his mind about Croesus and assigned him a comfortable position in the Persian administration. Croesus' ability to gain the ear of Cyrus was also said to have saved the Lydian people from certain destruction when Cyrus advised a policy of demilitarization of Lydian rebels rather than their mass execution.

It is often suggested that Croesus may have minted the first ancient coins. While it seems indisputable that coinage had an origin in Asia Minor, the association with Croesus himself is difficult to establish.

Bibliography: L. Kurke, *Coins, Bodies, Games, and Gold: The Politics of Meaning in Archaic Greece*, 1999.

Daniel Smith-Christopher

CTESIAS (late fifth century B.C.)

Ctesias was a historian and a Greek doctor in the service of Persia.

Ctesias was a doctor trained at the medical school of Cnidos. He is most famous for the years that he spent in the Persian court of *Artaxerxes II (c. 415–398) as a prisoner of war. There is some doubt about *Diodorus' account, however, that Ctesias was actually a prisoner originally, since Greek doctors were in great demand in the Persian courts, mainly by honorable invitation rather than capture. According to tradition, Ctesias wrote a series of twenty-three books called *The Persica*. Unfortunately, the work has not survived, although Photius, a Byzantine Christian scholar, discovered a complete copy of it in the ninth century. Most of what we now know of the work of Ctesias is abridged in the extant writings of Photius. Ctesias rather arrogantly claims to be better informed about the Persians than the great historian *Herodotus, a near contemporary.

Among his sources, he names the wife of Darius II (424–405), with whom he claims to have frequently spoken as a court physician. However, where events can be compared between the inscriptions of *Darius I, Herodotus, and Ctesias, Ctesias is revealed to have been either mistaken or intentionally fraudulent. An oft-cited example is Ctesias' claim that the Behistun Inscription, placed by Darius as political propaganda to support his seizing of the Achaemenid throne, was a monument to Semiramis, a legendary Assyrian queen. The Inscription, of course, has nothing to do with the Assyrians.

It is presumed that he spent most of his time in Babylon, and some scholars have suggested that he picked up a considerable amount of his material in the markets and streets, rather than in actual observation. Among some recent scholars, however, there has been a revival of interest in Ctesias as a reliable reporter of court gossip, or popular history, which would be an obviously important source for the understanding of popular attitudes and opinions, even if he is not a reliable source for reproducing the details of major historical events.

Bibliography: J.M. Bigwood, "Ctesias as Historian of the Persian Wars," *Phoenix* 32 (1978): 19–41; J.M. Cook, *The Persian Empire*, 1983; M. Dandamaev, *A Political History of the Achaemenid Empire*, 1989.

Daniel Smith-Christopher

CUNOBELINUS (?–A.D. 43)

Labeled *rex Brittanorum* by *Suetonius and regarded by some modern historians as the greatest ancient British king, Cunobelinus (or Cunobeline) was immortalized as William Shakespeare's Cymbeline.

Evidence for the period between *Julius Caesar's initial conquest of Britain in 55–54 B.C. and the Romans' return under *Claudius (the Emperor) in A.D. 43 is limited, much coming from modern finds of Roman trade goods and Celtic coins. These suggest that Cunobelinus was the son of Tasciovanus, ruler of the Catuvellauni and probably the Trinovantes. Scholars disagree about whether Tasciovanus and Cunobelinus were descendants of Cassivellaunus, the Celtic ruler who suffered defeat at Caesar's hands, and about whether Cassivellaunus ruled the Catuvellauni. Cunobelinus ruled both the Catuvellauni and Trinovantes in a region including much of modern Essex and Hertfordshire, though he had to oust a rival (and possible relative) named Dubnovellaunus from rule of the latter tribe (and possibly both). Whereas Tasciovanus had reigned from the Catuvellauni center at Verulamium (St. Albans), Cunobelinus based his reign in Camulodunum (Colchester), the royal seat of the Trinovantes, named for the Celtic war god Camulos; however, he minted coins at both sites.

Cunobelinus' ascendancy began early in the first century A.D. during the Emperor *Augustus' troubled final years, when he was probably in his twenties or early thirties, and continued through the reigns of *Tiberius (14–37) and *Gaius "Caligula" (37–41). Unlike tribes south of the Thames River, he was friendly to the Romans, providing them with gold, silver, iron, grain, cattle, hides, hunting dogs, and slaves, though Druid-influenced anti-Roman elements in Britain may have tempered his pro-Roman stance. His kingdom grew for most of his reign, perhaps extending into Kent. Trouble began around 39 or 40, when Cunobelinus expelled his son Adminius, who sought refuge on the continent, possibly prompting Caligula's abortive invasion of Britain. Cunobelinus' death (c. 40–43) or loss of control left his anti-Roman sons Togodumnus and Caratacus in power north and south of the Thames, respectively. Claudius' successful invasion meant that

Cunobelinus' legacy and his sons' reign in southeast Britain were short-lived. Cunobelinus may be buried in the Lexden Tumulus north of Colchester.

The king Shakespeare portrayed in *Cymbeline* bears no resemblance to the real Cunobelinus. As he often did, the bard based his play loosely upon Raphael Holinshed's *Chronicle*, which in turn is highly inaccurate regarding Cunobelinus. Cymbeline is not even the main character in the tragicomic romance that bears his name and that features deceit, disguise, and mistaken identity in a typically complicated Shakespearean plot that defies brief summation. Not the least of Shakespeare's departures from reality is the ending, in which Cymbeline is reunited with two sons stolen from him in infancy, the Britons defeat the invading Romans, and the royal family lives happily ever after. Still, Shakespeare's completely fictionalized Cymbeline is far better known than Cunobelinus, who is largely forgotten outside the circle of scholars interested in Britain in the first century.

Bibliography: P. Salway, *Roman Britain*, 1981; G.A. Webster, *The Roman Invasion of Britain*, 1980.

William B. Robison

CYLON (c. 630 B.C.)

Cylon was an Athenian nobleman who tried unsuccessfully to set himself up as tyrant at Athens.

Son-in-law of the tyrant of Megara and victor in the Olympic games, Cylon tried to capitalize on his fame and connections by seizing control of the government. He and his followers occupied the Acropolis, but the Athenian people did not rise up to support him as he had hoped. Cylon finally agreed to leave the city after the authorities promised that he and his followers would not be harmed. Once they had left the protection of the Acropolis, however, they were captured and killed. The treacherous way in which Cylon was killed caused a scandal. The magistrates, led by Megacles of the family known as the Alcmaeonids, were considered accursed as a result. Several generations later the reputation of this curse was still being used to embarrass Megacles' descendants, which included some of Athens' most famous leaders, such as *Cleisthenes and *Pericles.

Cylon's attempted coup is frequently seen as symptomatic of the general political instability that would soon necessitate the wholesale restructuring of Athenian government by *Solon. Our ancient sources, however, are more interested in it as the origin of the curse of the Alcmaeonids.

Bibliography: R. Osborne, *Greece in the Making: 1200–479 B.C.*, 1996.

William Hutton

CYMBELINE
See **Cunobelinus**.

CYPRIAN, SAINT (Thascius Caecilius Cyprianus, c. 200–258)

Bishop of Carthage during imperial persecution, Cyprian was instrumental in setting policies for the reintegration of lapsed Christians into the Church and providing a systematic theology of the Church.

Little is known of Cyprian's life before his tenure as bishop, and that little is largely taken from references in a large corpus of surviving letters. Cyprian converted to Christianity c. 255–256. His conversion was radical and transforming, for he adopted not only the faith of Christianity but also the disciplines of celibacy and poverty. Selling his inheritance and giving the proceeds to the poor, he dedicated himself to the study of theology, most especially the work of *Tertullian. He quickly rose in prominence and was ordained bishop in 248–249. This rapid ascension provoked jealousy that would later haunt him in his theological and administrative disputes. In January 250, Cyprian fled in the face of Emperor *Decius' persecution of Christians and attempted to govern his church through the use of letters and messengers. A major issue that soon arose was how to regard Christians who had escaped persecution either by bribing officials, by making some small anti-Christian gesture, or by renouncing the faith entirely. Some wanted to reinstate these Christians relatively easily; others not at all. Cyprian tried to hold the middle ground, allowing the reinstatement of the lapsed only after considerable penance. Partly because of his treatment of the lapsed and partly because of earlier jealousy, rival Christian factions emerged in Carthage. The broader unity of the Church was also threatened because of an increasingly acrimonious dispute between Cyprian, bishop of the principal city in North Africa, and the bishop of Rome, who claimed primacy over the entire Church. Exiled in a renewed persecution in 257, Cyprian was recalled to Carthage and beheaded on 14 September 258.

Of Cyprian's several treatises, his most important are *On the Lapsed* and *On the Unity of the Catholic Church*. In these works he articulates an ecclesiology that highlights the activity of the Holy Spirit in the Church, the visible unity of the Church in its bishops, and the principle of apostolic succession. While at first willing to argue for papal primacy, he backed away from this during his later disputes with Rome.

Bibliography: G.W. Clarke, ed., *The Letters of St. Cyprian of Carthage*, 4 vols., 1984–1989.

Steven D. Driver

CYRIL OF ALEXANDRIA, SAINT (c. 378–444)

Cyril of Alexandria was an important Christian Greek theologian and a major protagonist in the great Christological crisis of the fifth century.

Cyril was born some time near 378. His uncle Theophilus became the archbishop of Alexandria in 385 and brought Cyril to that city. In 403, when he was twenty-five years old, Cyril was ordained lector of the Alexandrian church and was closely attached to his uncle's court. In the same year he attended Theophilus at the notorious Synod of the Oak, which deposed *John Chrysostom. At his uncle's death, Cyril was consecrated archbishop on 18 October 412.

He inherited leadership of a turbulent Christian faction. Some troubles of his early administration include his seizure of sectarian churches, Christian mob violence directed against Jewish elements who had purportedly burned a Christian church, and the infamous murder by a Christian mob of the philosopher *Hypatia. In 416 an imperial investigation into Alexandrian affairs determined to reduce the size of his unofficial bodyguard, the *parabalam*, but within two years Cyril arranged the reversal of this policy, a mark of high imperial confidence.

At the same time we find him engaged in the active process of the evangelization of an Egypt still strongly devoted to the old cults, especially the religion of Isis. In his strong attempts to undermine the old religion, Cyril portrayed himself as both "holy seer" and powerful lord. His aggressive policy of evangelization was sometimes advanced by marauding monastics, such as those communities under the control of Shenoudi of Atripe.

After 428 Cyril's life changed dramatically, for he was drawn into conflict with *Nestorius, the archbishop of Constantinople, and a major dispute over the significance of the person of Christ arose, which resulted in settlement (in Cyril's favor) at the Council of Ephesus in 431. The main lines of argument, simply stated, were that Nestorius emphasized two centers of operation simultaneously present in the life of Christ: one human and one divine, with one sometimes predominating over the other. Cyril, on the other hand, insisted that the Christian faith demanded a vision of Jesus who was wholly and completely divine (only one single person, and that person God). For Cyril, Christ was none other that the Divine Word of God who inhabited the human form. There was no human Jesus alongside the divinity, and therefore everything that Jesus did, whether it was a human act such as sleeping or a powerful act such as raising the dead, was equally a work of the single divine lord. The divine power now present in the humanity, however, was also an archetype of how God had intended to "divinize" the human condition in the act of incarnation. Thus Christ is the pattern of the world's salvation.

The Council of Ephesus caused great bitterness in its aftermath, and the emperor's negotiators had to work for several years to restore Church communion, especially between Alexandria and Syria. Eventually in 433 a compromise was agreed on where important points of the Antiochene position (Christ had two authentic natures—both human and divine) could be reconciled with Cyril's insistence that Christ was a single reality—one divine person. However, the precise ramifications of that agreement still needed much clarifying, and without this, it was inevitable that the intellectual argument would soon break out again with even greater force. It did so with greater bitterness in the following generation.

Bibliography: J.A. McGuckin, "The Influence of the Isis Cult on St. Cyril of Alexandria's Christology," *Studia Patristica* 24 (1992): 191–199; J.A. McGuckin, *St. Cyril of Alexandria and the Christological Controversy: Its History, Theology, and Texts*, 1994.

John A. McGuckin

CYRIL OF JERUSALEM, SAINT (c. 315–c. 387)

Cyril was a bishop known for his strong stance against Arianism.

Very little is known of Cyril's early life, and the whereabouts and date of his birth are open to conjecture. He was a priest in Jerusalem when the bishop Maximus died in 348. Soon after, Cyril was ordained bishop of Jerusalem. In 357 he was deposed by a local council, primarily because of his opposition to the Arian bishop Acacius of Caesarea and his wish that Jerusalem have primacy over Acacius' metropolitan see. The Council of Seleucia reinstated him in 359. In 360 he was again deposed at the Council of Constantinople, returning to Jerusalem after the emperor Constantius' death in 361. His third banishment came in 366, under the Arianizing emperor *Valens, who opposed Cyril's appointment of Gelasius as bishop of Caesarea. Upon Valens' death, in 378, Cyril once again returned home, where he remained until his death. Cyril was surely anti-Arian and orthodox throughout his episcopal career. Nevertheless, given the complexity of the issues, some had their doubts. *Gregory of Nyssa examined Cyril's doctrinal position in 379 and found it sound. The Council of Constantinople in 381 also judged him to be in conformity with the Nicene position.

Cyril is known principally for his *Catechctical Lectures*, twenty-four talks delivered in 348 or 350, mostly for the preparation of catechumens about to be baptized. They are an important source for Cyril's theology and for liturgical practices of the time. His famous *Letter to Constantius* was written to the emperor about a vision of a cross in the sky over Jerusalem in 351.

Bibliography: P.W.L. Walker, *Holy City, Holy Places?* 1990.

Mark Gustafson

CYRUS THE GREAT (c. 580–529 b.c.)

Cyrus was the first Persian emperor, founder of the Archaemenian dynasty.

Cyrus founded the Persian Empire by uniting two Iranian peoples, the Medes and the Persians. While noted as a conqueror who assembled one of the largest empires in history, he is best known for his tolerance and magnanimity toward conquered peoples. The son of Cambyses, a Persian, and Mandare, daughter of Median King Astyages, who was warned by a portent that his grandson would depose him, Cyrus was ordered destroyed. The servant responsible for the task instead gave him to shepherds to raise. At a young age, his exploits brought him to the attention of Astyages, who returned him to his father but punished the servant by feeding his own son to him. As foretold, Cyrus, who led a Persian revolt against the Medes, captured and overthrew his grandfather in 549. Having united the Iranian peoples, he extended his empire throughout Asia Minor (with his defeat of *Croesus) and into Central Asia before conquering Babylon and Egypt. The Hebrew people held captive in Babylon saw him as their liberator, who in 537 allowed more than 40,000 Jews to return to the Promised Land of Palestine and rebuild their temple.

The Greeks, traditional enemies of the Persians, nevertheless considered him to be the model ruler. Indeed, the sheer size of the Persian Empire required innovative governance. Though tolerant of local customs, he appointed regional governors to represent him and to ensure that his edicts were obeyed. The need to communicate with many people across so great an area perhaps led him to begin the first postal system. He probably died in battle and was succeeded by his son, Cambyses.

Bibliography: M. Mallowan, "Cyrus the Great (558–529 B.C.)," in *Cambridge History of Iran*, 1985, 2:392–419.

Ron Harris

D

DARIUS I, KING OF PERSIA (r. 522–486 B.C.)

Darius was the Achaemenid ruler of Persia who initiated the Persian Wars against Greece.

The beginning of the reign of Darius I is filled with drama. As he was not a direct descendant of the great *Cyrus, Darius seems to have been concerned with defending his right to the throne. His famous Behistun Inscription tells us of the events (from his official perspective) leading to his rise to power, and copies circulated throughout the empire as official propaganda. Darius claimed that a usurper rose in revolt on 11 March 522. It appears that this usurper had considerable support, especially in the region of Babylonia. Darius eventually killed him and seized the throne on 1 July before his predecessor Cambyses had died. *Herodotus tells us stories about how Cyrus foresaw in dreams that Darius would later arise but later speaks of the plot of "the Seven" (prominent aristocratic families among the Persians) to name Darius the new emperor over the conspiratorial religious leaders whom Herodotus calls the "Magi." Darius' rule, in many ways as important and formative of Persian polity as Cyrus himself, continued to involve cooperation between the aristocratic families that were responsible for his rise to power in the first place.

Darius faced a challenge to his power throughout his empire in the opening years of his long reign. The Persian militia had to pacify the Babylonian region three times, and Egypt remained virtually semiautonomous throughout Persian rule. In response to the challenge of administering his vast territories, Darius imposed a system of local authorities ("satrapies") that were under the leadership of trusted Persian officials—often family members of the aristocratic families. Darius could furthermore impose varying forms of taxation on each satrapy, requiring constant supervision throughout his bureaucracy. Darius was also a reformer with regard to law. His occasional nickname "Lawgiver" comes not so much from codifying one law throughout the empire as putting imperial strength behind agreed local legal traditions compatible with Persian rule, even if they inevitably varied from region to region.

By 518, Darius was moving to consolidate his rule in Egypt, but his approach was more conciliatory—and longer lasting—than the rather heavy-handed approach to conquest of Cyrus and Cambyses. Darius, in fact, was "welcomed" to Egypt and dealt respectfully with local tradition after being named "Pharaoh" by Egyptian religious leaders.

Perhaps the most important legacy of the rule of Darius, however, was not so much his form of rule over the Persian Empire itself as his conflicts with Greece. As a result of the Ionian Revolt, Darius attempted to punish the Greeks for their assistance to the rebels. Darius is remembered in classical sources as the Persian leader who began the long history of conflict between Greece and Persia that forms so central a part of Greek and Near Eastern history.

Bibliography: J.M. Cook, *The Persian Empire*, 1983; M. Dandamaev, *A Political History of the Achaemenid Empire*, 1989.

Daniel Smith-Christopher

DARIUS III, KING OF PERSIA (r. 336–330 b.c.)

Darius III was defeated by the Macedonian *Alexander the Great, thereby ending the two-century-old Persian Achaemenid empire.

Artashata (also known as Codomannus in Greek sources), who took the throne name of Darius III (Persian, Darayavaush), was the great nephew of *Artaxerxes II (r. 405–359) and was placed on the throne by Bagoas, a powerful eunuch who had murdered two previous Persian kings (*Artaxerxes III and IV). Darius had some governmental experience, as he had been a satrap of Armenia. He was successful in restoring Persian rule in Egypt but did not, at first, realize the seriousness of the threat of Alexander the Great and thus did not actively support Athens against Macedon. He was defeated by the Macedonian king at Issus in Cilicia in 333 and rushed back to Babylon, leaving his royal family and retinue to be captured. Although he equipped a very large and diverse army, he was again defeated two years later at Gaugamela in northern Mesopotamia (331). After the second defeat, he once again fled east, probably in the hope of mounting another defense, but was killed by Bessus, the Persian satrap of Bactria, who proclaimed himself king of Persia. Darius was about fifty years old at his death.

Because of his defeat, Darius' reputation has suffered in Greek sources in comparison with Alexander's, and he has been considered weak, cowardly, and susceptible to poor counsel, although Greek sources admit that he had won fame before he became king by killing an enemy champion of the Kadousioi. Contrary to popular belief, his strategy against Alexander appears to have been sound, as he tried to raise revolts against Alexander and prudently pooled his resources in order to campaign against the Macedonian.

Knowledge of his reign is gleaned primarily through somewhat hostile Greek historical sources (e.g., *Arrian, *Plutarch, *Diodorus Siculus, *Strabo, and numerous fragments).

Bibliography: P. Briant, *From Cyrus to Alexander: A History of the Persian Empire*, trans. P. Daniels, 2 vols., 1997.

Mark W. Chavalas

DECIUS, GAIUS MESSIUS QUINTUS ("Trajan," c. 195–251)

Decius was the Roman emperor who initiated the first state-sponsored persecution of Christianity.

Decius was appointed by the emperor Philip in 248 to return stability to the Danube frontier, which was plagued by the Goths and mutinies of Roman legions. His success had the not uncommon result that his soldiers declared him emperor. Shortly after his defeat of Philip at Verona in 249, the new emperor issued an edict that required universal compliance with Roman religion by public sacrifice to the state gods. The edict may have been an attempt to stop a perceived weakening in Rome's position. Although its effect was limited geographically and short-lived, there was some apostasy, some martyrdom, and some flight (most famously, that of *Cyprian, bishop of Carthage). Decius also attempted to legitimize his power by adopting the name "Trajan." His attentions were soon again focused on the Goths, by whom he was defeated and killed in 251 at Abrittus. Thus Decius was the first emperor to die at the hands of a foreign enemy, which *Lactantius and other Christian writers saw as a clear sign of God's punishment of a persecutor.

Bibliography: R.L. Fox, *Pagans and Christians*, 1987.

Mark Gustafson

DEMETRIUS I POLIORCETES (336–283 b.c.)

Macedonian general and sometime king, Demetrius was a very colorful character and major player in the wars of the Successors of *Alexander.

Demetrius was the son of the old general *Antigonus and associated with him in military and political affairs at an early age. He and his father jointly assumed the title "King" after Demetrius sailed into Athens and removed the garrison and officials of *Cassander and then defeated a Ptolemaic fleet off Salamis in Cyprus in 306. He earned his nickname Poliorcetes ("City-Besieger") after his siege of Rhodes in 305/304, during which he used the largest and most complex siege equipment yet seen. In addition to siege warfare, he was also famous for developing and deploying huge warships. Indeed, he can be said to have started a fifty-year "naval arms race" between the Antigonid and Ptolemaic dynasties.

He restored the democratic government of Athens and was generally very popular in the city, partly for defense against the renewed attacks of Cassander but also because he was reputedly the most handsome man alive and fond of revelry. Perhaps too fond, because his excesses soon put him out of favor with the city.

In 302, all of the other kings formed a coalition against Antigonus and Demetrius, culminating in the Battle of Ipsus in 301 (one of the largest battles in antiquity) in which Antigonus was killed and Demetrius escaped with only part of his forces. He was unwelcome to return to Athens.

In 295, he seized upon an opportunity to murder the young and inexperienced son of Cassander and proclaimed himself king of Macedonia. He was not a particularly effective ruler, diverting most of his attention to creating a military and naval force for an invasion of Asia. He seemed about to duplicate the feat of *Alexander the Great. In 287 he was expelled from Macedonia by an invasion of *Lysimachus and *Pyrrhus. His long-suffering wife Phila, a daughter of *Antipater and sister of Cassander, committed suicide, but Demetrius soon regained sufficient loyal troops and a fleet and proceeded with his invasion of Asia. Within a few years, his invasion lost momentum, and he surrendered to *Seleucus I, who was married to his daughter, and ended his life in comfortable captivity. He gave himself over to intense revelry and drinking and died in 283.

He had several wives and innumerable concubines, but only one legitimate son, *Antigonus II, who would immediately claim the title of king of Macedonia. His line continued until 167.

Bibliography: N.G.L. Hammond and F.W. Walbank, *A History of Macedonia*, vol. 3, 336–167 B.C., 1988.

Janice J. Gabbert

DEMETRIUS II OF MACEDONIA (c. 276–229 B.C.)

Demetrius was the son of *Antigonus II Gonatas and the father of *Philip V.

Demetrius early gained distinction by defeating and dethroning Alexander of Epirus in 264. Upon his accession (239), he attempted to continue his father's policy of making peace in Greece by means of alliances. However, in 239 the Aetolian League allied with the Achaean League and tried to annex Acarnania in Epirus. Demetrius intervened, and the Demetrian Wars followed. Though Demetrius preserved Acarnania, he weakened himself greatly throughout Greece.

Demetrius was called north to fend off an invasion of the barbarian Dardanians in 229. After his defeat on the northern frontier, he died. His cousin *Antigonus III Doson succeeded him.

Demetrius II's reign has traditionally been seen as a very low point for the Macedonian monarchy.

Bibliography: N.G.L. Hammond and F.W. Walbank, *A History of Macedonia*, vol. 3, 336–167 B.C. 1988.

Andrew G. Traver

DEMETRIUS OF PHALERUM (c. 345–280 b.c.)

Demetrius was an Athenian peripatetic philosopher, statesman, orator, and later Librarian at Alexandria.

Demetrius studied with *Aristotle and *Theophrastus and supported the latter with a grant of land near the Lyceum, perhaps its Peripatos. Prominent from 325 in the pro-Macedonian faction (with other pupils of Aristotle, the tutor of *Alexander the Great), he was appointed by *Cassander in 317 to govern Athens on his behalf as *epimeletes* (governor) and *nomothetes* (lawgiver). He put in place a social reorganization and a new legal code, of which fragments remain on contemporary inscriptions. These were based on Theophrastus' collection of *Laws* with the ideal of avoiding excess and arrogance in all things. He reestablished Athens as the cultural capital of the world and was friends with the comic playwright *Menander. He supported Cassander in his war with *Antigonus but had allowed the Athenian empire and naval power to fall into disarray. Democratic elements in Athens, accusing him of a luxurious and unbridled private life, appealed to Antigonus, who in 307 sent his son *Demetrius I Poliorcetes to liberate that city and expel Demetrius. All but 1 of the 360 statues erected in his honor were destroyed, and he fled to *Ptolemy I Soter in Egypt, where he served on the legislative commission. Director of the new Library in Alexandria, he advocated the foundation of the Museum and making the new capital a cultural center to rival Athens and to draw on the many Eastern cultures revealed by Alexander's conquests, including Jewish. He did not live to see the fruition of his dreams. For opposing the succession of *Ptolemy II Philadelphus, he was put under guard in the country, where he mysteriously died in his sleep of snakebite.

The last great Attic orator, writing in a sweet, ingratiating style appropriate to his position under Cassander and Ptolemy and introducing the use of figures to disguise his meaning, he published his speeches, the results of his lawmaking, and many philosophical treatises, all now lost. Healed of blindness in Alexandria, he wrote paeans for the new Temple of Serapis and may also have sponsored the Septuagint. He became a model for *Cicero in the union of philosophy and statesmanship and in the figured style. The important peripatetic treatise *On Style* attributed to him is certainly later but probably reflects his views as known to Cicero.

Bibliography: W.W. Fortenbaugh and E. Schühtrumpf, eds., *Demetrius of Phalerum*, 1999.

Robert Dyer

DEMOCRITUS (mid-fifth–fourth century b.c.)

Democritus was a Greek philosopher and cofounder with *Leucippus of the atomic theory of matter.

Little is known of Democritus' life, but he was born at Abdera and is said to have visited Athens and to have known *Socrates. He is reported to have written a large number of works of very broad scope, including astronomy, biology, ethics, mathematics, epistemology, and a cosmological work, the *Lesser World-System* (lesser in contrast to Leucippus' *Great World-System*). His work survives only in fragments quoted by doxographers, and our knowledge of his doctrines comes most importantly from *Aristotle and his school.

Democritus developed his atomic theory of matter into a full philosophic system, including ethics, cosmology, epistemology, and theology. However, unlike modern atoms, Democritean atoms are indestructible minimum units of matter, and all matter derives from different combinations of atoms, organizing themselves randomly and eventually producing the total plurality of material phenomena, without the need for any divine organizing principle. Matter is composed of a mixture of atoms and void, and Democritus claimed that these two are all that really exist. Although the Democritean system does away with divine teleology, it implies physical determinism: Every event has a prior determinable physical cause, and thus, given full knowledge of physical laws, the future is knowable and determined.

The influence of Democritus has been immense. Much of the tradition of Greek rationalist views of anthropology and prehistory may derive from Democritus, and Atomism has characterized antiteleological thinking from ancient times to the present day. It was revived in the seventeenth century by Gassendi and has dominated scientific thinking since Dalton in the nineteenth century.

Bibliography: D.J. Furley, *The Greek Cosmologists*, 1987.

Gordon Campbell

DEMOSTHENES (384–322 B.C.)

Demosthenes was the most famous of the Athenian orators.

Demosthenes was still a boy when his father died; his estate was given over to trustees. Later after study in rhetoric and legal procedure, inspired it is said by his hearing the successful defense of the general Callisthenes, Demosthenes brought a successful action against the trustees. He then began work as a legal speechwriter for litigants and was sufficiently successful soon to be employed in a public capacity. So began a life in public affairs that aimed primarily at a united defense of Greece and the preservation of Athenian independence in the face of the threat of *Philip II of Macedonia.

His *First Philippic* (351) sounded a note of warning about the rising power of Macedon. It was soon followed by three *Olynthiacs* as Philip attacked and destroyed Olynthus in 346. Demosthenes was one of the Athenian ambassadors who negotiated the Peace of Philocrates that followed. Back in Athens, he began to attack the peace. There followed other *Philippics* demanding action against Philip. In the war that Demosthenes sought Macedon was victorious at the Battle of Chaeronea in 338. In spite of this, Demosthenes returned to lead the defense of Athens, proving to be such a pivotal character that he was chosen to deliver the funeral oration for the dead of Chaeronea. Indeed, so vigilant was he in the defense of Athens that in 336 the orator Ctesiphon proposed that he be awarded a golden crown for his services. *Aeschines later prosecuted Ctesiphon, but Demosthenes, at the height of his powers, successfully defended him in 330 with his acknowledged masterpiece *On the Crown*. Meanwhile Philip had been murdered, and his son *Alexander had marched on Asia. Demosthenes continued his fight for the independence of Athens but was convicted by the Areopagus of stealing twenty talents of the money brought to Athens by Alexander's treasurer, Harpalus. He went into exile, and after the Macedonian victory at Crannon (322), he was condemned to death. He took his own life at Calauria in 322.

Politically Demosthenes' life was a failure, but as an orator he was second to none. As a youth he struggled with physical difficulties, not least of which was a weak voice. Overcoming this through strict training, he eventually reached the peak of a rhetorical career. The content of his orations provides important details about the administration of fourth-century Athens, and his style was very influential.

Bibliography: R. Sealey, *Demosthenes and His Time*, 1993.

                                                                    Karen McGroarty

DIDYMUS CHALCENTERUS (C. 80 B.C.–A.D. 10)

Didymus was the last great Alexandrian scholar.

He belonged to the school founded by *Aristarchus of Samothrace two centuries earlier. He was nicknamed *Chalcenterus* (the "brazen-gut") because he was extremely productive; he is said to have written 3,500 or even 4,000 works. He was also nicknamed *bibliolathas* (the "one who has forgotten [his] books"), because of occasional statements in his later books that contradicted what he wrote in earlier works. Didymus' own works do not distinguish him as an original researcher. His contribution to the transmission of classical scholarship, however, was of great significance, since he diligently compiled and copied verbatim a great amount of excerpts from the commentaries of the most important Alexandrian grammarians of the previous two and a half centuries. His work on the reconstruction of Aristarchus' Homeric text was much used by later scholars. Also, among his compilations, prominent position occupied his work on *Aristophanes, a detailed and very rich collection of literary, historical, biographical, and prosopographical information. He also compiled commentaries on the lyric poets and the tragedians, Attic comedy, and selected speeches of *Demosthenes.

Didymus devoted himself to the preservation and transmission of the highlights of the scholarly works of his predecessors. Being the last in line of the Alexandrian scholars that started with *Callimachus, Didymus' productivity, favored by the establishment of *Augustus' peace all around the Mediterranean world, captured in his summaries the spirit of Hellenistic scholarship. Thus he succeeded in addressing the needs of a new era that was looking for shortcuts in the intellectual heritage of their ancestors.

Bibliography: R. Pfeiffer, *History of Classical Scholarship: From the Beginnings to the End of the Hellenistic Age*, 1968.

Sophia Papaioannou

DINOCRATES (or Deinocrates, c. fourth century B.C.)

Dinocrates was an architect who planned and undertook the building of Alexandria for *Alexander the Great. He also directed the building of the funeral pyre of Alexander's comrade Hephaestion.

Little is known about Dinocrates except from summaries of *Vitruvius and *Pliny the Elder. According to the sources, Dinocrates planned to sculpt Mount Athos in the likeness of Alexander the Great. The figure was planned with one hand holding a city and the other hand holding a basin with water flowing through the basin. Although the idea of sculpting a mountain was novel for his time, the sculpture was never undertaken.

Dinocrates did, though, apparently plan and supervise the building of Alexandria in an orthogonal (perpendicular) street system, a method employed for quickly establishing control over an annexed area. The plan of Alexandria is considered to have been similar to the plans of the cities of Piraeus and Rhodes. He also is remembered for the elaborate funeral pyre of Hephaestion and restoring the temple of Artemis at Ephesus after it was burned to the ground.

Specialized studies are lacking on Dinocrates because of the scarcity of available primary and secondary material.

Bibliography: F. Castagnoli, *Orthogonal Town Planning in Antiquity*, 1971.

Roger W. Anderson

DIO CHRYSOSTOM (first century A.D.)

Dio Chrysostom was an orator and philosopher of the first century A.D.

Dio Chrysostom was born to a wealthy family in the Prusa. He spent his early career in Rome, but he was later banished because of his opposition to the emperor *Domitian. After this, and even after his punishment was lifted by the emperor Nerva, he traveled throughout the Mediterranean world.

Dio Chrysostom's writings include some eighty works; most of them are epideictic speeches on mythic and other subjects, whereas a few were written for delivery before a political body. Dio Chrysostom's work reflects both the ideas and the practice of rhetoricians during the Second Sophistic.

Bibliography: C.P. Jones, *The Roman World of Dio Chrysostom*, 1978.

Jeff Rydberg-Cox

DIOCLES OF CARYSTUS (c. 375–295 B.C.)

Diocles was a Greek physician influential in the development of anatomy and physiology.

Diocles, a younger contemporary of *Aristotle, was the most important medical writer within the Lyceum. The Athenians considered him "a younger *Hippocrates." According to *Galen, Diocles was the first to write a treatise on anatomy. He was also the first physician to use a collection of Hippocratic writings. Diocles made significant contributions in physiology by bringing the four-element theory of *Empedocles (the body is composed of fire, water, air, and earth) into conformity with the Hippocratic theory of four humors (blood, phlegm, yellow bile, and black bile). He maintained that health and illness are independent of outside causes. The proper balance of the four elements is necessary for health. Illness and disease result from phlegm or bile blocking the movement of *pneuma*, the vital element for sense perception and bodily movement that flows through the veins from the heart to all parts of the body. Diocles was also the earliest scientist to write a pharmaceutical treatise on the nutritional and medical use of plants.

Bibliography: J. Longrigg, *Greek Rational Medicine: Philosophy and Medicine from Alcmaeon to the Alexandrians*, 1993.

Michael Anderson

DIOCLETIAN (Gaius Aurelius Valerius Diocletianus, c. 235–310/311)

Diocletian was a Roman emperor who instituted a comprehensive set of reforms and, in so doing, ensured the empire's survival and prosperity into the fourth and fifth centuries.

Diocletian, originally Valerius Diocles, was born in or near Salona in Dalmatia. One tradition asserts that his family was of slave origin, his father having been a freedman of the senatorial family of the Annullini. Like many able young men from the Pannonian provinces, Diocles joined the army. The nature of his progress through the military is uncertain, other than to say that by the year 283 he had obtained the command of the *protectores*, the elite corps of officer cadets, who also had the task of guarding the emperor's person.

At that time, the emperor was Carus (282–283), a military man whose two sons Carinus and Numerian formally shared power with him. In 283, Carus was killed under unusual circumstances while on campaign in Persia. Following the equally obscure death of Numerian, Diocletian was hailed as emperor by the army of the east on 24 November 284 and assumed his regnal name.

A brief civil war followed, culminating at a battle near the Margus River (the contemporary Morava River) in 285, in which Carinus was killed and by which Diocletian's authority over the entire empire was confirmed. He was immediately confronted with an insurgency in Gaul, and weakened European frontiers, as well as an uncertain situation in Persia. He responded by naming a fellow officer, Maximian, as Caesar to deal with the Gallic revolt. Diocletian was careful to retain his own primacy in the empire by raising Maximian to only junior rank. After a few months he raised Maximian to the rank of Augustus and soon afterward began employing the epithet "Iovius" (like Jupiter), while Maximian became "Herculius" (like Hercules).

Diocletian and Maximian ruled the empire between them between 284 and 293. For most of that time, they were busy campaigning to secure the empire's frontiers. One problem that they were not able to solve was the usurpation of General Carausius in Britain. He ruled the island and part of the mainland as a breakaway state after 287. It might have been this that prompted Diocletian and Maximian to arrange marriages between their daughters and their praetorian prefects in about 289. Four years later (March 293), their sons-in-law Constantius I and Galerius were raised to imperial rank as Caesars, and the dyarchy became a tetrarchy.

With Maximian and the Caesars now bearing the brunt of the military campaigning, Diocletian was able to concentrate upon a series of administrative and economic reforms. He divided the provinces into smaller units, which he then grouped together in regions, each of which was called a diocese. Each diocese was overseen by a deputy (*vicarius*) of the praetorian prefect. These administrative reforms resulted in an increase in the size of the imperial bureaucracy, which was paid for by a reformed and regulated tax system. Taxation was both in cash and in kind and supported by regular property assessments. The economy was stabilized by the abolition of the increasingly devalued silver-washed coinage that had served for most of the third century and the substitution of a new and stronger silver currency.

Two particular failures marred Diocletian's attempt to provide a comprehensive set of reforms. At one point, in order to prevent price inflation and to stabilize the army's costs for the procurement of supplies, Diocletian ordered that maximum prices be set for a vast range of commodities. People who charged more than the edict specified became guilty of a capital crime. Such a demand was unrealistic: A black economy grew, and goods were stockpiled rather than sold. Eventually, he relented and the law was no longer enforced, but the attempt itself indicates the degree to which Diocletian sought to bend all areas of life to his control.

The second failure was in the area of religion. In reforming the empire, Diocletian also sought to reassert Rome's traditional religious language. The imperial ideology that he expressed in his legislation looked to the immortal gods for approval and blessing. He therefore sought to limit religious diversity by forbidding the practice of both Manichaeism (cf. *Mani) and Christianity. In this he was frustrated. Many Christians and Manichaeans clung tenaciously to their beliefs, preferring imprisonment, torture, and death to apostasy.

Perhaps Diocletian's most remarkable achievement was his abdication. In May 305, he resigned from power, compelling an unwilling Maximian to do likewise. They were succeeded by their Caesars: Constantius in the west became the senior Augustus; Galerius in the east became the junior. Caesars were nominated for each of them, although both of the new appointees, Severus and Maximian, were clearly loyal to Galerius rather than Constantius.

After his retirement, Diocletian returned to the coast where he had been born. A vast fortified villa had been constructed for him. This later became the core of the medieval town of Split. At his villa, Diocletian left the affairs of the empire to his successors while he lived a life of leisure. When urged by Maximian to resume his role in public affairs, Diocletian refused, praising the joy he found in growing cabbages.

Diocletian did return briefly to public life in 308. By that time, the tensions between his successors had resulted in a series of conflicts, especially after the premature death of Constantius in 306. Elevated to the consulship by Galerius, he presided over a conference of the imperial rivals at the town of Carnuntum, then returned to the obscurity of retirement. The arrangements reached at Carnuntum did not endure, but Diocletian was never again invited to intervene. The date of his death is uncertain but was probably soon after that of Maximian in 310. The execution of his former colleague by *Constantine may have depressed him; certainly his statues were overthrown with those of Maximian. He was entombed in a mausoleum in the courtyard of his villa, which, in one of the ironies of history, subsequently became the cathedral for the town of Split.

Bibliography: T.D. Barnes, *The New Empire of Diocletian and Constantine*, 1982; S. Corcoran, *Empire of the Tetrarchs*, 1996; B. Leadbetter, " 'Patrimonium Indivisum'? The Empire of Diocletian and Maximian, 285–289," *Chiron* 28 (1998): 213–228.

William Leadbetter

DIODORUS SICULUS (c. first century B.C.)

Diodorus was the author of a universal history, written in Greek, in forty books, entitled the *Bibliotheke Historike (Library of History)*.

All that can be established about Diodorus' life is that he was born in Agyrium in the Sicilian interior, visited Egypt, settled in Rome, and composed the *Bibliotheke* approximately between 56 and 26. Six books dealing with mythology and ethnography, both Greek and non-Greek, until the Trojan War were followed by fourteen books that ended with the death of *Alexander the Great. The last twenty books concluded with the year 60/59. Only books one to five and eleven to twenty are fully extant. The remaining books survive in a fragmentary state, reproduced in Christian and Byzantine sources. Diodorus presented his narrative of historical as opposed to mythological times in annalistic fashion, synchronizing Olympiads and Athenian archon and Roman consular years. Though Diodorus followed closely his sources of information, at the same time, he presented a highly personal and broadly based moral thesis, influenced superficially by Stoicism, on the expediency of virtue as opposed to vice affecting the vicissitudes of men and nations.

Diodorus' testimony is particularly valuable as the only full source for the history of Greek Sicily and for the wars of the successors of Alexander the Great and as the only substantial, chronologically detailed account of Greek history between the Persian and Peloponnesian Wars.

Bibliography: K. Sacks, *Diodorus Siculus and the First Century*, 1990.

Lionel Sanders

DIOGENES LAERTIUS (c. 250 A.D.)

Laertius composed *The Lives of the Philosophers*, a series of biographies in ten books, spanning the sixth to the third centuries B.C.

Nothing is known for certain concerning Laertius. He probably came from Asia Minor and was either a sceptic, who examined all philosophies dialectically—or an eclectic litterateur. He is often unacquainted with the works of his biographees, using later interpretations of them instead. Thus, the value of each biography is dependent on his sources and citations. He quotes widely, but eclectically, probably utilizing some great library as that at Alexandria or Pergamum. Although he has a penchant for unhistorical anecdotes, he does append useful lists of his subjects' works, sometimes summarizing their thought. The biographies are generally arranged as follows: (1) by philosophical school and grouping for each book; (2) by chronological order (within each book); and (3) by succession of school leaders (within each section).

Book One is an introduction to the precursors of philosophy and a discussion of the Seven Wise Men. Book Two examines the early Ionian philosophers, *Socrates and his minor pupils (e.g., *Xenophon, Aristippus), grouped by school (e.g., Megarians, Cyrenaics). Some of these are mere sketches based on Hellenistic forgeries (e.g., Crito, Simon). Book Three examines *Plato's philosophy, combining early material about his life, later summaries of his views, and classifications of his works. Book Four is devoted to the succession at the academy: Plato's pupils in the Old Academy and *Arcesilaus and his successors in the Middle and New Academies. Although brief references are made to later figures, these biographies end with the second century B.C. Book Five turns to *Aristotle and his successors at the Lyceum, and it, too, is based on learned Hellenistic discussions. However, Book Six is mostly anecdotal, devoted to *Antisthenes, *Diogenes of Sinope, and the Cynics (followed down to the late third century B.C.). Book Seven examines the Stoa, starting with a serious discussion of its founder, *Zeno, and tracing his succession only as far as *Chrysippus (a section on the latter's successors may be lost). Book Eight deals with *Pythagoras and other philosophers from Greek Italy who were considered to be derived from him. There is no mention of the Neo-Pythagoreans of Laertius' period. Book Nine examines the pluralist-monist controversy (*Heraclitus, *Parmenides), including sections on the atomists and sceptics. Book Ten is devoted to *Epicurus, citing long excerpts from his letters and original summaries of his teaching.

Laertius incorporates much from the learned Alexandrian tradition of Greek biography as well as the earlier Peripatetic doxography. Often, his discussion is more literary and anecdotal than philosophical. Nonetheless, he is the most important source for many early thinkers as well as for their interpretations in the Hellenistic period.

Bibliography: J. Mejer, "Diogenes Laertius and Greek Philosophy," *Aufstieg und Niedergang der römischen Welt* 2 (1992): 3556–3602.

Menahem Luz

DIOGENES OF SINOPE (c. 412/403–324/321 b.c.)

Diogenes was founder of the Cynic movement.

Diogenes' family was expelled from Sinope for canceling the value of the state currency. Taking up residence in Athens and Corinth, he turned his circumstances into a philosophy of life: as a stateless, homeless, exiled beggar calling himself a citizen of the world (*kosmopolites*) and preaching the need to cancel (*paracharattein*) its moral and social values. He was probably acquainted with *Antisthenes' philosophy that true wealth belonged to the soul but went one step further, renouncing all property on principle, preaching the value of self-sufficiency (*autarkeia*) and possessing only the minimum for a wandering life: a single piece of clothing, a satchel (*pera*) for food, and in old age, a walking stick (*bakteria*). These fast became the standard kit for all Cynics, who survived on what came to hand. Diogenes preached a return to nature, recommending the example of a canine (*kynikos*) life, thus acquiring the name "Cynic." Like dogs and the homeless of Athens, he slept in a large funerary jar (*pithos*). His way of life demanded a hardiness of body and mind, encapsuled in his theory of education of double training for body and soul. The Cynic did not expect the rest of mankind to follow in his steps but saw himself as a watchdog barking at the wicked and fawning on the good. Diogenes compared himself to a choir master who set the choir one tone higher than what was required. Despising the dialectic of the philosophical schools, he employed the moral "diatribe," in which he upbraided his audience with outspokenness (*parrhesia*) at any public gathering. As such, Cynic philosophy criticized much in standard and philosophical education. In his dialogue the *Republic*, he went further than *Plato, recommending the abolition of state institutions such as marriage, religion, and accepted norms. From his teaching stems the subversive and antisocial element in the Cynic movement.

Diogenes left letters, dialogues, and plays that are now lost. Today, he is chiefly remembered for his role in anecdotes telling of his fictitious encounters with famous men, like Alexander the Great, or of his deliberating shocking antics in the marketplace. Among his most famous were Crates (c. 368/365–288/285) and his Cynic wife, Hipparchia (c. 336/333). The founder of the Stoa, *Zeno of Citium was influenced by his thought. Comparisons have been made between Diogenes' lifestyle and that of Christian mendicant as well as the more recent hippie movement.

Bibliography: R.B. Branham and M.-O. Goulet-Cazé, eds., *The Cynics*, 1996; L.E. Navia, *Classical Cynicism*, 1996.

Menahem Luz

DION (c. 408–354 b.c.)

Dion was the son of Hipparinus, a supporter of *Dionysius I of Syracuse, and brother of Aristomache, who married Dionysius in 398.

Married to Dionysius' daughter, Arete, Dion achieved fortune and renown in

Dionysius I's service. In 388 B.C., Dion met *Plato whose political ideology he later attempted to impose upon Syracuse. After Dionysius I's death in 368/367, Dion became embroiled in a power struggle with *Dionysius II's chief minister, the historian Philistus, and was banished for alleged treason with Carthage in 367/366. Dionysius II's confiscation of Dion's estate and forced marriage of Dion's wife to another man induced Dion to attack Dionysius in 357 with the support of 1,000 mercenaries and a mere twenty-five or thirty Syracusan exiles. Dion speedily captured all of Syracuse except the citadel of Ortygia, which remained in Dionysius' hands. Friction between Dion and the Syracusan populace, led by Dion's colleague Heracleides, forced Dion to retreat temporarily to Leontini. After Dion's return, Dionysius was forced to flee to Locri. Dion's haughty and austere demeanor, antidemocratic and despotic tendencies, financial rapacity, and attempt to impose a Platonic constitution on Syracuse provoked civil strife between Dion and Heracleides. Following Dion's capture of Ortygia and reconciliation with Arete, Dion had Heracleides assassinated. This act provoked the assassination of Dion in 354 by a faction led by Callippus, an associate of Dion at the Academy.

The conflict between Dion, Dionysius II, and Heracleides was disastrous for Sicily, engendering the collapse of the Syracusan empire, the rise of local despots, and internal discord in the Greek cities of Sicily.

Bibliography: M.I. Finley, *Ancient Sicily to the Arab Conquest*, 2nd ed., 1987.

Lionel Sanders

DIONYSIUS I (c. 430–367 B.C.)

Dionysius I was tyrant of Syracuse from 405 to 367 B.C.

Capitalizing on the Greek failure against Carthage in 406/405, Dionysius succeeded in having himself elected general and later sole general (*strategos autocrator*) with a bodyguard. He then made peace with Carthage, from whom he gained recognition as tyrant of Syracuse. Dionysius' fundamental policy as tyrant was to secure his personal supremacy over Syracuse, Sicily, and *Magna Graecia*. To this end, he turned the Syracusan citadel Ortygia into his personal fortress, quelled opposition decisively and generally ruthlessly, entered into alliances and hostilities with both Greek and non-Greek peoples of Sicily and southern Italy, and above all, posed as a Greek nationalist, unifier, and avenger against Carthage, against which he waged wars in 398–396, 393–392, 383–378, and 368–367. At its height, Dionysius' empire included most of Sicily, with the exception of the northwestern Punic sector, and a part of the Italian peninsula to the south of Tarentum. In addition, Dionysius exercised control over Ancona, the mouth of the Po, and the Adriatic coastline in the area of Split. He had allies in Epirus and northwestern Greece and among the Gauls, utilized the services of Campanian, Lucanian, and Iapygian mercenaries, and raided Etruscan territory. Dionysius' sphere of influence lacked a unified structure and consisted of a mixture of subject and allied states as well as colonies. Dionysius sought a high profile in mainland Greece and was closely allied to Sparta and, at the end of his reign, to Athens.

To sustain his militaristic efforts, he imported wood from Aetna and southern Italy, secured craftsmen from abroad, and introduced noteworthy military and naval innovations. To finance these endeavors, Dionysius resorted to both direct and indirect forms of taxation. The population of Syracuse was considerably enlarged with Dionysius' granting of land and citizenship to freed slaves and populations uprooted from Sicily and *Magna Graecia*. While Dionysius summoned the popular assembly, decision making was essentially in the hands of Dionysius and his kinsmen. Marriage alliances involving himself and his three daughters cemented political agendas. Though Dionysius adopted Persian-style dress and ceremonial, his power was based on the generalship. Athenian inscriptions refer to him simply as "archon of Sicily."

Dionysius wrote dramas that were generally ridiculed and entered into a relationship with significant cultural figures of his age, including *Plato, *Isocrates, and *Xenophon. His close friend and adviser until his exile in the mid-380s was the historian Philistus. The overall breadth of Dionysius' imperialistic vision, his military innovations, establishment of military colonies, use of mercenaries, and transference of populations rendered Dionysius a forerunner of *Alexander the Great and the Hellenistic dynasts.

Bibliography: B. Caven, *Dionysius I: War-Lord of Sicily*, 1990; L.J. Sanders, *Dionysius I of Syracuse and Greek Tyranny*, 1987.

Lionel Sanders

DIONYSIUS II (fourth century B.C.)

Dionysius II was the son of *Dionysius I of Syracuse and his Locrian wife Doris. Upon his father's death in 368/367 B.C., he became tyrant of Syracuse.

Of a less vigorous and militaristic disposition than his father and more inclined toward hedonistic pursuits, Dionysius immediately ended the war with Carthage inherited from his father and waged a halfhearted war with the Lucanians in southern Italy. He planted three colonies in Italy: two in Apulia and another on the site of Rhegium, named Phoebia. He wrote poetry and philosophical tracts, cultivated a friendship with Archytas and the Pythagoreans of Tarentum, and drew to his court notable philosophers—*Plato, Aeschines the Socratic, Aristippus of Cyrene, *Xenocrates, and Speusippus.

Dissension between court factions, headed by the Platonically inclined *Dion, Dionysius II's brother-in-law, and the historian Philistus culminated in Dion's honorary exile in 367/366 for alleged intrigues with Carthage. Dionysius' confiscation of Dion's property and forced marriage of Dion's wife, Arete, to another man led to open hostilities between Dion and Dionysius. Dion's initial successes in 357, including the capture of Syracuse with the exception of the citadel Ortygia, induced Dionysius to withdraw to Locri, leaving, temporarily, the Syracusan citadel Ortygia in the hands of Dionysius' son, Apollocrates.

At Locri, Dionysius exercised a brutal tyranny and hedonistic lifestyle before returning, after Dion's death in 354, to recapture Syracuse in 346 from Dionysius' half brother Nysaeus. Blockaded in Ortygia by Hicetas, tyrant of Leontini, Dionysius made a secret treaty with *Timoleon and escaped to Corinth in 344, where he continued his dissipated way of life and ended his days. Anecdotal evidence reports that, while at Corinth, Dionysius became a schoolteacher and devotee of Cybele and entered into dialogue with *Philip II of Macedonia.

Bibliography: M.I. Finley, *Ancient Sicily to the Arab Conquest*, 2nd ed., 1987; A.W. Lintott, *Violence, Civil Strife and Revolution in the Classical City*, 1982.

Lionel Sanders

DIONYSIUS OF ALEXANDRIA, SAINT (c. 200–265)

Also called Saint Dionysius the Great, Saint Dionysius of Alexandria was bishop of the Christian community in Alexandria and opponent of Sabellianism. The feast day for Dionysius is 7 November (west) or 3 October (east).

Dionysius of Alexandria was a convert to Christianity and studied in the school headed by *Origen in Alexandria. In 231–232 Dionysius became the head of the school. Dionysius became bishop in 247–248, continuing through the persecutions of the Emperors *Decius (249–251) and *Valerian (253–260), even though he fled into the desert to escape death. He favored restoring penitent apostates instead of banning them from the Church and against rebaptism of converts from heretical movements. He opposed Millenarian and Sabellian movements. He was vocal in the Trinitarian controversies, insisting that the Trinity was composed of three inseparable persons.

Although most of Dionysius' works are known in references from *Eusebius, *Athanasius, and others, a few fragments are available. Among his writings are works questioning the common authorship of the Gospel of *John and the Book of Revelation (*On the Promises*), refuting Epicurianism (*De Naiura*), arguments against a literal interpretation of the Book of Revelation (Revelation), and a defense of his position on the Trinity (*Refutation and Apologia*).

Bibliography: J. Quasten, *Patrology*, 4 vols., 1950–1986.

Roger W. Anderson

DIONYSIUS OF HALICARNASSUS (born c. 60s B.C.; fl. 30–8 B.C.)

Dionysius of Halicarnassus was a Greek historian of Rome, where he taught rhetoric.

Born in the Greek city of Halicarnassus, Dionysius journeyed to Rome around 30 B.C., after Octavian's (the future *Augustus) victory over *Marc Antony (31) put an end to the civil wars. In Rome he taught rhetoric and wrote, in Greek, several critical works and *Roman Antiquities*, the history of Rome for which he is best known, the first books of which appeared twenty-two years after he settled in Rome. Nothing is known of his life previous to his coming to Rome, nor of his death. *Roman Antiquities* was written in twenty books, covering the origins of Rome (he thought Rome was originally a Greek city) through the First Punic War. The first eleven books (up to 443 B.C.) are extant; only excerpts survive from the rest. His moralizing history is essentially a panegyric to Rome, which he believed to be the culmination of world history. This history provides, along with *Livy, much of what is known of early Rome. His sources include both written and oral traditions about Rome's beginnings. His historical writing features a full description in order to allow the reader to participate in a conversation with the past. Hence, he not only mentions the event and its outcome but as well details the causes, the development of events, and the intentions of the individuals involved. His other writings include treatises on rhetoric and evaluations of individual orators, as well as a study of *Thucydides.

Bibliography: E. Gabba, *Dionysius and the History of Archaic Rome*, 1991.

Ron Harris

DIOPHANTUS OF ALEXANDRIA (c. 250 A.D.)

Diophantus of Alexandria was of tremendous importance to the development of algebra and had great influence on later European number theorists.

Though there is some tenuous evidence that he may have been a contemporary, or near contemporary, of *Heron of Alexandria (c. 65–125), most historians tend to place him in the third century. Beyond the fact that he flourished at Alexandria, nothing certain is known about him, although there is an arithmetic epigram that purports to give some details of his life.

Diophantus wrote three works. His most important one, *Arithmetica*, originally comprised thirteen books. It still partially survives in Greek (six books) and in an Arabic translation (four books). A fragment of his *On Polygonal Numbers* is extant, but his treatise *Porisms* no longer survives. A translation of *Arithmetica*, along with a commentary, was made by Xylander (the Greek name assumed by Wilhelm Holzmann, a professor at the University of Heidelberg) in 1575. This edition was used in turn by the Frenchman Bachet de Méziriac, who in 1621 published the first edition of the Greek text along with a Latin translation and notes. A second edition of the *Arithmetica* was produced in 1670, which contained Pierre de Fermat's famous marginal notes and helped to stimulate number theory research.

The *Arithmetica* is an important text as in it Diophantus introduces symbolism into Greek algebra. This work is an analytical treatment of algebraic number theory, which marks Diophantus as a genius in the field.

Bibliography: T.L. Heath, *Diophantus of Alexandria: A Study in the History of Greek Algebra*, 2nd ed., 1964.

Cecilia Saerens

DIOSCORIDES (c. 40–90)

Dioscorides was a Greek physician, pharmacologist, and writer.

Dioscorides' life must be largely inferred from his work. His birthplace and hometown was Anazarbus, a town in southeastern Asia Minor. Though never attaining the size and status of Tarsus, its nearby rival, it was located along two important trade routes. As a young man, he studied botany and pharmacology in Tarsus and Alexandria. He may have served for a short time in the Roman legion, perhaps even giving medical service. But he was, by education and profession, a physician. Dioscorides was trained by Areios, a famous Tarsus medical practitioner and thinker, known for now-lost works on drugs and *Hippocrates.

Dioscorides attained renown for his five-book study called *De materia medica*, or *The Materials of Medicine*. This work was composed between 60 and 78. It contains data about more than 1,000 naturally derived drugs, mostly from plants, though a few from animals and minerals. There are several things that set this work apart from others of its ilk. First, as a result of his living in a highly trafficked area between East and West, Dioscorides had knowledge of plants in both regions. Second, this compiler not only described the medicinal remedy but also the subsequent effects on the patient. And third, rather than becoming embroiled in the medical controversies and theories of his day, Dioscorides recorded only his empirical observations. During the Hellenistic era, medicine was as much of a philosophy as a practical art. Dioscorides, however, disagreed with most of the contemporary medical theory. His work remains focused on observation, which gives it a timeless usefulness. It was the first compilation and analysis of its kind, and it retained its preeminence for hundreds of years following its initial composition. It still fascinates and informs today.

Bibliography: J.M. Riddle, *Dioscorides on Pharmacy and Medicine*, 1985.

Jennifer L. Koosed

DOMITIAN (Titus Flavius Domitianus, 51–96)

Domitian was Roman emperor from 81 to 96.

The second son of *Vespasian and Flavia Domitilla, he narrowly escaped death when his father rebelled against the emperor Vitellius in 69. When Vespasian became emperor he gave Domitian imperial titles but clearly favored his eldest son *Titus.

After Titus died (81), Domitian became emperor without any practical experience in governing. He had absolutist tendencies and had himself appointed consul every year for the first eight years of his reign. In all, he held the consulship seventeen times. In 85, he named himself censor for life, thus enabling him to control the composition of the Senate.

The Senate resented Domitian, as he owed his position to his father and did not have a distinguished career. As a result, Domitian freely allowed members of the equestrian class and provincials into the Senate. He rarely relied on the

Senate for advice and instead used a body of personally chosen advisers, his *consilium principis*. His personal apparel offended the senators as he dressed as a *triumphator*, including a laurel, scepter, and crown, and was accompanied by twenty-four licitors, whereas other emperors had only twelve.

After the revolt of L. Antonius Saturninus, governor of Upper Germany (88), Domitian became more suspicious of the Senate. He encouraged informers and had many senators exiled or executed. He disliked philosophers, as they supported the Senate, and had them expelled from Rome in 89 and from Italy six years later. Various plots were contrived against Domitian, and the last three years of his reign (93–96) turned into a veritable reign of terror. Domitian was assassinated in 96 through a plot devised by his wife, the Praetorian Guard, and several senators.

In foreign policy, Domitian was able to defeat the powerful Germanic tribe the Chatti. He also successfully concluded a peace agreement with the Dacian king Decabulus. However, he recalled *Agricola from Britain in 84, possibly because he was jealous of the general's successes.

History has rendered Domitian a harsh verdict and *Tacitus, *Suetonius, *Martial, and *Pliny the Younger were all very critical of him.

Bibliography: B.W. Jones, *Domitian and the Senatorial Order*, 1979.

Andrew G. Traver

DONATUS, AELIUS (fourth century A.D.)

Donatus was a famous Latin grammarian, teacher, and author of a standard Latin grammar textbook.

Donatus was a highly respected teacher in Rome; his most famous student, *Jerome, remembered him fondly. An abridged version of Donatus' commentary on *Terence, noteworthy for its discussion of issues of staging and comparisons with Greek models, survives as *scholia* (glosses). Of his commentaries on *Virgil's poems, which were written as a resource for other grammarians, a few introductory parts are extant; material from his original commentaries also survives in the two versions, especially the longer, of *Servius Honoratus commentary. Donatus was best known, however, for his two grammars. The *Ars Minor* was an elementary text, dealing with the parts of speech in the usual question and answer format. The *Ars Maior*, a more advanced text, also followed the standard format of introductory definitions and explanations of basic terms, questions and answers relating to the parts of speech, and brief definitions and examples of various vices (e.g., barbarism and solecism), poetic terms, and figures of speech.

His grammars, which were noteworthy for their conciseness, soon became the object of numerous commentaries and were used by such other writers as Alcuin, Cassiodorus, and Priscian. His works dominated the study of the Latin language until the twelfth century. Some monks were even said to prefer his rules to those of Benedict. His *Ars Minor* was translated into Greek by the thirteenth- or fourteenth-century Byzantine scholar Planudes. Donatus' influence was so pervasive that his name was used in Old French and Middle English as a synonym for "grammar," "textbook," "lesson," or "basic introduction."

Bibliography: E.J. Kenney and W.V. Clausen, eds., *Latin Literature. Cambridge History of Classical Literature*, vol. 2, 1982.

Rebecca Harrison

DONATUS OF CASAE NIGRAE (?–355 A.D.)

Donatus led most Christians of Roman Africa into schism against the Church. The movement is named Donatism after him.

The seeds of the controversy were sown long before Donatus' birth. In 256 a council of African bishops headed by *Cyprian of Carthage determined that the ministrations of an unworthy clergyman were invalid. The bishop of Rome objected to making the effects of God's grace dependent on its human intermediary, but as fresh persecutions overwhelmed the Christians, the disagreement between the churches of Rome and Africa was allowed to stand. It was able to come to the fore again when, in the wake of *Diocletian's Great Persecution (303–311), the government finally extended toleration to Christians (313). Moreover, ministerial unworthiness was then a pressing issue. The Great Persecution had induced many of the clergy to become inactive, and their resumption of priestly duties afterward offended the faithful. When the bishop of Carthage died in 311 and his successor, Caecilian, was rumored to have been an accommodationist, a furor erupted. A council of hard-line African bishops deposed Caecilian, and eventually Donatus, a priest from Casae Nigrae in Numidia, was chosen to replace him. Caecilian, however, refused to step aside.

In the years 313 to 316 Emperor *Constantine personally intervened and tried to resolve the dispute before tribunals, both ecclesiastical and civil. It was certainly not to his advantage to have a major controversy arise in the very religion whose interests he was busy promoting. However, since attempts to force Donatus' followers to recognize Caecilian were also unsuccessful, Constantine ordered toleration of the Donatists in 321, perhaps in the hope that, as the years went by, the dispute would die down.

It did not. Donatus was able to rally most of Christian Africa behind his stand for a heroically rigorous Christianity. Although Emperor Constantius sent Donatus into exile in 348, Donatism continued to be the majority sect in Roman Africa until the early fifth century when internal dissent, renewed imperial coercion, and the activity of *Augustine of Hippo combined to weaken its hold.

Bibliography: W.H.C. Frend, *The Donatist Church*, 3rd ed., 1985.

John Quinn

DRACO (seventh century B.C.)

Draco was an early Athenian lawgiver known for the severity of his laws.

Although Draco is an important figure in Athenian history, the details of his life and most of his laws are lost. The Aristotelian *Constitution of the Athenians* and *Aristotle's *Politics* both report that in 621 Draco enacted new laws for the Athenians, but the exact nature of these laws is unclear. The only laws that can be firmly attributed to Draco are those dealing with homicide. The Aristotelian *Constitution of the Athenians* suggests that Draco's reforms included the franchise of hoplites and the creation of a council and provided for elected officials. These sections are, however, generally rejected as spurious.

All of Draco's laws are consistently noted for their severe penalties. *Plutarch's *Life of Solon* reports that the punishment for most offenses was death. Perhaps because of their severity, most of these laws were replaced some thirty years later by *Solon except for the homicide laws.

Draco's importance lies, at least in part, in the respect that public speakers and politicians gave him in the fifth and fourth century. Orators invoked Draco (along with Solon) both as a model statesman and as a guiding spirit for laws in the fourth-century Athenian democracy.

Bibliography: M. Gagarin, *Drakon and Early Athenian Homicide Law*, 1981.

Jeff Rydberg-Cox

DRUSUS, MARCUS LIVIUS (C. 123–91 B.C.)

Drusus was a plebeian tribune in 91 whose actions led directly to the Social War (91–87).

He was the son of M. Livius Drusus (consul, 112; censor, 109), the tribune of 122 who had championed the cause of the Senate against *Gaius Gracchus. His early offices include a military tribunate, a quaestorship (in Asia), and possibly an aedileship. He is included by *Cicero in a list of young men who aligned themselves with the Senate to oppose the tribune *Saturninus in 100.

Drusus was a prominent figure in the distinguished senatorial group favoring reform at the end of the 90s. He was an accomplished public speaker, noted for his outstanding wealth and virtuous lifestyle. Elected to the tribunate in 91, his principal aim was to reinforce senatorial authority through a judicial measure that ended the equestrian monopoly in the extortion court (and probably other courts as well), establishing (it seems) that future jury panels should be recruited from a Senate enlarged by the addition of 300 equestrians. In an attempt to secure the backing of the plebs for his judicial proposal, Drusus also sponsored grain and agrarian legislation. A currency law debasing the silver coinage was probably designed to facilitate the financing of his popular program.

Drusus' legislation was carried with violence, a great number of noncitizens entering Rome on the day of the vote. In exchange for Italian support for his legislative package and to compensate for allied land losses under his agrarian legislation, Drusus offered to bring forward a bill granting the Italians Roman citizenship, a privilege upon which they now pinned their long-standing demand for equality of treatment within the Roman system.

Growing opposition from within the Senate led by the consul L. Marcius Philippus, from equestrian ranks, and from Etruscans and Umbrians disgruntled by the agrarian legislation, coupled with the death of one of Drusus' most influential supporters, L. Licinius Crassus, culminated in the annulment of Drusus' legislation by the Senate on technical grounds. Though still a tribune (and therefore sacrosanct) Drusus was subsequently stabbed to death by an unknown assassin, a murder that signaled the beginning of armed revolt for those Italians disappointed in their hopes of enfranchisement. His political defeat and assassination and the consequent frustration of allied hopes were the catalysts for the outbreak of the Social War.

Bibliography: P.A. Brunt, *The Fall of the Roman Republic and Related Essays*, 1988.

Lea Beness

DURIS (or Douris, active c. 500–460 B.C.)

Duris was a potter and red-figure painter in fifth-century Athens.

Nothing of Duris' life is known beyond what is supplied by the pots themselves. His signature appears on more than fifty (mostly as painter but occasionally as potter), and hence scholars have attributed to him the decoration of more than 300 vessels, mostly drinking cups intended for symposia, which he painted inside and out with figural scenes (myths, symposia, athletics, and battles) and patternwork (florals, spirals, meanders, crosses). Scholars divide his career into various phases. Although he painted pots manufactured by others, most were produced by Python. A prolific artisan, Duris has been described as "a painter of considerably efficiency, charm, and dullness." His best painting is excellent, and he had a knack for devising circular compositions appropriate for the interiors of cups, but much of his work (not often illustrated) is "mechanical and shallow." His energetic figures are often foreshortened, and he seems to delight presenting back views of figures as well as transparent drapery. His influence has been discerned in the work of contemporary and later pot painters: Epictetus, the "Berlin Painter," "Triptolemos Painter," and "Euaion Painter," among others.

Bibliography: J. Boardman, *Athenian Red Figure Vases: The Archaic Period*, 1975; D. Buitron-Oliver, *Douris: A Master-Painter of Athenian Red-Figure Vases*, 1995.

Kenneth D.S. Lapatin

E

EGERIA OF SPAIN (fl. 381–417)

Egeria was a fifth-century pilgrim, traveler, and author of the *Itinerarium Egeriae*.

Although it is tempting to believe that Egeria herself was a nun, scholars are more inclined to view her as a member of some kind of consecrated community. Clearly, Egeria was a devout, well-educated, and well-to-do woman who traveled to Asia Minor, Palestine, and Egypt in the late fourth and early fifth centuries. Her *Diary* focuses on her trip to Jerusalem and to various places in Holy Scripture and biblical tradition. It is a first-person account, written in the form of a letter and addressed to "Ladies, reverend sisters."

According to the *Diary*, she went first to Mount Sinai and then retraced the route taken by the Jews as described in Exodus. Then she visited Mount Nebo, which is believed to be the site of Moses' death. Next, she visited the tomb of Job at Carneas in Hauran; detoured to see St. Thomas the Apostle's tomb in Edessa; and went to the house of Abraham in Carrhae. However, Egeria's *Diary* is not just a list of places; it is a description of her pilgrimage, reflecting her fascination with and faith in the truths of Scripture. She characterizes herself as "somewhat curious," and every page of the *Diary* reveals her preoccupation with the physical sites of the Bible and her desire to meet and pray with her fellow Christians, wherever they may be.

Bibliography: G. Gingras, int. and trans., *Egeria: Diary of a Pilgrimage*, 1970.

Jana K. Schulman

EMPEDOCLES OF ACRAGAS (c. 493–433 B.C.)

Empedocles was a Sicilian pre-Socratic philosopher, wonder healer, and magician who taught the transmigration of souls and explained the universe as consisting of four material elements and two driving principles.

Very little is known about Empedocles' life, and his work survives only in fragments. He was born in Acragas in Sicily. Although he came from an aristocratic family, it is known that he promoted democratic tendencies in politics and that for that reason had to go into exile. There are several versions about his death. According to one of these, he ended his life by jumping into Mt. Etna. In antiquity, he was known not only as a philosopher but also as a thaumaturgist, healer, and prophet. He traveled and taught throughout the Greek world. He wrote two poems. The first (*On Nature*) was a theoretical cosmological explanation of the world; the second (*Purifications*) was a religious and mystical description of a soul's journey through various incarnations. According to *Aristotle, Empedocles was also the inventor of rhetoric.

As a philosopher, Empedocles belongs to the Ionic philosophical tradition, to which he introduced important Pythagorean and Orphic elements. He explained the Universe as a result of the mixture of four material principles, "roots" or elements (water, earth, fire, and air, assimilated with divinities), which are eternal and indestructible. What mortals call birth and death is nothing but the union and separation of these four original material principles. The different qualities of things consist of the different mathematical proportions of the elements. Empedocles postulated two other principles to explain the ongoing process of mixture and separation: Love and Strife. Through Love, things gather together into a perfect mixture, the original Sphere. Through Strife, the elements separate into each other again. The process of the world consists of a cosmic cycle of successive periods of domination by Love and then Strife.

Empedocles was a polemical figure who inspired poets and historians. His doctrine of the four elements exercised a lasting influence on medicine and physics.

Bibliography: P. Kingsley, *Ancient Philosophy, Mystery, and Magic. Empedocles and Pythagorean Tradition*, 1995.

Fernando Oreja

ENNIUS, QUINTUS (239–169 B.C.)

Ennius was a Roman poet who principally wrote dramatic and nondramatic verse.

Born in Rudiae in Calabria of an upper-class family, Ennius, having met *Cato the Elder while stationed in Sardinia, was introduced by him at Rome, where he was received by the foremost families. In his house on the Aventine, he taught Greek and Latin grammar to the sons of the Caecilii, the Cornelli, the Fulvii, and the Sulpicii, and there also composed his verse. In 184 he was granted Roman citizenship through his patron, G. Fulvius Nobilior.

Ennius' poetic works ranged over drama and the dramatic form known as *fabulae praetextae*, history, satire, mixed verse, philosophy, mock-heroics, and biography. His one prose composition, the *Euhemerus*, proposed that the gods were not divine beings but important men honored in an exceptional way after their deaths.

It is for his drama and his history that Ennius is primarily known. Of his tragedies twenty titles remain (e.g., *Achilles, Andromeda, Erechtheus, Hecuba*), of which twelve can be said to be based on *Euripides and three on *Aeschylus. The three comedies (*Caupunculus, Pancratiastes*, and *Telestis*) appear, from the few lines remaining, to be in the Greek New Comedy style. His other main work is the *Annales*, eighteen books on the history of Rome from the fall of Troy to contemporary affairs, of which 600 lines remain. He wrote this history in somber albeit halting hexameters, styling himself *Homer reborn.

Considered by the Romans to be the father of their poetry, Ennius' works were studied by such men as *Cicero and *Virgil, and quoted through the republic and empire, losing currency only after the fifth century.

Bibliography: O. Skutsch, ed., *The Annals of Q. Ennius*, 1985.

Deborah Eaton

EPAMINONDAS (c. 410–362 B.C.)

Epaminondas was a Theban statesman and general who was largely responsible for ending Spartan military predominance in Greece.

Epaminondas was the son of a Theban aristocrat. At a young age, he took an interest in philosophy and was a pupil of the Pythagorean philosopher Lysis. From 379 to 371 Athens and Thebes allied together and fought against Spartan supremacy; it is unclear what role Epaminondas played in this alliance. He was elected *boeotarch* (one of the federal magistrates of the Boeotian League) in 371. In that year, he represented Thebes in a peace conference with Sparta. At this conference, Athens and Sparta demanded that each city in Boeotia should sign as a separate party to the treaty. Epaminondas, however, refused to allow other Boeotian cities to sign independently. As a result, Thebes was excluded from the peace and left to face Sparta alone.

The Spartans then invaded and met Epaminondas' forces at the Battle of Leuctra (371). This battle was a Theban victory due to Epaminondas' usage of new tactics. He massed his troops an unprecedented fifty men deep on the left wing against a Spartan depth of twelve. The defeat of the Spartan army made Epaminondas immediately famous. He followed up this victory in the next year by invading the Peloponnese and freeing Arcadia and Messenia from Spartan domination. He founded a new city at Megalopolis to serve as a capital of a new Arcadian League. For the first time in two centuries an enemy force was near Sparta.

In the following years he campaigned both in Thessaly and the Peloponnese (369–368, 367) to maintain Theban predominance in Greece. In 364, he challenged Athenian supremacy at sea but was forced to return home to face a revolt in Arcadia. In 362 he invaded the Peloponnese for the fourth time and won an inconclusive victory at Mantinea. He died there of battle wounds, after advising the Thebans to make peace.

Epaminondas' reputation is based primarily on his skill as a general. His military strategies ended Spartan supremacy and anticipated the innovations of both *Philip II and *Alexander the Great.

Bibliography: J. Buckler, *The Theban Hegemony, 371–362* B.C., 1980.

Andrew G. Traver

EPHIALTES (?–461 B.C.)

Ephialtes was an Athenian politician of the early fifth century B.C. who was allied with *Pericles against *Cimon and involved in the reforms of the Areopagus.

Very little is known about Ephialtes. He was an opponent of Cimon in Athenian politics and probably involved in his ostracism in 461. He is best known for participation with Pericles in the democratic reform of the Areopagus. The Aristotelian *Constitution of the Athenians* describes how Ephialtes reformed the Areopagus by reducing its size and making members accountable for their actions. More important, he transferred many of its political functions to other Athenian institutions, including the assembly, the council, and the law courts.

Ephialtes was also known for his honesty. *Plutarch, in his *Life of Cimon*, claims that in the early fifth century Cimon, *Aristides the Just, and Ephialtes were the only political figures who were not becoming rich on account of their public service. Similarly, the *Constitution of the Athenians* describes Ephialtes as incorruptible.

Ephialtes' democratic reforms earned him many enemies. Plutarch describes Ephialtes as "the scourge of the oligarchs and relentless in his prosecution and scrutiny of those who did wrong to the people." Because of this, Ephialtes was assassinated. One of these enemies—a certain Aristodicus from Tanagra—murdered Ephialtes after Cimon's ostracism in 461.

Although so few details are known about Ephialtes, it is clear that he was an important figure in the politics of fifth-century Athens and that his reforms played a key role in the evolution of the Athenian democracy.

Bibliography: C.W. Fornara and L.J. Samons, *Athens from Cleisthenes to Pericles*, 1991.

Jeff Rydberg-Cox

EPHORUS OF CYME (c. 405–330 B.C.)

Ephorus was a Greek historian of the fourth century B.C.

Though born in the Anatolian city of Cyme, he studied in Athens with the great philosopher and orator *Isocrates. As is appropriate for a student of Isocrates, the bits of Ephorus' work that we have show a flair for rhetoric, drama, and vivid characterizations. He also seems to share Isocrates' pro-Athenian bias and his yearning for unity among the Greek cities.

His most important work was a universal history that encompassed both Greek and non-Greek history from the earliest historical times down to his own day. Apart from a few quotations by later writers, Ephorus' work has been lost, but his history served as an important source for ancient historians whose writings do survive.

Although the length (thirty volumes) and the ambitious scope of his history were unprecedented, he does not seem to have made any substantial advances over his predecessors in the methods of researching and writing history. He does, however, show a healthy respect for the distinction between myth and history and for the importance of eyewitness evidence.

Ephorus was highly regarded in antiquity, and his account became the standard account for many historical periods. For this reason, several later historians whose works still survive depended heavily on Ephorus. In particular, *Diodorus Siculus is thought to have relied on Ephorus almost exclusively for large parts of fourth-century history and for parts of fifth-century history not covered by *Herodotus or *Thucydides.

Bibliography: G.L. Barber, *The Historian Ephorus*, 1935.

William Hutton

EPICHARMUS (c. 530–440 B.C.)

Epicharmus was a Greek dramatist active at Syracuse in the first half of the fifth century.

Epicharmus was probably a native of Syracuse, but other Greek cities such as Megara Hybaea in Sicily also laid claim to him. He was the earliest prominent writer of the type of comedy known as Dorian farce, a mythological burlesque that satirized gods and heroes. His plays featured many of the persistent features of ancient comedy such as the parody of myths, the use of great heroic figures in farcical situations, and stock figures. Although he seems to have used musical accompaniment, his plays had no chorus. Today, only fragments and about thirty-five titles of Epicharmus' plays survive.

In antiquity, a large number of ethical and medical works were attributed to Epicharmus, but even as early as the third century B.C., they were regarded as forged. *Aristotle mentioned Epicharmus as one of the first to form proper plots, and *Plato called him the comedic equivalent of *Homer. One tradition claimed that Epicharmus was a student of *Pythagoras.

Bibliography: A. Pickard-Cambridge, *Dithrymb, Tragedy and Comedy*, 2nd ed., 1962.

Andrew G. Traver

EPICTETUS (c. 55–135)

Epictetus was a prominent teacher of Stoic philosophy in Rome, at Nicopolis in Epirus, and perhaps finally in Rome again.

Epictetus was born a slave in Phrygia. He was sold to a master in Rome and ultimately gained his freedom. His teacher was the prominent Roman Stoic Musonius Rufus. He left Rome in 89 when *Domitian issued an edict against philosophers, taking up residence in Nicopolis. Traditions that he was on intimate terms with *Hadrian, transmitted by the emperor's biographer, among others, would put him back in Rome before his death. A legend that the philosopher emperor *Marcus Aurelius was his student is probably not true, though Marcus said that he had studied the *Discourses*. No writings by Epictetus survive. Knowledge of his teaching is transmitted in the *Discourses* (originally eight books, of which four are extant) and *Enchiridion* ("Handbook" or "Manual") compiled from lecture notes by his student, the Roman aristocrat *Arrian.

Stoicism was established by *Zeno of Citium and *Chrysippus. Stoics, like most late classical religions and philosophies, offered a way to personal salvation, which for them took the form of a good life. The trick was to bring one's personal reason (*logos*) into harmony with the cosmic Logos that permeated Nature, the universe. To do so, one had to overcome all desires, passions, and attachments and maintain one's equanimity in the face of inscrutable fate, which though benevolent was also frequently cruel. Epictetus put special emphasis on ethics (the natural moral law was accessible to reason) and on practical moral training, including personal cleanliness. Mental life was in the subject's control and hence free. All external things, including pleasure and pain, are beyond control and irrelevant to morals. Knowledge and reason serve virtue. The wise person learns to manage desires and aversions and to control one's own assent. All people fail on occasion, but that is no excuse to quit trying. On occasion Epictetus spoke of Nature as Zeus, almost as a personal deity. He criticized Epicureans for hedonism and Platonists for scepticism. He admired Cynic freedom while rejecting their extreme behavior.

Several tales about Epictetus, even if apocryphal, contribute to a grasp of his life and teaching. One said his master was torturing him by twisting his leg. Epictetus calmly observed, "If you twist it any further it will break. See? I told you so." Another told of a summons from *Nero that Epictetus ignored. The emperor then sent a death threat. "Oh, so he's going to kill me? Go ask him what he plans to do to me after that." Epictetus remains a lively and relevant figure. He was the subject of stories in *USA Today* and the *Los Angeles Times* during 1998–1999. Novelist Tom Wolfe's wronged protagonist in *A Man in Full* found solace in his teaching. Author Sharon Lebell has made Epictetus the subject of two recent books.

Bibliography: A.A. Long, *Hellenistic Philosophy*, 1974.

Chris Hauer

EPICURUS (341–271 B.C.)

Epicurus was a Greek philosopher, founder of the Epicurean school that, along with the Stoics, was one of the two most important and influential systems of Hellenistic philosophy. His physics was based on the atomic theory of *Democritus, and the ethics placed pleasure as the goal of human action.

Epicurus was born on Samos, the son of an Athenian colonist, Neocles. The spur to the development of his philosophy came when he was taught by the Democritean physicist Nausiphanes. Epicurus rebelled against Democritean physical determinism, which, he felt, removed free will and moral responsibility from humans and bound us in an endless predetermined chain of causation. Therefore, he introduced a minute random "swerve" in atomic motion, by which an atom may, at no predetermined time or place, depart from its former course by the minimum possible amount, thereby breaking the chain of causation and ensuring that atomic motion is chaotic. Although Epicurus insisted on the existence of the gods, he denied them any influence or interest in the world or human affairs. Fate, predestination, and divine teleology were denied, and similarly, physical determinism was rejected, granting humans free will. Epicurus founded his first school at Mytilene, then a second school at Lampsacus, and moved to Athens in 306, where he set up the school famous as "The Garden."

The Epicureans were unusual in that they lived and taught in the seclusion of their garden, in contrast to their main rivals the Stoics, who taught in public in the agora. Indeed, the two schools held almost diametrically opposed worldviews, and there was intense rivalry between them. Epicurus is credited with writing 300 books, but only 4 of his works survive complete: the epitomes of the system in the letters to Pythocles, Herodotus, and Menoeceus and the "Principal Sayings."

Epicureanism has had an extraordinary influence on Western thought as the chief representative of an antiteleological view of the world, in which everything happens by an interaction of chance and necessity and where there is no room for fate, predestination, or divine guidance of the world. Epicureanism, mainly through *Lucretius, had a seminal influence on the development of Renaissance Humanism, and successive revivals fueled further liberal and radical thinking in science, ethics, and politics. The Epicurean denial of divine sanction for worldly status or the divine right of kings, and the liberating doctrine of free will, has made the philosophy popular with radical and socialist thinkers. The Epicurean concept of justice as a pact between friends strongly informed the political theories of John Locke and the "Social Contract" theories of John Stuart Mill and others, and Epicureanism can be seen as the well-spring of much of the liberal temper in Western thought.

Bibliography: A.A. Long and D.N. Sedley, *The Hellenistic Philosophers*, 1987.

Gordon Campbell

ERASISTRATUS OF CEOS (c. 304–250 b.c.)

Erasistratus was a Greek physician in Alexandria who helped establish the foundations for the scientific study of anatomy and physiology.

Erasistratus, whose father, uncle, and brother were also physicians, studied medicine in Athens and in Ceos. He was a younger contemporary of *Herophilus in Alexandria, where the two pioneered the use of human dissection (and possibly vivisection) in anatomical and physiological research. Erasistratus was responsible for advances in knowledge about the anatomy of the brain, the heart, and the vascular system. He distinguished the cerebrum from the cerebellum, described the cavities within and membranes that cover the brain, and succeeded in tracing the nerves into the interior of the brain. Erasistratus described the valves of the heart and recognized the heart's pumping function. He also described (in a rudimentary way) the way that air is taken into the body through inhalation and passes from the lungs to the heart and then (as vital *pneuma*) to the whole body through the arteries. Erasistratus rejected the widespread Hippocratic theory of humoral medicine. Instead, he attributed disease to "plethora," an excess of blood that produces inflammation and blocks the flow of *pneuma*. He rarely practiced bloodletting, preferring carefully regulated exercise and diet as preventive and therapeutic treatments.

Bibliography: J. Longrigg, *Greek Rational Medicine: Philosophy and Medicine from Alcmaeon to the Alexandrians*, 1993.

Michael Anderson

ERATOSTHENES OF CYRENE (c. 276–197 b.c.)

Eratosthenes was a gifted scholar who served as the director of the Library of Alexandria.

Eratosthenes was born in Cyrene but spent most of his early adulthood in Athens before being called by *Ptolemy III to Alexandria, where he remained for the rest of his life serving as tutor to *Ptolemy IV and director of the Library. He was an acquaintance and correspondent of *Archimedes of Syracuse and excelled in several diverse academic fields, working fruitfully in mathematics, geography, cartography, poetry, history, and philosophy. Reaching an old age and in despondency over his increasing blindness, Eratosthenes committed suicide by deliberate starvation.

Eratosthenes' most famous contribution to mathematics is a method by which the prime numbers can be found by separating them from the nonprime numbers. This method, named for him, is called the Sieve of Eratosthenes. He also solved the problem of the duplication of the cube and wrote the treatise *On Means*. Turning his mathematics to more physical application, he wrote *On the Measurement of the Earth*, wherein he describes the method by which he calculated the diameter of the earth. Noting the distance between and the relative angles of the sun from two locations on the same meridian, he was able to ascertain the polar diameter of the earth to within 1 percent of its true value.

Though Eratosthenes is most commonly known for his Sieve and calculation of the earth's diameter, he was also successful in many other scholarly endeavors. He wrote a commentary on *Plato's *Timaeus*, exploring the essential mathematical notions inherent to Plato's philosophy. In his poem *Hermes*, Eratosthenes gives a descriptive astronomy. In *Geographica*, he recorded the history of geography and proposed a spherical geography for the earth, and he was the first to draft a map of the world based on lines of longitude and latitude.

Bibliography: T.L. Heath, *A History of Greek Mathematics*, 1921.

Michael Labranche

EUCLID (C. 365–300 B.C.)

Euclid, author of the *Elements*, is the most famous geometer since ancient times.

The historical sources of Euclid's birth and early life are incomplete and uncertain, but it is known that Euclid was born the son of Naucrates either in Tyre or in Alexandria. It is also recorded that Euclid studied under the students of *Plato and later founded the Alexandrian School of Mathematics, where he taught for many years. In his professional life he was a traditional and accomplished scholar more interested in promoting his favorite discipline than in winning distinction for himself.

Ironically, Euclid is the most famous geometer of all time, and his lasting fame rests largely on just one of his major works, the *Elements*, though he wrote at least nine other major works. In this work, Euclid organized and rigorously presented all the basics of mathematics known in his time. Indeed, his work is so remarkably clear and thorough that it supplanted all previously written books on the subject. The *Elements* has remained a pivotal work in mathematics since that time. Scarcely any other book except the Bible has been more widely studied and edited. Moreover, no other book has had a greater influence on the development of scientific and mathematical thought. In this work, Euclid mapped out a rigorous method that built up the subject matter through successive definitions, propositions, and proofs. This method is still used today in the mathematical sciences.

Although Euclid is referred to as "the Geometer" and the *Elements* is commonly thought of purely as a geometry text, Euclid presents in it a collection of thirteen books treating the basic development of several areas of mathematics. Books I–IV deal with plane geometry and include the axioms on which everything else is based; Books V–VI present a new theory of proportions; Books VII–IX are given to basic number theory, including prime numbers; Book X is about irrational quantities, applying rigorous rules to the earlier work of Theaetetus; and Books XI–XIII form a presentation of solid geometry, including the construction of the five Platonic polyhedra.

Euclid's other works include major texts on conic sections, astronomy, and optics. He even wrote a text called the *Elements of Music*, which is a mathematical study of the Pythagorean theory of music and harmony. Unfortunately, many of these other works have been lost, but Euclid's *Elements* will always stand as a monument to his greatness as a mathematician and educator.

Bibliography: T.L. Heath, *A History of Greek Mathematics*, 1921; T.L. Heath, *The Thirteen Books of Euclid's Elements*, 2nd ed., 1956.

Michael Labranche

EUDOXUS OF CNIDOS (C. 398–345 B.C.)

Eudoxus was a mathematician, astronomer, geographer, and legislator who was probably the first person to attempt a mathematical description of the celestial plane.

We have no precise dates for the life of Eudoxus, but he is said to have flourished in the 103rd Olympiad (368–365) and to have died at the age of fifty-three, a few years after *Plato. Eudoxus studied geometry with the Pythagorean Archytas and came to Athens to hear the Socratics. He later spent sixteen months in Egypt with the priests at Heliopolis, where he made observations of the stars and may have written a celestial calendar entitled *Eight Year Cycle*. He then founded a school of his own at Cyzicus where, with the benefit of a good observation point, he made further observations of stars. These observations probably formed the basis of his *Phaenomena*.

In the course of a second visit to Athens, Eudoxus had the opportunity to discuss his mathematical model of planetary movements with both Plato and *Aristotle. Finally, Eudoxus retired to Cnidos, where he was held in great honor, and continued his astronomical research. It was here that he probably wrote his second work on the constellations and celestial circles called *Mirror of the Sky*, which was in some respects a revision of his *Phaenomena*. He also drew up laws for the city of Cnidos.

The Greeks deduced the sphericity of the sky and the earth in the fifth century. Fourth-century philosophers established the classical system of a rotating spherical cosmos with a stationary spherical earth at its center. In his *Phaenomena*, Eudoxus described the geometry of this cosmos, with its axis and two poles, and the forty-eight Greek constellations. There is also a tradition that he had the use of a star globe.

Bibliography: M.R. Wright, *Cosmology in Antiquity*, 1995.

Cecilia Saerens

EUMENES II (King of Pergamum, 197–158 B.C.)

Eumenes II was the greatest king of the Attalid dynasty, responsible for the cultural flowering of the city between 181 and 168.

In 190 he helped the Romans defeat *Antiochus III at Magnesia and lobbied the Senate for the conquered territory. By the Treaty of Apamea (188) he received all of the Seleucid territories west of the Taurus Mountains except Caria and Lycia, which were granted to Rhodes. He formed an alliance with Ariarathes IV of Cappadocia by marrying his daughter Stratonice and attacked and defeated Prusias of Bithynia in 184, who was supported by *Hannibal and the Galatians. Grateful for removing the Galatian menace the Greek cities hailed him as Soter (savior). He confronted Pharnaces I of Pontus and, with Rome's help, forced a favorable treaty in 179. In 175 he placed an ally, *Antiochus IV, on the Seleucid throne.

By now the dominant figure in Asia Minor, he elevated the festival of Athena Nikephoros to Panhellenic status in 181 and enlarged her sanctuary on the acropolis. On a terrace below he constructed the Great Altar of Zeus, one of the seven wonders of the ancient world, now partially reconstructed in the Berlin Museum. The great frieze, 446 feet long, represents the Battle of the Giants and was completed in 170. He introduced a second Panhellenic festival for Asclepius and Heracles and fostered the cults of Dionysus, whose ritual basket appears on the royal coinage, and Sabazius, Stratonice's family god. The gymnasium became a famous educational institution; the library attracted scholars such as *Crates of Mallos and his pupil *Panaetius, both of whom influenced Roman culture. These institutions had close links to the Athenian Academy, which Eumenes I had supported under *Arcesilaus. Eumenes' geopolitical usefulness to Rome ended with Rome's defeat of *Perseus at Pydna in 168. In 166 he crushed a Galatian revolt; when Rome unsuccessfully ordered him to grant them freedom, he became a symbol of resistance. In 164 the Romans retaliated by publicly collecting accusations against him. In his failing years he gave gifts to his new friends in Delphi, Miletus, and Rhodes.

Bibliography: E.V. Hansen, *The Attalids of Pergamon*, 2nd. ed., 1971.

Robert Dyer

EUMENES OF CARDIA (361–317 B.C.)

Eumenes served first *Philip II of Macedonia, perhaps as secretary, then *Alexander the Great as chief secretary, companion, and close adviser. In these capacities, Eumenes kept the *Ephemerides* (*Royal Journals*) until 324 and shared Alexander's secrets.

While en route with Alexander, Eumenes earned two military commands, one of which was in India. However, his skill as a general was not revealed until after Alexander's death. When Alexander died, Eumenes used his influence to support *Perdiccas as legitimate regent. Perdiccas conquered Cappadocia and appointed him satrap. Quickly raising and training a large cavalry he defeated Craterus and Neoptolemus. After Perdiccas' death, he supported *Olympias, Alexander's mother, and was named general of Asia by Polyperchon but was twice defeated by *Antigonus and eventually killed in captivity. Throughout his life, he had remained loyal to the idea of a united empire.

His character emerges from the *Lives* of *Nepos and *Plutarch. Wily and persuasive, a good leader of men, he used his closeness to Alexander to enhance his power after the king's death but was mistrusted as a Greek. While he was alive to defend Alexander's intentions, no successor dared call himself king. The *Ephemerides* were used by *Ptolemy I and must have been available in the Library of Alexandria, for Strattis wrote an elaborate commentary and *Arrian used them for his *History*.

Bibliography: N.G.L. Hammond, *The Macedonian State*, 1989.

Robert Dyer

EUPHORION (c. 275–200 B.C.)

Euphorion was a Greek lyric poet.

Born at Chalcis on Euboea, Euphorion studied philosophy at Athens. Around 220 *Antiochus III appointed him chief librarian in Antioch. He wrote several works on grammar and history in addition to epigrams and epics; his work only survives in fragments today. These fragments reveal that he wrote in a very difficult language on often obscure mythological themes and frequently plagiarized his predecessors, especially *Callimachus and *Apollonius of Rhodes. Nevertheless, Euphorion influenced later Greek poets such as *Nicander and *Parthenius. The Roman poets *Catullus, *Gallus, and *Virgil admired and imitated him.

Bibliography: B.A. van Groningen, *Euphorion*, 1977.

Andrew G. Traver

EUPHRONIUS (or Euphronios, active c. 520–490 B.C.)

Euphronius was a potter and red-figure painter in late sixth- and early fifth-century Athens.

Euphronius was one of the so-called Pioneer Group who revolutionized the depiction of the human figure on Athenian pots. Although a marble relief from the Athenian Acropolis might have been dedicated by him, nothing of his life is known beyond what is supplied by the pots themselves. His signature (as painter early in his career and later as potter) appears more than fifteen times, and hence scholars have associated him with more than sixty surviving vessels, ranging from large mixing bowls and cups intended for symposia to small perfume jars. His work is marked by great originality, a manifest delight in the detailed depiction of human anatomy, and the irrepressible urge to render the body in complex poses, and back views. Employing to full advantage the combination of heavy relief lines and fine dilute washes of the recently invented red-figure technique, he not only depicted bones, muscles, and sinews from multiple angles but also included such minute features as fingernails and eyelashes. Clothing, too, is painstakingly rendered, and his best work has no equal.

Bibliography: L. Giuliani et al., eds., *Euphronios: Pittore ad Atene nel VI secolo a. C.*, 1991; M. Robertson, *A History of Greek Art*, 2 vols., 1975.

Kenneth D.S. Lapatin

EURIC (r. 467–484)

Euric was king of the Goths of Gaul (anachronistically called "Visigoths") who took control of much of the province as Roman power collapsed in the West.

After the western imperial government settled the remnants of the Goths of *Alaric in southwestern Gaul around Toulouse, the kingdom was ruled by Theoderic I (418–451), who died supporting *Aetius against *Attila's attack on Gaul; then by his sons Thorismund (451–453), Theoderic II (453–467), and Euric. The latter two both murdered their predecessor. Euric sought to extend control over Roman Gaul and Spain, perhaps exploiting civil conflict in the western empire between *Ricimer and the emperor Anthemius. The emperor Nepos ceded the southern Gallic region of the Auvergne to Euric (475/476), to the distress of provincials such as *Sidonius Apollinaris. By capturing the provincial capital of Arles, Euric assumed control of Roman administration in the Gallic provinces. With the collapse of the western empire, Euric was the strongest power in the West, a position inherited by his son Alaric II. In 507, however, Alaric II was defeated and killed in battle in Vouillé by the Frankish king Clovis, whereupon the Gothic kingdom contracted to Spain.

Euric is recalled for his expansionism, exacerbating the collapse of Roman power in the West, and for his portrait by Sidonius as an aggressive Arian persecutor of Catholics. That rhetorical portrait, however, should be balanced by Sidonius' letters to cultured Roman provincials serving Euric's court and pursuing literary interests.

Bibliography: A. Gillett, "The Accession of Euric," *Francia* 26.1 (1999): 1–40.

Andrew Gillett

EURIPIDES OF ATHENS (c. 484–406 b.c.)

Euripides was the youngest of the three great Athenian tragedians who, according to *Aristotle, was "the most emotionally moving of the poets."

Euripides was born on the island of Salamis of Athenian parents. His father was a merchant, and his mother was of a noble family. He participated from his childhood on in the rituals of Athens. He carried a torch in religious festivals and poured wine for dancers. He won prizes as an athlete; turned his hand to painting; and collected books, eventually possessing a large library. He may have been a pupil of *Anaxagoras and a close friend of *Protagoras. Because of his appearance in several of *Aristophanes' satires, we know more about Euripides than other poets. Aristophanes characterizes him as a recluse, a bookworm, somewhat eccentric, and famous for disguising his heroes in the attire of those of lesser stature.

In 455, Euripides was permitted to compete for the tragic prize at the Great Dionysia. He won first prize in 441, but that play has not survived. While Euripides wrote between eighty and ninety plays, only nineteen of them survive. The ones for which we have more or less certain dates are *Alcestis* (438); *Medea* (431); *Hippolytus* (428); *Andromache* (c. 426); *Hecuba* (c. 424); *Heracles* (c. 421); the *Trojan Women* (415); *Iphigenia at Taurus* (c. 414); *Ion* (c. 413); *Electra* (c. 413); *Helen* (412); the *Phoenician Women* (412–408); *Orestes* (408); the *Bacchae* (405); *Iphigenia at Aulis* (405). The others are the *Heracleidae*; the *Suppliant Women*; *Cyclops* (a satyr play); and *Rhesus* (which some critics believe to be spurious).

Euripides' plays tended to be provocative in their subject matter, shocking his contemporaries, which might explain why he won first prize only a few times. In many of his plays, he sought to reveal to the audience just how much of an illusion their religion was in their day-to-day lives. In addition, Athenian conservatives regarded him as a troublemaker because, while he believed in democracy, he questioned political practices. Unlike *Aeschylus and *Sophocles, Euripides focused on people who were not the usual subject matter of tragedies, that is, women and slaves. Fascinated not only by "socially insignificant" people but also by stories of violence (Medea), unusual passion (Phaedra in *Hippolytus*), and madness (Heracles), Euripides created his own voice, moving away from what Aeschylus and Sophocles had done. He presented people the way they are, with all their vices; his insight into the psyche of his characters resulted in his ability to move the audience emotionally. In addition, by recasting traditional myths and challenging the depictions of the renowned heroes of antiquity, Euripides was able to criticize society, questioning the policies and injustices of Athens in his own day.

As Athens declined, Euripides became more and more pessimistic. In the play *Orestes*, he condemned the abuse of political power, which resulted in his exile from Athens; he went to Macedonia at the invitation of King Archelaus in 408, where he remained an honored member of the Macedonian court until his death in 406. Then, the Athenians, who wished to honor Euripides in Athens, requested his body, but King Archelaus refused to return it. As a result, the Athenians erected a cenotaph to Euripides' memory on the road between Athens and Piraeus, the chief port of the city.

Bibliography: S. Melchinger, *Euripides*, 1973; R. Seaford, ed., *Euripides: Bacchae*, 1996.

Jana K. Schulman

EUSEBIUS, PAMPHILIUS (c. 260–339)

Eusebius was a biblical scholar who wrote important sources, in Greek, on *Constantine, and propagated two new genres of historical writing: the chronicle and the ecclesiastical history.

Eusebius, born in Caesarea in Palestine, was from c. 280 a follower of Pamphilius (d. 310), a priest dedicated to preserving and studying the works of *Origen. Eusebius appears to have been adopted by Pamphilius. Many of Eusebius' writings concern historical and allegorical interpretation of the Bible. Besides two biblical commentaries, he produced the first biblical gazetteer, and the first division of the gospels into numbered sections for scholarly reference, as part of a concordance. His textual scholarship resulted in a commission from Constantine to provide fifty copies of the Bible for use in the new capital, Constantinople. Christianity was tolerated in the Roman Empire during Eusebius' youth, but under the persecutions of the time of *Diocletian, Pamphilius was imprisoned and martyred. Eusebius, briefly imprisoned, continued his work and became bishop of Caesarea in 313. He recorded contemporary martyrdoms in *Martyrs of Palestine*, and wrote several antipagan apologetics, including the *Preparation for the Gospel* and *Proof of the Gospel* against *Porphyry. A proponent of the views of *Arius, Eusebius escaped excommunication at the

Council of Nicaea (325) but nonetheless later wrote a tract attacking an opponent of Arius. Two other works established essentially new genres with long lives in Christian historiography. The *Chronicle* comprised two parts: a mostly lost historiographic introduction (the *Chronology)* and the *Canones* ("tables"), which set out in parallel columns datable events for the history of the ancient Near Eastern and Mediterranean kingdoms, concluding with the Roman Empire.

The *Ecclesiastical History* is an institutional history of the Church from apostolic times to the 290s in the first edition, 324/325 in the last. Both were published originally in the 290s and revised several times before their final publication in 324/325 to coincide with celebrations for Contantine's twentieth anniversary of rule. Eusebius delivered an extant *Panegyric to Constantine* in 336 and left a *Life of Constantine* unfinished at his death.

Contrary to the self-portrait in this last work, Eusebius was not an adviser or official historian to Constantine, though he preserves Constantinian propaganda. Greek continuations of the *Ecclesiastical History* appeared from the fourth to sixth centuries. Rufinus translated it into Latin in the 390s, whereby it was known to the medieval West, and three fifth-century Greek continuators were also translated into Latin at the request of Cassiodorus, but no other Latin church history appeared until Bede. Eusebius remained the main source for the early Church until the twentieth century. His use of copious direct quotations from official documents and other sources, unprecedented in classical historiography, is the origin of modern scholarly conventions of the use and acknowledgment of sources. The *Chronicle* was translated into Latin and continued to 376 by *Jerome, leading in turn to many further continuations, in more simplified formats, establishing the chronicle as the main medieval genre of history writing.

Bibliography: T.D. Barnes, *Constantine and Eusebius*, 1981.

Andrew Gillett

EUTYCHES OF CONSTANTINOPLE (c. 378–454)

Eutyches was the head of an important monastery in fifth-century Constantinople and was heavily involved in the Christological arguments that occurred in the aftermath of the controversial Council of Ephesus in 431.

Eutyches, as a younger theologian, had been one of the main opponents of the newly appointed archbishop of Constantinople, *Nestorius. By 449, Eutyches was one of the few leading figures left alive from the turbulent doctrinal period in which *Cyril of Alexandria's Christological theology had triumphed over that of the Syrians. He enjoyed an immense prestige as a defender of orthodox Christology. The current archbishop of Constantinople, Flavian, showed a tendency that was to be increasingly marked after the death of the emperor *Theodosius II (408–450), to give a greater role to the doctrine of the "two natures" of *Jesus Christ than had hitherto been allowed. Rome stood allied with Alexandria throughout the Christological controversy until the pontificate of *Leo I (440–461). By Leo's reign, the Romans had taken time to study all the texts, and they had realized that much of their own tradition was closer to that of the Syrians than it was to the Egyptians.

Eutyches deeply opposed the current policies of doctrinal reconciliation, which he saw merely as an attempt to soften and displace the Cyrilline doctrines, and so he allied himself with the cause of Dioscorus, Cyril's hard-line successor in Egypt. When Flavian disciplined the aging abbot, Eutyches appealed to Egypt for support and won the backing of the Church of Alexandria, along with much support from the aristocracy in the capital.

His ecclesiastical trial devolved into a major ecumenical synod (Council of Ephesus 449), which, to the great anger of the Syrian and Roman churches, vindicated him and condemned Flavian instead. The conduct of the synod was very tumultuous. It rejected the evidence of the Roman delegates, and their bitter protests led to the summoning of a further council held in Chalcedon, a suburb of Constantinople, in 451 (shortly after the death of Theodosius II). This was to be one of the most momentous international synods of the early Church, which in many ways established a "classical" theology of the person of Christ. The Council of Chalcedon deposed and condemned both Dioscorus and Eutyches, and the theology they stood for, but the victory brought in its aftermath the secession of the churches of Egypt (and Ethiopia), and the marks of the divisions remain to this day in the Eastern Church. Eutyches is perhaps more important as a catalyst of great international events in this period than as a theologian in his own right. He represented the early "One Nature" theology of Cyril of Alexandria, as did Dioscorus, but taken to an unacceptable pitch that Cyril had warned against in his lifetime.

Eutyches' misfortune was, eventually, to win no friends at all, for he finally tried to emphasize the transcendent deity of Jesus by teaching that his humanity was not consubstantial with that of ordinary human beings. This idea shocked the rest of the pro-Cyril movement in the Egyptian churches and led them to abandon him as a heretic just as decisively as did the West.

Bibliography: W.H.C. Frend, *The Rise of the Monophysite Movement*, 1972; J.A. McGuckin, *St. Cyril of Alexandria and the Christological Controversy*, 1994.

John A. McGuckin

F

FABIUS MAXIMUS VERRUCOSUS, CUNCTATOR, QUINTUS (?-203 B.C.)

A conservative patrician of the old order, Fabius' leadership and advice guided Rome through the nadir of the republic's fortunes during the Second Punic War (219–201) and earned him the title Shield of Rome.

Before the war with Carthage, Fabius had already served twice as consul and once as both dictator and censor. He also took part in the fruitless negotiations with Carthage on the eve of hostilities. After the defeats at the Battles of the Trebbia (218) and Lake Trasimene (217), Fabius was elected dictator a second time, and he immediately instituted a strategy based upon the avoidance of pitched battles and the destruction of the countryside to hamstring Carthaginian logistics. When *Hannibal marched past Rome and moved into the southern areas of Campania and Apulia, Fabius shadowed the Carthaginian army with his own. Hannibal was looking for foodstuffs, port facilities, and allies among the non-Latins of the area. Fabius responded by laying waste to the land in an effort to deny it to the enemy. His exertions earned Fabius the derogatory nickname *Cunctator* (the Delayer) and the ill will of the soldiers and citizens of Rome. At the end of his dictatorship he was not reelected, and his successors rushed blindly into oblivion at Cannae in 216. With the wisdom of his policy now made manifest, he went on to serve as consul three more times and *Cunctator* became a badge of honor. Fabius' strategy wore down the Carthaginians and allowed his colleague *Marcus Claudius Marcellus to fight a series of actions around the city of Nola (216–214). In 209, Fabius retook the city of Tarentum, which had gone over to Hannibal in 213. Fabius' later career featured his return to the Senate, where he became the leader of the resistance to *Publius Cornelius Scipio (later "Africanus") plan to invade Africa (205). Fabius' adamant stance against such a venture most probably stemmed from the natural caution of old age. Yet jealousy might also figure in the assessment. In 215,

Fabius manipulated the augurs to block the election of Marcellus to the consulship, which then went to Fabius. This was done as Hannibal marched unhindered through Italy.

While Fabius could not produce the victories of Scipio that laid Carthage low, his strategy bought the time needed to reorganize the Roman military and keep the Carthaginians at bay. His patrician bearing and keen adherence to Roman traditions also went far in sustaining Roman morale in her hour of crisis.

Bibliography: J.F. Lazenby, *Hannibal's War*, 1978.

Cyril M. Lagvanec

FABIUS PICTOR, QUINTUS (c. 210 B.C.)

Fabius Pictor was the first Roman historian.

He was a senator and went with an embassy to Delphi in 216; little else is known about him. He was a member of the patrician Fabius family (descended from a painter of frescoes—hence the cognomen Pictor) noted for its commitment to the common good. He was the first Roman to write a history of the city and was frequently cited by subsequent historians. His history is now lost except for a few quotations by other authors. Remarkably, he wrote in Greek, significant from a literary standpoint because it suggests that he consciously applied the traditions of Greek historiography to Rome; from a political standpoint, he might be seen as defending Roman policy to the Greek-speaking world in order to counter Greek historical writing sympathetic to Carthage during the Second Punic War.

Like many other early historians of Rome, he seems to have devoted great emphasis to the origins of the city and its institutions, then moved quickly to more recent events, paying scant attention to the in-between. He erroneously attributed responsibility for the Second Punic War, arguing that *Hannibal's attack on Rome was not sanctioned by the Carthaginian government but was a renegade act made in collusion with Hamilcar, a brother-in-law and the commander of Carthaginian forces in Spain. The error, based on his eyewitness observation of Senate debates in Rome, offers insight into contemporary political concerns and public sentiments surrounding the war, if not its true cause. His account of the First and Second Punic Wars provided the basis for *Polybius' history. He is quoted by *Livy, especially in the first ten books, but it is not certain whether Livy knew his account firsthand.

Bibliography: C.S. Kraus and A.J. Woodman, *Latin Historians*, 1997.

Ron Harris

FAVORINUS (c. 80–150)

Favorinus was a Latin philosopher, orator, and writer.

*Philostratus writes in his *Lives* that Favorinus boasted of his anomalous identity: "a Gaul who spoke Greek, a eunuch who was prosecuted for adultery, a man who had quarreled with the emperor and was still alive." Favorinus was born without testicles in Arles to an aristocratic family. He was a prodigy in Greek and rhetoric, left Gaul to study philosophy with *Dio Chrysostom, and then traveled throughout Greece and Asia as a public lecturer. Eventually, he settled in Rome and was a part of the Second Sophistic. As a member of the aristocracy, Favorinus was elected High Priest in Arles in absentia. He attempted to extricate himself from this position by appealing to an unsympathetic Emperor *Hadrian. At some point, a quarrel with the emperor resulted in his exile to Chios. The sources are vague, and it could have been this quarrel, or his prosecution for adultery, that led to the exile.

As a Sophist, he was well known during his lifetime. Most of his writings and orations are not extant, but his adept verbal sparrings appear in the writings of his declaimers and admirers alike. The two pieces that he is best known for are the *Corinthian Oration* and *On Exile*.

Bibliography: M.W. Gleason, *Making Men*, 1995.

Jennifer L. Koosed

FELICITY
See **Perpetua, Vibia, and Felicity, Saints**.

FLAMINIUS, GAIUS (?–217 B.C.)
G. Flaminius was a new man whose populist practices challenged the old senatorial order and presaged later conflicts between the *populares* and the *optimates*.

As a tribune in 232, Flaminius came to prominence in republican politics by agitating for the distribution of the *ager gallicus*, the Adriatic coastal district south of the Po River taken from the Senones Gauls. Flaminius wanted the land to be given to the veterans of the First Punic War (264–241) against the wishes of lease-holding senators. Flaminius overcame the opposition by carrying the proposal through the plebeian council and circumventing the Senate. This unprecedented move demonstrated that policy could be made outside the Senate, and others followed in Flaminius' way. Whether he undermined the republic or struck a blow for the underclass, Flaminius' land allotment probably triggered the last great Celtic invasion, which was defeated at the Battle of Telamon (225).

Elected consul in 223, Flaminius led an army north across the Po River in direct contradiction of a senatorial command to return to Rome. Flaminius' insubordination contributed to the conquest of the Insubres Gauls, and he celebrated a triumph at the people's wish and again over the objections of the Senate. As censor (220) he built the Via Flaminia and the Circus Flaminius. In 217, Flaminius was reelected consul in response to the defeat at the Trebbia the year before, which was laid at the feet of the Senate. As *Hannibal threatened Rome and ravaged Etruria, Flaminius moved to stop the Carthaginians. Outmaneuvered by Hannibal, Flaminius led his army into a trap at Lake Trasimene, where almost all of it was either killed or captured by the Carthaginians. Flaminius fell in the battle, with one tradition attributing his death to an Insubres cavalryman.

Although hostile historical tradition often paints Flaminius as an opportunistic demagogue and a general of no real merit, such depictions do not do justice to the man. Despite whatever political opposition he aroused, Flaminius still worked within the republic's constitution. As to the judgments concerning his military skill, Flaminius' campaign against the Insubres represented no mean feat, and the destruction of his army and his own death came at the hands of the greatest general of the age.

Bibliography: M. Grant, *History of Rome*, 2nd ed., 1978.

Cyril M. Lagvanec

FLAMINIUS, TITUS QUINCTIUS (?–174 B.C.)

T.Q. Flaminius was a powerful and influential Roman whose military acumen brought *Philip V to heel and whose diplomatic efforts marked the height of Rome's philhellenic policies.

Flaminius began his career as a military tribune under *Marcus Claudius Marcellus during the Second Punic War (219–201). Assigned to garrison duty at Tarentum in 205, it was here that Flaminius learned to read and write Greek. Whether this experience sparked his philhellenism or merely fueled his admiration for Greek philosophy, literature, and art is unclear. However, Flaminius went on to challenge even *Scipio Africanus in his pro-Greek sentiments and actions. Flaminius' record of service, deep interest in the Greek world, and a good bit of personal ambition earned him the consulship in 198. His task was to bring to a victorious conclusion the Second Macedonian War (201–197). Flaminius bested Philip V in a series of smaller actions that eventually culminated in the Battle of Cynocephalae in 197. There the legions carried the day and dashed Philip's dream of Macedonian hegemony in Greece. Flaminius thought well of the Antigonid king and succeeded in keeping Philip on the Macedonian throne as an ally to Rome and a bulwark against northern barbarian hordes. In the following year, at the Isthmian Games at Corinth, Flaminius proclaimed the freedom of Greece. He kept to his promise with the evacuation of the Roman army by 194 and by trying to block *Antiochus III's diplomatic designs on the area. In 193–192, Flaminius suppressed the revolutionary machinations of Nabis, king of Sparta. After the defeat of Antiochus III at Thermopylae in 191, Flaminius promulgated a truce in Greece that returned the area to a relative calm. After his time in Greece, Flaminius returned to further service in Rome. He died in 174.

As a member of the senatorial class, Flaminius was able to serve two masters at the same time. He diligently advanced Roman influence in the east while scrupulously catering to Greek sensibilities. The great irony for Flaminius lay in the fact that by thwarting Antigonid and Seleucid designs on Greece, he prepared the war for eventual Roman domination of the region.

Bibliography: F.W. Walbank, *Philip V of Macedon*, 1940.

Cyril M. Lagvanec

FLAVIUS, CNAEUS (fl. fourth century B.C.)

Cnaeus Flavius is credited with publishing the first manual containing the procedural rules governing civil actions in Roman law.

Few concrete details exist concerning Flavius' life. He was probably the son of a freedman and served as secretary to *Appius Claudius Caecus, who was censor in 312. Flavius himself was elected tribune, made a senator by Appius Claudius, and elected curule aedile in 304.

According to tradition, while curule aedile Flavius published the previously secret formulae needed to pursue civil actions; this became known as the *Ius civile Flavianum*. Flavius also made public a calendar of the *dies fasti*, days of which when legal business could be pursued. Because it was now possible for plebeians to pursue legal actions without the patronage of a patrician, Flavius' acts were considered important steps in removing the Roman judicial system from the exclusive control of the pontifical priesthood and the patricians. The publication of the *Ius civile Flavianum* and the calendar occurred not long before the promulgation of the *Lex Ogulnia* (300), which opened the pontifical priesthood to plebeians and thus further expanded their participation in the Roman legal system.

Bibliography: H.F. Jolowicz and B. Nicholas, *Historical Introduction to the Study of Roman Law*, 3rd ed., 1972.

Karen Wagner

FLORUS (fl. 115)

Florus wrote a summary history of Rome, highlighting events from its foundation to the zenith of *Augustus. This work is now conventionally entitled *Epitome*.

Nothing certain is known of Florus' life. Since *Trajan receives praise in the preface, whereas all other emperors, Augustus excepted, are criticized and their names suppressed, it is likely that Florus wrote during Trajan's reign. He is possibly the same Florus who exchanged jesting poems with the Emperor *Hadrian and still another Florus who composed a dialogue, *Virgil: Rhetorician or Poet?*, whose opening pages alone survive.

The summary form of history was destined to become a popular genre in late antiquity, when authors freely borrowed from Florus' *Epitome*. The medieval world admired the concision of the work; Renaissance critics such as Petrarch praised the rhetorical coloring of Florus' style. Both traits have combined to endear his work less to modern historians. However, one instance of his rhetoric was destined to make a lasting impression: Florus elaborated a comparison between a nation's history and the Ages of Man. Just as a person moves in stages from infancy to old age, so Rome was subject to a similar periodization.

Bibliography: J.M. Alonso-Núñez, *The Ages of Rome*, 1982.

John Quinn

FRONTINUS, SEXTUS JULIUS (c. 30–104)

Frontinus held high posts in the imperial administration and composed technical treatises.

Frontinus achieved the consulship c.74 and thereafter served a term as governor of Britain, during which he successfully conducted a war against the Silures. His exemplary supervision of Rome's water supply system helped earn him consulships again in 98 and 100.

A practical man of affairs, Frontinus wrote on the practical subjects with which he was familiar. Treatises on surveying sprang from his oversight of public works projects; now lost, they influenced later Roman books on the subject. Still surviving is his *Aqueducts of the City of Rome*, which details the history, route, and capacity of each of the city's water lines. Reflecting a self-definition of the Romans as master engineers, he boasted that the aqueducts supplying Rome were more impressive than the pyramids of Egypt or works of Greek art.

The four volumes of *Stratagems* remain Frontinus' most important work. Intended as a supplement to a (lost) book of military science, it is a compendium of examples arranged to illustrate specific courses of action, such as how to arrange an ambush. Almost all of the examples are drawn from the distant Roman and Greek past. Frontinus clearly belonged to the realist school; the only military trickery that he condemns on moral grounds is the hiring of a traitor to assassinate an enemy general.

Bibliography: E. Wheeler, *Stratagem and the Vocabulary of Military Trickery*, 1988.

John Quinn

FRONTO, MARCUS CORNELIUS (c. 95–c. 167)

Marcus Cornelius Fronto was the most honored orator of the second century and a teacher of the future emperors *Marcus Aurelius and Lucius Verus.

Fronto was born at Cirta in Roman Africa but moved to Rome for rhetorical studies. He possessed great wealth and, in fact, was proud that he owned the ancient mansion of *Maecenas on the Esquiline Hill. Fronto entered the Senate shortly after 120 and soon was the leading lawyer in Rome. He believed that public speakers should search out archaic words with which to lend elegance to their speeches, and this opinion won the day, as the archaizing tendencies of younger contemporaries such as *Apuleius illustrate. Shortly after becoming emperor in 138, *Antoninus Pius made Fronto a tutor to the two young men he was grooming for the throne. He was awarded the consulship in 143 and lived well into the joint reign of his charges.

Only a few fragments of Fronto's orations survive. More significant is a collection of his correspondence. These letters reveal details of life in the imperial circle, as letters of recommendation jostle with notes on rhetoric, solicitations for good health, and reports on daily routine.

Bibliography: E. Champlin, *Fronto and Antonine Rome*, 1980.

John Quinn

G

GAIUS (c. 115–180)

Gaius was an influential Roman jurist, teacher, and author of the *Institutes*, which became the standard textbook for students of Roman law.

It is ironic that the Roman jurist whose work is best known to modern scholars has left few traces of his own life. Gaius was probably born early in the second century A.D. in an eastern province of the empire. He seems never to have held public office, and it is not even clear whether he lived in Rome.

Gaius' chief contribution to Roman legal studies was the *Institutes*, a textbook on the elements of Roman private law completed around 161. The discovery in Verona in 1816 of a nearly complete manuscript from the fifth century makes this the only classical legal work that survives in substantially its original form. The *Institutes* is arranged in four books: one on the law of persons, two on the law of things, and one on legal actions. Gaius' interest in legal history sets this work apart from other classical legal scholarship. Gaius also published commentaries on Rome's first codified law, the Twelve Tables, the *Lex Papia Poppaea* of *Augustus, and both the Provincial and Urban Edicts.

Gaius' influence on Roman jurisprudence was not immediate, but over time the *Institutes* in particular came to achieve an esteemed place in legal studies. In his *Law of Citations* (426) Emperor Valentinian named Gaius one of the five jurists whose opinion was to be followed by imperial judicial officers when they heard cases. An abridgment of the *Institutes* in two books was preserved in the *Lex Romana Visigothorum* of Alaric II, promulgated in 506. Most notably, the plan and arrangement of Justinian's *Institutes*, as well as much of its content, were copied from the *Institutes* of Gaius.

Bibliography: A.M. Honoré, *Gaius*, 1962.

Karen Wagner

GAIUS, THE EMPEROR
See **Caligula**.

GALEN OF PERGAMUM (c. 130–200)

Author of the *Ars Medica*, surgeon, and man of letters, Galen's medical philosophy served for generations of physicians as the foundation of knowledge that would remain unchallenged until the seventeenth century.

Galen's birthplace, Pergamum, had been important since the third century B.C. due to its proximity to a famous medical temple, Asclepion; its importance was validated by Galen, who, despite his scientific training, believed in its healing cures. Galen came from an educated family and received a good liberal arts foundation before beginning his anatomical studies under Satyros; he eventually relocated to Alexandria, where he added medicine to his inquiries.

By 158, he had been studying medicine for twelve years; on his return to Pergamum, he was appointed physician to the gladiators, a post that provided invaluable observational opportunities. After a sojourn in Rome ended badly due to controversy over his medical theories, he returned to Pergamum, where he was enlisted in the fight against the plague that had struck the city, surviving a bout with the malady himself.

Galen then took up an assignment as surgeon to the legions fighting in the Germanic wars in Aquileia; his service there brought him to the notice of the emperor *Marcus Aurelius, who named him as physician to his son and heir, *Commodus, in 171. When Commodus became emperor himself in 180, Galen was made court physician, but his duties were such that he was able to devote a significant amount of time to study and writing; unfortunately, much of his work during this period was lost during a fire.

The brutality of Commodus and his threats against scholars led Galen to return to Pergamum in 192. He devoted his remaining years to meditation and writing before dying at the age of seventy around the year 200. His general ideas about medicine were set forth in his great work *Ars Medica* in which he brought together the strands of thought of other physicians upon whose works he had built, adding his own original research and observations. Galen never identified himself as being of a particular "school" of medical thought, and his wide-ranging interests were evident in his books on animal dissection, physiology, pathology, and pharmacopia. His long experience as a physician to gladiators and soldiers was captured in his work *De methodo medendi*, which remained the standard reference work for the treatment of wounds for generations. Galen also placed great emphasis on the importance of diet, hygiene, and exercise in the maintenance of health. His pragmatic approach to medicine thus served as a spiritual beacon for the doctors who followed him.

Bibliography: G. Sarton, *Galen of Pergamon*, 1954.

Connie Evans

GALLUS, GAIUS CORNELIUS (70–27/26 B.C.)

Gallus was an innovator among the Latin poets of the first century B.C.

Born in Cisalpine, Gaul (the Po valley in modern Italy), and educated there by the Greek poet *Parthenius of Nicaea, perhaps along with *Virgil, Gallus was a leader among the fashionable newer Latin poets who imitated Hellenistic Greek poetry. His love elegies to Vipsania Cytheris (his Lycoris), mistress of *Marc Antony and *Brutus, established the conventions of that genre. Virgil treats him as a friend in *Eclogues* 6 and 10 and probably cites lines from his poetry, otherwise known to us chiefly from a papyrus fragment first published in 1979. He was active in administration, first in the commission distributing land to *Caesar's veterans, later as aide-de-camp to Octavian (later *Augustus) in Egypt, where he negotiated with *Cleopatra before her suicide. He also served as prefect of the new imperial province of Egypt, suppressing a revolt there and leaving boastful inscriptions (still extant) on the pyramids and elsewhere. Rebuked by the emperor and indicted by the Senate, he committed suicide in 27/26. According to *Servius Honoratus, Virgil was then forced to remove his "praises of Gallus" from the end of the *Georgics*, where he may linger as the singer Orpheus, in the new allegorical style appropriate to imperial censorship.

Bibliography: D.D. Ross, *Backgrounds to Augustan Poetry*, 1975.

Robert Dyer

GELASIUS I, POPE (?–496)

Gelasius I was a fifth-century pope and creator of the theory of the two swords.

Gelasius was born in Rome of African descent and served as archdeacon and secretary to Pope Felix II. He became pope himself from 492 to 496 and was an effective administrator, using his own money to help the poor. He also relaxed the criteria for ordination in order to increase the number of clergy, who were in short supply.

Gelasius is most famous for his articulation of the theory of the two powers (swords) that govern the world, the "consecrated authority of bishops" and the "royal power." The first is wielded by the pope, the second by the emperor; though both powers come from God, the spiritual authority, in Gelasius' eyes, is more important because it has to provide for the salvation of the temporal. This formulation, used for centuries, was included in a letter to Emperor Anastasius I during the Acacian schism (484–519), in which he defended orthodoxy against the Byzantine emperor. The dispute started during the reign of Pope Felix II (483–492) and arose over attempts in the eastern church to placate the supporters of Monophysite Christology, who opposed the orthodox position that Christ had both a human and a divine nature as set out at the Council of Chalcedon (451). Pope Felix wrote to Emperor *Zeno to protest the elevation of a Monophysite as bishop of Alexandria and to demand a restoration of the terms of Chalcedon. His complaints not only had no effect, but Acacius, the patriarch of Constantinople, went so far as to include the names of several Monophysites in the diptychs (a list of those living and dead to be included in public prayers).

Incensed at this affront to his authority, Felix excommunicated Acacius, thus starting the Acacian schism. The schism continued into the reign of Gelasius, who refused to reconcile with the East until the offending names had been removed from the diptychs, which did not happen in his lifetime.

Bibliography: J. Taylor, "The Early Papacy at Work: Gelasius I (492–496)," *Journal of Religious History* 8.4 (1975): 317–332.

Kimberly Rivers

GELLIUS, AULUS (c. 128–180?)

Gellius was a Roman miscellanist and author of the *Noctes Atticae* (Attic Nights).

It is only from his writing that any details of his life can be drawn. He lived mostly at Rome, studying with the scholar Sulpicius Apollinaris, who also taught the emperor Pertinax (193). He was influenced by both the orator *M. Cornelius Fronto, and the rhetor *Favorinus. Gellius spent at least one year in Greece as both student and tourist, using this time to finish his education under Calvenus Taurus, having some contact also with the sophist and patron of learning *Herodes Atticus in Cephisia.

The *Noctes Atticae* are called such because, according to Gellius, he devised the plan of transforming his study notes into a more literary form during the long Attic winter nights. They consist of twenty books in a short-chapter format, and fortunately only part of the preface, the end of the last book, and all of book 8, bar the chapter headings, are missing. He covered subjects ranging from philosophy, law, and history through grammar to textual and literary criticism, showing a greater knowledge of things Latin than Greek. Although his thought is logical rather than penetrating, and although his style shows no consistency, varying from archaic to classical to the new, modern scholarship is yet indebted to him for many thousands of passages from works and authors no longer existing today.

Read by, among many others, the historian *Ammianus Marcellinus, and the writer *Ambrosius Theodosius Macrobius, quoted often in the Middle Ages, Gellius flowered again in the Renaissance, serving as a model for the humanist writers.

Bibliography: L. Holford-Strevens, *Aulus Gellius*, 1988.

Deborah Eaton

GELON (c. 540–478 b.c.)

Gelon, an ordinary citizen of Gela, became the tyrant of that city and Syracuse through carefully planned and executed military operations.

Gelon's rise to the position of tyrant began when he was appointed Calvary-commander under the tyrant Hippocrates. As a cavalry leader, Gelon showed a acute ability to direct troops and execute battle plans during field operations, proving himself several times in battle against Sicily and various Greek cities. After Hippocrates' death in a Sicilian battle, Gelon assumed supreme power by stripping Hippocrates' sons of their inheritance and using military threat to seize control of Gela. Shortly after his self-appointed rule over Gela, the noblemen of Syracuse appealed to him for aid during a slave revolt. The slaves had been successful in exiling their masters from the area. The aristocrats desperately needed assistance to win back their estates and once again gain governmental control. Gelon, recognizing the possibility of putting Syracuse under his rule, readily offered his assistance to the noblemen. As soon as Gelon proved victorious over the slaves, he once again used his army to muscle his way into power. Syracuse gave little resistance.

Gelon's reputation as a shrewd military mastermind quickly spread throughout the region. The Greeks, aware of Gelon's military prowess, appealed for his assistance in fighting against an invasion from the Persian *Xerxes. Gelon agreed to help the Greeks for the price of being supreme commander, but the Greeks refused to accept him on such terms. At the same time that the Greeks were defending themselves against Xerxes, Gelon took his forces into battle against Carthage. Despite the fact that the Carthaginian fielded an army of 300,000 men, Gelon proved to be the conqueror by means of military stratagems. Two years after defeating the Carthaginian forces, this popular ruler died and left his brother, *Hieron I, with full control over Gela and Syracuse.

Bibliography: A.G. Woodhead, *The Greeks in the West*, 1962.

Richard Draper

GERMANICUS JULIUS CAESAR (15 B.C.–A.D. 19)

Germanicus was the nephew and adopted son of Emperor *Tiberius.

Germanicus was the son of Nero Claudius Drusus, *Augustus' stepson, and Antonina, Augustus' niece. In A.D. 4, Augustus had Tiberius adopt Germanicus, although Tiberius already had a son of his own. Around the same time, Germanicus married Augustus' granddaughter, *Agrippina the Elder. A quaestor at age twenty-one, Germanicus served Tiberius in Pannonia (7–9) and along the Rhine (11). Elected consul in 12, in the following year he was given command of the Gallic and German provinces. Following the death of Augustus in 14, his legions mutinied because they wanted him emperor. His personal popularity enabled him to quell the mutiny and demonstrate his loyalty to Tiberius.

In a series of three campaigns lasting between 14 and 16, Germanicus crossed the Rhine and inflicted heavy casualties on the Germans. Tiberius, perhaps jealous of these victories, recalled Germanicus to Rome, where he was honored with a triumph (17) and elected consul a second time (18). Germanicus was then entrusted with the eastern frontier bordering Parthia. He left for the East in 18 and rapidly settled a disputed Armenian succession, negotiated with Parthia, and reduced Cappadocia and Commagene to provinces. He annoyed Tiberius in the following year by visiting Egypt—a province forbidden to all Romans of senatorial rank. Germanicus also came into conflict with Gnaeus Calpurnius Piso, whom Tiberius had appointed governor of Syria. After Germanicus demanded that Piso leave the province, he suddenly fell ill. Germanicus soon died, and Agrippina accused Piso of having poisoned him. When prosecuted by the Senate on that charge, Piso committed suicide, thus preventing any substantiation of the crime.

Agrippina and Germanicus had nine children, including the future emperor *Caligula and *Agrippina the Younger, the mother of *Nero. Emperor *Claudius was Germanicus' brother. In addition to his military talent, Germanicus was also an author. He wrote comedies in Greek and epigrams in both Greek and Latin and translated *Aratus of Soli's *Phaenomena* into Latin.

Germanicus was a successful and popular general, and if it were not for his premature death, he probably would have become emperor himself.

Bibliography: H.H. Scullard, *From the Gracchi to Nero: A History of Rome from 133 B.C. to A.D.*, 5th ed., 1982.

Andrew G. Traver

GLAUCIA, GAIUS SERVILIUS (c. late 2nd century B.C.)

Glaucia sponsored a law restoring equestrian control of the juries in the extortion court and died violently in 100 B.C. after the passage of the so-called last decree of the Senate.

Glaucia appears to have lacked illustrious forebearers in recent generations. He was an orator of merit whose performances were characterized by shrewdness and wit. He was quaestor by 109 and in 102 survived an attempt by the censor Q. Caecilius Metellus Numidicus to expel him from the Senate. He held the tribunate in 101 and the praetorship in 100 and in one of those years (more probably 101) successfully proposed an antisenatorial measure restoring to equestrians their former monopoly as jurors in the extortion court and making the prosecution of miscreant magistrates more comprehensive and effective. During these years Glaucia cooperated with the reformist *L. Appuleius Saturninus, securing the exile of mutual opponent Metellus Numidicus. Tensions in the alliance are nevertheless suggested by a public incident in which Glaucia's curule chair was smashed by Saturninus.

Though still praetor, Glaucia stood for the consulship in 99. His candidature was disallowed by the presiding consul *C. Marius, after the murder of a rival consular candidate. In response to growing civil unrest and the occupation of the capital by Glaucia and his associates, the Senate passed the *senatus consultum ultimum*, the so-called ultimate decree authorizing the use of force. After surrendering to Marius, who had given an official promise of safety, Glaucia, though still a praetor in office, was killed along with Saturninus in the Senate house by a lynch mob containing senators and equestrians.

This was the first time that the ultimate decree was used against a tribune of the plebs and magistrates in office. Glaucia usually receives negative treatment in the mostly conservative ancient source tradition.

Bibliography: J.L. Beness, "The Urban Unpopularity of Lucius Appuleius Saturninus," *Antichthon* 25 (1991): 33–62.

Lea Beness

GORGIAS OF LEONTINI (c. 485–380 b.c.)

Gorgias was a Greek sophist and rhetorician.

Gorgias was born in Leontini, Sicily, and went to Athens in 427 on a diplomatic mission. Although he traveled throughout the various Greek cities teaching rhetoric, he eventually settled in Athens. Later writers attributed philosophical doctrines to him, especially the maxim that "there is nothing, if there were we could not understand it, and if we could, we could not communicate it." Gorgias' extant works are *The Economium of Helen* and *The Apology of Palamedes*.

Gorgias is the chief character of *Plato's dialogue of the same name, which deals with true and false rhetoric. His prose influence can be seen in *Antiphon and *Thucydides, and in his pupil *Isocrates.

Gorgias was one of the first sophists and one of the most influential of the Greek rhetoricians.

Bibliography: G.B. Kerferd, "Gorgias on Nature or That Which Is Not," *Phronesis* 1 (1955): 3–25.

Andrew G. Traver

GRACCHUS, TIBERIUS SEMPRONIUS (163/162–133 b.c.)

The tribunate and violent death of Gracchus in 133 serve as a historical milestone, marking the first eruption of large-scale civil strife in Rome and the first major challenge to the authority of the Senate.

He was the son of Ti. Sempronius Gracchus (consul, 177, 163; censor, 169) and *Cornelia, the younger daughter of *P. Cornelius Scipio Africanus. In his mid-teens Gracchus served at Carthage under his cousin *P. Cornelius Scipio Aemilianus, who had married his sister Sempronia, and during that campaign he distinguished himself for being among the first to scale a wall. In 137 he served in Spain as quaestor and, utilizing the respect with which his father was held after earlier military service there, arranged a peace treaty with the Numantines that saved the army of the consul C. Hostilius Mancinus. The Senate refused to ratify this treaty.

As tribune of the plebs in 133, and with the backing of a number of eminent politicians including his father-in-law and *princeps senatus* Ap. Claudius Pulcher, the consul P. Mucius Scaevola, and the latter's brother P. Licinius Crassus Dives Mucianus, both distinguished jurists, Gracchus proposed a land law that was designed to solve a number of Rome's interrelated problems: the displacement and depletion of the peasantry, the consequent difficulties of finding willing and able military recruits, and the dangers posed by increasing numbers of slaves and urban crowding.

Gracchus' law reaffirmed a limit of 500 *iugera* (140 hectares) of arable public land in the possession of one person. Compromise provisions offering recompense to those who would be forced to abandon some of their illegal acquisitions (such as an allowance of 250 additional *iugera* for each child) appear to have been withdrawn in the face of opposition. The law also provided for the institution of an agrarian commission equipped with judicial powers to locate and confiscate surplus public land and distribute it in inalienable small plots to the poor who would pay the state a rent for their use. It is possible that the beneficiaries of Gracchus' law included not only Roman citizens but Italians as well.

In an unusual though not unprecedented move, Gracchus submitted the law to the popular assembly without prior discussion in the Senate. It was vetoed by fellow tribune M. Octavius, taken to the Senate for adjudication, and rejected. Octavius persisted in vetoing the law when it was taken back to the people, an action that went against a tradition of not pushing legal powers to their extremes. In order to end the impasse Gracchus took the unprecedented step of proposing the removal of his colleague Octavius from office. When this was accomplished the agrarian law was passed. Tiberius, his brother *Gaius, and his father-in-law Ap. Claudius Pulcher were elected to the agrarian commission.

When news was brought that Attalus III of Pergamum had died (133) and left his estate to the Roman people, Gracchus proposed to appropriate the bequest, possibly in the form of equipment grants for the holders of new allotments, also announcing that he would bring the question of settling Attalus' kingdom to the people, in so doing ignoring the Senate's traditional prerogative in the areas of finance and foreign affairs.

Gracchus then sought reelection to the tribunate. This controversial action, while probably motivated by Gracchus' desire to avoid prosecution as a private citizen, served to fuel accusations of tyranny from his opponents. In the absence of some of his rural supporters who were occupied with the harvest, Gracchus organized for the voting area on the Capitol to be occupied and physically barred to his opponents. When the consul Scaevola refused to use force against Gracchus and his supporters, the chief priest P. Cornelius Scipio Nasica Serapio, employing the formula that in earlier times had been used to summon citizens to arms when the enemy was at the gate, called upon those who wished for the salvation of the state to follow him. He led a group of senators and their retainers armed with clubs, staves, and broken benches against the Gracchans. The latter, standing in awe of the senators, refrained from physically assaulting them. Gracchus, though still a tribune (and therefore sacrosanct) was killed on the Capitol along with 200 or 300 supporters. The bodies of the victims were thrown into the Tiber by night.

In the following year special courts of doubtful legality were established by the Senate and conducted under consular authority to try surviving Gracchans. A number were found guilty and executed. The land commission, however, continued its work unhindered until 129.

The source tradition on Tiberius Gracchus is pervaded by prejudice and propaganda. The civil strife that erupted during Gracchus' tribunate marks the beginning of the so-called Roman Revolution.

Bibliography: E. Badian, "Tiberius Gracchus and the Beginning of the Roman Revolution," *Aufstieg und Niedergang der römischen Welt* 1 (1972): 668–731; A.H. Bernstein, *Tiberius Sempronius Gracchus. Tradition and Apostasy*, 1978.

Lea Beness

GRACCHUS, GAIUS SEMPRONIUS (154/153–121 B.C.)

Gaius continued his brother's challenge to the authority of the Senate through an extensive program of reform and met a similarly violent death.

He was the son of Tiberius Sempronius Gracchus (cos. 177, 163; cens. 169) and *Cornelia, the younger daughter of *Publius Cornelius Scipio Africanus. He married Licinia, the daughter of P. Licinius Crassus Dives Mucianus (cos. 131), one of the distinguished supporters of his brother's agrarian reform. In 133 Gaius was elected as one of the commissioners to implement *Tiberius' land law but at the time of the latter's violent death in that year was probably serving in Spain at Numantia under his cousin and brother-in-law *P. Cornelius Scipio Aemilianus.

Gracchus was an outstanding orator, and a number of fragments from his speeches survive. In 131 or 130 he publicly supported C. Papirius Carbo's bill concerning repetition of the tribunate, and in the mid-120s he opposed the proposal of M. Iunius Pennus to expel noncitizens from Rome. He served for two years as quaestor under L. Aurelius Orestes in Sardinia and upon his return to stand for the tribunate in 124 successfully defended himself before the censors when he was arraigned for returning home before his commander. He was elected tribune for 123 and again for 122.

During his two years as tribune he was responsible for a far-reaching and complex program of reform. Citizen rights, the political system, the food supply of Rome, agrarian, colonizing, and construction projects, public finance, the legal system, the army, provincial government, and the political status of Latins and Italians were among the areas encompassed by his legislation.

His earliest proposals were apparently those that related to the crisis of 133 and its aftermath. One such measure, banning from future office anyone who had been removed from public office by the people and so threatening M. Octavius, was withdrawn or perhaps rescinded. Another sought to prevent the kind of proceedings that had been used against his brother's supporters in 132; only the Roman people themselves could authorize a capital sentence against a Roman citizen, and any magistrate transgressing such a law should himself stand trial before the people. A law against judicial corruption may belong to this context.

Some of Gracchus' other more important measures included: (1) a law providing for distributions of grain to Roman citizens at a fixed price; (2) laws providing for land distribution and the foundation of colonies; (3) laws providing for public works such as the building of roads and granaries, the execution of which Gracchus himself personally supervised; (4) a law or laws regulating army service; (5) a law to establish farming of the tax in the newly established province of Asia through contracts leased by the censors in Rome; and (6) a law requiring the Senate to nominate consular provinces before the consular elections. Gracchus also concerned himself with legislation regarding the composition of jury panels, a result of which was the enrollment of members of the equestrian order in extortion cases at least, a development that saw the introduction of the wealthy classes outside the Senate onto the public stage.

Gracchus' proposals to alter the voting procedure in the centuriate assembly, to offer citizenship to the Latins and voting rights to the Italian allies, threatened substantial changes to the voting system and to the political dominance of the wealthy within that system. The measure concerning the Latins and allies was opposed by C. Fannius, the consul for 122, who appealed to the selfish interests of the Roman people, and by the senatorially supported tribune M. Livius Drusus, who proposed a rival popular program. In the face of such opposition the bill concerning the Latins and allies was unsuccessful, and Gracchus failed to be reelected to a third successive tribunate.

When the consul L. Opimius and one of the tribunes of 121 set out to repeal parts of Gracchus' legislation, a fracas developed during which an attendant of the consul was killed. The Senate then passed for the first time a formal declaration of the kind that in the modern scholarly literature is usually designated as *senatus consultum ultimum*, the "final decree of the Senate," in effect authorizing a forcible solution of the crisis. In response, Gracchus and his associate M. Fulvius Flaccus (cos. 125; trib. pleb, 122) occupied the Aventine with a body of armed men, a move designed both to win them a bargaining position in negotiations with the Senate and to evoke the memory of a secession of the plebeians for the defense of the people's liberty during the early days of the republic. Opimius called upon senators, equestrians, and their servants to take up arms and took two unprecedented steps: He secured the services of foreign auxiliary troops, namely, a body of Cretan archers, and offered rewards for the taking of citizen heads, those of Gracchus and Flaccus. The Gracchans were eventually overwhelmed, and Gracchus himself, on the point of capture, according to most versions, ordered a personal slave to kill him. More than 3,000 of his followers were executed without trial.

The bodies of Gracchus and his companions were thrown into the Tiber and various posthumous sanctions imposed: Gracchus' property was confiscated and his widow Licinia forbidden to mourn and to recover her dowry. A number of Gracchus' laws neverthless remained operative, some with far-reaching consequences.

The source tradition on Gaius Gracchus, as for his brother Tiberius, is infused with distortion and propaganda. The tribunates of Gaius Gracchus fundamentally challenged the rule of the Senate in the area of policymaking. His challenge and the conservative efforts to counter it further destabilized the Republic.

Bibliography: D. Stockton, *The Gracchi*, 1979.

Lea Beness

GREGORY OF NAZIANZUS, SAINT (c. 330–390)

One of the three Cappadocian Fathers, Gregory also bears the title "theologos," an honor shared only with the evangelist *John in Christian tradition.

Gregory was born in Cappadocia to Nonna and Gregory the Elder, who became bishop of Nazianzus in 325. After studies in Caesarea where he met *Basil (later bishop of Caesarea), Gregory studied at Alexandria and Athens and gained a formidable reputation as an orator. When Basil came to study in Athens, they developed a close friendship and planned to dedicate themselves to Christian philosophy, an ascetic and contemplative commitment to the faith. Basil left Athens in 356 for a tour of ascetic groups. Gregory was at first tempted to stay in Athens and take up a prestigious teaching appointment. Nonetheless, around 358 he joined Basil in Pontus. One of the fruits of their fellowship was the *Philocalia*, a synthesis of *Origen's writings that sought to preserve Origen's insights while at the same time avoiding his less tenable speculations. Family obligations kept Gregory from engaging fully in Basil's enterprise, and in 361 Gregory's father induced him to be ordained into the priesthood. Basil, too, became increasingly involved in ecclesiastical affairs. In 372 Basil, now bishop of Caesarea, appointed his friend bishop of Sasima, a postal station, in order to assert Nicene Christianity against neighboring Arian Christian authority. The office, its insignificant location, and the political motivation hurt Gregory deeply; he never took up the position.

Instead, until his father's death in 374, Gregory helped run the church at Nazianzus. Thereafter Gregory withdrew to an ascetic community in Seleucia in Isauria. Following the death of the Arian emperor *Valens in 378, Gregory agreed to pastor a beleaguered Nicene church in Constantinople where he solidified his reputation as a Nicene leader who eloquently articulated Nicene Trinitarian and Christological theology in opposition to Apollinarianism and Arianism. The Council of Constantinople elected him as its president after Meletius of Antioch died suddenly in 381. However the factions that necessitated the council wrangled over Gregory's election so bitterly that he resigned. Gregory returned to serve the church at Nazianzus and retired in 383 to Arianzus, the family estate, where he edited his life's work. He died in 390.

The five *Theological Orations* on the Trinity, presented in 380, left Gregory's mark on the eastern church, for which he was accorded the title "theologos." Gregory's orations (44), letters (c. 345), and poetry (ca. 17,000 verses) were also prized by Byzantine and Renaissance scholars as literary models. Gregory hoped to provide Christians with literature that could rival and replace dependence on non-Christian classics. Although overshadowed in the West by *Augustine's *Confessions*, Gregory's autobiographical poems are important for their style and personal revelation.

Bibliography: C. White, trans., *Gregory of Nazianzus, Autobiographical Poems*, 1997.

Lisa D. Maugans Driver

GREGORY OF NYSSA, SAINT (c. 335/340–post 394)

Gregory, the youngest of the Cappadocian Fathers, was a mystical theologian whose works display a marked integration of ancient philosophical traditions into Christian theology.

Gregory's family boasted an extensive Christian pedigree, including survivors of persecutions and several saints. Gregory at first avoided the ascetic path initiated by his sister Macrina and followed by his mother Emmelia and brothers *Basil, Naucratius, and Peter. His education combined local study, directed in part by Macrina and Basil, and advanced self-study in both classical and Christian writings. Gregory was ordained lector around 360 but decided against a church career; instead, he married and followed his father's profession as a teacher of rhetoric. Basil's election to the episcopacy in Caesarea (370) eventually involved Gregory, whom he appointed bishop of the village of Nyssa in 372. Basil organized this appointment and that of his friend *Gregory of Nazianzus in hopes of increasing support for Nicene orthodoxy during a period when Arians were ascendant in eastern politics and Christianity. Unfortunately Gregory early on suffered from some administrative inadequacies that Arian opponents used as a basis for exiling him from Nyssa during 376–378.

The coincidence of the deaths of Basil (379) and the Arian emperor *Valens (378) contributed to Gregory's prominence among Nicene leaders. During the Council of Constantinople (381), the new Nicene emperor *Theodosius I insisted that communion with Gregory, among others, be a condition for those who claimed to be orthodox. Gregory engaged in ecclesiastical missions and the defense of Nicene theology against both Eunomians, who denied the divinity of Christ, and the Apollinarians, who denied Christ's humanity. Gregory made further visits to Constantinople defending the divinity of the Son and the Holy Spirit (383) and later (385) delivering funeral orations for Theodosius' young daughter Pulcheria and wife Flaccilla. Gregory died sometime after attending a synod in Constantinople in 394.

Much of Gregory's reputation rests upon his books against Eunomius, a culmination of Cappadocian theology, and his mature works on Christian life, such as *On the Song of Songs* and *Life of Moses*. He was an esteemed spiritual adviser and viewed life in Christ to be a lifelong journey leading progressively toward a fuller participation in God and accompanied by increasing imitation of Christ. Gregory was influenced by *Origen as he sought to synthesize Platonic thought into a fully Christian philosophy. Furthermore, he emphasized the negative way (apophatic) of coming to know God, a method whereby the believer gradually strips away all positive statements about God. Since God is beyond all that humans mean by such statements and conceptions, ultimately He becomes known in "darkness" where He reveals his presence beyond the capability of human physical and intellectual senses. Such theology was influential on eastern theologians such as Pseudo-Dionysius and Gregory Palamas and through Latin translations of Pseudo-Dionysius in the western Middle Ages.

Bibliography: W. Jaeger, *Two Rediscovered Works of Ancient Christian Literature: Gregory of Nyssa and Macarius*, 1954.

Lisa D. Maugans Driver

GYGES (c. 680–645 b.c.)

Gyges was king of Lydia and founder of the Mermnad dynasty. He is the earliest known foreign ruler to seek domination over the Greek cities of Asia Minor.

Gyges usurped the Lydian throne by murdering his predecessor and marrying the queen. He extended Lydian power to the shores of the Propontis to the north, westward to the Ionian Greek cities on the Aegean Sea, and south as far as the Menander River. He was famous for his wealth and sent expensive gifts to Apollo's oracle at Delphi. Gyges formed alliances first with the king of Assyria, Assurbanipal, and then with the Egyptian pharaoh, Psammetichus I, to further his ambitions. He was killed fighting against Cimmerian invaders. His son Ardys succeeded him on the Lydian throne.

Bibliography: A. Andrewes, *The Greek Tyrants*, 1956; G.M.A. Hanfmann, *Sardis from Prehistoric to Roman Times*, 1983.

Carl A. Anderson

H

HADRIAN (Publius Aelius Hadrianus, c. 76–138)

Hadrian was a popular emperor of the early second century (r. 117–138) known for his love of Greek civilization.

Hadrian was born around 76 into the gens Aelia, one of the first families of Spain to enter into the senatorial aristocracy. After his father's death, Hadrian was entrusted to the care of his father's cousin the future emperor *Trajan and a man named Publius Acilius Attianus. During his youth he developed a passion for all things Greek, which earned him the nickname *Graeculus* (Greekling). Indeed, the beard he wore as an adult was rumored to hide his poor complexion but was in all likelihood a Greek affectation. In 100 he married Vibia Sabina, Trajan's great-niece, further cementing his relationship to the emperor under whom he served as quaestor in 101. In 112 he was archon of Athens but left in 113 to serve under Trajan in the Dacian campaigns, finally becoming governor of Syria in 114. Hadrian's adoption as successor was announced the day after Trajan's death in 117 amid rumors that Trajan's wife Plotina had staged the posthumous adoption.

Much of Hadrian's career was spent traveling, especially in Greece. Relations between Hadrian and Sabina were poor; most of his affection was directed toward his young male companion from Bithynia named Antinous. Born about 110, Antinous accompanied Hadrian on many of his travels, including a fateful trip down the Nile, where Antinous drowned in the river. Hadrian's mourning for Antinous was intense; he established a hero cult for him and erected shrines and statues for him throughout the empire as well as founding the city of Antinoopolis in his memory.

Hadrian is perhaps best known for his building legacy, especially in Athens, where he completed the Olympieion (Temple of Olympian Zeus), which had been begun in the sixth century B.C., the Library of Hadrian, and the Arch of Hadrian, which demarcated the old Greek and new Roman cities. He adopted

*Antoninus Pius in 138, the same year in which he died at Baiae and was deified by the Senate.

Bibliography: A.R. Birley, *Hadrian: The Restless Emperor*, 1997.

Katrina M. Dickson

HAMILCAR BARCA (c. 275–228 B.C.)

Hamilcar was a Carthaginian general during the First Punic War (264–241) and the father of *Hannibal.

Although the family background of Hamilcar is unknown, he probably belonged to the Carthaginian aristocracy with family estate in the region of Leptis Minus. He first appears on the historical scene in 247, the year his eldest son Hannibal was born, as commander of the Carthaginian fleet. After eighteen years of war with Rome, Carthage had lost most of its possessions in Sicily. Nevertheless, Hamilcar was successful in ravaging the southern coast of Italy at Bruttium. He then attacked the north coast of Sicily and seized the stronghold of Heircte. From this base, he was able to attack the Romans at Panormos and the Italian coast as far as Cumae. In 244, he succeeded in capturing Eryx and provided some relief from the Roman siege of Drepanum. However, after the Punic fleet was defeated by the Romans off the Aegates in 241, Hamilcar was ordered to negotiate a peace settlement with the Roman consul C. Lutatius Catulus.

Upon completing the peace settlement with Lutatius, Hamilcar resigned his command and left Sicily. However, his former mercenaries revolted under the leadership of Spendios and Matho (Truceless War, 241–238). When Hanno, his political adversary, was unsuccessful at suppressing this rebellion, the Carthaginian Council of Elders reappointed Hamilcar as commander in chief. Although Hamilcar succeeded in defeating Spendios, the successes and long duration of the rebellion ultimately forced Hamilcar to cooperate with Hanno in defeating Matho in 238.

In 237 Hamilcar was sent to Spain with the primary objective of exploiting the silver and gold mines of Sierra Morena to pay off the Carthaginian war debt to Rome. Taking his son-in-law Hasdrubal and his young son Hannibal with him, he settled at Gades, "re-establishing the Carthaginians' affairs in Iberia." In order to secure his control over lower Andalusia, he campaigned from 235 to 231 against the Iberian peoples eastward as far as Cape de la Nao. At some time during this period he founded a city at a place named Acra Leuce (Alicante), though its precise location is unknown. Hamilcar appears to have died during the winter of 229–228. *Diodorus claims that he drowned in a river while retreating from laying siege to Helice, but other accounts of his death are known.

Bibliography: S. Lancel, *Hannibal*, 1998.

Ronald A. Simkins

HANNIBAL BARCA (247–183 B.C.)

Hannibal Barca was a Carthaginian nobleman whose campaigns against Rome in the Second Punic War (219–201) almost brought down the republic. In consequence, he is reckoned one of the greatest captains in military history.

Hannibal was born the first son and fourth child of *Hamilcar Barca, hero of the First Punic War (264–241) and the Truceless War (241–238). From Hamilcar's experiences in his dealings with Rome, Hannibal cultivated a deep antipathy toward the rival republic. Hannibal traveled with his father to Spain in 237, as Carthage moved to extend its control over the Iberian peninsula. Here Hannibal was immersed in the camp life of a soldier and after the death of his father and brother-in-law, Hasdrubal the Fair, he was elected to command the army in Spain in 221. In this position, Hannibal continued to extend Carthaginian influence over Spain while making preparations for a possible war with Rome. He also had to deal with opposition in the Carthaginian Senate led by Hanno the Great.

War with Rome soon became a reality. The conflict arose over the fate of the city of Saguntum, which lay on the border between the portions of Spain dominated by Carthage and Rome. After a period of civil disorder, Hannibal besieged and took the city in 219, an act that the Romans considered a violation of an agreement concluded in Carthage in 228. Hannibal moved quickly and energetically once war was declared. He prepared the Carthaginian defenses in north Africa, left his younger brother Hasdrubal in command of Spain, and married a Spanish woman to strengthen his ties with the Iberian tribes. In the spring of 218, Hannibal marched out of Nova Carthago, passed through southern Gaul, and crossed the Alps with an army of 26,000 Libyans, Iberians, and Numidians. By the autumn of 218, Hannibal and his army, joined now by a growing number of Gauls, moved into the Po River Valley. Beginning here, he would campaign in the Italian peninsula for the next fifteen years. With very little support from Carthage in the way of men, money, or supplies, Hannibal would nonetheless shake the Roman republic to its foundations.

To meet this threat, Rome sent its armies against the Carthaginian invader. During the next three years, through the superior generalship of Hannibal, Rome suffered three consecutive military disasters: First at the Trebbia River in 218, then Lake Trasimene in 217, and culminating in the greatest Roman defeat in Roman history at Cannae in 216, Hannibal and his army annihilated over a dozen legions.

Despite such spectacular successes, the Carthaginian leader could not force Rome into a negotiated peace. Roman resources proved nearly inexhaustible, most of Rome's Italiot allies remained loyal, and Carthage directed most of its support to its defense of Spain. From 215 until his departure in 203, Hannibal concentrated his efforts in southern Italy. In 215 he concluded an alliance with *Philip V of Macedonia, but little good came of it. Through a series of battles, sieges, and stratagems, Hannibal was able to maintain his army in southern Italy and keep the Romans at bay. This, however, marked the extent of Hannibal's successes. During this twelve-year period the Romans effected the conquest of Spain and defeated both major attempts by Carthage to reinforce Hannibal. At the Metaurus River in 207, Hasdrubal Barca's army was destroyed and Hannibal's brother was slain. Four years later Mago Barca's army was defeated in the Po River Valley, and Mago soon after succumbed to his wounds. When *Publius Cornelius Scipio led an invasion of the North African coast near Carthage in 204, Hannibal resolved to return with his army to defend his homeland.

Hannibal successfully transferred his army back to North Africa in 203. Scipio's campaigning meanwhile had weakened greatly the Carthaginian position, and peace talks had begun. Now with Hannibal's return, both sides girded for one last great battle. At Zama in 202, Scipio overbore Hannibal, and an exceedingly harsh peace treaty resulted the next year.

In the aftermath of the Second Punic War, Hannibal strove to rebuild Carthaginian fortunes. Elected suffete in 196, he helped to administer a postwar prosperity and attacked the corrupt practices of the ruling oligarchy. This latter endeavor encouraged his opponents to denounce him to Rome as a conspirator with the Seleucid monarch *Antiochus III, with whom tensions had mounted with Rome. Rather than submit to the mercy of his enemies, Hannibal fled to Tyre and met with Antiochus III in 195 at Ephesus. Hannibal remained at the Seleucid court as an adviser to the king, and when the Syrian War (192–189) broke out between the Seleucids and Rome, Hannibal took an active role. As an admiral he lost the Battle of Side (190) to a Rhodian fleet allied to Rome. The following year, Hannibal was at Antiochus III's side at the decisive Battle of Magnesia, but the king failed to make use of the great captain's talents. Denounced as an implacable enemy of Rome in the peace treaty that followed, Hannibal went into exile, wandering through Asia Minor and the reaches of the Eastern Mediterranean. He eventually joined the court of King Prusias of Bithynia, but the Romans came to demand that Hannibal be turned over to them at Libyssa in 183; as Bithynian soldiers came to seize him, Hannibal took poison and died.

Hannibal's legacy was twofold. Although he lost the Second Punic War and Carthage only outlived him by another thirty-seven years, the dire threat that he posed to Rome led to numerous and critical changes to the Roman republic. With the practice of multiple and consecutive consulships for the more talented commander, the idea of the interchangeability of leadership was undermined. The war provoked an agrarian crisis in Italy because of the length and destructiveness of the conflict. Changes in industry and commerce led to the rise of the social class known as the *equites* (knights). Roman coinage was reorganized, while the Roman victory opened the way for Roman imperialism and guaranteed the hegemony of the Latin culture over the Greek in Italy.

His second legacy rests with his reputation as a military genius. With a heterogeneous and polyglot force, Hannibal marched into Italy, and although outnumbered and regularly neglected by the powers in Carthage, he almost humbled the republic of Rome. In terms of his tactical skill, strategic sense, diplomatic endeavors, and cunning ruses, Hannibal had few equals and no master.

Bibliography: S. Lancel, *Hannibal*, 1998.

Cyril M. Lagvanec

HECATAEUS (late sixth and early fifth century B.C.)

Hecataeus was a geographer and writer from the island of Miletus.

Very little is known about the life of Hecataeus. He was born on the Ionian island of Miletus, and according to *Herodotus, he traveled through Egypt and the Mediterranean. He was also active in the Ionian resistance to the Persians in the early fifth century.

Hecataeus is known to have written two major works, a geographical and ethnographical work, the *Periegesis*, and chronicle of different familial myths. We possess only fragments or quotations in other authors from these works. The geographical work appears to have been organized as a travel log, describing both the places and people that Hecataeus encountered in his journeys around the Mediterranean world. The mythological work appears to have taken a rationalizing approach to mythic stories.

Despite our lack of detailed knowledge about his life and his works, Hecataeus was clearly an important figure in the intellectual environment of the late sixth and early fifth centuries. Herodotus, for example, was familiar with and influenced to some degree by Hecataeus' works.

Bibliography: L. Pearson, *Early Ionian Historians*, 1939.

Jeff Rydberg-Cox

HELENA AUGUSTA, SAINT (c. 250–330)

Helena was a Christian Roman empress and mother of Emperor *Constantine.

Born in the Bithynian town of Drepanum (later Helenopolis) in about 25, she is described as having been of low occupation (a tavern maid) until she formed a relationship with the young officer Constantius, to whom she bore Constantine. The difference of their social status makes it unlikely that they were ever formally married. Even so, they remained together until Constantius put her aside to contract a dynastic match with the daughter of Maximian.

After Constantine became emperor, she returned to public life. She became a Christian, converted, according to one story, by her son. In 325, she was raised to the rank of Augusta. Granted a palace in Rome (the Sessorian Palace, now the site of Sancta Croce in Gerusalemme), she lived there for most of the rest of her life. In 326, she protested the execution of Constantine's son Crispus, and it may have been her intrigues that ensured the execution of Constantine's wife Fausta. After the death of Fausta, Helena went on pilgrimage to Palestine, where she is said to have located the True Cross, a fragment of which she brought back to Rome. Under her oversight, construction of the great basilicas of the Holy Sepulchre and the Holy Nativity were commenced.

She died soon after her return from Palestine and was entombed in a great mausoleum attached to the basilica of Saints Peter and Marcellinus in Rome that was originally intended for her son.

Bibliography: H.J.W. Drijvers, *Helena Augusta*, 1992.

William Leadbetter

HELLANICUS OF MYTILENE (c. 490–405 B.C.)

Hellanicus was one of the earliest Greek chroniclers to establish a common chronology for Greek history.

Hellanicus was one of several fifth-century B.C. Ionian "logographers"—those who first began using prose as a Greek literary form. He wrote works of mythography, ethnography, and universal and local chronicles. His five works of mythography, for which fragments survive, provided genealogical narratives concerning the ancient Greek heroes and related the local histories of Greek cities during the heroic age. His ethnographic treatises explored the foundations of Greek settlements in Thessaly, Boeotia, and Lesbos and the origins and customs of foreign lands such as Egypt, Scythia, and Persia. With his chronographic writings, Hellanicus created a system for dating events of Greek history by using the list of the priestesses of Hera at Argos and the list of the victors at the Carnea, the national Spartan festival. In the *Atthis*, a local history of Athens from the earliest times down to the author's own day, Hellanicus introduced the chronological innovations of ordering the succession of mythical kings and using the list of eponymous magistrates.

Bibliography: C.W. Fornara, *The Nature of History in Ancient Greece and Rome*, 1983.

Michael Anderson

HERACLIDES OF PONTUS (c. 390–c. 322 B.C.)

Born in Heraclia on the Pontus, Heraclides studied philosophy at *Plato's Academy (c. 367/366–339/338). He is chiefly remembered for his innovative theories of subatomic structure, heliocentric movement of the planets, and discussion of extraterrestrial life.

Heraclides was a senior member of the Academy when its members sought a rational explanation for celestial movement. His proposals are attempts to solve problems arising from Plato's *Timaeus* much as did *Aristotle in the *Metaphysics*. Very little evidence survives concerning his thought, and there is still scholarly controversy concerning much of it. Although Heraclides continued to hold that the sun and outer planets revolved around the earth, he solved the mystery of the movement of Venus and Mercury by proposing their revolution around the sun. He suggested that the earth rotated daily on its axis so that the fixed stars seemed to move nightly. Much like *Anaxagoras, he proposed that the cosmos was infinite but that each star contains an entire cosmos within it. The moon was likewise an inhabited world with earth and air, from which a man once fell to earth.

In his opinion, material bodies are made up of empty pores and ever-moving particles. The latter are either qualitative bodies or nonqualitative elementary fragments. Unlike *Democritus, he held that these were liable to change in a world that was governed by divine providence. While accepting Plato's theory of the immortal soul, he nonetheless maintained that it was made of material *aether*.

Heraclides' cosmology is sometimes seen as an intermediate system, paving the way for *Aristarchus of Samos and Tycho Brahe. His physical theory is also seen as an alternative to those of Anaxagoras and Democritus, although still descended from the Pythagorizing of Plato's *Timaeus*. *Cicero was an admirer of Heraclides' style of dialogue, copying several of his ideas in his *Republic*.

Bibliography: H.B. Gottschalk, *Heraclides of Pontus*, 1980; W.K.C. Guthrie, *A History of Greek Philosophy*, vol. 5, 1978.

Menahem Luz

HERACLITUS OF EPHESUS (c. 544–478 B.C.)

Heraclitus was a reclusive aristocratic philosopher in the Ionian city of Ephesus. Heraclitus is most famous for promoting the claim that all is flux, becoming, and changing.

As is true with many of the pre-Socratic philosophers, little is known about the life of Heraclitus. *Diogenes Laertius claims that Heraclitus was the son of Bloson (though he admits that others claimed he was the son of Herakon) of Ephesus. Heraclitus is also believed to have been from a wealthy trading family, which should not be surprising considering the importance of Ephesus as a trading center in the sixth century B.C. According to legend, however, Heraclitus did not continue the public, merchant life of his family but withdrew to the hills and immersed himself in philosophical reflections. Diogenes Laertius claims that Heraclitus later fell ill and returned to the city to seek help. The efforts of the doctors were futile, however, and Heraclitus died at the age of sixty. Whether Diogenes Laertius' (c. 250 A.D.) account is accurate or not (some scholars argue that Heraclitus never fled the city to the hills to become a reclusive thinker), the scant few fragments of the one book Heraclitus is believed to have written were widely quoted and extremely influential.

The surviving fragments of Heraclitus' book, the title of which is said to have been "On Nature," display a style that is difficult to interpret due to the frequent paradoxes and vague symbols and metaphors Heraclitus uses. This writing style led Heraclitus' contemporaries, as well as later commentators on Heraclitus, to refer to him as "the obscure." Despite the obscurity and apparent difficulty of Heraclitus' fragments, one position is clear: He believes that conflict and flux/becoming are the natural state of the cosmos. It was Heraclitus who is often credited with the well-known statement: "You cannot step into the same river twice." This statement is not found precisely stated as such in the surviving fragments, though it is certainly within the spirit of Heraclitus' philosophy, and many of Heraclitus' successors and followers often credited this statement to him. *Plato and *Aristotle would later reject Heraclitus' obscure, paradoxical utterances as examples of a failure to reason, though the Stoics would later rediscover and reemphasize Heraclitus. Even in the nineteenth and twentieth centuries, important philosophers such as Friedrich Nietzsche and Martin Heidegger have stressed the enduring significance of Heraclitus.

Bibliography: G.S. Kirk, J.E. Raven, and M. Schofield, *The Presocratic Philosophers*, 2nd ed., 1983.

Jeffrey A. Bell

HEROD THE GREAT (r. 37 B.C.–A.D. 4)

Herod was born the son of Antipater in the late 70s B.C. and ruled in Palestine as a client-king to Roman patrons. He was a complex and conflicted figure whose reign was marked by political shrewdness, effectiveness in the public arena, personal insecurity, and palace intrigues.

His rise to the throne was particularly contentious. Many of the Jewish aristocracy rejected him because he, a descendant of a non-Jewish family, claimed a title historically associated with Davidic lineage. Others rejected him because Roman authority had legitimated both him and his father. Herod's rule was filled with power struggles and continuous efforts to solidify his kingship. With the marriage to his first wife Mariame, he attempted to establish ties with his former enemies, the Hasmoneans. Later, he established close ties with Octavian (*Augustus) who, after defeating *Marc Antony at Actium (31), became the first emperor of the Roman world. Augustus increased Herod's kingdom and granted him the status of friend and ally to the Roman Empire. Even as he gained the favor of the empire abroad, in Judaea, rumors of treason, assassination attempts, and Herod's own insecurities resulted in the executions of his wife Miriame, much of her family, two of his sons, and anyone whom he believed threatened his rule. The Gospel of *Matthew highlights this aspect of Herod's attitude in its legendary account of the slaughter of the innocents.

Despite hostilities with the Jewish aristocracy and troubles within his household, several events attest to Herod's benevolence and political savvy. During a severe drought and plague c. 24 B.C., he reportedly minted coins from his personal vessels of silver and gold to purchase grain from Egypt, which he distributed throughout his kingdom. *Josephus also claims that he distributed clothing to the needy. During another drought he is reported to have removed one-third of the tax burden from the populace. Herod's greatest achievements were his building projects, at that time unsurpassed by any one ruler in the ancient world. In his capital Jerusalem, he built the Antonia Fortress in honor of Marc Antony. His Central Palace, the largest and most elaborate of Herod's Palaces, could accommodate affairs of hundreds of guests. By far, his most prestigious architectural accomplishment was the Temple Mount. This rebuilding of the Jewish temple enlarged the mount and an impressive royal basilica on its south face.

He built several fortresses in the Judaean desert, including Masada, Hyrcania,

Alexandrium, and Cypros. In Caesara Maritima, he built a magnificent city with streets intersecting at right angles, an underground drainage system, a hippodrome, and theater where games were held every five years honoring Augustus. Finally, Herodium, constructed within a mountain, was the culmination of Herod's buildings. It included a palace complex, a fortress monument, and his royal tomb.

Herod's reign ultimately was full of ambiguities as evidenced by the circumstances surrounding his death. In order to ensure mourning after his death, he ordered the deaths of the elders in cities throughout his kingdom so that even if the populace did not mourn his death, they would mourn upon his death.

Bibliography: N. Kokkinos, *The Herodian Dynasty: Origins, Role in Society and Eclipse*, 1998; S. Perowne, *The Life and Times of Herod the Great*, 1956.

Herbert Marbury

HEROD ANTIPAS (first century A.D.)

Herod Antipas is the name by which most scholars identify the son of *Herod the Great and the tetrarch of Galilee from 4 B.C. to A.D. 39. However, on his own coins he is known simply as Herod.

Much of what we know of Antipas' life derives from *Josephus' historiography. According to Josephus, Antipas and his brother Archaelus were Herod's two sons by Malthace, the Samaritan. Antipas is best known for his two appearances in the Gospels. First, he is criticized by *John the Baptist for divorcing his first wife, the King of Nabatea's daughter, and marrying Herodias, his niece. This second marriage, considered unlawful by many Jews, worsened Antipas' public image, an image already tarnished by the general perception that he was more loyal to Rome than to Judaea and more wedded to Hellenistic culture than to Jewish culture. Either for his criticism or at the request of his new stepdaughter, Antipas had John the Baptist arrested and beheaded. Second, the Gospel of *Luke reports that Antipas participated in the trial of Christ, since as a Galilean *Jesus was under his jurisdiction. Although his portrayal in the Gospels is negative, Antipas is reported to have shown respect for Jewish customs by attending holy feasts in Jerusalem and by minting aniconic coins.

Like his father, Antipas is known for his building projects. He fortified the city of Livias, renaming it in honor of *Augustus' wife *Livia. He also constructed an entirely new city, Tiberius, and populated it. Nonetheless, his reign ended with accusations of treason against Rome and subsequent exile by Emperor *Caligula.

Bibliography: N. Kokkinos, *The Herodian Dynasty: Origins, Role in Society and Eclipse*, 1998.

Herbert Marbury

HERODAS (fl. c. 270 B.C.)

Herodas, or perhaps Herondas, was a famous Hellenistic composer of *mimiamboi*, literary mimes in iambic scazons. His poems dealt with everyday experiences, many of which were often of a sexual nature.

Herodas combined the stock material of popular *mimos* with the choliambic meter associated with the seventh-century iambic poet *Hipponax. He was little more than a name until the discovery of a number of his poems on a papyrus roll first published in 1891. The poems, seven of which are relatively well preserved, have been transmitted with individual titles. There are a few references in the mimes to historical events. For example, mime one mentions the fraternal cults that *Ptolemy II established for himself and his wife Arsinoe in 272/271. References in another mime to the two artists *Praxiteles and *Apelles establish a range of 280–265 for the poem's dramatic date. Herodas was therefore roughly contemporary with *Theocritus and *Callimachus. Because Alexandria is mentioned prominently in the first mime and another of his mimes is concerned with literary programmatics, Herodas has often been linked with other poets from the city of Alexandria. There is, however, no certain evidence about his place of origin.

The influence of Herodas' *mimiamboi* is not directly attested, as it is with other Hellenistic poets. However, mimic elements in the Roman poet *Ovid bear similarity to elements in Herodas, and the Roman writer *Pliny the Younger considered Herodas as being the best poet of his genre.

Bibliography: G.O. Hutchinson, *Hellenistic Poetry*, 1988; G. Mastromarco, *The Public of Herondas*, 1984.

Carl A. Anderson

HERODES ATTICUS (Tiberius Claudius Atticus Herodes, c. 101–177)

Herodes, as orator, politician, and public benefactor, was a major figure in the rhetorical and philosophical movement known as the Second Sophistic.

Herodes Atticus lived at the height of the Second Sophistic during the prosperous second century. Schooled in rhetoric by prominent teachers, he himself tutored *Aelius Aristides and the young *Marcus Aurelius and Lucius Verus. He was a wealthy man of great distinction who put his talents and resources to public purposes. He was consul in Rome in 143. His public benefactions included many buildings and monuments, particularly in his home city of Athens (he was born at Marathon). The theater or "Odeon" that he built on the south slope of the Acropolis survives in a good state of restoration and is still the scene of plays and concerts. Like his pupil Aelius Aristides, Herodes espoused a purely Attic style of rhetoric. His voluminous writings ranged from letters and diaries to lectures and set speeches. None survives except for a Latin rendition of a *fabula* (fictitious narrative). He figures importantly in the *Lives of the Sophists* by *Philostratus.

Bibliography: A. Lesky, *A History of Greek Literature*, 1966.

James Holoka

HERODIAN (c. 170–240)

Herodian was the author of eight books that recounted the history of the Roman Empire from *Marcus Aurelius through Gordian III.

Though Herodian was a historian, the details of his own life are rather obscure. The dates of both his birth and death are unknown, but it appears that he was born in Syria and lived between 170 and 240. Because Herodian claimed to have been an eyewitness to all of his historical accounts, it is assumed that he worked as an officer for the Roman emperors. The length of the time his record covers has led some scholars to believe that he lived a long, healthy life.

Herodian's eight volumes chronicled a seventy-year history of the Roman Empire from 180, the death of Marcus Aurelius, to 238, the beginning of the reign of the emperor Gordian III (238–244). Although Herodian's histories are well written and interesting, it is very apparent, through various details found in his writings, that his knowledge of geography was extremely limited. Even though he struggled with the nature of the outlying terrain and the location of various places, his writing style betrays a sincere and sober attempt to be accurate in his reporting. He can be faulted in that his accounts are superficial, rhetorical, and often full of moralizing. In spite of these, the contemporary nature of his accounts makes them of considerable value in understanding this period of the Roman Empire.

Bibliography: M. Grant, *Greek and Roman Historians: Information and Misinformation*, 1995.

Richard Draper

HERODOTUS (c. 484–c. 430 B.C.)

Often referred to as the "Father of History," Herodotus was the first of the Greek writers to record history in a narrative form, as evidenced by his great *History*, the story of the conflict between the Greeks and the Persians.

Probably born in the second decade of the fifth century B.C., Herodotus came from the Greek-Carian community of Halicarnassus, on the Mediterranean coast of Turkey. A member of a prominent family, Herodotus counted the poet Panyassis among his relatives. Lacking alliances, Halicarnassus afforded Herodotus the opportunity to develop unbiased opinions about both the Greeks and the Persians.

The city was ruled by a female tyrant, Artemesia, and Herodotus and Panyassis got involved in a plot to oust her successor around 455. For their troubles, Herodotus was exiled to Samos, and Panyassis was killed. Samos was part of the Athenian empire, and it was there that Herodotus began his historical researches. With the backing of Athens, he returned home and avenged his expulsion by kicking out the tyrant Lygdamis, but his efforts were not well received, and he relocated to a new community in southern Italy, Thurii, and established citizenship there around 443. Thurii later allied itself to Sparta, despite Athenian claims to the city.

The *History* grew out of observations that Herodotus made during his travels, which were wide-ranging; besides Italy, he was known to have ventured to Egypt, Babylon, Ukraine, and Greece and may have visited Africa. While Herodotus often wrote down what he saw, he just as frequently relied on his memory as he compiled his work. In between his travels, he supported himself mostly through lecturing, though he might have engaged in trade and diplomacy at various times. While in Athens, he made the acquaintance of writers, among them the playwright *Sophocles.

Herodotus lacked a concrete historical theory, but his works seem to take a cyclical approach, in common with other Near Eastern or Eastern peoples. He displayed a rather ambiguous attitude toward war, which was surprising, given that the *History* focused on that very topic. Herodotus did not confine himself to collecting only his own observations; his work contains the comments of others whom he met in his travels, and many of his conclusions are simply inferences proceeding from other sources. While Herodotus viewed his work as the recording of experience, the scientific historian *Thucydides dismissed him as simply a storyteller whose work could not be conclusively relied upon.

His great contribution, the *History*, was a narrative account of the conflict between the Greeks and Persians, but it is also a recounting of the process of Persian expansion, which culminated in the invasion by *Xerxes of the Greek mainland in 480–479. Though it is written from a Greek perspective, it is rather unbiased in its observations. The work also includes descriptions of his travels and the peoples that he encountered on those travels. The date of publication of the *History* is uncertain, though it is assumed that the publication was a gradual process, probably beginning around 430 and continuing for about six years, ending as late as 421. Sometime around the end of the fourth century, the work was divided into nine books and further separated into sections and subsections. Despite its nonscientific approach, the *History* is an invaluable resource for any student of the ancient world.

There is no evidence of the date of Herodotus' death, nor his place of burial. It is generally conceded, however, that his travels came to an end around 447, and he spent the remainder of his years completing the *History* and giving lectures. Since he had relocated to Thurii, it is believed that he is buried there, though he may have chosen to go elsewhere toward the end of his life. The obscurity surrounding the man, however, does not detract from his enormous contribution to the historical record, a contribution that certainly earns his sobriquet the "Father of History."

Bibliography: J.A.S. Evans, *Herodotus*, 1982; J.B. Gould, *Herodotus*, 1989.

Connie Evans

HERON OF ALEXANDRIA (c. 65–125)

Heron of Alexandria, sometimes known simply as Hero, was a mathematician who worked chiefly in geometry and mechanics.

Heron was born in Alexandria but little else is known of his life besides his accomplishments in the mathematical and physical sciences. He wrote numerous books on sundry mathematical and physical topics, but most of Heron's works put greater emphasis on practicality than on theoretical rigor. Consequently, many of his treatises were popular and subjected to continual alteration and augmentation and have been transmitted to the present day in Greek, Latin, and Arabic.

Metrica, Heron's most important geometrical work, encompasses mensuration in two and three dimensions. One particularly renowned result, known as Heron's Formula, gives the area of any triangle in terms of the lengths of its three sides. *Metrica* also contains a method for approximating square roots. Among his other purely mathematical treatises are *Definitiones*, *Geometrica*, *Geodaesia*, and *Commentary on Euclid's Elements*, which enumerates special cases of Euclid's propositions and employs alternative, semialgebraic proofs for the first time.

As an engineer, Heron excelled in devising many ingenious mechanical devices, which he cataloged in several books. *Pneumatica* contains descriptions of about 100 toys and machines, including siphons, fountains, steam engines, automatic doors, and coin-operated automata. Other inventions were of a more serious nature. *Belopoeica* concerns the construction of engines of war, while *Dioptra* and *Catoptica* explain the proper use of mechanism for surveying land and focusing mirrors. All of Heron's mechanical developments indicate a keen insight into and clever use of the basic principles of physics.

Bibliography: T.L. Heath, *A History of Greek Mathematics*, 1921.

Michael Labranche

HEROPHILUS OF CHALCEDON (c. 320–260 b.c.)

Herophilus, a Greek physician in Alexandria, was one of the earliest practitioners of systematic human dissection for anatomical research.

Herophilus, who was a pupil of *Praxagoras of Cos, practiced and taught medicine in Alexandria during the early years of the Ptolemaic kingdom. He was considered one of the great physicians of antiquity by the second-century medical writer *Galen. Herophilus' practice of human dissection (and possibly vivisection) produced important anatomical discoveries concerning the brain, eye, nervous and vascular systems, abdominal cavity, and reproductive organs. He was the first to distinguish and describe the ventricles of the brain. His demonstration that the nerves originate in the brain convincingly refuted the widespread conception of the heart as the central organ of sensation and the seat of the intellect. One ancient source claims that he distinguished between the sensory and motor nerves. Herophilus gave the first accurate description of the size, position, shape, and texture of the human liver. He also applied the name "duodenum" to the first part of the small intestine. He was the first to make an anatomical (as opposed to a functional) distinction between arteries and veins, noting that the coverings of arteries are thicker than those of veins. In terms of therapeutics, Herophilus was rather conventional, adhering to the theory of humoral medicine and treating patients with contrary remedies, bloodletting, and the liberal use of drugs. He did, however, further develop the pulse theory of Praxagoras and employ the measurement of pulse as a major diagnostic and prognostic tool.

Bibliography: H. von Staden, *Herophilus: The Art of Medicine in Early Alexandria*, 1989.

Michael Anderson

HESIOD (c. 700 b.c.)

Hesiod was one of the oldest known Greek poets and is a key source of information on early Greek values and theology.

The biography of Hesiod, the writer of the *Theogony* and *Works and Days*, is sketchy, and his existence has been challenged by recent scholarship. The internal evidence of the texts themselves depicts humble beginnings for the poet. Hesiod's father moved from Aeloian Cyme to Ascra in Boeotia near Mt. Helicon and, in the process, gave up sea-trading for agriculture. In Chalcis, Hesiod won a prize for poetry at the funeral games for Amphidamas. *Works and Days* records a conflict with his brother Perses over their inheritance. The tale, recorded in *Certamen Homeri et Hesiodi*, of a poetic contest between Hesiod and *Homer, with Hesiod declared the winner, may have more to do with perceptions of the poetic traditions they came to represent than with historical fact. Two other works, *The Shield of Hercules* and *The Catalogue of Women*, which previously have been attributed to Hesiod, were probably written over a century later. Scholars have also questioned the reports of his death in Locris and of a tomb at Orchomenus.

Hesiod's mode of composition continues to be debated: Whether it was oral or written, Hesiod, like Homer, was working from an oral tradition. Both the *Theogony* and *Works and Days* follow epic conventions and are written in dactylic hexameters. The *Theogony* is an account of the origin and genealogies of the gods and is an essential source of early Greek theology. The poem begins with a hymn to the Muses followed by the Creation as Chaos comes into existence. Hesiod proceeds to cover the genealogies of some 300 gods. The poem ends with the marriage of Zeus and various affairs of Zeus and other gods and goddesses.

In *Works and Days*, Hesiod offers his brother Perses moral and practical advice on living. This didactic work employs myth as well as proverbs and allegory. It is this work in particular that seems to be responsible for the traditional division of genres between Homer and Hesiod: Homer representing the heroic epic and Hesiod the didactic verse. Hesiod's significance is particularly apparent in ages interested in mythology. From the first Latin translation of *Works and Days* in 1471 to John Milton to Ezra Pound, Hesiod's influence is apparent.

Bibliography: G. Nagy, *Greek Mythology and Poetics*, 1990.

Christine Cornell

HIERON I (late sixth–fifth century B.C.)

Hieron was the brother of *Gelon, tyrant of Gela and later of Syracuse. When Gelon seized Syracuse in 485, he gave Hieron the suzerainty of Gela. Upon Gelon's death in 478, Hieron became tyrant of Syracuse, while Gela passed to another brother, Polyzalus.

To ensure his control of Syracuse, Hieron employed the services of a secret police. In 476, he transported the Naxians and Catanians to Leontini and re-founded Catana as Aetna, filling Aetna with 10,000 Dorians. He appointed his son, Deinomenes, tyrant of Aetna. Hieron's interest in southern Italy was manifested by his help to Sybaris against Croton, his success in persuading Anaxilas, tyrant of Rhegium, to desist from attacking Locri, and above all, his support of Cumae against the Etruscans. Hieron's great victory over the Etruscans in 474 was crucial for the subsequent Etruscan decline and was equated by *Pindar with Gelon's victory over Carthage at Himera in 480.

Hieron cemented ties with other tyrants, Anaxilas of Rhegium and Theron of Acragas, by marrying Anaxilas' daughter and the daughter of Theron's brother Xenocrates. Yet his relationship with other tyrants never became totally harmonious. With his brother, Polyzalus of Gela, he maintained a hostile relationship and inflicted a major defeat upon Theron's son and successor, Thrasydaeus, which expedited the onset of democracy at Acragas.

Sensitive to contemporary opinion, Hieron laid no claim to the royal title and referred to his position on coins and inscriptions as simply "Hieron and the Syracusans." Courting popularity in the Greek world, he sent chariots and gifts to Olympia and Delphi. Hieron's court became a significant cultural center and attracted prominent literati, including Pindar, *Simonides, *Epicharmus, *Bacchylides, *Xenophanes, and *Aeschylus.

Hieron, after long suffering from gallstones, died in 466 and was succeeded by his son, Thrasybulus. Later Greek assessments of Hieron were divided, ranging from *Timaeus' extreme negativity to *Xenophon's and *Plutarch's more positive appraisals.

Bibliography: R. Hackforth, "Sicily," in *The Cambridge Ancient History*, 1983, V:145–164.

Lionel Sanders

HIERON II (306–215 B.C.)

Hieron II was the long-lived tyrant of Syracuse who gave the city two generations of peace, prosperity, and cultural advancements.

Hieron was a Syracusan officer serving in the army of *Pyrrhus of Epirus. From there he moved to the command of the Syracusan army, and in that capacity he defeated the Mamertines in 270. Upon his victory, Hieron was acclaimed king, a situation supported by his marriage to Philistis, a descendant of *Dionysius I. In the First Punic War (264–241), Hieron originally sided with Carthage in the struggle for Sicily, but after being bested by Rome in 263, the tyrant concluded a peace treaty that left Syracuse a Roman ally for the next fifty years. This alliance with Rome, coupled with a complete eschewing of any expansionist schemes, allowed Syracuse to enjoy years of unbroken peace and plenty as the city came to dominate the eastern half of Sicily.

During the same time, Hieron added to Syracuse's already lustrous reputation. Upon his rise to power, Hieron found Syracuse a well-administered city and a center of trade, wealth, literature, science, and art, where luxury and extravagance were the norm. As tyrant he continued the trends with his adherence to sound government and unstinted support for the arts. Hieron executed great public works, such as the rebuilding of Syracuse's magnificent theater and the construction of probably the greatest altar in the classical world. Cut from living rock, the altar was 650 feet long and 40 feet high. Under the direction of *Archimedes, who might have been related to Hieron, Syracuse's defenses became the strongest in the Mediterranean. Hieron also maintained a strong fleet, which at one point included a massive galley of over 5,000 tons. Hieron sponsored many artistic and intellectual activities and even authored a book on agronomy. The Syracusan dekadrachma of Hieron II is regarded by many as the finest coin in the numismatic record. Interestingly, one of the few artists not to receive Hieron's patronage was the famed poet *Theocritus, himself a native of Syracuse.

Hieron's long reign was also marked by a civil administration of the highest order. His tax code, the Lex Hieronica, copied in part from the laws of *Ptolemy II, was so thorough and effective that Rome later adopted it. Hieron accumulated huge surpluses of grain, which he used to great effect in diplomatic negotiations. The riches of the Syracusan treasury allowed Hieron to send 100 gold talents to assist Rhodes, as the city rebuilt after a terrible earthquake (225), and upon his death at ninety, Hieron left the city's coffers full. Remarkably, the tyrant accomplished all of this without recourse to bloodshed or brutality. One tradition related that Hieron tried to abdicate several times but was brought back by popular supplications. Another tradition had Hieron considering a democratic constitution for Syracuse but was turned from such designs by the intervention of his daughters. After his death in 215, his incompetent grandson, Hieronymus, took Syracuse over to Carthage during the Second Punic War (218–201). After its fall to Rome in 211, the city became a part of the growing Roman sphere of control.

Hieron II was arguably the greatest tyrant of the classical age. His long and wise reign produced a golden era for Syracuse, where the city's status and power were only exceeded by its wealth and culture.

Bibliography: M. Grant, *From Alexander to Cleopatra*, 1982.

Cyril M. Lagvanec

HIERONYMUS OF CARDIA (c. 360–260 B.C.)

Hieronymus was a Greek historian who recorded events in his own lifetime, beginning with the death of *Alexander the Great in 323. Though his account is now lost, it served as the basis for many later accounts that still survive.

Hieronymus was a participant in some of the events that he recorded, and he set a new high standard for objectivity and careful research in a period when history writing tended to be excessively dramatic and rhetorical. Hieronymus was a townsman and perhaps a relative of *Eumenes of Cardia, Alexander's Greek secretary. Eumenes became a leading figure in the tumultuous succession crisis that followed the death of Alexander, and Hieronymus joined his entourage when he was leading royalist armies in Anatolia. In 317, after Eumenes was defeated and killed by his rival *Antigonus (later Antigonus I), Hieronymus joined Antigonus and served both him and his descendants, who in time became the kings of Macedon. Hieronymus is said to have died at the age of 104 as a member of the court of Antigonus' grandson, *Antigonus II Gonatas.

Hieronymus supplemented his eyewitness testimony with documentary evidence, a practice that was rare for historians of his day. Later writers sometimes charged him with bias toward Eumenes and Antigonus, and their accusations have some merit. Still, his favoritism seems to have been tempered by a genuine regard for the truth. Perhaps the experience of following two patrons who were enemies of one another tempered the enthusiasm he might have shown for either patron separately.

Charges of favoritism aside, Hieronymus was well regarded in antiquity, and his account became the standard account of the crucial period of the Successors of Alexander. He was the main source for later accounts that survive, including *Plutarch's biography of Eumenes and the account of *Diodorus of Sicily.

Bibliography: J. Hornblower, *Hieronymus of Cardia*, 1981.

William Hutton

HILARY, SAINT (Hilarius, c. 315–368)

Sometimes designated as the "*Athanasius of the West," Hilary was a bishop of Poitiers and an important opponent of Arianism in western Europe.

Little is known of Hilary's early life except that he was born to pagan parents in Poitiers, spent some time studying Neoplatonic philosophy, and converted to Christianity as an adult. He became bishop of Poiters c. 353. Throughout his adult life Hilary was a participant in the controversy over the doctrinal definition of the nature of Christ. Supporters of *Arius argued that Christ was created by God to be God's son and an instrument of God's will but that Christ and God were not equal. Trinitarians, including Athanasius and Hilary, argued against this position, asserting that God and Christ existed together, coequal throughout eternity. Later, with further theological development, the latter position would become the orthodox doctrine of the Western church, but that outcome was not certain during Hilary's lifetime. In 356 when the Eastern emperor Constantius

II ruled alone, Hilary and other supporters of the Trinitarian position were exiled to remote parts of the empire.

While in exile in Phrygia, Hilary wrote his most famous work *De trinitate*, which articulates his orthodox position and his opposition to Arian doctrines. Other works by Hilary include: *De synodis*, *Opus historicum*, commentaries on the Psalms and the Gospel of *Matthew, and hymns. Although Hilary's discussions of the nature of God and Christ do not always accord with the orthodox position of the Western church as it was determined in succeeding centuries, in 1851 Pius IX declared Hilary a "Doctor of the Church" in recognition of his committed opposition to Arianism.

Bibliography: G.M. Newlands, *Hilary of Poitiers: A Study in Theological Method*, 1978.

Olivia H. McIntyre

HIPPARCHUS OF NICAEA (c. 180–125 b.c.)

Hipparchus was an astronomer, a mathematician, and one of the founders of trigonometry.

Hipparchus was born in Nicaea and spent his life working there, in Alexandria, and in Rhodes. He is sometimes referred to as Hipparchus of Rhodes. He made several important contributions to the study of astronomy, discovering the precession of the equinoxes, calculating the length of the year and lunar month, investigating the motion of the planets, and cataloging the position of the fixed stars. Hipparchus was the first to use trigonometry systematically, and he compiled books of tables of values for chord lengths that were based on the division of the circle into 360 degrees, a work that is equivalent to modern trigonometric tables for all angle measures in half-degree increments. He devised methods for solving spherical triangles and used a system of latitudes and longitudes for specifying location on earth and in the heavens.

Hipparchus made significant improvements to the instruments used in astronomy, and his calculations and observations show great accuracy. His calculation of the year's length is correct to within 6.5 minutes, and his value for the length of the lunar month differs from the currently accepted value by less than one second. He also produced more accurate estimates for the diameters of the moon and sun and further refined a system of epicycles to model the motion of the planets. The star catalog made by Hipparchus lists the position and magnitude of 850 stars with such accuracy that it was even used by Halley in the seventeenth century.

Bibliography: T.L. Heath, *A History of Greek Mathematics*, 1921; O. Neugebauer, *A History of Ancient Mathematical Astronomy*, 1975.

Michael Labranche

HIPPIAS (late sixth century b.c.)

Hippias was a tyrant of Athens in the late sixth century who came to power after the death of his father *Pisistratus.

Hippias was the son of Pisistratus, a sixth-century tyrant of Athens. He and his brother Hipparchus took power in Athens after Pisistratus' death in 527. These two leaders appear to have been patrons of the arts; Hipparchus is said to have invited poets such as *Anacreon and *Simonides to Athens and to have established the recitation of Homeric poetry at the Panathenaic festivals.

Hippias and Hipparchus, however, also had political enemies. In 514, Harmodius and Aristogeiton—wanting revenge for a series of romantic slights—plotted to murder the two tyrants at the Panathenaic festival. When they believed that their plot was about to be revealed, the two abandoned their original plan to kill both leaders and murdered only Hipparchus. After Hipparchus' murder, both *Herodotus' history and the Aristotelian *Constitution of the Athenians* report that Hippias' reign became even more harsh. During this time, the opposition of the Alcmaeonids—*Pericles' ancestors—to Hippias also intensified. After failing to remove Hippias by force, the Alcmaeonids built a temple at Delphi and contrived to have the oracle command the Spartans to free Athens every time they approached with a question. In 510/509, the Spartans under *Cleomenes I agreed, invaded Athens, and deposed Hippias.

According to Herodotus, Hippias escaped Athens to Sigeum and eventually to the Persian empire, where he hoped to persuade the Persians to help restore him to power. He returned to Greece as a guide and ally for the Persians at Marathon.

Bibliography: O. Murray, *Early Greece*, 2nd ed., 1993.

Jeff Rydberg-Cox

HIPPIAS OF ELIS (mid-fifth century B.C.)

Hippias was a sophist of the first generation.

Very little is known about Hippias. He was an ambassador of his native city Elis. Like other sophists, Hippias traveled extensively as a professional teacher. He was famous in antiquity for his mnemonic skills and mastery of all the sciences and arts. *Plato wrote two dialogues ridiculing him (*Hippias maior* and *Hippias minor*). Hippias was a polymath and wrote extensively in almost every literary genre, but nothing more than a few references to his work exist.

History seems to have been of particular interest to Hippias. He composed a complete list of Olympic victors, an important presupposition for dating events in history, and wrote a work called *Synagoge* that seems to have been the first systematic doxographic survey of previous writers. This work probably constitutes the base for the Platonic and Aristotelian accounts of earlier philosophy. Another book, *Names of Peoples*, may have been an ethnographic study. He was probably an original mathematician, too: It is known that he discovered the quadratrix and attempted to square the circle. Hippias set law in opposition to nature by claiming that the first is a tyrant establishing, against natural filiation, differences between humans.

Bibliography: G.B. Kerferd, *The Sophistic Movement*, 1981.

Fernando Oreja

HIPPOCRATES (c. 460–370 b.c.)

Hippocrates was a famous physician and founding father of Greek empirical medicine at the school of Cos.

We have little today but his name and countless theories and myths of his life and accomplishments. From his contemporary *Plato we know that he based treatment of local symptoms on general physical examinations and regimen, "treatment of the whole." Before 419 he left Cos to practice in Thessaly and perhaps Macedonia. It is to his sons and students in Cos that we owe some, probably most or all, of the sixty treatises written in the years 430–330, collected under his name in the third century b.c. and known today as the *Corpus Hippocraticum*. His work clearly constituted a revolution against the dream therapy and mind healing of Asclepiadean medicine (of which the tragedian *Sophocles was a priest and, to judge from his writings, practitioner) and against the basing of medical practice on speculative philosophical hypotheses.

His school described medicine as a *techne*, scientific skill, and required students to learn the nature of man and the individual and the symptoms of each disease before examining in detail the physical characteristics of any given. It laid emphasis on food, in particular undigested food and gas, and the digestive system, tracing the effects of the "salty, bitter, sweet, acidic, astringent, and insipid" and seeking digestive cures by a particular empirical procedure, the testing of the chemical effect of various drugs on substances outside the body. It adhered to the theory of four elements or constituents of the physical body, which it named "bile, black bile, phlegm, and blood," and sought a proper balance between them. Much of its practice was simple prognosis, for example, of the causes and anticipated progress of a high fever, from accumulated evidence of symptomatic histories in past cases and physical examination of the whole body. *Thucydides adopted this method in recounting the history of the Peloponnesian War and justifying the use of such histories.

Hippocrates was greatly revered by *Galen, whose works dominated Roman and medieval, even comparatively modern, medicine and were well known in Arabic medicine. The Hippocratic oath remains a model for medical ethics today. Aphorisms attributed to him had a wide vogue, including the famous "Life is short, science long, opportunity brief, experiment dangerous, judgment difficult." Because of his great fame and the lack of firm historical evidence, many legends about him later circulated—for example, that he burned the temple of Asclepius on Cos and healed King Perdiccas of Macedon of lovesickness. All our evidence combines to suggest that he was a practicing doctor engaged in amassing medical evidence from his own experience and left teaching and writing to others.

Bibliography: J. Jouanna, *Hippocrates*, 1999; G.E.R. Lloyd, *Magic, Reason and Experience*, 1979; W.D. Smith, *The Hippocratic Tradition*, 1979.

Robert Dyer

HIPPODAMUS OF MILETUS (c. 500 b.c.)

Hippodamus, known as the "father of city planning," is considered one of the most famous town engineers and architects found in Greek history.

It is unlikely that Hippodamus was responsible for the creation of the "grid-iron" planning found in Greek cities, but he did advance the idea of replacing broad straight streets that crossed each other at right angles for narrower streets that employed angular crossings. He is also credited with successfully promoting the idea of grouping homes and dwellings together in an organized fashion.

He planned the port city of Athens, the Piraeus, during the midportion of the fifth century. After that he moved to the colony of Thurii and, with the help of other colonists and architects, implemented the rectangular-shaped plan that gave him a place in history. It is because of Hippodamus' help in planning Thurii that he became known as "Thurian." Some time after completing the Thurii colony project, ancient authorities credit him with planning and helping to build the city of Rhodes. The idea has been questioned in modern times because the city was not founded until 408, thus making Hippodamus a very old man at the time. Even so, it is not impossible he had direct influence. Certainly the city bears at least an indirect influence because of the rectangular street patterns that are connected to his style of city planning.

Toward the end of his life, Hippodamus became increasingly interested in physical sciences and, for that reason, was ranked among the sophists. His political theories and foppish appearance brought him under the ridicule of *Aristotle.

Bibliography: F. Castagnoli, *Orthogonal Town Planning in Antiquity*, 1971.

Richard Draper

HIPPOLYTUS, SAINT (?–c. 235)

Hippolytus was a leader in the Roman church of the third century, and many Christian texts circulated under his name.

Hippolytus came to prominence in Rome following a controversy over the city's ecclesiastical organization. Callistus, one of Rome's bishops, had moved to establish himself as the sole authority. Such a monarchical episcopate had developed in the eastern churches more than a century earlier but was not a feature of the church of Rome. Callistus therefore faced bitter opposition. Although Hippolytus is sometimes regarded as the major antagonist to Callistus, he in fact seems to have been receptive to monarchianism and promoted reconciliation between the factions.

It is very difficult to distinguish the genuine writings of Hippolytus from the works later attributed to him. Certainly his are a commentary on the Bible's Daniel, a study of the doctrine of the Antichrist, and a treatise against patripassianism, a heresy that held that *Jesus was the incarnation of God the Father, not of God the Son. He did not write, but may have edited, the *Refutation of*

All Heresies. Preserved within its section on Greek philosophy are extracts from the writings of the Pre-Socratics, which would otherwise be lost.

Bibliography: A. Brent, *Hippolytus and the Roman Church in the Third Century*, 1995.

John Quinn

HIPPONAX (fl. c. 540 B.C.)

Hipponax was a Greek poet whose iambic works are characterized by invective and satirical attack.

Hipponax is said to have invented a variation of the iambic line, which ends the normal alternation of short and long syllables with three longs. His ending gives the line the name scazon ("limping") or choliambic ("lame iambic") verse. Hipponax was reportedly banished from his birthplace Ephesus and moved to Clazomenae. His poetry pioneered mythological parody and presented the rough-and-tumble existence of the poor. He describes a life of drunken brawling and sex with original, obscure, and obscene vocabulary. Later poets characterized him as a wasp, bitterly stinging his foes. Foremost among his enemies were the sculptor Bupalus and his brother Athenis. It is said the enmity arose out of a mocking sculpture of Hipponax that emphasized his ugliness. The rivalry with Bupalus and his love affair with Arete both figure prominently in the extant fragments. Of course, these may be ahistorical literary invention. How his poems were performed is not known, but *aulos* (pipe) accompaniment seems likely. Hipponax's poetry (both form and content) was admired and imitated by later poets including *Callimachus, *Herodas, and *Persius.

Bibliography: D.E. Gerber, ed., *Greek Iambic Poetry*, 1999.

C.W. Marshall

HISTIAEUS OF MILETUS (late sixth century–489 B.C.)

Histiaeus was tyrant of Miletus and among those Greek tyrants of Asia Minor who aided the Persian king *Darius I in his campaign against the Scythians in 515. He is better known as the instigator of the Ionian revolt at 499, the prelude of the Persian Wars (490–479).

During the Scythian expedition the Greek tyrants of Ionia were furnishing the fleet and were in charge of the construction and maintenance of the bridges that would assist Darius to cross the Hellespont and the Danube. Although urged by the Scythians to desert the Persians and destroy the bridges to hinder Darius' retreat, Histiaeus persuaded the other tyrants to observe their loyalty to Darius. He asserted that if they embraced the Scythian proposals to desert and then cause their cities to revolt, they would all fall from sole power. As reward for his guarding of the bridge over the Danube for the Persian troops, Histiaeus asked and received permission to rule and fortify the Thracian city Myrcinus, on the Strymon river. Soon, however, Darius suspected that Histiaeus might take advantage of his new settlement in Thrace and rebel against Persia and thus invited him to Susa and detained him at his court. This detention did not hinder Histiaeus from communicating to his son-in-law *Aristagoras the signal for the outbreak of the revolt of the Ionian cities against Persia in 499 by means of a tattoo of the phrase "cause Ionia to rebel" printed on the head of a slave. At the outbreak of the revolt, Histiaeus fled Susa and, in charge of a fleet, patrolled the area around Byzantium. Eventually, soon after the crushing of the rebellion by the Persians, Histiaeus fought on land near Miletus, where he was arrested by the Persians Artabanus and Harpagus and subsequently put to death (impaled). Histiaeus' ingenuity, especially his trick involving the tattooed slave, has given rise to scholarly arguments that doubt the historical identity of Histiaeus and support instead the existence of a folkloristic nucleus that turned into a biographical account.

Bibliography: G.B. Gray and M. Cary, "The Reign of Darius," in *The Cambridge Ancient History*, 1977, IV: 173–227.

Sophia Papaioannou

HOMER (fl. eighth century b.c.)

Homer is the poet to whom the composition of the two ancient Greek epics the *Iliad* and the *Odyssey* is ascribed.

What little we know about the poet himself comes from references within the poems. Although the poet does not introduce himself specifically, his portrait of the blind poet Demodocus in the Odyssey has been taken to be somewhat of a self-portrait. The language of the poems, a mixed dialect with Ionic predominant and Aeolic second, suggests that Homer lived in Ionia, an area of Greek settlements on the western coast of Asia Minor and the adjacent islands. The two most probable locations for his birth are Chios and Smyrna, and the ancient biographers of Homer agree that he died in Ios.

Although these ancient critics debated as to whether one poet or two composed the *Iliad* and the *Odyssey*, modern scholarship recognizes Homer as the poet of both texts. There is also agreement that the *Iliad* predates the *Odyssey*; both are dated to the second half of the eighth century—the former to 750 and the latter to 725. Both poems are composed in hexameter, the so-called "heroic meter." Both are divided into twenty-four books, and the poems share characters as well as poetic technique.

The *Iliad*, the longer of the two poems, tells the story of the wrath of Achilles, as the opening lines demonstrate. This story is set against the backdrop of the Trojan War. The Greeks, led by Agamemnon, had sailed to Troy to retrieve Helen, the wife of Agamemnon's brother, whom Paris, a Trojan prince, had spirited away. The poem begins, like epic poems do, *in medias res* (in the middle of things), some years after the Greeks had arrived in Troy.

Book I opens with the quarrel between Agamemnon and Achilles, provoked by Agamemnon, which results in Achilles' decision to remove himself from the fighting until his honor is restored. The poet never loses sight of the subject— Achilles' wrath—even as he describes the Greek and Trojan heroes and fighters in detail. Books II–VIII provide character analyses of Agamemnon (II), Diomedes (V), and Hector (VI), among others, at the same time as they depict the change in fortune of the Greeks. In Book IX, Homer reminds us of Achilles' anger and his reasons for it as he rejects Agamemnon's embassy. After the death of Patroclus, Achilles transfers his anger from Agamemnon to Hector and pursues him relentlessly (Books XVIII–XXII), killing him in Book XXII. The last two books resolve Achilles' wrath by showing him rejoining the Greek community and celebrating Patroclus' funeral (XXIII) and by consoling Priam, Hector's father, and himself (XXIV).

The *Iliad* is a tragedy that focuses on honor and the devastation of war. The Greeks have come to Troy to recapture Helen and restore Greece's honor. Theirs is the offensive position and theirs, more often than not, are the heroic victories. The Trojans fight to preserve their city, their women and children, and their homeland; theirs is the defensive position. However, Homer characterizes both Greeks and Trojans similarly, thereby emphasizing their common origins and the tragic stupidity that underlies the war.

In the *Odyssey*, the genre changes from tragedy to romance, the theme from honor to survival. The opening lines of this poem once again announce its subject: Odysseus' attempt to return to Ithaca and to reunite with his wife Penelope and son Telemachus. This poem, too, begins *in medias res*; the *Odyssey* begins ten years after the fall of Troy, when all the Greeks have returned home with the exception of Odysseus. The action opens in Ithaca, but not with Odysseus; rather with his son, recently come to manhood and forced to deal with 108 hostile suitors of his mother.

Like the *Iliad*, the *Odyssey* also has a theme that unifies it: reunion. However, unlike the *Iliad*, which unfolds linearly, the *Odyssey*'s structure is more complicated. The first four books, often called the *Telemachia*, narrate the adventures of Telemachus and his visits to Nestor and Menelaos to find out news of his father. Book V introduces us to Odysseus, marooned on Calypso's island; the next three books (VI–VIII) bring him to the island of Skheria and the hospitality of the Phaeacians. In Book IX, Odysseus identifies himself to the Phaeacians and relates his adventures from the time he left Troy, ten years before, up to the present day (IX–XII). The second half of the poem focuses on Odysseus' return home. In Book XV, the two strands of the narrative merge when father and son are reunited, and the poem ends with the killing of the suitors and Odysseus' reunion with his wife (XXIII) and father (XXIV).

Unlike the *Iliad*, the *Odyssey* focuses far more on one character. Odysseus is a master of dissembling, a master mariner, a master warrior, and a teller of tales. The story, like the ones Odysseus himself tells, is a blend of epic and folklore. The monsters Odysseus meets terrify his crew and evoke deep fears in his audience. It is not surprising that the *Odyssey* has been called the first psychological study as it details Odysseus' experiential quest for identity and knowledge in addition to his quest to return home. If Achilles represents the physical hero, the fighter, then Odysseus is the thinking man's hero. Given the choice, Odysseus will think his actions through, although he is more than able to fight heroically and win. It is, perhaps, due to this redefinition of heroism that scholars regard the *Odyssey* as the work of the older, more mature poet.

Both the *Iliad* and the *Odyssey* are the works of a master craftsman. Homer's poems are longer—as far as it is known—than any other epics of the period, but he has narrowed down the time frame of each poem and created or recreated each poem as a unified whole. They reveal his ability to choose and vary the stories, vocabulary, and epithets available to him; this ability, in turn, identifies him as a composer of oral poetry. A performing bard knew the stories that his audience would find entertaining, and the better the bard, the more he would imprint each story with his own style. That style derives from his knowledge and use of the techniques of oral composition, which include, among others: synonyms of different metrical shapes (allowing for easy insertion within a line), formulaic expressions (epithets like "the white-armed Hera"), type scenes (like the arming of the hero), and repetition (of a word, a line, or even an entire scene).

Homer's skill as an innovative poet made him the focus of ancient critics who turned to him to provide examples of rhetorical strategies. His poems, however, do more than simply provide fertile ground for a rhetorical examination of language, figures, and tropes. The *Iliad* and the *Odyssey* still excite and delight readers of all ages and backgrounds today.

Bibliography: M.W. Edwards, *Homer: Poet of the Iliad*, 1987.

Jana K. Schulman

HORACE (Quintus Horatius Flaccus, 65–8 B.C.)

Horace was a Roman poet who introduced Greek literary forms into Latin literature and developed an influential theory of poetry.

The son of a freedman, Horace was born in Venusia in Apulia (modern Venosa), where his father, an auctioneer, owned land. The family was wealthy enough for Horace to be educated in Rome and Athens, after the manner of upper-class Romans of the time. While in Athens, Horace joined the army of *Brutus, whose fall brought the loss of the family's property. Allowed to return to Rome (unlike many of his comrades), his poetry brought him into contact with the poets *Virgil and Varius Rufus, who introduced him to *Maecenas, a wealthy patron of poets and friend to *Augustus Caesar. The patronage of Maecenas (who gave him the famous Sabine Farm) allowed Horace the financial stability to devote his energies entirely to poetry.

His poems include the *Epodes*, *Satires*, *Odes*, and *Epistles*. The *Epodes* were his earliest writings, in which he introduced into the Latin language both the metrical form and subject matter of Greek iambic poetry. The two books of *Satires* offer an alternative to the aggressive and sometimes abusive tone of Menippean satire. Horace's satiric criticism is almost always intended to correct vice by calling attention to it, rather than to abuse the person in error. The *Odes* represent his lyric poetry. The first three books probably were published around 23; the fourth book, written at the request of Augustus, appeared several years later. The *Odes* introduced into Latin language the metrical forms and subject matter of the Greek ode, adapting both to the concerns of Augustan Rome. The *Epistles*, letters in the form of verse, offered him a vehicle for philosophic speculation on how one ought to lead one's life and for giving advice to friends. *Ars Poetica* (*The Art of Poetry*, also called *The Letter to the Pisones*) outlines Horace's influential theory of poetry, part of which asserts that poetry teaches by entertaining.

Bibliography: D. Armstrong, *Horace*, 1989.

Ron Harris

HORTENSIUS, QUINTUS (r. 289–286 B.C.)

One of Rome's most famous dictators, Q. Hortensius brought an end to the struggle between the orders.

During the 300s B.C., the Roman peasants had suffered increasingly because of debts. While overpopulation prevented all the sons of a farmer from obtaining farmland and deterioration of the soil in Latium also contributed to their economic plight, the peasants incurred the most debt when they engaged in their obligatory service in the army. Their frequent absence from their farms while on service made it difficult for their families to raise sufficient crops to sustain themselves and pay taxes.

Matters came to a crisis after the conclusion of a lengthy war with the Samnites. As the senators were the primary creditors, they refused to approve the relief legislation that the tribunes had demanded and that the Tribal Assembly had passed. Exasperated, the plebeian soldiers marched over the Tiber River to the Janiculum Hill and threatened to secede from the state. In response, the Senate appointed the plebeian Hortensius as dictator, who managed to alleviate the debt situation of the plebeians. He then passed the *Lex Hortensia* that stated that any plebiscite passed by the Tribal Assembly should become law independent of the Senate's approval. As a result of this law, the Tribal Assembly held more legislative independence than did the Centuriate Assembly. Nonetheless, the power of these assemblies remained fairly limited, for the assemblies could meet only when summoned by a magistrate, who might not share the interests of the plebeians. Furthermore, the assemblies could not initiate any measures but only vote on issues or candidates proposed to them.

Hortensius also altered the calendar in some way, perhaps by introducing the prescribed days on which assemblies might be held (*dies comitiales*). According to *Macrobius, Hortensius also authored a second *Lex Hortensia* that allowed lawsuits to be held on market days.

Bibliography: E. Staveley, *Greek and Roman Voting and Elections*, 1972; L.R. Taylor, *Roman Voting Assemblies*, 1966.

Judith Sebesta

HYPATIA (c. 370–415)

Hypatia was a mathematician, astronomer, and Neoplatonic philosopher who was brutally murdered by a mob of rioting Christians in Alexandria.

Daughter of the mathematician Theon, Hypatia revised the third book of his *Commentary on the Almagest* and wrote on the *Arithmetica* of *Diophantus and the *Conics* of *Apollonius of Perge, although none of her writings survive. She was also credited with inventing several scientific instruments including a hydrometer and a device for distilling water. Hypatia was most famous among her contemporaries as a teacher and for her leadership of the Neoplatonic school in Alexandria. She had many famous students including Synesius of Cyrene, later bishop of Ptolemais, whose letters to her survive. Considered beautiful, learned, and eloquent by her friends, Hypatia faced the bitter opposition of *Cyril, patriarch of Alexandria, who considered her the embodiment of pagan corruption and an enemy of the Christian community. In particular Cyril feared her friendship with the pagan prefect of Alexandria, Orestes. While Cyril's part in Hypatia's death has never been ascertained, it has long been held that Cyril encouraged a Christian mob to attack Hypatia and drag her through the streets while skinning her alive. After her death, many intellectuals left Alexandria for safer areas.

Little known for centuries, Hypatia emerged in the nineteenth century as a symbol for feminists of the historical suppression of women's accomplishments. In the twentieth century, *Hypatia* became the title for the leading English-language journal for women in philosophy.

Bibliography: M. Dzielska, *Hypatia of Alexandria*, 1995.

Olivia H. McIntyre

I

IBYCUS OF RHEGIUM (c. sixth century B.C.)

Ibycus was a Greek erotic and lyric poet of the sixth century B.C.

Ibycus was a lyric love poet in the court of *Polycrates of Samos, perhaps about 530 B.C., who invented the *sambyke*, a triangular cithara. He also wrote an encomium for Polycrates and mythological narratives on loves such as that of Zeus for Ganymede and Thalos for Rhadamanthos.

There are few surviving fragments other than isolated phrases or tiny bits of papyrus. These fragments are marked by the consistent use of Homeric language and the intense beauty of their images, often densely packed. From *Stesichorus he inherited the choral tradition of mythological narrative.

Two proverbs derive from events or legends of his life: "more foolish than Ibycus," because he refused the opportunity to become tyrant of Rhegium, and "the cranes of Ibycus," from the story that the birds who witnessed his murder led to the arrest of his murderers.

Bibliography: D.A. Campbell, ed., *Greek Lyric*, vol. 3, 1991.

Robert Dyer

ICTINUS (fifth century B.C.)

Ictinus was a Greek architect who helped build the Parthenon in Athens.

Ictinus was one of a number of architects who worked at Athens during the time of *Pericles under the supervision of *Phidias. According to *Vitruvius, Ictinus designed the Parthenon with *Callicrates, though there is some speculation that they were rivals and that Ictinus finished what Callicrates had already begun. Ictinus worked on the Parthenon between 447 and 438. He also designed the Odeum of Pericles and was involved in the rebuilding and enlargement of the Telestrion Hall at the Temple of Demeter and Persephone at Eleusis. According to *Pausanias, Ictinus designed the Temple of Apollo Epicurius (c. 430–

420) at Bassae in Arcadia. *Scopas claimed that it was the most beautiful temple in the Peloponnese, after the Temple of Athena at Tegea.

Ictinus was one of the most celebrated architects of Athens.

Bibliography: A.W. Lawrence, *Greek Architecture*, 5th ed., 1996.

Andrew G. Traver

IGNATIUS OF ANTIOCH, SAINT (?–c. 107)

Ignatius, who also bore the name Theophorus, was a bishop of Antioch martyred in Rome.

Little is known of Ignatius' life before he was condemned to death during the reign of *Trajan. While he was transported across Asia Minor to Rome as a condemned prisoner, he wrote letters of exhortation to Christian communities along the route. Seven of these letters are extant. The most frequently recurring admonition is the call for Christians to recognize a threefold hierarchy of clergy in their local congregations: bishop, priests, and deacons. Ignatius insisted that a bishop must be obeyed as if he were God himself; this is our earliest evidence for the development of the monarchical episcopate. However, addressing a letter to *Polycarp of Smyrna, he made it clear to the young bishop that the holder of such an office must be a diligent servant of his flock.

Ignatius was anxious to suppress the docetist heresy, which denied that *Jesus had a genuinely human existence, and had no sympathy for those Christians who wished to retain Jewish customs. He regarded the Eucharist as the actual body of Jesus and its celebration as the focal point of Christian assembly. Ignatius' letters reveal a special fondness for striking imagery. In a passage often quoted by later Patristic authors, Ignatius described how the Devil had been tricked into overlooking the incarnation and death of Jesus by the inscrutable silence of God's activity.

In all the letters, but especially in the *Letter to the Romans*, Ignatius exulted in his impending martyrdom. Comparing himself to a lover awaiting his beloved, he asked the Christians of Rome not to prevent his appointment with death by interceding with the authorities. Such a resolute stand inspired many generations of Christian martyrs.

Bibliography: W. Schoedel, *Ignatius of Antioch*, 1985.

John Quinn

IRENAEUS OF LYONS, SAINT (c. 130–200)

Irenaeus is one of the more important early Christian thinkers.

Irenaeus was born in Asia Minor, possibly at Smyrna (modern Izmir), where he saw and heard the martyr *Polycarp. After studying at Rome, he settled in Lyons, which had a sizable community of Asia Minor merchants, and he was soon elected as a presbyter of the Christian community there. The Church of Lyons sent him as a delegate to Rome, to intercede for "Montanist" Christians of the Asia Minor homeland who had been coming under increasing opposition from the episcopate. While he was in Rome, in 177, a short but bitter attack was made upon the Christians of Lyons, which cost the bishop Pothinus his life. When Irenaeus returned he was elected as bishop in his place, c. 178. His work as a theologian came into its own from this time onward, for his writings show how pastoral responsibility for the larger community tends to shape and govern most of his positions. Later in his life he again interceded for Asia Minor Christians at the tribunal of the Roman Church, when he advised Pope Victor, in 190, to take a more tolerant line with the so-called Quarto-Decimans, who followed a variant liturgical dating of Easter.

Irenaeus is most well known for the subsequent impact of his teachings about the Church. He lived in a time when the so-called Gnostic crisis was in full flow. Until modern times, his summation of the Gnostic theologians was one of the few major sources that scholars had for knowledge of their teachings, and Irenaeus himself was a hostile opponent to their doctrines. Since 1947 primary sources (the Nag Hammadi documents) have again become available, and the entire Gnostic question has been reassessed. Irenaeus regarded the Gnostic systems as all of a piece and hopelessly mired in mythic superstition. He saw them as driving a wedge between materiality and spiritual truth, of advocating a dualistic, pessimistic, and antimaterialistic view of reality, and of representing such a chaos of organization and teaching authority that they posed a grave danger to the continuity and coherence of the Christian movement. In fact, most of his anti-Gnostic apologetic survived to become the classical view of the Gnostic "heresy."

In arguing against the Gnostic teachers he had encountered, Irenaeus, somewhat like *Ignatius before him, turned to stress the importance of the role of the bishops as custodians, guardians, and teachers of the churches over which they presided. The bishops, he argued, were the direct successors of the apostles, who in turn were the direct successors of the teachings of Christ himself. Only in this pure lineage of historically provable teachers would the authenticity of the message of *Jesus be preserved. In other words, the succession of bishops was synonymous with "apostolic succession" and, in turn, with evangelical authenticity. Irenaeus also gave a strong role in his system of thought to the canonicity of the Bible. The biblical text was, for him, like a canon (standard rule of measurement) by which all true and false doctrines might be assessed. What was not present in the four gospels was not to be received by the churches. He stressed the central role of the Incarnation in the redemption of the cosmos and, against many of his Gnostic rivals, emphasized the importance of the appearance of the Logos of God within the flesh. The principle of Incarnation was highly important to him, and in this he had a major effect on the subsequent intellectual tradition of the Great Church. Little or nothing is known about his last days, though some sources recorded that he died as a martyr.

Bibliography: D. Minns, *Irenaeus*, 1994.

John A. McGuckin

ISAEUS (c. 420–c. 340 b.c.)

Isaeus was an Athenian orator who specialized in litigating cases involving wills and inheritance.

Little is known about Isaeus beyond his speeches. Of the more than sixty known speeches thought to be by Isaeus in antiquity, twelve survive. Of these speeches, eleven deal with matters of inheritances and estates. These works are known for their detailed exposition of the laws and circumstances surrounding the case. Because of the nature of the cases that Isaeus deals with, these works also provide valuable insights into social relationships in classical Athens.

Isaeus wrote in a plain style like that of *Lysias. Despite the personal nature of many of his cases, Isaeus did not attempt to portray the characters of his litigants and their opponents vividly in the same way that Lysias did in his speeches.

Isaeus is an important figure in the history of ancient rhetoric because of his technical mastery of the details of his cases and because of his style. He was also thought to have influenced and to have been influenced by several other important orators; he is said to have been a student of *Isocrates and a teacher of *Demosthenes.

Bibliography: G.A. Kennedy, *The Art of Persuasion in Greece*, 1963.

Jeff Rydberg-Cox

ISOCRATES (436–338 b.c.)

Isocrates was a Greek pamphleteer and teacher of rhetoric. He is perhaps most famous for his work the *Panegyricus*, which first encouraged the unification of the Greek city-states under the leadership of Athens and Sparta against the threat of Persia.

Isocrates was born in Athens into a wealthy family but lost his inheritance in the Peloponnesian War. In his youth he studied under the Sophists, notably *Gorgias of Leontini, and was also a follower of both *Socrates and *Plato. He began work as a speechwriter but soon became a teacher of rhetoric instead. At some point he opened a school of rhetoric on the island of Chios but returned to Athens c. 403 and soon after founded a school there. The curriculum in his Athenian school is a matter of some debate. It seems he not only provided just a theoretical training in oratory but also concentrated on preparing pupils for engagement in practical affairs and the politics of the day. The school was successful, and Isocrates regained his wealth. With the emergence of *Philip II of Macedonia and Greek resistance to him, Isocrates renewed his appeal for Greek unity and war against Persia. The *Philippus* published in 346 reiterates the sentiments of the *Panegyricus*. This was not to be, and when Philip crushed the Greeks at Chaeronea in 338, Isocrates' dream lay in ruins. He starved himself to death in the same year.

Although Isocrates never addressed the public as an orator, his written speeches give us a valuable insight into the political affairs of fourth-century

Greece. The orators Hyperides, Lycurgus, and *Isaeus, the historians *Theo-pompus and *Ephorus, and the general Timotheus were all pupils of his. His distinctive prose style was copied throughout the Greek world, and his tech-niques would later, through *Cicero and *Quintilian, make their way into the Latin West.

Bibliography: Y. Too, *Rhetoric of Identity in Isocrates*, 1995.

Karen McGroarty

J

JEROME, SAINT (Eusebius Hieronymus, c. 347–419/420)

One of the four doctors of the early Christian church, Jerome was a prolific translator, biblical commentator, and author of a wide range of ascetic, theological, and polemical works.

Born near Aquileia, Jerome studied at Rome and then pursued a career in the imperial court at Trier. He soon abandoned his chosen career, however, in order to take up a Christian ascetic life. At first he settled with like-minded friends at Aquileia, but about 374 this protomonastic group was shattered by internal disputes. He then left Aquileia for Palestine, eventually settling in Calchis, Syria. At Calchis, Jerome attempted to live as a Christian hermit, but in the end he proved unsuited to the solitary life. He was never able to forget the world he had left behind and instead maintained a lively correspondence and became enmeshed in a local ecclesiastical dispute. Jerome eventually abandoned his hermitage and traveled to Constantinople, where, in 381, he witnessed the proceedings of the Council of Constantinople and associated with one of the principal Greek theologians of the day, *Gregory of Nazianzus. Jerome then traveled to Rome, where he befriended and became secretary to Pope Damasus (366–384). He also began to associate closely with a group of aristocratic women, especially Paula and her daughters Blandina and Eustochium.

While at Rome, Jerome championed Christian ascetic life in such a way that he offended many. He used his considerable literary skill to ridicule Roman Christians, especially the clergy, for what he regarded as their lax moral character. He also praised celibacy in a way that denigrated Christian marriage. After the death of his protector Damasus and the scandal of Blandina dying at least partly from excessive fasting, Jerome found it necessary to leave Rome in 385 in order to avoid growing hostility toward him. Jerome then embarked on a roundabout journey to Bethlehem. In the course of this journey, Paula, who also had left Rome, joined him, and together they visited pilgrimage sites in Egypt and Palestine. The two eventually settled in Bethlehem and established a monastery for men ruled by Jerome and a monastery for women ruled by Paula. At Bethlehem, Jerome could not refrain from entering into further controversy. He argued bitterly with Rufinus, an old friend from Aquileia then residing in Jerusalem, over some of *Origen's theological propositions. In the course of this argument, Jerome also fell out with John, the bishop of Jerusalem. Toward the end of his life, Jerome participated in disputes with *Pelagius, unwisely attempting to link the views of Pelagius with those of Origen.

Jerome began his translation of the Bible when Damasus asked him to correct Latin versions of the four gospels, originally written in Greek. When he turned to the Latin Old Testament, Jerome made the inspired decision to use the Hebrew original rather than relying on Greek translations then in use. When completed, Jerome's translation of the Hebrew Bible came to serve as the standard text for the Latin West. This text, when combined with new translations of the Greek New Testament in which Jerome also had a hand, came to be known as the Vulgate. Jerome's interest in the Bible led him to comment on many biblical books. At first he relied heavily on the commentaries of Origen, but as some of Origen's theological propositions became increasingly suspect, Jerome attempted to distance himself from this early influence. It was perhaps Jerome's own heavy reliance on Origen that led him to become such a strident anti-Origenist crusader late in his life. Jerome's literary output was prolific in other areas as well. He has left more than 150 letters noted for their excellent Latin style. He contributed to our knowledge of history by continuing *Eusebius' *Chronicle* to 378 and composing a series of short biographies entitled *On Illustrious Men*. Jerome also composed three lives of saints, the most famous being *The Life of Paul the First Hermit*. Finally, Jerome contributed to the West's vision of the Christian ascetic life, both through his letters and biographies and through his translation of a monastic rule and other material from the Pachomian communities (cf. *Pachomius). Though more often derivative than original, Jerome gathered into one corpus an immense body of Christian literature that was to have enormous impact on the future of western Europe.

Bibliography: S.D. Driver, "The Development of Jerome's Views on the Ascetic Life," *Recherches de théologie ancienne et médiévale* 62 (1995): 44–70; J.N.D. Kelly, *Jerome: His Life, Writings and Controversies*, 1975; P. Rousseau, *Ascetics, Authority and the Church in the Age of Jerome and Cassian*, 1978.

Steven D. Driver

JESUS OF NAZARETH (C. 4 B.C.–A.D. 30)

Jesus of Nazareth was an itinerant Jewish teacher who after his death became the focal point of Christianity.

The most detailed accounts of the life of Jesus are four first-century Christian biographies (known as "gospels") that challenge readers to accept Jesus' unique relationship with God. These were written in the first century, at a time when eyewitnesses to Jesus' life were beginning to die. The earliest, *Mark, is also a primary source for *Matthew and *Luke: The overlap of material and "common perspective" leads to the term "Synoptic" Gospels. *John was written after these, probably in the 90s, and offers a different but not incompatible selection of material. Controversies surrounding the merits of these as historical sources for the life of Jesus provide a great range of opinion, from excessively skeptical approaches that deny any certainty to unquestioning and literal acceptance of the gospel accounts. Though the interpretative stakes are high, it is worth applying no stricter standard of proof than that used for other individuals from antiquity. So, for example, accounts of Jesus' birth, present in Matthew and Luke, which date the event to the time of King *Herod the Great (who died in 4 B.C.) need not be doubted, though it has been suggested that placing the birth in Bethlehem is an added detail, better to accord with Jewish expectations of the place of the Messiah's birth. First-century Judaism was filled with a diversity of movements, some of which were actively expecting a Messiah, an "anointed" descendant of King David who would spearhead the deliverance of the Jews from Roman occupation (similarly, the word "Christ" derives from the Greek word meaning "anointed," and it came to be used also as a proper name for Jesus in the decades following his death). While it might be right to question the interpretation of certain details in the gospels given the explicit ideological purpose of the works, many historical details are corroborated by contemporary Jewish and Roman sources, and the gospels clearly do contain historical data about Jesus.

Most of Jesus' life was spent in the village of Nazareth in Galilee, where he most likely lived with his parents *Mary and Joseph and his siblings, including one called James, and worked in Joseph's profession as a craftsman or carpenter (the word can also be used for a shipwright, which if relevant might explain the prominent place held by fishermen among Jesus' followers). The gospel accounts are largely unconcerned with Jesus' daily life before the beginning of his ministry. As a practicing Jew, his first language was Aramaic, though he probably also knew Hebrew and some Greek. Sometime c. 27–28 Jesus became associated with *John the Baptist, who urged piety and repentance because divine judgment was imminent. Following his baptism by John, Jesus began an itinerant ministry centered around the town of Capernaum in Galilee. His message initially was not significantly different from John and his followers, though it seems likely that Jesus saw himself as the climactic fulfillment of the hopes of Israel, actually inaugurating God's judgment. To this end, there are indications that Jesus actively sought to fulfill certain Messianic prophecies from the Jewish scriptures. His call for repentance and an immediate personal response was accompanied by teaching that inverted social norms. Jesus' teaching emphasized God's love for the disenfranchised and the humble and promised forgiveness for any wrongdoing for which there was sincere repentance. Sincerity, humility, and selflessness seem to have been prized above strict adherence to Mosaic law; however, he seems not to have explicitly opposed the law. Along with some contemporary Jewish thought, Jesus' teaching promised God's mercy and love to Jews and non-Jews (or "Gentiles") alike. His teaching appealed to the rural masses, and around him developed an inner circle of followers, which came to be known as "the Twelve." A distinctive form of teaching used by Jesus was the parable, a short metaphoric narrative describing otherworldly realities (such as "the kingdom of God") in everyday, rural terms using farming and shepherding images. As with *Homer's similes, the parables relate the remote to the audience's everyday experiences. The kingdom of God was promised to any that wanted it, and it was not to be established through political or military force. Wonder-working, of particular types paralleled in first-century Judaism, complemented this teaching. The majority of the miracle accounts describe healings and exorcisms, both of which are well established in first-century thought and practice. Jesus' actions are therefore exceptional, but not unique, as the gospels acknowledge. Jesus was both a teacher and a wonder-worker, and these two aspects cannot be separated from his perception of the fulfillment of God's purpose.

Late in his ministry, Jesus transferred his activities to Jerusalem, perhaps in anticipation of the Passover in the year 30 (33 is also a possibility, though less likely); he had hitherto avoided large cities. Jesus created a disturbance in the Temple grounds, apparently enacting a symbolic judgment on Israel. The high priest Caiaphas arranged for Jesus' arrest following this incident and passed him for trial to *Pontius Pilate, the Roman military prefect in Judaea. The transfer to the political authority allowed for capital punishment, and the charge was presented as a political one, drawing on the Jewish associations made with the title Messiah, from which it was understood that Jesus was claiming to be "King of the Jews." This claim may have been implicit in Jesus' teaching and in his deliberate attempt to fulfill Messianic prophecies, but there are indications he avoided the term in reference to himself, preferring instead the ambiguous term "Son of Man." This expression primarily means "human" but has Messianic associations in Judaism (cf. Daniel 7:13). Jesus was crucified as an insurrectionist on a Friday, during Passover celebrations in Jerusalem, and was given a hurried burial before the Jewish Sabbath. In the weeks following his death, many of his followers experienced something that gave rise to accounts of a resurrected Jesus, and for this they were prepared to be killed.

After his death, ideas about Jesus developed significantly. He became a theological figure whose death was seen by believers (now known as "Christians") to be the central act of human history, an atoning sacrifice for the sins of humanity by an individual who was somehow both fully human and fully divine: Christians traditionally view Jesus as the Son of God and await his return. Early Christians embraced many countercultural practices that probably originated with Jesus himself, including ritual foot washing among equals or even by social superiors. A letter by *Pliny the Younger describes the activities of the Christian church in Bithynia c. 111. This group included male Roman citizens, which makes the presence of female slaves in positions of authority (they are *ministrae*, or "deaconesses") all the more troubling to Pliny. It is hard to imagine an individual whose life and death have had an impact on Western culture as much as has Jesus. In three centuries, Christianity became the official religion of the Roman Empire, and Islam continues to honor Jesus as one of its prophets. A sixth-century dating of Jesus' birth by Dionysius Exiguus is used as the base point for Western calendars, dividing eras Before Christ (or Before the Christian Era) and *Anno Domini* ("In the Year of Our Lord . . ." or Christian Era).

Bibliography: E.P. Sanders, *The Historical Figure of Jesus*, 1993; E.P. Sanders, *Jesus and Judaism*, 1985.

C.W. Marshall

JOHN THE BAPTIST, SAINT (fl. 20s–30s)

John was the son of Zacharias and Elizabeth and is known as "The Forerunner of *Jesus Christ."

Outside of *Josephus' accounts and the reports in the gospels, little is known about John the Baptist. Josephus reports that John admonished his community to act justly and to practice piety. He baptized those believers or adherents who wished to be cleansed or reborn. According to Josephus, *Herod Antipas was threatened by John's popularity and executed him. Among the people of Judaea, Herod's defeat by Aretas, king of Retia, was popularly considered divine retribution for unjustly killing John. The Marcan (cf. *Mark) story adds that John lived an ascetic life in the wilderness, that Jesus was baptized by him and began preaching after his arrest, and that Herod had him killed at the instigation of his wife Herodias. John had criticized Herod for the divorce of his first wife and his marriage to Herodias. The Matthean (cf. *Matthew) narrative adds that John criticized the Pharisees, Sadducees, and the aristocracy of Jerusalem. His message did, according to the narrative, garner a following among the marginalized, the outcasts, and the tax collectors. The Lucan (cf. *Luke) tradition claims that John the Baptist and Jesus were related because their mothers were cousins.

Scholars reconstruct the balance of historical knowledge about John using sociohistorical methods. John most likely came from a family of rural priests, who were alienated from society and who shared enmity toward the aristocracy typical of the large peasant class of his day. Many argue that John was an "oracular" prophet in the tradition of Jeremiah. John's mission of "prophecy" is understood best when considered in the long tradition of ancient Hebrew and later Jewish prophets who pronounced judgment upon the aristocrat-peasant socioeconomic dialectic in Syria-Palestine.

John appeared in public as an apocalyptic prophet, preaching that the judgment of God would descend upon Israel. His message critiqued harshly the status quo and probably anticipated God's ultimate reordering of society.

Bibliography: C. Kazmierski, *John the Baptist: Prophet and Evangelist*, 1996.

Herbert Marbury

JOHN THE EVANGELIST, SAINT (first century A.D.)

John, the son of Zebedee, is the traditional author of the New Testament Gospel of John and the first, second, and third Letters of John, a disciple of *Jesus, a prominent leader in the early Church, and according to legend, the longest lived of the apostles.

John, the son of Zebedee, along with his brother James, was among Jesus' first disciples (late 20s). They had been partners with their father in a Galilee fishing business. They were apparently a prosperous family since they had their own boat and hired servants (Mk. 1:20). Some think their mother was a sister of Jesus' mother, and hence the brothers would have been Jesus' cousins. Jesus made them members of the Twelve, a select group of disciples representing the Twelve Tribes of Israel. They also constituted, along with *Peter, an inner circle of three, who were present at several significant events, including the Transfiguration (Mk. 9:2, Mt. 17:1, Lk. 9:28). Jesus called the brothers "sons of thunder" because of their aggressive natures. They angered the other disciples by requesting prominent places, perhaps cabinet posts, in the messianic kingdom, declaring themselves ready to face any ordeal (Mk. 10:35–41; Mt. 20:20–24 suggests their mother initiated the request for royal favors).

Following the Resurrection, both brothers were prominent leaders in the early Jerusalem Church. James was one of the first martyrs among the apostles, being executed on the orders of the Roman client Herod Agrippa (Herod III). His place in the inner circle of three was taken by James, the brother of Jesus, so it continued to consist of Peter, John, and (a new) James. At the time of the Jerusalem Council, probably in the 40s or early 50s (Gal. 2:2–10; cf. Acts 15: 4–30), *Paul named James, Cephas (Peter), and John as the "pillars" of the Jerusalem community. James, the brother of Jesus, was by this time the most influential Christian leader in Jerusalem. Traditionally, John, the son of Zebedee, made his way to Ephesus where he became a prominent leader in the Church there. Legend says he lived on into the 90s when he died of natural causes, the last of the apostles. *Irenaeus claimed *Polycarp for his report on the subject, and *Eusebius claimed other authority for it. Another tradition says John suffered early martyrdom in the homeland, but its erroneous identification of the agent of James' death renders it suspect. Some confusion may arise from the fact that *John* was a popular Jewish name. Papias named John the Apostle and John the Presbyter as prominent early leaders, and to them may be added John the Seer, author of the Revelation to John, among others. That the son of Zebedee was the evangelist may go back to an early tradition, or it may rest upon the identification of John as the anonymous "beloved disciple" whose testimony is claimed for the authority of the gospel (Jn. 21:24).

The Gospel of John is written in simple but fluent koine Greek. "The Fourth Gospel" is unique among the canonical gospels, as recognized by *Clement of Alexandria in his observation that John wrote "a spiritual gospel," as opposed to the more literal approach of the Synoptics. There is no evidence that John knew or used any of the Synoptic sources, though they share some stories, such as the Feeding of the 5,000 (Jn. 6:1–15; Mk. 6:32–44; Mt. 14:13–21; Lk. 9:10–17), the only wonder tale recounted in all four gospels. Rather, John seems to have had independent sources, including a tradition of seven signs that disclosed the glory of the Father, beginning with the transformation of water to wine at the wedding in Cana and ending with the raising of Lazarus (Jn. 2–12). John's literary style is unique. He embodies Jesus' teachings and his own thoughts upon them in long reflective discourses, unlike the aphorisms and parables of the Synoptics. John also differs from them in matters of chronology. John lacks the birth and infancy narratives of *Matthew and *Luke. Like *Mark he begins his narrative with *John the Baptist and with Jesus as an adult. But he has affixed prior to that a prologue that is a mystical midrash or meditation on Genesis 1:1–4, the first day of creation. It shows affinities with the Creation school of early Jewish mysticism. The Light of the first day of creation is the Logos, God's creative wisdom, which has "become flesh," a real human person, Jesus the Messiah. This incarnationism strikes a powerful blow against Gnosticism and other forms of Hellenistic dualism that were appealing to Gentile Christians. John drops the term *Logos*, which has obsessed many interpreters, after the prologue. But the contrast between light and darkness is utilized through the gospel (cf. Jn. 3:1–21). John also makes extensive use of ceremonial symbolism, especially the bread and wine of the Passover and the Christian Eucharist and the water of the Jewish *miqvah* (ritual bath) and Christian baptism. At Cana, Jesus made the best wine (Jn. 2:10). Baptism with the laying on of hands ("water and the Spirit") is new birth, birth from above (Jn. 3:5). Jesus is the bread of life (Jn. 6:35). On the Feast of Tabernacles with its water libation, Jesus offered "living water" (Jn. 7:37–39; cf. 4:13–15), and since it was also a feast of light, declared, "I am the light of the world" (Jn. 8:12). John seems to suggest that through profound acts of worship the ordinary person may know in a dramatic and symbolic way what the mystic experiences directly. Similar language and thought, including a strong love doctrine, have convinced many readers the gospel and the three Letters of John are from the same hand. Similarly, the radically different apocalyptic thought of Revelation and its less fluent Greek suggest that its author was another John.

Bibliography: R.E. Brown, *An Introduction to the New Testament*, 1997; C.E. Hauer and W.A. Young, *An Introduction to the Bible: A Journey into Three Worlds*, 4th ed., 1998.

Chris Hauer

JOSEPHUS (37–100)

Josephus was a Jewish diplomat, historian, and soldier in the first century A.D.

Details of Josephus' life are known from his *Life*, the earliest known autobiography from the ancient world, which is in essence a defense of his conduct in the war against Rome (66–70) and which contains relatively few autobiographical details. He was evidently an aristocrat, as he was descended from the Hasmonean dynasty of Jewish kings, and was also a priest. He claims to have been a very precocious child and spent time with the three main sects of Judaism (Pharisees, Sadducees, and Essenes). At the young age of twenty-nine, he became a general on the Galilean front in the Jewish war against Rome. Upon his surrender to the Romans at Jotapata, he became a Roman citizen, received a tract of land outside Jerusalem, and acquired a Roman surname, Flavius. He then resided in *Vespasian's palace in Rome and devoted his time to writing four main works in Greek (*Life*, *History of the Jewish War*, *The Jewish Antiquities*, and *Against Apion*).

Josephus' *History of the Jewish War*, an account of the Jewish revolt against Rome, emphasized the power of Rome and the foolhardy nature of Jewish resistance. *The Jewish Antiquities* was a massive history of the Jewish people from their biblical beginnings to his present. It is especially important because of the light it sheds on the postbiblical periods and on first-century Palestine. However, he rationalized many of the supernatural elements in biblical history, presumably to cater to a Hellenistic audience. *Against Apion* was an apologetic work where Josephus defended the Jews against anti-Semitic charges, while he attempted to show their superior ethics.

Josephus considered himself a historian in the classical tradition in spite of having many personal biases and occasionally contradicting himself (especially when it came to discussing his behavior during the Jewish War). Although his writings were rarely cited by Graeco-Roman authors, and were virtually ignored by Jewish authors, they were preserved by the early church fathers who were interested in them because they provided a context for early Christianity.

Bibliography: M. Lebel-Hadas, *Flavius Josephus: Eyewitness to Rome's First Century Conquest of Judea*, 1993.

Mark W. Chavalas

JUGURTHA (c. 160–104 b.c.)

Jugurtha was an African prince whose military successes against Roman armies precipitated a political crisis in Rome.

Jugurtha was a member of the royal family in Numidia, a north African region in which Rome had considerable business interests. He traveled to Spain and fought alongside the Roman army in 134, earning praise from Roman officers. Upon his return to Africa, his uncle Micipsa, king of Numidia, adopted him and promoted him to the status of his own two sons. After Micipsa died in 118, Jugurtha murdered one brother and forced the other to flee, thereby compelling the Roman Senate, concerned with commerce in the region, to mediate the dispute. The two brothers nevertheless remained rivals, and in 112 Jugurtha executed his remaining brother and some of his Italian supporters. Rome now lost patience with Jugurtha, and they dispatched to Africa over the next several years a series of armies led by aristocratic generals, but the Numidian prince maintained a successful guerrilla campaign against his better-equipped and -trained opponents. A political crisis developed in Rome as opponents of the aristocrats questioned the competence and motives of the generals waging the war, and eventually the lower classes succeeded in appointing their champion *Marius as commander (107). After three additional years of campaigning, Marius' lieutenant *Sulla captured Jugurtha, who was brought back to Rome and executed in 104.

Our primary source for Jugurtha is the historian *Sallust. His *Jugurthine War* depicts the Numidian prince as an imposing enemy whose military talents exposed the incompetence and corruption of the Roman aristocracy. Above all, Sallust argued, the episode of Jugurtha illustrated the political struggle between the Roman aristocrats and their rivals, which would be revisited most spectacularly in the careers of Sulla and *Caesar.

Bibliography: G.M. Paul, *A Historical Commentary on Sallust's Bellum Iugurthinum*, 1984.

David Christiansen

JULIA DOMNA (?–217)

Julia Domna was the wife of the emperor *Septimius Severus and mother of the emperors Caracalla and Geta.

Julia Domna was born in Emesa (Syria) of a humble background and married Septimius Severus after his first wife died. She was one of the most influential and public empresses, effecting her husband's foreign policy and active in domestic affairs. Domna's role in government was emphasized by her presentation on coins and in public sculpture where she appeared at the side of the emperor, as his equal and mother of his children. On coins her title "Augusta" often is emphasized rather than her relationship to the emperor. She is represented both on the Arcus Argentarius in the Forum Boarium and on the Severan arch at Leptis Magna. One of her contributions in Rome seems to have been a restoration of the Temple of Vesta. Julia Domna committed suicide by self-induced starvation in 217.

Bibliography: D. Baharal, "The Portraits of Julia Domna from the Years 193–211 C.E. and the Dynastic Propaganda of L. Septimius Severus," *Latomus* 51 (1992): 110–118; H. Benario, "Julia Domna Mater Senatus et Patriae," *Phoenix* 12 (1958): 67–70.

Lisa Auanger

JULIAN THE APOSTATE (Flavius Claudianus Julianus, 331–363)

The Roman emperor Julian, a former Christian, rejected Christianity and tried to reestablish traditional Greco-Roman religion.

The political environment of the mid-fourth century deeply marked Julian's life. As a member of the Constantinian family (cf. *Constantine), Julian experienced the execution of his father and brothers and virtual house arrest for much of his early life as his cousin, the emperor Constantius II, attempted to consolidate power. Even into adulthood survival remained precarious; Julian's elder brother Gallus was made Caesar (351), then executed by Constantius (354). Exiled to Athens, Julian studied philosophy together with future Christian leaders *Basil of Caesarea and *Gregory of Nazianzus. In 355 Julian married Constantius' sister Helena and was then commissioned as a military representative to Gaul. Julian demonstrated exceptional administrative and military ability in reorganizing the province after defeating the encroaching Germanic tribes. In 360 Julian's troops revolted against Constantius' orders to supplement the army on the eastern frontier. The army in Gaul proclaimed Julian emperor, and only Constantius' death in 361 prevented a civil war. After a two-year reign, Julian died in battle against the Persians in June 363.

Julian pursued his intellectual and ascetic predilections within Christianity, being baptized and ordained a deacon. Neoplatonic philosophers in Athens influenced Julian's embrace of traditional religion and his rejection of Christianity. As emperor, Julian sought to reform taxes, corruption, and religion—policies that made him unpopular from the start. The aristocracy resented attacks on their privileges. Christians worried about persecution and civil limitations (e.g., Christians were forbidden from teaching classics since they did not believe in the gods). In response, Julian tried to create a pagan "church" that imitated Christian charity and organization in hopes of reclaiming those who had been duped into Christianity through its social services. An able orator, Julian delivered two scathing speeches against Christians, *Against the Galileans* and *Beard-hater* (Julian sported a philosopher's beard). In general, pagan intellectuals were wary of Julian's revival, especially given its emphasis on ascetic simplicity and charity, which clashed with traditional pagan values of honor and wealth.

Bibliography: G.W. Bowersock, *Julian the Apostate*, 1978.

Lisa D. Maugans Driver

JULIANUS SALVIUS (L. Octavius Cornelius P. Salvius Julianus Aemilianus, c. 100–169)

Julian was the leading figure in the reorganization of jurisprudence, including revision of the praetorian edicts, under *Hadrian and one of the jurists most cited by fellow jurists.

Julian was born in the Roman province of Africa (modern Tunisia). He became a member of the imperial councils of the emperors Hadrian, *Antoninus Pius, *Marcus Aurelius, and Lucius Verus. Because of Julian's exceptional learning, Hadrian gave him double the usual salary for the office of quaestor, assigning him the responsibility of composing a definitive edition of the praetorian edicts. Julian's edition, which became known as the *Edictum perpetuum*, replaced the annual versions of each official and permanently set the governance of legal proceedings by which praetors, and probably aediles, could carry out their office. Julian, characteristic of the new type of jurist, held a series of offices, including consul (148), pontifex, governor of Lower Germany, Nearer Spain (c. 161–164), and Africa (167/168), and prefect of the state and military treasuries. He was also head of one of the two juridical "schools."

His *Digest*, a collection in ninety volumes of his own *responsa*, authoritative legal opinions, in various forms, was an inspiration and source for many other jurists and was used extensively in the compilation of the *Digest* of Justinian. Justinian's *Digest* lists Julian and *Papinian separately at the head of the chronological index of sources. Julian was especially known for his originality of thought and for his interest in cases involving ethical questions; he was and is considered one of the foremost, if not the foremost, jurists of the classical period of Roman law.

Bibliography: O. Tellegen-Couperus, *A Short History of Roman Law*, 1993.

Rebecca Harrison

JUSTIN MARTYR, SAINT (?–c. 165)

Justin was an early Latin apologist for Christianity.

Born in Flavia Neapolis (now called Nablus) in Samaria, probably of Greek parents, Justin studied philosophy at Ephesus with teachers of a variety of sects: Stoic, Peripatetic, Pythagorean, and Platonist. He was seeking religious truth, and until he met an old man by the sea at Ephesus, Justin thought he had found it in Platonism. The old man undermined Justin's confidence in his philosophy and pointed to the fulfillment of Old Testament prophecies in the life of *Jesus Christ. Already impressed by the courage of the martyrs, Justin converted to Christianity and became a Christian philosopher. He taught in Ephesus in the 130s and then moved on to Rome, where he became an active propagandist for his faith, disputing with pagan philosophers, Jews, and heretical Christians. His criticism of the Roman judicial system for persecuting Christians because of "the name only" drew down the wrath of the state on his own head, and he was arrested and beheaded around 165.

Justin is best known for his three surviving works, the *First* and *Second Apology* and *The Dialogue with Trypho the Jew*. In them, he tried to present an accurate picture of his religion to a pagan audience and to reconcile faith and reason. Some have seen his faith as a "corrected Platonism." His works are an important witness to the life and thought of the Christian Church in the second century.

Bibliography: H. Chadwick, "Justin Martyr's Defense of Christianity," in *The Early Church and Greco-Roman Thought*, 1993, 23–45.

Kimberly Rivers

JUVENAL (Decimus Iunius Iuvenalis, c. 60–130)

Juvenal was a Roman satirist known for his biting attacks on Roman life and society.

Little is known about Juvenal himself. There have been attempts to glean biographical information from his *Satires*, but the use of a satiric persona thwarts such efforts. We do know that *Martial addressed three epigrams to him, and it is possible that Juvenal was of high social status since he did not name a patron and had been educated in rhetoric. Evidence from the *Satires* provides loose dating: Book 1 was published around 112 during the reign of *Trajan (98–117), and Book 5 dates from shortly after 127 during the reign of *Hadrian (117–138). Juvenal wrote sixteen *Satires* in all, which are divided into five books and were probably published this way. The final poem, *Satire 16*, is unfinished.

In the *Satires*, Juvenal employs wit, indignation, irony, pithy epigrams, and exaggeration while drawing on forms and language from epic and other genres in his wide-ranging satire. In Books 1 and 2 he employs an angry persona who takes on public life and men in the first book and private life, especially women, in the second. Books 3 and 4 are marked by a calmer, more detached persona, whereas Book 5's persona rejects anger and views humanity with cynical superiority. Juvenal's example was influential in the Renaissance and beyond. John Dryden was one of his translators, and Samuel Johnson one of his imitators. Juvenal's name has been given to satire of a particularly biting, critical nature (as opposed to the gentler Horatian satire).

Bibliography: S.H. Braund, *Roman Verse Satire*, 1992.

Christine Cornell

L

LACTANTIUS, LUCIUS CAECILIUS FIRMIANUS (c. 240–320)

Lactantius was a Christian Apologist and was known during the Renaissance as the "Christian *Cicero."

Lactantius was born in North Africa and was a pupil of the rhetorician Arnobius the Elder. During the reign of *Diocletian, he was summoned to Nicomedia to teach rhetoric there. It is uncertain when he converted to Christianity, but he was a Christian by 303 and lost his position when the persecution began that year. He moved to the West in 305, he may have lived in Gaul, and he returned to the East c. 311. By 317 he was in Trier in the capacity as tutor to *Constantine's son Crispus.

Lactantius wrote many works, but the only ones that survive are connected with Christianity. His *Human and Divine Institutions* (304–311) sought to defend Christianity against the attacks of the philosopher and imperial official Hierocles; he also uses this work to commend Christianity to men of erudition. *De opificio Deo* (303–304) is an attempt to prove the existence of God by recourse to human anatomy. *De ira Dei* (c. 314) treats the divine punishment of evil, and *De moribus persecutorum* (c. 318) describes the evil fate of those who had persecuted Christianity. Lactantius also wrote a poem *The Phoenix* and an *Epitome* of his *Institutions*.

Of all the early Christian writers, Lactantius is the most classical in style. He uses pagan authors, namely, *Lucretius, *Virgil, and especially Cicero. While Lactantius wrote to support Christianity, he has little to say about the details of doctrine and organization.

Lactantius was the first Christian writer to combine Latin rhetoric with the defense of Christianity.

Bibliography: E.D. Digeser, *The Making of a Christian Empire: Lactantius and Rome*, 1999.

Andrew G. Traver

LARS PORSENA
See **Porsena, Lars**.

LEO I, POPE (c. 400–461)

Leo I was the most dynamic pope of the fifth century and the first to assert Petrine supremacy.

Leo was born around 400, probably in Rome to Tuscan parents. He was a deacon in Rome under Celestine I and served as adviser to both Celestine and Sixtus III. Away in Gaul when Sixtus died, Leo was called back to Rome and chosen as bishop of Rome in 440.

The most characteristic aspect of Leo's pontificate was his unwavering insistence on the primacy of the pope over the Christian church. To Leo, this primacy was based on the transferal of authority over the Church, which had been originally conferred on *Peter by *Jesus Christ, to each succeeding pope as Peter's heir. Just as Peter had had more authority than the other apostles, so the pope had greater authority than the other bishops. Leo's assertion of Petrine supremacy was upheld in the western half of the Roman Empire. In the East, however, he encountered opposition, most notably in the dispute over Monophysitism. In 448, the abbot *Eutyches was deposed by Flavian, the patriarch of Constantinople, for teaching the Monophysite doctrine that Christ had only one nature, as his human nature had been absorbed by his divine nature. In full agreement with Flavian, Leo sent him a letter (the *Tome*), condemning Eutyches and setting out the orthodox position that Christ has two permanent and distinct natures in one person. To his surprise, it was Eutyches' doctrine that was upheld at the Council of Ephesus in 449. Furious, Leo denounced the synod as a "robber council" and eventually saw his position prevail at the Council of Chalcedon in 451. However, he remained unreconciled to canon 28 of Chalcedon's decrees, which stated that Constantinople had primacy over the Church in the East.

Besides his theological formulations, Leo was also important for filling the vacuum of declining civil government in Rome. In 452 Leo met *Attila the Hun near Mantua and persuaded him to withdraw his forces. In 455 he met Gaiseric the Vandal outside the walls of Rome on a similar mission. Although he did not prevent Gaiseric from attacking the city, Leo did persuade him to spare it from the worst excesses of ancient warfare.

Bibliography: H. Jedin and J. Dolan, eds., *History of the Church*, vol. II, 1980.

Kimberly Rivers

LEONIDAS (?–480 B.C.)

Leonidas was a Spartan king and the Spartan general in the Persian War (490–479) who was made famous for holding the pass at Thermopylae against the Persians.

Leonidas was the Spartan given the command of the allied Greek land forces in 480. This was part of Greek strategy to use army and fleet together: The army was posted in the Pass of Thermopylae, on the Gulf of Malia, while the fleet was held nearby at the headland of Artemisium. Leonidas and his troops of Spartans and allies held the Persians in the pass for two days and inflicted heavy losses on them, while the main body of the Greek army was delayed by the festival of Carnea. But Leonidas' contingent was betrayed by Ephialtes, a Malian, who showed the Persians a mountain path that turned the Greek position. On learning what had happened, Leonidas dismissed his allies and gave battle with only his 300 Spartans. They died in this heroic last stand, and their famous epithet was written by *Simonides: Tell them in Lacedaemon, passerby/ That here obedient to their words we lie.

Leonidas and his Spartans are an emblem of Spartan devotion to duty, toughness, and courage, but his example inspires all heroic last stands.

Bibliography: E. Bradford, *The Year of Thermopylae*, 1980.

Andrea Schutz

LEPIDUS, MARCUS AEMILIUS (c. 90–12 B.C.)

Lepidus was a Roman politician and general remembered primarily for being a member of the Second Triumvirate.

Lepidus was born within the prestigious Aemilian family, whose ancestors had been active in Roman politics for centuries. He sided with *Caesar in the civil war, who rewarded his support by granting him a command in Spain (48–47) and a consulship (46). Caesar also arranged for Lepidus to succeed *Antony as "master of the horse," a position reserved for the chief lieutenant of the dictator. Following Caesar's assassination in 44, Lepidus became the chief priest of Rome and was assigned an army to campaign in Spain and Gaul. He supported Antony when the aristocratic Senate declared him a public enemy, and later he, Antony, and Octavian (*Augustus) used their armies to compel the Senate to grant them supreme authority in all political affairs. Relying on the power of this command, the "Second Triumvirate," the three men divided the legions and provinces among themselves, and they encouraged their countrymen to assassinate some 2,300 political opponents (43). Lepidus oversaw the interests of the Triumvirate while his colleagues traveled to Greece the following year to confront the armies of *Brutus and Cassius. After Antony and Octavian defeated the opposition forces in the Battle of Philippi, they lessened Lepidus' role by assigning him only the province of Africa, but still Octavian required his assistance in 37 in his war with *Sextus Pompey. Lepidus' failed attempt to seize Sicily for himself in the aftermath of the campaign provided justification for his complete removal from the Triumvirate, and Octavian banished him to the countryside. According to some sources, Octavian took pleasure in humiliating Lepidus until his death in 12.

Our chief sources for Lepidus' career are the accounts of the Romanized Greeks, *Cassius Dio, and *Appian. Historians are generally unanimous in their opinion that Lepidus' talents and political acumen were not equal to his pedigree.

Bibliography: R.E. Weigel, *Lepidus: The Tarnished Triumvir*, 1992.

David Christiansen

LEUCIPPUS (fl. 440 B.C.)

Leucippus was a pre-Socratic philosopher who founded the Atomist School of philosophy in Abdera.

So little is known about Leucippus' life and work that already in antiquity there were doubts about his existence. It is uncertain whether he was born in Elea, Abdera, or Miletus. Sources almost always mention him in connection with his disciple *Democritus, and it is not always possible to distinguish between the two. It is almost certain that he founded the Atomist School of philosophy in Abdera and that he established the principles of the old Atomist theory later developed by Democritus. He quite probably wrote a book entitled *The Great Cosmology*.

According to Leucippus, the world consists of an indefinite number of very little nongenerated and indestructible particles called atoms moving in all directions in the infinite void. Atoms are compact and are equated with the Being, while the void is the non-Being. Birth and death are only the conjunction and separation of atoms.

Leucippus has to be seen as the first in postulating a consequent mechanistic and materialistic theory of the world that exerted a decisive influence from antique to modern conceptions about the nature of matter.

Bibliography: D.J. Furley, *Two Studies in the Greek Atomists*, 2 vols., 1967.

Fernando Oreja

LIVIA (Livia Drusilla, 50s B.C.–A.D. 29)

Livia was the wife of the emperor *Augustus and the mother of *Tiberius and Drusus and assisted in the continuation of the Julio-Claudian dynasty as rulers of the new Rome.

Livia was first married to Tiberius Claudius Nero but was forcibly divorced from him to marry Octavian (Augustus) c. 38 B.C. By her first husband she was the mother of the emperor Tiberius and Drusus. For Octavian/Augustus, Livia was the ideal wife, active in cult and publicly supporting his governmental philosophy. In his will, Augustus specified that she be given the title "Julia Augusta" and adopted into the Julian family. Livia ruled almost jointly with Tiberius at the beginning of his reign, but Tiberius soon forced her to retire. She died in A.D. 29 of natural causes and was made *diva* under the Emperor *Claudius.

Livia was the first woman in Roman history to have her image systematically produced in portraits that were situated in public places. Many of these were posthumously produced and recognize her as a genitor of the ruling family. Livia herself was active in public building in Rome. She built a shrine to Divus Augustus, may have built or dedicated a temple of Concord (perhaps the same as the Porticus Liviae), played a role in the construction of the Macellum Liviae, dedicated the Porticus Liviae with a shrine to Concord with Tiberius, restored a temple of Bona Dea on the Aventine, and had a connection with the altar of Ceres Mater and Ops Augusta.

Bibliography: E. Bartman, *Portraits of Livia: Imaging the Imperial Woman in Augustan Rome*, 1999; R.A. Bauman, *Women and Politics in Ancient Rome*, 1992; N. Purcell, "Livia and the Womanhood of Rome," *Proceedings of the Cambridge Philological Society* 32 (1986): 78–105.

Lisa Auanger

LIVIUS ANDRONICUS, LUCIUS (c. 284 b.c.)

Livius Andronicus was regarded as the first Latin poet and playwright.

The preferred tradition puts Livius' birth around 284 in Tarentum, a Greek colony in southern Italy. He was probably at least part Greek, as his name "Andronicus" indicates; his full name is that of a freed slave. Livius was brought to Rome and served as a tutor to his master's children. He also taught other children as the earliest known *grammaticus*, teaching Latin and Greek literature at the second level of education. His translation of the *Odyssey* from Greek into Latin (in native Latin meter) was the first Latin epic, serving also as the first Latin literary textbook. In addition, Livius is credited with the first written Latin tragedy and comedy, based on Greek plots and meters, produced in Rome in 240. He subsequently acted and directed as well as composed. His hymn, commissioned by the Senate for public performance at a religious ceremony in 207, led to official recognition of his professional association of playwrights and actors, the first known granting of such status for literary activity.

Livius was influential as an innovative author and teacher, who introduced Greek literature to the Roman world and influenced the development of a separate, formal, Latin literary style. His works, though criticized by classical authors as archaic, remained a part of the standard syllabus for two centuries and continued to be studied by grammarians through the seventh century. Today, fragments of his *Odyssey* and of about thirteen of his plays are extant.

Bibliography: G.B. Conte, *Latin Literature: A History*, 1994.

Rebecca Harrison

LIVY (Titus Livius, 59 b.c.–a.d. 17)

Livy was a Roman historian whose account covered all of Rome's history from its origins.

Livy was born and lived in the northern Italian city of Padua. Although it is not known when, or for how long, he visited Rome and was on good personal terms with *Augustus. Little is known of his life. A daughter married a rhetorician named Magius, and his son may have been a writer. Besides his monumental history of Rome, he also wrote philosophical dialogues and a letter advising his son on rhetoric.

Although he has been called the historian of the Augustan age and, at times, his history has been described as Augustan propaganda, he was of independent mind as a historian and, relatively speaking, discriminating in his discussion of events. He gave special attention to major episodes of Rome's early history, constructing a national history in a lively style and with an emphasis on the importance of cultural memory. His attitude toward the past was necessarily ambiguous: Rome of the late Republic had fallen from the ideals and morals of its founding legends, yet had become a great power, an "empire without end." Livy's criticism of Roman morals in the late Republic, then, serves not as Augustan propaganda but rather as a sign of general dissatisfaction with a form of government that had run its course. Hence, Livy's book helps to explain the causes of the social reforms under Augustus. Most of the 142 books of his *Ab urbe condita* (From the Foundation of the City) have been lost. Only 35 survive: 1–10 (the arrival of Aeneas through the Roman subjugation of Italy), 21–30 (the Second Punic War), and 31–45 (the Macedonian and Syrian Wars). The books were divided into groups of five (pentads) or ten (decades). The first five books recount traditional legends of Rome's founding, up through its conquest by the Gauls in about 390 B.C. Roman tradition holds that the Gauls destroyed what written historical records the Romans possessed, an idea modern historians dispute. Although Livy ostensibly acknowledges this date as the boundary between "history" and "prehistory," marking the division between books 5 and 6, he makes no qualitative change in narrative mode but continues to recount the names, dates, speeches, and events just as before the break. Books 21–30, on the Second Punic War, owe much to *Polybius, and a comparison of the two authors does much to illustrate features of Livy's originality and style.

Bibliography: C.S. Kraus and A.J. Woodman, *Latin Historians*, 1997.

Ron Harris

LUCAN (Marcus Annaeus Lucanus, 39–65)

Lucan was a Neronian poet who wrote the ten-book Latin epic *De bello civili* (On the Civil War).

Born in Corduba, Spain, Lucan moved to Rome at an early age and was given an elite education, perhaps supported by his uncle M. Annaeus Seneca (*Seneca the Younger), who was tutor to the future emperor *Nero. Lucan was trained in Stoic philosophy by L. Annaeus Cornutus alongside the poet *Persius and in the late 50s went to Athens, until he was recalled by Nero to join his *cohors amicorum* ("band of friends") in 59. Lucan was honored for his encomium of the emperor at the newly established Neronia in 60 and was appointed quaestor and augur. None of his early poetry survives. Following these honors, Lucan began composing *De bello civili* (also called in modern times the *Pharsalia*), an epic, perhaps left unfinished, describing the beginning of the civil war between *Julius Caesar and *Pompey (49–48 B.C.), including the Battle of Pharsalus (48 B.C.). Lacking any clear hero and minimizing the role of the gods, the poem continually subverts allusions to *Virgil's *Aeneid*: The dismemberment of the epic genre parallels the dismemberment of the Roman Republic. The emperor's reported jealousy of Lucan probably stems from recitations and circulation of the first three books in 62 or 63. In 64 Nero banned Lucan from recitation. He then became involved in the unsuccessful Pisonian conspiracy against the emperor and in 65 took his own life. His wife Polla Argentaria survived him.

While Lucan was a model for Latin authors until the sixteenth century and his was the first classical poem printed with a press, his epic has not fared well since, typically suffering in comparison to Virgil. Christopher Marlowe translated the first book, and Shelley admired the poet, as had Dante centuries before.

Bibliography: J. Masters, *Poetry and Civil War in Lucan's Bellum Civile*, 1992.

C.W. Marshall

LUCIAN (c. 117–?, fl. 161–169)

In addition to philosophical works and essays in Greek, Lucian pioneered the writing of comic prose dialogues and can legitimately be said to have invented science fiction.

What is known about Lucian's life derives from his works, and since the works are comic in tone, there can be no certainty about any of the details. Nevertheless, it seems that he was born in Samosata, in Syria. His native language was probably Aramaic, though all his works are in Greek. In an allegory ("The Dream") he describes two women fighting over him, Sculpture, his uncle's profession, and *Paideia* ("Education"), with the latter being victorious. Lucian pursued higher education, and, after a foray as a lawyer in Antioch, became a sophist, traveling and giving oratorical displays. The learning displayed by Lucian embodies the spirit of the Second Sophistic period, drawing on classical models to present contemporary philosophical ideas in a witty and learned style. The variety of his works is immense: Pamphlets, biographies (both sincere and scornful), short talks, rhetorical exercises, a lighthearted treatise on historiography, and a short novel ("True Histories," often referred to by the Latin title *Vera Historia*) all demonstrate Lucian's cleverness, imagination, and appreciation of various philosophies. Further, the genre of short prose comic dialogue is first attested in Lucian. Lucian's dialogues include the collections *Dialogues of the Gods*, *Of the Sea-Gods*, *Of the Dead* (in which the Cynic philosopher Menippus is a prominent character), and *Of the Courtesans* (which reflect the same world often presented in New Comedy), plus there are several individual dialogues. He died sometime after 180.

The influence of Lucian's prose on subsequent European humorists is extensive. Perhaps most striking are the echoes of "True Histories," with its description of a moon voyage, on Thomas More, Cyrano de Bergerac, Daniel Defoe, Jonathan Swift, Jules Verne, and H.G. Wells.

Bibliography: C.P. Jones, *Culture and Society in Lucian*, 1986.

C.W. Marshall

LUCIUS
See **Paullus, Lucius Aemilius**.

LUCRETIA (?–509 B.C.)

Lucretia's rape and death, according to Roman tradition, precipitated the events leading to the expulsion of King Tarquinius Superbus (*Tarquin the Proud) and the establishment of the republic.

While Lucretia's husband Lucius Tarquinius Collatinus, the king's son Sextus Tarquinius, and other young men were besieging Ardea, they amused themselves by boasting about the excellence of their wives. To settle the argument as to whose wife was the most virtuous, they made a surprise visit to their homes in Rome. They found all their wives engaged in various amusements, except for Lucretia, who remained virtuously at home with her maidservants, spinning.

Sextus, however, became inflamed with love for Lucretia and came back alone a few days afterward. Lucretia offered him, as her husband's friend, hospitality, but during the night Sextus crept into her room. While she resisted him, he forced her to comply by threatening to kill her, murder a slave, and place his body in bed with him. To avoid this shame, Lucretia submitted to him.

After Sextus left the next day, she summoned her father, her husband, and her husband's cousin, Lucius Junius Brutus, and told them what had happened. She asked them to swear vengeance and then stabbed herself, saying that this was the only way she could prove her innocence. The men then told the whole story to the Roman people who, outraged, expelled the Tarquin family.

The story is most likely fictitious, being modeled upon similar Greek stories that link the expulsion of tyrants to moral outrages. In *Livy's account, Lucretia is presented as the model of the Roman matron, resolute in proving her chastity.

Bibliography: I. Donaldson, *The Rapes of Lucretia*, 1982; P.K. Joplin, "Ritual Work on Human Flesh: Livy's Lucretia and the Rape of the Body Politic," *Helios* 17.1 (1990): 51–70.

Judith Sebesta

LUCRETIUS (Titus Lucretius Carus, c. 94–c. 55 B.C.)

Lucretius was a Roman Epicurean philosopher and poet, author of a six-book hexameter poem *De Rerum Natura (D.R.N.*; On the Nature of the Universe).

Very little is known directly about his life. The only contemporary reference to him is in *Cicero's letter of February 54 to his brother Quintus in which he praises the poems of Lucretius for showing flashes of genius and great artistry. This suggests strongly that *D.R.N.* was already published by this date.

D.R.N. has been one of the most influential of all works of ancient philosophy in the Western world and was for a long time the main source for knowledge of Epicureanism. In this work, he expounds Epicurean physics, based on the atomic theory of matter, and ethics, which seek to free the human mind from fear of the gods, death, and fate, caused by superstition (*religio*). This is the single most important source for Epicureanism and ranks as one of the greatest achievements of both Roman philosophy and Latin poetry. Generally Lucretius is ranked with, or second to, *Virgil, as one of the finest of all Latin poets, and indeed Virgil, himself a former Epicurean, was heavily indebted to him as an inspiration and a source. *D.R.N.* has been one of the chief representatives of the anti-teleological view of the Universe: a view that denies any purpose in the world and removes from the gods any authority or role in human affairs. In Epicureanism, there is no fate or predestination, and any divine plan for the world is denied. All things happen through chance and physical necessity, but even physical determinism is rejected and free will placed at the center of the ethics. Thus, Lucretius has been one of the foremost influences in the development of the liberal temper in Western thought. He was deeply involved in the rise of Renaissance Humanism and later strongly informed the work of Erasmus, Montaigne, Rousseau, Gassendi, and others. Lucretius' fiercely anti-religious polemics and his antiteleological account of Creation inspired many anti-Lucretian Christian works, among them Sir Richard Blackmore's *Creation* of 1712 and Cardinal Polignac's *Anti-Lucretius* of 1745.

His account of the origin of life by the random formation of creatures without any divine plan, and adaptation of species by extinctions in a struggle for life, remained the chief opponent of the creationist view until supplanted in the role by Darwin's *Origin of Species* in 1859.

Bibliography: D. Clay, *Lucretius and Epicurus*, 1983.

Gordon Campbell

LUCULLUS, LUCIUS LICINIUS (c.118–57/56 B.C.)

Lucullus was a Roman statesman and general whose name became synonymous with luxury.

Lucullus was one of the rising generation favored by the dictator *L. Cornelius Sulla, under whom he had served. As consul in 74, he received command against King *Mithridates VI of Pontus with whom the Romans had been intermittently at war since 88. He regained Asia and Bithynia and forced Mithridates out of Pontus. He then returned to the province of Asia where he attempted debt relief (71), incurring the wrath of Roman financial interests that would lead to agitation at Rome against his continuing command. In 69 he routed Mithridates' ally, King Tigranes of Armenia at Tigranocerta, *Livy reporting that the Romans had never entered into battle so overwhelmingly outnumbered. His further invasion of Armenia (and the opening of hostilities with Parthia) was thwarted by a mutiny of his troops in their winter quarters at Nisibis (68/67), the soldiers' discontent having been fanned by his brother-in-law *Clodius. This gave Mithridates the opportunity to regroup. Lucullus' thunder was stolen by the subsequent campaigns of *Pompey (who replaced him in 66); and even his formal triumph was delayed three years by political infighting. He consequently set himself in bitter political opposition to Pompey, and his divorce of Clodius' sister and remarriage to *Cato the Younger's sister Servilia marked his conservative alignment. However, disappointment in the political sphere led to his virtual retirement c. 59, and he was chiefly remembered in the Roman tradition for his gardens in Rome, his style of dining, and the entertainments he enjoyed. His luxury became proverbial, the grandiose architecture of his seaside Campanian properties winning him the sobriquet "*Xerxes in a toga." He also amassed a large library that he made accessible to scholars.

Bibliography: A. Keaveney, *Lucullus*, 1992.

Tom Hillard

LUKE (first century A.D.)

Luke was a physician who accompanied the Apostle *Paul on his journey to Rome and wrote about one-quarter of the New Testament (the Books of Luke and Acts).

Details of Luke's life are sparse indeed. In biblical sources he is described by the Apostle Paul as a "beloved physician" (Colossians 4:14) and a fellow worker and companion of Paul (Philemon 24 and 2 Timothy 4:11). Moreover, the book of Acts contains a number of passages written in the first-person plural that describe events from the standpoint of a companion of Paul. These events included Paul's vision that requested his aid in Macedonia (16:10–17), Paul's imprisonment at Philippi (20:5–38), meeting with the Jerusalem council (21:1–18), and the Mediterranean shipwreck and journey to Rome (27:1–28:16).

Although the works are anonymous, early church tradition attributes the Books of Luke and Acts to Luke. Furthermore, they describe him as coming from Antioch in Syria and that he died at the age of eighty-four in the Greek province of Boeotia without having been married. Scholars have argued that he was either a Gentile Christian or a Jewish Christian of the diaspora.

The literary style of Luke and Acts betrays that the author was well educated and knew both Hebrew (Old Testament) and classical traditions. The terminology used in Luke-Acts (often seen as two volumes of a single work) is similar to that used in Graeco-Roman historical and biographical works. Although the Book of Luke contains details of *Jesus' life, Luke does not (like *Plutarch) write an exhaustive biography but concentrates on certain aspects of his life that best portray Christ's character. The Book of Acts, a description of the early church after Christ's resurrection, is primarily concerned with the deeds of Paul and his travels. It contains detailed speeches that are similar to those found in the Greek historian *Thucydides and the Roman historian *Sallust. However, Luke's intense interest in theological concerns causes his writing to be considered the work not only of a historian but of a theologian as well.

Bibliography: I.H. Marshall, *Luke: Historian and Theologian*, 1989.

Mark W. Chavalas

LYCOPHRON (third century B.C.)

Lycophron was a Greek poet and scholar.

A native of Chalcis in Euboea, Lycophron went to Alexandria c. 284. *Ptolemy II commissioned him to organize the Library's manuscripts of the comic dramatists. As a dramatist himself, he was included in the Pleiad, the elite group of seven Hellenistic tragedians. According to *Ovid, Lycophron was killed by an arrow.

While Lycophron was credited with writing many tragedies, only fragments of his work remain today; only a few lines exist of his satyric drama *Menedemus*. Lycophron was also a grammarian and a glossographer of the comic poets, and some of his glosses do survive.

Lycophron may have also written a dramatic dialogue entitled the *Alexandra*. This poem contains 1,474 iambic lines consisting primarily of Cassandra's prophecies about the heroes of the Trojan War. His authorship of this work was questioned in antiquity and has been more recently attributed to Pseudo-Lycophron.

Bibliography: T.B.L. Webster, *Hellenistic Poetry and Art*, 1964.

Andrew G. Traver

LYCURGUS (c. eighth–seventh century B.C.?)

Lycurgus was a legendary Spartan lawgiver and constitutional reformer. He was said to have founded the system of military training for which Sparta later became renowned and to have established *eunomia*, or "good order."

The existence of a historical personage named Lycurgus is a topic that has been debated since antiquity itself. Accounts of Lycurgus' life differ in various details, including dating and the specific reforms attributed to him. Our most complete account, by the second century A.D. biographer *Plutarch, probably represents a synthesis of traditions that had existed for centuries. Like other legendary lawgivers of archaic Greece, Lycurgus was rumored to have traveled widely and to have associated with the foremost sages of the day. Some writers believed that he borrowed his constitutional framework from Crete. After returning from his travels, Lycurgus sought confirmation for his reforms from the Delphic Oracle. Plutarch quotes a document, known as the Great Rhetra, that is an alleged recording of the oracle's response. During the visit, the priestess also reportedly called Lycurgus a god. Lycurgus was subsequently worshipped as a divinity in Sparta.

Lycurgus' reforms can be divided into three categories: constitutional, military, and social. Constitutionally, he is said to have established the board of elders known as the Gerousia. This council acted as a check against the power of both the kings and people. Some (but not all) writers also attribute to Lycurgus the establishment of the ephorate, the board of five overseers to the kings. Militarily, Lycurgus may have first enacted a redistribution of land that gave to each Spartan citizen an equal-sized plot. The allotment was designed to produce just enough food to keep a man and his wife physically healthy. Lycurgus also established a system of common messes known as *phiditia*. The messes formed the basic units upon which the Spartan military system was based. Each member was expected to contribute a share of his household's produce to the common mess. Boys, who were reared by the state rather than their parents, were admitted into the messes so that they might learn from the example of elders. Boys were also expected to undergo a hierarchical system of physical training, known as the *agoge*. Lycurgus enacted laws that were designed to complement the military structures he had established and to keep the city in a constant state of preparedness against its subject population, the helots. For instance, in order that they might devote their full attention to military matters, citizens were prohibited from practicing manual crafts. He outlawed many forms of luxury including, possibly, money. Perhaps his most interesting reform was his program of eugenics, aimed at producing the best possible warriors. Unlike throughout the rest of Greece, women in Sparta were encouraged to exercise in order to produce strong babies. Babies born with deformities were abandoned. Men were allowed to share wives, and married couples rarely saw each other; this created a mutual state of desire that was thought to result in stronger offspring.

According to Plutarch, Lycurgus died after securing a promise from the Spartan people that they would not change his laws. The legend of Lycurgus is part of an idealization of Sparta that occurred during antiquity years after Lycurgus reportedly lived. While there may have been a reformer named Lycurgus in the early history of Sparta, it would be difficult to attribute to him alone the many features for which Sparta was later admired.

Bibliography: R.J.A. Talbert, int. and trans., *Plutarch on Sparta*, 1988.

Luis Molina

LYSANDER (?–c. 395 b.c.)

Lysander was a Spartan general who aided Sparta in reestablishing the primacy of its naval forces and also became commander of the Spartan troops.

Lysander commenced his lifelong occupation as a Spartan army officer and statesman when he served as an admiral for the Spartan forces near the end of the Peloponnesian War. As a young admiral, Lysander's character was described as severe, strong-willed, and determined. It was because of his passionate qualities that he was appointed to lead the naval fleet. Lysander immediately magnified his office by reforming the Spartan fleet into an efficient and effective navy. Once the outfitting and training were complete he tested the navy in actual battle. He work proved effective in the battle at Notium (407), which precipitated the collapse of *Alcibiades.

Soon after Alcibiades' withdrawal, Lysander went to battle with the Athenians and defeated their fleet. Although it was against Spartan law to appoint the same officer to command a fleet twice in a row, Lysander was granted the privilege because of his extraordinary military talent. He moved against a powerful Athenian fleet and, by using superior naval skills, succeeded in capturing 170 of their ships at the Battle of Aegospotami (405). His tactics broke the back of the

Athenian fleet and brought the war to an end. Lysander subsequently besieged Athens and installed decarchies or boards of ten pro-Spartan officials throughout Athens' old allies in the Aegean. After Athens fell, a new government was created there, consisting of a board of thirty Athenian citizens sympathetic to Sparta (Thirty Tyrants).

After Lysander's victory over Athens, he lost touch with Spartan law and politics and became more involved in the Athenian lifestyle. Though he did not apply himself directly in the proceeding of Spartan politics and power, he still remained a powerful influence in governmental issues. In fact the election of Sparta's monarch, *Agesilaus II, is entirely credited to Lysander's efforts and influence in supporting Agesilaus' political campaign. After Agesilaus was placed on the throne, Lysander returned to Sparta where the Spartan government turned to him for help with the Corinthian War (395–386). The Spartans desired to receive aid from northern allies in order to defeat Corinth. Because of Lysander's popularity and fame, the Spartan government selected him to persuade these states to help Sparta in its plight. Lysander was successful in his endeavors in recruiting other forces to aid Sparta. While trying to rejoin his detachment with the Spartan army, he was surprised and killed by the Thebans.

Because of his arrogant and self-aggrandizing attitude, he was unpopular with many of his peers. His lack of popularity is reflected by the unsympathetic perspective found in the ancient literary sources.

Bibliography: A.H.M. Jones, *Sparta*, 1967.

Richard Draper

LYSIAS (c. 460–c. 380 b.c.)

Lysias was a speechwriter who was active during the late fifth and early fourth centuries in Athens.

Lysias was the son of Cephalus, a Syracusan who lived in Athens. During his youth, Lysias took up residence in Thurii, a Panhellenic colony in Italy where he studied rhetoric with Tisias of Syracuse. After the Athenians' expedition to Sicily, Lysias left Thurii for Athens to live as a resident alien. In Athens, Lysias and his brother operated a successful business until their property was confiscated by the Thirty Tyrants in 403. At this time, Lysias began work as a speechwriter, composing speeches for others to deliver in the assembly, the council, and the law courts.

Lysias was a prolific writer; it is probable that he wrote more than 100 speeches. Of these, 34 works survive. Twenty-three were written for delivery in the law courts, 8 were written for delivery in the assembly, the council, or before the Areopagus, and 3 were written for display or public performance.

There are two particularly noteworthy aspects of Lysias' style. First, he vividly portrays the character of those involved in his cases. Second, Lysias writes in a plain style with few rhetorical devices or complex sentences.

Bibliography: C. Cary, ed., *Lysias: Selected Speeches*, 1989.

Jeff Rydberg-Cox

LYSIMACHUS (c. 360–281 B.C.)

Lysimachus was a Macedonian general, satrap, and king who, as one of the successors to *Alexander the Great, came to rule a portion of his divided empire.

Lysimachus was a citizen of Pella in Macedonia, although his father was said to have been a Greek from Thessaly. He distinguished himself as a bodyguard for Alexander and came to prominence during the eastern campaigns in India. Following Alexander's death (323), Lysimachus received the satrapy of Thrace. He spent the next few years consolidating his position there and originally took a limited role in the wars between Alexander's successors. In the General Peace of 311, *Antigonus I recognized Lysimachus as satrap of Thrace. In 309 Lysimachus founded the strong capital city Lysimachia on the Hellespont; in 306, following the murder of Alexander's son Alexander IV, he took the title of king.

In 302, Lysimachus renewed an alliance with *Cassander, *Ptolemy I, and *Seleucus I and invaded Asia Minor to attack Antigonus. He and Seleucus defeated and killed Antigonus at Ipsus in 301, and Lysimachus received most of Asia Minor.

In 298 Lysimachus concluded an alliance with Ptolemy that ended in an exchange of brides. Lysimachus accepted Ptolemy's daughter Arsinoe as his third wife, while Ptolemy's younger son, *Ptolemy II, accepted Lysimachus' daughter, also named Arsinoe, as wife. When faced with this new alliance, Seleucus allied himself with Antigonus' son *Demetrius I Poliorcetes, who occupied Athens in 295 and seized control of Macedonia in the following year. While Demetrius prepared for an invasion of Asia, Lysimachus joined with King *Pyrrhus of Epirus to occupy Macedonia. Demetrius was defeated and died under house arrest in 283.

However, a bitter succession dispute threatened Lysimachus' control over Thrace. Due to court intrigue, and accusations of treason, Lysimachus had his popular son and heir apparent Agathocles executed. Agathocles' supporters fled to Seleucus and urged him to support their cause, thereby leading to a resumption of hostilities. Although both kings were now over eighty years old, Seleucus invaded Lysimachus' territory in Asia Minor. In 281, Seleucus defeated and killed him at Corupedium (Field of Crows) in Phrygia.

Lysimachus was a brilliant general and a patient statesman. After his death, Seleucus hoped to reunite the Asian and European portions of Alexander's empire. Seleucus' dream, however, remained unfulfilled as he, too, died in the following year.

Bibliography: H. Lund, *Lysimachus: A Study in Early Hellenistic Kingship*, 1992.

Andrew G. Traver

LYSIPPUS OF SICYON (or Lysippos, active c. 370–315 B.C.)

Lysippus was a prolific Greek sculptor in bronze, who gained renown as the favorite of *Alexander the Great.

Greek and Latin authors record his (i.e., his workshop's) prodigious output in various genres including portraits of athletes and public figures, heroes, gods, action groups, and animals. Many of his works were transferred to Rome. No originals by his hand survive, apart from inscribed bases, but many statue types have been identified, often overoptimistically, in Roman versions in diverse media. The most reliable attributions are the *Kairos*, *Eros*, *Apoxyomenos* (*Athlete Cleaning Himself*), *Alexander*, and *Heracles* (Farnese type), all supported by the detailed descriptions of ancient authors. This preserved visual evidence and copious written tradition indicate that Lysippus experimented with motion, space, proportion, naturalism, and scale. *Pliny the Elder praised Lysippus' scrupulous attention to detail and reports that he made the heads of his figures smaller and their bodies taller and leaner than did previous sculptors, giving them the appearance of greater height. His statement that *Polyclitus was his teacher appears to have been ironic, and while other ancient writers state that he was nobody's pupil, but looked to Nature, his illusionism is reflected in the remark of *Xenocrates that "he made men as they appeared to be." Lysippus' brother, Lysistratus, is said to have been the first to take plaster molds from live models for use in bronze-casting.

Bibliography: A.F. Stewart, *Greek Sculpture: An Exploration*, 2 vols., 1990.

Kenneth D.S. Lapatin

M

MACCABEUS, JUDAS (or Judah Maccabee, ?–161/160 B.C.)

Judas was a Jewish guerrilla leader who fought *Antiochus IV's policy of forced Hellenization.

Judas was the third of five sons of the Jewish priest Mattathias of the Hasmonean family. When Antiochus attempted to impose Hellenistic culture and religion on the Jews, Mattathias fled to the mountains and organized military resistance. Judas took over the rebel leadership upon his father's death and proved to be a formidable military talent, defeating four Seleucid armies in succession. In 165, he restored the Temple of Jerusalem by purifying it from its desecration by the Seleucids. To commemorate this event, Judas instituted the Jewish festival of light, Hannukkah. On Antiochus' death in 164, the Seleucids offered the Jews freedom of worship. However, Judas continued to fight, hoping to free his people both politically and religiously. Although he himself was killed a few years later, his brothers continued the fight, and his youngest brother, Simon, eventually secured the independence of Judaea.

Bibliography: B. Bar-Kochiva, *Judas Maccabeus. The Jewish Struggle against the Seleucids*, 1989.

Andrew G. Traver

MACROBIUS, AMBROSIUS THEODOSIUS (fl. c. 430)

Macrobius was a high-ranking Roman official and writer of the influential encyclopedic works the *Saturnalia* and the *Commentary on the Dream of Scipio*.

Little is known about Macrobius' life, though it is now fairly certain that he was writing in the 430s, not the 390s as was long believed. Some biographical details can be deduced from his writings: that he was probably born in Africa and became a Roman senator and later praetorian prefect in Italy in 430; that he was very well educated and proficient in Latin and Greek; and that he was probably a pagan.

Macrobius was the author of three works: (1) a discourse on Greek and Latin verbs (now lost, though a medieval abridgment is available); (2) the *Saturnalia*, a digest of classical learning for his son, cast as a series of Platonian dialogues with a focus on *Virgil; and (3) the *Commentary on the Dream of Scipio*, a discussion of the intellectual, moral, and scientific topics (particularly those relating to Neoplatonic philosophy) raised in a brief section of *Cicero's *Republic*. In the latter two works, Macrobius demonstrates his technique as an antiquarian: He idealizes the past and recasts key ideas into a form palatable to his readers, who are probably unfamiliar with the original Greek and Latin texts that are his sources.

Although they appealed to Christians throughout late antiquity and the Middle Ages, Macrobius' works do not refer to Christianity. They display instead an interest in Greek and Roman philosophy, religion, literature, and science. Because they were widely read and frequently cited, Macrobius' writings were important transmitters of much classical knowledge that might otherwise have been lost. Medieval writers recognized the *Saturnalia* and *Commentary* as convenient repositories of classical learning of relevant topics such as dreams, numerology, the soul, astronomy, and geography. As an important source of Neoplatonic and scientific ideas, the *Commentary* in particular became an influential text in the rise of scholasticism and the development of medieval philosophy and science.

Bibliography: W.H. Stahl, int. and trans., *Commentary on the Dream of Scipio by Macrobius*, 1952.

Antonina Harbus

MAECENAS, GAIUS (?–8 B.C.)

Maecenas was a leading adviser to Octavian (later *Augustus) and a patron of letters.

Maecenas descended from a prominent Etruscan family. His grandfather had been a leading member of the equestrian class, in the 90s; his mother could trace her ancestry back to the ancient rulers of the city of Arretium.

In the early years of the Second Triumvirate between Octavian, *Marc Antony, and *Marcus Lepidus, Maecenas became a firm supporter of Octavian. He accompanied Octavian on the campaign at Philippi (42), negotiated his marriage to Scribonia, and represented him on numerous diplomatic missions including those to *Sextus Pompey (40) and to Antony and his agents (40, 38). He was the intermediary in the renewal of the Triumvirate in 37. Although he never held a public office, Octavian entrusted him with the principal responsibility of maintaining order in Rome when he fought Sextus Pompey in 36 and during his final defeat of Antony (32–30). In 30, Maecenas detected and crushed the conspiracy of Marcus Lepidus.

Maecenas' most enduring mark on the Augustan Age lies in his patronage of letters. He himself wrote many prose works and poetry and established a reputation for his grandiose verses; these works only survive in fragments today. He subsidized *Virgil and supported the publication of his *Georgics*. He likewise sponsored both *Horace and *Propertius.

A rift seems to have occurred between Maecenas and Augustus later in his life. Augustus ceased to use him in diplomatic capacities and may have had an affair with his wife Terentia. When Maecenas died, he left all of his property to the emperor.

Through his patronage, Maecenas created a literary flowering that reflected well on the Age of Augustus.

Bibliography: K. Galinsky, *Augustan Culture*, 1996.

Andrew G. Traver

MAELIUS, SPURIUS (mid-fifth century B.C.)

Maelius was a wealthy plebeian who, after having relieved a famine at Rome at his own expense, aimed at tyranny.

Maelius was a wealthy member of the equestrian order and of plebeian origin who was reputed to have alleviated a famine in Rome in 440–439 by free distribution of corn at his own expenses. This generosity gained him popular support and encouraged him to seek election to the consulate, his ultimate ambition being to attempt a coup against the state and become a tyrant (*rex*). He failed, however, to be elected to the consulate.

At the same time, the famine situation in Rome called for state of emergency and led to the appointment of *Cincinnatus as dictator, soon to be followed by transferring to the control of the Roman government the food-shortage problem with appointment of Minucius as official undertaker of the food supply. This resulted, first, to the discovery of Maelius' conspiracy against the Roman state and, second, to Maelius' own death by C. Servilius Ahala, who was serving at the time as *magister equitum* (master of the horse) under Cincinnatus' dictatorship.

The historical kernel of Maelius' biography has been seriously doubted by modern critics, who attribute the conception of the entire conspiracy of Maelius to inspiration by events of the later Republican period (more specifically, the similar accusations against the *Gracchi brothers resulted in their persecution and tragic death). Moreover, it was becoming common practice among politicians in the later republic to distribute free grain to the people of Rome in exchange for their vote. Maelius' mention, on the other hand, in the work of the pre-Gracchan historian Cincius Alimentus cautions against complete rejection of the historicity of this early piece of Roman history.

Bibliography: R.M. Ogilvie, *A Commentary on Livy Books 1–5*, 1965.

Sophia Papaioannou

MANETHO (third century B.C.)

Manetho was an Egyptian scribe and priest of Serapis at Heliopolis who wrote a series of historical and religious works in Greek concerning Egypt during the reign of *Ptolemy II.

Details of Manetho's life are scanty at best. He appears to have been born in Sebennytus (the main city of Dynasty XXX) in the Delta region of Egypt. Although eight works were attributed to Manetho in antiquity, modern scholars only credit him with a history of Egypt (*Aegyptica*) and some unnamed cultic texts mentioned by *Plutarch. The original *Aegyptica*, which most likely contained historical narratives, is no longer extant, although portions were preserved by the Jewish historian *Josephus. Moreover, an abridgment of the *Aegyptica* made in the early Christian era that contained dynastic lists and annotated notes was preserved in part by Christian writers such as *Eusebius. Manetho's *Aegyptica* is significant in that it was the first historical work by an Egyptian written to instruct foreigners about the history and religion of his native land.

Bibliography: G. Verbrugghe, *Berossos and Manetho: Native Traditions in Ancient Mesopotamia and Egypt*, 1996.

Mark W. Chavalas

MANI (216–276)

Mani was a Persian religious visionary and the founder of Manichaeism.

From his early childhood in southern Mesopotamia, Mani was subject to visions and gained an awareness of his own heavenly protection. At age twenty-four, in reaction to another vision, he broke away from his religious attachments to the Elkesaites, austere Jewish-Christian Baptists, and answered the call to be an apostle, in the manner of *Paul, of a new message of light. His missionary journeys took him first through northwestern Iran, then to India. Other missionary preachers were sent at his behest, across the border into Roman territory. When Mani returned home after two years he found favor with the Sassanid king Shapur, so that Manichaeism enjoyed tolerance for thirty years. Though Mani wrote widely, only fragments remain. In 276 he was detained and executed upon the orders of the new Persian king Vahram. Manichaeism was nearly destroyed in Persia, but having gained even more appeal through Mani's martyrdom, it grew in central Asia and across the Mediterranean. In 297, the emperor *Diocletian's edict against the Manichees outlawed the religion and persecuted its followers. Manichaeism came to be viewed as a Christian heresy. Nevertheless, it continued to flourish, with varying success, and was observed in China as recently as the 1930s.

Mani combined Jewish, Christian, Buddhist, and Zoroastrian ideas into a doctrine with universal aims. It was a system based on the dualism of light and darkness and the effort to free the divine particles of light trapped in the various evil material bodies of this world. The few Elect devoted their lives to this salvific work through extreme ascetic practices including vegetarianism, fasting, celibacy, and avoiding ownership and the usual forms of work. They preached and studied and copied manuscripts (of Mani's letter and books, and a new book of Acts), waited on by the Hearers, who in turn confessed their sins to the Elect and received absolution from them. Manichaeism had wide appeal across the normal societal divisions. Famously, as he records in his *Confessions*, *Augustine spent nine years as a Hearer before rejecting that faith.

Bibliography: R.L. Fox, *Pagans and Christians*, 1987.

Mark Gustafson

MANILIUS, MARCUS (first century A.D.)

Manilius was the author of *Astronomica*, a didactic poem about astrology.

Apart from speculation that Manilius was either African or Asiatic Greek by birth, nothing is known of his early life. The poem implies that Manilius was both a Roman citizen and a resident of Rome. The *Astronomica* survives in five books, the fifth one incomplete. The latest event referred to in the poem is the defeat of Varus by Arminius in the Teutoburg Forest (9 A.D.) during the reign of *Augustus, and it appears that the fifth book was not written until the time of *Tiberius.

The *Astronomica* presents advanced views on astrology. Book one describes the creation of the heavens; book two, the zodiac signs; book three, the divisions of the signs; book four, their influence on men; and book five, their effect on children. Manilius occasionally imitates *Lucretius. The poem itself was probably never published and was neither quoted nor mentioned by ancient authors.

Although neglected in antiquity, Manilius' *Astronomica* has attracted the attention of modern Latin scholars.

Bibliography: M.R. Wright, *Cosmology in Antiquity*, 1995.

Andrew G. Traver

MANLIUS CAPITOLINUS, MARCUS (early fourth century B.C.)

Manlius was the Roman political and military figure of the early Republican period reputed to have averted the sack of the Roman citadel by the Celtic Gauls in 386.

Under Manlius' consulship, in 392 the Romans defeated the Aequi, an Italic tribe with whom Rome had frequently clashed. It was his association with the miraculous salvation of Rome in 386, however, that caused Manlius' name to become a legend for generations to come. According to popular tradition, Manlius was at the time a commanding officer of the Roman guard on the Capitolium, the ancient citadel of Rome. He discovered and repulsed a night attack of the Gauls against the citadel after being awakened by the crackling of the geese, the birds sacred to Juno; he subsequently assumed the name *Capitolinus*.

Critical opinions regarding the historicity of the incident are divided. Most explain it as aetiological myth, created and communicated by a branch of the Manlii family that lived on the Capitolium to explain their assumption of the cognomen Capitolinus. Others believe that the originality of Manlius' adventure should be received as guarantee of its historical authenticity, since the only detail challenging its credibility is the fact that geese were never known in Roman antiquity as birds sacred to Juno.

Manlius is also reputed to have supported the people (plebs) of Rome, despite his patrician origins, and even to have been impeached for tyranny. Yet this piece of information is of suspicious credibility, since the case of a prominent Roman politician and military leader who appropriates the support of the plebs in order to seize absolute power becomes a standard narrative motif in the earlier books of *Livy's Roman history.

Bibliography: R.M. Ogilvie, *A Commentary on Livy Books 1–5*, 1965.

Sophia Papaioannou

MARCELLUS, MARCUS CLAUDIUS (?–208 B.C.)

Marcellus was one of a handful of senators to hold repeated consulships during the Second Punic War (219–201) and whose martial skills and dogged determination earned him the sobriquet "Sword of Rome."

Marcellus served in the First Punic War (264–241) and held several governmental posts prior to his election as consul in 222. As consul he contributed significantly to the defeat of the Insubres Gauls, which earned him a triumph. Although recognized as one of Rome's best generals, Marcellus was not called upon when *Hannibal crossed the Alps. An underestimation of the Carthaginian's abilities coupled with constitutional tradition led to Marcellus being passed over. Only after the disasters at Trebbia (218) and Lake Trasimene (217) was Marcellus given a new command. In 216 he took over a band of marines and the disgraced survivors of Cannae and moved them into Campania. For the next two years, Marcellus threatened and harassed Hannibal, fighting three separate battles in the vicinity of Nola. In these engagements, the Romans fought their enemy to a draw. That Marcellus could meet Hannibal in the field and not get his army annihilated attests to the senator's abilities. In addition, these battles revived Roman morale and forced the Carthaginians into a war of attrition that they could not win.

Marcellus' successes in Campania earned him the consulship again in 214 with the mission to secure Sicily. *Hieron II had died in 215, and his grandson took Syracuse over to the Carthaginians. At the same time, Carthage dispatched an army to the island. Marcellus sailed to Sicily and undertook a three-year siege of Syracuse, which the Romans took in 211 despite the best efforts of *Archimedes to preserve the city. Marcellus also beat a Syracusan army at Acrillae (213) and cleared most of Sicily of Carthaginians.

Recalled to the mainland, Marcellus fought Hannibal again at Numistro in Apulia (210), which ended in another bloody stalemate. Thereafter, Marcellus harassed Hannibal in fine Fabian style (cf. *Fabius Maximus) until the Carthaginians went into winter quarters. After being elected to a fifth consulship in 208, Marcellus died in an ambush set by Numidian cavalry near the town of Bantia, near Venusia. This was on the eve of Marcellus' overseeing the combination of two consular armies.

Until he met *Publius Cornelius Scipio at Zama (202), Hannibal's greatest opponent was Marcellus. His tenacity and skill afforded the Carthaginians little respite in the campaigns of southern Italy or Sicily. Marcellus' exertions stymied Hannibal's plans and bolstered Roman spirits. If Hannibal admired Fabius Maximus as a tutor, he considered Marcellus his adversary.

Bibliography: J.F. Lazenby, *Hannibal's War*, 1978.

Cyril M. Lagvanec

MARIUS, GAIUS (c. 157–86 b.c.)

The historian *Sallust associates the rise in Marius' fortunes with the first challenge to the insolence of the Roman nobility. He became the supreme example in Roman republican politics of what the Romans called a *novus homo*, a "new man," achieving no less than seven consulships despite his nonaristocratic origins.

Marius was born into a wealthy equestrian family of high municipal standing from the territory around Arpinum. His first recorded military experience was gained under *P. Cornelius Scipio Aemilianus at Numantia in Spain, Marius reportedly attracting his commander's attention by his conspicuous bravery. He advanced in his early political career under the patronage of the influential family of the Caecilii Metelli but with dramatic displays of independence. He held the quaestorship c. 123, the tribunate in 119, and the praetorship in 115. After a successful command in Spain, Marius returned to Rome to marry Iulia from the patrician family of the Iulii Caesares, thereby forging a useful link with an established family.

In 109–108 he served in Africa under Q. Caecilius Metellus (Numidicus) against the Numidian king *Jugurtha. When Metellus rebuffed Marius' request to seek the consulship at Rome the latter denounced his commander's conduct of the war. After an unusual demonstration of support from the artisan class and peasantry and with the backing of the equestrian class, Marius secured election to the consulship for 107, persuading the people to overrule regular procedure and assign him the command in Africa against Jugurtha in place of Metellus. The two men remained bitter enemies. Having removed the property qualification for military service, Marius recruited volunteers for the campaign in Africa, in effect formalizing a process that had seen increasing numbers of *proletarii* enter the Roman citizen militia over the previous century.

In 105 Marius achieved victory after the capture of Jugurtha with the help of his subordinate officer *L. Cornelius Sulla. Because of the ongoing threat of migratory northern tribes, the Cimbri, Ambrones, and Teutones, Marius was elected in absentia to a second consulship for 104 and to an unprecedented succession of consulships for the four following years. During his northern campaigns Marius also adopted a number of changes to the equipment and tactical organization of the Roman army, in effect making it more professional. After eventual success against the northern tribes, Marius was hailed as the third founder of Rome and accorded quasi-religious veneration by Roman householders.

In 100 Marius' sixth consulship was marked by a falling out with the reformers *L. Appuleius Saturninus and *C. Servilius Glaucia, who had secured land grants for his veterans and the exile of his enemy Numidicus. After the murder of a consular candidate and the passage of the so-called ultimate decree of the Senate, Marius used force to suppress his former political allies. Despite their surrender and a pledge of safety from Marius, they were murdered by a lynch mob. The following decade appears to have witnessed a reduction in Marius' immense prestige and stature.

After limited service in the Social War (91–87) against Rome's Italian allies, Marius associated himself in 88 with the tribune *P. Sulpicius, who organized for the transfer of the command against *Mithridates VI from the new consul Sulla to Marius. This provoked Sulla's unprecedented march on Rome with an army and the realization of the revolutionary potential of Marius' creation of a client army with strong personal loyalty to its commander. When Sulla took the city and had Marius and Sulpicius declared public enemies, Marius fled to join his veterans in Africa. Subsequently assembling a fighting force and in collaboration with the deposed consul of 87, *L. Cornelius Cinna, Marius followed Sulla's example and took Rome by force. After the massacre of a number of his political opponents, Marius entered a seventh consulship in 86, dying during his first month in office.

After Sulla's victory in the ensuing civil war (c. 82) he ordered the remains of Marius exhumed and scattered as well as the destruction of the public monuments that had commemorated Marius' victories over Jugurtha and the northern tribes. The ancient source tradition, based on the memoirs of a number of political enemies (including Sulla), is generally hostile to Marius.

Marius' tenure of multiple consulships, five of them held consecutively, altered the political landscape. His enlistment of landless volunteers for the army, more an institutionalization of earlier developments than an outright innovation, recognized the changing nature of Roman society and its military needs but had in turn far-reaching implications for the role of the military on the Roman political scene.

Bibliography: T.F. Carney, *A Biography of C. Marius*, 2nd ed., 1970; R.J. Evans, *Gaius Marius. A Political Biography*, 1994.

Lea Beness

MARK THE EVANGELIST, SAINT (first century A.D.)

John Mark is the traditional author of the New Testament Gospel of Mark and a prominent figure in early Church tradition.

John Mark was the son of a woman named Mary who owned a house in Jerusalem, where she hosted early Church meetings. Theirs must have been a cosmopolitan Jewish family, since the son bore both a Hebrew (John) and a Latin (Mark) name. He is referred to as John in Acts (13:3, 13) but most often by the double name or, out in the Roman world, his Latin name. He first appears as a companion of his kinsman, Barnabas, and *Paul, on the "first missionary journey," probably in the early 40s (Acts 12:25, 13:1, 5). Mark did not stay the course but returned home, causing Paul to reject him as a companion on the "second missionary journey" (Acts 13:13, 15:38). This ended the Paul-Barnabas partnership, with Barnabas and Mark heading to Cyprus, while Paul and Silas embarked together for Syria, Cilicia, and beyond (Acts 15:36–41). The estrangement was resolved. Paul spoke highly of Mark as a coworker in some late letters (Col. 4: 10; Philem. 24: 2; Tim. 4:11) He was also associated with *Peter by I Peter 5:13. Legend identifies Mark as the youth who lost his loincloth and ran away naked during the arrest of *Jesus (Mk. 14:51–52). The fourth-century historian *Eusebius, reported a tradition from Papias (second century), which he got from "the elder," that Mark, who had been Peter's translator (i.e., from Aramaic into Greek), wrote down Peter's account of what Jesus had said and done "accurately, but not in order." Mark's was therefore widely regarded as a Petrine Gospel, though few modern scholars accept the tradition fully at face value. That this was an early tradition is confirmed by *Justin Martyr's reference (second century) to Peter's memoirs in citing material from Mark 3:16–17. Mark was also regarded as the founder of the Church in Alexandria. Venetian merchants are said to have transferred his relics from Alexandria to the cathedral of St. Mark in Venice (832). The lion is his symbol in Christian iconography.

The Gospel of Mark is believed by a majority of mainstream scholars to have been the earliest of the canonical gospels and to have been used as a source by *Matthew and *Luke, the other two "Synoptic" Gospels (i.e., gospels that share an implied chronology and take a like view of Jesus' career, in contrast to the Gospel of *John). At the beginning of Mark, Jesus is a mature adult. He receives baptism from *John the Baptist. At John's arrest, Jesus launched his public activity, announcing, "The Kingdom of God is at hand; repent and believe the gospel" (i.e, the good news of the Kingdom). Mark has been characterized as "the urgent gospel" because of the haste Jesus exhibited; Mark uses the term "immediately" eight times in his first chapter and forty times in all. It has also been called "a gospel of power" because the triumph of God's power over demonic forces is an important theme. Finally, it is "a gospel of suffering." It emphasizes not only that the Messiah must suffer to achieve his work but that his followers must also suffer (most appropriate if Mark wrote for Roman Christians after *Nero's persecution and the martyrdom of Peter and Paul). An intriguing note in Mark is "the Messianic Secret." Jesus forbade beneficiaries of his mighty works and even the disciples at the Transfiguration from prematurely disclosing his messianic identity, a prudent precaution in the revolutionary atmosphere of the time.

The best texts of Mark end at 16:8, with the bewildered and frightened women at the empty tomb. Scholars are divided over whether the gospel originally ended thus. Some think the original ending is lost. Few fully embrace any of several longer alternative endings, the most popular of which (Mk. 16:9–20, endorsed by the Council of Trent and followed by the King James Version) contains the words invoked by snake-handling sects (16:18). Codex W in the Freer Library, Washington, D.C., adds a passage after 16:14 in which the disciples offer an alibi for their failures and the Risen Christ promises an early end to the dominion of Satan.

Bibliography: R.E. Brown, *An Introduction to the New Testament*, 1997; C.E. Hauer and W.A. Young, *An Introduction to the Bible: A Journey into Three Worlds*, 4th ed., 1998.

Chris Hauer

MARTIAL (Marcus Valerius Martialis, 38/41–101/104)

Martial wrote almost 1,500 extant Latin epigrams, characterized by wit, pithiness, and at times vulgarity.

Martial was born in Bilbilis, Spain, and in 64 moved to Rome, having received a good education in Latin and Greek. Early associations with fellow Spaniards including *Seneca the Younger were cut short by the Pisonian conspiracy, though Martial maintained in association with *Lucan's widow. He worked as a poet and client and in 80 published a book of epigrams that now survives in fragments, commemorating the opening of the Flavian amphitheater, the Coliseum (this work is commonly called the *Liber de spectaculis*, or Book on the Spectacles). He aggressively cultivated the favor of *Titus and *Domitian, and was granted the *ius trium liberorum* (Right of Three Children) and an honorary tribunate, which conferred equestrian status and had other financial rewards. In 85 he had two books of witty mottoes published as Saturnalia gifts (books 13 and 14). Subsequent collections of epigrams appeared between 86 and 96 (books 1 through 11), and some were reedited. Most of these poems are occasional verse, written for real or fictional addressees, and subsequently gathered for publication. Martial owned a farm in Nomentum that produced some wine, but he lived unmarried in Rome. With the accession of *Trajan, Martial returned to Bibilis in 100, where he lived the remainder of his life. A final collection written in Spain (book 12) acknowledges the patronage of a woman, Marcella. Another of his patrons, *Pliny the Younger, mentions his death in a letter datable to 104.

Martial's verse is pointed and learned, drawing on the epigrammatic tradition of *Catullus. Since the Renaissance, Martial's poetry has been variously emulated by European vernacular writers and subjected to censorship, expurgating some of the poet's most brutal barbs.

Bibliography: D.R. Shackleton-Bailey, ed., *Martial, Epigrams*, 3 vols., 1993; J.P. Sullivan, *Martial: The Unexpected Classic*, 1991.

                                                                            C.W. Marshall

MARTIANUS CAPELLA (Martianus Minneus Felix Capella, fl. after 410)

Martianus was the author of *The Marriage of Philology and Mercury*.

Martianus was educated in north Africa, possibly at Carthage, and was an official in the provincial administration of the Roman Empire. He wrote sometime after the sack of Rome by the Visigoths in 410, perhaps as late as the 470s. Nothing else is known of his life.

His reputation rests on *The Marriage of Philology and Mercury*, one of the most influential educational works of the Middle Ages. Written partly in prose and partly in meter, *The Marriage* is an allegorical account of the heavenly ascent of the mortal Philology and her marriage to Mercury, the messenger of the gods and the god of eloquence. The first two books set out the background myth in a difficult and florid Latin style. The other seven books provide an introduction to each of the seven liberal arts: grammar, dialectics, rhetoric, geometry, arithmetic, astronomy, and music. Each art is presented by an elaborately described female personification. The work as a whole was thought to symbolize the union of eloquence and learning.

Although Martianus' perspective is pagan, his depiction of the heavenly ascent and of the arts was compatible with Christianity. His work also made the ancient teachings available in convenient form and was first appreciated by the third generation of Carolingians. In the twelfth century, writers like William of Conches and Thierry of Chartres admired Martianus for his views on cosmology. By the thirteenth century, his reputation as a scientist had begun to wane, but the allegorical setting of his work kept him in style until the fourteenth century.

Bibliography: W.H. Stahl, R. Johnson, and E.L. Burge, trans., *Martianus Capella and the Seven Liberal Arts*, 2 vols., 1971.

                                                                          Kimberly Rivers

MARTIN OF TOURS, SAINT (c. 316–397)

Martin was the bishop of Tours and the patron saint of France.

Martin was born in Pannonia to a pagan Roman military family. He was educated in Pavia, Italy, where he first encountered Christianity, and he became a catechumen. Drafted in the Roman army, he served his military service in Amiens. There he gave half of his cloak to a beggar, later revealed to him in a dream to have been *Jesus Christ. After this experience, he received baptism, obtained discharge from the army, and sought a religious vocation. *Hilary of Poitiers ordained Martin an exorcist following his discharge. Martin then traveled to Pannonia, Italy, and Illyricum. In 360, Martin returned to Gaul and, together with Hilary, founded the first monastery there at Ligugé. Martin resided at this monastery until 372, when the people of Tours chose him for their bishop. As bishop, he encouraged monasticism in Gaul and founded the monastery Marmoutier-les-Tours (Martini monasterium) outside of Tours. Moreover, Martin did much to evangelize the hitherto neglected countryside; he helped extirpate idolatry and introduced a rudimentary parochial system in the rural areas of Gaul.

When the dualist heresy of Priscillianism appeared in Gaul and Spain, Martin objected to turning heretics over to the state for punishment, as he felt that excommunication was sufficient punishment. Martin occasionally met with Emperor Maximus (383–388) at Trier and received a pledge from him that he would not execute the heretic Priscillian. When he put Priscillian to death (386), Martin protested vigorously and refused to hold fellowship with those bishops who sanctioned the execution of heretics. Martin died on a pastoral procession at Candes.

The *Confessio* attributed to Martin is not authentic. The primary source for Martin's life is Sulpicius Severus' *Vita*. Gregory of Tours, Martin's successor as bishop 200 years later, also composed a collection of miracles about him.

Martin was one of the most popular saints throughout the Middle Ages and was seen as the spiritual father of France.

Bibliography: J. Matthews, *Western Aristocracies and Imperial Court* A.D. *364–425*, 1990.

Andrew G. Traver

MARY (c. 22 B.C.–A.D. 35)

According to Christian tradition, Mary is the mother of *Jesus and son of God who, over the ages, has come to represent the ultimate in devoted motherhood.

What is known of Mary comes from the Bible and oral tradition. Born in Nazareth near the hills of Galilee in present-day Israel, then under the Roman Empire, Mary (born Miriam) belonged to a very traditional Jewish family. Of peasant stock, Mary's family probably made their living from agricultural pursuits. In accordance with Jewish tradition, Mary was betrothed at an early age—between twelve and fifteen—to a carpenter named Joseph.

Before the marriage could take place, however, Mary was found to be with child. Mary had conceived a child whose coming was announced to her by the angel Gabriel in an event called the Annunciation; according to Catholic tradition, she was chosen for this task as she had been born free of Original Sin—a privilege that made her the Immaculate Conception. Joseph decided to repudiate the betrothal quietly, but an angel appeared to him as well and told him the child was the son of God and would be the savior of his people.

As Mary neared her time, she and Joseph were called to Bethlehem to participate in an imperial census, and it was there Mary gave birth to Jesus, sometime between 7 and 4 B.C. He was acknowledged as the Messiah at his presentation, while Mary was told that a great sword would pass through her. As Jesus grew to manhood, Joseph taught him the art of carpentry, but Mary passed on to him the stories and practices of their faith.

According to Catholic tradition, Jesus was the only child of Mary, who remained pure despite his birth, but Protestant tradition holds that she and Joseph went on to have four more sons, and at least two daughters, and lived a rather normal life despite the extraordinary occurrence of Jesus' birth.

Mary was a guest at the wedding at Cana where Jesus turned the water into wine, and it is believed this miracle occurred at her instigation. She was among the four women who were present at the foot of the cross when Jesus was crucified; he addressed her as "woman" to show her as a disciple who would carry on his message.

It is believed that Mary did indeed spread the message of her son's teachings in her remaining years, about which almost nothing is known. The absence of biographical information about Mary in the New Testament led very early to the production of apocryphal accounts such as The Gospel of Mary. According to Catholic doctrine, after having completed her earthly life, Mary was in body and soul assumed into heaven. This event is referred to as the Assumption.

In the years since, Mary has come to represent many things to many people—the ultimate mother, the mother of sorrows, steadfast faith, virginity, and purity. Reputed appearances in connection with miracles have been associated with her over the centuries, and she has become one of the most recognizable and enduring images in art. She has thus become an icon for the Christian faithful.

Bibliography: S. Cunneen, *In Search of Mary*, 1996.

Connie Evans

MASINISSA (c. 238–148 B.C.)

Masinissa was king of Numidia and an important ally of Rome in the last stages of the Second Punic War (219–201).

The historical sources for the life of Masinissa are generally concerned with Roman affairs, and so they present his career chiefly in terms of his relationship with Rome. He first appears as an ally of Carthage in campaigns against the western Numidian chieftain Syphax (c. 213). In 211 he went to Spain as the commander of Numidian cavalry. There Masinissa distinguished himself as a skillful commander and tactician, especially of cavalry. His loyalty to Carthage, however, was based on national self-interest, and when the Romans defeated Punic forces at the Battle of Ilipa in 206, effectively ending the Carthaginian presence in Spain, Masinissa defected to the Roman side. In 204 he joined forces with the Roman commander *Publius Cornelius Scipio Africanus, who had landed his troops in Africa. He helped Scipio to defeat and capture Syphax, and he contributed significantly to Scipio's victory over *Hannibal at the Battle of Zama (202). The following year the Roman Senate rewarded Masinissa for his services by naming him king over the unified realm of Numidia. Masinissa continued to be a loyal supporter of Rome in its wars in Spain, Macedonia, and Greece. By provoking Carthage into invading his territory in 150, he set the stage for Rome to declare war on Carthage for the third and final time in the Third Punic War.

Masinissa was one of the earliest and best known "client kings" who, in return for service and loyalty toward Rome, ruled their kingdoms with Rome's support. He emerged from Rome's struggle with the Carthaginians with a kingdom that stretched in modern terms from Libya to Algeria. His son Micipsa succeeded him on the Numidian throne.

Bibliography: T.A. Dorey and D.R. Dudley, *Rome against Carthage*, 1971.

Carl A. Anderson

MATTHEW THE EVANGELIST, SAINT (c. first century A.D.)

Matthew is one of the twelve disciples of *Jesus and the traditional author of the first gospel in the New Testament.

According to the Gospel of Matthew, Matthew was a Galilean tax collector working at a toll booth in Capernaum when Jesus called him to become a disciple (Mt. 9:9). Matthew is also called "the tax collector" in the Gospel's list of the disciples (Mt. 10:3). However, in the parallel accounts in *Mark 2:14 and *Luke 5:27 the tax collector is named Levi, and Matthew is not identified as a tax collector in the lists of the disciples (Mk. 3:18; Lk. 6:15). Numerous solutions to the confusion between Matthew and Levi are possible. Traditionally, these two accounts have been harmonized, and commentators have assumed that Jesus changed Levi's name to Matthew after he became a disciple. A more likely solution is that the author of the first gospel had a list that identified Matthew as a tax collector and assumed that he should be identified with the Levi of the earlier Gospel of *Mark.

The name of Matthew was not attached to the first gospel until the latter half of the second century. Perhaps Matthew was a patron of the community from which the gospel originated. The reason why Matthew was associated with the first gospel is unknown. Church tradition maintains that Matthew preached first to Hebrews. In the first half of the second century Papias wrote, according to *Eusebius, that Matthew "collected the sayings in the Hebrew language, and each interpreted as he was able." Although the precise meaning of the Greek is unclear, most scholars have discounted the Papias tradition. Later traditions claim that Matthew preached in Ethiopia and in the East. Some traditions claim he was stoned at Hierapolis along the Euphrates, but others claim he died a natural death. None of these traditions, however, are historically reliable.

Bibliography: D. Guthrie, *New Testament Introduction*, 3rd ed., 1970.

Ronald A. Simkins

MEGASTHENES (350–290 B.C.)

Megasthenes was a Greek ambassador sent by *Seleucus I to the court of Chandragupta, ruler of the Mauryan kingdom in India. Megasthenes wrote the *Indica*, which served as the best contemporary source for India and was used for centuries by various authors, such as *Strabo, *Diodorus Siculus, and *Arrian.

Chandragupta reconquered northwest India and the Indus valley region following the death of *Alexander the Great. This conquest prompted Seleucus to think about expanding into the wealthy region to regain the territory Alexander once held. Seleucus invaded the region around 306 but soon realized Chandragupta's strength. Seleucus formally ceded the Indus valley, Gandhara, Swat valley, and east Arachosia to Chandragupta, but he kept west Arachosia. Megasthenes was serving as the ambassador to the satrap of west Arachosia when Seleucus asked him to serve as ambassador to Chandragupta. Following the tradition of Alexander, Seleucus sent Megasthenes to Pataliputra, the royal residence of the Mauryan empire, to gather information regarding the strength of Chandragupta. Megasthenes probably stayed in Pataliputra from 304 until 299, the time of Chandragupta's death.

The information gathered by Megasthenes presented Chandragupta as an absolute monarch, fully in control of his empire. He spent most of his day hearing cases in court, his palace was always open to visitors, and the people enjoyed relative freedom. Mauryan society was divided into classes (caste system) with each class performing a specific role. The majority of the population cultivated the land, while a class of professional soldiers served in the military. The Mauryan empire also had a class of bureaucrats who performed duties on a national and local level.

Megasthenes described Seleucus' eastern neighbor in a very favorable and possibly exaggerated light. Mauryan society seemed to match Greek society, and Chandragupta's army was certainly a formidable opponent. Seleucus may have used Megasthenes' information to forgo any attempt at invasion and establish diplomatic ties with the powerful Mauryan empire. Seleucus used the pretense that Chandragupta's people respected the idea of freedom; therefore Seleucus chose not to invade out of respect for their beliefs. The reality of the situation was that invading India was a difficult task, and there was a good chance of failure.

Although the information Megasthenes gathered may have been somewhat exaggerated, subsequent travelers to the Mauryan empire brought back similar stories, prompting the successors of Seleucus to maintain diplomatic ties with the successors of Chandragupta. Megasthenes' importance lies in the detailed information, used for many centuries, about a supposedly barbarian region that proved to be not too unlike Greek society.

Bibliography: R.K. Mookerji, *Chandragupta Maurya and His Times*, 4th ed., 1966; S. Sherwin-White and A. Kuhrt, *From Samarkhand to Sardis*, 1993.

Paul Miller

MELEAGER (early first century B.C.)

Meleager was a poet, anthologist, satirist, and Cynic philosopher of considerable ability.

He summarizes his life in four mock epitaphs telling of his birth in cultured Gadara ("an Athens in Syria"), adolescence in once Phoenician Tyre, and old age in the cosmopolitan island of Cos, where he received citizenship. As an itinerant Cynic sophist, his early works were Menippean satires (now lost), in which he expressed mockery at the foibles of mankind in a mixture of prose and poetry. His outlook resembles the cosmopolitanism upheld in the Cynic movement. Some of this philosophy is found in his epigrams, often full of self-deprecating humor. Others are love poems dedicated to the girls and boys of Tyre, describing his torturous emotions with great vividness. Yet others are whimsical nature poems spoken to the cicadas and grasshoppers of the countryside. His writing is famous for attaining great beauty through few words, composed in a simple and lucid style, though conforming to the structure of the traditional epigram to which he added greater depth.

Meleager is also famous for composing one of the earliest anthologies of Greek poetry, *The Garland*, which is the basis of our surviving Byzantine *Greek Anthology*. The poems are excerpted from the early lyric poets of Lesbos down to close before his own time. His list of contents survives, written in the form of a poem, in which he compares each author to a separate flower (*anthos*). Many of his own poems are also preserved in the *Greek Anthology*.

Bibliography: K.J. Gutzwill, *Poetic Garlands: Hellenistic Epigrams in Context*, 1998; P. Whigham and P. Jay, trans., *The Poems of Meleager*, 1975.

Menahem Luz

MENANDER (342/341–c. 292/291 B.C.)

After his death, Menander was considered the leading playwright of Greek New Comedy.

Menander was born to a good family in Athens and c. 321 produced his first play, *Orgê* (Anger). He is said to have written over 100 plays, though he only won eight victories. If he was this prolific, many of his plays must have been presented outside of Athens and at minor festivals. It is said he was taught by *Theophrastus and the comic playwright Alexis, but this may be extrapolation based on perceived influences. He is also associated with *Demetrius of Phalerum, the pro-Macedonian governor of Athens from 317 to 307. In 316, *Dyskolos* (The Angry Old Man) was victorious at the Lenaea. This is the only play to survive complete, though substantial fragments also exist of *Samia* (The Samian Girl), *Epitrepontes* (The Arbitration), *Aspis* (The Shield), and several other plays. The plays are typically set in Athens and deal with young lovers overcoming obstacles to be united with one another. Menander displays a delight in elegantly balanced plots and gentle humor. His wit appears in dramatic structure, word play, and the secularization of Euripidean motifs: For example, *Epitrepontes* adapts a plot device from *Euripides' lost tragedy *Auge*. *Aristophanes of Byzantium famously praised the natural feel of Menander's dialogue, "O Menander! O Life! Which of you copied the other?" The exaggeration here is underlined when it is remembered that Menander's plays were in verse, acted by male, masked actors. Menander seems to have been considered good-looking but had a squint.

The Romans idealized Menander's comedy. *Plutarch's hyperbole says there is no reason to go to the theater except to see Menander. *Plautus and *Terence adapted his works in their drama, and imperial theatrical mosaics show the esteem in which Menander was held. Many short excerpts were preserved due to their sententious quality, but the absence of substantial passages has made any evaluation of the ancient claims impossible until the twentieth century. Papyrus finds, particularly of the Cairo Codex in 1905 and the Bodmer papyrus in the 1950s, have led to significant reappraisals of Menander's dramaturgy and place in literary history.

Bibliography: W.G. Arnott, ed., *Menander*, 3 vols., 1979–2000.

C.W. Marshall

MICON (or Mikon, fl. c. 470–450 b.c.)

Micon was an Athenian painter.

Like his contemporary and colleague *Polygnotus, Micon is known through literary sources, rather than physical remains. His lost works, however, are described in considerable detail by Greek and Roman authors and may be reflected in contemporary painted pottery. He painted *Theseus and Minos* and probably an *Amazonomachy* and *Centauromachy* in the Thesion at Athens; in the Peisianakteion (a.k.a. "Painted Stoa") was another *Amazonomachy*, and some ancient authors also attribute to him the famous depiction of the *Battle of Marathon* there. His treatment of space, like that of Polygnotus, was considered innovative: in his *Argonauts* in the Anakeion he positioned the hero Butes so that only his head and eye appeared above a hill.

*Pausanias praises his rendering of horses, but some found fault with them as he included eyelashes on the lower lid, where they do not occur in nature. Like Polygnotus, he probably painted with hot wax on wooden panels. Pausanias credits him with producing a statue of Callias, an Olympic victor in the pankration in 472. According to *Pliny the Elder, his daughter Timarete was also a painter.

Bibliography: M. Robertson, *A History of Greek Art*, 2 vols., 1975.

Kenneth D.S. Lapatin

MIDAS (c. 760–696/695 b.c.)

Midas was the historical king of Phrygia, known to the Greeks as Midas and as Mita of Mushki to the Assyrians; he is also a legendary figure.

In 709/708 the Assyrians defeated him in the Taurus region of Anatolia and later forced him to offer tribute to *Sargon II. During his tenure as king, Midas introduced slavery, the first stamped gold coins, and (perhaps) the alphabet to Phrygia. He married the Greek daughter of King Agamemnon of Cyme, the birthplace of his contemporary *Homer, and, according to *Herodotus, dedicated a golden throne at Delphi. He died during the Cimmerian massacre of the Phrygians in 696/695 by drinking bull's blood, perhaps under duress.

Midas may be the man in his sixties buried in state in a *tumulus* at his capital, Gordion. Archaeological excavations of these *tumuli* reveal woven woolen carpets, exquisite woodwork (often boxwood inlaid with juniper), metalwork, and carving. His culture was marked by gold, music, horsemanship, sheep rearing, the Phrygian peaked cap, monumental sculpture, the cult of Cybele and Attis, and the trees sacred to them. Homer's Hecuba, queen of Troy and mother of Hector and Paris, is Phrygian; Athena appears in his Phaeacia as if she were Phrygian.

The Midas of legend represents a type of irrational greed for gold and forbidden knowledge; these legends, however, confuse the historical Midas with Phrygian tales of their first King Midas, who established the nation near his mines on Mt. Vermion in Macedonia. There in his rose garden Midas trapped Silenus by putting wine in the fountain and extracted from him the secret of life. For restoring him to his master, the god Dionysus, he was granted that everything he touched should turn to gold. Unable to feed himself, he was cleansed by Dionysus in the river Pactolus, which thereafter bore gold for his people. According to *Ovid, he also judged a musical contest between Pan (or Marsyas) and Apollo; the latter punished him by giving him an ass's ears, which he hid under his peaked cap, although the reeds whisper his secret.

Bibliography: C.H.E. Haspels, *The Highlands of Phrygia*, 2 vols., 1971.

Robert Dyer

MILTIADES (c. 554–c. 489 b.c.)

Miltiades is best known to history as the victorious Athenian general at the Battle of Marathon.

Miltiades was a member of the wealthy, aristocratic Philaid family at Athens. He was archon, one of the nine chief magistrates, in the year 524/523. He spent some twenty years as governor representing Athenian interests in the Chersonesus area (modern Gallipoli), where he married the daughter of the Thracian king, Olorus. He participated in *Darius I's expedition into Scythian territory but later joined the Ionian revolt of 499–494. After the failure of the revolt, he returned to Athens and was elected to the panel of ten *strategoi* (generals) each year from 493 to 489. The historian *Herodotus credits him with the decision to make a stand at Marathon against the Persian invasion force led by Datis and Artaphernes in 490.

At Marathon, Miltiades, enjoying the confidence of his colleagues, made several critical decisions regarding the timing and location of the battle, as well as Greek troop dispositions. He is thought by some modern historians to have arranged his forces, the famous 10,000 heavy infantrymen (hoplites), in a line that featured a thin center and extra depth on the wings as a shrewd offensive tactic. Others believe this arrangement was purely defensive, dictated by the need to avoid envelopment by the longer Persian battle line. In any case, the unorthodox deployment of forces enabled the Athenians to repulse the opposing lines of the numerically superior Persian army and then to turn on its center in a classic pincer movement. The battle ended in a spectacular Athenian victory (6,400 Persian dead as against 192 Athenians). The Persian forces abandoned their assault on Attica and did not return till the expedition led by King *Xerxes a decade later.

The following year (489), Miltiades was dispatched with a large fleet to conquer islands that had apparently sided with the Persians. In the course of an unsuccessful attack on the island of Paros, Miltiades was severely wounded in the leg. For his failure in this mission he was tried, convicted, and fined fifty talents, an enormous sum. He died of gangrene in prison not long afterward. Responsibility for payment of the fine was assumed by his son *Cimon, who was the leading military and civil leader at Athens for some fifteen years following the defeat of Xerxes' invasion force in 480/479.

Bibliography: R. Sealey, *A History of the Greek City-States, ca. 700–338* B.C., 1976.

James Holoka

MIMNERMUS (fl. c. 632–629 B.C.)

Mimnermus was an elegiac poet and musician.

A prolific elegiac poet, Mimnermus belonged to those Colophonians exiled from their city who controlled Smyrna for 200 years until its destruction by Alyattes of Lydia c. 600. Extant only in fragments, his poems were collected in two books. In one book, *Smyrneis*, he wrote elegies on the earlier battle between Smyrna and *Gyges of Lydia that he had heard "from the elders," probably to urge his city to a renewed effort against Alyattes. His other collection, *Nanno*, is named from his love-songs for a Lydian flute-girl and probably contained songs for symposia that later influenced *Horace. As themes, Mimnermus treats the brevity of youth and the brevity of life; his poems also contain exhortations to enjoy youth. His "Homeric" (cf. *Homer) vocabulary reflects a common origin from the hexameter oracles of Claros at Colophon; he is otherwise unHomeric. *Nanno* was later admired by *Callimachus of Cyrene.

Bibliography: D.E. Gerber, ed., *Greek Elegiac Poetry*, 1999.

Robert Dyer

MINUCIUS FELIX, MARCUS (fl. 200–240)

Minucius Felix was a Christian apologist, probably from north Africa, and author of the *Octavius*.

Any facts of his life must be inferred from his one known literary work (corroborated by *Lactantius and *Jerome). The narrator of the *Octavius* is Minucius Felix, an advocate at Rome, who recalls the debate of his two lawyer friends, Octavius, a Christian, and Caecilius, a pagan. While vacationing in Ostia, a dialogue ensued on the merits of paganism and Christianity. The discussion is philosophically rather than biblically based, showing the influence of *Cicero and *Seneca, as well as a probable dependence (though this is a matter of scholarly disagreement) on *Tertullian's recent *Apology*. The consequence of the learned debate is the conversion of Caecilius. The *Octavius*, an elegant defense of Christianity and a hearty attack against paganism, is, despite its obvious bias, valuable for its portrayal of Christian thought in the religious and social setting of upper-class Rome in the early third century. There are various indications that may link Minucius Felix to Africa, but none of them are definitive.

Bibliography: G.W. Clarke, *The Octavius of Marcus Minucius Felix*, 1974.

Mark Gustafson

MITHRIDATES VI EUPATOR DIONYSUS (113–63 B.C.)

Mithridates was the king of Cappadocia on the Pontus (Black Sea) who fought three "Mithridatic Wars" with Rome.

A minor when his father Euergetes was assassinated in 120, he returned from exile to overthrow his Greek mother Laodice, the regent, and his brother Phraates I. He inherited a multicultural kingdom, rich in iron and silver, ship timber, olives, and horses. This realm was ruled by an ancient Persian nobility, to which he belonged, from their castles and the Greek cities Amisus, Amaseia, and his capital Sinope. His royal emblem, an eight-rayed star and the crescent moon, represented the dynasty's patron gods, Zeus Stratios, or Ahuramazda, and Men Pharmacou, a Persian form of the native moon goddess.

Preoccupied with regional intrigues and expanding his kingdom around the Black Sea, he followed his parents' policy of avoiding conflict with Rome until 89, when, under provocation, he defeated Nicomedes IV of Bithynia and the Roman commissioner Aquillius with his famous scythed chariots. With 400 ships he entered the Aegean Sea and was quickly welcomed as liberator by most of western Asia Minor and Greece. Rome appointed *Sulla general and declared war. Mithridates responded by ordering the massacre of all Romans and Italians in the Greek cities. Perhaps 80,000 died in these so-called Ephesian Vespers. In 87 Sulla recaptured Athens and won the Battle of Chaeronea, forcing the Treaty of Dardanus in 85 and recovering all Roman territory, on which he imposed ruinous fines. After various skirmishes, Nicomedes' gift of Bithynia to Rome in 75 provoked the third war in 73. *Lucullus was initially successful and conquered Pontus, but Mithridates counterattacked in 68 and again enlisted the overtaxed Greek cities. *Pompey, arriving in 66, routed him to the Crimea, where his son Phamaces staged a military coup in 63, and he died, by suicide or assassination.

The Greek cities and their neighbors thought they had found a savior from the ruinous Roman taxation system. Mithridates was a lesser man than his myth, inadequate to unify this resistance or defeat Sulla and Pompey. Rome exacted savage reprisals on those who fought longest for independence and altered its cultural history through the influx of educated Greek slaves from among Mithridates' supporters, committed to principles of liberty and human rights to which he had never subscribed.

Bibliography: B.C. McGing, *The Foreign Policy of Mithridates VI Eupator King of Pontus*, 1986.

Robert Dyer

MYRON (fl. mid-fifth century B.C.)

Myron was a Greek sculptor of the early Periclean Age.

Myron was a native of Eleutherae in Attica. Along with *Polyclitus, he was a pupil of Ageladas, the head of an Argive metal casting school. He was a slightly older contemporary of Polyclitus and *Phidias, and was held to have been one of the greatest sculptors of his time. Myron worked principally in bronze, and although he made some statues of heroes and gods, his fame rested primarily upon his representation of athletes. His activity is dated around 450 by the victories of three athletes for whom he made statues in 456, 448, and 444.

Myron contributed much to the theory of symmetry and the development of the classical style. He eliminated the harshness of early classical sculpture to achieve a greater sense of realism. Of Myron's works mentioned in sources, only two exist and both in Roman copies: his *Discobolus* (Discus Thrower) and *Athena and Marsyas*. The original of the latter once stood on the Acropolis of Athens. Both of these works illustrate his interest in the arrested movement of the body.

Although a gifted sculptor, knowledge of Myron today is based on literary sources, primarily *Pliny the Elder and *Lucian.

Bibliography: G.M.A. Richter, *The Sculpture and Sculptors of the Greeks*, 4th ed., 1970.

Andrew G. Traver

N

NAEVIUS, GNAEUS (third century B.C)

Naevius was an early Roman poet, author of tragedies, comedies, and an epic entitled *Punic War*.

Naevius was the first known native Roman poet, possibly from Campania. He served in the First Punic War and began his career as a playwright around 235, without any apparent patronage, despite his plebeian status. He wrote tragedies, including the first known Latin ones based on original Roman rather than borrowed Greek themes. He was better known for his comedies and helped establish the form of the genre in Latin, freely adapting and/or combining Greek models or sometimes using original Roman themes. His *Punic War*, a relatively short epic (following Hellenistic practice) in native Latin Saturnian meter, was the first national Latin epic with a Roman theme. Written during the Second Punic War, it narrated the early histories of Carthage and of Rome (including the legend of Aeneas) and the history of the First Punic War. Naevius is noteworthy for his use of contemporary events as subjects, and he was known for his invectives, reminiscent of *Aristophanes, against contemporary noble figures; these may have led to an imprisonment and/or exile. He died in Utica, Africa, sometime after 204.

His works show a blend of classical Greek, Hellenistic, and native Latin influence. His innovative language, figures of speech, and plots influenced later Roman poets, especially *Plautus, *Ennius, and *Virgil. Naevius' epic, which was divided into seven books by the grammarian Lampadio, was the subject of at least two commentaries. Today, titles and/or fragments of about forty of his works survive.

Bibliography: G.B. Conte, *Latin Literature: A History*, 1994.

Rebecca Harrison

NEBUCHADNEZZAR II (r. 605–562 b.c)

Nebuchadnezzar II was the greatest ruler and builder of the Chaldean kings of the Neo-Babylonian empire and is well known as the destroyer of Jerusalem and the kingdom of Judah.

When Nebuchadnezzar (Akkadian, Nabu-kudurri-usur) succeeded his father Nabopolassar as Babylonian monarch in 605, he had already established his reputation as a great military commander by his victory over the Egyptians at the decisive Battle of Carchemish in the same year. As with his Assyrian predecessors, Nebuchadnezzar was preoccupied with his western border in Syro-Palestine. In 601 he campaigned against Egypt, a war that ended in a draw, with severe losses on both sides. Many of the Syro-Palestinian states rebelled against Nebuchadnezzar, including Jehoiakim of Judah, who renounced his allegiance to Babylon. According to both cuneiform and biblical sources, the Babylonian king subsequently laid siege to and captured Jerusalem, appointed a new king (Zedekiah), deported much of the local population, and imposed a heavy tribute. Ten years later, however, Zedekiah switched allegiance to Egypt, incurring Nebuchadnezzar's wrath (see 2 Kings 24–15, Jeremiah 39, and 2 Chronicles 36). This time, Jerusalem was not spared. Not only were Zedekiah and his sons killed, but the city, its fortifications, the Solomonic temple, and temple accessories were all destroyed. Thus, Nebuchadnezzar was responsible for ending the Jewish state and the Davidic royal line.

Although little is known of Nebuchadnezzar's other military activities, he was renown as a builder in Babylon itself. He conducted extensive renovation projects, rebuilt the city walls, constructed a bridge to bring together the two halves of the city separated by the Euphrates River, and restored the Babylonian temple tower and other holy places. At the end of his long reign the Babylonian empire was virtually the same size as its predecessor Assyria.

Although cuneiform sources give a fragmented picture of Nebuchadnezzar's reign, he appears in later biblical (e.g., Daniel), rabbinic, and Arabic commentaries, in books of the Apocrypha, and in classical (e.g., *Strabo, *Diodorus Siculus, and Berossus) and medieval authors. Though the Hebrew sources understandably bemoan his conquest and destruction of Jerusalem and the temple, other sources describe his great building projects, and some even credit him with superhuman achievements.

Bibliography: D.J. Wiseman, *Nebuchadrezzar and Babylon*, 1991.

Mark W. Chavalas

NEPOS, CORNELIUS (c. 99–24 b.c.)

Nepos is the earliest Latin biographer whose works are extant.

Nepos was born in Cisalpine Gaul and migrated to Rome, where he flourished as a writer and cultivated friendships with *Cicero, *Atticus, and *Catullus. Nepos' literary output included love poetry, a world history in three volumes (the *Chronica*), a geography, a book of anecdotes (the *Exempla*), large-scale biographies of *Cato the Elder and Cicero, and the *Biographies of Famous Men* (the *De Viris Illustribus*). Only sections of the biographies dealing with the lives of *Foreign Generals* and of Cato and Atticus and some fragments from the biographies of Greek and Roman historians survive from Nepos' total output. Two editions of the *Biographies* appeared: the first before the death of the work's dedicatee, Atticus, in 32; the second somewhat later.

Though Nepos utilized the works of major historical sources such as *Thucydides, *Theopompus, and *Timaeus, the biographies were not intended to serve as serious historical accounts but as works designed to entertain and instruct. Greatly influenced by rhetorical and peripatetic precedents, the biographies exhibit moralizing and anecdotal tendencies and are conspicuous for glaring factual errors. Offering a jaundiced assessment of the generalissimos and civil discord of his own era, Nepos championed the ideals of political liberty and of the rule of law and professed a great admiration for Atticus for his ability to compromise and espouse neutrality in hazardous times. As an author of Roman and non-Roman, especially Greek, biographies, Nepos exercised an important influence upon *Plutarch, who emulated Nepos in his own parallel lives of Greeks and Romans. The simplicity of Nepos' language has rendered the biographies ideal school texts for students initiating their acquaintance with Latin.

Bibliography: J. Geiger, *Cornelius Nepos and Ancient Political Biography*, 1983.

Lionel Sanders

NERO (Nero Claudius Caesar, 37–68)

Nero was the fifth emperor of Rome. During his reign the city of Rome was consumed by a huge fire that Nero blamed on the Christians, whom he subsequently persecuted.

Born Lucius Domitius Ahenobarbus on 15 December 37, Nero was the child of Gnaeus Domitius Ahenobarbus (consul in 32) and *Agrippina the Younger. Shortly after Agrippina's marriage to the Emperor *Claudius, Nero was adopted by the emperor, becoming Tiberius Claudius Nero Caesar in 50. When Claudius died on 13 October 54, Nero became emperor and declared his adoptive father deified. His early years as *princeps* are described positively by ancient authors, though they often accuse his mother Agrippina of dominating him. In March 59, after several unsuccessful attempts on her life, Nero had Agrippina murdered at her villa near Baiae. In 62, he married Poppaea Sabina, his mistress of four years, and in 63 she bore him a daughter who only lived for a few months.

The most notorious event of Nero's reign occurred in 64, when a great fire destroyed much of Rome. Nero countered accusations of having set the fire himself by blaming it on the emerging Christian sect. The upper classes reviled Nero for taking advantage of the fire's destruction to rebuild a huge villa-palace complex for himself in the center of Rome, but he consistently remained popular with the lower classes. After the fire he enacted improved building codes for the reconstruction of the city of Rome and forced all ships delivering supplies into the city to carry out debris from the fire in order to facilitate cleaning and rebuilding efforts.

In 65 Nero shocked the citizenry by appearing on stage and singing, which led to the formation of an assassination plot to replace Nero with Gaius Calpurnius Piso. Following the Pisonian conspiracy several prominent citizens were forced to commit suicide, including *Lucan, *Petronius, *Seneca, and Tigellinus. Poppaea died in 66, and in 67, Nero took an extensive literary tour of Greece, where he competed in all of the Panhellenic and Panathenaic games. Following several revolts, Nero committed suicide in 68.

Bibliography: M.T. Griffin, *Nero: The End of a Dynasty*, 1984.

Katrina M. Dickson

NESTORIUS OF CONSTANTINOPLE (?-c. 451)

Nestorius was a monk from Antioch who became archbishop of Constantinople in 428 and founded the heresy that subsequently became known as the Nestorianism.

Nestorius had been selected as archbishop by the imperial court as an outside candidate, brought in as an attempt to resolve internal factionalism that was rife in the capital. From the moment of his arrival he had great difficulty establishing his leadership in the city. The powerful camps of the Empress Pulcheria, the monks, and many of the aristocracy were opposed to him, and a large section of the people resisted the introduction of Syrian Christology for what they felt was its foreign "novelty."

Nestorius emphasized in his teaching that *Jesus Christ had two distinct centers of operation in his life. He was human, and he was divine. These two circles of operation, however, must not be confused; otherwise, the resultant vision of Christ would be confused: someone who was properly neither God nor man but some form of myth. For Nestorius exact language was very important in this process of keeping to a pure faith. The Godhead, present in Christ, worked signs of great power, such as the raising of the dead, while the humanity in Christ showed the usual signs of weakness and need (e.g., hunger, thirst). The Word of God was the proper grammatical subject of the divine acts, the man Jesus was the subject of the human acts, and if one wished to connote the mysterious way the Scriptures spoke of the "union" of the two factors, one should use the grammatical subject "Christ." He was especially vehement in denying the legitimacy of phrases that evoked the union (such as *Mary as the "Mother of God"). But as these phrases were a strong staple of popular piety, he was bent on trouble.

Many of those who heard him took him to be suggesting that there were two personal subjects in Christ: a man and a god. It was by no means what he meant, but it was how a large section heard him and has become, ever after, the popular meaning of the heresy of "Nestorianism": the doctrine that a man, Jesus, dwelt simultaneously alongside the Divine Word in the person of Christ.

Nestorius was summoned to the Council of Ephesus in 431 to answer charges of heresy. There he met with the powerful opposition of *Cyril, the archbishop of Alexandria, and the majority of bishops who found his language unacceptable. Although he had the support of the Syrian theologians, he was condemned and held under house arrest for a while; then, late in 431, he was deposed as archbishop and sent back to his monastery in disgrace. He disobeyed an imperial order not to continue his theological propaganda and was sent into exile to Petra. There he still refused to cease an active campaign of writing against Cyril and the Council of Ephesus and so was transferred yet again to one of the most severe penal colonies of the Byzantine state, the Great Oasis in Upper Egypt. It was here that he stayed until his death, sometime in the early 450s.

Bibliography: J.A. McGuckin, "The Christology of Nestorius of Constantinople," *The Patristic and Byzantine Review* 7.2–3 (1988): 93–129.

John A. McGuckin

NICANDER OF COLOPHON (second century B.C.)

Nicander was a Greek poet and grammarian.

Nicander was born at Claros, near Colophon, where his family held the hereditary priesthood of Apollo. Nicander wrote didactic poems on scientific themes but was not a scientist himself. Two lengthy hexameter works of his survive complete, both of which by internal dating favor a date in the second century. The first, *Theriaca*, dedicates its 958 lines to remedies against the bites of snakes and other poisonous creatures. The second, *Alexipharmaca* (360 lines), lists vegetables, minerals, animal poisons, and their anecdotes. In his facts, Nicander followed the physician Apollodorus the Iologus (third century B.C.), but he often intermixed superstition with precise details about botany and medicine.

Nicander also wrote six epics, a treatise on apiculture, and a poem on hunting. Among Nicander's lost works is the *Heteroeumena*, a mythological epic used by *Ovid in his *Metamorphoses*, and *Georgica*, said by *Quintilian to have been imitated by *Virgil. *Cicero praised Nicander's works, and *Pliny the Elder quoted them.

While Nicander was lauded and imitated by his later contemporaries, his two extant works probably do not reflect the full range of his literary abilities.

Bibliography: A.S.F. Gow and A.F. Scholfield, eds., *Nicander: The Poems and Poetical Fragments*, 1953.

Andrew G. Traver

NICIAS (c. 470–413 B.C.)

Nicias was an Athenian politician and military leader who emerged as one of the leading opponents of *Cleon after *Pericles' death. He was an advocate of a quick but favorable peace with Sparta during the Peloponnesian War, and he was the leader of the ill-fated Sicilian expedition.

Nicias was a wealthy Athenian who came to power after Pericles' death. *Plutarch reports that he lacked Pericles' political acumen and therefore had to rely on his wealth and use it for public spectacles to counter Cleon's popular appeals to the Athenian people.

During the early part of the Peloponnesian War, Nicias fought several minor battles. He is also known for negotiating a peace treaty with the Spartans to temporarily end the hostilities in 421. This temporary peace is commonly referred to as the Peace of Nicias.

Nicias gained a more infamous position in history after the resumption of the war with Sparta. At this time, *Alcibiades favored an expansion of the hostilities with an expedition to Sicily. Although Nicias initially opposed this undertaking, he, along with Alcibiades, was chosen to lead the expedition. Alcibiades was quickly recalled to Athens to answer for his suspected role in the affair of the Herms—an act of vandalism the night before the Athenian fleet left for Sicily. This left Nicias solely in charge of the fleet in Sicily, where he was firmly defeated.

Despite his role in the Sicilian disaster, Nicias is well spoken of in both the Aristotelian *Constitution of the Athenians* and *Thucydides' history. The former describes Nicias among those who were not only good and noble men but also politically active and servants of the whole state.

Bibliography: W.R. Connor, *Thucydides*, 1984.

Jeff Rydberg-Cox

NICOLAUS OF DAMASCUS (first century B.C.)

Nicolaus of Damascus was *Herod the Great's court philosopher and historian who compiled a universal history in 144 books and an encyclopedia of Greek Aristotelian learning.

Born in 64 B.C., the same year *Pompey was in Syria, Nicolaus was an exact contemporary with the well-known geographer and historian *Strabo. Nicolaus was first patronized by Herod the Great. His students included the twin children of *Marc Antony and *Cleopatra (b. 40 B.C.), and so it is thought that when *Augustus gave over to Herod the former territories of Cleopatra connected to Judaea that Nicolaus joined Herod's court. He twice accompanied Herod to Rome and represented him before the Roman authorities. After Herod's death (4 B.C.), he served for Herod Archelaus. It was in his service or in retirement that Nicolaus died later in Rome.

Some of Nicolaus' life, including his studies in grammar, poetry, rhetoric, music, and philosophy, is recorded in an autobiography he wrote; however, it only survives in a fragment. Only fragments of Nicolaus' *Ecumenical History* survive today, but portions are incorporated into *Josephus' *Jewish Antiquities*. Nicolaus was also commissioned to write a biography of Augustus, which he apparently completed after the emperor's death (A.D. 14). He also wrote a treatise entitled *On the Philosophy of Aristotle*, which seems to have been written near the end of his life in Rome. This work, later translated into Syriac and Arabic, treats *Aristotle's physical works in the *Metaphysics* and *On the Soul*.

Bibliography: H.J.D. Lulofs, *Nicolaus Damascenus on the Philosophy of Aristotle*, 1965.

Brannon Wheeler

NUMA POMPILIUS (c. 715–673 b.c.)

Numa was the second king of Rome and is traditionally remembered for his religious reforms.

It is most likely that Numa is a historical figure, but much that is ascribed to him was probably the result of a long period of development. Though the name "Numa" is of Etruscan origin, it is commonly believed that he was a Sabine. Numa received his appointment to the office of king when the people of Rome became restless with senatorial oppression and brought him to the throne through a show of strength. According to tradition, the people found him attractive because of the intelligence and wisdom he had gained from his Pythagorean studies.

Roman lore ascribes to Numa the standardization of the Roman religion, especially prescriptions of activities that would bring the favors of the gods upon the Roman people. One radical religious reform attributed to Numa was the prohibition of blood sacrifices upon the altar. In addition, he discouraged costly sacrifices and outlawed creating graven images. Other religious reforms that are ascribed to him include the organization of the priestly colleges and a calendar system. Instead of relying on the ancient ten-month calendar, Numa created a twelve-month timetable that defined seasons and festivals in a more efficient manner.

Tradition credits Numa with serving as king for thirty-nine years. Throughout his reign, it was maintained, Rome never experienced war, being able to negotiate peacefully through the skill of her king. Numa died from old age and was buried on the Janiculum. Near his burial plot lay another tomb containing his books, laws, and policies. It is from Numa's Sabine origin and religious influence as king that historians attribute the striking correlation between early Roman religion and the Greek cults from southern Italy.

Bibliography: R.M. Ogilvie, *Commentary on Livy Books 1–5*, 1965.

Richard Draper

O

OCTAVIA (?–11 B.C.)

Octavia was the sister of Octavian (later *Augustus) and the wife of Marcellus and then of *Marc Antony.

Octavia lived in Rome with Gaius Claudius Marcellus, with whom she had three children, until his death in 41. With the Senate's permission, since she was pregnant, she soon married Marc Antony and later bore him two children. She assisted Antony in maintaining the triumvirate. Octavia attempted to be active in foreign affairs in her marriage with Antony, traveling extensively with reinforcements to help her husband, who was not always appreciative.

Octavia was active in official building in Rome. Augustus refurbished Porticus Metelli and renamed it the Porticus Octaviae after her. Perhaps her most notable contribution to Rome was the Bibliotheca Porticus Octaviae, which she commissioned in 23 after the death of Marcellus. When she died in 11, she was buried in the Julian mausoleum with a public funeral at which Augustus gave a speech.

Bibliography: R.A. Bauman, *Women and Politics in Ancient Rome*, 1992.

Lisa Auanger

OCTAVIAN/OCTAVIUS

See **Augustus**.

ODOACER, FLAVIUS (or Odovacer, c. 433–493)

Odoacer was the general of the western Roman army who deposed Romulus "Augustulus," the last western emperor.

Odoacer was of indeterminate barbarian background. His father Edeco was a senior follower of *Attila; after the collapse of Attila's empire, Edeco led a minor barbarian confederacy in central Europe. Odoacer, too, first appears as a freebooter, commanding a group of Saxons in post-Roman northern Gaul in the 460s against Franks under Childeric (father of Clovis). By 471/472, he was in Italy commanding imperial forces under *Ricimer. Following the failure of the brief emperors Glycerius and Nepos (installed by Constantinople), Odoacer took charge of rebellious barbarian contingents seeking land grants and pensioned off the last emperor, Romulus, nicknamed "little emperor."

Odoacer sought to rule Italy as the nominal viceroy of the eastern emperor, but his constitutional position was very ambiguous: The eastern emperor *Zeno gave him the honorary title *patricius*, though he is not attested as *magister utriusque militum* (master of military forces) unlike *Aetius and Ricimer; his coins have his name but no title; in a few papyri and in literary sources he is called *rex* ("king"). Odoacer provided defense and stable government for Italy from the sometime imperial capital of Ravenna, honoring the Roman senatorial aristocracy and promoting the civil bureaucracy. In 489, Zeno sent Theodoric to depose Odoacer. After several battles, a siege of almost three years, and an attempt to raise his son Thela as caesar, Odoacer surrendered but was murdered by Theodoric in 493. Theodoric's own stable rule, however, was a continuation of Odoacer's policies.

Odoacer advanced from a checkered career as war leader to become the first postimperial ruler of Italy, though many contemporaries still referred to "the empire." Byzantine writers of the time of Justinian's "reconquest" (Procopius, Jordanes) first construed 476 as the end of Roman rule in the West.

Bibliography: J. M. O'Flynn, *Generalissimos of the Later Roman Empire*, 1983.

Andrew Gillett

OLYMPIAS (c. 375–316 b.c.)

Olympias was the wife of *Philip II of Macedonia and the mother of *Alexander the Great.

She was the daughter of King Neoptolemus of Epirus and claimed descent from the Homeric hero Achilles. Her name was originally Myrtale, but she changed it to Olympias in recognition of Philip's victory in the Olympic Games of 356. She married Philip in 357; she was Philip's fourth wife. Her son Alexander was born in 356; a daughter Cleopatra followed in 355.

Philip's other brides had been Thessalian, Thracian, Illyrian, and Scythian. However, in 337 Philip married a young woman also named Cleopatra who hailed from a powerful Macedonian family. Olympias now felt her position at court threatened and withdrew to Epirus. After Philip's death (336), Olympias returned to court and had Cleopatra and her infant daughter Europa killed.

While Alexander seemed to have enjoyed good relations with his mother, his regent in Macedon *Antipater did not. Olympias once again withdrew to Epirus. After the death of Antipater in 319, his successor as regent in Macedon, Polyperchon, was faced with a grand alliance consisting of *Antigonus, Antipater's son *Cassander, *Lysimachus, and *Ptolemy. In desperation, Polyperchon turned to Olympias for assistance and invited her to act as regent for Alexander's young son, Alexander IV. She declined until 317, when Cassander established Philip's son and Alexander's half brother Philip III Arrhidaeus as king of Macedon. Allied with Polyperchon, Olympias gained the support of the Macedonian army. However, after she ordered the execution of Arrhidaeus, his wife Eurydice, Cassander's brother, and 100 of Cassander's partisans, Olympias quickly fell from grace. Cassander's Macedonian Assembly condemned her to death, but his soldiers refused to carry out the sentence. Instead, the relatives of those whom she had executed killed her.

Olympias was a powerful woman who played important roles in the power struggles following the deaths of both Philip and Alexander. While she strove to preserve Alexander's territory for his son, Cassander's imperial ambitions ensured that the empire would not remain intact.

Bibliography: M. Grant, *From Alexander to Cleopatra*, 1982.

Andrew G. Traver

ORIGEN (c. 185–254)

Despite a posthumous condemnation, Origen remains a giant among Christian theologians; his scriptural commentaries and speculative theology influenced both eastern and western Christianity for centuries.

Origen's life centered around teaching and preaching first in Alexandria and later in Caesarea, Palestine. Origen enjoyed a dual education in the regular Hellenistic curriculum and in Christian scripture and doctrine. A persecution in 202 claimed the life of Origen's father Leonides. Origen supported his family by establishing a school of rhetoric. Concurrently he was appointed head of the catechetical school in Alexandria. He practiced an increasingly ascetic Christianity, eventually dedicating himself solely to teaching in the church. Origen's ardor led to a rash act of self-castration in a literal interpretation of *Matthew 19:12, an act he appears to have regretted later in life. Aside from this overly sensationalized event, Origen's reputation as a teacher and defender of Christianity grew. Julia Mammaea, the mother of emperor Alexander Severus (r. 222–235), even brought Origen to court in Antioch in order to learn more about Christianity. Around 231 Origen was exiled from Egypt, stemming from his lay preaching and ordination to the priesthood, both conducted without consultation with Demetrius, bishop of Alexandria. Origen set up a new life in Caesarea, where he continued to write, teach, preach, and dialogue with pagans, Jews, and heretics. His also presented Christian approaches to philosophy for curious non-Christians. Origen's *Against Celsus* was an important cultural and intellectual defense of Christianity in response to a well-informed critique of Christianity, *Celsus' *True Doctrine*. The Decian (cf. *Decius) persecution (250–251) contributed to Origen's death. His position as a leading voice for Christianity in the empire won him imprisonment and severe torture in an attempt to have him deny the faith. Released after Decius' death, Origen died in broken health c. 254.

Origen's focus on the Bible grew from his belief that Christ the Word of God underlies the whole of scripture. He was the first theologian to write homilies and commentaries which spanned the bulk of the Old and New Testaments. Employing aspects of Neoplatonic philosophy, he explored the multiple ways whereby Christ communicates through the "word" of scripture. Origen's biblical and Christ-centered approaches formed the foundation for *On First Principles*, which explored beliefs about God, creatures, rational souls and free will, and Scripture. Some aspects of this work, taken out of context both from his writings as a whole as well as from the theological context of his time, led to a condemnation in 553 in conjunction with the Three Chapters controversy. While this caused the loss of many of Origen's works, it did not prevent the continued presence of Origen's ideas and methods through other theologians.

Bibliography: H. Crouzel, *Origen*, trans. A.S. Worrall, 1989.

Lisa D. Maugans Driver

OROSIUS, PAULUS (early fifth century A.D.)

A priest and native of Braga, Orosius was commissioned by *Augustine to provide supporting evidence for the *City of God* but instead wrote the first world history from a Christian perspective.

Orosius first appeared in 414 when he traveled to Africa to meet Augustine. Augustine sent him to *Jerome in Palestine to help fight against the Pelagian heresy (cf. *Pelagius), and Orosius was present at the Council of Diospolis in 415. Orosius returned to the West in 416, bringing with him the relics of St. Stephen the proto-martyr. He first landed on Minorca, where the presence of Stephen's relics incited Christian hostility against the Jewish population. Fearing the Visigoths, Orosius left Minorca for Africa instead of returning to Spain. When composing the *City of God* in response to the capture of Rome by the Visigoths, Augustine commissioned Orosius to draw up a list of past disasters, probably in the hope of setting defeat in proper perspective. Orosius instead produced the first universal Christian history, the *Seven Books of History against the Pagans*. Nothing is known about his career after this point.

Contrary to Augustine, Orosius argued that God had established and overthrown empires in a clearly discernible pattern from the very beginning of human history. Drawing on the traditional image of four world empires in the Book of Daniel and on the coincidence of *Jesus having been born during the reign of *Augustus, the first Roman emperor, Orosius argued that the Roman Empire served as the culmination of God's plan for humanity. Thus, rather than representing the complete collapse of pagan glory, the Christianization of the Roman Empire heralded the kingdom of God on earth. This triumphal view of Christian history was to remain dominant throughout much of the Middle Ages.

Bibliography: W.H.C. Frend, "Augustine and Orosius on the Fall of the Roman Empire in the West," *Augustinian Studies* 20 (1989): 1–38.

Steven D. Driver

OVID (Publius Ovidius Naso, 43 B.C.–A.D. 17)

Ovid was an Augustan poet whose most famous works are the *Heroides* and the *Metamorphoses*. He was married three times and had one daughter by his second wife.

Ovid was born at Sulmo, some ninety miles outside of Rome, to an ancient but impoverished equestrian family. His father expected him to take up a career in public office, but Ovid found that poetry not only appealed to him much more than did politics, but it seemed to be natural for him. He soon became popular among Rome's literati, becoming the friend of both *Horace and *Propertius.

Ovid's first work was the *Amores*, a collection of love poems about a relationship with a woman named Corinna. They are probably not autobiographical poems, but they were so successful that many Roman women claimed to be Corinna. Ovid next published the *Heroides*, letters from deserted legendary heroines to their faithless lovers. These poems demonstrate Ovid's sympathy for women and his knack for creating vibrant character. The *Ars amatoria*, a handbook on love, depicts pleasure-loving Roman society; the *Remedia amoris* soon followed, perhaps as a response to outraged moral Roman society. Ovid then began to experiment: His tragedy on the story of *Medea* (now lost) was very well received. But the *Metamorphoses* was his most ambitious project. This work is commonly held to be Ovid's foray into epic. It is a long poem (fifteen books of hexameters) on a grand subject: The history of the world is told from the creation of the cosmos to the apotheosis of *Julius Caesar, all in a seamless fabric of transformation tales. However, the poem seems to undercut the usual civic purposes of Roman epic; not all the transformations are glorious, moral, or despite the praise of *Augustus at the end, even tactful. Nevertheless, the *Metamorphoses* is an astonishing collection of classical mythology, a tour de force of psychological insight, and a most artistic tapestry of narrative.

Although the *Metamorphoses* finishes in praise of Augustus, the emperor was not pleased. For reasons that remain cryptic, Ovid was exiled to the shores of the Black Sea. He remained there for the rest of his life, leaving the *Fasti* (a poem on the myths behind the Roman calendar) only half finished. While in exile, Ovid continued to write, appealing for clemency and a return to Rome and composing the *Tristia*, poems about his melancholy life among barbarians, and the *Epistulae ex Ponto*, letters of lament. Ovid insists throughout his writings that he was guilty of no more than indiscretion and likens himself to Actaeon, which has prompted numerous scholarly detectives to surmise that he was guilty of having seen something he should not have seen: a plot against Augustus; Augustus' daughter, the notorious Julia, involved in some affair; or Augustus himself involved in something scandalous, like incest with his daughter or grand-daughter. We will probably never know the truth and are left with the touching image of the poet in exile who even learned the native language so he could continue writing.

Ovid's contribution to Western culture is considerable. His accounts of classical mythology fueled imaginations from the twelfth century onward. His ability to write pictorially inspired painters and sculptors, like Velasquez and Bernini. His convincing characters and powerful images provided the sources and models for Chretien de Troyes, Guillaume de Lorris, Jean de Meung, Chaucer, John Gower, Dafydd ap Gwilim, Shakespeare, Spenser, and Ezra Pound, to name a few writers.

Bibliography: S.K. Myers, *Ovid's Causes: Cosmogony and Aetiology in the Metamorphoses*, 1994.

Andrea Schutz

P

PACHOMIUS, SAINT (c. 292–346)

Pachomius is credited in Christian tradition with being the founder of communal (cenobitic) monasticism.

Born a pagan in southern Egypt and conscripted into the Roman army, Pachomius benefited from the charity Christians traditionally offered those who were sick or otherwise suffering. This experience led him to be baptized upon his discharge in 313. For a while he lived an ascetic life under the tutelage of the hermit Palaemon and later with his brother. About 320, Pachomius had a vision in the deserted town of Tabennisi to establish a monastery to which many would come. The monastic community grew quickly, and others were soon established or recruited. At his death, Pachomius was the head of nine monasteries for men and two for women, which combined contained some 3,000 religious.

Pachomius' greatest impact lay first in the very idea of monks assembled as a community and second in the monastic rules that circulated under his name. Pachomius organized his monks into austere and thoroughly regimented communities oriented toward works of charity, evangelization of the countryside, and the cultivation of holiness. Perhaps as a result of his military training, Pachomius exercised harsh discipline and required sublimation of personal will. Initially, this rigor seems to have been an attempt to eliminate the class distinctions that dominated ancient society and to build a strong sense of community and mutual support. The rigor of the rule tends to hide Pachomius' emphasis on discernment, purity of heart, and charity that are revealed so clearly in his biographies. As the monasteries evolved, however, they tended to become more inward looking and isolated from the larger world. After Pachomius' death, his monasteries played an increasing role in Egyptian ecclesiastical affairs and even in the economy of the Nile, as the monastic farms participated both in relief of the poor and in agricultural trade.

Bibliography: P. Rousseau, *Pachomius. The Making of a Community in Fourth-Century Egypt*, 1986.

Steven D. Driver

PANAETIUS (c. 185–c. 110 B.C.)

Panaetius was a Greek Stoic philosopher, credited with the founding of "Middle Stoicism." He was especially influential in Roman thought and was closely associated with many prominent Romans.

He was born on Rhodes and came to Athens, where he was a pupil of *Chrysippus' former student Diogenes of Babylon in the 150s. He became head of the Stoic school c. 130, and *Posidonius was his most famous pupil. His extensive writings are now lost, but his *On Duty* served as a model for *Cicero's *On Duties*, his *On Providence* as a source for Cicero's *On the Nature of the Gods*, and his *On Equanimity* influenced similar works by *Plutarch and *Seneca. He was an adviser to *Scipio Aemilianus, and he was influential in Roman political circles where his ethical emphasis on public service and the duties of power helped to provide an ideology for aristocratic rule.

Panaetius broadened the appeal of Stoicism by focusing on practical issues of conduct rather than theoretical notions of virtue and moderated Stoic asceticism by formulating systematic rules for the pursuit of worldly things such as wealth and position. Thus, he was in a great degree responsible for enabling Stoicism to become the dominant philosophy of Rome.

Bibliography: A.A. Long and D.N. Sedley, *The Hellenistic Philosophers*, 2 vols., 1987.

Gordon Campbell

PAPINIAN (Aemilius Papinianus, c. 150–212)

Papinian was an influential jurist and praetorian prefect during the reigns of *Septimius Severus and Caracalla.

The early life of Papinian is obscure; he is believed to have been from Syria and possibly a relative of *Julia Domna, the second wife of Septimius Severus. He served as an assessor, or chief legal adviser, to the praetorian prefects during the reign of *Marcus Aurelius and stepped into higher office with the accession of Severus. Papinian was praetorian prefect from 205 and employed the jurists *Paulus and *Ulpian as his assessors. He was with Severus in Britain (208–211), and the dying emperor reputedly placed his two sons, Geta and Caracalla, under his care. However, when Caracalla had Geta murdered and seized power in 212, Papinian was executed.

Papinian's contributions to Roman legal studies were extensive. His most influential works were a collection of *Quaestiones* in thirty-seven books and *Responsa* in nineteen books; both of these works cover a wide range of problems in both public and private law. His legal reputation was so esteemed that in Valentinian's *Law of Citations* (426), Papinian was named as the jurist whose judgment was to prevail when the other four—*Gaius, Ulpian, Paulus, and Modestinus—offered contradictory opinions. By the fifth century his *Responsa* comprised the third year of legal studies at Berytus, and nearly 600 excerpts of his works were incorporated into Justinian's *Digest.*

Bibliography: A.R. Birley, *The African Emperor: Septimius Severus,* rev. ed., 1998.

Karen Wagner

PARMENIDES OF ELEA (c. 515–445 b.c.)

Parmenides was an important philosopher who was reputed to have conversed with *Socrates when the latter was very young. Parmenides is most famous for his hexameter poem, *On Nature*, in which he claims that All is Being, or that reality is an eternal and unchanging Being.

Parmenides was born in Elea, in what is now the Italian island of Sicily. Little is known about his life, but according to *Diogenes Laertius, Parmenides, *Zeno of Elea, and Socrates met in Athens when Socrates was young (i.e., approximately 450, or when Socrates was roughly twenty years old). Whether or not they did indeed meet, Socrates and *Plato were heavily influenced by Parmenides' poem *On Nature*. Plato wrote a dialogue entitled "Parmenides," and Plato's own theory of the forms is itself largely an effort to reconcile Parmenides' idea that Being simply is with the everyday experience of change. This is quite a challenge for Plato, for Parmenides argues that Being simply is what it is and cannot not be, and thus becoming, and change is illusory for it implies that something is not before it comes into being. But to say that Being is not, or that something that is, is not, is contradictory for Parmenides and is therefore not true. With Plato's theory of the forms, therefore, we have an attempt to reconcile the reality of something that is eternal and unchanging with the apparent flux and becoming of daily life. The theory of forms is Plato's attempt to do just this, and to the extent that Plato's philosophy has had a profound influence within Western culture, we can also say that, by extension, so too has Parmenides' thought had an implicit and profound influence.

Bibliography: G.S. Kirk, J.E. Raven, and M. Schofield, *The Presocratic Philosophers,* 2nd ed., 1983.

Jeffrey A. Bell

PARRHASIUS (fl. 430–390 b.c.)

Parrhasius was one of the greatest painters of Greece.

A native of Ephesus where he was the pupil of his father Evenor, Parrhasius worked mainly in Athens and later became an Athenian citizen. His period of activity can be roughly fixed by *Pliny the Elder. As *Xenophon's *Memorabilia* records a conversation between Parrhasius and *Socrates on the subject of art, Parrhasius must have therefore been a prominent painter by 399. *Seneca's story that Parrhasius bought one of the Olynthians whom *Philip II of Macedonia had sold into slavery as a model is without chronological foundation.

Another tale relates a contest between Parrhasius and *Zeuxis. Zeuxis painted some grapes so perfectly that birds came to peck at them. But when Zeuxis asked Parrhasius to draw aside the curtain to show his picture, he realized that his rival's painting was the curtain itself. As Zeuxis tricked the birds, so Parrhasius tricked Zeuxis.

Parrhasius is known to have painted more than twenty pictures, all of them now lost. His painting of *Theseus is said to have adorned the Capitol in Rome. Most of his themes were mythological, and his depictions of gods and heroes became models for later artists. His greatest skill was to make his figures appear to stand out from the background. Many of his drawings on wood and parchment were preserved and valued by craftsmen even in Pliny's day. He also wrote a lost treatise entitled *On painting*.

Bibliography: M. Robertson, *A History of Greek Art*, 2 vols., 1975.

Andrew G. Traver

PARTHENIUS OF NICAEA (first century B.C.)

Parthenius was a Greek poet enslaved in Bithynia about 80 after the war against *Mithridates VI.

During the Third Mithridatic War, Parthenius was taken by the family of the poet Helvius Cinna (immortalized in Shakespeare's *Julius Caesar* as a victim of mistaken identity) to their property in Cisalpine Gaul (the Po Valley), near Cremona, where he was later freed. He taught *Virgil and his fellow student *Gallus, for whom he wrote a series of *Erotika Pathemata*, plots of stories to be used in poetry, exemplifying women's obsessive love. Virgil based one on the suicide of Dido in the *Aeneid*. Parthenius' poetry was in the Alexandrian style, influenced by *Callimachus and *Euphorion, whom he may have introduced to Italy. We seem to owe to him the curiously morbid and perverse view of female sexuality in the circle of younger poets, scorned by *Cicero as "singers of Euphorion."

Bibliography: R.R. Dyer, "Where Did Parthenius Teach Vergil?" *Vergilius* 42 (1996): 19–24.

Robert Dyer

PATRICK, SAINT (fl. fifth century)

Patrick was the bishop traditionally credited with permanently establishing Christianity in Ireland, of which he is the patron saint, and whose life story has grown to mythological proportions, making him one of the best known figures in British and American popular culture.

The only accurate sources for Patrick's life are his *Epistle to the Soldiers of Coroticus* and his *Confession*. Muirchu's *Life*, other *Lives*, the Irish annals, and later works have contributed much to his legend but nothing additional to a factual account of the real man. Because of the vast body of myth and speculation surrounding Patrick (or Patricius) and the remoteness of fifth-century Ireland, both geographically from the Rome of his day and chronologically from our own time, there have been fierce debates in the modern era about the details of his life, with some scholars even claiming that there were two "Patricks" and others that there was none. Though scholars now generally accept his existence, disagreement continues about the dates of his birth, mission, death, and other events, and both Catholics and Protestants claim his legacy. Even today it is widely assumed that Patrick was Irish, when in fact he was a Romanized Briton.

The dates for Patrick's birth in respectable works range from c. 373 to c. 415, and those for his death from c. 460 to c. 493. What is certain is that he was born in Britain and that his grandfather Potitus was a Christian priest (clerical celibacy not then being universal) and his father Calpurnius a prosperous deacon in a place Patrick calls Bannaventa Burniae. This was somewhere in western Roman Britain (many locations have been suggested but none substantiated). When he was about sixteen, Irish raiders carried him off to northern Ireland, where he became the slave of a chieftain named Miliucc in a place called Voclut (probably near Killala in county Mayo), working as a herdsman and experiencing great hardship for the next six years. Though by his own admission he was irreligious prior to his capture, in Ireland he began to pray and became devout. After hearing a voice in a dream telling him to return home, he escaped and took ship, to Gaul as it turned out, with a cargo of Irish wolfhounds. A few years later he finally made it back to Britain and his family. There he had a vision of a man named Victoricus who pleaded with him to return to Ireland, and subsequently he had visions of *Jesus Christ.

Sorely lacking in education, something that caused him shame throughout his life, Patrick apparently returned to Gaul to obtain training for the priesthood, but though his works show that he was quite familiar with Scripture, his Latin is very peculiar. Thereafter he was consecrated as bishop of Ireland. The date and duration of his appointment are other points of controversy, but it must have been after 431, for Patrick was preceded as bishop by Palladius, whom Pope Celestine I appointed in that year, and some scholars place his return to Ireland much later. Clearly Patrick assumed leadership of an already existing Christian community that he then dramatically expanded, but he was one of the first ecclesiastics to emphasize spreading the gospel beyond the boundaries of the Roman Empire. It appears that he conducted much of his missionary activity in northern Ireland, working through local chieftains. Though the Irish church in later centuries was to be heavily based on monasteries, Patrick relied upon an episcopal form of organization. By his own account he converted thousands, but he remained unsatisfied because he had not achieved more. His letter to Coroticus takes that obscure British king to task for his soldiers' murder of Irish missionaries. His *Confession*, the more revealing of his works, has inspired many generations of believers and continues to do so.

No Christian saint has been more altered by popular culture than Patrick except perhaps for St. Nicholas of Myra, but even his modern incarnation Santa Claus remains associated with Christmas, a genuine holy day for millions, while the feast of St. Patrick (17 March) has been almost entirely secularized in most places where it is observed. Modern celebrations of St. Patrick's Day have less to do with his achievements as bishop than with the expression of patriotism in Ireland or Irish ethnic pride in America, and those considerations in turn are often eclipsed by leprechauns, green beer, gratuitous display of shamrocks, and rather unsaintly revelry. Myths abound, for example: that he wrote the hymn called "St. Patrick's Breastplate," that he drove all the snakes out of Ireland, that he called fire down from heaven, that he ran over his sister with a chariot because she was unchaste, and that even now he can release souls from purgatory. The story that he used the shamrock to illustrate the concept of one God in three persons could be true but is a late addition to his mythology.

Yet the real Patrick is worthy of remembrance. While the claim that "the Irish saved civilization" may be somewhat exaggerated, the early church in Ireland that Patrick helped to found contributed much to preserving classical and Christian culture and to converting and civilizing the pagan "barbarians" who threatened it. Because sixth-century Ireland is so poorly documented, it is difficult to assess the extent of his influence on the subsequent flowering of art and learning in early medieval Ireland or the Irish monks' evangelization of Scotland and northern England, which in turn led to Anglo-Saxon monks' evangelization of the Franks and other Germanic peoples on the continent. Still, it is safe to say that without Patrick's achievement the history of Christianity in western Europe would be significantly different.

Bibliography: T. Cahill, *How the Irish Saved Civilization: The Untold Story of Ireland's Heroic Role from the Fall of Rome to the Rise of Medieval Europe*, 1995; T. O'Laughlin, *St. Patrick: The Man and His Works*, 1999; E.A. Thompson, *Who Was St. Patrick?* 1985.

William B. Robison

PAULINUS OF NOLA, SAINT (Pontus Meropius Articius, c. 354–431)

Paulinus was a poet and politician who later became a bishop.

Paulinus was born in Bordeaux in Aquitaine to a well-connected senatorial family. He was a successful student of *Ausonius there. In 378 he was consul suffect of Rome, and in 381 governor of Campania. Soon after, he met *Ambrose, and was eventually baptized in 389. Paulinus and his wife Therasia then went to Spain, and in 394, in Barcelona, Paulinus became a priest. After renouncing the life of aristocrat and politician, and having given away his vast wealth, in 395 Paulinus and Therasia went to Nola (in Campania, Italy). There, next to the sanctuary of the third-century martyr Felix (to whom Paulinus was dedicated) at Cimitile, they and others lived a monastic life of poverty. In 409, Therasia died, and Paulinus became bishop of Nola. He remained there until his death on 22 June 431. Paulinus had a vast number of friends and correspondents, including many leading Christians of his day, such as Ausonius, Ambrose, Sulpicius Severus, *Martin of Tours, *Jerome, Rufinus, *Augustine, Niceta of Remesiana, Victricius of Rouen, Julian of Eclanum, and others.

The details of Paulinus' life are known largely from his letters, over fifty of which survive. They also provide a useful insight into the character of religious life and piety in the late fourth and early fifth centuries and into early Christian ideas of friendship. Paulinus was also an important Christian poet of his day (if not of the same stature of *Prudentius). Some thirty-five poems are extant, written mostly in hexameter. Fourteen of them reflect the cult of St. Felix, for whom Paulinus wrote a special birthday poem (*carmen natalicium*) every 14 January.

Bibliography: J.T. Lienhard, *Paulinus of Nola and Early Western Monasticism*, 1977.

Mark Gustafson

PAULLUS, LUCIUS AEMILIUS (c. 229–160 B.C.)

Paullus was a Roman statesman and general. His victory at Pydna put an effective end to the Macedonian monarchy and established Rome's position as the leading power in the Mediterranean.

Paullus was the son of the homonymous consul of 216 who died, in that year, at the Battle of Cannae. His early political career was marked by an aloof style but singular success. As praetor in 191 and then proconsul in 190, he won victories in Spain; and as consul in 182 victories over Ligurian tribesmen. After initial failure in canvassing for a second consulship, he found himself reelected by popular demand during the war against *Perseus of Macedonia (171–168), the prosecution of that war being voted to him rather than assigned, as was traditional, by lot. As consul in 168, he brought that war to a close at the Battle of Pydna. In 167, by authority of a senatorial resolution, he allowed his troops to pillage seventy cities on a single day, 150,000 people being enslaved. His return to Rome (166), where he enjoyed a resplendent triumph (possibly his third), was marred by discontent among his soldiery, their threatened vote coming close to denying him the honor (and presaging such an influence in the assembly as a potential force in the political process), and by the death of his two youngest sons within days of the triumph. His older sons (by an earlier marriage) had been adopted out to other families, the eldest becoming Q. Fabius Maximus Aemilianus, the younger, *P. Cornelius Scipio Aemilianus. Consequently Paullus was the last of his line. One of his daughters married the son of *Cato the Elder. He was elected to a censorship in 164, at which time he may have initiated a landscaping of the eastern side of the Roman forum in an innovative architectural program that advertised the glories of his clan. This would have set an example for more extravagant enterprises in the next century. As an augur, he was noted for his meticulous attention to the minutiae of augural science, and as a commander for a similarly strict discipline, counting victory as a mere accessory to the training of citizens.

Paullus was lionized by a conservative historical tradition that simplified a complex personality. He was a willing participant in the exploitation of victory (as seen in Epirus), a "philhellene" (as seen in the education of his sons and his tour of Greek cultural and historical sites in 168), committed to an austere Roman traditionalism and famed for his chosen "poverty" in later life.

Bibliography: E.S. Gruen, *The Hellenistic World and the Coming of Rome*, 1984.

Tom Hillard

PAUL OF TARSUS, SAINT (?–mid-60s)

Paul, whose Jewish name was Saul, was the prominent early Christian missionary and "Apostle to the Gentiles" whose letters to fledgling Christian communities comprise more than one-fourth of the New Testament canon.

Paul was born into a religiously observant Jewish family of Tarsus in Cilicia in the first decade of the first century A.D. His family likely came from Gischala in Galilee and traced its descent from the tribe of Benjamin; hence, Paul was given the name of the most illustrious ancestor of his tribe, Saul, the first king. Paul inherited Roman citizenship, practiced the trade of tentmaking, and received both Jewish and Greek education, including training in rhetoric. His later studies took him to Jerusalem, where he studied under Gamaliel and became a Pharisee. As a zealous Pharisee he persecuted his fellow Jews who believed in *Jesus as the Messiah. On the way to Damascus in pursuit of those fleeing the persecution, Paul experienced what he described as a revelation by God of the risen Jesus. The experience effected in Paul a change of attitude toward Jesus and his followers and his conversion from Pharisaic to Messianic Judaism. Believing himself called to be the instrument by which the biblical promises about the eschatological ingathering of the nations would be fulfilled, Paul spent the remainder of his life preaching the gospel among Gentiles. Following the trade routes and earning his living by his trade, Paul embarked on missionary journeys to urban centers of the Mediterranean basin. His early efforts in Arabia, Syria, and his native Cilicia were conducted in cooperation with the church at Antioch of Syria. His later endeavors extended to Galatia, Macedonia, Greece, and eventually, according to Clement, to Spain. His preaching resulted in the establishment of numerous churches, hence his designation as "second founder of Christianity." During these journeys, he maintained contact with and directed the communities he had established by means of letters, some of which are preserved in the New Testament.

In 50/51 Paul participated in the Jerusalem conference, convened to address a conflict generated by the success of the Gentile mission. The newly acquired status of Gentiles as members of the People of God had raised the question of their relation to Jewish Law, including circumcision. Paul was an outspoken advocate of what proved to be a controversial decision, that Gentiles were free from the obligations of the Law. The conflict and its aftermath undoubtedly served as the catalyst for the development of his doctrine of justification by faith alone. Before returning to his mission territory, in what was an astute diplomatic

gesture, Paul agreed to the request of the leaders of the mother church in Jerusalem that he take up a collection from his Gentile churches for the needy of
the Jerusalem church. Upon return to his missionary work, Paul vigorously pursued the collection, regarding it as a means to bind the Gentile churches more
closely to the mother church more and as testimony to the Jerusalem leadership
of the divine blessing on his Gentile mission.

In the late 50s, Paul returned to Jerusalem with representatives of the Gentile
churches to deliver their collection for the poor. At the instigation of opponents
who accused him of sacrilege for polluting the Temple precincts by bringing
Gentiles into it, Paul was arrested, imprisoned at Caesarea, and upon exercising
his prerogative as a Roman citizen to appeal his case to Caesar, was sent to
Rome, where he remained under house arrest. According to *Eusebius, Paul was
beheaded in Rome during *Nero's reign. Widely venerated as a saint, apostle,
and martyr soon after his death, he was accorded the honor of being declared,
with *Peter, the joint founder of the prestigious Church of Rome.

Paul's enduring influence was assured by the Acts of the Apostles, in which
he is the most prominent character, and the publication of his letters. Of the
thirteen letters attributed to Paul in the New Testament, seven are generally
agreed to be written by him: 1 Thessalonians, Galatians, 1–2 Corinthians, Philippians, Philemon, and Romans. Through these letters, which contain the earliest Christian theology, Paul has exerted enormous influence on subsequent
Christian thought and practice. In the early centuries alone his influence is visible in the writings of *Clement, *Ignatius, *Polycarp, *Irenaeus, *Origen,
*John Chrysostom, and *Augustine. Later, his doctrine of justification by faith
as articulated in Galatians and Romans inspired the reforms of Luther and Calvin
and the emergence of Protestantism.

Bibliography: J. Murphy-O'Connor, *Paul. A Critical Life*, 1996.

Susan Calef

PAULUS, JULIUS (fl. late second–early third century)

Julius Paulus was a prominent Roman jurist and state official during the Severan dynasty.

Julius Paulus is another of the classical Roman jurists who have left very few
traces of their personal lives. Nothing is known of his birth or life until he is
mentioned as a student of *Quintus Cervidius Scaevola. Paulus served as an
assessor, or legal adviser, for *Papinian while the latter was praetorian prefect
and was a member of the imperial *consilium* of *Septimius Severus and Caracalla. He may have been praetorian prefect under Alexander Severus (222–235).

Paulus' legal writings are numerous and notable for their clarity and logic.
The most important of his writings were the *Responsa* (twenty-three books) and
Quaestiones (twenty-six books); these were collections of cases handled by Pau-
lus in his own legal practice. He also wrote a commentary on the civil law, *Ad
Sabinum*. Paulus also published *Decreta*, reports of cases heard by Severus, and

wrote extensive commentaries on the works of earlier jurists. The influential *Sententiae* was probably not written by Paulus but rather a much later compilation of extracts from his major works. Paulus' prestige is best demonstrated by the fact that by the fifth century his *Responsa* was the fourth-year text in the law curriculum at Berytus, and excerpts from his works amount to approximately one-sixth of Justinian's *Digest*.

Bibliography: F. Schulz, *History of Roman Legal Science*, 2nd ed., 1967.

Karen Wagner

PAUSANIAS OF MAGNESIA AD SIPYLU (?) in Asia Minor (c. 115–180)

Pausanias was a Greek periegetic writer of the Roman period whose *Description of Greece* survives in ten books.

Although Pausanias claimed to describe "all things Greek," his detailed guide treats only the cities and sanctuaries of the Greek mainland, that is to say, the Roman province of Achaia. Numerous digressions, however, address material further afield and attest to his travels in Italy, Anatolia, the Levant, and Egypt. As Pausanias was chiefly concerned to convey the local histories of Greek states, he concentrates on the architecture, sculpture, and painting of the Archaic and classical periods, recounting myths as well as sacred and political histories. Being a keen judge of artistic styles and no fool, he often qualifies the accounts of local guides, rejecting their stories or distinguishing their opinions from his own. Apparently writing for a sophisticated Panhellenic audience unfamiliar with Greek homeland, he pays little attention to postclassical monuments, except those associated with notable Romans, particularly *Hadrian, whom he praises especially.

His style, for the most part, is simple and unpretentious, though he does occasionally echo earlier Greek prose writers. Despite, or perhaps because of, the wealth of information his work contains, it does not appear to have been especially popular in antiquity but was copied in the Renaissance. Although his accounts of particular sites sometimes appear to be confused, his accuracy has been confirmed by excavation, and he provides valuable testimony for now lost and damaged buildings and artworks, as well as Greek history, mythology, and religious practices.

Bibliography: C. Habicht, *Pausanias' Guide to Ancient Greece*, 1985.

Kenneth D.S. Lapatin

PELAGIUS (c. 350?–c. 418)

Pelagius was a theologian whose controversy with St. *Augustine of Hippo over free will and related issues led the Church to condemn him as a heretic.

Pelagius was born between 350 and 360 in Britain or Ireland (probably the former). Some scholars contend that he was a monk or studied law, but there is little evidence for either. In the early 380s he traveled to Rome, where he remained until 409, when the Goth *Alaric's approach forced him and his chief disciple Celestius to flee, first to Sicily and then to north Africa. Up to this point his theology had developed in isolation from doctrinal currents outside of Italy, but he became embroiled in a dispute with Augustine after Celestius bluntly advocated Pelagian views while seeking ordination from Bishop Aurelius of Carthage in 411 and was excommunicated. Meanwhile, Pelagius had moved to Palestine, where he enjoyed considerable support but became involved in further strife with St. *Jerome and *Orosius. A council at Diospolis in 415 vindicated Pelagius, but this carried little weight in north Africa, where in 416 a council at Carthage asked Pope Innocent I to condemn Pelagius and Celestius. In 417 he did so, but his successor Pope Zosimus initially exonerated the two men before reversing himself in 418 after Emperor Honorius and another council at Carthage denounced them again. Pelagius died that same year or shortly thereafter, probably in Egypt. Pelagianism became sufficiently widespread in Britain that in 429 Pope Celestine I sent St. Germanus of Auxerre there to combat it, and he may have made a second trip prior to his death c. 448. The Council of Ephesus condemned Pelagius' teachings in 431.

Pelagius' enemies and supporters both have often exaggerated or misrepresented his views. His two major treatises, *On Nature* and *On Free Will*, are no longer extant (though Augustine quotes them extensively), while his surviving works include only a commentary on St. *Paul's epistles, a confession of faith, and five letters. However, existing sources lead modern scholars to conclude that Pelagius was a practical moral reformer concerned about Christians' routine behavior and wished to be orthodox. Still, he did have distinct differences with Augustine. Pelagius believed that Adam was mortal even before his fall from grace, that his sin was not passed to future generations, that infants are not born with Original Sin and do not require immediate baptism, that man has free will and does not need prevenient grace to live a completely good life, and that there were good men before the coming of Christ. Augustine won the battle, becoming the most influential molder of Christian theology between St. Paul and Thomas Aquinas. Nevertheless, Pelagianism survived as the most pervasive heresy other than Arianism, and many Christians probably have shared some Pelagian beliefs. Had Pelagius not appeared when the Christian church confronted a welter of other heresies, and had he not encountered Augustine fresh from his struggle against the Donatists and falling again into Manichean dualism that stressed transmission of Adam and Eve's sin through the concupiscence of successive generations, he might be regarded as the purveyor of an alternate theology— like, for example, *Clement and *Origen on certain issues—rather than as a heresiarch.

Bibliography: J. Ferguson, *Pelagius: A Historical and Theological Study*, 1956; B.R. Rees, *Pelagius: A Reluctant Heretic*, 1988.

William B. Robison

PELOPIDAS (c. 405–364 b.c.)

Pelopidas was a military and political leader from the city of Thebes. In the 370s and 360s Pelopidas and his close friend *Epaminondas were responsible for turning Thebes, briefly, into the most formidable military power in Greece.

Pelopidas became a hero to his fellow Thebans when he led a daring effort to assassinate the pro-Spartan magistrates of his city and get rid of the Spartan garrison that occupied the citadel. He was eventually made leader of the Sacred Band, a unit of 300 specially trained infantrymen that was instrumental in many of Thebes' military successes. At the Battle of Leuctra in 371, Pelopidas and his Sacred Band held a crucial position in the left wing of the Theban army commanded by Epaminondas. In this battle the Thebans thoroughly routed the Spartans and ended forever Spartan dominance in the Greek world.

After Leuctra, Pelopidas was sent on a series of campaigns in Thessaly to check the growing power of the Thessalian leader Alexander of Pherae. On one of these campaigns, Pelopidas was captured by Alexander and had to be rescued with much effort by Epaminondas. A few years later (364), Pelopidas met Alexander again at the Battle of Cynoscephalae. Pelopidas won the battle but died in the fighting.

Pelopidas and Epaminondas were examples of an innovative and quasi-professional breed of military leader that arises in the fourth century. *Philip II of Macedonia, as a youth, spent time as a hostage in Thebes and seems to have learned much from Pelopidas and Epaminondas, which he later passed down to his son, *Alexander the Great.

Bibliography: J. Buckler, *The Theban Hegemony, 371–362* b.c., 1980.

William Hutton

PERDICCAS (c. 370–320 b.c.)

Perdiccas was a Macedonian military leader. During *Alexander the Great's Asian campaign Perdiccas rose through the ranks to become one of Alexander's chief lieutenants. For a brief time after the king's death, Perdiccas was the most powerful man in the world.

By 323, the year that Alexander died, Perdiccas held the position of commander of the royal Bodyguards. It was claimed, probably by Perdiccas himself, that Alexander had given his signet ring to him before he died. While Perdiccas argued that this signified Alexander's wish that he be regent, other generals were not so ready to yield to his authority. One immediate problem was to determine who was going to be the next king. While Perdiccas and the cavalry supported the unborn son that Alexander's wife Roxane was expecting, the infantry preferred Alexander's half brother Philip Arrhidaeus. Eventually a compromise was worked out involving a joint kingship between the two, with Perdiccas serving as protector for the kings and the others taking up important positions throughout the empire.

Perdiccas soon lost the trust of the other generals, who began to believe that he coveted the kingship for himself. Perdiccas' behavior did nothing to assuage such fears. For instance, he turned down a promising marriage alliance with the daughter of *Antipater, viceroy of Macedonia, in favor of Alexander's sister Cleopatra. Eventually a broad coalition teamed up to oppose Perdiccas, but before they came to battle, Perdiccas was killed in a mutiny of his soldiers in Egypt in 320.

Had Perdiccas succeeded in maintaining the arrangement he worked out after Alexander's death, the empire might have remained united under the kingship of Alexander's descendants. After his death, however, the remaining generals felt less compulsion to respect the legitimacy of the royal family's claim.

Bibliography: W. Heckel, *The Marshals of Alexander's Empire*, 1992.

William Hutton

PERICLES (c. 495–429 B.C.)

Pericles was one of the leading politicians in Athens in the fifth century B.C. He was responsible for many important changes in the Athenian democracy, the construction of many of Athens' public buildings, and the architect of the Athenians' strategy during the early years of the Peloponnesian War.

Pericles' father was Xanthippus and his mother was Agariste. Agariste was the niece of *Cleisthenes and a member of the Alcmaeonid family who had been active in Athenian politics since the late seventh century. As a young man (in 472), Pericles was the *choregos* who was responsible for funding the production of *Aeschylus' tragedy the *Persians*. He rose to prominence in the 460s in alliance with *Ephialtes against *Cimon. After Ephialtes' death in 461, he participated in military campaigns, and he helped consolidate Athenian power as the leader of the Delian League.

During the 450s Pericles was responsible for several important reforms in the Athenian democracy. Early in his political career, Pericles—in alliance with Ephialtes—was probably involved in a reform of the Areopagus (some recent scholars, however, have argued that Pericles' allies and later historians associated him with Ephialtes' attack on the Areopagus after the fact). No source survives that reveals the exact nature of these reforms, but *Aristotle's *Constitution of the Athenians* suggests that they involved the transfer of some judicial and administrative functions from the Areopagus to the council, the assembly, and the law courts. The intent of these reforms appears to have been the expansion of the number of people participating in the Athenian democracy. Sometime after Ephialtes' death, Pericles also introduced pay for jury service—and perhaps also for other public services—to expand the number of people able to participate in political institutions of democratic Athens. Pericles is also credited with limiting Athenian citizenship to only those people who were legitimate children of a citizen mother and father.

During this period, Pericles was also active in the execution of the public building projects in Athens including the Parthenon, the Propylaea, and the fortification of the route from Athens to port in the Piraeus.

Pericles' personal life was somewhat scandalous. During the 450s, Pericles left his wife to live with the *hetaira* *Aspasia, with whom Pericles had a son. Aspasia was active in Athenian political and intellectual circles. She is said to have been a teacher of rhetoric, and *Plato, in the *Menexenus*, claims that she was the author of Pericles' famous funeral oration. Despite the fact that Pericles passed a law limiting the privileges of citizenship to the legitimate children of two citizens, Pericles' son was granted citizenship long after his father's death.

Both Pericles' political power and his personal lifestyle attracted the ridicule of Athenian comic poets. For example, Aspasia was a target in comedy both because of her unorthodox relationship with Pericles and because of her presumed influence on Athenian policy. *Plutarch's *Life of Pericles* also reports that comic poets would attack Pericles more generally for his sexual license. It claims, for example, that Pericles would commission the famous sculptor *Phidias to create works of art to help him convince women to meet with him. Ridicule of Pericles was not confined solely to his personal life; he was also mocked for the control he exercised over Athenian politics. Plutarch reports that Pericles was compared unfavorably to Zeus because both were capricious absolute rulers and that he was also mocked as a new *Pisistratus.

The end of Pericles' career coincides with the outbreak of the Peloponnesian War. Pericles was the author of the Athenian strategy for the first part of the war. Aristotle reports that as early as the 440s and 450s, Pericles focused on developing Athens' naval power. This had important implications for the battle with Sparta because they possessed a superior land army. Pericles' strategy was for the Athenians to remain within their city walls and allow the Spartans free reign in the surrounding countryside. At the same time, the Athenian navy would keep the Spartan forces in check by attacking coastal areas in Sparta's territories. According to *Thucydides, this strategic configuration would allow Athens to outlast Sparta in a war of attrition.

At the end of the first year of the war, the Athenians gathered to bury those who had died in battle. Thucydides reports that Pericles delivered the now-famous eulogy for these war dead. Thucydides' version of this funeral oration is now considered one of the most important pieces of Greek literature from the classical period. In 429, just over two years after the outbreak of the Peloponnesian War, a plague struck Athens, and Pericles was among its victims.

Pericles' influence on classical Athens was far-reaching. Thucydides credits him with being a great leader, and the Aristotelian *Constitution of the Athenians* suggests that Pericles made Athens a much more democratic city. This period also saw the production of some of the great works of Greek literature in the tragedians and Greek art and architecture on the Acropolis and in the Parthenon. The age of Pericles, in fact, is traditionally considered the golden age of Athenian democracy.

Bibliography: C.W. Fornara and L.J. Samons, *Athens from Cleisthenes to Pericles*, 1991; A.J. Podlecki, *Perikles and His Circle*, 1998.

Jeff Rydberg-Cox

PERPETUA, VIBIA (c. 181–203), and FELICITY (?–203), SAINTS

Saints Perpetua and Felicity were Christian martyrs from Roman Carthage who challenged Roman and Christian patriarchal authority.

While Perpetua is famous as the first female Roman martyr, her importance derives from her challenge to Roman and Christian patriarchal authority. Her public disobedience toward her father and Hilarianus, the proconsul, violated the Roman doctrine of the father's absolute authority, while her dream visions established her as an authority over the male leaders of the Christian church in Carthage.

What little is known about Perpetua comes from *The Passion of Saints Perpetua and Felicity*, an account assembled shortly after their martyrdom in the arena. Perpetua was an educated Roman citizen who could read and write; she could speak both Latin and Greek. From the *Passion* we know that she was married and had recently given birth to a son; nothing is known of her husband. Rather, Perpetua's father was the major male figure in her life. Contrary to his wishes, Perpetua converted to Christianity and joined a church in Carthage. Before she had taken her final vows of Christianity, she was arrested and imprisoned along with the other converts. Brought before Hilarianus, she publicly disobeyed orders from him to perform a sacrifice to the health of the emperor. Her refusal humiliated her father, who begged her to sacrifice and who was in turn beaten as a result of her refusal. While in prison, she had dream visions. She recorded these visions in a writing that is included in the *Passion* and that constitutes one of the earliest surviving examples of women's writing.

In the first dream, she envisions her own salvation, seeing herself climb a ladder into heaven. In the next vision, she sees her deceased brother Dinocrates, at first dirty and bearing the facial cancer that caused his death at age seven, unable to reach a pool of water to drink. In a subsequent vision, she sees him as well dressed with his faced healed, able to drink. She understands the visions to mean that her martyrdom will save her brother.

In the next vision, she sees herself, changed into a man, wrestling against an Egyptian in an arena. When she defeats the Egyptian, she understands that her death in the arena will represent her victory over the devil. Saturus, another condemned Christian, dreams that he and Perpetua, having been martyred, join in the heavenly host, advising their church leaders, thereby establishing the martyrs as authorities over the earthly church.

Felicity, a slave, was eight months pregnant when arrested and thus ineligible to be martyred in the arena with the others. Miraculously, she gave birth early, permitting her also to be thrown to the beasts on 3 March 203 in games held to celebrate the birthday of the emperor *Septimius Severus' son, Geta. While imprisoned, the Christians' faith was evident to their guards, many of whom converted. When thrown into the arena near Carthage, Saturus was gored by a wild boar, while Perpetua and Felicity were gored by a heifer. Still alive, the bloodied and wounded Christians were taken to a stage in the center of the arena to have their throats slit by young gladiator recruits. Perpetua's attacker missed, striking her collar bone and causing her to howl in pain. She in turn guided the sword into her own body as if she could die only by her own will. Her death act not only served as further witness to her faith but also signaled a reassertion of female authority in both the secular and Christian realms.

Bibliography: J.E. Salisbury, *Perpetua's Passion: The Death and Memory of a Young Roman Woman*, 1997.

Ron Harris

PERSEUS (213/212–166 B.C.)

Eldest son to *Philip V, Perseus was the last Antigonid ruler, and his failed efforts at reestablishing Macedonian authority in the Balkans led to his downfall and the end of an independent Macedon.

Perseus was born about 213–212 to Polycrateia, a Greek noble woman whom Philip had seduced and abducted. Brought up half-Greek and half-Macedonian, Perseus regularly showed himself very indulgent in matters dealing with the Hellenic world. He served his father ably and well in the Second Macedonian War (200–197), where he displayed real energy and skill as a general. In the aftermath of the Roman victory at Cynocephalae (197), Perseus, too, rankled at the offhand treatment of Rome. Over time this led him into a series of personal and policy conflicts with his younger half brother, Demetrius, since the latter more and more espoused a pro-Roman stance that also seemed to threaten Perseus' ascension to the throne. Philip eventually ordered Demetrius' death in 181. Philip died two years later, leaving Perseus king of Macedon.

Perseus inherited a kingdom that had been rebuilt by Philip following the defeat at the hands of the Romans. With this, he began to extend his authority into the northeast and northwest areas of the Balkans traditionally associated with Macedonian imperialism. In addition, Perseus forged an alliance with the Seleucids by marrying Seleucus IV's daughter. Rhodes, too, joined the pact, and all of Greece began to see Perseus as the bulwark against Roman encroachment. Fearing for the independence of Pergamum, *Eumenes II appealed to Rome to intervene. Seeing its authority in Greece challenged, Rome initiated the Third Macedonian War in 171. Despite his marriage alliance and his pro-Hellenic attitudes, only Epirus, Illyria, and the Odrysae Thracians came to Perseus' aid. With a determination born of desperation, Perseus led his army against Rome, and at first he held his own. The Romans finally broke the Illyrians and reinforced their army in Macedon. In 168, they also elected *Lucius Aemilius Paullus consul, and he immediately set about training his army until it was in a high state of military readiness. In late June, Paullus brought Perseus to battle at Pydna. The Macedonians nearly carried the day, but rough ground broke up the phalanx and allowed the legionnaires to regroup, counterattack, and sweep the field of Perseus' army. Although he escaped the battle, Perseus was captured and adorned Paullus' triumph in Rome. He died two years later while imprisoned at Alba Fucens, the victim of Roman maltreatment.

Perseus stands as a rather tragic figure, the last Antigonid monarch, and the last best hope for any sort of Hellenistic renaissance. Pydna gave final proof of the superiority of the Roman military system over the phalanx, and with the fall of Perseus, the remaining Hellenistic empires and kingdoms could but bide their time until Rome would bring them down.

Bibliography: F.W. Walbank, *Philip V of Macedon*, 1940.

Cyril M. Lagvanec

PERSIUS FLACCUS, AULUS (34–62)

Persius was a Latin Stoic poet.

Persius was born at Vollaterrae in Etruria to an equestrian family. After his father's death, he was educated in Rome by L. Annaeus Cornutus alongside the poet *Lucan. This Stoic influence lies behind the moralizing tone in the short book of poetry that survives. Dense with literary allusion, the six satires (written in dactylic hexameters) and brief prologue are filled with aggressive, idiosyncratic imagery. The prologue (written in choliambics, a meter used by *Hipponax and *Callimachus) ironically distances Persius' work from a popular contemporary preference for Callimacheanism and instead allies itself with the verse satire of Lucilius and (especially) *Horace. The programmatic Satire 1 surveys the bleak state of the contemporary literary scene with passion and concision. Subsequent poems discuss hypocrisy in prayer (2) and the use of Stoicism for self-improvement (3), present *Socrates and *Alcibiades in conversation on the need to "know thyself" (4), provide a tribute to Cornutus with a Stoic sermon (5), and urge contentment with one's possessions (6). Cornutus published these poems after Persius died of a stomach ailment.

Christian writers through the late classical and medieval periods praised the moral tone of Persius' work. While more recent authors have picked up the voice of the angry young man, it is typically mediated through Persius' successor, *Juvenal.

Bibliography: G. Lee, trans., and W. Barr, int., *The Satires of Persius*, 1987.

C.W. Marshall

PETER, SAINT (?–mid-60s)

Peter, also referred to as Simon Peter and Cephas (Aramaic), was one of the twelve apostles of *Jesus and a leading figure in the life and mission of the early church, to whom two New Testament letters are attributed. He is traditionally regarded as the first pope and bishop of Rome.

Peter, whose original name was apparently Simon Bar-Jona (son of John), was a fisherman from the village of Capernaum in Galilee. He had a brother Andrew, was married, and in his missionary activity after the death of Jesus, apparently traveled with his wife. He was among the first called by Jesus to be a disciple and clearly belonged to the inner circle commonly referred to as the Twelve, serving as the group's spokesman. Only in the Gospel of *Matthew is Simon renamed as the "rock" (*petros*) of the new church and given keys of authority. One cannot know for certain whether the name change to Peter and the assignation of authority took place during the ministry of Jesus or only after the Resurrection, although the latter seems more likely. If after the Resurrection, the change occurred early, since *Paul regularly refers to him not as Simon but Cephas, a grecized form of the name derived from the Aramaic word for "rock." It is probable that Peter made a confession of Jesus as the Messiah during Jesus' lifetime but that his understanding of Jesus' messiahship, being inadequate, called forth Jesus' rebuke. Peter's denial of Jesus during the Passion further suggests the apostle's flawed understanding of Jesus.

Peter clearly played a major role in the apostolic church. He is depicted as the most prominent leader of the Jerusalem church in the first fifteen chapters of Acts of the Apostles. His leadership role is corroborated by Paul's testimony that the Risen Jesus appeared first to Peter, an experience that may have contributed to Peter's stature in the early church, and that he functioned as a "pillar" of the mother church in Jerusalem and as the leader of the mission to the circumcised. Although a leader of the Jerusalem church and involved in the Jewish Christian mission, there is evidence that Peter exercised some sort of bridging role to the Gentile churches as well, although the nature and extent of that activity are difficult to determine.

With the exception of an echo of his martyrdom in the Gospel of *John, the New Testament provides nothing on Peter's life beyond the period of Paul's activity. Numerous early noncanonical texts attest his eventual presence and martyrdom in Rome, probably during the Neronian persecution. These sources provide no information on how Peter got to Rome, nor do they agree on the length of Peter's stay in Rome, the motive and nature of his martyrdom, or his involvement in the leadership structure of Roman Christianity. *Clement, a leader of the Roman church, describes Peter's trials in Rome, and the historian *Eusebius reports an ancient story about Peter's crucifixion in Rome during *Nero's persecution. Peter's function in the Roman church is unattested, but it is clear that the papacy as we know it today did not exist in first-century Rome. The singular devotion to Peter by the Roman community was a late development. Until the third century, Peter and Paul jointly bore authority in Rome and elsewhere. *Ignatius of Antioch assumed that both Peter and Paul exercised authority over the church in the imperial capital, and *Irenaeus claimed that together they founded the church there and inaugurated the succession of bishops. The tradition identifying Peter as the first bishop of Rome emerges only in the late second or early third century, due in part to the efforts of Roman bishops to claim universal leadership of the Christian community on the basis of the tradition of Peter as "rock of the church" in the Gospel of Matthew. This unique tradition continues to serve as the basis for the Petrine office of the papacy in Roman Catholicism.

It is unlikely that Peter wrote either of the two letters that bear his name in the New Testament. The attribution of these and numerous second- to sixth-century texts to the apostle (e.g., Apocalypse of Peter, Gospel of Peter, Acts of Peter, Martyrdom of Peter) indicates a widespread appreciation of his stature in the early church and a desire to claim the authority of Peter for one's views.

Bibliography: R.E. Brown, K.P. Donfried, and J. Reumann, eds., *Peter in the New Testament*, 1973.

Susan Calef

PETRONIUS ARBITER, GAIUS (?–65)

Petronius was the author of the *Satyricon*, a bawdy, picaresque narrative satirizing Roman society in the age of *Nero.

Despite speculation, most agree that the author of the *Satyricon* was identical with Petronius Arbiter, a governor of Bithynia and a consul who was admitted into Nero's inner circle, where his refined tastes, voluptuary nature, and administrative energy earned him a position as "arbiter of taste" and arranger of entertainments. According to *Tacitus, however, when a rival spread false rumors about Petronius, he fell into disfavor with the emperor and committed suicide to avoid a worse death.

Because only fragments of books 14–16 exist, the *Satyricon* remains as mysterious as its author. These fragments suggest that the *Satyricon* was once an immense work, close in size to the Homeric epics that it frequently mocks. The *Satyricon* concerns the sexual misadventures of Encolpius, Ascyltus, and their young slave Giton as they wander around the Greek colonies of southern Italy. During their travels, Encolpius suffers the wrath of the god Priapus, and as a result he finds himself not only in frequent sexual trouble but also impotent. While trying to overcome his sexual curse as well as find meals and lodging, he meets witches, eunuchs, pimps, slaves, nouveau riche freedmen, and other characters who demonstrate the unsavory, excessive side of the new Roman Empire. In addition, he encounters characters whose classical names, such as Agamemnon and Circe, lend the story a mock-heroic air. The central, most complete fragment involves the dinner of Trimalchio, an immensely rich, vulgar, former slave who treats Encolpius and his friends to an extravagantly tasteless meal. During the meal, which is filled with images of death, money, and artifice, Petronius captures the voices of a new class of Roman citizen.

The *Satyricon* is considered a wholly original Roman hybrid, a comic novel as well as a Menippean satire. While brilliantly mocking traditional narrative forms such as the Greek romance and epic, it uses realistic detail, outrageous sexual situations, and playfully obscene language to criticize excess (*luxuria*) in Roman society.

Bibliography: C. Connors, *Petronius the Poet: Verse and Literary Tradition in the Satyricon*, 1998.

Richard Louth

PHEIDON (c. 650 B.C.)

Pheidon was an early ruler of the Greek city of Argos. He is credited with a number of important innovations and with making Argos into one of the leading powers of Greece in his time.

Although he held the kingship legitimately as a descendant of the royal house of Temenos, many later writers called Pheidon a tyrant because of the harsh nature of his rule. His most notorious act was an invasion of Olympia and his subsequent usurping of the running of the Olympic games. Many modern historians also credit him with defeating the Spartans at the Battle of Hysiae in 669, but our sole ancient source for this battle does not mention Pheidon in connection with it. He is said to have introduced a new system of weights and measures and to have minted the first coinage on the island of Aegina. Many scholars doubt this last achievement because there is no archaeological evidence for coinage in Greece before c. 600. Still, it is conceivable that Pheidon was responsible for introducing fixed standards for the weights of precious metals, which would have been an important step on the way to a standardized system of coinage.

Pheidon was an important figure in a period of great political, military, and economic transition in Greece. His influence stretched from Olympia in the west to Aegina in the east, and under his leadership, Argos had the upper hand, for once, in its long-lasting rivalry with Sparta.

Bibliography: L.H. Jeffery, *Archaic Greece: The City-States c. 700–500 B.C.*, 1976.

William Hutton

PHIDIAS (or Pheidas, c. 490–430 B.C.)

Phidias, considered the most influential sculptor in classical Athens, directed building projects on the Acropolis and created monumental statues of Athena and Zeus. While his most legendary statues no longer exist, the frieze of the Parthenon still demonstrates his talents.

The son of a painter, Phidias had already created two famous bronze statues for the Acropolis when, according to *Plutarch, *Pericles chose him to supervise the rebuilding of this site. The Athena Promachos (470–460) was so huge that its spear could be seen from the sea, and the Athena Lemnia (c. 450) was celebrated for its beauty. As supervisor of the Acropolis, Phidias directed a group of artists including *Ictinus and *Callicrates, who constructed buildings and carved decorative sculptures such as the pediments, metopes, and frieze of the Parthenon. He also created the Athena Parthenos (438), a forty-foot chryselephantine (gold and ivory) statue standing inside the Parthenon. Although it no longer survives, *Pausanias left a description of it, a Hellenistic copy was made for the main hall of the royal library in Pergamum c. 160 B.C., and it appeared on Roman coins from the time of *Hadrian.

In 432, Pericles' enemies accused Phidias of having stolen gold from the Athena Parthenos. Although he was cleared of this charge, he was later accused of impiety by depicting both Pericles and himself on the shield of Athena Parthenos. Moving to Olympia, he formed another workshop and created a magnificent seated statue of Zeus, considered one of the Seven Wonders of the World. He died either in Elis or while imprisoned in Athens.

Phidias is credited with guiding an entire generation of artists in his Athenian and Olympian workshops as well as with influencing a second generation of sculptors who venerated his work. His awe-inspiring cult statues of Athena Parthenos and Zeus captured the detached majesty of these gods, while his reliefs for the Parthenon demonstrated his ability to represent the natural, fluid movement of humans. Phidias' work on the Acropolis embodied the spirit of Periclean Athens as well as the balance, idealism, beauty, and grandeur of the High Classical style.

Bibliography: M. Robertson, *A History of Greek Art*, 2 vols., 1975.

Richard Louth

PHILEMON (c. 363–264 B.C.)

Philemon was a Greek comic poet.

Philemon left his native Syracuse and became an Athenian citizen in 307/306. He also spent some time at the court of *Ptolemy I in Egypt. He contributed ninety-seven plays to the stage of New Comedy, and sixty of their titles are known. Some of these plays, however, may have been written by his son, the younger Philemon, who is said to have also been a playwright.

Philemon won at least four first-place prizes, sometimes defeating his rival *Menander. In the end, however, Menander proved victorious, as only fragments and adaptations of Philemon's work survive. The general sense of his dramatic style can be derived from *Plautus' *Mercator* (The Merchant), *Trinummus* (Threepenny Day), and probably *Mostellaria* (The Haunted House), which are Latin adaptations of plays by Philemon. Philemon's style is thought to have been livelier than Menander's, involving less complicated plots, more wit, and more farcical situations.

Philemon's comedies were revived in Athens after his death, and in the second century A.D., a statue was erected there in his honor. *Apuleius drew comparisons between him and Menander, and *Quintilian assigned him second place among the poets of the New Comedy.

Bibliography: T.B.L. Webster, *Studies in Later Greek Comedy*, 2nd ed., 1970.

Andrew G. Traver

PHILIP II OF MACEDONIA (382–336 B.C.)

Philip became king of Macedonia in 359 at the age of twenty-three. He reformed the army organization, its tactics, and its weapons and converted Macedonia from an undistinguished backward collection of tribes into a major world power. Philip's efforts made possible the world conquests of his son, *Alexander the Great.

One of his early important actions was to gain control of the gold mines at nearby Mount Pangaeus; that wealth would enable him to buy power and influence whenever possible, backed up by the threat of a formidable army. Philip was a capable diplomat as well as military commander. The combination of money, military force, and persuasion enabled him to gain control of neighboring Celtic tribes as well as independent Greek cities. His "alliances" with them were decidedly unequal but generally fell short of outright control or annexation.

His control of the north Aegean sea coast was a matter of great concern to the city of Athens, which depended on imports of grain and timber from the area. Indeed, the entire region had been part of the Athenian empire fifty years earlier. Philip had an ally among Athenian politicians, *Aeschines, but fierce opposition from the famous orator *Demosthenes, whose First Philippic was delivered in 351.

Philip inserted himself into the affairs of central Greece during the "Third Sacred War" from 356 to 346, when he agreed to pursue and punish the Phocian mercenaries who had taken control of the sacred site of Delphi. In return, he received the votes of the Phocians on the influential Amphictionic Council; he had previously gained the votes of Thessalian cities. During this war, he used bolt- and stone-throwing catapults for the first time.

Demosthenes succeeded in persuading Athens to declare war on Philip in 341 while he was besieging Byzantium, a city that was an ally of Athens, and he also arranged an alliance with the city of Thebes, a former ally of Philip. In the Battle of Chaeronea in 338, the Athenians and Thebans were soundly defeated by the Macedonians under Philip and his eighteen-year-old son Alexander. Thebes was severely punished and garrisoned, but Philip sent his son to Athens to negotiate a treaty of friendship and alliance. He was about to invade Persia and needed the support of the Athenian fleet. In the following spring, all the Greek cities were invited to a meeting at Corinth (it was an invitation that only Sparta refused), where Philip announced the creation of the Hellenic League, under his direction, which would mount a joint invasion of Persia.

An advance force was sent across the Hellespont into Persian-controlled Anatolia in the spring of 336, but before the main invasion could be launched, Philip was assassinated. He was attending the wedding of his daughter, Cleopatra, when one of his bodyguards leaped forward and stabbed him. The assassin, Pausanias, was immediately killed by Alexander and other bodyguards. His motive was apparently a private grievance with Philip, and his action was perhaps encouraged by *Olympias, Philip's estranged wife. Alexander was immediately hailed as king in his place.

The major ancient source of information for Philip is the orator Demosthenes, whose speeches portray Philip in the darkest possible terms. Demosthenes was correct in the analysis that Philip brought about the end of the free and independent Greek polis; Greece would remain largely under Macedonian control thereafter. Others saw Philip as the first to unite Greece. In both diplomatic and military matters, Philip prepared the way for his son, Alexander the Great.

Bibliography: E.L. Borza, *In the Shadow of Olympus*, 1990; N.G.L. Hammond, *Philip of Macedon*, 1994.

Janice J. Gabbert

PHILIP V OF MACEDONIA (238–179 B.C.)

Philip V was the penultimate Antigonid monarch whose forty-two years on the throne represented a series of unsuccessful bids to extend Macedonian hegemony.

Philip V succeeded to the kingship in 221, upon the death of his stepfather and guardian, *Antigonus III. Although a brave and resolute soldier and possessing adequate diplomatic skills, Philip lacked the vision to bring to fruition any of his long-range plans. He also regularly demonstrated a ruthlessness that went far in frustrating his efforts. This probably stemmed from his propensity to inject his personal emotions into Macedonian policy.

In his early days as king, Philip V was seen as the one man who could unite the Hellenic world and prevent its subjugation. He soon showed himself as a conqueror, and the Aetolian League, Sparta, and Elis successfully resisted Philip in the Social War (221–217). Balked in his efforts to control the Greeks, Philip struck a treaty with *Hannibal in 215 and moved against Rome in Illyria. Mutual distrust between the two opponents of Rome and Graeco-Roman resistance finally led to the Peace of Phoenice in 205, which left Philip's westward schemes unfulfilled. Since 218, he had worked to revivify the Macedonian fleet, and with it Philip tried to control much of the Aegean Sea and Anatolia. He aroused the states of Pergamum and Rhodes, which combined to defeat him at the major naval battle of Chios (201), and later led them to call for Roman intervention. Alarmed by Philip's expansionist ways, Rome declared war in 200. The Second Macedonian War came to an end at the decisive Battle of Cynocephalae (197), where *Titus Quinctius Flaminius led his legions in a smashing victory over the Hellenistic phalanx.

After the defeat, Philip actively collaborated with Rome in their wars with Nabis of Sparta and *Antiochus III of the Seleucid empire. Despite cordial relations with Flaminius and *Scipio Africanus, Philip received shabby, offhand treatment from Rome. Even as he rebuilt his ravaged kingdom and focused his energies to the north, the only compass point where he had not yet met with failure, Philip continued to submit to the arbitrations and pronouncements of Rome. His final years were marked by frustrations and setbacks, even to the point of ordering the murder of his younger son, Demetrius, in 180 when the prince seemed too eager to ally himself with Rome. Defeat, grief, and old age finally felled the king the following year. He left the realm to his eldest son, *Perseus.

A man of real talents, Philip V could never formulate a coherent foreign policy. All of his efforts to extend Macedonian power and influence collapsed and only facilitated the extension of Roman control eastward.

Bibliography: F.W. Walbank, *Philip V of Macedon*, 1940.

Cyril M. Lagvanec

PHILODEMUS (c. 110–c. 40 B.C.)

Philodemus was a Greek Epicurean philosopher and poet who was influential in Roman circles, being the friend and adviser of L. Calpurnius Piso Caesoninus, father-in-law of *Julius Caesar. *Cicero esteemed him, and the Roman poets *Virgil and *Horace were in his circle.

He was born at Gadara, southeast of Galilee, and studied under Zeno of Sidon, head of the Epicurean school. He came to Italy in the 70s and settled at his patron Piso's villa at Herculaneum. Unlike his contemporary fellow Epicurean philosopher poet *Lucretius, he seems not to have been much interested in physics but wrote widely on ethics, the arts, and theology and also epigrammatic poems on love.

His works have survived mainly in the papyrus fragments recovered from his library in Piso's villa at Herculaneum, which was destroyed in the eruption of Vesuvius in A.D. 79. This was first excavated in the 1750s and has yielded charred fragments of several works, including *On Signs, On Piety, On Frankness, On the Good King According to Homer, On Poems,* and *On Music,* among others. Now the reconstruction and editing of fragments undertaken by the Philodemus Project is one of the most important endeavors in classical scholarship.

Philodemus was a vigorous defender of Epicureanism against contemporary attacks of other schools and helped to interpret the philosophy for a Roman audience. He was not particularly an original thinker but can be seen developing Epicurean doctrine in response to other schools, especially the Stoics, while retaining a strong concern for establishing Epicurean orthodoxy.

Philodemus' learning and sophistication helped make Epicureanism more respectable in his own day—witness Cicero's (who was no admirer of Epicureanism) high regard for him. Today, with the recovery and reconstruction of more of his works, Philodemus is becoming one of the most important sources for Hellenistic philosophy.

Bibliography: E. Asmis, "Philodemus' Epicureanism," *Aufstieg und Niedergang der römischen Welt* 2 (1990): 2369–2406.

Gordon Campbell

PHILO OF ALEXANDRIA (Philo Judaeus, c. 30 B.C.–A.D. 45)

Philo was a scholar and a leader of the Jewish community in Alexandria.

Philo was born in Alexandria where he rose to prominence in the Jewish community. He led a delegation to Rome to the Emperor Gaius (*Caligula) in A.D. 40 to protest the persecution of Jews and the restrictions on their religious practice. In his writings, he attempted to incorporate Hebrew religion with Greek philosophy by means of allegory. Most of his writings survive in Greek, although there are a few Armenian translations. He is the most important representative of Hellenistic Judaism.

Philo's extant works can be divided into three groups. The first group contains treatises on recent events including *Against Flaccus*, a denunciation of Flaccus, the Roman governor of Alexandria, and *On the Embassy to Gaius*, an account of the Jewish delegation sent to Caligula. Both of these works were very influential in early Christian communities as they presented the idea that persecutors would inevitably be punished by God's judgment. The second group consists of general philosophical and religious essays. The third group consists of twenty-five essays and homilies to elucidate the Pentateuch, in particular Genesis. In one work of this group, *The Exposition*, Philo attempts to explain the Mosaic Law to the Gentiles; in another, *The Allegory of the Laws*, Philo explains Mosaic Law to the Jews through recourse to allegory. In his scriptural expositions, Philo relied exclusively on the Greek translation of the Hebrew Scriptures.

Like *Plato, Philo's doctrine man is dualistic, treating the body as a prison for the soul that seeks to rise to God. Ethically, man's aim is to seek deliverance from the world of sense to return to God. Philo's view of the Logos, which the Stoics had defined as the Godhead, was that of an immanent intelligence of the transcendent God, distinguished though not separate from God. Similarities exist here to the Gospel of *John, and this conception of the Logos influenced the early Church Fathers. Many early Christian writers, such as *Clement and *Origen, used Philo's allegorical method.

While Philo had a minimal effect on Judaism, his writings had a lasting influence on early Christian literature.

Bibliography: S. Sandmel, *Philo of Alexandria: An Introduction*, 1979.

Andrew G. Traver

PHILOPOEMEN (253–182 B.C.)

Philopoemen was a statesman of the Achaean League.

Philopoemen was born into a wealthy family of Megalopolis. Although educated by Platonists, he preferred military studies.

In 223 Philopoemen persuaded his citizens against an alliance with *Cleomenes III of Sparta, who had recently annexed the cities of Mantinea, Tegea, and Orochomenus. He successfully evacuated Megalopolis before Cleomenes' assault and then decisively defeated the king in the following year at the Battle of Sellasia. Philopoemen spent his next ten years fighting as a mercenary in Crete. Upon his return, he was elected commander of the Achaean League's cavalry. Two years later, he was appointed the League's chief commander. He reorganized the cavalry and infantry of the League and twice defeated Sparta (207, 202–201).

Philopoemen opposed the League's entry on the Roman side against *Philip

V in the Second Macedonian War and once again left for Crete in 198. He returned in 193 and successfully led the Achaeans against Sparta but was prevented by *T.Q. Flaminius from taking the city. Philopoemen incorporated Sparta and Messene into the League but had to crush a Spartan revolt in 188. Philopoemen demilitarized the city and abolished the remnants of any Lycurgan institutions.

He continued to dominate League policy in the face of growing Roman power. Philopoemen was captured when Messene revolted in 183/182 and was given poison. *Polybius participated in the funeral and carried his ashes. Our chief authority for his life is Polybius, and *Plutarch, *Pausanias, and *Livy all used him as a source.

Although considered a hero of the League, Philopoemen was never able to balance the interests of the Greek states with those of Rome in a successful manner.

Bibliography: R.M. Errington, *Philopoemen*, 1969.

Andrew G. Traver

PHILOSTORGIUS (c. 368–c. 435)

Philostorgius was an Arian ecclesiastical historian.

Philostorgius was born at Boryssus in Cappadocia. He made his way to Constantinople by age twenty, where he took up residence. His profession is unknown. At some point he made the acquaintance of Eunomius, the radical (anomoean) Arian.

Philostorgius is known for his *Ecclesiastical History*, which concerns events from 320 to 425, but he differs markedly from the other continuators of *Eusebius of Caesarea because he was not a supporter of Nicene orthodoxy. Probably for this reason his work did not survive but is recoverable only partially, mainly through the summary and excerpts in the ninth-century epitome of Photius. Philostorgius is plainly biased, defending *Arius, favoring Aetius and Eunomius, praising the Emperor Constantius, while condemning *Theodosius I and II. But he uses sources not used by the other church historians, portrays Arian leaders and perspectives in a favorable light, and thus is very valuable for his representation of the losing side in the Arian controversy.

Other works, including the life of Lucian of Antioch and an encomium on Eunomius, are lost.

Bibliography: J. Quasten, *Patrology*, 4 vols., 1950–1986.

Mark Gustafson

PHILOSTRATUS OF LEMNOS (c. 230)

Philostratus was a Sophist and biographer, best known for his work on Apollonius of Tyana.

Philostratus was a biographer and does not give any detailed information about his own life, but his biographies do provide glimpses of his education and philosophy. He was born on the island of Lemnos to a literary family. He plied his rhetorical trade in Athens and then in Rome. There he came into the circle of the Empress *Julia Domna. Julia Domna had turned her talents and energies to cultivating a literary salon. There she commissioned Philostratus to write a biography of Apollonius, the first-century wonder-worker and "man of God." His second work, *The Lives of the Sophists*, begins with a survey of the late fifth- and early fourth-century B.C. Sophists, then traces an intellectual genealogy from that time to his own time. The remainder of the work then provides biographies of Philostratus' teachers and contemporaries. Through his writings he was both a part of and a chronicler of a renaissance experienced in the Hellenistic world under Roman rule. Specifically, he participates in the revival of Sophism and records this revival, naming the period the "Second Sophistic."

Philostratus' *Life of Apollonius* has had a lasting effect on Christianity and the study of Christianity. Apollonius was a philosopher who performed miracles and healings, gathered disciples, and is called by some of his followers the Son of God. The parallels between Apollonius and *Jesus were first developed by Hierocles, a governor under *Diocletian, as part of an anti-Christian track. By the end of the fourth century, Apollonius was a key component in the debate between pagans and Christians. Today, he remains a subject of study in New Testament and historical Jesus scholarship.

Bibliography: G. Anderson, *Philostratus*, 1986.

Jennifer L. Koosed

PHOCION (c. 400–318 B.C.)

Phocion was an Athenian general and statesman.

Though Phocion was the son of a lathe worker, he received an extremely good education, which enabled him to become a celebrated Athenian war hero. While attending lectures from *Plato and *Xenocrates as part of his educational experience, Phocion developed moral fervor toward and desire for peace. In order to promote ideas of peace, Phocion became involved in promoting the welfare of Athens through activity in both civil and military affairs.

As a statesman he commanded great respect supporting *Aeschines, Eubulus, and Demades against *Demosthenes and Hyperides. He vigorously opposed the anti-Macedonian policies of Demosthenes and thought that cooperation with *Philip II of Macedonia was in the best interest of Athens. But his greater fame was as general at which he was considered a military mastermind. In fact, Phocion was elected general forty-five times without ever attending an election. It was through his powerful service against Persia (350 and 344), his campaigns in Euboea (348), his expulsion of Cleitarchus from Eretria (341), and his defense of Byzantium (340/339) that he gained his reputation.

After *Alexander the Great's death (323), Phocion opposed Athenian participation in a revolt against Macedonia (Lamian War). *Antipater quashed the revolt and severely limited Athens' franchises. Phocion's popularity began to decline when he served as diplomat to Antipater. In 319, Antipater's son *Cassander directed the Macedonian commander in Athens to seize the Piraeus, the port of Athens. Phocion made no attempt to stop him, because the commander had lied about his intentions. Many Athenians viewed Phocion's role in the Piraeus affair as treasonous, and when a new Athenian democracy was formed, Phocion was immediately condemned to death.

*Plutarch presents a very favorable view of Phocion, comparing his life to *Cato the Younger's and his death to that of *Socrates.

Bibliography: P. Green, *Alexander to Actium: The Historical Evolution of the Hellenistic Age*, 1990.

Richard Draper

PHYLARCHUS (third century B.C.)

Phylarchus was a Greek historian.

The area from which Phylarchus came is uncertain but is usually identified as Athens or Naucratis. Nothing is known about his life, and only a few fragments of his work are extant except in references in writings of later historians. He wrote a twenty-eight-volume *Histories* covering the period from the death of *Pyrrhus c. 272 until the death of *Cleomenes III of Sparta c. 220. A few fragments of this work remain.

*Polybius in the second century B.C. criticized Phylarchus' writing style and content as arbitrary and erroneous. However, Polybius' evaluation was due to his opposition to Phylarchus' sympathetic perspective of Sparta. Apparently Phylarchus used supernatural or miraculous stories, anecdotes, love affairs, and other illustrations that were deemed to be sensational in his writing. It appears that Phylarchus adopted this style from Duris of Samos, who dealt with the preceding period in a similar way. *Plutarch, like Polybius, also took issue with Phylarchus' historical presentations. However, both Polybius and Plutarch used Phylarchus' historical presentation as the basis for their history of the period since Phylarchus' works were apparently the most comprehensive on the period available.

Bibliography: T.W. Africa, *Phylarchus and the Spartan Revolution*, 1961.

Roger W. Anderson

PINDAR (c. 518–c. 445 B.C.)

Pindar was a poet from the territory of Boeotia in central Greece. His most famous poems are odes written for victors in great athletic competitions like the Olympic games.

Pindar specialized in choral lyric poetry, which was poetry performed by a chorus with dancing and musical accompaniment. He wrote his poems for hire, and his patrons included some of the most prominent people in the Greek world, including the tyrants of the prosperous Greek cities of Sicily and noblemen from

Corinth, Athens, Cyrene, and Thebes. Forty-six of Pindar's victory odes, called *epicinian*, survive and are almost all that remain of the large and diverse body of poetry that he is known to have written. In a typical victory ode Pindar celebrates not only the victorious athlete but also his family, his city, the gods, and the aristocratic ideals of athletic achievement. Most of the *epicinian* odes also include extended mythical narratives that reflect somehow on the victor or his community. Pindar's style is characterized by intricate rhythmical structures, complex and abruptly shifting trains of thought, elaborate metaphors, and esoteric allusions. Although his works were performed at public celebrations, only a highly sophisticated audience could have appreciated his poetry.

The expense, preparation, and artistry that went into the composition and performance of Pindar's odes show the high regard in which both athletics and poetry were held in ancient Greece. He was revered, though seldom imitated, by the ancients. When *Alexander the Great destroyed the city of Thebes, he ordered that the house of Pindar be left standing. The obscurity of Pindar's poetry, and the fact that it was composed for specific occasions, made it less popular in later centuries. Nevertheless, poets throughout the ages have turned to Pindar as a model for earnest and lofty poetry of praise.

Bibliography: W.H. Race, *Pindar*, 1986.

William Hutton

PISISTRATUS (c. 610–527 B.C.)

Pisistratus established a lasting tyranny at Athens after the Battle of Pallene in 546. He retained that position until his death at an old age in 527. He was a beneficent tyrant, and his reign was regarded as a golden age.

Pisistratus seems to have first come to the attention of the Athenians by distinguishing himself by capturing the port of Nisaea in a war against Megara c. 565. Out of the unrest that followed *Solon's political reforms Pisistratus created a power base among the hill farmers of northeast Attica. Pisistratus' first two attempts to gain control of Athens ended in failure and a ten-year exile. He then set about building strong connections throughout the Greek world that would enable him to establish himself as tyrant at the third attempt. He appears to have settled in Eretria and with Eretrian helped to establish the city of Rhaikelos on the Thermaic Gulf. He then gained access to the gold and silver mines around Mount Pangaeus and also established connections with Thebes and Argos. This network of support enabled him to win the Battle of Pallene and to establish himself as tyrant of Athens. Pisistratus reigned as tyrant until his death in 527 when the tyranny was passed on to his sons *Hippias and Hipparchus.

Pisistratus' reign was known as a golden age. Through a skillful manipulation of the aristocrats in the political arena Pisistratus brought peace to Athens. He redistributed confiscated land to the poor and gave loans to them. He appointed traveling judges to take administration of the law away from local aristocrats.

Attic coinage was improved, and under his guidance, the economy boomed. The Agora became the hub of Athenian life. Pisistratus strengthened the Athenian position in the Cyclades by installing Lygdamis as tyrant of Naxos. Sigeum, near the entrance to the Hellespont, was also captured and control of it given to one of his sons. Athens took advantage of these new safe trade routes and markets, and Attic black figure pottery began to dominate the export market. Pisistratus united Attica, and through a carefully orchestrated religious policy, Athens emerged as its cultural center. Athena was adopted as a national symbol, and her head became a permanent symbol on Attic coinage. He established the festival of the City Dionysia at which plays were performed. Under his guidance Athens developed a sense of national identity. He did not implement new political reforms; he allowed Solon's constitution to operate, and under him the people gained experience in the art of politics. This experience left them ready to embrace the political reforms of *Cleisthenes that ultimately developed into the first democracy in western Europe.

Bibliography: B.M. Lavelle, *The Sorrow and the Pity*, 1993.

Karen McGroarty

PLACIDIA, GALLA (c. 388–450)

She was the dowager empress of the western half of the Roman Empire, responsible for many early Christian monuments of Ravenna.

The daughter of the emperor *Theodosius I and sister of the emperors Honorius and Arcadius, Galla Placidia was kidnapped by the Goths of *Alaric during the siege of Rome (410) and carried with them to Gaul, where she later married Alaric's successor, Athaulf, in a Roman ceremony (414). Her son to Athaulf, Theodosius, died in infancy. After Athaulf's death (415), the general Constantius defeated the Goths (416), securing Placidia's release, and married her (417); it was not reputed to be a happy union. Their two children included the future emperor Valentinian III (419–455). Constantius was elevated as co-emperor with the childless Honorius in 421 but died a few months later. The widowed Placidia, now with the title *augusta* (empress), soon fell out with Honorius and departed to Constantinople, ruled by Arcadius' son *Theodosius II. Following Honorius' death (423), Theodosius II appointed Placidia's infant son Valentinian as western emperor and sent them with an army to suppress an Italian usurper, John (425). Initially, Placidia presumably acted as regent for Valentinian, but *Aetius soon dominated the court. The court resided at Ravenna until the 440s but relocated to Rome in 450, where, after reinterring her firstborn son at the basilica of St. Peter's Vatican, Placidia died.

During her long residence at Ravenna, Placidia patronized the construction of important churches and other buildings, beginning a tradition of church building and especially of mosaic decoration (continued by later bishops of Ravenna, Theodoric, and the Byzantine exarchs after the conquest of Italy by Justinian) that influenced Western architecture and art throughout the Middle Ages and produced the best-preserved early Byzantine mosaic art.

Bibliography: S.I. Oost, *Galla Placidia Augusta*, 1968.

Andrew Gillett

PLATO (c. 428/427–347 b.c.)

Plato was a Greek philosopher who continued and developed *Socrates' inspiration of philosophy as dialectical research at once rational and ethical, against the claims of the Sophists.

Born in Athens in 428/427 into an aristocratic family—his parents were important supporters of *Pericles—Plato came into contact with Socrates' circle while still a boy and cultivated political interests together with philosophical studies. Socrates' execution in 399 urged him, as reported in one of the *Letters* attributed to him, to deepen his philosophical investigations on the decline of democracy and political systems in general, which, in classical Greece, were identified with the city and its territory. A period of intense work and travel followed. Around 388 Plato visited the Greek colonies of Sicily, met some members of the local Pythagorean school, and became friends with *Dion, brother-in-law of Syracuse's tyrant *Dionysius I; this circumstance prompted his projects of political reform. Upon his return to Athens, Plato opened a school in proximity to a sanctuary of the hero Academus (hence the name Academy), at which he and his associates frequently lectured on philosophy, mathematics, and astronomy. Furthermore, the Academy nurtured studies in natural sciences, jurisprudence, political sciences, and the humanities in general. Plato himself considered the foundation and organization of the school his greatest personal achievement, and the Academy was to become the most important center of advanced learning in the classical world until its suppression in A.D. 529. Asked by Dion to be tutor of the young tyrant of Syracuse *Dionysius II, Plato in 367 sailed back to Sicily; however, his hopes of realizing his political program for a government held by a statesman trained in science and philosophy, instead of a demagogue, were crushed within two years. A third journey to Sicily in 361 was again fruitless. Plato spent the rest of his life teaching at the Academy until his death in 347.

Owing to the continuity of the Academic tradition, all the writings attributed to Plato from antiquity have been handed down to posterity. Modern scholarship determined that a large majority of the dialogues, but probably few of the *Letters*, are genuine Platonic productions. The dialogues are well-refined literary writings that reflect in dramatic form Socrates' teachings and the discussions at the Academy. Plato himself did not consider them to be the main vehicle of the transmission of his thought but rather subsidiary and introductory to the teaching activity at the Academy. They are representations of conversations and speeches of certain characters, often Plato's own friends and associates, above all Socrates, exchanging questions and answers on disparate subjects, sharing different philosophical views, and recounting myths and various religious beliefs. Plato never introduces himself among the protagonists, and it is difficult at times to determine which of the persons portrayed in the dialogues holds Plato's own views and doctrines. The dialogues' literary form, however, allows Plato to promote the notion of philosophy as a dialogical process and exchange of ideas, instead of a set of definitive conclusions, and constitutes a constant stimulus for the reader's own thinking.

Some dialogues, such as *Apology*, *Crito*, and *Euthypro*, were probably composed early: They vividly portray the personality of Socrates while standing trial and awaiting death and his moral, political and philosophical views. *Protagoras*, *Meno*, *Cratylus*, *Symposium*, *Phaedo*, *Phaedrus*, and the *Republic* are the works of an exceptionally developed and energetic philosophical mind and must belong to the central part of Plato's life. *Parmenides*, *Theaetetus*, *Philebus*, *Critias*, *Timaeus* (Plato's only work known directly to the Latin middle ages), and *Laws* display a didactic inclination, appropriate to a more mature writer.

Plato never exposed his doctrines systematically, but all his dialogues deal variously with several broad areas of interest focused on five related philosophical themes: (1) the doctrine of the Ideas or Forms; (2) the identification of virtue with knowledge; (3) the opposition between true knowledge, which is recollection, and opinion; (4) the theory of the tripartite soul, and (5) the necessity that philosophers be the rulers of the city.

Plato frequently narrates myths in order to provide a figurative elucidation of philosophical doctrines. In the *Republic*, for instance, man's condition is likened to that of prisoners chained since birth in a cave and facing the back wall. Behind them burns a pyre, and other men walk between the prisoners and the fire, carrying statues of animals and things; yet the prisoners cannot turn their heads, and all they can see are the shadows of themselves and of the objects projected on the back wall. Like the prisoners, the ordinary man is chained by his own passions and prejudices and knows only shadows of reality. He has no true knowledge but mere conjecture (Gr. *eikasia*). If he were freed, he could not initially endure the brightness of the fire and recognize the reality of the objects in front of him and would strive to return to his chains. If, however, he were forced to look toward the fire, which represents the visible sun, he would gradually discern the different statues, representing the objects of commonsense cognition, and the chained prisoners. His knowledge would be limited at this stage to the ever-changing sensible world (Gr. *pistis*). These two lower degrees of cognition are concerned with what is sensible and opinable, which, according to Plato, does not still possess true reality. Rather than of knowledge they are degrees of opinion (Gr. *doxa*). When dragged out of the cave into open daylight, the man would have even greater problems in adjusting his sight, but he will eventually be able to see the real things in the world, which symbolize the objects of moral, intellectual, and mathematical knowledge, or Ideas. He would have attained at this stage knowledge (Gr. *dianoia*) of these unchangeable, ungenerated, and eternal (and therefore fully true) realities. Finally, he would be able to gaze directly at the sun, representing the highest of the Forms, the Idea of the Good, which is the origin and the cause of what is real, true, beautiful, and right. The knowledge then acquired would be absolute (Gr. *noesis*), and the man would properly be a philosopher, capable of distinguishing Ideas from sensible changing things. *Dianoia* and *noesis* are for Plato the terms of true science (Gr. *episteme*). The philosopher should therefore educate his former fellow prisoners about the real world outside the cave, that is, show them true knowledge against their prejudices; but Plato, not forgetful of Socrates' fate, adds that someone returning to the cave would not be able to see in the dim light and would almost certainly fail to convince the prisoners to free themselves; they would rather put him to death. For Plato, the Ideas are the objects of true knowledge but are not mere thoughts; they exist in a region of heaven where the souls of men see them before birth. After birth, through the repeated perceptions of the sensible and changing "reflections and shadows" of the Ideas, man is able to "remember" or "recollect" the intellectual and unchanging originals and have true knowledge. This is why the particular geometrical figures found in nature are defined by the unchanging and ideal figures and why men can refer to the ideas of temperance and justice in their conduct.

In the later *Timaeus*, Plato gives a mythical account of the creation of the sensible world by a divine Demiurge, who takes the eternal Ideas as models for his creation. Through the doctrine of the Ideas, Plato opposes epistemological skepticism and moral relativism. The doctrine of recollection supports the thesis of the immortality of the human soul, which passes through a succession of many lives. The human soul is described as divided into three parts: the judgmental or rational element, located in the head, which aims towards the general good; the appetitive element of the stomach, searching for immediate gratification; and the spirited element of the heart, which provides energy. The spirited soul should always be ruled by reason, lest the blind appetites take over the whole soul.

In the *Republic*, Plato extends this psychological tripartition to society, where the true philosopher-statesmen, who possess knowledge, should rule, while the ordinary people attend to agriculture, crafts, and trade, and the military class serves for the protection of the city. In this organization, education lies at the very foundation of society. Art and literature must serve the education of the citizens and not be goals in themselves.

Recent scholarship debates the extent to which Plato's own teaching is actually fully represented in the dialogues on three points. First, the character of Socrates stands up as the leading proponent of many philosophical doctrines, such as the theory of the Forms, which was indeed considered a Socratic teaching in the tradition of the Academy. Second, there is Plato's attitude toward his own writings, since he makes several references to the superiority of oral communication over written words in philosophy. In the *Phaedrus*, for example, Socrates remarks that writing is supposed to improve people's intelligence and to convey knowledge; in fact, writing can only give a pretense of knowledge and a shadow of the truth, because it would produce in the reader ideas and images already thought of by someone else and not "remembered" by the reader. Written words are not alive like spoken words, which can "defend themselves" in the discussion and "engage" in the process of question and answer. The philosophers do not write in order to communicate their knowledge of what is beautiful, right, and good—that is reserved to the art of discussion or dialectic— but only to amuse themselves or to help their memory in old age. According to his own observations, Plato, then, would not have committed his philosophical views to a medium that he represented as a pastime. Finally, *Aristotle gave an account of Plato's philosophy that was very different from anything found in the dialogues and close to the Pythagorean notion that the ultimate reality is made up of numbers; this account led some critics to believe that Plato's original philosophy was consigned to esoteric oral teachings inside the Academy.

One of the greatest philosophical personalities of all times, Plato contributed significantly to the foundations of Western metaphysics and epistemology, and his search for stable and permanent grounds for man's conduct and thought deeply influenced such fields as psychology, moral and political philosophy, and aesthetics.

Bibliography: P. Friedländer, *Plato*, 2nd ed., 2 vols., 1973; W.K.C. Guthrie, *A History of Greek Philosophy*, vol. iv: *Plato. The Man and His Dialogues: Earlier Period*, vol. v: *The Later Plato and the Academy*, 1975, 1978; G. Reale, *Towards a New Interpretation of Plato*, 1997.

Roberto Plevano

PLAUTUS, TITUS MACCIUS (fl. c. 205–184 B.C.)

Plautus was the foremost comic playwright in Rome and remains the best-attested dramatist from antiquity.

"Titus Maccius Plautus" is probably a stage name, evoking associations with Athenian Old Comedy, improvisational Italian rustic farces (the *fabulae Atellanae*), and Hellenistic mime. Each of these genres has influenced Plautus' extant plays, which themselves are adaptations of a fourth genre, Greek New Comedy (they are therefore *fabulae palliatae*, plays in Greek dress). Plautus was born in Sarsina in Umbria and by c. 205 was the head of a theatrical troupe that performed on contract at *ludi* ("games") in and around Rome. The only certain dates for his productions are 200, when *Stichus* was produced, and 191, when *Pseudolus* was presented at the Megalesian Games to commemorate a new temple to Cybele, though it is likely he had a career in the theater before this. *Varro recognized twenty-one authentic Plautine plays, and twenty-one plays survive more or less complete, although *Vidularia* is largely fragmentary and other titles and fragments exist. Papyrus discoveries of *Menander over the past century have demonstrated how free the translation from New Comedy at times can be. Plautus drew on the above-mentioned comic traditions and his own literary genius to create exuberant verse comedies filled with slapstick, puns, exaggerated stock characters, and polymetric songs. Much of the humor is metatheatrical, explicitly acknowledging the fictionality of the dramatic world, and is based on social inversions, with clever slaves ordering their young masters to aid in the deception of their own father or a pimp.

Plautus' plays are the earliest complete literary works to survive in Latin, and he is the earliest Roman professional playwright attested. After his death, his plays continued to be performed, influencing medieval comedy and Renaissance drama in continental Europe. *Miles Gloriosus* provided the prototype for many subsequent braggart soldiers. Shakespeare adapted *Menaechmi* (with elements of *Amphitruo*) in his *Comedy of Errors*, and *Aulularia* inspired Molière's *L'Avare* (The Miser). More recently, elements from several plays were combined to produce Gelbart and Shevelove's *A Funny Thing Happened on the Way to the Forum*.

Bibliography: G.E. Duckworth, *The Nature of Roman Comedy*, 2nd ed., 1994; N.W. Slater, *Plautus in Performance*, 1985.

C.W. Marshall

PLINY THE ELDER (Gaius Plinius Secundus, 23–79)

Pliny was a prolific Roman writer and active public official, best known for his encyclopedic *Natural History*.

Pliny was from Novum Comum (now Como) in northern Italy. He was from a wealthy family that was likely part of the municipal governing class. His career in public service began in the army as an equestrian stationed in Germany. This was followed by time in the legal service as a pleader during the reign of *Nero, then a series of procuratorships and council membership under *Vespasian and *Titus. Finally, Pliny served as commander of the Misenum fleet. His investigation of the eruption of Vesuvius on 24 August 79 resulted in his death likely from asphyxiation. His nephew and adopted son, *Pliny the Younger, is our primary source for this biographical information. Pliny's varied and active career allowed him opportunities to travel in Germany, Spain, and probably Africa, experience reflected in his writings.

Pliny's works reflect a wide range of interests and an impressive dedication to knowledge. His publications included works on the cavalry, on the development of an orator, and on the study of language. He wrote a memorial biography of Quintus Pomponius Secundus, who was likely his patron. He also wrote the twenty-book *Bella Germaniae*, which is a history of Rome's Germanic campaigns. Pliny's *A Fine Aufidii Bassi* in thirty-one books continues the history of Rome begun by his contemporary Aufidius Bassus. Of greatest significance, though, is the thirty-seven-book *Natural History*.

Despite its title the *Natural History* is more than a natural history. Drawing on the sources of information available to him, Pliny created an encyclopedic work on life and nature. He brought together information on ancient medicine, biology, botany, agriculture, astronomy, mineralogy, and metallurgy. Recently critics have argued that despite earlier judgments to the contrary the work does give evidence of deliberate organization and methodology, although clearly inclusiveness was a dominant principle. Pliny's work was a model and influence for later Roman, medieval, and Renaissance writers and scientists. His work continues to be a valuable (if fallible) source of information on the ancient world.

Bibliography: M. Beagon, *Roman Nature: The Thought of Pliny the Elder*, 1992.

Christine Cornell

PLINY THE YOUNGER (Gaius Plinius Caecilius Secundus, c. 61–c. 112)

Pliny was a prominent Roman politician and man of letters in the early Roman Empire best known for his collection of correspondence.

Pliny was born into a wealthy family in the town of Comum in northern Italy. He was adopted and raised by his uncle, *Pliny the Elder, a well-known public official of equestrian social rank and author of the encyclopedic *Natural History*. He received a first-rate education at Rome; *Quintilian was one of his teachers. He followed a stint as a junior legionary staff officer with a distinguished, if unspectacular, career as lawyer, public official, and senator. Significant administrative posts included treasury prefectures, the Tiber drainage curatorship, and the governorship of Bithynia-Pontus, where he evidently died while still in office. In the course of his life, he was the friend of the historian *Tacitus and a trusted public servant under emperors as different as the autocratic, unstable *Domitian and the competent, fair-minded *Trajan (a contrast highlighted in Pliny's sole surviving public oration, the *Panegyric*).

Pliny's collection of *Letters*, published in ten books over the last decade or so of his life, is a valuable window into the lives of men and women of a specific social and political status in the early second century. Since they were prepared for publication by their author, the letters do not afford the sort of genuine and unguarded revelations to be found in *Cicero's letters. Nonetheless, they do illustrate the concerns and occupations of an educated, personally genial, sincerely well-intentioned Roman administrator. Subject matter includes: commentary on official and unofficial matters of politics, law, and the courts; personal advice to friends and associates concerning, for example, career and marriage plans; philanthropic measures, including matching-funds support for a school in Comum; and descriptions of topographical and natural phenomena, including an eyewitness account of the eruption of Vesuvius in 79, which took his uncle's life. Book 10 of the collection comprises exclusively correspondence between Pliny and the emperor Trajan, most notably an exchange regarding problems Pliny experienced in dealing with Christians in his province. Throughout, the impression given is of a man of high (more or less Stoic) moral standards and a genuinely strong sense of civic responsibility.

Bibliography: A.N. Sherwin-White, *The Letters of Pliny: A Historical and Social Commentary*, 1966.

James Holoka

PLOTINUS (205–c.269/270)

Plotinus, the founder of Neoplatonism, is the leading philosophical figure of late antiquity.

He was born in Lycopolis in Egypt into a Greek, or Hellenized, family. At twenty-eight he became a student of philosophy in Alexandria, then a center of advanced learning, and associated, for eleven years, with *Ammonius Saccas, who, despite writing nothing, was an accomplished late-Platonic teacher and had a deep influence on third-century philosophy. In 242 he joined a military expedition against Persia in order to learn about the philosophies of the Persians and Indians, but he did not go farther than Mesopotamia. Upon the expedition's failure, he settled in Rome, where he created his own very successful school of philosophy.

Plotinus considered himself primarily a follower of *Plato, although in his lectures he showed considerable syncretism by referring to authors and commentators of the Stoic, Pythagorean, and especially the Peripatetic school, such as *Alexander of Aphrodisias, and did not see himself as the founder of a further philosophy. However, Plotinus established the Neoplatonic tradition, which greatly influenced contemporary paganism, and the later Christian and Moslem theologies. The activity in his school reflected Plato's preference for oral teaching over writing; he began to write only ten years after the opening of the school and never arranged his treatises systematically or published them for a wide audience. These tasks were accomplished thirty years after Plotinus' death by *Porphyry, Plotinus' disciple, editor, biographer, and friend, with the edition of the *Enneads*. He died c. 269/270, widely regarded for his austere conduct of life and his kind and caring personality.

For Plotinus, philosophy must provide man with the knowledge of his true self and his place with regard to reality and to its first and supreme principle, the Good. In general, only what is immaterial, unchanging, and eternal is real; in man, these are the attributes of the intellectual soul, which does not concern itself with the ever-changing conditions of the body, or even with the conscious awareness of them. Once united with the body, the intellectual soul is "contaminated" with matter and must follow a path of ethical ascent that would lead it first to "regain" itself through beauty and knowledge and eventually to mystical union with the supreme principle. The Good, also called One and God, is absolutely transcendent, beyond any determination and form. Reflecting on the Aristotelian doctrine of the self-thinking intellect as first principle, Plotinus concludes that its absolute simplicity requires the absence of any duality and distinction: The Good/One is therefore, first above all, beyond being. Plotinus explains the production of plurality from the One with the term *emanation*, implying that it is not a free act of creation but rather a necessary procession of distinct realities that does not affect the One. The first emanation is Intellect, identified with the Platonic Demiurge, which contains the most perfect of beings, the Forms, which are finite in number. From Intellect proceeds Soul, which provides a link with the natural world and from which individual human souls emanate.

Bibliography: L.P. Gerson, ed., *The Cambridge Companion to Plotinus*, 1996.

Roberto Plevano

PLUTARCH (c. 50–120)

Plutarch was a Greek philosopher, biographer, and miscellaneous writer.

Plutarch was born at Chaeronea in Boeotia. He was trained in philosophy and rhetoric at Athens and traveled to Asia, Egypt, and Italy. He lectured on philosophy at Rome during the reign of *Vespasian and perhaps longer; according to one tradition, Plutarch undertook the education of the future emperor *Hadrian. Another tradition states that *Trajan bestowed consular rank upon him, and Hadrian appointed him procurator of Greece.

For at least thirty years of his life he was a priest at Delphi. He is known to have written about 227 books, of which 78 miscellaneous works (*Moralia*) and 50 biographies survive. The *Moralia* comprise treatises on a wide range of philosophical, rhetorical, and antiquarian subjects, as well as dialogues that discuss various philosophical and theological issues. Philosophically he was influenced by *Plato, and has been seen as a forerunner of Neoplatonism. In the realm of practical philosophy, Plutarch was chiefly interested in ethics. No other ancient author wrote more than Plutarch did on moral subjects.

Plutarch's biographies are of great interest. His *Bioi Paralleloi* (*Parallel Lives*) are biographies of fifty prominent Greeks and Romans. Plutarch arranged his *Lives* in an approximate chronological order, pairing together a Greek and a Roman and finally comparing the two. Although he does present some internal variations, within each biography Plutarch usually treats the subject's birth, youth, character, deeds, and death. Plutarch's objective was to glorify the subject, entertain the reader, and present a moral lesson. Nevertheless, the *Lives* contain much information of historical value and were used for centuries as a prime source for knowledge about the ancient world. William Shakespeare used Sir Thomas North's translation of Plutarch as his major source in *Julius Caesar*, *Antony and Cleopatra*, and *Coriolanus*.

Although a prolific writer and a significant figure of the literary milieu of the first century, Plutarch's fame rests today primarily as a biographer.

Bibliography: C.P. Jones, *Plutarch and Rome*, 1971; D.A. Russell, *Plutarch*, 1973.

Andrew G. Traver

POLLIO, GAIUS ASINIUS (76 B.C.–A.D. 4)

Pollio was a statesman, historian, and man of letters.

A grandson of the Asinius who led the Marrucini against Rome in the Social War (91–87), he fought for *Julius Caesar in almost all the major campaigns of the Civil War including Pharsalus (48), Thapsus (46), and Munda (45). Praetor in 45, governor of Further Spain in 44, he joined *Marc Antony, for whom he governed Cisalpine Gaul in 41 and, as consul in 40, negotiated the short-lived Treaty of Brundisium with Octavian (see *Augustus). He celebrated a triumph over the Balkan Parthini in 39 and retired to use his spoils on a public library and devote himself to literature.

He had been part of urbane literary society since his youth. *Catullus described him as a "lad packed with wit," and Helvius Cinna wrote a *Propempticon* (Travel Companion to Greece and Asia) for him in 56. *Horace dedicated an ode to him, probably a pastiche of his terse, bold style and gift for anecdote, known to us from a letter to *Cicero of 43 and quotations in *Seneca the Elder. He is also mentioned by *Virgil, but not as a patron, and *Gallus was a mutual friend. He was a leading orator, giving public declamations, tragedian and critic of style, feared for his "strict, harsh judgment" of Cicero, *Livy, and others.

Pollio's lost eyewitness *Histories* of the Civil War were his crowning achievement and a source of *Plutarch and *Appian. We probably owe him Caesar's phrase "The die is cast" and the negative coloring of Cicero in history.

Bibliography: R.G.M. Nisbet and M. Hubbard, *A Commentary on Horace, Odes Book I*, 1978.

Robert Dyer

POLYBIUS (c. 200–c. 118 b.c.)

Polybius was a Greek historian who wrote a *Universal History* in forty books of the Roman conquest mainly of the Greek eastern Mediterranean between 200 and 146 b.c.

Polybius was born at the end of the third century b.c. at Megalopolis in Arcadia where his father Lycortas was a leading member of the Achaean League. The young Polybius witnessed the League's failure to negotiate favorably with the Romans, and when the Macedonian monarch *Perseus was defeated by the Romans at Pydna in 168, Polybius was one of a number of prominent Achaeans taken hostage to Italy and detained there for sixteen years. When in Rome, Polybius had the good fortune to meet and befriend the young *Scipio Aemilianus. He became a part of Scipio's circle and through him met members of the leading Roman families. When Scipio went to Spain and North Africa in 151, Polybius went with him and made his return to Italy in *Hannibal's footsteps over the Alps. His status as hostage ended in 150, but soon after his return to Greece, he rejoined Scipio at the siege of Carthage and witnessed its sacking in 146. Back in Greece a war had broken out between the Achaean League and Rome; the League was quickly defeated and Corinth was sacked. Polybius returned home after the events and acted as a mediator between the League and Rome. A precise chronology of his movements becomes difficult after 145. He visited Alexandria and Sardes and may have accompanied Scipio on his command against the Spanish city of Numantia in 133. The precise date of his death is unknown.

The purpose of Polybius' *Universal History* was to explain how and why

Rome came to world domination in the short space of fifty-three years. His aim, using a variety of sources, was to present a rigorous history that attempted to understand and explain the events related. He hoped that this might be of benefit to aspiring politicians and might help his Greek audience come to terms with the vagaries of the fortune that had befallen them.

Bibliography: F.W. Walbank, *Polybius*, 1972.

Karen McGroarty

POLYCARP, SAINT (c. 69–c. 155)

Polycarp, the bishop of Smyrna for nearly fifty years, was martyred at age eighty-six.

Later tradition soon asserted that Polycarp had been a disciple of the Apostle *John, but the first reliable indication of his career comes from the letters of *Ignatius. These record the mutual admiration of the bishops who met when Ignatius was being taken to martyrdom in Rome. Ignatius, in fact, figures prominently in Polycarp's only extant writings, two letters (already merged into one document in antiquity) to the Christians of Philippi. In the one, Polycarp appealed to the welcome given Ignatius by the Philippians as an example of the righteousness of the church there; in the other, he recorded that he was forwarding copies of Ignatius' letters, as the Philippians had requested. More significant than his letters is Polycarp's reputation. Before the end of the second century, Polycarp came to be regarded as a symbol of orthodox belief. The story was told that when the heretic Marcion demanded to be recognized by Polycarp, the bishop responded that he recognized him only as the firstborn of Satan. Knowing that the western churches calculated the date of Easter by a reckoning different from that which prevailed in Asia Minor, Polycarp is said to have traveled to the capital to discuss the matter with Anicetus, one of Rome's bishops. Although neither man convinced the other, they agreed that their differing opinions did not compromise Christian unity.

Most significant of all, however, is the impression made by Polycarp's death. An eyewitness account, *The Martyrdom of Polycarp*, is the oldest Christian martyrology. Many features mentioned in the work, such as the commemoration of the day of martyrdom as the "birthday" of the saint, became standard in both the practice and literature of the early Church.

Bibliography: C. Jefford, K.J. Harder, and L.D. Amezaga, *Reading the Apostolic Fathers*, 1996.

John Quinn

POLYCLITUS (or Polycleitus, fl. late fifth century B.C.)

Polyclitus was the leading sculptor of the Argive school and a rival of *Phidias.

Polyclitus was a native of Argos and a student of Ageladas. He was known throughout antiquity for his bronze statues of athletes and for his aesthetic sense.

Polyclitus developed a new sculptural style, setting mathematical proportions for the parts of the human body to give harmony a visible form. He wrote a work on his technique, *The Canon*, which emphasized rhythm and proportion in his statutes, particularly his *Doryphorus*. Although this text only survives today in fragments, it influenced successive generations of artists.

Polyclitus' most famous statues were *Diadumenus* (youth binding a fillet on his head, c. 430) and *Doryphorus* (spear thrower, c. 450–440). His other statues include *Discophorus* (discus thrower), a Hermes, and a Hercules. Polyclitus also sculpted a Hera (420) in ivory and gold for her temple near Argos; it was said to equal Phidias' Athena in Athens. Polyclitus' Amazon, sculpted as an entry in a competition at Ephesus, was selected over those of Phidias and *Cresilas.

Although his works are only known today through Roman copies or literary sources such as *Pausanias and *Strabo, Polyclitus helped set the standards for the ideal classical style of the male athletic form.

Bibliography: M. Robertson, *A History of Greek Art*, 2 vols., 1975.

Andrew G. Traver

POLYCRATES (c. 575–522 b.c.)

Polycrates was the tyrant of the Aegean island of Samos. Under Polycrates Samos enjoyed unprecedented power and prosperity, but his reign and his fate came to exemplify to the Greeks the dangers and excesses of one-man rule.

Polycrates became tyrant c. 540. He built up the Samian navy and began carving out a seaborne empire for himself in the eastern Aegean. He developed ties with foreign powers and dealt not only with other Greek leaders but also with the king of Egypt and the representatives of the Persian Empire as equals.

Polycrates' wealth, fueled by trade, tribute, and piracy, reached legendary proportions. He spent some of it in ambitious building projects, including a new temple for the goddess Hera and an aqueduct cut directly through a mountain. Polycrates was also a patron of the arts: He invited the lyric poets *Anacreon and *Ibycus to Samos.

As tensions began to build between the Greeks and the Persian Empire, Polycrates was a major actor on the Mediterranean stage. In the 520s, he lent some of his warships to the Persians to aid in their conquest of Egypt. This act probably made other Greeks nervous, and soon afterward the Spartans and Corinthians sent an expedition to Samos in an attempt to oust Polycrates. The attempt was unsuccessful, but in the meantime Polycrates had incurred the suspicion of Oroites, the Persian governor of westen Anatolia. Oroites invited Polycrates to visit him in his capital of Sardis, but when Polycrates arrived, in hopes of receiving monetary aid for his imperial plans, he was seized and put to death.

Polycrates was a typical Greek tyrant in many respects: resourceful and innovative, popular with his people, lavish in his public expenditures. After his ignominious death he became the paradigm for the Greeks of the pitfalls of tyranny, since at the height of his greatest fortune he was cut down by his own ambition and recklessness.

Bibliography: G. Shipley, *History of Samos 800–188* B.C., 1987.

William Hutton

POLYGNOTUS (or Polygnotos, fl. c. 475–450 B.C.)

Polygnotus was a painter, a son and pupil of Aglaophon of Thasos; he was active on the Greek mainland, particularly Athens, where he reputedly obtained citizenship.

Polygnotus became prominent in Athens apparently by painting free of charge, in contrast to his collaborator *Micon, the *Mupersis* (*Troy Taken*) in the Peisiankteion ("Painted Stoa"). In that painting, according to *Plutarch, he depicted the mythological Laodike with the features of his lover Elpinike, sister (or half sister) of the Athenian statesman *Cimon, who may well have sponsored his other works. Polygnotus also painted *The Wedding of the Leucippidai* in the Athenian Anakeion and *Achilles in Skyros* and *Odysseus with Nausikaa*, both later in the "Pinakotheke" in the Propylaia to the Athenian Acropolis. Outside of Athens he painted *Odysseus Having Slain the Suitors* at Plataea, and another *Iliupersis* and a *Nekyia* (*Underworld*) in the Lesche (Clubhouse) of the Cnidians at Delphi.

Although none of his work survives, ancient authors, notably *Pausanias and *Pliny the Elder, describe in detail his innovations, including the abandonment of the baseline and the uneven distribution of figures over a variable groundline. These seem to be reflected on contemporary Athenian painted pots. *Aristotle and *Lucian credit Polygnotus with painting more animated and expressive faces, while Pliny attributes to him the first representations of women in transparent drapery, of open mouths showing teeth, and of faces varying from the "rigidity that had existed previously." (Surviving painted pottery, however, demonstrates that all of these features actually appeared earlier.) According to Aristotle, Polygnotus is also said to have represented men better than they were, and he seems to have conveyed ethos by choosing to depict revelatory narrative moments of decision or aftermath, rather than the height of action. *Quintilian refers to simplicity of his colors, and *Cicero states that he only used four. His paintings were probably executed in hot wax on wooden panels, and Pliny, among others, reports that he employed the encaustic technique. It is more difficult to credit the same author's statement that Polygnotus was also a sculptor.

Bibliography: D. Castriota, *Myth, Ethos, and Actuality. Official Art in Fifth-Century Athens*, 1992; M. Stansbury-O'Donnell, "Polygnotos' *Iliupersis*. A New Reconstruction," *American Journal of Archaeology* 93 (1989): 203–215; M. Stansbury-O'Donnell, "Polygnotos' *Nekyia*: A Reconstruction and Analysis," *American Journal of Archaeology* 94 (1990): 213–235.

Kenneth D.S. Lapatin

POMPEIUS MAGNUS, GNAEUS (Pompey the Great, 106–48 B.C.)

Pompey the Great was a highly skilled Roman general and a member of the First Triumvirate.

From an early age Pompey was immersed in the world of the soldier. While still in his teens he accompanied his father on campaign during the Social War (91–87), even putting down a rebellion of the army while his father cowered in his tent. While only twenty-three he raised a private army to support the aristocratic *Sulla in the civil war, and he won a major battle against three experienced generals. Sulla recognized the young man's talent and assured his allegiance by compelling him to divorce his wife in order to marry Sulla's stepdaughter (though she also was married and about to give birth). For the remainder of the civil war Pompey served with distinction in Italy, Sicily, and Africa, and Sulla granted him a triumph in 81, although he lacked the prerequisite political and social standing. He also received from the Senate the cognomen *magnus* ("great"), thereby associating himself with *Alexander the Great. *Crassus, a fellow general of Sulla, resented the indulgence shown to Pompey, and a feud ensued.

For most of the next decade Pompey subdued rebellious Romans who took advantage of the unsettled political conditions following Sulla's death in 78. After suppressing the insurrection of Lepidus (father of *Lepidus, the future triumvir) by executing his ally, Brutus (father of *Brutus, assassin of *Caesar), he campaigned against Sertorius, a Roman exile attempting to form an opposition Senate in Spain. Successful after several years of difficult fighting, he marched west in time to destroy the remnants of *Spartacus' defeated slave army fleeing from Crassus (71). When Pompey demanded a second triumph for ending the slave insurrection, the Senate capitulated, fearing that he might use his seasoned army to march on Rome. Once again Crassus objected to the honors bestowed on his rival, and as a result their joint consulship of 70 was contentious. Pompey's military successes and the popular legislation he passed as consul won the admiration of the public but angered the aristocracy, and so the conservative Senate objected in 67 to a popular law that granted Pompey a three-year command to rid the Mediterranean of pirates. He displayed at sea the same military efficiency he had demonstrated on land, clearing the seas of pirates in a mere eighty-nine days. As he was completing this campaign, he was given the additional task of waging war against the Pontic king *Mithridates VI Eupator, who had been interfering with Roman interests in the eastern Mediterranean for more than two decades. He quickly defeated the Pontic army and spent 66–63 abroad in the east, adding Pontus and Syria as Roman provinces.

Returning to Italy in 62, Pompey was at the height of his popularity with the public. He had expanded Rome's presence in the eastern Mediterranean without consulting the Senate, acting essentially as a monarch and acquiring a vast fortune for himself. The Senate nervously awaited his return, fearing that he might follow the precedent of his mentor Sulla by using his veteran legions to establish himself as dictator. Yet Pompey disbanded his army and made three requests: land for his troops, ratification of his actions in the East, and a third triumph for himself. The conservative members of the Senate, led by *Cato the Younger, refused to grant the first two requests, and so Pompey sought political support elsewhere. He allied himself with the populist Caesar by marrying his daughter (Julia) and was reconciled with his rival Crassus, (60–59). The three men formed a political coalition termed the "First Triumvirate," and with the support of his two colleagues, Pompey obtained land to reward his soldiers as well as a formal endorsement of his activities in the eastern Mediterranean.

For the next decade he remained in Rome, serving as consul in 55 and overseeing the interests of the triumvirate while Caesar campaigned in Gaul. However, his alliance with Caesar collapsed following the deaths of Julia and Crassus. Amid the political violence of 52 he was appointed the sole consul, supported even by his foe Cato. This support from the conservative leader underscored a growing sentiment in the Senate that a strong political role by Pompey was preferable to an authoritarian government under Caesar. After Caesar invaded Italy in 49, Pompey and many aristocratic senators withdrew to Greece to train an army to meet the veteran legions of the Gallic wars. After several months of maneuvering, the two armies met near the town of Pharsalus, where Pompey was decisively defeated (48). After he fled to Egypt, Ptolemy XIII ordered him murdered, perhaps to ingratiate himself with Caesar.

The career of Pompey has interested many authors, particularly his struggle against Caesar. *Tacitus and *Seneca doubted his character and motives, but *Velleius Paterculus and *Plutarch generally spoke highly of him. In the *Pharsalia*, *Lucan's epic recounting Pompey's battle with Caesar, he is depicted as a tragic figure of the Republic, the victim of Caesar's mad rush toward authoritarianism.

Bibliography: P. Greenhalgh, *Pompey: The Republican Prince*, 1981; P. Greenhalgh, *Pompey: The Roman Alexander*, 1980; R. Seager, *Pompey: A Political Biography*, 1979.

David Christiansen

POMPEIUS MAGNUS, SEXTUS (Sextus Pompey, c. 67?– 35 B.C.)

The general Sextus Pompey, son of *Pompey the Great, challenged the authority of Octavian (later *Augustus).

Although Sextus Pompey did not equal his father's illustrious military career, he was a highly skilled general. After *Caesar's victory over the Republican forces at Pharsalus, Sextus accompanied his father to Egypt and witnessed his murder (48). He joined *Cato the Younger and other leaders in Africa, but he fled to Spain after Caesar routed the Republican army at Thapsus (46). He joined his brother's army, succeeding him as general, and by 45 Sextus was the sole Republican commander whom Caesar had not yet defeated. Following the dictator's assassination in March 44, he began cooperating with the Senate, which entrusted him with command of the Roman fleet. By late 43, however, Octavian and *Antony declared him an outlaw and sentenced him to death. For the next seven years Sextus virtually controlled the western Mediterranean with his ships, overcoming fleets loyal to Octavian on several occasions. After blockading Rome and cutting off its grain supply, he agreed to a truce with Octavian in 39 and was appointed the governor of Sicily and Sardinia. But by the next year the agreement had collapsed, and Sextus resumed his harassment of shipping and raids on Italian towns. Eventually he succumbed to the superior resources of Octavian and fled to the East, perhaps seeking the protection of Antony. There he was instead put to death by one of Antony's generals.

Some scholars have viewed Sextus as the final champion of the Republic, a hero who carried on the struggle against authoritarianism long after Pompey, Cato, *Cicero, and *Brutus had died. For others, his support of the irretrievable republican cause was disingenuous and merely a pretext for ensuring his own political authority.

Bibliography: M. Hadas, *Sextus Pompey*, 1930.

David Christiansen

PONTIUS PILATE (governor 26–36)

Pontius Pilate was governor of Judaea, under whom *Jesus was crucified.

Little is known of Pilate's early life. The emperor *Tiberius, whose policy was to maintain peace in the provinces, appointed him governor of Judaea with the title of *prefect* (from an inscription, correcting the anachronistic title *procurator* of some literary sources). The most famous event in Pilate's long tenure was the case of Jesus, who was turned over to Pilate by the Jews. Although he protested Jesus' innocence, "washing his hands" of blame, Pilate yielded to the crowd's demand for his crucifixion and the release of Barabbas.

The Jewish authors *Philo and *Josephus, recorded other incidents involving military standards bearing the image of the emperor, the use of sacred funds for construction of an aqueduct, gilded shields, and finally, his use of force against a Samaritan gathering. This led to the Samaritan council's appeal to the Syrian legate, Pilate's superior, who ordered Pilate to go to Rome and give an account to the emperor. By the time Pilate arrived in 37, Tiberius was dead. Some sources indicate that he was later exiled in Gaul.

The earliest Christian sources were sympathetic to Pilate; the earliest Christian creeds included Pilate for historical dating rather than blame. An abundance of apocryphal literature arose, including a letter of an essentially Christian Pilate to Tiberius and an account of his martyrdom. The Greek Orthodox Church canonized his wife, whose name is given in the *Acts of Pilate* as Procula; the Coptic church celebrates the feast day of St. Pilate and Procula. *Eusebius in the fourth century reported a tradition of Pilate's suicide, and Western legends told of his possessed corpse. Many modern accounts have been colored by an assumed association between Pilate and Tiberius' prefect of the Praetorian

Guard, Sejanus, whose anti-Jewish stance was given by Philo, probably, however, to shift blame from Tiberius. Pilate has been a frequent subject in art (e.g., Rembrandt's *Ecce Homo*) throughout the ages.

Bibliography: P.L. Maier, *Pontius Pilate*, 1968.

Rebecca Harrison

PORPHYRY (232/233–c. 305)

Porphyry was a Neoplatonic philosopher of great learning and ease of communication.

Porphyry was born in c. 232 into a rich Syrian family; he grew up in the cosmopolitan and thriving Phoenician capital Tyre and later moved to Athens. There he associated with Longinus, an extraordinarily learned Platonist who, like *Plotinus, had followed *Ammonius' lectures in Alexandria and who won Porphyry over with his particular brand of Platonism, in which the Ideas were thoughts of mind possessing an independent reality. In 263 he went to Rome and became a member of Plotinus' circle. He was very close to the master himself; they had frequent conversations, after which Porphyry modified his own views. Plotinus also provided moral support for his younger friend, helping him out of a severe bout of depression and inviting him to travel for distraction. Porphyry then moved in 269 to Sicily, where he wrote extensively on *Plato's dialogues, on Aristotelian logic, and on the similarities between the two philosophies; only a few fragments of these works survive.

His didactic introduction to *Aristotle's *Categories*, the *Isagoge*, had enormous success. Translated into Latin by Boethius, it became, in the Middle Ages, the standard textbook on the controversy over the universals. He also engaged in polemical exchange in the work *Against the Christians*, which did not survive the later Christian censorship; his support for the traditional religion seems to have stemmed from an allegoric and philosophical interpretation of pagan myths. He returned to Rome only several years after the death of Plotinus and assumed the direction of the School in order to continue the work of his mentor. Porphyry was instrumental in the diffusion of Plotinian Neoplatonism; his exegetical efforts concerning Plotinus' writings culminated with their complete edition, in around 398, under the title of *Enneads*, together with Porphyry's own biography of the masters.

Porphyry's stature as a philosopher is difficult to assess, since most of his works are lost. He seems to have followed Plotinus' footsteps, sometimes simplifying him, for instance, by denying the superessential character of the One and downplaying the differences between Intellect and Soul. Philosophy had, for him, a practical end: the purification of the wise man's soul from passions and affections through knowledge and ascetic practices; he recommended, for instance, the following of a strict vegetarian diet. In his later years he married a widow, to whom he addressed a still extant philosophical treatise (*Ad Marcellam*). The exact date of his death is not known but must have occurred around 305.

Bibliography: A.C. Lloyd, "The Later Neoplatonists," in *The Cambridge History of Later Greek and Early Medieval Philosophy*, 1967, 272–325.

Roberto Plevano

PORSENA, LARS (r. 508–504 B.C.)

When King Tarquinius Superbus (*Tarquin the Proud) was driven out from Rome, he fled to Lars Porsena, the Etruscan king of Clusium, north of Rome.

According to Roman legend, Porsena's troops occupied the Janiculum Hill, on the far bank of the Tiber. While he lay siege to Rome, two acts of Roman heroism occurred. When Porsena's troops tried to gain the Sublician Bridge over the Tiber in order to enter Rome, Horatius Cocles, Spurius Lartius, and Titus Herminius held off the whole Etruscan army while the Romans broke the bridge up behind them. As the demolition neared its end, Horatius sent his two comrades back to safety. As the last bridge timber fell, Horatius dove into the Tiber and swam over to the Roman bank. The second hero, Gaius Mucius Scaevola, volunteered to kill Porsena. Upon stealing into Porsena's camp, Scaevola misidentified Porsena's royal secretary as the king and killed him instead. Captured and threatened with torture, Scaevola defiantly thrust his right hand into the fire of an altar to demonstrate how little he regarded pain. Scaevola proclaimed that 300 Roman youths had sworn to kill Porsena and that he, Scaevola, was the first to make the attempt. Struck with Scaevola's fortitude, Porsena thereupon released him. Porsena, however, was so impressed by this display of Roman courage and resolve that he made peace.

Some historians, following a variant Roman tradition, now think it more likely that Porsena took Rome and either ruled as its king or established a government subject to himself until he withdrew from Rome, perhaps due to his defeat by the Latin League at Aricia in 504.

Bibliography: A. Alföldi, *Early Rome and the Latins*, 1965; R.M. Ogilvie, *A Commentary on Livy, Books 1–5*, 1965.

Judith Sebesta

POSIDONIUS (c. 135–c. 50 B.C.)

Posidonius was a Greek Stoic philosopher who was one of the most important intellectual figures of his day. He is considered the most scientific of the Stoics and was especially influential in Roman thought.

He was born in Apamea in Syria and studied at Athens under the Stoics *Panaetius and Antipater. He founded his school in Rhodes, becoming a Rhodian citizen, and held the highest office, representing Rhodes in two embassies to Rome in 87–86 and 51.

Posidonius wrote extensively on physics, cosmology, divination, psychology, geography, meteorology, and anthropology, among other subjects, but his work now survives only in fragmentary quotations. He was orthodox in some parts of Stoic theory but innovative in others, insisting on the close connection between the three parts of Stoicism, physics, logic, and ethics, in an analogy with the human body, with physics as the flesh, logic as the bones, and ethics as the soul. His physical investigations were famous. In these, he sought to explain the causes of celestial, terrestrial, and marine phenomena as part of an interconnected cosmic system. He took a Platonizing approach to psychology, explaining the passions with reference to the motions of the soul, positing one rational and two irrational faculties of the soul, thus arguing against *Chrysippus' idea of the passions as false judgments of the rational faculty of the soul. This informed his ethics, in which he argued, against Chrysippus, that evil does not arise from external forces but from the effects of the irrational faculties of the soul. Therefore, he emended the earlier Stoic doctrine of "living in accordance with Nature" to living contemplating the truth and order of all things together, while not being led by the irrational faculties of the soul.

Posidonius had a strong influence on Roman thought (*Cicero attended his lectures) and was once thought, especially in the nineteenth century, to be the originator of many of the ideas to be found in the works of Cicero, *Virgil, *Seneca, *Varro, and others (pan-Posidonianism). More recently, his direct influence has been disputed. He was known later by *Strabo and others, especially for his geographical and meteorological works.

Bibliography: L. Edelstein and I.G. Kidd, eds., *Posidonius*, 3 vols., 1972–1999.

Gordon Campbell

POSTUMIUS, ALBIUS (early fifth century B.C.)

Postumius was a Roman dictator, of plebeian origin, who led the Romans in the war against the Latins in the first decade of the fifth century and under whose dictatorship the Romans fought and won the battle at Lake Regillus (496).

This Latin war was an aggressive one for Rome, part of the strategy adopted by a series of powerful plebeian leaders to secure Rome from becoming subject to harassment by the neighboring Latin people in the future. Postumius was the second dictator of Rome following T. Larcius, who inaugurated the office a year earlier. The early Roman tradition is not unanimous with regard to the exact date of Postumius' dictatorship, and the dates of 499 and 496 are presented as equally possible. The later date seems preferable, since it follows the appointment of Postumius at the consulate in 496; according to part of the tradition, Postumius resigned his consular office protesting the doubtful loyalty of his colleague at the consulate and became dictator later in that year. If one accepts 499 as the correct year of his service as dictator, then one must also accept that Postumius was appointed dictator without having held the consular office yet, which (the consulate), according to the sources, was a necessary qualification for the dictatorship.

Bibliography: R.M. Ogilvie, *A Commentary on Livy Books 1–5*, 1965.

Sophia Papaioannou

PRAXAGORAS OF COS (fl. fourth century B.C.)

Praxagoras was a Greek physician and surgeon credited with differentiating between veins and arteries and identifying the pulse in the arteries.

Praxagoras was from the island of Cos, off the coast of Asia Minor. This major center of Greek medicine was also the home of *Hippocrates, the "Father of Medicine." Though other physicians, including his father Nicarchus, may share the discovery, the distinction between veins and arteries was usually attributed to Praxagoras. He was the first to determine that only arteries pulsate and classified differences in pulse as early, observable diagnostic indicators of pathological conditions. He believed that the veins originated in the liver and carried blood, whereas the arteries, which narrowed into vessels called "nerves," carried *pneuma*, a special kind of air, involved in voluntary motion. Diet and its relation to bubbles (a by-product of digestion), *pneuma*, humors (products of abnormal digestion), and disease were central to his theory. Praxagoras, who was one of three physicians credited with perfecting dietetics, stressed prevention and the need to individualize diet and therapy according to the particular nature of each person.

We know the titles of nine of his writings, of which only fragments survive; his *Anatomy* is among the first works known on this topic. Regarded as the last of the great Coan physicians, Praxagoras served as a bridge to the Alexandrian period in medicine, known for its advances in anatomy. His students included *Herophilus, one of the most significant of the Alexandrian physicians.

Bibliography: P. Prioreschi, *A History of Medicine*, 2 vols., 1996.

Rebecca Harrison

PRAXITELES (fl. 364 B.C.)

Praxiteles was a fourth-century Greek sculptor whose images of divinities were famed for their grace, beauty, sensuality, and *phantasia*.

Virtually nothing is known about the life of Praxiteles beyond his art. It is possible that the sculptor Cephisodotos was his father. Praxiteles worked in both bronze and marble, though his reputation mainly resulted from his works in marble. His most famous work, and that which is most frequently commented on by ancients, may have been the *Aphrodite of Cnidos* (Knidos), a nude image that was meant and displayed to be viewed from both front and back. In addition to the famed Cnidian Aphrodite, he also produced the *Aphrodite of Cos*, Erotes (nude and other), a Flora, a Triptolemos, a Demeter, a Bonus Eventus (Good Fortune), Maenads, Caryatids, Sileni, Poseidon, a Leto with her children, a Chloris, an Artemis, and a Hermes with the Baby Dionysus.

Among his works in bronze were the *Rape of Persephone*, *Dionysus with Drunkenness*, a satyr, a woman putting on a garland, a woman putting on an arm band, possibly an Autumn (possibly a wine-bearer), Apollo Suaroktenos, a Matron Weeping, a Lady Smiling (based on his girlfriend Phryne), a charioteer, and a Herm. His work was copied even in antiquity.

Praxiteles' style was one of exquisite naturalism that seemed to bring works of art to life, with an ability to change bronze to flesh and instill the soul into stone. According to *Philostratus, *phantasia* was in attendance while he worked, allowing him to represent what was not visible by the eyes. Praxiteles used live models, including Phryne, his girlfriend, who also served as model for *Apelles' Aphrodite and to whom he gave his statue of Eros.

Bibliography: C.M. Havelock, *The Aphrodite of Knidos and Her Successors: A Historical Review of the Female Nude in Greek Art*, 1995; A.F. Stewart, *Greek Sculpture: An Exploration*, 2 vols., 1990.

Lisa Auanger

PROCLUS (410/412–485)

Proclus is considered the last important pagan Greek philosopher and influential in spreading Neoplatonic ideas throughout the Byzantine, Islamic, and Latin worlds.

According to the biography of his disciple, Marinus, Proclus was born in Constantinople in 410 or 412 into a wealthy Lycian family and spent his childhood in Xanthus (Lycia). His early philosophical education occurred in Alexandria under Olympiodorus the Elder. He then moved to Athens at the age of twenty and associated with the Platonists, especially Syrianus, under whom he completed his *curriculum studiorum* at the Academy. He later became the head of the Academy and held this position until his death (485).

Proclus was a hardworking scholar; he commented on *Plato's *Dialogues*, and besides philosophical treatises, he wrote on astronomy, mathematics, and geometry and also composed poetry. He considered himself a follower of the Neoplatonist Iamblichus (c. 250–325) and opposed Christianity in defense of traditional Paganism; he was, however, interested in all religious beliefs and superstitions. Like other Neoplatonists he was strictly vegetarian, never married, was initiated to the Chaldean mysteries, and thought himself to have received communications from the gods. Proclus considered his philosophy to be the exposition of the secret doctrines of Plato and the Pythagoreans. For him, human thinking must deal with realities, and material things are such only to a certain degree—they are rather appearances. The One or Good is the ultimate reality and unifies philosophy, ethics, and theology; the human soul can ascend to union with the One only through the exercise of virtue, knowledge, and faith. From the One proceeds a class of participated forms, called *henads*, which are present in Intellect and Soul and in all successive emanations; the *henads* are at the same time qualities and substances and carry the divine properties of the One to all real things, however remote. In places he identified the *henads* with the gods of the Greek pantheon.

Proclus' metaphysics is a complex systematization, by the constant use of triadic structures of Neoplatonic doctrines. His ideas and methodology found an echo in the works of Dionysius the Areopagite and with them were channeled into the Latin West. Furthermore, Proclus' *Elements of Theology* was translated and abridged in Arabic under the title *Liber de causis*, which, once translated again into Latin in the twelfth century, was believed to be one of *Aristotle's writings until William of Moerbecke's Latin version of the complete *Elements* from the original Greek, which reestablished Proclus' authorship of the *De causis*.

Bibliography: L. Siorvanes, *Proclus: Neo-platonic Philosophy and Science*, 1996.

Roberto Plevano

PROPERTIUS, SEXTUS (c. 50–after 16 B.C.)

Propertius was a Roman poet who wrote four books of elegies that are striking in their imagination, tending to vary abruptly in mood and thought.

Propertius was born of a prominent family in Assisi, and when his father died early, his property, like *Tibullus', was reduced by the confiscations of Octavian (later *Augustus). However, Propertius had sufficient income to be able to abandon a law career in favor of composing poetry. By the time he had started his second book of poems, Propertius had become a member of the literary circle of *Gaius Maecenas, principal counselor of Octavian, and patron of *Horace and *Virgil. Despite this connection, Propertius showed impudence toward Octavian/Augustus throughout his poetry, probably as a result of the confiscation of his family property. However, as the constraints imposed by the Augustan regime became more severe, he was forced to become less direct in his attacks.

From internal evidence it appears that Propertius' four books were published no later than 28, 26, 23, and 16 B.C., respectively, Book 2 being thought to be a grouping by a later person of two separate books. The prime focus of his work in the first book is his love affair with his mistress, Cynthia, the pseudonym, according to *Apuleius, of one Hostia. Book 2 conveys less of a creative spirit than the first, covering a variety of topics in a general, withdrawn way. Propertius' claim to be a new *Callimachus in Book 3 only comes into focus in Book 4, which contains several well-crafted poems on Roman themes based on Callimachus' *Aetia*.

Bibliography: J.P. Sullivan, *Propertius: A Critical Introduction*, 1976.

Deborah Eaton

PROTAGORAS (c. 490–420 B.C.)

Protagoras was the most important Sophist of classical Greece. He proposed a form of relativism and subjectivism popular in Greek democracies.

Protagoras was born in Abdera but wandered from state to state, amassing wealth by teaching rhetoric and political philosophy. Requested to draw up a constitution for the colony of Thurii in 444/443, he based it on principles common to all parties. Athenian youth, aspiring to excel in the democracy, studied rhetorical theory under him: To every argument (*logos*) there is a counterargument (*antilogos*), truth being decided by the most persuasive speaker. In *Truth, or The Wrestlers' Throw*, Protagoras claimed that the subjective opinion of the individual is the measure of all things both qualitatively and existentially. Although social norms are likewise subjective—and no society is more correct than another—the individual will adhere to the conventions adopted by the society in which he lives in order to avoid punishment. In *On the Gods*, he raised doubts concerning their existence—the individual does not have enough information to decide. For this he was allegedly punished himself by expulsion from Athens and the burning of his books. In *A Great Argument*, he stated that study needs natural ability and practice in addition. Similarly, he based his theory of social progress on the natural ability of the human race to learn and invent.

Protagoras was one of the first teachers of the classical era to supply a need for education beyond basic letters. He laid the foundations for methods of disputation in later schools of rhetoric and law. His work lies at the basis of the rhetorical schools of the Second Sophistic during the Roman era. In the classical period, the Sophist *Gorgias developed a theory of nihilism from Protagoras' subjectivism. *Socrates and *Plato were critical of Protagoras' relativistic morality and influence on society. His dialogue *Protagoras* describes an imaginary conversation between Socrates and the Sophist. *Aristotle even criticized the logical contradiction that the same thing can be and not be, depending on the subject. Even later sceptics who accepted Protagoras' theory of counterargument criticized his claim that the individual is absolute measure for all things. Protagoras' works survive in very few brief fragments. Up to recently, his historical contribution was thus often misjudged.

Bibliography: W.K.C. Guthrie, *The Sophists*, 1971; E.A. Havelock, *The Liberal Temper in Greek Politics*, 1964; G.B. Kerferd, *The Sophistic Movement*, 1981.

Menahem Luz

PRUDENTIUS, AURELIUS CLEMENS (c. 348–c. 405)

Prudentius was one of the greatest poets of the early Latin Christian Church.

The only surviving biographical data are given in the forty-five line preface to the edition of poems that he published in 405 at the age of fifty-seven. He was born in 348 in the region of Tarragona, Spain. He does not speak of his own conversion, though he does of other Christian notables, which may suggest he was born into a Christian family.

He was educated in the manner customary to Roman gentlemen (grammar and rhetoric) and was then active as a lawyer. He says that "bitter experiences" led him away from law, into public administration. At the end of his career, he governed two important cities as Urban Prefect. His reputation for good government was such that he was finally offered a post as diplomatic attaché to the imperial court. It was at court that he experienced a crisis of meaning of some kind that led to his retirement from public life—though this may simply have been consequent on the death of *Theodosius I in 395. A key element in this transition was his journey to Rome, which profoundly impressed him with its monuments to Roman civilized values and Christian achievement.

After this visit, sometime between 401 and 403, he took up poetry with a vigorous aim to represent Christianity in its struggle with "paganism"—though the level of his command of metre suggests he was already a skilled writer. Nothing is known of him after 405, when he published the *Cathemerinon*, and the date of his death is uncertain. His "conversion" to the retired life is depicted as a turning to "simplicity"—the life of perfection. It is coterminous with his adoption of poetry as expressive medium. His withdrawal to his estates (sometime after 395) marks the high point of his compositions and editing work. His works offer a round of hymns for Christian daily prayer (*Cathemerinon*), celebrate the feats of Christian martyrs (*Peristephanon*), and also offer synopses of Christian doctrine on salvation and the incarnation of Christ. His *Psychomachia* was a highly influential allegory of the virtues and vices. His master theme is that *Jesus Christ is the true destiny of all Roman civilization and its highest moral and cultural values. He exercised an immense influence on the literary imagination of the Western early medieval Church, and many digested passages of his works made their way into the Roman breviary as office hymns.

Bibliography: F.J.E. Raby, *A History of Christian Latin Poetry*, 1997.

John A. McGuckin

PTOLEMY I SOTER (c. 367–282 b.c.)

Ptolemy served as a general under *Alexander the Great and subsequently became first satrap and later king of Egypt.

After Alexander the Great's death in 323, Ptolemy, the former satrap of Egypt under Alexander, arose in Egypt as the founder of one of the most stable and long-lasting of the Hellenistic regimes that followed Alexander's amazing conquests. Already in the struggle between the successors, Ptolemy showed his political wile by turning up with the body of Alexander, which he placed in state in Egypt before planning to give him a pharaoh's burial. Such activities implied a great deal of traditional authority; it was the task of kings to bury their successors. However, Ptolemy showed even further cleverness in strategically turning down many opportunities to extend his influence beyond Egypt as a conqueror, thus preventing his regime from engaging in the deadly overreach that was the doom of many other successor regimes of the Hellenistic period.

Already in 312, Ptolemy defeated *Demetrius, son of *Antigonus I (the latter hoping to consolidate some semblance of Alexander's vast territory) in Gaza, and reached an agreement with *Seleucus I of Babylon that would vary between bloody feuding and temporary alliances. In another struggle with Demetrius, this time over Rhodes, Ptolemy earned the name Soter ("Savior") by supplying the Rhodians with food and supplies during the long siege initiated by Demetrius.

The great "Colossus" at Rhodes, a statue of Helios, was erected there to honor Ptolemy's assistance.

It is clear that Ptolemy, based on his years as satrap, came to understand many of the difficulties of ruling Egypt. Egypt's considerable agricultural wealth depended on a centrally organized system based on the annual flooding of the Nile. This required strong centralized leadership. But this was a leadership that also depended, as Ptolemy knew, on the support of the Egyptian religious establishment. Ptolemy cultivated the latter by supporting the cult of Sarapis, restoring the temples of the pharoahs, and through generous gifts to the religious establishment.

However, Ptolemy also used his considerable economic resources to maintain foreign mercenaries as a hedge against local opposition. This was a wise policy, given that after 217, when indigenous Egyptians themselves were armed to support the Ptolemaic forces at the Battle of Raphia, there followed a constant stream of uprisings among the indigenous population.

The fate of Alexandria as one of the great ancient cities of the Near East is directly connected to its patronage by Ptolemy, who established his Egyptian base of operation here. Ptolemy seemed early determined to make Alexandria not only a political center but a cultural center as well. Thus, Ptolemy conceived of a center for philosophy that would evolve into the famous Library, considered one of the ancient wonders of the world, and contributed greatly to Alexandria's reputation. Ptolemy even invested imperial funds in the securing of personnel to populate his cultural center with famous philosophers. Ptolemy was not only a patron of the arts; he was also an author, and in the latter years of his life, he wrote a history of Alexander's campaigns. Although this work is lost, it was used as a chief source by the historian *Arrian.

Ptolemy knew, however, that what really drove Alexandria was commerce, not high culture. In this regard, the Ptolemies famously ran Egypt as a dictatorship and maintained strong monopolies on the production of oil, papyrus, and perfume. Furthermore, the trade tariffs on imports were so exorbitant (at times 50 percent or higher), and their use of native weights and measures contributed to a Ptolemaic Egyptian economic isolation from the rest of the Near East. Widespread wealth from Egypt's impressive resources and agricultural potential was never encouraged under Ptolemaic rule.

Moreover, despite making appearances of taking on local customs and religious pageantry, there are an interesting variety of sources that suggest that indigenous Egyptian attitudes toward Ptolemaic rule were severely critical and resented. The Ptolemies ruled Egypt with the racism typical of Aristotelian xenophobia, and the number of actual Egyptians serving in the central administration remained, it appears from our available sources, to be less than 5 percent.

Ptolemy also engaged in considerable, and complex, international negotiations via his own marriages and the marriages of his daughters. After Ptolemy repudiated his wife Eurydice to marry her niece Berenice, he named his son from the latter marriage as the successor, the future *Ptolemy II Philadelphus.

Bibliography: W.M. Ellis, *Ptolemy of Egypt*, 1994; P. Green, *Alexander to Actium: The Historical Evolution of the Hellenistic Age*, 1990; R.A. Hazzard, *Imagination of a Monarchy: Studies in Ptolemaic Propaganda*, 2000.

Daniel Smith-Christopher

PTOLEMY II PHILADELPHUS (c. 308–246 b.c.)

Ptolemy II was the youngest son of *Ptolemy I Soter and succeeded him as king of Egypt.

Ptolemy II's political career started when he was named coruler by his father, Ptolemy I, in 284. After his father died (282) and he was named sole ruler of Egypt, he had his father deified. In 280 Ptolemy instituted the *Ptolemaieia*, a festival in honor of his father and the house of Ptolemy. Ptolemy II had two wives during the tenure of his reign as pharaoh. The first marriage was a strictly political affair as Ptolemy married Arsinoe, the daughter of the king of Thrace, *Lysimachus, whereas the latter married Ptolemy's sister, also named Arsinoe. After the death of Lysimachus and the banishment of his own wife, Ptolemy married his own sister. This was seen as a clever political move because the marriage was done in keeping with traditional Egyptian culture. This gave even more validation to the reign of the Ptolemies in Egypt. It was after this marriage to his sister that he was given the title Philadelphus ("Brother-loving").

Ptolemy II was probably best known for his architectural and literary advances. It was during his reign that the famous lighthouse and Library of Alexandria were completed. He also built many cities, temples, and canals along the coast of the Red Sea. Most of these cities were set up as trade towns that were used to enhance and supplement the economy of Egypt.

Ptolemy's two largest undertakings in the realm of literature are *Manetho's *History of Egypt* (*Aegyptica*) and the Septuagint. At Ptolemy's request a priest named Manetho set about the work of recording a written history of Egypt. This body of work was originally written in Greek so that Ptolemy could read it. The only remaining part of the work we have left is a list of kings, although portions of it survive in *Josephus and *Eusebius. The second great undertaking was the writing of the Septuagint, the Greek translation of the Torah. Ptolemy already had many Jewish people living in Alexandria by the time he was made coruler. Many of these Jewish people had been so integrated into Greek culture they had lost the knowledge of how to read Hebrew. As a result of this they were becoming removed from their sacred writings. Ptolemy had seventy-two Jewish elders brought into Alexandria, and there they translated the Hebrew of the Torah into Greek. In addition to these two great literary enterprises, Ptolemy was well known as a generous sponsor to the arts and surrounded himself with poets, most notably *Callimachus and *Theocritus.

Militarily, Ptolemy met with little success in either the Chremonidean War

(266–261) against *Antigonus II Gonatas or the Second Syrian War (260–253) against *Antiochus II and Gonatas. Nevertheless, through skillful diplomacy, Ptolemy was able to assert his influence in the Aegean, Asia Minor, and Syria.

It can be argued that the efforts put forth by Ptolemy I and Ptolemy II were so effective that the entire line down to *Cleopatra VII were able to reap the bounty of Egypt without the need of much change in administration. The combinations of increased trade, traditional marriage, increased emphasis on learning, architecture, and the deification of Ptolemy I Soter gave the Ptolemy dynasty a link to the culture and people of Egypt. It was this link and these achievements that allowed the Ptolemaic dynasty to be one of the most stable and long-lasting of any of the Hellenistic states.

Bibliography: P. Green, *Alexander to Actium: The Historical Evolution of the Hellenistic Age*, 1990; R.A. Hazzard, *Imagination of a Monarchy: Studies in Ptolemaic Propaganda*, 2000.

James A. Cook III

PTOLEMY III EUERGETES ("Benefactor," c. 288–221 B.C.)

Ptolemy III was the third in the line of Macedonian kings of Egypt and ruled that country from 246 to 221.

Ptolemy III, the eldest son of *Ptolemy II, was the brother of Berenice, one of the ill-fated wives of *Antiochus II. When Antiochus II died in 246, his wife Laodice had Berenice and her son murdered, and Ptolemy III arrived in Antioch too late to save them. There ensued the so-called Third Syrian War (246–241). Ptolemy was a particular strong ruler and even occupied Antioch itself for a time. After Antioch, Ptolemy III turned eastward and occupied Babylon, penetrating as far as Susa. Part of the success of his campaigns may be attributed to his widespread international support as a result of the general abhorrence of the Greeks at the murder of Berenice and her child. The main result of this successful eastern incursion was that he was able to recapture a number of Egyptian statues and icons originally taken by the Persians and return them to Egypt in their appropriate sanctuaries. By retrieving these sacred statues, Ptolemy earned considerable popularity at home—popularity that was needed because of insurrections that were breaking out during his absence.

Reports about the rule of Ptolemy III indicate that he was praised in Egyptian texts as a strong ruler, one who provided funds for temples and the encouragement of Egyptian religious centers and who even provided grain in times of inadequate irrigation from the Nile. As was *Alexander the Great, Ptolemy was proclaimed pharaoh. When there was a severe silver shortage in Egypt, it was Ptolemy III that introduced a bronze coinage.

Ptolemy was noted for maintaining his grandfather's interest in the famous Library at Alexandria, and enacted the interesting law that all books that arrived

328 PTOLEMY IV PHILOPATOR

in the ports of Alexandria be seized and held until copies were made. It has been reported that often it was the copies, rather than the originals, which were returned. Ptolemy III even kept the originals of the famous tragedians (*Aeschylus, *Sophocles, and *Euripides), losing the hefty deposit that Athens insisted upon before "loaning" them.

Bibliography: P. Green, *Alexander to Actium: The Historical Evolution of the Hellenistic Age*, 1990.

Daniel Smith-Christopher

PTOLEMY IV PHILOPATOR ("Loving His Father," c. 244–205 B.C.)

Ptolemy IV was the fourth in the line of Macedonian kings of Egypt.

After his father died in 221, Ptolemy, under the influence of his advisers, had his brother, mother, and uncle assassinated and then ascended to the throne of Egypt. The classical source tradition is generally hostile to his reign, which has been characterized as a continual drunken revelry. Ptolemy neglected the affairs of state, which allowed *Antiochus III to threaten the Ptolemaic possessions in Coele-Syria. In 219, Antiochus seized several coastal towns in that area, and while Ptolemy's adviser Sosibus engaged in negotiations intended to delay Antiochus' advance, Ptolemy had the Egyptian army reorganized. Antiochus' attack posed such a danger to Ptolemy that, for the first time, the Macedonian kings of Egypt enrolled the native Egyptians in the infantry and cavalry and trained them in phalanx tactics.

By 218 Sosibus' negotiations had collapsed, and Antiochus resumed his offensive. In spring 217, Ptolemy's new army met the Seleucid forces at Raphia in southern Palestine and, with the help of the Egyptian phalanx, was victorious. At Sosibus' advice, he negotiated a peace with Antiochus, and the latter withdrew from Coele-Syria. After Raphia, Ptolemy married his sister Arsinoe, who bore him a successor in 210; his son was immediately named coruler. As Ptolemy fell under the further influence of his advisers, native Egyptians, realizing their own military potential and the need that Ptolemy had for them in the army, broke into open revolt. By 205 this revolt had spread throughout most of Egypt. Ptolemy died mysteriously in that same year; his advisers Sosibus and Agathocles killed Arsinoe in the following year and produced a will that proclaimed them the guardians of Ptolemy's infant son.

*Strabo and *Polybius highlight the degeneracy and corruption rampant during Ptolemy's reign. Nevertheless, Ptolemy's victory at Raphia kept Egypt at least temporarily out of Seleucid control. After the ascension of his infant son, the possessions of Ptolemaic Egypt would once again be threatened by *Philip V and Antiochus.

Bibliography: F.W. Walbank, A.E. Astin, M.W. Frederiksen, and R.M. Ogilvie, eds., *The Hellenistic World*, vol. 7.1 of *The Cambridge Ancient History*, 2nd ed., 1984.

Andrew G. Traver

PTOLEMY OF ALEXANDRIA (Claudius Ptolemaeus, c. 85– 165)

Claudius Ptolemy was a mathematician, astronomer, and geographer.

Few details are known concerning the life of Claudius Ptolemy. He was born either in Alexandria or Ptolemais and worked in Alexandria until at least 141. While in Alexandria, Ptolemy made astronomical observations and wrote his most famous work, *Syntaxis*, now almost universally known by the name *Almagest* after the Arabic translation.

The *Almagest* is an important mathematical and scientific work for several reasons. Its Table of Chords is one of the first instances of a table of trigonometric values and corresponds to a modern sine table for angles from 0.25 degrees to 90 degrees in steps of 0.25 degrees. The book fully presents all the methods necessary for deriving the values in the Table of Chords, including the sum, difference, and half-angle identities. He found the sine of half a degree with the equivalent of six decimal places of accuracy. The trigonometric values thus discovered are used along with his astronomical observations to present a theory of planetary motion. In his theory of eccentrics and epicycles, he extends the work of *Hipparchus and others to explain the motion of the five planets. Other topics covered in the *Almagest* are spherical geometry, the motion and sizes of the sun and moon, the length of the lunar month, the occurrence of eclipses, and the construction of the astrolabe.

Ptolemy wrote works, both theoretical and applied, on several other topics. His *Analemma* was an explanation of the representation of celestial locations by means of orthogonal projection, that is, three coordinates. In this work he describes the position of the sun at any time of the day, a problem linked to the construction of accurate sundials. Ptolemy's *Optics* treats the theory of convex and composite mirrors and the theory of refraction. He also wrote at least one work on mechanics and attempted to prove the parallel postulate of *Euclid. As a geographer, Ptolemy's fame rests on his *Guide to Geography*. This work influenced Western cartography until the eighteenth century.

The *Almagest* holds a prominent place in the history of mathematics and astronomy and was used as primary resource for many hundreds of years. Indeed, it was not supplanted as the preeminent text until Copernicus wrote *De revolutionibus* in 1543. It has recently been suspected by some scholars that a portion of the data reported by Ptolemy is either spurious or specifically invented in order to support his own hypotheses concerning the motion of the heavenly bodies. If such is the case, the data sets of the *Almagest* may well be the earliest example of academic dishonesty.

Bibliography: T.L. Heath, *A History of Greek Mathematics*, 1921; R.R. Newton, *The Crime of Claudius Ptolemy*, 1977.

Michael Labranche

PYRRHON OF ELIS (360–270 B.C.)

Pyrrhon was a Greek philosopher who founded the ancient Sceptic School.

Little is known about Pyrrhon of Elis, and what is known is doubtful. He was born in Elis, where he was first an apparently mediocre painter. He was a disciple of Bryson of Megara and later of Anaxarcos of Abdera. With Anaxarcos he participated in *Alexander the Great's campaign to India, where he had contact with the so-called gymnosophists. On returning to Elis he founded his school. He admired *Democritus and was probably influenced by *Protagoras. He abstained from participating in politics. Elis honored him with the position of high priest and, in consideration to him, exempted philosophers from paying any taxes.

He did not write any works, except for a lost poem dedicated to Alexander. Information about his doctrine comes principally from the few fragments conserved of the works of his disciple Timon, from *Diogenes Laertius, and from *Sextus Empiricus. It is difficult to determine how much of the Sceptic doctrine can be attributed to Pyrrhon.

His philosophy, like other Hellenistic schools, is determined by an ethical finality: the achievement of happiness, understood as apathy or impassivity and ataraxy or quietness of the mind. For Pyrrhon there is no criterion for the truth: There are only phenomena relative to the dispositions (or *tropoi*) of each person and always in contradiction to each other. Thus the supposed nature of things always remains obscure. Consequently the wise will refrain from making dogmatic affirmations. This aphasy, the suspension of affirmations, is followed as a natural consequence by apathy and ataraxy. According to some sources, his indifference to the senses went so far that he did not care about external dangers such as precipices or dogs, others claim his guiding principle for his conduct was "common life."

Pyrrhon's school seems to disappear with the few disciples of his successor Timon. But his principles were reelaborated and enriched by *Aenesidemus and later by Sextus Empiricus. Both saw themselves as only further developing Pyrrhon's doctrines.

Bibliography: M. Burnyeat and M. Frede, eds., *The Original Sceptics. A Controversy*, 1997.

Fernando Oreja

PYRRHUS OF EPIRUS (c. 319–272 B.C.)

Pyrrhus was king of the Molossians in Epirus by hereditary right, but for most of his life he struggled with rival claimants in a collateral line. He was related to *Olympias, mother of *Alexander the Great, and attempted to equal or rival Alexander as a world conqueror.

At the age of seventeen, while temporarily out of power in Epirus, he joined with *Demetrius I Poliorcetes and was with him at the Battle of Ipsus in 301 and was later placed in command of various Greek holdings by him. He later transferred his allegiance to *Ptolemy I. When *Cassander died in 297, Pyrrhus was called to aid one of his sons against his brother, as was Demetrius. Demetrius murdered the young man and proclaimed himself king of Macedonia, a position that Pyrrhus also coveted. In 286 he joined with *Lysimachus and Ptolemy to drive Demetrius from Macedonia and agreed to share rule of Macedonia with Lysimachus. He was, however, driven out by Lysimachus in 283 after the death of Demetrius in Asia. While frequently in conflict with *Antigonus II Gonatas, son of Demetrius, Pyrrhus was looking for new opportunities and found one in a request for aid from the city of Tarentum in south Italy, which had entered a war with Rome.

Pyrrhus is most famous for his war against the Romans (282–274), in which he won several battles but at great cost in casualties, which he could not easily replace. On being congratulated by his staff for another victory, he is said to have remarked, "One more such victory and I am finished"—hence the term "Pyrrhic victory." He removed most of his forces to Sicily to respond to requests for help, and to seek further conquests, but was ultimately unsuccessful. He returned to Italy briefly and finally withdrew to Epirus in 274. He acquired another army, mostly Gauls as mercenaries, and invaded Macedonia and temporarily drove Antigonus II Gonatas to the seacoast. But while plundering the countryside, his Gauls desecrated royal tombs at Aegae (modern Verghina) and enraged the local population. It was an opportune time for Pyrrhus to seek yet another opportunity for conquest, this time against Sparta, ostensibly aiding an exiled king. Sparta defended itself vigorously, and aid from Macedonia at the last minute caused Pyrrhus to withdraw. In the meantime, a faction in the city of Argos sought his aid; the other faction sought help from Antigonus. During fierce fighting in the city, Pyrrhus was hit on the head by a roof tile thrown by an old woman who observed her son in danger from Pyrrhus. While he was stunned, a Macedonian soldier recognized him and attempted (sloppily) to cut off his head; the severed head was presented to Antigonus.

Pyrrhus' soldiers admired him for his boldness and considerable combat skills, while rivals universally considered him one of the best generals who ever lived.

Bibliography: N.G.L. Hammond and F.W. Walbank, *A History of Macedonia*, vol. 3, 336–167 B.C., 1988.

Janice J. Gabbert

PYTHAGORAS OF SAMOS (c. 570–?)

Pythagoras was the charismatic leader of an intellectual/religious society known for its strict vegetarian diet and for its work in abstract disciplines such as geometry. Pythagoras is probably most known for the theorem that bears his name.

Pythagoras was born on the Ionian island of Samos somewhere around 570. Pythagoras later left Samos as a result of his disagreements with the Samian tyrant *Polycrates. Pythagoras emigrated to Crotona in southern Italy. It was while he lived at Crotona that Pythagoras founded a society that sought to pursue religious, political, and philosophical ends. Pythagoras was apparently an extremely charismatic, endearing, and intelligent person, and he quickly and easily attracted many followers. The extreme nature of this society, however, such as strict rules of behavior and diet (e.g., sexual abstinence, vegetarianism), aroused suspicion and mistrust among nonmembers. It was perhaps this mistrust that led Cylon (who he was is uncertain) to lead a revolt against Pythagoras' society, and many of its members were killed. Pythagoras himself fled Crotona to Metapontum, where his society later regained its influence until another persecution occurred in the middle of the fifth century.

Determining exactly what Pythagoras believed, or what the activities and doctrines of his society were, is extremely difficult. This is so because the society members were sworn to secrecy regarding their beliefs, and Pythagoras himself did not write down his doctrines. We are left, then, to the writings of Pythagoras' contemporaries or near contemporaries (e.g., *Xenophanes) when assessing Pythagoras' philosophy. From the evidence that is available, however, a few conclusions can be drawn. First, the Pythagoreans believed that philosophy should be a way of life—and a way that assured the salvation of one's soul. Of the Greek gods the Pythagoreans worshipped, Apollo was the most important. As the traditional Greek god of moderation and temperance, Apollo fit well with the Pythagoreans' concern for self-control, moderation, and abstention from eating flesh and beans. Pythagoras was even considered to be the living incarnation of Apollo. The other important belief among the Pythagoreans, and a belief that *Plato and many others since have taken quite seriously, is that the universe is numbers, or that through an understanding of mathematics we acquire the keys with which we can understand the cosmos. It was this emphasis on mathematics and geometry that led Pythagoras and his followers to attempt to uncover mathematical relationships in nature. In music and in geometry, the Pythagoreans discovered consistent mathematical relations (e.g., the well-known Pythagorean theorem). This idea would find its greatest proponent and supporter in Plato and in the Neoplatonists, yet many scientifically and mathematically minded individuals continue to find in Pythagoreanism the beginnings of a tradition of which they feel they are still a part.

Bibliography: G.S. Kirk, J.E. Raven, and M. Schofield, *The Presocratic Philosophers*, 2nd ed., 1983.

Jeffrey A. Bell

PYTHEAS OF MASSILIA (fourth century B.C.)

Pytheas completed a unique scientific and commercial sea expedition extending to the North and Baltic Seas.

Pytheas, from the Greek colony of Massilia (modern Marseilles), was a navigator, astronomer, and mathematician who studied under *Eudoxus. In the last quarter of the fourth century, during a gap in Carthaginian control of the straits, Pytheas sailed around Spain, up the western coast of France, and across to Cornwall, which he had learned was a source of tin; there he observed the mining process. He was the first Greek to circumnavigate Britain and determine its triangular shape. Having learned of an island called Thule (Iceland or Norway), he proceeded north past Scotland in search of it. He observed the influence of the moon on tides, noted the short length of daylight, recorded reports of a place where the sun never set in the summer and where the sea was solid, and determined that the pole star was not above the true north. He then proceeded east across the North Sea, seeking amber, another valuable trade item. He found Scandinavia, writing the first description of it, and its amber regions, but deemed a sea route impractical for trade. He went as far as the mouth of what is probably the Vistula River in Poland. Having reached what he thought was the Don, the boundary between Europe and Asia, he sailed back to Marseilles.

Although many of his observations were dismissed as unbelievable, quotations from his account, *About the Ocean*, have survived in other writers. Pytheas determined the latitude of Massilia, and his further observations were important for *Eratosthenes' work and for determining parallels of latitudes through northern Europe. His report on Thule led to the literary use of the term "Ultimate Thule" for the most remote end of the world. He also dispelled the myths of monsters in the Atlantic and may have opened up an alternative route for tin trade from Massilia.

Bibliography: C.F.C. Hawkes, *Pytheas: Europe and the Greek Explorers*, 1977.

Rebecca Harrison

Q

QUINTILIAN (Marcus Fabius Quintilianus, 35–100)

Quintilian was the most famous rhetorician of first-century Rome. The rediscovery of his work in the fifteenth century led to the revival of classical Latin rhetoric during the Renaissance.

Born in Spain, Quintilian came to Rome first as a youth to study with Domitius Afer, returned to Spain, then returned to Rome again c. 68 as a student of Servius Sulpicius Galba. In addition to his work in the law courts, Quintilian himself soon became sought after as a teacher of rhetoric. Among his students were *Pliny the Younger and two grandnephews of the Emperor *Domitian. So great was Quintilian's talent and fame that he became the first rhetorician to be given a salary from the state. Several of Quintilian's works mentioned by his contemporaries are now lost, including *De causus corruptae eloquentiae*, a speech *Pro naevio arpiniano*, and two books on rhetoric compiled (without his permission) from his students' class notes. Above all, Quintilian's lasting fame rests on a single book, the *Institutio oratoria*, a study of Latin rhetoric in twelve books. In the *Institutio*, Quintilian discusses the training of an orator from infancy to mature adulthood, examining various genres of writing as well as practical techniques for effective speech making. He defends the value of Roman rhetoric against critics who would make it subordinate to the Greek and directs his readers to good exemplars from whom they can learn. Above all, he defends the Ciceronian ideal that rhetoric, whether written or spoken, is a moral force that must be used for the good of the community.

Quintilian's reputation survived into the Middle Ages, but only fragments of his work were known until Poggio Bracciolini discovered a complete text of the *Institutio oratoria* at the monastery of St. Gall in 1416. Copied and spread across Europe, the *Institutio oratoria* became the primary rhetorical textbook among Renaissance humanists, leading to the revival of classical Latin as the *lingua franca* of the educated elite of Europe.

Bibliography: G.A. Kennedy, *The Art of Rhetoric in the Roman World*, 1972.

Olivia H. McIntyre

R

RICIMER, FLAVIUS (c. 418–472)

Ricimer was a barbarian-born general of the western Roman army who dominated western politics from 456 to his death.

The son of the barbarian royal families of the Gothic kingdom (in southern Gaul since 418) and Suevic kingdom (in western Spain since 411), Ricimer nonetheless pursued a career in the Roman army, serving under *Aetius. Like the earlier "generalissimos" *Stilicho and Aetius, Ricimer held the office of *magister utriusque militiae* (master of military forces, from 456) and the high honorary title *patricius* (from 457) but was consul only once (459). He was an Arian Christian (cf. *Arius). He emerged as the most powerful western general, in part because of his large personal wealth and ties to the Burgundian kings of southeastern Gaul. The Theodosian imperial dynasty was extinguished with the death of the emperor Valentinian III in 455; thereafter, western imperial succession was determined by complex, violent politics involving the army, the Senate of Rome, the eastern emperors in Constantinople, and the barbarian kings. Ricimer caused the overthrow of the Gothic-supported Gallic usurper Avitus (455–456); the installation and deposition of the general Majorian (457–461); the elevation of Libius Severus (461–465); the deposition of the eastern nominee Procopius Anthernius, a Constantinopolitan general and noble whose daughter, Alypia, Ricimer had married (467–472); and the installation of Anicius Olybrius, a noble Roman senator and son-in-law of the late Valentinian III, supported also by the Vandal king Geiseric (472). A month later, Ricimer died (August 472); Olybrius died the following November. Only three emperors—elevated by the army or the eastern emperor—followed briefly before *Odoacer deposed the last western emperor.

Ricimer is the last attested western figure to dominate politics over a prolonged period. His barbarian connections and manipulation of puppet emperors have been seen as symptomatic of the collapse of the western empire.

Bibliography: J.M. O'Flynn, *Generalissimos of the Later Roman Empire*, 1983.
Andrew Gillett

RIOTHAMUS (fl. 468)

Riothamus (Rigotamus, Riotimus) was an obscure king of the Britons who historian Geoffrey Ashe claims was the real King Arthur.

Riothamus may have succeeded in the 450s the semi-legendary Vortigern, whom tradition credits for inviting the Germanic barbarians Hengist and Horsa into Britain in 449. According to the sixth-century historian Jordanes, in 468 the western Roman emperor Anthemius sought Riothamus' assistance against the Gothic king *Euric's invasion of Gaul. Riothamus led a force said to comprise 12,000 men across the sea into Armorica; his presence is attested by a letter written to him by *Sidonius Apollinaris, a Roman aristocrat in Gaul. Anthemius' deputy Arvandus attempted to betray Riothamus but was caught; nevertheless, Euric defeated the Britons at Bourg-de-Déols (perhaps in 470), a battle mentioned by the sixth-century chronicler Gregory of Tours. Having lost much of his army, Riothamus fled into Burgundy and disappeared from history. Though some historians claim that Riothamus and his men were "Bretons" (i.e., from Brittany), Ashe and others disagree.

Ashe compares this story to the highly suspect twelfth-century chronicler Geoffrey of Monmouth's account of Arthur, who led an army of Britons to Gaul, was betrayed by a deputy, was last known to be among the Burgundians, and disappeared after his last battle, headed for Avallon (there was a real site called Avallon in fifth-century Burgundy). He offers plausible, though by no means conclusive, explanations for the discrepancies between Riothamus' story and Geoffrey's tale, including the different names ("Rigotamus" may have been a title); different foes, that is, Goths for Riothamus and Romans for Arthur (dramatic license); and different dates for their disappearance, that is, Riothamus in 470 and Geoffrey's Arthur in 542 (a different system of dating plus clerical error). He also cites other sources that place Arthur in the fifth century, including the *Legend of St. Goeznovius* (c. 1019) and chronicles by Alberic (a thirteenth-century Cistercian monk), Martinus Polonus (quoted by Jean des Preis, 1338–1400), and Jacques de Guise (a fourteenth-century Franciscan).

Critical reaction to Ashe's study has been mixed, but the book has attracted a wide readership, influenced popular opinion about the legendary king, and stirred considerable controversy among hard-core Arthurians. In the end, however, Ashe bases his identification of Arthur with Riothamus not only upon some interesting parallels but also upon a significant amount of unproved (and as yet unprovable) speculation. Nevertheless, all attempts to identify Arthur, who may not ever have existed in fact, are based upon speculation, and Riothamus perhaps has as good a claim as any of the other candidates.

Bibliography: G. Ashe, *The Discovery of King Arthur*, 1985.
William B. Robison

ROMULUS (c. 753 b.c.)

Romulus and Remus, twin brothers, were the legendary founders of Rome.

The myth of Romulus and Remus, whose origin is controversial, takes many forms. All versions, however, tell the story of Rome's founding in a way that conjoins native Italian traditions with the legend of Troy. Numitor, king of Alba Longa and descended from Aeneas, was deposed by his younger brother, Amulius. To protect his claim, Amulius killed Numitor's sons and placed the daughter, Rhea Silvia, in the convent of the Vestal Virgins to prevent heirs. Ravished by Mars, Rhea Silvia gave birth to twins, Romulus and Remus. Amulius ordered the twins to be drowned in the Tiber River, where instead of drowning they were saved and nursed by a she-wolf. Faustulus, the king's chief herdsman, found the twins and took them home to raise with his wife, Acca Larentia. The twins grew into strong, bold men, leaders of a small band of daring and plundering youth. During one adventure, Remus was captured and taken before Numitor. When Romulus came to his brother's rescue, their identities became known, and the brothers led an uprising against Amulius, whom Romulus killed, and restored Numitor as king. The twins left Alba Longa to found the city that would become Rome. In a dispute over who would rule, Romulus walled his area and, according to one version of the myth, in a fit of anger, killed Remus, who had lept the wall. Romulus reigned for about forty years, having developed the city and increased its population in two ways: by offering asylum to fugitives and by kidnapping and marrying the daughters of the neighboring Sabines, who had been invited to a festival. Romulus vanished during a storm, never to be seen again, and was deified as Quirinus (originally an ancient Sabine god), whose assimilation to Romulus intertwines Italian and Trojan myths of origin.

Bibliography: J.N. Bremmer, "Romulus, Remus and the Foundation of Rome," in *Roman Myth and Mythography*, 1987, 25–48.

Ron Harris

RUFUS, QUINTUS CURTIUS (first century a.d.)

A rhetorician and historian, Curtius wrote a history of *Alexander the Great in ten books.

Scholars have vigorously debated both the date and the identity of Quintus Curtius Rufus. Although it is still not certain when he lived, the prevailing theory is that he wrote during the principates of *Augustus, *Claudius, or *Vespasian. He may be the same Quintus Curtius Rufus mentioned in the index of *Suetonius' *De Grammaticis et Rhetoribus* and is thought to have lived during the early years of the Roman Empire.

Quintus Curtius Rufus is the author of the *History of Alexander*. This work is the only full-length Latin history of Alexander to survive. Curtius based his work on a number of earlier sources, among which he mentions Cleitarchus, *Ptolemy, and Timagenes. Other likely sources include *Livy, the *Historiae Philippicae* of *Pompeius Trogus, *Virgil's *Aeneid*, and perhaps *Herodotus.

He uses Livian models and usually writes as a moralist. Scholars have found echoes of Herodotus in his work, but unlike him, Curtius favors the use of speeches, in the manner of *Thucydides.

Bibliography: J. Yardley, trans., and W. Heckel, int., *Quintus Curtius Rufus, the History of Alexander*, 1984.

Brannon Wheeler

S

SALLUST (Gaius Sallustius Crispus, 86–35 B.C.)

Sallust was a public official and major Roman historian, author of monographs on the war with *Jugurtha and the conspiracy of *Catiline.

Gaius Sallustius Crispus was born at Amiterrium (San Vittorino), Italy. In the course of his political career, he sided with *Julius Caesar against *Pompey in the Civil War that broke out in 49. Though Sallust's service in governmental and military posts was undistinguished, Caesar did appoint him the first governor of the province of Africa Nova in 46. Afterward, Sallust was charged with (but not convicted of) extortion and embezzlement; the scandal forced him into an early retirement. The wealth Sallust had amassed in office bought him a palatial villa at Tivoli and, in Rome, an elegantly landscaped complex of parklands surrounding a fine mansion, later the possession of Roman emperors.

Sallust's firsthand knowledge of the gradual disintegration of the Roman political system in the late republican period informs the historical works he wrote in his retirement. The *War with Catiline* (c. 42) is devoted to the failed conspiracy of a disgruntled aristocrat who tried to recoup electoral and financial losses by an armed insurrection, quashed by *Cicero during his consulship in 63. *The War with Jugurtha* (c. 40) recounts the conflict between Rome and an upstart king of Numidia in 111–105. This was an apt subject because of Sallust's familiarity with north Africa and the opportunity it afforded to expose and dissect mismanagement and corruption among the ruling elite. Sallust's other major work, the *Histories* (begun c. 39), survives only in fragments.

Sallust has been most influential as a stylist and moralist. Forced out of an active political life, he became an analyst of the moral decline in the ruling elite of a great imperial power. *Tacitus emulated his terse and acerbic style of writing, and St. *Augustine's approval of his ethical stances ensured his popularity in the Middle Ages. Erasmus preferred Sallust to *Livy and Tacitus in recommending school curricula. More recently, Sallust has appealed to readers, including many Marxists, who have found in his work a congenial indictment of a corrupted ruling aristocracy.

Bibliography: R. Syme, *Sallust*, 1964.

James Holoka

SALONINA (fl. 242)

Salonina was wife of the later Roman emperor Gallienus (253–268) and an important woman of state.

Little is preserved of the life of Salonina. She may have been of Hellenic origin and was frequently represented in the coinage both in Rome and in the provinces. Her images in the coinage show her patronage and connection to several cults that formed the state religion. She was associated with the traditional goddesses: Ceres, Juno, Venus, and Vesta. She also was connected with the cults of several virtues and qualities that showed the benefits that her family brought. These include Aequitas, Concordia, Fecunditas, Felicitas, Fortuna, Pietas, and Victoria. An arch on the Esquiline was rededicated jointly to her and Gallienus by an Aurelius Victor. Reportedly Salonina witnessed the death of Gallienus before the walls of Milan in 268.

Bibliography: A.S. Robertson, *Roman Imperial Coins in the Hunter Coin Cabinet, University of Glasgow*, 1962–1982.

Lisa Auanger

SALVIUS JULIANUS

See **Julianus Salvius**.

SAPPHO OF MYTILENE (c. 612–c. 558 B.C.)

One of the earliest of the Greek poets whose work only survives in fragments, Sappho was also a female role model whose literary contributions have sometimes led her to be referred to as the "Tenth Muse."

As a young girl, Sappho lost her father in a war with Athens, and the family moved to the city of Mytilene on Lesbos, an island off Asia Minor in the Aegean Sea, for greater safety. Her earliest poetic works were done in response to a romantic pursuit, and by the age of seventeen, her work was drawing some interest. The women of Lesbos had great personal freedom, and Sappho soon became an informal leader of the young girls there, to whom she felt strong emotional ties.

Her poetic influences were many and varied, mostly the lyrical poets, but her writing reflected a certain wild and orgiastic quality as well while retaining a sense of simplicity and naturalness. When the war ended in 596, Sappho's involvement in a plot to overthrow the island's leaders led to her ejection from the city and eventually from Lesbos. Only twenty-one, she went into exile, settling in Syracuse. Sappho found the city much to her liking, but for reasons of protection, she decided to take a husband, Cercolas; she eventually gave birth to a daughter, Cleis, and was widowed soon after.

As a wealthy widow, Sappho emerged as a social, literary, and artistic leader, and her work was recognized as brilliant. At age twenty-six, she was permitted to return to Lesbos, where she began to gather a more formalized circle of aristocratic girls around her and taught them gracious living; together, they wrote verses, played music, and danced, often to Sappho's poetry set to music. Their mothers were happy to have their daughters under Sappho's tutelage, and she functioned as their role model. Sappho did engage in several tempestuous affairs with some of the girls, a practice that slowly gave her an unsavory reputation, but her position as a leader of society remained unchallenged. Sappho continued to lead a rather luxurious lifestyle, writing marriage songs for bridal couples and some hymns, though she preferred the former, and she found comfort in her music and poetry and in her female acolytes. She was the object of admiration for the wise men of her day, including *Solon, and her own wisdom was evidenced by her aphorisms, such as "You cannot bend a stiff mind."

In 560, at the age of fifty-two, Sappho embarked on a passionate affair with a young sailor, Phaon, to whom she wrote many of her most romantic poems. When Phaon broke off the affair and left without saying goodbye, Sappho boarded a ship bound for Sicily to find him but stopped off at Apollo's temple on a hill at Corfu. Perhaps realizing her pursuit of Phaon was hopeless, she decided to commit suicide by leaping off the cliff. In his *Heroides*, *Ovid wrote about her legendary love for Phaon.

The people of Lesbos honored her memory and her work for generations, and though only fragments of her work survive, later generations have learned of her through the praise of others. Regardless of any controversies about her personal life, however, her work as a poetess remains a great achievement.

Bibliography: A. Weigall, *Sappho of Lesbos: Her Life and Times*, 1932.

Connie Evans

SARGON II (r. 721–705 B.C.)

Sargon II was king of Assyria during its formative empire years and also completed the conquest of Samaria, the Israelite capital, and deported many of its leading citizens.

Sargon seized the throne of Assyria when his predecessor, Shalmaneser V, was killed in a palace revolution. He was apparently a usurper, a fact partly shown by his throne name, Sargon (Akkadian, Sharru-kin, "true king"). He also left an account of his accession to the throne, justifying the removal of Shalmaneser.

Vassal states in Syro-Palestine rebelled against Assyria because of its internal problems. Sargon quickly met a coalition (which included the cities of Damascus, Hamath, Samaria, and Arpad) at Qarqar in 720, which he defeated. He subsequently marched through Palestine and claimed to have defeated an Egyp-

tian army near the Egyptian border. In the wake of this campaign, Sargon deposed numerous rulers and deported large amounts of the local populations from
this area. Included in this campaign was Sargon's successful completion of the
siege of the Israelite capital of Samaria, which had been commenced by Shalmaneser. He is mentioned only once in the Old Testament (Isaiah 20:1), although it is clear that he played a major role in Israelite affairs. He subsequently
deported large numbers of important Israelite families to other parts of the empire.

Sargon also campaigned in eastern Turkey against Mita (the classical *Midas)
of Phrygia and against Urartu (located in Armenia), successfully weakening both
of these states and creating a peaceful frontier. Like his predecessors, Sargon
continued to have problems with Assyria's southern neighbor Babylon. The
Chaldean, Merodach-Baladan, seized the Babylonian throne during the succession problem in Assyria in 721 and held it until Sargon deposed him in 710.
Like his predecessor *Tiglath-Pileser III, Sargon took the title of king of Babylon, although Merodach-Baladan was able to flee to Elam in the east.

In spite of numerous military campaigns during his reign, Sargon found the
time to build a new capital, Dur-Sharrukin, nearby to Nineveh, and repopulated
it with many of the deported peoples.

Sargon died in battle in 705, campaigning in the north. Since the death of the
king in battle was considered an evil omen, Sargon's successor *Sennacherib
had to endure a major revolt throughout the empire.

Bibliography: P. Albenda, *The Palace of Sargon, King of Assyria*, 1986.

Mark W. Chavalas

SATURNINUS, LUCIUS APPULEIUS (c.132–100 b.c.)

As tribune in 103 and 100 Saturninus embarked upon a program of reform,
the most significant since that of *Gaius Gracchus in the 120s, and like Gracchus, died violently after the passage of the so-called ultimate decree of the
Senate.

As quaestor at Ostia (probably 104) he was replaced in his supervision of the
grain supply by the leading man in the Senate, M. Aemilius Scaurus, bespeaking
an exceptional situation. This humiliation reportedly induced Saturninus to identify himself with the popular cause.

Saturninus was the only individual during the historical period to be elected
three times to the plebeian tribunate (for the years 103, 100, and 99). He used
the office in a number of ways, most notably to legislate for the land settlement
of recently demobilized soldiers. This legislation, which appropriated certain
features of the Gracchan program (such as transmarine colonization), alienated
a substantial section of the urban plebs, which was hostile to its Italian beneficiaries, and serious civil conflict between the urban and rural citizenry resulted.

Saturninus challenged the senatorial establishment by proposing legislation
for the provision of subsidized grain to the people and involved himself in the

popular prosecutions of senatorial commanders for incompetence on the battle-field. He also sponsored a popular law making any attempt to diminish the majesty of the Roman people an indictable offense, one aim of which was probably to safeguard himself and his legislation.

Saturninus further alienated conservative opinion through his political meth-ods, such as his disregard of unfavorable auspices, the imposition of an oath compelling senators to abide by his legislation (perhaps an innovation), and his continued resort to violence. One of his competitors was murdered by soldiers at the tribunician elections in 101, and the killing of a consular candidate in the following year led to a break with his ally, the consul, *Gaius Marius, and to the passage of the *senatus consultum ultimum*, or ultimate decree of the Senate. Though a tribune (and therefore sacrosanct) and despite a formal guarantee of safety from Marius, Saturninus was lynched in the Senate house along with his praetorian associate *C. Servilius Glaucia by a mob containing senators and equestrians.

The violent suppression of Saturninus and his associates in 100 involved the second use of the so-called ultimate decree of the Senate (dormant for more than two decades) and its first use against a tribune of the plebs and magistrates in office.

Saturninus was the first Roman politician to exploit the support of demobil-ized soldiers in the political sphere, support that at times manifested itself in the form of violence. In the tradition of C. Gracchus he alienated senatorial sym-pathies by seeking to direct policy from the assembly. He countered the violence and obstructive tactics of conservative opponents with further violence. He has consequently received a mostly negative portrayal in the senatorially dominated source tradition.

Bibliography: J.L. Beness, "The Urban Unpopularity of Lucius Appuleius Saturninus," *Antichthon* 25 (1991): 33–62.

Lea Beness

SCAEVOLA, QUINTUS CERVIDIUS (fl. late second century)

Cervidius Scaevola was the chief legal adviser of *Marcus Aurelius.

Although Quintus Cervidius Scaevola is a major figure in Roman legal his-tory, both as an adviser to Marcus Aurelius and as teacher of *Julius Paulus and possibly *Papinian, there is little extant biographical information on him. His birthdate and birthplace are unknown, as is the date of his death. His only known official position was head of Rome's police force, *praefectus vigilum*, c. 175–179.

Cervidius Scaevola's legal writings leave much clearer traces. He wrote a *Digesta* of forty books, twenty books of *Quaestiones*, and a *Regulae* in four books. The *Responsa*, a six-book epitome of his *Digesta*, was circulated after his death. Scaevola enjoyed an unrivaled reputation in his own time but was later overshadowed by the jurists of the Severan Age, Papinian, Paulus, and *Ulpian.

Bibliography: F. Schulz, *History of Roman Legal Science*, 2nd ed., 1967.

Karen Wagner

SCIPIO AEMILIANUS AFRICANUS NUMANTINUS, PUBLIUS CORNELIUS (185/184–129 B.C.)

Scipio Aemilianus was the Roman statesman and general who destroyed Carthage.

Scipio was a patrician by birth and adoption. The son of *L. Aemilius Paullus and Papiria, he was adopted by the son of *Scipio Africanus. He married his cousin Sempronia (a childless and unhappy union). Actively present at Paullus' victory in Macedonia (168), Aemilianus then further distinguished himself in his early military career (and was highly decorated), in his devotion to cultural pursuits (enjoying connections with *Terence, Lucilius, *Panaetius, and *Polybius), and in the antique discipline of his private life. In 147, after having served as a junior officer in the war against Carthage (the Third Punic War), and while standing for the relatively junior office of aedile (for which he was eligible), popular pressure arose in favor of his tenure of the consulship to which the establishment bowed, the laws being suspended to allow the anomaly. Assignment of the province of Africa (and the war against Carthage) was made by popular vote rather than by the customary use of the lot. In 146, as consul, he took Carthage, destroying it utterly. During the city's sack, according to Polybius, he shed tears, quoting a line of *Homer that evoked the vulnerability of civilizations.

He was probably sympathetic when his intimate friend Laelius proposed land reform and when the latter withdrew that proposal in the face of conservative concerns. He sought the censorship of 142, which he won as a popular candidate but exercised with socially conservative rigor. In 134, because of the continuation of the war against Numantia in Spain, which had been waged since 153 (with many Roman reverses), he was called again to the consulship, although, at that time, a law forbade the second tenure of that office. He introduced a strict military discipline, recalling the spirit of his censorship, and proceeded to besiege Numantia. In 133, his capture and destruction of the city brought to a close the Numantine war and marked the end of any concerted Celtiberian resistance to Rome.

Having returned to Rome and compelled by popular demand to cast judgment on the fate of his cousin (and brother-in-law) *Tiberius Gracchus, Scipio expressed guarded criticism and, subsequently, more substantial concerns about the alienation of the property-owning Italian allies that had resulted from Gracchus' land reforms. These stands brought Scipio into unpopularity at loud public gatherings. In 129, on a morning on which he was to deliver a speech on the subject of Italian concerns, he was found dead in his bed. No investigation was made into the death, though subsequent allegations of foul play involved his mother-in-law *Cornelia, his wife Sempronia, his brother-in-law *Gaius Gracchus, and political associates of the Gracchi.

Scipio was remembered in Roman tradition as the destroyer of Carthage, one of the last heroes of the "old Republic." Although he died expressing grave reservations about the path of reform advocated by members of his own family, his own career reveals an individual ready to seize opportunities that would have far-reaching political consequences, the precedents set by him being cited in arguments in favor of the multiple consulships of *Marius and the cumulative commands of *Pompey.

Bibliography: A.E. Astin, *Scipio Aemilianus*, 1967.

Tom Hillard

SCIPIO AFRICANUS, PUBLIUS CORNELIUS (236–184/183 B.C.)

Publius Cornelius Scipio was a Roman senator who through his military and diplomatic genius defeated Carthage in the Second Punic War (219–201) and prepared the way for the rise of the Roman Empire.

Born into the ranks of the Roman nobility, Scipio served with distinction under his father Publius Cornelius Scipio, after the latter was elected consul in 218. Later, at the titanic disaster at Cannae (216), the younger Scipio was credited with rallying many of the Roman survivors at Canusium. In 211, at the twin battles of Castulo and Ilorca in Spain, the Carthaginians destroyed two Roman armies and slew Scipio's father and Gnaeus Cornelius Scipio Calvus, his uncle. In the following year, the younger Scipio was appointed by the people to the command in Spain and invested with proconsular imperium. He would go on to break the Carthaginian hold over Spain and avenge his family's deaths.

Scipio's subsequent campaigns in Spain represented an almost unbroken string of successes during the next five years. This stemmed from Scipio's superior military and diplomatic skills. He thoroughly trained his troops and broke with standard Roman doctrine by encouraging high levels of personal initiative among his men, increasing the tactical flexibility of the individual units and making greater use of the *triarii*, the last line of soldiers of a deployed army. Scipio also insisted on taking the offensive and bringing the war to the enemy. These tactical innovations and clear strategic insight were coupled with a real talent for battlefield command and led to numerous victories in Spain. Scipio also demonstrated a keen diplomatic spirit in his dealings with his opponents. While he could prove a remorseless foe, as at the destruction of the Spanish town of Ilurgia in 206, where Scipio ordered the inhabitants massacred, he generally showed himself a humane and trustworthy individual. Through his diplomatic efforts, Scipio succeeded in detaching a number of Spanish tribes from their allegiance to Carthage.

Scipio opened his campaigning in Spain with the taking of Carthago Nova (209). Carthago Nova was Carthage's premier city and port in Spain, and its loss cost them access to a large manpower pool, a good portion of the region's silver mines, and a superior base for future operations. The Romans gained the same, and Scipio used Carthago Nova to stage his next move into Spain. With his improved army, Scipio campaigned in the interior of south-central Spain, where he first defeated Hasdrubal Barca at Baecula (208). Then, two years later at Ilipa, Scipio broke the back of Carthaginian resistance in large part because of his tactical innovations instituted within his army. With the fall of Gades (206), Roman control of Spain was complete. Scipio established a colony with some veterans at Italica, approximately seventy-five miles north of Gades, before returning to Rome.

In 205, Scipio was elected consul, and this allowed him to carry forth his plans for invading north Africa and threatening Carthage. In this plan he was opposed by many senators, led by *Quintus Fabius Maximus Verrucosus, who argued that a direct move against Carthage would not draw *Hannibal and his army out of Italy. Scipio landed in Africa in 204, besieged the city of Utica, and won over to the Roman side the Numidian prince *Masinissa. A superior cavalry general, Masinissa brought with him a large number of the vaunted Numidian light cavalry. With these new and valuable allies coupled to Scipio's most capable army and directed by Scipio's genius, the Roman forces proceeded to defeat every Carthaginian or loyal Numidian army sent against them in 204–203. Scipio swept away Carthaginian resistance and drew ever closer to Carthage itself. These successes eventually led to the recall of Hannibal in 203. After peace negotiations proved abortive, the last clash between Rome and Carthage played itself out at Zama (202). Here, the two great captains faced off against each other. Scipio successfully countered each of Hannibal's moves with the superiority in cavalry provided by Masinissa's Numidians, and the Romans carried the day. In the aftermath of Zama, even Hannibal counseled peace, and the Second Punic War ended the next year.

Following the humbling of Carthage, Scipio returned to Rome for a magnificent triumph and the conferring of the title Africanus. He then settled into a career of political and diplomatic service and was elected censor (199) and consul for the second time in 194. He was also honored with the title and position of *princeps senatus*, which he held for twelve years. A deeply committed philhellene, he strove to maintain a balance of power between the Hellenistic kingdoms, various leagues, and individual city-states, with Rome as a final arbiter. In the Syrian War (192–189), Scipio, constitutionally barred from serving as consul, accompanied his brother Lucius as a legate, but illness kept him out of the decisive Battle of Magnesia (190) that ended *Antiochus III's Hellenic aspirations. Despite honors, offices, and a conscientious attention to duty, Scipio's postwar career failed to recreate the accomplishments scored against Carthage. His philhellenic tendencies, remarkable record of successes, and the undivided loyalty of the people of Rome generated a remarkably bitter and ungrateful cabal of senatorial enemies who strove to hamstring Scipio in his efforts at governance and diplomacy. Withdrawing from the Roman political scene, Scipio died in 184–183.

Scipio's legacy was widespread and mixed. He broke Carthage and saved

Rome from Hannibal, arguably the finest soldier of the age. Scipio won for Rome control of the entire western Mediterranean, while his military reforms made it possible for the Roman army to humble the powerful Antigonid and Seleucid kingdoms and extend its influence into Greece and Asia Minor. These successes did not, however, come without a price. To achieve these victories and conquests, Scipio fashioned an army of well-trained, semiprofessional soldiers who would serve for many years under his personal command. This undermined the tradition of a citizen-militia and the older systems of annual commands. Such changes boded ill for the future of the republic. While Scipio was too honorable and scrupulous to use these advantages to seize power, those who followed him were not.

Bibliography: H.H. Scullard, *Scipio Africanus: Soldier and Politician*, 1970.

Cyril M. Lagvanec

SCOPAS (fl. 395–330 B.C.)

Scopas of Paros was a Greek sculptor and architect who produced several cult images and worked on the Mausoleum in Halicarnassus.

Little is known of the life of Scopas; he may have been born around 395/390. He may have been the third generation of a family of artists whose work there has been substantial difficult differentiating. He worked in Tegea, Halicarnassus, Ephesus, and Thebes.

Scopas' style demonstrated substantial naturalism, but his main contribution seems to have been making stone seem to come to life, appearing to express intense emotion. His rendering of movement in art was remarkable among the ancients; according to Callistratus, his Maenads even seemed to wave their hands. Scopas worked in different media. His architectural sculpture included the carving on the east side of the Mausoleum at Halicarnassus. His architectural design is said to have included the Temple of Athena Alea at Tegea; it is possible that he worked on the pedimental sculpture of this temple, or had an influence on, showing the Calydonian Boar Hunt. The sanctuary included sculptures of Asclepius and Hygieia, which appear to be his work. In addition, he produced several images of divinities and figures of myth. His works include an Aphrodite and a Pothos (Yearning), an Apollo, a seated Hestia, a Kanepheros (Basket Bearer), a Marine Thiasos including a Poseidon, Thetis, Achilles, and Nereids, a colossal seated Ares, a nude Aphrodite, possibly the Dying Children of Niobe, Aphrodite on a goat (Aphrodite Pandemos), Eumenides of Furies (two of three), Apollo Smintheus, a Maenad, and a Heracles. *Pliny the Elder and *Pausanias are the major literary sources for his work.

Scopas ranked with *Praxiteles and *Lysippus as one of the major sculptors of the fourth century B.C.

Bibliography: A.F. Stewart, *Skopas of Paros*, 1977.

Lisa Auanger

SELEUCUS I NICATOR (358–281 B.C.)

Seleucus was a general of *Alexander the Great and the founder of the Seleucid dynasty.

Seleucus was the son of Antiochus, a Macedonian nobleman and general of *Philip II. Although he distinguished himself as a general under Alexander the Great, Seleucus received no portion of the empire on the first division in 323 after Alexander's death. However, after aiding the Diadochi in the murder of *Perdiccas, the general and future king *Antigonus rewarded Seleucus by appointing him over the satrapy of Babylon in the second division of the empire in 321. Seleucus remained as the satrap of Babylon until 316. Although Seleucus had sided with Antigonus in his struggle with *Eumenes of Cardia for control over Asia, Antigonus attacked Seleucus and drove him from Babylonia. He took refuge with *Ptolemy in Egypt.

Antigonus' aspirations for control of Alexander's empire were challenged by Ptolemy, *Lysimachus, and *Cassander with the demand that Seleucus be returned to his position over Babylonia. Antigonus refused this and other demands, and appointed his son *Demetrius over Syria-Palestine in anticipation of an assault on Egypt. With the insistence of Seleucus, Ptolemy attacked and defeated Demetrius at Gaza in 312. While Antigonus had to concentrate his forces against the advance of Ptolemy, Seleucus was free to march into Mesopotamia and reclaim his position over Babylonia. Ptolemy soon made peace with Antigonus, but because Antigonus was unwilling to relinquish his claim over "all Asia," Seleucus remained at war until 309/308.

By 308 Seleucus was the indisputable ruler of Mesopotamia and Iran. He had come to terms of peace with Antigonus, apparently after defeating him in an important battle. Seleucus now directed his attention to the east and engaged in a series of battles with the Chandragupta, the Mauryan ruler of India. When Antigonus usurped the Macedonian crown in 305 after the murder of Alexander's son and Demetrius' defeat of Ptolemy in Cyprus, Seleucus followed the other Diadochi in claiming the royal title *basileus* for himself. Sometime between 305 and 303, Seleucus made peace with Chandragupta, ceding to him far eastern territories and receiving elephants in exchange. Seleucus joined the coalition against Antigonus' ambitions in Greece, and in 301 he and Lysimachus defeated him at Ipsus. With the death of Antigonus, Seleucus added Asia Minor east of the Taurus mountains and northern Syria to his kingdom. Ptolemy, who had not participated in the Battle of Ipsus, had occupied southern Syria and refused to surrender it to Seleucus. Out of respect for his old friend, Seleucus did not press his claim to all of Syria, but this conflict laid the foundation for a series of Syrian wars in the following generations.

Following the Battle of Ipsus, Seleucus' orientation turned west. He founded the four Syrian cities that were to become the center of his kingdom: Antioch-on-the-Orontes, Seleuceia-in-Pieria, Laodicea-on-the-Sea, and Apamea. Near the end of his reign he appointed his son *Antiochus I as co-regent and gave him jurisdiction over the upper satrapies. In the following decades, Seleucus allowed himself to be drawn into conflict with Lysimachus, who had made advances into Macedonia. Seleucus invaded Asia Minor and defeated Lysimachus at Corupedium (Field of Crows) in Phrygia (281). Having inherited all of Asia Minor from Lysimachus, Seleucus appeared intent on claiming the Macedonian throne for himself. However, after crossing the Straits, he was murdered by Ptolemy Ceraunus, the estranged son of Ptolemy I.

Bibliography: F.W. Walbank, A.E. Astin, M.W. Frederiksen, and R.M. Ogilvie, eds., *The Hellenistic World*, vol. 7.1 of *The Cambridge Ancient History*, 2nd ed., 1984.

Ronald A. Simkins

SELEUCUS II CALLINICUS (r. 246–226 B.C.)

Seleucus was the eldest son of *Antiochus II and Laodice and the father of *Antiochus III the Great.

Born c. 265, Seleucus took the Seleucid throne in 246 when Antiochus II died in Ephesus under mysterious circumstances. The former queen Laodice claimed that Antiochus had designated Seleucus on his deathbed to be his heir. However, the current queen Berenice had her son (who is unnamed) proclaimed king and appealed to her brother *Ptolemy III for help. Under the pretext of supporting the legitimate heir of Antiochus, Ptolemy campaigned into Syria (the Third Syrian or Laodicean War) and took the imperial city of Antioch. Although Berenice and her son were soon murdered, probably by Laodice, Ptolemy maintained the pretext and marched into Mesopotamia. His sudden return to Egypt to suppress an uprising enabled Seleucus to consolidate his hold on Asia, and by 245, he was recognized as king in Babylon. Conflict between Seleucus and Ptolemy continued until 241 but was limited primarily to the regions along the Mediterranean coast. Ptolemy continued to control Antioch until the reign of Antiochus III.

When Seleucus marched east to reclaim his kingdom, he appointed his brother Antiochus Hierax as his co-regent in Asia Minor. In 241 Antiochus, with the help of Galatian mercenaries, rebelled against Seleucus and claimed sole rule of the Seleucid kingdom. In 240 Antiochus claimed a decisive victory over Seleucus in a battle near Ankyra but was not able to follow up his victory further east. By 236 at the latest, Seleucus had made peace with his brother, relinquishing Asia Minor to Antiochus.

The remainder of Seleucus' reign was spent fighting in the east. The satrap of Bactria, Diodotus, rebelled against Seleucid rule in 239. By 238 *Arsaces I and the Parni had invaded Parthia and Hyrcania. He repelled Seleucus' campaign to reclaim these regions in 228. Seleucus died in 226 as a result of a fall from his horse.

Bibliography: F.W. Walbank, A.E. Astin, M.W. Frederiksen, and R.M. Ogilvie, eds., *The Hellenistic World*, vol. 7.1 of *The Cambridge Ancient History*, 2nd ed., 1984.

Ronald A. Simkins

SENECA THE ELDER (Lucius Annaeus Seneca, c. 55 B.C.– 40 A.D.)

Seneca was a Latin rhetorician and the father of the more famous *Seneca (the Younger).

Seneca was born of an equestrian family at Corduba in Spain and went to Rome as a young boy to study public speaking. Little is known of his life except that he taught rhetoric in Rome and fathered three sons: Novatus Gallio, a governor of Achaea; Seneca the Younger; and M. Annaeus Mela, the father of *Lucan.

Seneca wrote a work entitled *Oratorum sententiae divisones colores* and dedicated it to his sons. This work originally contained ten books of rhetorical exercises known as *controversiae*, of which five books are still extant. These *controversiae* were speeches for the prosecution or the defense in imaginary court cases and pertained to criminal, civil, and social issues. Although Seneca originally wrote seventy-four of these fictitious cases, only thirty-five of them survive today. This work also included two books devoted to *suasoriae*, or practice speeches, which offered advice to historical or mythological figures as they faced crucial decisions; only seven of these exercises in imaginary advice are extant.

Seneca's work provides valuable evidence about the training in rhetoric in the early empire, especially with respect to declamation. His works also recalled the oratory of *Cicero's day.

Bibliography: J. Fairweather, *Seneca the Elder*, 1981; L.A. Sussman, *The Elder Seneca*, 1978.

Andrew G. Traver

SENECA (THE YOUNGER) (Lucius Annaeus Seneca, c. 4 B.C.–A.D. 65)

Seneca was an author, Stoic philosopher, orator, politician, and the tutor of Emperor *Nero.

Lucius Annaeus Seneca was born between around 4 B.C. in the city of Corduba in southern Spain. He was the second son of *Lucius Annaeus Seneca the Elder, also an author, and Helvia, of a wealthy equestrian family originally from Italy. He was taken to Rome by his mother's stepsister to be educated for the law and an official career. His early years were spent studying grammar, rhetoric, and his favorite subject, philosophy. Seneca preferred Attalus the Stoic and followers of the Roman Sextius, who practiced what Seneca described as a form of Italian Stoicism. Another influence was Demetrius the Cynic, though it is not certain when Seneca met him. He and his wife Pompeia Paulina had one son, who died in 41.

His skills as an orator were so good that during 39, according to *Cassius Dio, his success offended Emperor *Caligula and nearly cost Seneca his life. From 41 to 49, during the reign of the Emperor *Claudius, he was exiled for alleged adultery with Iulia Livilla, sister of Caligula. He was recalled at the behest of *Agrippina the Younger, another sister of Caligula and Claudius' new wife, to serve as praetor and as tutor to her young son Nero. When Nero became emperor in 54, Seneca became one of his advisers and, along with the praetorian prefect Burrus, guided Nero for five years of successful government. When Nero effectively severed his ties with Agrippina by having her murdered in 59, Seneca's influence was on the wane. When Burrus died of throat cancer in 62, Seneca retired and offered his wealth to Nero in a placatory gesture.

Seneca is most famous for his role as Nero's adviser and for his literary works, most of which are philosophical in nature. The extant prose works include the *Dialogi, De clementia, Natural Questions,* and the *Epistulae Morales.* His tragedies include *Hercules, Troades, Phoenissae, Medea, Phaedra, Oedipus, Agamemnon, Thyestes,* and *Hercules Oetaeus.* Seneca is often mentioned as the author of *Octavia,* based on the events of 62, but many scholars do not think this is possible since he is also a character in the play. The same objection is often raised to his authorship of the *Apocolocyntosis,* a mixture of prose and poetry describing the deification of Claudius.

Bibliography: M. Griffin, *Seneca: A Philosopher in Politics,* 1991.

Katrina M. Dickson

SENNACHERIB (r. 705–681 B.C.)

Sennacherib, one of the major rulers of the Late Assyrian Empire, is best known for his campaign in Syro-Palestine in 701, where he threatened the existence of Jerusalem.

Sennacherib (Akkadian, Sin-ahhe-eriba) succeeded his father *Sargon II as king of Assyria in 705. He was immediately confronted with a rebellion of his vassals in Syro-Palestine, apparently led by Hezekiah of Judah. This rebellion is known from both Assyrian and biblical sources (2 Kings 18–19, 2 Chronicles 32, and various portions of Isaiah). Sennacherib invaded the area in 701, claiming to have "caged Hezekiah in Jerusalem like a bird." There is archaeological evidence of massive destruction by the Assyrians in Judah. However, the Assyrians may have been diverted from capturing Jerusalem by an Egyptian/Ethiopian army led by Tirhakah to the south. Instead, Sennacherib demanded harsh terms from Judah. All fortified cities and outlying areas (including some cities in Philistia and Phoenicia) were seized, Hezekiah's treasury was emptied, and some of his daughters were sent as concubines to Nineveh, Sennacherib's capital. The biblical writers claimed that the Assyrian army was destroyed by divine intervention, however.

Even more serious was Sennacherib's Babylonian problem. Assyria's neighbor to the south had been tributary to Assyria for the past half century. Merodach-Baladan, the Chaldean chieftain of Babylon, also rebelled against Assyria at Sennacherib's accession and enlisted Hezekiah's support, which he received according to 2 Kings 20. However, the revolt culminated in Babylon's utter destruction by the Assyrians in 689.

Sennacherib conducted many urban renewal projects in Nineveh, including a new palace complex, parks, irrigation projects, and massive fortifications. The Assyrian king was assassinated by one or more of his sons in 681 and was succeeded by another son, Esarhaddon.

Bibliography: J.M. Russell, *Sennacherib's Palace without Rival at Nineveh*, 1991.

Mark W. Chavalas

SEPTIMIUS SEVERUS, LUCIUS (146–211)

As emperor of Rome, Severus founded a personal dynasty and turned Rome into a military monarchy.

Severus was born in Leptis Magna in North Africa and came from an equestrian family that included senators. He himself entered the Senate around 173 and became consul in 190. At the time of the murder of Emperor *Commodus (192), Severus was governor of Upper Pannonia and commander of the largest army on the Danube River. After the subsequent murder of Commodus' successor, Pertinax, Didius Julianus purchased the title of emperor from the Praetorian Guard. Soon afterward, Severus' troops declared him emperor. While Severus marched on Rome, Julianus rapidly lost his support and was murdered by his own soldiers. Severus then entered the city without resistance.

Severus disbanded the Praetorian Guard and replaced it with troops loyal to him. He first placated his rival in Britain, Decimus Clodius Albinus, by granting him the title of *caesar* (junior emperor). In 194, he marched east and defeated yet another rival, the governor of Syria, Gaius Pescennius Niger. After defeating Niger, Severus marched against Albinus and defeated him near Lyon in 197. When he reentered Rome, he named Caracalla, his son by his Syrian wife *Julia Domna, as co-emperor and successor.

After a brief visit in Rome, Severus returned to the east to punish Parthia for its support of Niger. His successful campaigns ended in the annexation of Mesopotamia (199). After spending two years in Egypt (200–201), Severus spent the next six years in Rome and Africa. A rebellion in northern Britain called him there in 208. After initial successes with heavy losses in Caledonia, Severus retreated southward and rebuilt *Hadrian's wall. Severus died in York, succeeded by his two sons Caracella and Geta. Severus' descendants would remain in power until 235.

Under Severus' reign, the army obtained a dominant role in the state. Severus increased the soldiers' loyalty by increasing their pay, allowing them to marry, and providing them with certain benefits upon their discharge. Next, he reduced the number of legions under the control of each general, in order to prevent the rise of a new military rival.

Severus relied heavily upon the equestrian class to fill all levels of the state bureaucracy, and throughout his reign, the Senate gradually diminished in power. Severus also reformed the administration of justice by transferring Italian courts from senatorial jurisdiction to the praetorian prefect. The jurist *Papinian was named praetorian prefect in 205; the lawyers *Paulus and *Ulpian were also active during his reign.

Although Severus' reign was successful, it also paved the way for the rapid militarization of the Roman state.

Bibliography: A.R. Birley, *The African Emperor: Septimius Severus*, rev. ed., 1998; M. Grant, *The Severans: The Changed Roman Empire*, 1996.

Andrew G. Traver

SERVIUS HONORATUS, MARIUS (c. 360s–420s)

Servius was a Latin grammarian and author, known especially for his commentary on *Virgil.

Servius' full name is based on ninth-century manuscripts; both "Marius" and "Maurus" appear for his *praenomen*. He was a teacher in Rome, whose extant writings include a respectfully critical commentary on *Aelius Donatus' *Art of Grammar*, and works on the metrical quantity of syllables, on meters, and on the meters of Horace. Servius is best known for his line-by-line commentary on Virgil's poems. This survives in a shorter, more original form and as the basis of a longer, later version, known as *Servius Auctus* (Augmented) or *Servius Danielis* (named for its discoverer, P. Danielis, who published it in 1600), supplemented with material from other commentaries. Servius' commentary, which was written for students, emphasized linguistic aspects, such as grammar, rhetorical figures, analyses of Virgil's literary use of previous Latin and Greek authors, punctuation, and variant manuscript readings. There is often an underlying prescriptive attitude, with "corrective," standard prose alternatives given for Virgil's poetic usages. In literary interpretation, however, Servius often presents the reader with a choice. He also comments on earlier religious customs, institutions, geography, history, and mythology, providing us with valuable, though not always reliable, antiquarian material, especially from works now lost.

Servius was included as one of the participants in *Macrobius' *Saturnalia*, a literary dialogue on various topics, especially Virgil. Servius is represented there (anachronistically) as just starting his career, but with the reputation he later earned as the epitome of the fourth-century *grammaticus*. He is represented as a scholar, especially of Virgil, answering questions on the history and meanings of words and on aspects of Virgil's Latin. Servius' works continued to be used for at least 500 years and provide us insight into the role of the grammarian and how people of late antiquity read classical authors.

Bibliography: E.J. Kenney and W.V. Clausen, eds., *Latin Literature. Cambridge History of Classical Literature*, vol. 2, 1982.

Rebecca Harrison

SERVIUS TULLIUS (c. 578–535 B.C.)

Servius Tullius, sixth king of Rome, was most known for conceiving the treaty between Rome and the Latin League.

There are many discrepancies concerning the origin of Servius Tullius. For that reason some critics have claimed that his existence is purely mythical, but there is considerable evidence that he was a historical figure. Many ascribe Servius' life to Roman folklore because of obscurity concerning his origins and fabulous portions of his history. For example, tradition ascribes his maternity to a free house maid, a slave girl, or the household god. In addition, Roman accounts say that soon after Servius' marriage he had two daughters who matured at an extraordinarily rapid rate, and Servius married them off to his wife's brothers, to secure their loyalty.

It is relatively certain that as a historical figure he married the daughter of Tarquinius, monarch of Rome. When Tarquinius died, tradition states, competition broke out between Servius and the patrician body for the rights of the crown. Servius, through the inheritance of Tarquinius and the laws of the land, won the battle and became Rome's sixth king. Once in office, he spent a lot of energy militarily moving against the Etrurians. The most influential achievements attributed to Servius were constitutional reforms that assisted the plebs and, more important, negotiating a successful treaty between Rome and the Latin League. In addition to Servius' changes regarding the constitution, tradition credits him with erecting the walls that surrounded Rome, though this is highly doubtful, and for building the temple of Diana on the Aventine Hill, where the text of his treaty with the Latins was stored. Servius was known as a friend of the people because his government policies paved the way for the Republic.

Bibliography: A. Alfödi, *Early Rome and the Latins*, 1965; R.M. Ogilvie, *A Commentary on Livy Books 1–5*, 1965.

Richard Draper

SEXTUS EMPIRICUS (c. 160–210)

Sextus Empiricus codified the Sceptical philosophy of the ancient Greeks, in particular the philosophy of *Pyrrhon of Elis, which was discussed by Sextus in his book *Outlines of Pyrrhonism*.

Sextus Empiricus was a near contemporary of *Diogenes Laertius (who wrote about Sextus), who likely lived in Rome and Alexandria at various stages of his life. Sextus was a medical doctor who, according to Diogenes Laertius, studied medicine with the empiricist Sceptical doctor Menodotus of Nicomedia. It was perhaps the influence of Menodotus that led Sextus to study Greek Scepticism. Sextus' writings are our only source of information regarding the Sceptical tradition in Greek philosophy. In addition to his book *Outlines of Pyrrhonism*, Sextus also wrote *Against the Dogmatists (Adversus Mathematicos)*. The central argument to be found in these books is that true knowledge is impossible. Between errors in our perception and our ability to justify contradictory claims on any subject, the Sceptics, Sextus argued, show that the best we can have is a strong inclination to believe something based on its probability. The arguments found in these books were to be extremely influential upon the thoughts of

Michel de Montaigne and René Descartes. One could perhaps argue that Sextus Empiricus is in small part responsible for the empirical, scientific approach to knowledge that has come to characterize much of modern thought.

Bibliography: G.S. Kirk, J.E. Raven, and M. Schofield, *The Presocratic Philosophers*, 2nd ed., 1983.

Jeffrey A. Bell

SIDONIUS APOLLINARIS, GAIUS SOLLIUS (Modestus, c. 430–c. 480/490)

Sidonius was a Gallic landowner, an imperial official, and bishop of Clermont whose poems and letters are our best sources on fifth-century Gaul.

Sidonius was a descendant of a senatorial family of the southern Gallic region of the Auvergne whose members had occupied high imperial offices and that was connected with most other important Gallic families. Sidonius first appears as the panegyricist in Rome of his father-in-law Eparchius Avitus (emp. 455–456). Avitus had usurped the western imperial throne with the aid of the Gothic kingdom of southwestern Gaul (established around Toulouse several generations earlier, in 418), following the deaths of *Aetius and Valentinian III. When Avitus was overthrown by Majorian (emp. 457–461), Sidonius was briefly in disgrace but soon pardoned and held a court post (461). In 467 he led a provincial embassy to the emperor Anthemius in Rome and was awarded with the senior post of Prefect of the City of Rome for 468 and the honorary title *patricius*. After his return to Gaul, he was elected bishop of Clermont (469?). He opposed attempts by *Euric to annex the Auvergne, but the region was eventually ceded by the emperor Nepos, shortly before *Odoacer deposed the last western emperor (476). Sidonius was briefly exiled but soon returned to favor by Euric.

Sidonius' book of poems includes epic panegyrics to Avitus, Majorian, and Anthemius in the style of *Claudian, which are valuable as historical sources. His nine books of letters, modeled on *Pliny the Younger, illustrate many aspects of provincial society and of the usually cordial relations between provincials and the neighboring "barbarian" kingdom of the Goths. The letters and poems were admired and used as models throughout the Middle Ages.

Bibliography: J. Harries, *Sidonius Apollinaris and the Fall of Rome*, A.D. 407–485, 1994.

Andrew Gillett

SILIUS ITALICUS (c. 25–101)

Silius Italicus was a Roman public servant and a Latin poet who wrote *Punica*.

The details of Silius Italicus' life are primarily found in *Pliny the Younger. He served Rome as a proconsul of the province of Asia and was also a consul in the year 68—the year of *Nero's death. He turned to writing only after his retirement from political life. Pliny portrays Silius Italicus as rich, cultured, and happy. A great admirer of *Virgil, he bought his grave site in order to restore and maintain it. At the age of seventy-five he decided to end his own life through starvation because he was afflicted with an incurable ailment.

Silius Italicus left the world his work *Punica*, the longest poem written in Latin (approximately 12,000 verses). It is an epic about the Second Punic War and focuses on the career of *Hannibal. It contains passages about Anna (Dido's sister), Regulus (from the First Punic War), the grisly details of six of the war's battles, and numerous catalogs. *Punica* is usually dismissed as an inferior sort of work, but, as one commentator put it, it is more blamed than read.

The faults of the poem include its repetitiousness and its excessive variation of the names of the two main players: Rome and Carthage. Yet there are some fine moments in the poem, which are underappreciated because of the other criticisms.

Bibliography: A.J. Boyle, ed., *Roman Epic*, 1993.

Jennifer L. Koosed

SIMEON STYLITES, SAINT (c. 386–459)

Simeon (the Elder) was a Syrian monk and the first "pillar saint."

Simeon was born in northern Syria, the son of a prosperous Christian shepherd. He began, while still a young man, an ascetic life, spending a number of years at two monasteries. His extreme and eccentric self-discipline set him apart from the others. Simeon left the monastery to live as a hermit in a hut on a mountaintop. Finally he moved to a pillar at Telneshe. For nearly forty years he lived as a stylite—perched on a small platform atop three successive pillars increasing in height (to a maximum of approximately sixty feet). He stood and prayed on top of the columns, spending his days in a variety of tasks. He mediated disputes, defended the oppressed, preached to the gathered crowds, and regulated many of the routine daily concerns of the community, much like a rural patron or benefactor. He spent the rest of his time in prayer. Simeon's pillar became a site of pilgrimage. He healed the sick, heard confessions, witnessed the manumission of slaves, and dispensed advice, and his fame spread throughout the east and to the west, as far as Britain. Reportedly, large groups of pagans were converted, imperial policy was influenced (as when Simeon objected to the plan of *Theodosius II to return the synagogues in Antioch to the Jews, and the emperor complied), and thousands gathered annually for a celebration on the anniversary of a miracle by which he ended a drought.

Simeon is seen both as a representative holy man of late antiquity and as a model of the most extreme asceticism. His vocation gave rise to many imitators. The fifth-century monastery and church of Qal'at Sim'an marks the spot where Simeon's pillar stood. Three major hagiographical sources exist for Simeon: a contemporary account in Theodoret of Cyrrhus' *Historia Religiosa*; a Syriac life by his disciples, written just after his death; and a Greek life by Antonius, apparently another disciple.

Bibliography: S.A. Harvey, "The Sense of a Stylite: Perspectives on Simeon the Elder," *Vigillae Christianae* 42 (1988): 376–394.

Mark Gustafson

SIMONIDES OF CEOS (556/532–468 B.C.)

Simonides was a well-traveled and highly paid professional poet.

Ceos was famous for its boys' choirs, who sang at festivals on Delos and elsewhere. Simonides was the first poet to apply the high traditions of choral poetry to celebrating athletic victories. With this subject he could celebrate the struggle for excellence, *aretê* (which also implies moral excellence) and supremacy in all aspects of human life and use poetry to resist the otherwise transitory character of achievement. He offered in return for payment the hope of immortality to athletes, rulers (including Hipparchus of Athens, the Scopadae and Aleuadae of Thessaly, Xenocrates of Rhegium, the Oligaethidae of Corinth, and *Hieron I of Syracuse), and cities. He celebrated the Greek battles against the Persians at Thermopylae, Artemisium, Marathon, Salamis, and Plataea.

In the Plataea elegy, recently recovered from a papyrus roll that also includes symposia songs, he glorifies the victorious Spartans by invoking Achilles in a hymn and comparing them to the heroes at Troy. His account of how he was miraculously saved from the house that fell on his patron Scopas became a commonplace for the gods' protection of poets from the punishment prescribed for wrongdoers. His choral songs are marked by a tenderness and sympathy that reach a sublime simplicity in his sepulchral epigrams (of which many are believed inauthentic), such as that for *Leonidas and the Spartans fallen at Thermopylae: "Welcome stranger, tell them in Sparta we lie here still obedient to their commands."

Bibliography: D.A. Campbell, trans., *Greek Lyric*, vol. 3, 1991; M.L. West, *Greek Lyric Poetry*, 1993.

Robert Dyer

SIMON MAGUS (c. first century A.D.)

Simon was a magician in Samaria who became a follower of *Jesus at the preaching of Philip.

Little historical information is known about Simon Magus. The only first-century document to mention Simon is the Acts of the Apostles, and it presents a wholly Lucan (cf. *Luke) perspective. According to Acts 8:9–24, Simon had gathered a large following in Samaria by his practice of magic. The Samaritans identified him as "the power of God that is called Great." When Philip preached the gospel in Samaria, casting out demons and healing the sick, Simon converted and was baptized. Simon was amazed at the great miracles performed by Philip. When Simon saw that *Peter and *John were able to bestow the Holy Spirit on the Samaritan converts through the laying on of their hands, he offered the apostles money in exchange for a similar power. Peter rebuked Simon, who apparently repented.

By the second century, writers identify Simon as the founder of the Simonians, a gnostic sect, but their representation of him is polemical and largely legendary. *Justin Martyr claims that Simon was from the Samaritan village of Gitta, that he performed miracles in Rome (empowered by demons), and that he was accompanied by a former prostitute named Helena. *Irenaeus claims that Simon was the source of all heresies and that the Simonians worshipped Simon and Helena as Zeus and Athena. The legendary accounts of Simon describe his battles with Peter and *Paul, and present him as an anti-Christ. Simon's legacy survives in the term "simony" used to refer to the buying or selling of ecclesiastical positions.

Bibliography: W. A. Meeks, "Simon Magus in Recent Research," *Religious Studies Review* 3 (1977): 137–142.

Ronald A. Simkins

SOCRATES (c. 470–399 b.c.)

Socrates is perhaps the most influential and charismatic of the ancient Greek philosophers. Socrates' discussions with his fellow Athenians focus largely on moral matters, and these discussions would later become the model for *Plato and his written dialogues.

There is little known about the specifics of Socrates' life. Socrates never wrote, or at least his contemporaries (e.g., Plato and *Xenophon) claimed that he never wrote. Our only record of Socrates' life is therefore what Plato says of him in his dialogues and what Xenophon writes of him. It is thus difficult to determine precisely whether Socrates did indeed argue and philosophize in the manner in which this is portrayed by Plato. This difficulty is referred to as the Socratic problem, and there are two contrasting responses to the problem. At one end, some scholars argue that there was indeed a historical Socrates, and this is the Socrates as represented in Plato's dialogues. At the other end, some argue that Socrates is only a literary figure, or a literary character only loosely based (if at all) on an actual historical person. Complicating matters is the fact that Plato's dialogues, with only a few exceptions, consistently use Socrates as the primary interlocutor, and thus Socrates is likely only the mouthpiece for the philosophy Plato himself is putting forward. *Aristotle was aware of this problem and made a point of distinguishing between the Platonic and the historical Socrates. Aristotle would also claim, when he later fled Athens due to the persecution he was receiving because of his association with *Alexander the Great, that he was leaving because he did not want Athens to wrong philosophy a second time. This reference to Socrates, and to Socrates' trial and conviction for "not believing in the gods the state believes in" and for "corrupting the youth," supports the view that Socrates did indeed stand trial as Plato, in the *Apology*, and Xenophon, in his own *Apology*, both argued. As a result of these facts, the general consensus is that there was indeed a historical Socrates who stood in his own defense at his trial and who, in 399, was sentenced to death by the drinking of hemlock.

Socrates was reportedly a noteworthy individual for his day, for he actually lived as his philosophy said he should live. Life, Socrates believed, should be devoted to one of simple pleasures and simple needs. In this way, one can better come to know oneself; or, to put it another way, one can realize one's full potential. If one were to become obsessed with worldly pleasures and pursuits, one would then be constantly beyond oneself, constantly enslaved to the need to satisfy pleasures that can never be finally and ultimately satisfied. This concern for living a good life wherein the pleasures and desires are constrained by one's reason and intellect is precisely how Socrates is reputed to have lived. As examples of this lifestyle, Socrates was considered to be remarkable for his ability to walk in the snow without shoes; his ability to drink without apparent intoxication; and his refusal to be seduced by the flirtatious advances of young attractive men (e.g., *Alcibiades). Despite this life of simplicity, Socrates was nonetheless quite at home with the affluent, and his asceticism did not inhibit his ability to engage in philosophical disputation with the most respected and wealthy citizens of Athens. Socrates was also possibly connected with the Periclean circle of influence, perhaps as a result of the honorable and courageous manner in which he was reported to have fought as a hoplite during the Peloponnesian War.

Philosophically Socrates is understood by most to mark a turning point in Greek thought. Prior to Socrates, from *Thales to *Anaxagoras, the primary concern of the philosophers was to account for the Cosmos, and to do so on the basis of certain basic principles or elements (e.g., water for Thales and the seeds for Anaxagoras). With Socrates, however, the focus of attention shifts to understanding human beings themselves, such as how we should live, what is best for us. It is this turn to moral concerns that most influenced Plato (though Plato, in his *Timaeus*, also wrote on cosmological matters as well) and later Aristotle through Plato. It is for this reason that historians of philosophy will refer to the philosophers that precede Socrates by the generic term, pre-Socratic.

Socrates' most influential contribution to philosophy is his dialectical question-answer method. As a typical Socratic dialogue proceeds, at least as found in Plato, Socrates begins a conversation with someone who he assumes to be knowledgeable on a particular subject. Socrates would ask a poet about the nature of beauty, a politician about the nature of justice, and a sophist about the nature of knowledge. In each case, Socrates receives an answer to his question, which then leads to further questions. What inevitably happens is that the interlocutor contradicts his initial claim. Socrates then concludes that they did not truly know what they thought they knew, but, rather, they only have an opinion about knowledge. It is at this point where Socrates, and Plato, too, as he further develops this argument, belies the influence of *Parmenides on his thought. As Parmenides argued, ultimate reality is unchanging—it simply is and cannot not be. When Socrates uncovers a contradiction in someone's elaboration of the definition of the nature of something (e.g., justice, beauty), this cannot be true knowledge, for in contradicting themselves, they are saying it both is and is not something. The true definition simply is what it is, and it is noncontradictory and unchanging. Socrates' dialectical method is therefore an effort to uncover a noncontradictory truth by eliminating all truths that are contradictory. Socrates was in the end unsuccessful in this enterprise, and this led to Socrates' well-known conclusion as found in Plato's *Apology*: If Socrates is the wisest man, as the Oracle at Delphi said, it must only be in that Socrates knows that he knows nothing. In other words, Socrates at least admitted he did not know any ultimate, noncontradictory truths, whereas many of the people with whom he had conversations believed they did possess this knowledge.

Socrates' dialectical method has had a profound influence upon Western culture. One could even argue that science itself progresses by utilizing the method initially laid down by Socrates: That is, scientists put forward hypotheses and theories and accept such theories until contradictory evidence causes them to put forward a new theory, which is in turn embraced only so long as it does not encounter contradictory evidence. Plato and Aristotle largely extend Socrates' approach. Aristotle's logic, for example, and in particular his law of noncontradiction, is in many ways simply a formalization of Socrates' dialectical method. Furthermore, considering the influence Plato and Aristotle have had on Western philosophy and culture, it becomes obvious that it is perhaps impossible to overstate the significance and influence of Socrates.

Bibliography: J. Burnet, *Greek Philosophy, Thales to Plato*, 1914, G. Reale, *A History of Ancient Philosophy: From the Origins to Socrates*, 2 vols., 1985; A.E. Taylor, *Socrates*, 1953.

Jeffrey A. Bell

SOLON (sixth century B.C.)

Solon was an Athenian politician and revered in antiquity as a wise philosopher. He is best known for his reforms of Athenian law and the forgiveness of debt.

*Plutarch's *Life of Solon* reports that Solon was born to a noble family and that he was a cousin to *Pisistratus. He initially gained fame in Athens because of his role in the war against Megara for Salamis. At this time, Athens was beset with political tension between inhabitants of different regions and between the rich and the poor. Plutarch explains that the Athenian poor had fallen heavily into debt to the wealthy. Many poor cultivated the lands of the rich, paying them one-sixth of the harvest. Other segments of the poor, however, had offered themselves as collateral for debts; when this debt could not be repaid, their creditors could take them and offer them for sale as slaves either at home or abroad.

In these circumstances, Solon was elected archon to institute political reforms.

The Aristotelian *Constitution of the Athenians* describes how Solon canceled debts and banned the practice of using a person as collateral for a loan. He also created a new social organization, dividing the citizens based on their wealth and property. These *four* classes were called the *pentakosiomedimnoi*, the *hippeis*, the *zeugitai*, and the *thetes*. The highest offices were reserved for the upper two classes, lesser offices were given to the *zeugitai*, and the *thetes* were allowed only to serve in the assembly and trials.

In addition to his social reforms, Solon also reformed the laws previously established by *Draco with the exception of those dealing with homicide. Both the *Constitution of the Athenians* and Plutarch's *Life of Solon* report that these laws were inscribed and posted in the Athenian royal portico and the citizens took an oath to obey them. Solon perhaps also regularized the meetings of the assembly and established law courts for settling civil disputes. The ancient sources describe this as one of the most democratic of Solon's reforms because it gave great power to the common people since many important matters were addressed in the courts.

After undertaking these reforms, Solon contrived to leave Athens for ten years, and he established that his laws would not be changed during that time. During this time, Solon traveled the Mediterranean. *Herodotus reports that during his travels Solon met *Croesus, but chronological considerations suggest that this story almost certainly cannot be true.

Solon was revered as both a wise man and a lawgiver. During the fourth century, Athenian orators attributed almost all of their laws to Solon. In antiquity Solon was counted among the seven sages of the ancient world. Much of what we know about Solon is preserved in his poetry. Both the *Constitution of the Athenians* and Plutarch's *Life of Solon* cite his poetry as evidence of his deeds and character.

Bibliography: O. Murray, *Early Greece*, 2nd ed., 1993; A.M. Snodgrass, *Archaic Greece: The Age of Experiment*, 1980.

Jeff Rydberg-Cox

SOPHOCLES (c. 496–406 b.c.)

Sophocles was one of the three great Greek tragedians, the other two being *Aeschylus and *Euripides.

Only a general impression of the life of Sophocles is possible. His first contest is reported to have been a victory over Aeschylus in 468. Sophocles' popularity is evident in his high number of wins over fellow tragedians. He never placed last, was often second, and won at least twenty times. Of his 123 plays, only 7 have survived. In addition to his career as a playwright and a brief career as an actor, he also served as a public official. In 441/440 he was elected as a *strategos* (a general). He supported the establishment of the cult of Asclepius in Athens and was honored by a hero cult under the name of Dexion after his death. Of the 7 surviving plays, no chronology is possible. *Ajax, Antigone, Electra, Oed-*

ipus Tyrannus, and *Trachiniae* cannot be dated. Victories are recorded for *Philoctetes* in 409 and for *Oedipus at Colonos* in 401. The latter play was produced by his grandson of the same name after the playwright's death. Sophocles' plays are linked by his tragic vision, which recognizes both the heroic dignity of humanity and its helpless mortality.

Readers of Sophocles have been and continue to be fascinated by these plays that evoke ever-changing responses. Although *Antigone*, *Oedipus Tyrannus*, and *Oedipus at Colonos* are all associated with Thebes, they are not a trilogy and stand as independent plays. There are, however, thematic parallels between all seven of the surviving plays. At the center of each play is a heroic figure who stands apart from other mortals, and issues of pride, shame, and honor run through the plays. For *Aristotle the example of Sophocles' plays is central to an understanding of Greek tragedy. In the *Poetics*, Aristotle's notion of *anagnorisis*, or recognition, was strongly influenced by Sophocles' work, particularly *Oedipus Tyrannus*, which Aristotle used repeatedly as an example. For Oedipus, among other Sophoclean characters, the dramatic moment of recognition happens as he finally sees through critical misunderstandings, but clarity comes too late to avert tragic consequences. Knowledge for characters like Oedipus comes with pain and suffering. In these moments of recognition, both the characters' potential for greatness and their vulnerability are evident.

Sophocles' legacy is apparent in his impact on ancient Greek drama and in the following centuries of performance since the plays were first written. Readers like Sigmund Freud and Ezra Pound attest to the continued interest in these plays, as do the movies and performances seen in our own age.

Bibliography: P.H.J. Lloyd-Jones and N.G. Wilson, *Sophoclea: Studies on the Text of Sophocles*, 1990.

Christine Cornell

SPARTACUS (?–71 B.C.)

Spartacus led the last and greatest of slave revolts in the Roman world.

A Thracian of great physical strength and intelligence and having previous experience in the Roman army, Spartacus was elected one of three leaders when about thirty to seventy gladiators broke out of a gladiatorial training school at Capua in 73. After initial military successes, the gladiators were joined by fugitives, both slave and free, and defeated a number of praetorian armies. Increasingly disciplined but at the same time prone to splintering leadership, the slave army, which came to number, it is said, about 70,000, fell to ravaging Italy. In 72, although one of his colleagues (Crixus) suffered a crushing defeat, Spartacus overcame two consular armies (twice) and a proconsular one.

In the autumn of 72, *M. Licinius Crassus, who was appointed to take command against him with a large army, attempted with limited success to confine him to the toe of Italy and eventually (spring 71) defeated him in pitched battle. Spartacus died fighting, though his body was never found. Some 6,000 survivors of the battle were crucified along the Appian Way from Capua to Rome.

Although Spartacus' revolt was to mark the close of the era of great slave rebellions, its memory lingered as one that could evoke fear. The memory of Spartacus has also inspired political movements and revisionist artistic treatments in the modern world.

Bibliography: K. Bradley, *Slavery and Rebellion in the Roman World 140 B.C.–70 B.C.*, 1989.

Tom Hillard

STESICHORUS (c. 662–c. 556 B.C.)

Stesichorus was a Greek choral poet whose long mythological works, according to *Quintilian, "raised on the lyre the weight of epic song."

Stesichorus ("he who establishes the chorus"; his given name was perhaps Teisias) made his home in Himera, in Sicily. He was not the only poet who adapted heroic subjects to lyric metres—*Xanthus had done so previously—but he was most successful at doing so and is well represented in the papyrus record. His *Geryoneis* relates the killing of Geryon when Heracles is trying to capture his cattle. Stesichorus' elaborate and repetitive diction in narrative and reported speech is laced with Homeric allusion and establishes sympathy for the monster.

Other poems include *The Sack of Troy*, (Calydonian) *Boar-Hunters*, a two-book *Oresteia* (a significant source for *Aeschylus), and a lengthy fragment from a poem dealing with the family of Oedipus that most scholars believe to be by Stesichorus. It was said he went blind when he slandered Helen, and so he recanted in a *Palinode* that said an image went to Troy instead; this was a source for *Euripides' *Helen*.

Stesichorus' poetry is written in the Doric dialect and is triadic, consisting, like many tragic choruses, of three repeating metrical units: The *strophê* ("turn") and *antistrophê* ("counterturn") are metrically identical to each other, and these are followed by an *epô(i)dos* ("song that follows"). The combination of dialect and triadic structure was certainly performed by a chorus in tragedy, which, combined with the etymology of the poet's name, suggests that Stesichorus' works were also sung by a chorus, while a lyre-player, probably Stesichorus himself, provided accompaniment. Some have objected that certain poems would be too long for choral performance: the *Geryoneis*, with more than 1,300 lines, may have lasted over four hours. This would certainly be demanding for a chorus, but it is not impossible.

Bibliography: D.A. Campbell, ed., *Greek Lyric*, trans., vol. 3, 1991.

C.W. Marshall

STILICHO, FLAVIUS (c. 350–408)

Stilicho was the leading general of the western half of the Roman Empire from 395 to his death; he dominated the court of the emperor Honorius.

Stilicho was of Roman-Vandal birth, much pilloried by enemies. His early army career in the East under *Theodosius I included marriage to the emperor's niece Serena. After accompanying Theodosius to Italy in 394 against the usurper Eugenius, he was promoted to senior general in the West, *magister utriusque militiae* (master of military forces), an office he held thereafter and strengthened. In January 395 Theodosius died, leaving his young sons Arcadius (c. 377–408) and Honorius (384–423) to rule the East and West, respectively, and appointing Stilicho as Honorius' guardian (i.e., viceroy and effective ruler of the West). Stilicho's attempt to extend his authority to the East led to conflict with the court of Arcadius, and Stilicho was declared a public enemy in Constantinople (397). Nevertheless, Stilicho received high honors from Honorius. He was consul twice (400, 405), and Honorius married both Stilicho's daughters (Maria, 395– 407/8; Thermantia, 408). Stilicho suppressed rebellions against Honorius in Africa (under the general Gildo, 397) and Britain and Gaul (under a succession of usurpers, 406–411) and repelled barbarian raids. He defeated *Alaric three times, twice in the East (Greece in 395, the Peloponnese in 397, Italy in 402), but from 405 used him as an auxiliary. The costs involved were unpopular with the Roman aristocracy. Stilicho was executed in 408 during a palace coup. It was claimed, probably falsely, that he wanted his son Eucherius to succeed Arcadius (d. 408) as eastern emperor.

Stilicho's use of military power to dominate a weak court, imitated by the later western "generalissimos" *Aetius and *Ricimer, is seen as a fatal flaw of the late empire. Perhaps his most durable contribution to Western culture was his patronage of the poet *Claudian, whose epic panegyrics were imitated from late antiquity to modern times.

Bibliography: J.F. Matthews, *Western Aristocracies and Imperial Court* A.D. *364–425*, 1990.

Andrew Gillett

STRABO OF AMASEIA IN PONTUS (C. 64 B.C.–A.D. 21)

Strabo was the author of the lost *Hypomnemata* (Historical Notes) in forty-three books and the *Geographica* in seventeen books, both designed to complement the other.

His family was prominent in the Pontic capital before, during, and after the reign of *Mithridates VI. His grandfather rebelled and handed over several forts to the Roman general *Lucullus. Strabo was, from his name, a Roman citizen and visited Rome numerous times, first about 44 during his studies of philosophy, history, and geography. By the year 25 he seems to have been settled in Rome under the patronage of Aelius Gallus, on whose staff he served in Egypt in 25–24. He also moved, as did *Dionysius of Halicarnassus, in the hellenizing circle of the Aelii Tuberones that included (Aelius) Sejanus and *Tiberius Claudius Nero, the future emperor Tiberius, who claimed descent from Odysseus.

He called his *Geography* a *chorography*, a guide to places throughout the known world, and meticulously reported details from earlier writers, sometimes without regard for the passage of time. We read it today for its local history, resources, and customs. In fact, it is a political geography, concerned with the appropriation of the earth's resources for man's purposes and designed to assist Roman imperial administrators in governing: in achieving effective control of resources (perhaps for taxation) and communications and in understanding the peoples they ruled. Strabo admired Rome's culture and imperial destiny. He noted that the Romans had turned the conquest of Italy into "a springboard for leadership of the world" and claimed that "it would be difficult to administer such an empire except by turning it over to one man, as to a father." The "palace" that Tiberius would build on the Palatine would be its administrative capital, with the *Geography* as a useful tool.

Bibliography: G.W. Bowersock, *Augustus and the Greek World*, 1965; H.J.W. Drijvers, "Strabo on Parthia and the Parthians," in *Das Partherreich und seine Zeugnisse*, 1998, 279–293.

Robert Dyer

SUETONIUS TRANQUILLUS, GAIUS (c. 69–140)

Suetonius was a Roman author and imperial secretary who authored *The Lives of the Caesars* and other works on early and preimperial Rome.

Suetonius was born c. 69 during the civil wars that year between rival generals. His father served in the army of one of the defeated generals but later transferred his support to the victorious *Vespasian. The name *Tranquillus* is possibly in honor of the period of peace following Vespasian's victory. Suetonius' early life seems to have been spent in Rome, where he studied rhetoric and grammar under some of the most prestigious teachers of his day. After his schooling, he appears to have entered the law profession but later changed his focus to writing. His association to *Pliny the Younger was important for his career, and under Pliny's tutelage the young author began to serve in positions under Emperor *Trajan. He served Trajan as the emperor's head of the Roman libraries, chronicling archival records and serving as an adviser on cultural affairs. Following the ascension of Emperor *Hadrian, Suetonius received a promotion to the post of *ab epistulis*, or chief secretary of the emperor. During Hadrian's grand tour of the empire, Suetonius accompanied the emperor until he was dismissed from his post in 122 due to his disregard of court protocol toward the Empress Sabina. Following his dismissal, Suetonius devoted himself to writing and died around the year 140.

Although Suetonius wrote many works on subjects such as orators, the rise of bureaucracy, and the pastimes of the Greeks, his most famous works were biographies. In his *De viris illustribus* (Illustrious Men), which is only partially intact, Suetonius looked at former Roman authors of glory such as *Lucan, *Horace, and *Virgil. In his best and only work that is almost completely extant, *De vita Caesarum* (The Lives of the Caesars), Suetonius examined the personal and political history of the first twelve Caesars of Rome. In this work, he turned away from the former Greek style, as seen in Virgil, and wrote the first Roman biography that focused on reality as opposed to the role of the divine in everyday life.

Bibliography: A. Wallace-Hadrill, *Suetonius: The Scholar and His Caesars*, 1983.

Charles S. Paine III

SULLA FELIX, LUCIUS CORNELIUS (138–78 B.C.)

Sulla was a Roman aristocrat whose military talents and brutal repression of political rivals allowed him to become dictator.

Sulla came from the patrician family of the Cornelians, but his immediate ancestors were impoverished and undistinguished. Little is known of his youth other than his strong education in Greek and Latin literature, for which he was later praised. After he inherited the substantial fortunes of both his stepmother and Nicopolis, a courtesan, he was able to finance a political career. He was elected to his first public office in 107 and was attached to the army of *Marius, who was waging a campaign in Africa against *Jugurtha, prince of Numidia. Sulla distinguished himself on the battlefield and ended the campaign by intriguing with an African king to capture Jugurtha (105). He accompanied Marius to Gaul to defend the provinces against German invaders, but at some point he transferred to the army of Quintus Lutatius Catulus, perhaps because of a feud with Marius. Catulus handed over to his subordinate management of the army, and Sulla displayed his talents as a commanding officer by defeating the Germans (101). Buoyed by these successes he returned to Rome to stand for public office, and Sulla used his financial resources to be elected to the praetorship at some point between 98 and 93.

After this office the Senate sent him to Cilicia, a region in the modern nation of Turkey, and there he restored to power the king of Cappadocia, who had been expelled by *Mithridates VI Eupator, king of Pontus. While abroad he was influenced by a prophecy that he was fated for greatness, and his belief that he was favored by destiny is reflected in the name that he eventually took for himself, *felix* ("blessed"). By the time he returned to Rome in 92 or 91, his military successes over the last decade had elevated him to a leading role in the aristocratic party, which nominated him to lead an expeditionary force against Mithridates. His rival Marius was supported by the popular opposition, but before a final decision was made, Rome found itself at war with its Italian allies. Sulla took a leading military role in the Social War (91–87), which ensured that he was elected consul for 88 and granted command of the Mithridatic War. However, his political opponent *Sulpicius managed to have the generalship transferred to Marius, and Sulla, inspired by a vision that urged him to strike down his enemies, marched on Rome with his army, an action never before taken by a Roman citizen. Opposed by unarmed civilians, he seized the city, burned houses, and executed several political rivals. He filled government posts with his associates, hoping to safeguard his position while away on campaign against Mithridates, but soon after he departed at the end of 88, Marius and his allies regained control of the Senate.

For the next four years Sulla campaigned in Greece and Asia Minor, aware that his enemies once again were in control of Rome. On campaign against Mithridates he displayed once more his superior abilities as a general and a willingness to employ ruthless measures against his enemies. He drove the forces of Mithridates from Europe, but he slaughtered many civilians and plundered temples throughout Greece to finance his campaign. Eventually he reached an agreement with the Pontic king for his withdrawal from all the territory he had conquered in Asia Minor, but despite the success of Sulla's expedition, the hostile Roman Senate sent a second army to Asia Minor to challenge him. When Sulla marched against it, however, its soldiers deserted their commander to join him. By the end of 84 Sulla had reestablished Roman control in the eastern Mediterranean, and in the spring of the following year, he returned to Italy to confront his political enemies. The opposition party lacked strong leadership (Marius had died three years earlier), and so Sulla easily overcame two senatorial armies, defeating one in battle and winning over the other through bribery. His second march on Rome (82) was supported by many aristocrats, including *Pompey and *Crassus, and this time Sulla resolved to secure his position with more extreme measures. He massacred opponents in Rome and throughout Italy, and he ordered that his political rivals should be assassinated and their property confiscated (much of which he later obtained for himself through fraudulent public auctions).

After a compliant Senate declared Sulla dictator without naming a date for him to vacate the office (an unprecedented act in Roman history), he methodically restructured the government. He was primarily interested in strengthening the position of the Senate and the aristocratic party, institutions that he felt were necessary for the stability of the state. Toward this end he increased the number of political offices and law courts, putting them under the exclusive control of senators. For centuries the interests of the lower classes had been protected by tribunes, officers who were allowed to veto legislation they deemed detrimental to the general populace, but Sulla restricted this privilege, believing that ambitious tribunes were abusing their power to forward their own careers. He infused new blood into the Senate by enrolling supporters from the merchant class, thereby increasing the size of the institution to some 600 members, but he ensured the supremacy of the aristocratic families by reserving the leading offices for a small number of families. Once he instituted these measures, he surprised everyone by resigning the office of dictator and withdrawing to the countryside (79). He indulged himself in a luxurious lifestyle until his death in the following year.

Sulla's career transformed the nature of Roman politics for decades. His march on Rome provided an example for others aiming at absolute power, including *Caesar; his public call for the assassination of political rivals certainly inspired *Antony and Octavian (*Augustus); and later generals noted that Sulla's soldiers were more devoted to their commander than the state because of his willingness to indulge their desire for riches. Modern scholars are uncertain how to assess Sulla: Some condemn him for the brutality of his military campaigns and the repressive regime of his dictatorship, whereas others argue that he employed desperate measures to halt the collapse of the Roman republican form of government. While it may be true that he employed drastic measures to preserve the Republic, later politicians followed his example merely to achieve personal supremacy. Sulla himself recounted his career in twenty-two volumes of memoirs, but only fragments of these writings exist today.

Bibliography: A. Keaveney, *Sulla, the Last Republican*, 1982; H. Last and R. Gardner, "Sulla," in *The Cambridge Ancient History*, 1985, IX:261–310.

David Christiansen

SULPICIUS RUFUS, PUBLIUS (124/123–88 B.C.)

As plebeian tribune in 88 he attempted to secure the equitable enrollment of newly enfranchised Italians and freedmen in the Roman tribal system. His transference of the Mithridatic command from *Sulla to *Marius, provoked Sulla's epochal march on Rome and resulted in Sulpicius' violent death.

In the mid-90s he prosecuted C. Norbanus (trib. pleb. 103), a case that established his reputation as a speaker of considerable eloquence. He was a member of the distinguished political circle that included *M. Livius Drusus, the reformist tribune of 91, and L. Licinius Crassus (cos. 95), Rome's leading orator. He served as a legate in the Social War (91–87), probably as a senior officer under Cn. Pompeius Strabo (cos. 89).

He was elected as plebeian tribune for 88. It appears that he opposed the illegal consular candidacy of C. Iulius Caesar Strabo early in his term of office. He sponsored a revolutionary legislative program, proposing to enroll the newly enfranchised Italian citizens and freedmen in all the tribes (thereby guaranteeing a fair distribution of their votes throughout the tribal system), to recall exiles, and to regulate senatorial debt. The prospect of the equitable registration of Italians within the voting system led to serious street fighting between old and new citizens. The consuls Q. Pompeius Rufus and L. Cornelius Sulla responded by banning public business. Further violence ensued and the eventual enactment of Sulpicius' laws. Sulpicius' successful promulgation of a radical popular proposal to transfer the command against *Mithridates VI from Sulla to C. Marius (now only a private citizen) precipitated Sulla's march on Rome with six legions. Sulpicius was forced to flee the city. He and a number of his associates (including Marius) were declared public enemies, a disquieting precedent by which citizens could be pronounced guilty of crimes against the state and sentenced to death without trial. His legislation was annulled. Sulpicius, though a tribune in office (and therefore sacrosanct), was captured by Sullan agents and murdered. His head was later publicly displayed in the Forum and burial of his body forbidden.

Sulpicius appears to have abandoned the traditional tribunician role of protector and promoter of the interests of the Roman plebs in favor of the newly enfranchised Italians. The dictator Sulla's effective nullification of the power of the tribunate within the next decade may well have been prompted by his experience of Sulpicius in 88. The source tradition on Sulpicius is generally hostile.

Bibliography: A. Keaveney, "What Happened in 88?" *Eirene* 20 (1983): 53–86.

Lea Beness

SYAGRIUS (ruled c. 465–c. 487)

Syagrius was an independent Roman ruler in northern Gaul whose territory was conquered by Clovis.

Syagrius' father, Aegidius, was a senior general who served under *Aetius with Majorian (457–461). He commanded the army in northern Gaul. When Majorian, as emperor, was murdered by *Ricimer (461), Aegidius rebelled against Ricimer's puppet emperor Severus but was killed by Ricimer's machinations. Syagrius succeeded to his father's position, ruling northern Gaul from Soissons as a Roman commander but in rebellion against the western emperors. Comparable autonomous Roman "kingdoms" under generals are known, most notably in Dalmatia. Both Aegidius and Syagrius were closely tied to the Franks, then occupying northern Gaul; Gregory of Tours recalls Aegidius as "king of the Franks" for eight years and styles Syagrius "king of the Romans," perhaps in recognition of his autonomous status. Syagrius was defeated and killed by Clovis, who was consolidating control of the various Frankish groups; the autonomous postimperial Roman "kingdom" was absorbed into Frankish power.

Syagrius is recalled in early Frankish historiography as part of the irresistible rise to power of Clovis.

Bibliography: I. Wood, *The Merovingian Kingdoms*, 1994.

Andrew Gillett

T

TACITUS, CORNELIUS (c. 56–117)

Tacitus wrote histories of the Julio-Claudian and Flavian emperors and other historical and rhetorical works. His moralistic approach, psychological insights, and acerbic style were admired by later generations and became important contributions to Western historiography.

Tacitus was born in southern Gaul. He moved to Rome after being recognized as a gifted orator and pursued a career as a senator. Under the three Flavian emperors (*Vespasian, *Titus, *Domitian), Tacitus ascended the traditional senatorial career ladder, culminating in his election as consul in 97. He began his writing career in 98 with publication of *Agricola*, an encomiastic biography of his late father-in-law *Agricola. Tacitus used the biography to voice criticisms of Domitian and to show that even under tyranny good men could attain honor by steering a middle course between undignified servility and excessive but impractical displays of independence.

Later that year, Tacitus published *Germania*, an ethnographic treatise on the barbarian tribes to the north. As with *Agricola*, Tacitus used the *Germania* as a vehicle for expressing his political and moralistic beliefs. Here, Tacitus created an implied contrast between the simple and virtuous lifestyle of the Germans and the immorality of contemporary Roman society. In the *Germania*, Tacitus also continued to exhibit something of an antiimperialist mentality first detectable in the *Agricola*. The *Dialogue on Orators*, Tacitus' only rhetorical work, is dated around 102. This work discusses reasons for the decline of oratory in the age of emperors, including the suggestion that under a system of one-man rule, debate is no longer needed.

In 108, Tacitus issued his first complete historical account, the *Histories*. The work covered the years 69–96, the era of the three Flavian emperors. Little more than those sections covering the year 69 survives, but it represents the most detailed account of any period of Greek or Roman history we possess.

The *Histories* revealed that Tacitus was an able historian, capable of synthesizing large masses of documentary materials and of swiftly narrating a broad time frame. They also showcased his continued interest in moralistic assessment and a sophisticated political acumen. But it was not until publication of the *Annals*, around 117, that Tacitus could be described as a truly extraordinary historian. In this, his *magnum opus*, Tacitus brings to bear a penetrating psychological acuity and caustic wit to a year-by-year account of the last four Julio-Claudian emperors. Rather than analyzing their reigns from the standpoint of geopolitics or economic considerations, Tacitus turns to the intrigues of the palatial court and the unique and sometimes bizarre personalities of the emperors to explain events. His depiction of *Tiberius, for instance, a classic of Western literature, suggests that the emperor was at heart an evil man whose true personality only gradually emerged as he progressively disaffected those around him.

Because of critical comments regarding Christians and Jews, Tacitus was reviled and nearly forgotten in late antiquity. During the Renaissance, however, he experienced a revival. His antimonarchical views were embraced in a time of staunch republicanism, and his compressed style was seen as an interesting, if not refreshing, alternative to the glib eloquence of *Cicero. In subsequent centuries, after absolutist monarchs reestablished their authority throughout Europe, Tacitus' writings were seen as a useful guide for how to survive court life under an autocrat. In Reformation Germany, nationalists gravitated toward the *Germania* to support their claims of racial purity and moral superiority to the Italian papists. Tacitus also exercised an influence on the revolutionary politics of eighteenth-century France and America.

Bibliography: R. Mellor, *Tacitus*, 1993.

Luis Molina

TARQUIN THE PROUD (Lucius Tarquinius Superbus, 534– 510 B.C.)

Tarquin the Proud (Superbus) was the seventh and last king of Rome.

Though *Fabius Pictor identified Superbus as the son of Lucius Tarquinius Priscus (the fifth king of Rome), chronologically he is more likely to have been Priscus' grandson. As the seventh king of Rome, Superbus pursued an aggressive foreign policy that included the capture of several Latin towns and the reorganization of the Latin League into a military alliance under the leadership of Rome. He also negotiated the first treaty between Rome and Carthage that recognized Rome as the ruling power in Latium and as controller of the Italian coast south to Tarracina. To his reign also is attributed the completion of the Temple of Jupiter Capitolinus on the Capitoline Hill.

Later Roman historians characterize him as a harsh ruler whose tyranny led to his downfall. According to Roman legend, his son Sextus raped the honorable matron *Lucretia, thus turning public opinion against the Tarquin dynasty. Expelled from Rome, he and his sons fled to Caere and managed to persuade the towns of Veii and Tarquinii to attack Rome. Defeated at Silva Arsia, Superbus then appealed to the great Etruscan leader *Lars Porsena. When he attacked Rome, however, Porsena was so impressed by the courage of Calus Mucius Scaevola and Horatius Cocles that he made peace with the Romans.

A second historical tradition has Porsena taking Rome, after which he probably abolished the kingship and established the Republic. Superbus then united forces with his son-in-law Octavius Mamilius, only to be defeated at Lake Regillus (496). His hopes of restoration completely destroyed, Superbus took refuge at the court of the tyrant Aristodemus of Cumae, where he died in 495.

Archaeological excavation shows that Rome under the two Tarquin kings Priscus and Superbus was transformed from a small settlement to a city with strong Etruscan characteristics, especially in terms of urbanization and religion.

Bibliography: A. Alföldi, *Early Rome and the Latins*, 1965; R.M. Ogilvie, *A Commentary on Livy Books 1–5*, 1965.

Judith Sebesta

TERENCE (Publius Terentius Afer, fl. 166–160 B.C.)

Terence was a Roman playwright of comedies adapted from the Greek.

The details of Terence's life cannot be verified. According to *Suetonius, Terence was born in Carthage. Terence, as a slave, was brought to Rome by Terentius Lucanus, a senator, but was freed shortly thereafter. Suetonius reports in the *Life* that Terence died in 159 while still a young man. Although his plays were not always immediately successful, Terence had his supporters: His patrons included *Scipio Aemilianus, who commissioned Terence's final play, *Adelphoe*, for the funeral games of his father, *Lucius Aemilius Paullus. Terence's six plays have all survived: *Andria* (166), *Hecyra* (165), *Heautontimorumenos* (163), *Eunuchus* (161), *Phormio* (161), and *Adelphi* (160). *Hecyra* and *Phormio* are based on the Greek comedies of Apollodorus of Carystus and the others on the comedies of *Menander. Terence's comedies are not simply translations but are skillful adaptations that generally retain the ethos and outline of the originals. His additions to the plays included prologues that were addressed to the critics rather than used to provide expository information and new scenes that added lively comedy. Most important, his changes aimed for greater consistency and psychological realism in characterization.

Although Terence uses ornate language at times, he brought a far more naturalistic style to the drama than is seen in the works of *Plautus and other authors of the *fabulae palliatae* (Latin comedy adapted from Greek New Comedy). In addition to his influence on his own age, Terence provided a stylistic model for the ages that followed. He was widely read and imitated across Europe through the Renaissance and into the nineteenth century.

Bibliography: D.F. Sutton, *Ancient Comedy: The War of the Generations*, 1993.

Christine Cornell

TERTULLIAN (c. 160–c. 225)

A native of North Africa, Tertullian was the first significant Latin Christian writer whose works would serve as a foundation in the development of the Latin theological tradition.

The first reliable date we have for Tertullian is the appearance of his *To the Nations* and his *Apology* in 197, two apologetic works designed to defend Christian faith and morals against the accusations of pagans and to challenge pagans over their own lax moral character. Tertullian wrote many theological works, the most significant of which is *Against Marcion*. In these works Tertullian was concerned both to refute heresy and to define Christian doctrine. To accomplish the latter, it was necessary for him to articulate the nature of the true church and why it alone has the right to define doctrine and interpret Scripture. Among the theological propositions he championed were the incarnation of the Son of God, the full humanity of Christ, and the resurrection of the body, ideas especially repellent to the heretical Gnostics. Perhaps his most important theological contribution was his work on the relationship of the persons in the Trinity. Although he would later alter his views on this matter, his earlier work would provide a vocabulary that would shape later Latin Trinitarian theology. Finally, Tertullian also composed a series of treatises on the Christian moral and ascetic life. Later in his life Tertullian became enamored with a heretical sect called Montanist after its founder. He seems to have been attracted to this sect primarily because of its emphasis on strict adherence to a rigid moral code, a rather harsh ascetic discipline, and the immediate presence of the Holy Spirit in the midst of true believers.

Bibliography: T.D. Barnes, *Tertullian: A Historical and Literary Study*, 1971.

Steven D. Driver

THALES OF MILETUS (c. 620–560 B.C.)

Thales is considered by many to be the first Western philosopher. Thales is most known for his belief that all is ultimately constituted from water.

Very little is known about Thales' life, and nothing with any certainty. *Herodotus and *Democritus have said that Thales was from Phoenician ancestry, though this could in turn be simply because they sought to argue that philosophy was ultimately Eastern in origin. Thales was also credited with predicting the eclipse of 585. There is little proof of this claim, other than that there was indeed a solar eclipse in 585; however, by the time of *Plato and *Aristotle, this had come to be an accepted, even if an unsubstantiated, fact. Thales was also believed to have traveled to Mesopotamia during his lifetime and to have died where he lived most of his life—in Miletus.

The significance of Thales lies in his contribution to intellectual history. Thales is considered to be the first Western intellectual to attempt a nonmythological explanation of the cosmos. Rather than account for the order and workings of the cosmos in terms of gods and mythical creatures, Thales accounts for the cosmos on the basis of a primary substance, water. Although many today would reject such a claim, and most of Thales' own successors (e.g., *Anaximander) rejected it as well as being oversimplistic, Thales nonetheless initiated a program of explaining phenomena in a naturalistic, nonmythologizing way. Living in the seaport town of Miletus, a town that was actively involved in Mediterranean trade during Thales' lifetime, it should not be surprising that Thales' intellectual concerns would turn toward a more worldly explanation and that he would also be concerned with celestial matters (including both the reputed prediction of the solar eclipse in 585 and his supposed recognition of the importance of the North Star for navigating at sea). It is for this reason that Thales is often credited with being the first philosopher.

Bibliography: G.S. Kirk, J.E. Raven, and M. Schofield, *The Presocratic Philosophers*, 2nd ed., 1983.

Jeffrey A. Bell

THEMISTOCLES (c. 530–459 B.C.)

Themistocles was an Athenian politician who was prominent at the beginning of the fifth century. He is best known for his role in the defeat of the Persians at Salamis in the Persian Wars.

Themistocles was born to the Lycomid family, a family with no previous significant involvement in Athenian politics. He became an archon in 493/492 and devoted his efforts to strengthening the Athenian navy and fortifying the Athenian port at the Piraeus. In 483/482, when a large deposit of silver was discovered at Laurium, Themistocles convinced the Athenians to use the surplus to expand the Athenian navy to 200 ships. These ships played an important role in Athens' victories against the Persians at Artemisium and Salamis.

One of Themistocles' best-known exploits took place during the Persian Wars just prior to the battle at Salamis. According to *Herodotus, during the war the Athenians asked the oracle at Delphi how they could best defeat the invading Persians. The oracle responded that the Athenians would have a wooden wall for their sanctuary, and with its protection, they would be able to defeat the invading army. The interpretation of this oracle was a matter of some debate in Athens; some people claimed that the oracle meant that the Athenians should fortify the Acropolis, and others argued that the walls were a metaphor for Athens' wooden ships. Themistocles convinced all but a few Athenians that the wooden walls were their ships and that the oracle foretold their victory in a naval battle at Salamis. With the exception of a few people who did not believe Themistocles and set up wooden fortifications on the Acropolis, the Athenians abandoned the city and prepared to engage the Persians in a naval battle at Salamis. The Athenians were victorious at Salamis, and this victory led to the Persians' eventual withdrawal from Greece.

Throughout his career, Themistocles was a major player in the competitive arena of Athenian politics. One feature of fifth-century Athenian politics was the practice of ostracism, or exiling a person for ten years. In this procedure, the Athenian assembly would vote once a year to decide if they should hold an ostracism vote. If enough people agreed to this vote, the assembly would meet at a later time and vote for the person that they thought should be exiled. If 6,000 people had voted, the person who received the most votes was required to leave the city for ten years. After the ten years had expired, these exiles could return to Athens and keep their property. During the 490s and 480s, Themistocles regularly received votes for ostracism, and he may have been one of the instigators of *Aristides the Just's ostracism in 482. According to *Plutarch, Themistocles stirred public opinion against Aristides by spreading the story that he wanted to abolish the law courts and that, as a result, he was ostracized. After the Persian Wars, in the late 470s, Themistocles was himself ostracized and exiled from Athens.

*Thucydides reports that after Themistocles left Athens he took up residence in Argos and traveled throughout the Peloponnese. During this time, Themistocles was implicated in the intrigues of the Spartan Pausanias against his native town. When Sparta asked Athens to prosecute Themistocles, he fled Greece, and he eventually became a suppliant of the Persian king who appointed him governor of Magnesia in Asia Minor. Thucydides reports that there was some dispute about the manner of Themistocles' death; some say that he was murdered while in Magnesia, but Thucydides insists that he died of natural causes.

After his successes in the Persian Wars, fifth-century politics were not kind to Themistocles; Herodotus reports that he was suspected of having accepted a bribe, and he is generally ambivalent about the ways that Themistocles accomplished his political and military goals. Further, as governor of Magnesia, Themistocles was accused of helping the Persians plot against the Greeks. Time, however, dulled these suspicions and accusations. Themistocles' interpretation of the oracle about Athens finding protection behind wooden walls and his role in the battles at Artemisium and Salamis became the most important aspects of his legacy. Fourth-century orators praise Themistocles as a great statesman. Even by the late fifth century, Thucydides was able to praise Themistocles as a great Athenian leader and for his ability to effectively assess situations and form an appropriate plan of action.

Bibliography: C.W. Fornara and L.J. Samons, *Athens from Cleisthenes to Pericles*, 1991; A.J. Podlecki, *The Life of Themistocles: A Critical Survey of the Literary and Archaeological Evidence*, 1975.

Jeff Rydberg-Cox

THEOCRITUS OF SYRACUSE (320–250 B.C.)

Theocritus was a Greek poet who is credited with the invention of pastoral poetry.

There is no record of Theocritus' life and career; rather, his biography must be gleaned from his writings. The only biographical information from an external source is a passing reference to the names of his parents: Praxagos and Philinna. Although he was certainly raised in Sicily, and he always referred to himself as a Syracusean, his poetry indicates that he left his home early in his adult life. In his work, there are more indications of the eastern part of the Greek world than of Sicily. He was very familiar with Alexandria and may have ended up under the patronage of *Ptolemy II.

Theocritus' work is voluminous. It is one of the most remarkable extant corpora from the ancient world. Because of his innovative style, he has been hailed as the inventor of bucolic or pastoral poetry. His language is eclectic and always novel. His works are full of charming rural scenes and suffused with a yearning for an ideal pastoral past. Besides his characteristic bucolic verse, he also wrote hymns, epics, epigrams, mimes, and a love poem. Theocritus had a great and immediate impact on all subsequent poets. A tradition of bucolic poetry sprang up in his wake, and he influenced *Virgil profoundly. His influence has been felt—both through Virgil and directly through his own work—especially in the poetry of the Renaissance and the Romantic eras.

Bibliography: D.M. Halperin, *Before Pastoral*, 1983.

Jennifer L. Koosed

THEODORE OF MOPSUESTIA (350–428)

Theodore was a bishop and theologian whose scriptural exegesis attracted much attention.

Born at Antioch, Theodore studied under the pagan rhetorician Libanius and became friends with *John Chrysostom. At the latter's insistence, Theodore became an ascetic and remained at a monastery near Antioch for ten years. He became a priest around 383 and the bishop of Mopsuestia in 392.

In his exegesis, Theodore denied that many of the accepted "messianic" prophecies of the Psalms were predictions of *Jesus; he also interpreted the Song of Songs as a love poem with no allegorical significance. His approach was consistent with the other influential leaders of the so-called Antioch School, which opposed the allegorism of many Alexandrian theologians. These Antioch exegetes reacted strongly against eliminating the literal, historical meaning of the Bible for what they saw as an arbitrary allegorism based on Platonic philosophical ideas foreign to the text. Although Theodore's exegesis was primarily preserved in Syriac and Armenian translations, his tradition of interpretation was popularized in the Greek writings of Chrysostom.

In his Christological thought, Theodore insisted on Christ's humanity in the formula that the union of God and man in Christ formed a single person (*prosopon*), which in no way qualifies the permanent duality of the two uniting natures. In Christ was the "son of God" and the "son of David," the latter inhabited by the former. The two natures could be joined but not "fused" into one nature, as *Cyril, archbishop of Alexandria (412–444), held. Theodore's best-known disciple, *Nestorius, who was appointed archbishop of Constantinople in 428, further developed this Christology and was condemned at the Council of Ephesus in 431. Theodore himself was condemned posthumously at the Second Council of Constantinople (553).

Bibliography: J. Meyendorff, *Byzantine Theology, Historical Trends and Doctrinal Trends*, 2nd ed., 1983; J. Pelikan, *The Spirit of Eastern Christendom (600–1700)*, 1974.

Brannon Wheeler

THEODOSIUS I (c. 346–395)

Theodosius was the Roman emperor who rescued the eastern empire after the Battle of Adrianople and ensured its essential unity at the end of the fourth century.

Theodosius, born of Spanish parentage, was the son of a senior commander in the army of Valentinian (364–375). With the patronage of his father and other officers, he saw military service as a young man and was appointed as governor of the province of Moesia in the early 370s. In 375, Theodosius' father was suddenly arrested and executed at the order of Valentinian. Theodosius himself found it prudent to retire from public life to the family's estates in Spain.

After the defeat and death of *Valens at the Battle of Adrianople (378), Gratian recalled Theodosius and sent him to the East to conduct the war against the Goths. Early the following year, he was proclaimed emperor in the east, with Gratian exercising direct authority in the western provinces. Theodosius conducted the war against the Goths with great acumen, reaching a diplomatic agreement with them in 382, and also with the Persians in 386, after which the long-disputed territory of Armenia was partitioned.

Theodosius' diplomacy was tested in 383 when he was compelled by circumstance to recognize the usurpation of Magnus Maximus in the west, but in 388, he intervened when Maximus tried to overthrow Valentinian II in Rome. Maximus was bested in two battles, after which he was captured and executed. This brought Theodosius, briefly, to Milan, where he came into conflict with its bishop, *Ambrose. Later, after Valentinian died in 392, he defeated Eugenius, another claimant to the western provinces.

During his lifetime, Theodosius associated his two sons, Honorius and Arcadius, with him in imperial rule. Upon his sudden death in 395, they divided the empire between them.

Theodosius was also a great warrior for Catholic orthodoxy. Under his auspices, the Council of Constantinople was held in 381, and it was his law that mandated the Nicene faith as the only legal form of Christian practice. Moreover, through the same law, he also expressed the desire that all the people of the empire practice this faith, thereby ending any pretense of toleration of religious pluralism in the empire.

Bibliography: J. Matthews, *Western Aristocracies and the Imperial Court*, 1975; S. Williams and G. Friell, *Theodosius: The Empire at Bay*, 1994.

William Leadbetter

THEODOSIUS II (401–450)

Theodosius II was eastern emperor (408–450) and compiler of the Theodosian Code.

Theodosius II, only son of the emperor Arcadius (383–408), was born in 401 and succeeded to the throne in 408. Throughout much of his reign real political power was exercised by his praetorian prefects and his elder sister Pulcheria. His reign was marked by a policy of engagement with the western empire; Theodosius helped place his cousin Valentinian III on the throne at Ravenna in 425 and married his daughter Eudoxia to Valentinian in 437. During this time the empire was also beset by the growing threat of the Huns, which was met in the East by the lavish use of bribes and the construction of new defensive walls around Constantinople. Theodosius' domestic activities included establishing a university in Constantinople in 425 and calling the Council of Ephesus in 431, which condemned the theology of Nestorianism (cf. *Nestorius). A second Council of Ephesus in 449 addressed the problem of Monophysitism and resulted in strained relations between the emperor and Pope *Leo I.

Theodosius is best remembered for the Theodosian Code, which was promulgated in 438. Two separate commissions, the first appointed in 429, the second in 435, arranged and edited all valid imperial constitutions from *Constantine to Theodosius. The Code is divided into sixteen books, each book is divided into titles, and items in the titles are arranged chronologically. It was also promulgated in the western empire by Valentinian III and was later incorporated into the Lex Romana Visgothorum of Alaric II. The Code remained law until it was replaced by Justinian's Code in the sixth century. Theodosius II died in 450 and was succeeded by his sister Pulcheria and her husband Marcian.

Bibliography: J.B. Bury, *History of the Later Roman Empire*, 2 vols., 1923.

Karen Wagner

THEOGNIS OF MEGARA (c. 540 b.c.)

Theognis was a Greek elegiac poet.

Probably born at the beginning of the sixth century, Theognis lived during a time in which non-nobles were challenging the power of the Megaran aristocratic class. Theognis sided firmly with the aristocrats, despising democracy and the "new men" it produced. Theognis traveled throughout the Greek world and mentions visits to Euboea, Sparta, and Sicily. It is unknown when and how he died.

Theognis is credited with the authorship of about 1,400 lines of poetry that survive in a collection called the *Theognidea*. The collection reads like a moral handbook for aristocrats, praising the values of the wellborn and vilifying the lower classes. Most of the poems are short drinking songs written for the symposium. Some of them concern moralizing maxims; others deal with the love of boys.

There is little doubt that Theognis wrote an original core of poetry, but the

Theognidea is a compilation of poems written between the late seventh and early fifth centuries. Some of the couplets in the *Theognidea* can be attributed to *Mimnermus, *Tyrtaeus, and *Solon.

Theognis' poetry reflects the social divisions inherent in sixth-century Megaran society.

Bibliography: M.L. West, *Studies in Greek Elegy and Iambic*, 1974.

Andrew G. Traver

THEOPHRASTUS (c. 370–c. 287 B.C.)

Theophrastus succeeded *Aristotle as the head of the Peripatetic school in Athens, writing widely and making particular contributions to the study of botany.

Theophrastus ("the divine speaker"; his real name was Tyrtamus) is best known today for his *Characters*, a series of thirty descriptions of the exaggerated behaviors of often base individuals, which are perhaps drawn as models for New Comedy; this, however, is not representative of the bulk of his work. Theophrastus was born in Eresus on the island of Lesbos and may have studied with *Plato in Athens. He was probably associated with Aristotle by the time of the latter's move to Mytilene in 345/344 and accompanied him to Macedon when Aristotle was appointed *Alexander the Great's tutor two years later. He moved to Athens in 335 when Aristotle founded the Peripatos and took over the school's leadership in 323 until his death c. 287. Under his leadership the school flourished, acquiring property and reputedly having 2,000 students. Theophrastus wrote widely on almost every branch of knowledge—including important works on logic, psychology, ethics, rhetoric, politics, theology, human and animal physiology, music, and theology, which survive today only in fragments—but it was his works in botany that were particularly significant: His classification of plants parallels Aristotle's work on animals. Recent work has made significant progress on what can be learned of Theophrastus from classical Arabic sources.

Bibliography: W.W. Fortenbaugh et al., eds., *Theophrastus of Eresus: Sources for His Life, Writings, Thought, and Influence*, 2 vols., 1991.

C.W. Marshall

THEOPOMPUS OF CHIOS (c. 378–c. 320 B.C.)

Theopompus was an important Greek rhetorical historian.

Most of the biographical information about Theopompus comes from a biography or vita by the Byzantine scholar Photius. Theopompus was born on the island of Chios. With his father Damasistratus, he was exiled from Chios because of his father's sympathy for Sparta, an enemy of Chios. He traveled extensively at this time. He studied in Athens, most likely with *Isocrates. Later Theopompus spent several years at the court of *Philip II of Macedonia. Philip's son, *Alexander the Great, arranged for Theopompus to return to Chios about

333. He apparently had a political position for part of the next ten years. Upon Alexander's death (322), Theopompus was again exiled from Chios. He went to Egypt for refuge, although *Ptolemy I was not very receptive to his presence in Egypt. Shortly after his arrival in Egypt, he died.

Among Theopompus' writings are three historical works: the *Epitome of Herodotus*, *Hellenica*, and *Philippica*. *Herodotus* is the first epitome of an earlier work. The *Hellenica* continues the historical presentation of *Thucydides from 411 to 394. Theopompus' attention to details of the period is more dramatic than in *Xenophon's work. *Philippica* was a sympathetic portrayal of Philip but also included the deeds of Greeks and barbarians, making it appear as a universal history.

Theopompus had a universal historical conception. His writings dealt with military and political events but also included details in geography, ethnography, cultural history, history of religion, marvels, and myths. His work contains digressions as well as an emphasis on rhetoric. He also has a tendency toward moralizing.

Theopompus' works rely on firsthand observation from travels and the court of Philip. He also read many literary works, such as speeches and comedies, displayed in the breadth of style and apparent research in his writings.

Bibliography: M.A. Flower, *Theopompus of Chios*, 1994.

Roger W. Anderson

THESEUS

Theseus was the slayer of the Minotaur, a legendary king of Athens, and a lawgiver.

Theseus was the son of Aethra, princess of Troezen, and Aegeus, king of Athens, but some say that Poseidon was his real father. Theseus first made a name for himself by ridding the isthmus of its outlaws, among them Procrustes and Kerkyon. Procrustes insisted that all guests fit his bed. If the bed were too short, he would lop off any bits hanging over the edge; if too long, the guest would be stretched to fit. Kerkyon wrestled with all passers-by and killed them.

Theseus is most famous for slaying the Minotaur, the half man/half bull hidden in the labyrinth in Crete. Theseus was part of the group of youths and maidens sent as tribute to King Minos to be fed to the Minotaur. However, Ariadne, Minos' elder daughter, fell in love with Theseus, and he with her. She agreed to help him kill the Minotaur and lent Theseus a magic ball of twine to lead him through the labyrinth. Once the monster was dead, she and Theseus fled for Athens. En route, Theseus was ordered by the god Dionysus to leave Ariadne behind on the island of Naxos. Dionysus wanted her for his bride. Theseus was so flustered by this that he forgot to change the ship's sails: When Aegeus saw black sails instead of the white sails promising success, he threw himself off the Acropolis. Theseus was then proclaimed king.

Theseus' remaining adventures were in the company of his best friend Pirithoous and usually involved the capture of a woman: the Queen of the Amazons, Helen of Sparta, and the goddess Persephone. He eventually married Phaedra, Ariadne's younger sister, who fell in love with Theseus' son Hippolytus. Her overtures rebuffed, she claimed that Hippolytus tried to rape her. Theseus believed his wife, rather than his son, and exiled the boy, who was then killed by a mad bull. This tragedy left its mark on Theseus' kingship; he was eventually deposed and murdered. Despite this inglorious end, Theseus is best remembered as a slayer of monsters and a good king.

Bibliography: I. Scott-Kilvert, int. and trans., *Plutarch, the Rise and Fall of Athens*, 1960.

Andrea Schutz

THUCYDIDES (c. 460–400 b.c.)

Thucydides, son of Olorus, was a Greek historian who wrote a history of the Peloponnesian War fought between Athens and Sparta and their respective allies between 431 and 404.

Thucydides' *Histories* is quite impersonal, and as a result, very little is known about his life. In addition to a few personal references in the *Histories* we have some fragments from a biography written by a certain Marcellinus in the sixth century A.D. We know that he was an Athenian, and he himself tells us that from the start of the war he was of an age to be able to record the events accurately. From this we conclude that he was born c. 460. Most authorities agree that he was related in some way to *Miltiades, the Athenian general who fought at Marathon (490), and that through Miltiades he was connected with the leading families in Thrace. Thucydides' immediate background must have been aristocratic and conservative. He contracted and survived the plague that broke out in Athens in the summer of 430. In 424 he was elected to the post of general and with Eucles was sent to patrol the north Aegean. He was on the island of Thasos when news came that the Spartan general Brasidas was trying to capture Amphipolis. Thucydides attempted to prevent this but arrived too late. As a result he was exiled and spent the next twenty years traveling around the Greek world, during which time he collected much information from both sides that he used in his *Histories*. He did return to Athens after his exile, but since he displays no knowledge of the fourth century, he probably died a few years after his return, c. 400.

Thucydides' *Histories* contain what is generally accepted as a direct critical reference to the romantic and, by implication, inaccurate element in his predecessor *Herodotus. Thucydides' stated aim was to be accurate, and he makes it known that he made every attempt to verify his source material. His importance lies in his attempt to record history in a scientific manner. This claim has provoked many debates, because of the presence in the text of artificially constructed speeches. Nevertheless, his stated objectivity earned him a high reputation in the Greek world and later influenced such historians as *Polybius and *Ammianus Marcellinus.

Bibliography: G.L. Cawkwell, *Thucydides and the Peloponnesian War*, 1997.

Karen McGroarty

TIBERIUS CLAUDIUS NERO (42 B.C.–A.D. 37)

Son of *Augustus by adoption, Tiberius was Rome's second emperor (14–41). His awkward ascension to the throne and contentious relationship with the Senate eventually led to his semiretirement on the island of Capri, where he died.

Born on 16 November 42 B.C. to Tiberius Claudius Nero and *Livia Drusilla, Tiberius was a member of the eminent *gens Claudia*. Shortly before the birth of his brother Drusus in 38 B.C., Livia divorced his father and married Octavian (later the Emperor Augustus). Tiberius was his stepfather's last choice as successor after Marcellus, *Agrippa, Gaius, and Lucius, and when Augustus adopted Tiberius and Agrippa Postumus in A.D. 4, he forced Tiberius to adopt his own nephew *Germanicus at the same time. When Augustus died in 14 Tiberius became Rome's second emperor.

Unfortunately for Tiberius the legions in Pannonia and Germany took advantage of the upheaval created by Augustus' death and revolted. Tiberius sent his natural son Drusus and adoptive son Germanicus to quell the revolts. Later when Germanicus was sent east in 19 he accused a close friend of Tiberius', Gnaeus Calpurnius Piso, the governor of Syria, of having poisoned him. Germanicus was immensely popular with the people, and when his widow, *Agrippina the Elder, returned to Rome the next year with his ashes, she garnered immense public sympathy, which only added to Tiberius' problems. Piso was put on trial before the Senate and committed suicide.

At this time Tiberius allowed his Praetorian Prefect Lucius Aelius Sejanus to become closely involved in imperial affairs, further alienating Germanicus' family. In 30 Sejanus made public accusations of treason against Agrippina and her family, causing the exile of all except young Gaius (*Caligula). Sejanus was only eliminated when Tiberius realized that his next target for removal in his pursuit of power would be Gaius. In 31 Tiberius denounced Sejanus in a letter sent from Capri, clearing the way for Gaius as sole heir to the throne.

Tiberius' reign was characterized by good relationships with the provinces, on the one hand, and his increasing use of the charge of *maiestas* (treason) to attack his personal enemies, on the other. The picture that *Tacitus paints of Tiberius is that of a lonely, brooding man who was at times extremely ambivalent toward the exercise of imperial power and thus easy prey for unscrupulous friends and relatives.

Bibliography: B. Levick, *Tiberius the Politician*, 1976.

Katrina M. Dickson

TIBULLUS, ALBIUS (c. 55–19 B.C.)

Tibullus was a Roman elegiac poet, friend of *Horace and *Ovid, of equestrian rank who composed two books of elegies.

There is a corrupt and anonymous *Life*, but most that is known of him comes from his own writing. Tibullus was one of a group of poets who gathered around the patrician M. Valerius Messalla Corvinus, orator and patron of literature. Although he alleged that his patrimony was subject to Octavian's (*Augustus) confiscations in 41–40, he cannot be considered to be as poor as he implies, for his friend, the poet Horace, wrote of him as comfortable in a villa at Pedum.

Although the manuscripts of Tibullus' work, known as the *Corpus Tibullianum*, contain three books, only the first two are by Tibullus himself. The third contains poems by others in Messalla's circle, for example, elegies by Lygdamus and by Sulpicia, Messalla's niece, with one or two only possibly by Tibullus himself.

The emphasis in the poems of Tibullus is on romantic love and the pleasures of life in the country, expressed simply, without the decorations of mythology or an embellished vocabulary. Book 1, published c. 27, deals primarily with his love for his mistress, Delia (according to *Apuleius a pseudonym for one Plania), and also, contrastingly, for a boy named Marathus. In the second book, which comprises only some 400 lines and so perhaps either incomplete or published after his death, there is a new mistress, Nemesis, whose real identity remains unknown. In addition, these books contain poems on such subjects as rural fetes, his patron Messalla, and the blessing of a country at peace.

Bibliography: F. Cairns, *Tibullus: A Hellenistic Poet at Rome*, 1979.

Deborah Eaton

TIGLATH-PILESER III (r. 744–727 B.C.)

Tiglath-Pileser III was a powerful king of Assyria who laid the foundations for Assyria's massive empire of the eighth and seventh centuries B.C.

Tiglath-Pileser (a Hebrew form of the Akkadian phrase Tukulti-apil-Esharra) most likely came to the throne as a usurper in 744 when Assyria was in danger of being conquered by the kingdom of Urartu (in present-day Armenia). This Assyrian king was able to drive out Urartu from formerly Assyrian-held territories and even invaded Urartu itself. Tiglath-Pileser also invaded Syro-Palestine and defeated and made tributary many of the Aramean, Neo-Hittite, and Phoenician cites, such as Damascus, Tyre, and Byblos. In a later campaign (734) he conquered Phoenicia and Philistia, creating a trading center to link Assyria to Egypt. In fact, he laid siege to and conquered the city of Damascus in 732, thus ending the Aramean state centered there.

This Assyrian king is also known from Old Testament sources (2 Kings 15–16, 1 Chronicles 5, and 2 Chronicles 28) where he was also called Pul (Akkadian, Pulu, presumably a nickname derived from the element *apil* in his name). He invaded northern Israel on two occasions, once at the behest of Menahem of Judah, who was under siege by Pekah of Israel and Rezin of Aram-Damascus, and later during his Syro-Palestinian campaign of 734. In fact, Pekah, Pekah's successor Hoshea, Menahem, and Menahem's successor Ahaz are all listed in Assyrian sources as paying tribute to Assyria in this period.

Tiglath-Pileser also intervened militarily in the politics of Assyria's southern neighbor, Babylon. However, when the Babylonians rebelled against Assyrian involvement, the Assyrian king extended much effort to quell the revolt and subsequently took the unprecedented step of ascending to the Babylonian throne himself. However, the Babylonians continued to resist Assyrian direct control for the next century.

Tiglath-Pileser enacted major changes in Assyria, as he doubled the size of the army, revamped the provincial administration, and conducted a major campaign of deporting conquered peoples to other regions of the empire.

Bibliography: H. Tadmor, *The Inscriptions of Tiglath-Pileser III, King of Assyria*, 1994.

Mark W. Chavalas

TIMAEUS OF TAUROMENIUM (c. 346–250 B.C.)

Timaeus wrote a popular history of Magna Graecia to 264 B.C. in which he began the system of dating from the Olympiads; *Plutarch later used him as a source.

Timaeus of Tauromenium (a city of refuge for the dispossessed people of Naxos that his father Andromachus had founded when *Dionysius II had destroyed their city) was born in 346 and is said to have lived ninety-six years. Forced to leave Sicily by the tyranny of *Agathocles of Syracuse (usurped power 317), he went to Athens and spent fifty years there. In the course of his stay in Athens, he wrote his history, taking for his subject the events, real or imaginary, in Sicily and the adjacent countries from mythical times down to the 129th Olympiad (264).

Timaeus seems to have been one of the rhetorical historians of the Isocratean (cf. *Isocrates) school. He had read diligently all that the earlier writers could teach him concerning the West, and was not sparing of criticism, even of *Ephorus of Cyme, whose reputation stood high and survived his attacks. In his hatred of tyrants, he abused Agathocles furiously, and he was full of scorn for *Aristotle. Timaeus' lack of real critical sense made him unreliable, though a storehouse of curious information and good stories. He remained the chief authority for the times and places that he treated, and our knowledge of him comes from a mass of quotations and references in *Diodorus, *Polybius, and others.

Bibliography: L. Pearson, *The Greek Historians of the West. Timaeus and His Predecessors*, 1987.

Cecilia Saerens

TIMOLEON (c. 411–334 B.C.)

Timoleon was a Corinthian liberator of Sicily.

Timoleon first won recognition by liberating Corinth from the despotism of his brother. He lived in retirement until 345, when the aristocrats of Syracuse appealed to their mother city of Corinth against the tyrant *Dionysius II. Timoleon was selected by Corinth to lead a liberation force against Dionysius. By shrewd tactics, he freed Syracuse, forced Dionysius to abdicate, and defeated the Sicilian opposition supported by Carthage. Timoleon then instituted constitutional reforms and encouraged widespread immigration from Greece to Sicily. Timoleon removed the tyrants of other Sicilian cities and defeated Carthage at the Battle of the Crimson River c. 341. He retired to private life in Syracuse with extensive honors.

Timoleon brought peace to Greek Sicily and helped to revive its prosperity.

Bibliography: R.J.A. Talbert, *Timoleon and the Revival of Greek Sicily,* 1974.

Andrew G. Traver

TIMOTHEUS OF MILETUS (c. 450–c. 360 b.c.)

Timotheus wrote lyric poetry in Greek, to be accompanied by the cithara and in some cases the *aulos* (pipe), and was the leading exponent of the "new music."

A fragment of the comic playwright Pherecrates describes the music of Timotheus as "meandering ant-tracks," an image that evokes both the innovative flourishes and the winding melodies typified by Timotheus and the new music, which assigned multiple tones to single sung syllables (as is commonplace in music today). While Timotheus' early work was in hexameters, this later style embraced polymetric astrophic lyric, as is also found in late works of *Euripides. Timotheus wrote dithyrambs, preludes, hymns, and particularly nomes (solo songs accompanied by the cithara). He used as many as twelve strings on his lyre—the usual number was seven—which allowed the use of multiple tunings in the same song. One such poem is partly preserved on papyrus: "The Persians," performed c. 410 probably in Athens, was a prizewinning nome around 650 verses long (c. 240 surviving) on the victory at Salamis; Euripides wrote the hexameter prelude for this work. An epitaph proclaims Timotheus the "skillful charioteer of the lyre"; however, given the loss of the musical notation, it is his lyrics with their obscure kennings that are most striking today. "The Birth-Pangs of Semele" and "Scylla" were choral works to be accompanied by the *aulos.* While seen as effeminate by traditionalists of his day, the crowd-pleasing innovations made by Timotheus and others added complexity to music.

Bibliography: D.A. Campbell, ed., *Greek Lyric,* trans. vol. 5, 1993.

C.W. Marshall

TIRO, MARCUS TULLIUS (?–4 b.c.)

Tiro was *Cicero's chief secretary who is credited with developing a system of shorthand notes and who, by his publications, preserved some of Cicero's works for us.

Little is known of Tiro's early life; his original name, Tiro, is a Roman name. He was a slave of Cicero and acquired the first two parts of his name (Marcus Tullius) when his master freed him in 53. Tiro, who served as Cicero's secretary and literary adviser, is attributed with developing a system of shorthand signs for taking notes. After Cicero's death in 43, Tiro published some of Cicero's speeches, sixteen books of his letters to his friends, and perhaps, a collection of his jokes. Cicero's collection of letters includes twenty-six letters addressed to Tiro, and numerous others make mention of him, showing respect and affection by Cicero's whole family. Tiro himself composed a biography of Cicero, several works on grammar, and one on miscellaneous questions, all lost. He died in 4 B.C., reportedly at the age of ninety-nine.

Later Romans further developed Tiro's system of shorthand signs; it flourished during the later empire for imperial, ecclesiastical, and everyday use and during the Carolingian Age. A collection of letter and word signs known as "Tironian notes," as the system was called, survives.

Bibliography: J.E. Sandys, *A History of Classical Scholarship*, 3 vols., 1958.

Rebecca Harrison

TITUS (T. Flavius Vespasianus, 39–81)

Titus was Roman emperor from 79 to 81.

Titus was the eldest son of *Vespasian and Flavia Domitilla and the elder brother of the future emperor *Domitian. He saw military service in Germany and Britain, and in the reign of *Nero, when Vespasian was sent to Palestine to put down the Jewish rebellion, Titus went with his father and served as his chief military assistant. When Vespasian departed for Rome to claim the imperial title, Titus completed the suppression of the revolt, destroying Jerusalem in 70.

The Senate conferred Titus a triumph when he returned to Rome, and his list of honors continued to grow. Vespasian awarded him proconsular power, tribunician power (71), and the office of censor. Vespasian and Titus served as consuls together, and Titus held the consulship for seven years in succession. Vespasian also gave sole command of the Praetorian Guard to Titus.

Although Titus was popular in the army, many Roman civilians regarded him as cruel and were scandalized by his affair with his Jewish mistress Berenice. When Vespasian died in 79, Titus succeeded him uncontested, and his disposition rapidly changed. He put aside Berenice and initiated a period of great generosity by spending lavish sums of money on games and shows. Titus also completed the Flavian amphitheater (Colliseum) and constructed the baths that carry his name.

Titus had to grapple with three great disasters during his reign: the eruption of Mt. Vesuvius on 24 August 79, which buried Pompeii and Herculaneum, a great fire in Rome (80), and an outbreak of the plague (80). Titus used public funds to help alleviate the suffering of those involved in those disasters.

Titus never trusted his brother Domitian and was reluctant to give him an imperial position. Titus died unexpectedly in 81, and many suspected that Domitian had poisoned him. Titus was immediately deified.

Although Titus' reign was short-lived, he was one of Rome's most popular emperors.

Bibliography: B.W. Jones, *The Emperor Titus*, 1984.

Andrew G. Traver

TRAJAN (Marcus Ulpius Trajanus, 53–117)

Known as the *Optimus Princeps* (Best Emperor), Trajan reigned from 98 to 117, presiding over the Roman Empire at its greatest extent.

Born in 53 at Italica in Spain, Trajan was the son of a distinguished Roman family. His father, Marcus Ulpius Trajanus, had served with both *Vespasian and *Titus in Judaea, and when he was governor of Syria, young Trajan served with him. Continuing his distinguished military career in Germany, he was saved by his location in the provinces from any association with *Domitian's reign. Nerva (96–98) probably adopted Trajan precisely because of both his lack of association with Domitian and the considerable military forces under his command in Germany, both of which made him a potential challenger to Nerva's position as emperor. When Trajan reached Italy, Nerva was already dead, and Trajan dealt swiftly with the Praetorian Guards who had murdered him.

Many of Trajan's accomplishments are listed in *Pliny the Younger's *Panegyricus* of 100, including his aid to victims of child abuse and exposure, his continuance of Nerva's *alimenta* (a food welfare program), and his numerous building projects both in Rome and elsewhere. The year 101 marked the beginning of Trajan's campaigns against the Dacians, which are commemorated on the spiraling frieze of the massive column intended as his sepulcher and as the centerpiece of his forum in Rome. In 107 Trajan annexed Arabia, and from 114 to 116, he expanded eastward into Parthia and Mesopotamia so that under Trajan Rome controlled her widest expanse of territory.

In 114 the Senate officially bestowed the title *optimus* upon Trajan, and he died in 117 while returning to Rome from the eastern front of Selinus in Cilicia. Trajan's public works and career were celebrated by the Senate, who divinized him.

Both Trajan and his wife Plotina were praised for their virtue, simple tastes, piety, and dignity. Trajan and Plotina were childless, and it seems that though there were rumors of forgery surrounding the posthumous adoption of *Hadrian in Trajan's will, both of them wanted Hadrian to succeed Trajan as emperor.

Bibliography: A. Garzetti, *From Tiberius to the Antonines*, 1974.

Katrina M. Dickson

TROGUS, GNAEUS POMPEIUS (first century B.C.)

Trogus was the Roman historian who wrote the *Historiae Philippicae*.

Trogus was a Celt from the region of Vocontii in Gallia Narbonensis. His grandfather served in the war with *Pompey against the Roman exile Sertorius and received Roman citizenship. His father served under *Julius Caesar. Trogus himself wrote works on the natural history of animal and plants, all now lost but preserved as fragmentary quotations in *Pliny the Elder. But Trogus' chief claim to literary fame is his *Historiae Philippicae*. This work is a general history of the world in forty-four books. Its title derives from the fact that it covers those portions of the world that fell under the influence of *Alexander the Great and his successors.

Trogus begins this work with Ninus, the founder of Nineveh, and ends at roughly the same point as his contemporary *Livy. Trogus' work is noteworthy, as he does not treat the history of Rome until Rome came into contact with the East. As his work dealt with the peoples outside of Italy, it thus formed a useful complement to the Roman histories of Livy and others. For his sources, Trogus relied heavily upon the Greek historians. The work today survives only in an epitome and in quotations of *Jerome, *Augustine, and others.

Bibliography: A. Dihle, *Greek and Latin Literature of the Roman Empire: From Augustus to Justinian*, 1989.

Paul Miller

TYRTAEUS (fl. c. 630 B.C.)

Tyrtaeus was a Spartan elegiac poet. His poems, of which about 250 lines have survived, are characterized by martial themes and concern for public ethics, especially in wartime.

Tyrtaeus' biography is derived primarily from quotations and details in the poems, but this information is not very reliable. There are, however, references in the poems themselves to historical events. For example, the Second Messenian War, which Sparta successfully waged against her subject neighbor, situates the poet in the late seventh century. In addition, Tyrtaeus mentions Spartan civic unrest connected to constitutional reforms also dated to the late seventh century. He was contemporary with the elegiac poet *Callinus, who likewise wrote about military subjects.

As a poet, Tyrtaeus espoused Spartan warrior values. Nonetheless, his elegies provide important information for the Second Messenian War and for the historicity of the "Great Rhetra," the major document for early Spartan constitutional history. In addition to elegiac poetry, Tyrtaeus is said to have written anapestic and iambic chants that were performed by armed dancers at certain religious festivals at Sparta. There is, however, no precise information about these poems, and hence their attribution to Tyrtaeus is uncertain.

Bibliography: W.G. Forrest, *A History of Sparta*, 2nd ed., 1980; M.R. Lefkowitz, *The Lives of the Greek Poets*, 1981; M.L. West, trans., *Greek Lyric Poetry*, 1993.

Carl A. Anderson

U

ULFILA (c. 300/310–383)

Ulfila was a Gothic bishop who translated the Bible into Gothic.

The descendant of Romans captured in Gothic raids on Asia Minor in the 250s, Ulfila ("little wolf") lived among Goths adjacent the Roman Empire on the middle Danube. Since 322, Roman-Gothic relations were determined by a treaty imposed after military victory by *Constantine. Ulfila was consecrated bishop among the Goths at the command of either Constantine or his son Constantius II (he was not the first recorded bishop among the Goths). The Roman-Gothic conflict in the late 340s resulted in the exile of Ulfila and his followers to the empire, where they were received by Constantius and settled in the Balkans (modern Bulgaria). Ulfila developed a new script in order to translate the Bible into Gothic and wrote tracts in Latin, Greek, and Gothic. His translation was one of many into vernacular languages in the third/fourth centuries, including Syriac, Coptic, Armenian, and new Latin translations (cf. *Jerome). His creed (which is extant) was developed from the thought of *Arius rather than the creed of the Council of Nicaea, and he was involved in church politics between "Arians" and Nicenes. After the Nicene Creed was declared the exclusive Christian creed at the Council of Constantinople (381), *Theodosius I called a further council the following year to reconcile malcontents. Ulfila died in Constantinople after arriving for this council. Fifth-century church historians associated him with the Gothic appeals to the emperor *Valens in 376 to enter the empire, but this is dubious. His Arianism is symptomatic, not causal, of the nonorthodox Christianity of the later Gothic, Vandal, and other kingdoms.

The Gothic Bible is the earliest written Germanic language and so of great philological importance. The discovery of a substantial part of the Gospels in the mid-sixteenth century (the Codex *Argentium*) was very influential on the development of modern Germanic scholarship. Together with the *Germania* of

*Tacitus, the *Getica* of Jordanes, and the *Edda* of Snorri Sturluson, the Gothic Bible was construed as a monument to an ancient Germanic cultural continuity, rivaling classical antiquity.

Bibliography: P. Heather and J. Matthews, *The Goths in the Fourth Century*, 1991.

Andrew Gillett

ULPIAN (Domitius Ulpianus, c. 160–223)

Ulpian was an influential jurist and praetorian prefect under the Roman emperor Alexander Severus (222–235).

Ulpian was from Tyre, but little else is known of his birth, family, or training. His official career included a post as assessor, or legal adviser, for *Papinian while the latter was praetorian prefect. He also served as secretary of petitions under *Septimius Severus, and was a member of Severus' imperial *consilium.* Banished from Rome during the reign of Elagabalus, Ulpian returned by 222 to serve first as prefect of the corn supply and finally as praetorian prefect under Alexander Severus until the Praetorian Guard murdered him in 223.

Ulpian was one of a number of influential jurists who lived and wrote at the end of the second and beginning of the third centuries. He was a colleague of *Julius Paulus and a teacher of Herennius Modestinus. His numerous writings covered almost all aspects of public and private law. The most important were the *Ad edictum praetoris*, a commentary on the Praetorian Edict in eighty-three books, and his *Ad Sabinum*, an extensive commentary on the *Ius civile* of Massurius Sabinus in fifty-one books. Ulpian also wrote numerous works outlining the duties and powers of imperial officials, including *De officio consulis* (five books) and *De officio proconsulis* (ten books). Ulpian's reputation was second only to that of Papinian among later jurists. The *Law of Citations* (426) named him one of the five jurists whose opinions were to be followed by imperial judicial officials. By the fifth century his *Ad edictum* had become the text for the second year of legal studies at Berytus. Ulpian's writings were the principal source for Justinian's *Digest* and comprise almost one-third of that work.

Bibliography: A.M. Honoré, *Ulpian*, 1982.

Karen Wagner

V

VALENS (c. 328–378)

Valens was the Roman emperor who permitted the Goths to settle on Roman territory and was later defeated by them in battle.

Born in the town of Cibalae in Pannonia, his father Gratianus was a senior officer in the armies of *Constantine's sons. Both Valens and his elder brother Valentinian also became serving officers. In February 364, Valentinian was chosen by his colleagues to be emperor in succession to Jovian and proclaimed by the army. Within a month, Valentinian had nominated Valens to be his imperial colleague, also with the rank of *augustus*.

While Valentinian concentrated his efforts in ensuring the security of the western provinces, Valens concentrated in the eastern provinces. In the early months of his reign, he was forced into flight from Constantinople to Ankara through the revolt of Procopius, a relative of the emperor *Julian. Procopius was, however, captured and executed, which left Valens unchallenged in the east. This left him deeply suspicious of conspiracy, and there were a significant number of trials and executions for treason during his reign.

In 375, Valentinian died, leaving Valens as the senior emperor. He found himself distracted by the problem posed by the Goths who, pressed by the Huns and by famine, were seeking to resettle on the Roman side of the Danube. Valens first allowed them to cross but then later provoked them to conflict. In a great battle at Adrianople in 378, Valens and two-thirds of the Roman army (including many of its senior officers) were slain.

Valens was an Arian Christian (cf. *Arius), sufficiently intolerant of Nicene community to interfere consistently in ecclesiastical affairs during his reign.

Bibliography: A.H.M. Jones, *The Later Roman Empire*, 2 vols., 1964.

William Leadbetter

VALERIAN (Publius Licinius Valerianus, ?–260)

Valerian was a Roman emperor from 253 to 260 who instigated a new round of Christian persecutions and died as a Persian captive.

From old Roman patrician stock, Valerian was consul under Emperor Alexander Severus (222–235). Under Emperor Gallus (251–253), Valerian was the commander of the troops of the Upper Rhine. Gallus summoned him to suppress a revolt led by the rival emperor Aemilian. Gallus was murdered by his soldiers in 253, and Aemilian was proclaimed emperor. While Valerian arrived too late to save Gallus, he still managed to avenge him. Aemilian was assassinated by his soldiers in the same year, and Valerian, already recognized as emperor by his troops, was accepted as emperor in Rome.

In 258 Valerian resumed the persecution of Christians started by *Decius. In this year, he prescribed harsh penalties for Christian senators, knights, respectable women, and imperial slaves. He had both Bishop *Cyprian of Carthage and Bishop Sixtus II of Rome executed.

Valerian designated his son Gallienus *augustus* in the western portions of the empire in 253 so he could turn his attention eastward and confront the escalating problems there. The Goths were rapidly advancing into Asia Minor, and the Persians were invading Cappadocia. In 258/259 the Sassanid Persians surprised and captured Valerian. They held him captive until his death the following year.

Christian polemicists viewed Valerian's capture as the result of his persecutions. *Lactantius claimed that the Persians had flayed him and kept his skin as a trophy. The deaths of both Decius and Valerian were therefore seen in the Christian tradition as a direct result of imperial persecutions.

Bibliography: R.L. Fox, *Pagans and Christians*, 1987.

Andrew G. Traver

VARRO, MARCUS TERENTIUS (116–27 b.c.)

Born at Reate, northeast of Rome, Varro became the leading antiquarian of his generation.

He began his studies in Rome under Lucius Aelius, the first scholar of Latin literature and antiquities, before going to Athens to study with the Academic philosopher Antiochus of Ascalon. Commencing his political career, Varro rose to the rank of praetor. Having sided with *Pompey during the Civil War, he was pardoned by *Julius Caesar after the Battle of Pharsalus (48). Caesar then asked him to plan and organize the first public library at Rome, but these plans were never carried out. When *Marc Antony proscribed him, Varro fled into scholarly retreat.

By the beginning of his seventy-eighth year, he had written 490 books; at the time of his death, it is thought that he had written about 620 books, comprising seventy-six different works. His interests were varied, and his publications included almost all areas of knowledge, including geography, law, philosophy, rhetoric, music, medicine, religion, literary history, agriculture, the Latin language, and Roman social and political history. Unfortunately, only his works on the Latin language and on agriculture survive to any extent. Out of the 25 books of his work on Latin, *De lingua latina*, only books 5 through 10 are partially or wholly extant. This work covered etymology, inflections, morphology, and syntax. He dedicated this work in 43 to Caesar. His published his work on agriculture, *De re rustica*, in 37. Its 3 books, in the form of a dialogue, give advice on farming and stockbreeding.

Bibliography: J.E. Skydsgaard, *Varro the Scholar: Studies in the First Book of Varro's "De Re Rustica,"* 1968; D. Taylor, *Declinatio: A Study of the Linguistic Theory of Marcus Terentius Varro,* 1974.

Judith Sebesta

VEGETIUS RENATUS, FLAVIUS (late fourth century A.D.)

Vegetius was a late Roman military writer.

Scholars have vigorously debated both the identity and date of Vegetius. He was probably from Spain or southern Gaul. He bred horses, had traveled the Roman Empire, and was an imperial bureaucrat. He composed two works: *Epitoma rei militaris*, a manual on Roman military institutions, and *Digesta artis mulomedicinae*, a veterinarian work on horse and cattle ailments. In the *Epitoma*, he refers to the emperor Gratian (375–383) as *divus* and alludes to the Battle of Adrianople (378) but does not mention the sack of Rome in 410 or any of the military events of the early fifth century. Vegetius thus probably composed it sometime before the year 400.

Vegetius dedicated the *Epitoma* to an emperor, but scholars have disputed which one, advancing *Theodosius I (379–395), Valentinian II (375–392), Honorius (395–423), and Valentinian III (425–455) as possible candidates. The consensus today is that Theodosius was probably the most likely one and that Vegetius presented the work to him during the emperor's stay in Italy between 388 and 391.

In the *Epitoma*, Vegetius disclaims all military knowledge and claims that he compiled his information solely from books, not practical experience. The end result is an admixture of many different sources, including *Frontinus and *Cato the Elder as well as imperial edicts of *Augustus, *Hadrian, and *Trajan. Vegetius divided the book into four sections: Section one treats recruitment and training; two discusses organization; three handles logistics, tactics, and strategy; while four describes siege and naval warfare. The work was edited by Eutropius in Constantinople in 450.

The *Epitoma* was an extremely popular technical work that explained to medieval and Renaissance audiences the basics of Roman military thinking.

Bibliography: N.P. Milner, int. and trans., *Vegetius, Epitome of Military Science*, 2nd ed., 1996.

Andrew G. Traver

VELLEIUS PATERCULUS (C. 19 B.C.–A.D. 30)

Velleius was a soldier, a political figure, and a historian.

Velleius was of Campanian ancestry. He served as a military tribune in Thrace, Macedonia, Greece, and the East. He was the prefect of cavalry in Germany and Pannonia under the future emperor *Tiberius; he was quaestor in A.D. 7 and praetor in 15.

Velleius wrote a compendium of Roman history from its origins to 29 in two books entitled *Historiae Romanae*. There are many missing portions of book one, which originally covered the history of the East until the destruction of Carthage and Corinth (146 B.C.). Book two covers the period 146 B.C.–A.D. 30; Velleius treats the events from the death of *Julius Caesar to the reign of Tiberius very fully. This work today only survives in a single manuscript.

Historians often use Velleius' *Historiae* for its material on the reigns of *Augustus and Tiberius. In opposition to most historians, Velleius believed that Augustus had indeed reestablished the Roman republic. With respect to Tiberius, Velleius provides a useful counterbalance to the accounts of *Tacitus and *Suetonius, because unlike them, he admired the emperor.

Bibliography: M. Grant, *Greek and Roman Historians: Information and Misinformation*, 1995.

Andrew G. Traver

VERCINGETORIX (?–46 B.C.)

Known primarily from *Julius Caesar's *Commentaries on the Gallic Wars*, Vercingetorix led the Gauls in an uprising against Roman rule in 52 B.C.

Born the son of Celtillus, an Arvenian nobleman, Vercingetorix as a young man successfully united most of the Gallic tribes in opposition to Caesar. He took advantage of the growing conflict between Caesar and *Pompey, as well as uprisings in the north of Gaul, to attack Roman control in the south, near Narbonne. Having held against this attack, Caesar moved quickly to the north, bringing the conflict to Gallic strongholds in the Seine and Loire valleys. Rarely, however, did the two sides meet in open battle. More often fighting consisted of Roman sieges of Gallic strongholds and the Gauls' attacks on Roman supply lines. The disrupted supply lines along with Vercingetorix's scorched earth policy created major difficulties for the Roman troops. Nonetheless, Caesar pressed on, winning a siege at Avaricum but forced to withdraw from the siege at Gergovia. The decisive confrontation came near Alesia, where the two sides met in a cavalry battle before Vercingetorix's troops retreated to the hilltop safety of the fortified base itself. Caesar swiftly surrounded the hill and built an impenetrable barricade around it. Food supplies rapidly ran out. A Gallic assault force, numbered by Caesar at approximately 350,000 men, was unable to break through the Roman barricade to relieve the starving soldiers. Acknowledging defeat, Vercingetorix surrendered and was sent to a Roman prison. The Romans brutally completed their suppression of the Gauls' revolt, leaving devastation behind them. When Caesar returned to Rome for his triumphal entry in 46, the imprisoned Vercingetorix was forced to march in the parade as a conquered foe before being ritually executed.

In the nineteenth century, as France sought to create a national identity separate from that of the kings of France, Vercingetorix emerged as a national hero, a symbol of French unity and opposition to oppression. In 1865 Napoleon III funded a major archaeological project at Alesia, as well as commissioning a statue to commemorate Vercingetorix's stand against the Romans. The face on the statue was modeled on the visage of Napoleon III himself. Since then Vercingetorix has loomed large in the French pantheon of national leaders.

Bibliography: M. Dietler, " 'Our Ancestors the Gauls': Archaeology, Ethnic Nationalism, and the Manipulation of Celtic Identity in Modern Europe," *American Anthropologist* 96.3 (1994): 584–605.

Olivia H. McIntyre

VESPASIAN (Titus Flavius Vespanianus, 9–79)

Vespasian, the first Roman emperor of the Flavian dynasty, was largely responsible for restabilizing the empire and rebuilding Rome after the fire of *Nero and the confusion of 69.

Vespasian was born in Sabine Rieti. His father and grandfather had been tax collectors; his grandfather had fought for *Pompey at Pharsalus (48 B.C.). Vespasian gave service in Thrace, Crete, and Africa. He married Flava Domitilla and fathered two sons, *Titus and *Domitian, who would continue his dynasty. He served in Germany and in Britain under the Emperor *Claudius, and in Africa under Nero. In 66, Nero appointed Vespasian governor of Judaea when the great Jewish rebellion erupted. After the rapid deaths of Nero, Galba, and Otho, Vespasian's troops proclaimed him emperor in Alexandria in 69.

Vespasian was responsible for the preservation of historic information when he restored 3,000 burned bronze plates to the Capitol; he cleared Rome of astrologers and members of some cults by changing laws, and restored and added to the city architecturally, which had been devastated by the fire of Nero. His building activity in Rome included restoration and rebuilding. His first major project was the Temple of Jupiter Optimus Maximus. He completed the Temple of Divine Claudius and undertook the Temple of Peace, which he financed with the spoils from the triumph over Jerusalem. This complex essentially served as a museum as well as a sacred area, holding important painting and sculpture from around the world. It also may have housed an early marble map of Rome. He also appears to have contributed to the theater arts by restoring the scaena on the Theatre of Marcellus. He remodeled the Colossus of Nero into an image of the Sol, god of the Sun.

Vespasian established a stable dynasty whose members also made contributions in the arts.

Bibliography: R. H. Darwall-Smith, *Emperors and Architecture: A Study of Flavian Rome*, 1996; M. St. A. Woodside, "Vespasian's Patronage of Education and the Arts," *Transactions of the American Philological Association* 73 (1942): 123–129.

Lisa Auanger

VIRGIL (Publius Vergilius Maro, 70–19 B.C.)

Virgil was the chief Augustan poet, author of the *Aeneid*, *Eclogues*, and *Georgics*.

Virgil was born in Andes, near Mantua. His father was a farmer or a potter, and the family was sufficiently well off to educate Virgil at Cremona and Mediolanum (Milan). He eventually went to Rome and studied philosophy, rhetoric, and literature and became the friend of the historian *Pollio. He lived in Neapolis (Naples) for a time but was living in Rome again when his first work, the *Eclogues*, was published. By this time, he was a friend of *Maecenas, a literary patron, and *Augustus' trusted counselor. Virgil dedicated the *Georgics* to him. Virgil also introduced his friend *Horace to Maecenas, and the two poets accompanied Maecenas on a journey to Brundisium (Brindisi) in 37. After this trip, Virgil retired from Rome to Campania and spent eleven years writing the *Aeneid*. In 19, before it was quite completed, Virgil left Italy to travel in Greece and Asia Minor. He intended to spend three years there polishing the poem. He met Augustus in Athens, however, and the emperor wished him to return to Rome with him. Unfortunately, Virgil fell ill at Megara and died at Brundisium. He was buried outside Neapolis, where he had spent the greater part of his life. His tomb was greatly revered in later ages.

The first of his three works, the *Eclogues*, is a collection of ten short, unrelated poems in hexameters. They were composed between c. 42 and 37 and are largely on pastoral themes, as their alternate title the *Bucolics* would indicate. *Eclogae* means "selections" and was not the title Virgil chose. However unconnected the title would claim them to be, the poems in fact are linked by their utopian, bucolic scenery and by their dreamlike association of ideas. The poems established Virgil as one of the great nature poets, and they served as the models for much subsequent European poetry. Spenser, Milton, Rousseau, and Mallarme all demonstrate the influence of these poems, themes, and images.

The *Georgics*, Virgil's second work, written between 37 and 30 in Campania, is a didactic agricultural poem, divided into four books each on the subject of farming. This poem, too, is written in hexameters, a meter Virgil developed brilliantly. Book I deals with cultivation of crops and weather signs. Book II revolves around growing trees, particularly vines and the olive tree. Book III discusses the raising of cattle, and Book IV deals with keeping bees. Use of hexameters for agricultural poetry is a very ancient tradition, going back to the remote Greek past of *Hesiod. Virgil, in fact, claimed to be a Roman Hesiod and saw it as a patriotic endeavor to bring this Hesiodic spirit to Rome and to Latin. The four books therefore praise Rome and the Italian landscape. Italy was only recently united, and Virgil clearly saw it as a new, very emotional concept. The *Georgics* is in some measure a response to the recent civil wars, and a dominant theme is the need for a peace that is worked for. *Seneca deeply admired the poem, suggesting that "Virgil did not seek to instruct teachers, but to delight readers." That this poem did so is clear from its influence on Milton's *Paradise Lost* and the favor it found with Montaigne, Dryden, and Cecil Day-Lewis, to name but a few.

The *Aeneid*, unfinished at Virgil's death, is his best-known work. This is Virgil's most civic and patriotic work. It is the foundation legend of Rome, attached to the death of Troy. It picks up where other Troy narratives leave off and depicts the death throes of Priam's kingdom. More than anything, it is the story of Aeneas and the prophecies about the greatness of Rome. The story follows Aeneas from the ashes of Troy to the shores of Carthage, where Aeneas falls in love with the widowed Queen Dido. She thinks they have exchanged vows of fidelity; he obeys commands from Jupiter himself and leaves her. Upon realizing that she has been betrayed and shamed, and that she has shamed and betrayed everything she valued, Dido commits suicide, sparking enmity between Carthage and Rome that finds expression in the Punic Wars. But the rest of Aeneas' future promises glory, even if the present is hard. Aeneas journeys to the underworld, where his father tells him of the splendor of the line he will found with the Latin princess Lavinia. But even though this destiny is the will of the gods, it does not proceed without some conflict. Although Lavinia's father and his countrymen agree to the union with the newcomers, Juno incites one of Lavinia's former suitors, Turnus, to rebellion. The rest of the book is a sort of anti-*Iliad*, wherein Aeneas is the newcomer laying siege to an established kingdom, seeks for allies, faces Camilla, the warrior maid fighting for Turnus, and finally vanquishes Turnus. The story ends there, with promises of dynasty and empire hanging in the air.

Aeneas is a civic hero, and this sets him apart him from his legendary fellows. Whereas Achilles might be famous for his impassioned courage, and Odysseus for his agile brain, Aeneas is characterized throughout by his duty to family, by his moderation in all things, and by his humility to the gods' will for him. Although he encounters the same sorts of adventures as Odysseus, for instance, trips to the underworld and the Island of Cyclops, Aeneas is never in any danger of succumbing to temptations. Sometimes this is due to his mother, Venus, who steers him clear of physical dangers; sometimes this is because his commitment to his duty is stronger than his curiosity. His pursuit of Rome, particularly as his son's legacy and the gods' will, dominates the poem and Aeneas' character. The epic love affair with Dido of Carthage is compromised by Juno's and Venus' manipulation of her and the fact that Virgil repeatedly refers to her emotions as more like madness than the love that engenders dynasties. It is not just Aeneas' betrayal of Dido that sparks the Punic Wars; Virgil seems to argue that it is also a basic dissonance in culture.

The *Aeneid* is one of the most influential works in Western culture. *Augustine's *Confessions* not only make frequent reference to Virgil's work, but it is clear that Augustine himself understood his life as somehow following Aeneas'. Dante chose Virgil as his guide through the Inferno, and Virgil remains the quintessential voice of Rome as it wished itself to be.

Bibliography: K. Toll, "Making Roman-ness and the *Aeneid*," *Classical Antiquity* 16 (1997): 34–56.

Andrea Schutz

VITRUVIUS POLLIO, MARCUS (c. first century B.C./A.D.)

Vitruvius was a Roman military engineer and architect whose work *De architectura* influenced building design both in late antiquity and in the Renaissance.

Little is known about Vitruvius' life except that he designed and built only one building, a basilica at Fanum Fortunae. His long-lasting and widespread influence rests on his book *De architectura*, the only surviving Roman treatise on architecture. In this ten-book work, Vitruvius discusses many elements of the architect's craft including mathematics and measurement; the practicalities of using different types of building materials; the design of religious, civic, and domestic buildings; and above all, the interaction of a building with its environment. Throughout the treatise he draws on his own experience and the writings of others to create a work that is both practical and philosophical. It is not known exactly when Vitruvius wrote *De architectura*, although scholars agree that it was probably finished after the year 27 B.C.

Although an abridged version of *De architectura* survived into the Middle Ages, it was not greatly influential until Poggio Bracciolini discovered a manuscript of the complete work in the monastery of St. Gall in 1414. Copied and read by Renaissance humanists, the treatise greatly influenced the Florentine Leon Battista Alberti. Once published in 1485, *De architectura* influenced generations of Renaissance architects, including Michelangelo, Bramante, and Leonardo da Vinci.

Bibliography: I.D. Rowland, ed., *Vitruvius: Ten Books on Architecture*, 1999.

Olivia H. McIntyre

X

XANTHUS (C. 464 B.C.)

Xanthus is reputed to have been the first barbarian author to use Greek; he composed a history of his own country Lydia (*Lydiaca*).

Xanthus the Lydian, son of Canduales, is mentioned to have lived at the time of the capture of the city of Sardis. This reference, however, could refer either to its capture by *Cyrus during *Croesus' reign (c. 546) or its capture by the Greeks in the Ionian Revolt (c. 499). On the other hand, *Strabo says that Xanthus described a great drought in Asia Minor that took place during the reign of *Artaxerxes I Macrocheir (r. 464–424). This reference thus gives the year of Artaxerxes' accession, 464, as a *terminus post quem* for the publication of Xanthus' work. Furthermore, *Dionysius of Halicarnassus mentions Xanthus as one of the writers "living rather earlier than the time of the Peloponnesian War and extending as far as the age of *Thucydides." According to *Ephorus of Cyme, *Herodotus found inspiration in the work of Xanthus.

Xanthus' *Lydiaca* is originally said to have consisted of four books. It is, however, quite impossible to tell how he arranged his material within these four books. His history probably ended with the capture of Croesus and the end of Lydian independence. The anecdotal evidence leads one to believe that his historical arrangement was just as loose as that of Herodotus. Besides the *Lydiaca*, there is one reference to a work entitled *Magica* (a *magos* was a Persian priest) and another to a *Life of Empedocles*.

Although Dionysius of Halicarnassus in his *De Thucydide* speaks despairingly of the so-called historians prior to Herodotus, in his major work *Roman Antiquities*, he gives high praise to Xanthus for his wide range and authoritative character of his work.

Bibliography: L. Pearson, *Early Ionian Historians*, 1939.

Cecilia Saerens

XENOCRATES OF CHALCEDON (c. 396 to 314 B.C.)

Xenocrates was the head of the Platonic Academy from 339 to 314.

Not much is known about the life of Xenocrates, and of his numerous works we possess only a few fragments. He accompanied *Plato, as did Speusippus (407–339), in his second journey to Sicily. His seriousness and continence were proverbial, as much as his phlegmatic character. Plato, comparing him with *Aristotle, said he needed a spur for one and a rein for the other. After the death of Speusippus, Xenocrates led the Academy for twenty-five years.

Xenocrates wrote an extensive amount of theoretical works of which only a few fragments have been handed down to us. He is attributed with the traditional division of knowledge into logic, physics, and ethics. He developed and systematized the Platonic doctrines with a particular inclination to mathematics and Pythagorean (cf. *Pythagoras) conceptions. Xenocrates based his metaphysics on the principles of Unity and of the Dyad, from which he derived the numbers, considered at the same time as mathematical entities and as Ideas. He understood both principles as divinities that extend over the whole world. Identifying, in opposition to Speusippus, the Good with Unity and the Evil with Plurality, he came to the conclusion that the things of the world were both full of good and bad demons. He explained the nature of the (World-)soul as a self-moving number. Understanding the body as the prison of the soul, he maintained an ascetic position in ethics. In his opinion, the irrational parts of the soul survive death as much as the rational part.

His systematizing seems to have consisted mostly of threefold classifications. Apart from the three parts of the philosophy mentioned above, he distinguished three different substances in the world (the intelligible or supercelestial, the sensible or sublunar, and the celestial, both intelligible and sensible), three grades of knowledge (knowledge, sensibility, opinion,) and three grades of truth (complete, incomplete, mixed).

Bibliography: H.S. Schibli, "Xenocrates' Daemons and the Irrational Soul," *Classical Quarterly* 43 (1993): 143–167.

Fernando Oreja

XENOPHANES OF COLOPHON (c. 570–c. 475 B.C.)

Xenophanes was a Greek poet and thinker. Though classified as an Ionian philosopher, he lived most of his life in various cities in Sicily and Magna Graecia.

Like that of other pre-Socratic philosophers, Xenophanes' work is known to us only in fragments. From these we know that he wrote in a variety of poetic meters rather than prose. Two fragments, best looked at as purely literary productions, deal with the rules of behavior for drinking parties (*symposia*) and with the greater civic value of poets as compared with athletes.

Xenophanes' importance as a thinker lies chiefly in his criticism of traditional Greek notions of the Olympian deities. In particular, he attacked the depiction of the gods by *Homer and *Hesiod as immoral and in general utterly anthropomorphic in their physical and psychological makeup. He also observed that people of different cultures conceptualized their gods in ways peculiar to themselves and concluded that all such conceptions were subjective and, by implication, without any probative value. This sort of deduction from anthropological reflections on diverse societies anticipated an important strand of Greek thought, clearly evident in, for example, the *History* of *Herodotus. In the place of misguided customary ideas of the gods, Xenophanes substituted the notion of a single, nonanthropomorphic deity that in some sense pervaded and animated the physical universe.

Other fragments reveal Xenophanes' preoccupation with familiar subjects of pre-Socratic philosophy: the nature of the heavenly bodies; the extent of the earth; the importance of water and the sea as a basic element in the composition of physical objects, including human beings; and epistemological speculations about the nature and limitations of human knowledge.

Xenophanes was a poet who thought deeply about philosophical issues. His negative critiques of conventional religious thought and his often radical positive statements about the nature of the divine exerted a strong influence on such later thinkers and artists as *Heraclitus, *Aeschylus, *Euripides, *Plato, and *Aristotle.

Bibliography: J.H. Lesher, int. and trans., *Xenophones of Colophon: Fragments. A Text and Translation with a Commentary*, 1992.

James Holoka

XENOPHON (c. 430–c. 354 B.C.)

Xenophon was a Greek soldier and man of letters.

Xenophon was an Athenian who, having been born into a wealthy family, was not well disposed to democracy. He stayed in Athens during the reign of the Thirty Tyrants in 404 and fought those trying to restore the democracy in 404–403. He left Athens soon after and enrolled in the army of Cyrus, who was attempting to remove his brother *Artaxerxes II from the Persian throne. The expedition was soundly defeated at Cunaxa (401). When the Greek generals were treacherously murdered, Xenophon became the leading figure and led the survivors on an arduous journey back to the Greek colony at Trapezus on the Black Sea. Some say that he was exiled from Athens at this point and took service in the Spartan army, under the leadership of Thibron, which had arrived in Anatolia to make war on the Persians. As a mercenary he subsequently served under the Spartan commanders Dercylidas and *Agesilaus II. He became a personal friend of Agesilaus, and on his return to Greece, he fought on the Spartan side at Coronea against, among others, the Athenians. Xenophon was given estates by the Spartans at Scillus in Elis, probably at the behest of Agesilaus. Here he spent the next twenty years mostly engaged in writing the works that have come down to us. Not long after the Spartan defeat at Leuctra (371) by the Theban forces commanded by *Epaminondas, he was expelled from his estates. One tradition says he settled in Corinth where he lived out the rest of his days, another that he returned to Athens when relations between Athens and Sparta improved.

A prolific writer, Xenophon is famous for his *Hellenica*, a history of Greece from 411 to 362, and the *Anabasis*, an account of a mainly Greek mercenary expedition into Persia. He was a friend of the philosopher *Socrates and recorded his impressions of him in the *Memorabilia*.

In more recent times Xenophon's faults as a writer have become obvious. At times he is factually inaccurate, and he clearly carries a Spartan bias. Yet he still emerges as a man of much common sense. His clear style and exposition ensured that he enjoyed a high reputation in antiquity and with the rebirth of the classics in western Europe. Xenophon was often the first unadapted Greek text that schoolboys studied.

Bibliography: J.K. Anderson, *Xenophon*, 1974.

Karen McGroarty

XERXES, KING OF PERSIA (c. 519–465 b.c.)

Xerxes was king of the Persian empire when it suffered defeat against the Hellenic coalition in the second phase of the Persian Wars (480–479).

Xerxes succeeded his father *Darius I in 486 and appears to have continued his policy, at least concerning the western front, where the Persians were attempting to expand into the Balkans and Greece. However, Xerxes was soon confronted with rebellions in Egypt (486–485, which took a year to quell) and Babylonia (c. 481). Xerxes, however, failed to control the mainland of Greece, although some Greek city-states did in fact submit to Persian authority (Thessaly and Thebes). After some early victories in central Greece, Xerxes' navy lost a decisive battle at Salamis (480), and the Persian army was defeated on land at Plataea (479). Xerxes left abruptly after the naval battle, possibly to quell another Babylonian rebellion successfully; control of this centrally located area was crucial for the survival of the empire. The Greeks, however, followed up with a revolt of several Aegean islands against Persian rule and another Athenian naval victory against Persia in Pamphylia in Asia Minor (466). Xerxes was murdered along with his crown prince Darius in a palace revolt in 465.

Knowledge of his reign is derived from antagonistic Greek sources (stemming from *Herodotus), Jewish tradition, and scattered Persian inscriptions. Xerxes' reputation has suffered more than any other Achaemenid king. *Plato describes him as raised under the care of women in the royal harem, and thus he did not have the same hardened experience as his father Darius. Furthermore, Herodotus claims that he was put in power because of the influence of his mother, Atossa, and allowed himself to be persuaded to undertake the Greek expedition, where he acted with ruthless pride, made many irrational decisions, and angered the gods with his impiety. Both Herodotus and *Strabo claim that Xerxes violated the sanctuaries in Babylonia during the second insurrection, exhibiting a so-called intolerance, which appears to be confirmed by the Persian Daiva inscription. In addition, Xerxes was satirized as Ahasuerus in the biblical book of Esther as a king who makes irrational decisions and is dominated by women.

However, when put in historical perspective, a more balanced estimation of Xerxes' reign can be accomplished. Herodotus describes Xerxes more as a tragic figure who was divinely fated to fail in the Greek expedition, no matter what decisions he makes. This description of Xerxes as a weakling and womanizer is found in novelistic sections of Herodotus. Moreover, there is no evidence that Xerxes discontinued the worship of Marduk at Babylon in this period, nor that the king was intolerant of gods other than Ahura Mazda. Xerxes was also a prolific builder who consolidated the holdings of the empire, although he will forever be tainted by defeat in the Persian Wars.

Bibliography: P. Briant, *From Cyrus to Alexander: A History of the Persian Empire*, 2 vols., 1997.

Mark W. Chavalas

Z

ZENO (?–491)

Zeno was the emperor of the eastern Roman Empire from 474 to 491.

The man who became Emperor Zeno was originally called Tarasacodissa Rousoumbladeotes and was an Isaurian notable. During the reign of the emperor Leo (457–474), he was perceived as a useful counterbalance to the power of the chief of the army, Aspar, and his family. Assuming the name Zeno, he was married to Ariadne, Leo's daughter, and their son, also named Leo, was proclaimed successor to his grandfather.

When the emperor died, the younger Leo immediately associated his father with him in the empire and, soon after, died. As emperor, Zeno faced a number of major revolts, both from members of the family of Leo and of former adherents of his own. Despite one lengthy deposition, he survived through a mixture of his own skill and the mistakes of his enemies.

He sought to resolve two long-standing problems faced by the eastern empire: the problem of the Ostrogothic presence and the doctrinal dispute over Monophysitism. In the former, he was more successful, sending Theodoric and his people to Italy, where they displaced *Odoacer in northern Italy. In the latter he was less successful, negotiating a pastoral letter, the *Henotikon*, which the Patriarch of Constantinople issued. This document was accepted by neither side and had the effect of estranging the Papacy and the Patriarchate of Constantinople for over a generation.

Never popular, he died suddenly and was largely unmourned in 491 without clear arrangements for the succession. It was his widow, Ariadne, who settled the matter through her marriage to a young and able nobleman, Flavius Anastasius.

Bibliography: G. Ostrogorsky, *History of the Byzantine State*, 1980.

William Leadbetter

ZENOBIA (third century A.D.)

Zenobia was the queen of Palmyra who succeeded in leading a major revolt in the eastern Roman provinces.

Palmyra was an important commercial center on the caravan route between Syria and the upper Euphrates River. Odenath, Zenobia's husband, had ruled Palmyra as a client state of Rome, yet had enjoyed almost virtual independence under the emperor Gallienus. In 267, Odenath and his son from a previous marriage were assassinated; Zenobia had herself declared regent for her own son Vaballathus (Wabhallath "Gift of God").

After Gallienus was assassinated in 268, Claudius II Gothicus succeeded him and spent the majority of his reign fighting the Goths. Zenobia attempted to maintain the independence of Palmyra, and after Claudius died of the plague (270), she had Vaballathus proclaimed *augustus* and herself *augusta*. Not content to remain a Roman client, Zenobia had Palmyrene forces occupy and annex Egypt, Syria, and large parts of Anatolia.

After two years, Roman Emperor *Aurelian reclaimed Egypt, Anatolia, and Syria. He defeated Zenobia at Antioch, and she retreated to Palmyra, where he eventually captured her. Zenobia attempted to escape across the Euphrates to the Sasanians, but Aurelian seized her, brought her back to Rome, and paraded her in golden chains along with Tetricus, the last monarch of Postumus' splinter state in the West. Later, she was given a villa at Tivoli, where she died.

Some speculation exists that Zenobia had been planning on protecting Christianity, some forty years before *Constantine, as a counter to Roman hostility toward the movement.

Bibliography: F.F. Peters, *The Harvest of Hellenism. A History of the Near East from Alexander the Great to the Triumph of Christianity*, 1970; I. Shahid, *Rome and the Arabs: A Prolegomenon to the Study of Byzantium and the Arabs*, 1984.

Brannon Wheeler

ZENODOTUS (fl. 280 B.C.)

Zenodotus was the first superintendent of the Library at Alexandria and an originator of the discipline of textual criticism.

Zenodotus of Ephesus (born c. 325) probably began work on an edition of *Homer while employed as the tutor of young *Ptolemy II. When the latter ascended the throne in 288, Zenodotus was put in charge of the state-financed research library affiliated with the think tank known as the "Museum." He undoubtedly had a role in the acquiring and categorizing of books, though his system of classification is uncertain.

Zenodotus was known for his lexicographical work, a *Homeric Glossary*, and especially his critical editions. While direct evidence of the latter does not survive, some notion of their character emerges from the reactions of later scholars. We know that he devised the obelus as a symbol designating spurious lines and that his efforts at emendation were not based on the considered critical principles espoused by such later Alexandrian scholars as *Aristarchus of Samothrace. Zenodotus seems to have usually adopted the reading of only one manuscript when editing a text, consulting others only when in doubt about the authenticity of particular lines.

Zenodotus' place in the history of textual scholarship is secured by the primacy rather than the high quality of his textual criticism.

Bibliography: R. Pfeiffer, *History of Classical Scholarship: From the Beginnings to the End of the Hellenistic Age*, 1968.

James Holoka

ZENO OF CITIUM (c. 335–263 b.c.)

Zeno was a Greek philosopher, founder of Stoicism, which, along with Epicureanism, was one of the two most important and influential Hellenistic philosophical systems.

Zeno was born in Citium in southeast Cyprus, son of Mnaseas, a merchant, and was perhaps of Phoenician descent. He came to Athens around 312, where he is said to have studied under the Cynic Crates, the Socratic *Antisthenes, and the Academics *Xenocrates and Polemon. At first, his followers were known as Zenonians but later adopted the name Stoics when Zeno began teaching in the *Stoa Poikile* (Painted Porch) in the Athenian agora. He was a prolific writer, but his works now survive only as fragments.

Stoicism is divided into three parts: logic, physics, and ethics. Of these, logic, later greatly developed by *Chrysippus, is perhaps the greatest Stoic contribution to philosophy. In Stoic physics, matter is a continuum (contrast Epicurean atomism), ethics place virtue as the highest good, Stoic theology is pantheistic, and the Stoic Universe is anthropocentric. Like Epicureanism, it is an ethical philosophy in that it is intended as a guide to life, and Zeno's ethics are marked by a strongly Cynic influenced cultural primitivism.

Stoicism was a flexible philosophical system, much altered and developed by many thinkers over the years and practically refounded later by Chrysippus. In general, Stoicism is characterized by a teleological worldview in which the world is pervaded and controlled by a divine principle (the "creative fire"), which guides all things and ensures the outcome of all events will be for the ultimate benefit of the world as a whole. Thus, virtue consists of understanding and accepting the divine will and matching one's behavior to it: behaving according to Nature, which, for the Stoics, is equivalent to God. Stoicism was the most popular and influential of all philosophies in the Hellenistic world, especially at Rome. It influenced, directly and indirectly, the Church Fathers and was often seen as a precursor of Christianity. Stoicism played an important role in Renaissance thought, was a strong influence on Spinoza and Kant, and has been revived several times, recently as neo-Stoicism.

Bibliography: A.A. Long and D.N. Sedley, *The Hellenistic Philosophers*, 2 vols., 1987.

Gordon Campbell

ZENO OF ELEA (c. 490–? b.c.)

Zeno was an important student and defender of Parmenidean philosophy. Zeno is probably most famous for his paradoxes, which were used to defend the Parmenidean claim that motion and becoming are illusory.

Little is known about the life of Zeno except that he was a younger student of *Parmenides. Zeno was likely born sometime between 490 and 485. Zeno was born in Elea, on what is now Sicily. According to *Diogenes Laertius, Zeno spent his entire life in Elea, in part because he disliked the arrogance of Athenians. According to other reports, however, Zeno and Parmenides met with *Socrates in Athens about 450. Details of his life are therefore sparse, though we do know quite a bit about his paradoxes. Through the use of paradoxes, Zeno sought to defend Parmenides' philosophy from critics; in particular, Zeno attempted to show that Parmenides was right when he claimed that true reality, Being, simply is, and thus cannot be subject to becoming and change, for if this were so, Being would have to become something it now is not. Change, motion, and becoming are therefore illusory. To prove this point, Zeno put forth his famous paradox concerning motion. If motion from point A to point B is possible, Zeno argued, one must first reach the midpoint between A and B. Before reaching this midpoint, however, one must first reach the midpoint between A and the first midpoint, and so on, *ad infinitum*. Since there are an infinite number of such midpoints, and since it takes time to move from one point to another, any motion will therefore take an infinite amount of time and therefore is impossible—or, as Parmenides said, it is illusory. This paradox and others have been persistent challenges for philosophers and mathematicians to tackle, and it continues to be Zeno's legacy.

Bibliography: G.S. Kirk, J.E. Raven, and M. Schofield, *The Presocratic Philosophers*, 2nd ed., 1983.

Jeffrey A. Bell

ZEUXIS (fl. 424–397 b.c.)

Zeuxis was a Greek painter of exceptional technical merit who was known for his creativity in subject matter and synthetic style.

The details of Zeuxis' life are unclear. His origins were of Lucanian Heraclea, but he painted widely, taking commissions abroad. Zeuxis' style was noted in antiquity for its synthetic aspects: He took the best or most beautiful features from individual models and merged them to make a more beautiful whole. He believed that "nature had not refined to perfection any single object in all its parts" and tried to transfer the truth from the live model to the painting.

Zeuxis was recognized in antiquity for his rendering of the female body, in which he used the best features of live nude models. He apparently emphasized the body's limbs. In a contest with *Parrhasius, Zeuxis reportedly painted fruit with such accuracy that birds were fooled. Ancient descriptions suggest that he added a liveliness and emotion to his painting and as such was surely a forerunner to the Hellenistic phase. Zeuxis painted both in color and in monochrome white and also made statues of clay. Following his contemporary *Apollodorus, Zeuxis used shading to produce an early form of chiaroscuro. Zeuxis tried to find new, unusual, and strange subjects. His works included a Centaur family, an Alcmene, a Pan, a Helen, a Marsyas Bound, a Penelope, an enthroned Zeus, a Heracles Strangling the Snakes in the Presence of Alcmene, and an athlete. Sadly, none of these works survive.

Bibliography: V.J. Bruno, *Form and Colour in Greek Painting*, 1977.

Lisa Auanger

ZOROASTER (fl. 1200 B.C.?)

Zoroaster (or Zarathustra) founded Zoroastrianism, one of the great religions of the ancient Near East, which flourished in Persia (Iran) for centuries, influenced the development of Western monotheism, and remains alive today.

The primary source for Zoroaster's life and teaching is the collection of holy books called the *Avesta*, particularly the *Gathas* (hymns), the *Younger Avesta*, and various *Pahlavi* (Middle Persian) texts. There are two ancient traditions as to when Zoroaster lived, one dating his life to 5,000 years before the Trojan War (6000 B.C.) and the other to 258 years before *Alexander the Great (570 B.C.). Western scholars long accepted the latter, thereby placing Zoroaster in the same century as the Persian *Cyrus the Great, founder of the Achaemenian empire. More recent scholarship demonstrates that Zoroaster must have lived between 1500 and 1100 B.C., most likely around 1200 B.C. Controversy has also surrounded his teachings, with opinion ranging from those who accept the nineteenth-century scholar Martin Haug's contention that Zoroaster espoused a strict monotheism bereft of all ritual except prayer to others who regard early Zoroastrianism as traditionally polytheistic like most ancient religions, notably that of Vedic India. Again, modern scholarship has provided a different picture.

Zoroaster's homeland was probably northeastern Iran. Apparently he was born into a pastoral society, for his name means "he who can manage camels," that of his father Pourusaspa, "possessing gray horses," and that of his mother Dughdhova, "milkmaid." Zoroaster was destined from childhood to be a priest, for which he began training about the age of seven. He reportedly married three times, producing three daughters by his first wife and two sons by his second. Dubious legend says that he lived seventy-seven years and forty days; even more doubtful is the story that he was assassinated or died by some other violent means. Tradition maintains that he experienced revelation when he was thirty years old, which by ancient convention was when a man achieved full maturity (*Jesus Christ began his ministry at the same age). While attending a spring religious festival, Zoroaster went to a nearby river to get water for a morning ritual, and upon emerging from the stream, he had a vision of the god Ahura Mazda and the six Bounteous Immortals and thereby received spiritual enlightenment; he would later experience numerous similar revelations. In preaching the new doctrine revealed to him, Zoroaster initially encountered the well-known phenomenon that a prophet is not welcome in his own country; however, he eventually found a safe base at the court of a king named Vistaspa.

Zoroaster's teachings are complex, and no more than a brief outline can be given here. While rooted in earlier Indo-Iranian paganism, much of what he taught is strikingly original. First and foremost is the dualistic conception that in the beginning there was only one good god, Ahura Mazda (Ohrmazd), the Lord Wisdom, who was and is opposed by the evil god Angra Mainyu (Ahriman), the Hostile Spirit. To assist him in the battle of good versus evil, Ahura Mazda created the six Bounteous Immortals, or *yazatas*, lesser divinities who are not quite gods but are more exalted creatures than the angels of Western monotheism. With Ahura Mazda or his Holy Spirit, Spenta Mainyu, they form a divine heptad linked to the seven creations of the material world and with various forces or spirits. Spenta Mainyu is associated with man; the others are arranged in pairs: Asa Vahista linked with fire and order; Vohu Manah with animals and good intent; Khsathra Vairya with the sky, metals, and desirable dominion; Spenta Armaiti with the earth and holy devotion or obedience; Haurvatat with water and health; and Ameretat with plants and long life. There were also other lesser divinities, notably Mithra and Varuna. Paralleling the *yazatas* were the *daevas*, demons or evil spirits who served Angra Mainyu.

According to Zoroastrian eschatology, Ahura Mazda created the world as a stage upon which good will triumph over evil. Once this is accomplished, Ahura Mazda's creation will be restored to its original perfection, an event known as the *Frasegird*, or "making wonderful," and historic time will end. Meanwhile, there is already an afterlife in which the souls of the good (*asavan*) ascend to heaven, while those of the evil (*drugvant*) descend to hell. Before the end of time there will come a series of three *Saosyants*, or saviors (one near the end of each of the last three millennia, according to tradition), who will abet the defeat of Angra Mainyu. Once Ahura Mazda is victorious, the souls of the dead will be brought from heaven and hell to be reunited with their resurrected bodies and judged (perhaps by Mithra) in an ordeal by fire involving molten metal. Those who are saved will live forever in Ahura Mazda's restored realm, while the damned will be utterly destroyed along with Angra Mainyu and hell itself.

There is little record of the spread of Zoroastrianism in the first centuries of its existence, though clearly it had triumphed in Persia prior to the conquests of Cyrus the Great, whose family were probably devotees. From Zoroaster's day forward it appears to have involved extensive ritual, much of it conducted by a priestly class known as the magi and including sacrifice, fire worship, and a series of holy days known as *gahambars* that celebrated the various creations. Not surprisingly, Zoroastrianism gave rise to its own heresies, such as Zurvanism (which regarded Ahura Mazda and Angra Mainyu as literally twins), and produced important offshoots such as Mithraism (in which Mithra, linked with the sun, became the main focus of worship), Manicheism (featuring a radical dualism in which the spiritual realm is completely good and the created material world entirely evil, cf. *Mani), and various Gnostic cults. Zoroastrian influence on Judaism, Christianity, and Islam is so obvious as to require no explanation here. Zoroastrianism continued to thrive in the successive Persian empires until the coming of Islam in the seventh century A.D. Some adherents fled to India, where their descendants are still known as Parsis, though pockets of Zoroastrianism survive in Persia. Today it can also be found in Australia, Canada, Europe, the United States, and elsewhere.

Bibliography: M. Boyce, *A History of Zoroastrianism*, 2 vols., 1975–1982; M. Boyce, *Zoroastrianism: Its Antiquity and Constant Vigour*, 1992.

William B. Robison

Glossary

Academy. The school established by Plato in Athens c. 385 B.C.

Achaean League. A federation of cities in northern Greece. It had a presiding general and a cavalry commander and an assembly that decided a common foreign policy.

Achaemenids. The descendants of Achaemenes (Hakhamanish), the eponymous founder of the Persian royal house. According to Herodotus, Achaemenes was the ancestor of both Cyrus and Darius.

Acropolis. The upper city or citadel, notably the one at Athens.

aediles. Roman patrician (curule) and plebeian magistrates who superintended the provisioning of Rome, trade, markets (including weights and measures), public games, roadways, sanitation, and police.

Aetolian League. A federation of Greek cities in central Greece that gained in cohesion after a successful defense of the area against the Celts. After saving Delphi in 279 B.C., the Aetolians absorbed most of the cities of the Amphictyonic Council. As a federation, all men of military age met twice annually in an assembly; there was a chief magistrate and a council made up of representatives of the cities.

ager gallicus. Public domain in the territory of the Gauls in northern Italy.

ager publicus. Public domain.

Alcmaeonids. A noble Athenian family prominent in politics.

Amphityonic League. The governing body of an ancient league of Delphi's neighbors, the Delphic Amphictyony, that administered the oracle.

apotheosis. A ceremony whereby a mortal was admitted to the number of the gods (*divus*).

archon. A general title for an officeholder. At Athens it was given to the nine men, with their secretary chosen annually to the chief magistracy. One of the ten was president of the state and gave his name to the year, the "eponymous archon."

Areopagus. A hill near the Athenian Acropolis. The aristocratic council that met there and took its name was a development of the Homeric Council of Elders. This was the most powerful body in the Athenian state during the archaic period, but the radical reforms of 462–461 stripped it of political power and left it as a judicial court

Arianism. The theory of Arius that resulted in one of the first major doctrinal divisions in the early Church. Condemned as a heretic at the Council of Nicaea in 325, he asserted that Christ was a man, distinct from and subordinate to God.

Behistun Inscription. A carved inscription on a Behistun relief that relates in detail the struggles of Darius to secure the Persian throne.

boeotarch. A chief magistrate of the Boeotian League.

boule. The Council of Five Hundred at Athens.

censor (cens.). Roman magistrate charged with the task of conducting a "census" every five years of citizens and their possessions and of drawing up a list of senators.

choregia. The office of the *choregos*, whose duty it was to defray the expenses of producing the chorus for a play; the office was borne by individual citizens of sufficient wealth.

cleruchy. A colony, peculiar to Athens, planted in foreign soil and in which all the people (cleruchs) remained Athenian citizens.

Comedy (Greek), Middle. The phrase "Middle Comedy" was coined by Hellenistic scholars to describe the period between Old and New Comedy (c. 404–321 B.C.).

Comedy (Greek), New. The comedies produced at Athens during the last quarter of the fourth century B.C. and into the third century B.C.

Comedy (Greek), Old. The comedies produced at Athens during the fifth century B.C.

comitia centuriata. Roman assembly of the people, gathered for the election of senior magistrates, voting on laws and justice. Voting was by *centuria*, according to classes established on the basis of their wealth at the time of the census.

comitia curiata. Ancient Roman assembly of the people (voting was by curia, which retained only a religious role); it conferred the imperium on magistrates.

comitia tributa. Plebeian assembly charged with the election of aediles, tribunes, and quaestors and voting on plebiscites. Voting was by tribe.

consuls (cos.). Heads of state under the Roman republic; this system survived under the empire with reduced power. The office was annual, with two consuls under the republic.

Corinthian League. The term used by modern scholars to designate the alliance organized to implement the peace established by Philip II in 338 B.C.

dactyl. A poetical foot of three syllables, one long followed by two short.

Delian League. The modern name for the confederation organized by Athens after the end of the Persian Wars. Founded in 477 B.C., the League was slowly converted into an Athenian empire as Athens began forcing unwilling states to remain in the organization or to join if they were not already members.

deme. A township of Attica or a section of Athens. The demes' elected officials were known as demarchs.

Diadochi. The immediate successors of Alexander the Great.

Diadumenus. Specifically, Polyclitus' statue of a youth tying a fillet around his head.

dictator. Roman magistrate appointed legally with full powers but for a specified period (less than six months) and in order to accomplish a precise task, when grave danger threatened the state.

Discobolus. Specifically, Myron's statue of a youth throwing the discus.

Doryphorus. Specifically, Polyclitus' statue of a youth carrying a spear.

ecclesia. The assembly of citizens at Athens.

edictum (pl. *edicta*). General ordinance; official pronouncement of a magistrate.

ephor. One of the five chief magistrates at Sparta.

epinician. An ode in honor of a victor.

equites. Roman "knights," businessmen, and capitalists.

gens (pl. gentes). A Roman clan or group of families linked by a common name and by a belief in common ancestors.

Gerousia. The Spartan Council, consisting of twenty-eight elders and the two kings.

graphe paranomon. A constitutional safeguard at Athens under which an indictment was possible for bringing before the assembly measures in conflict with the laws.

helot. Term given particularly to the non-Dorian inhabitants of Laconia and Messenia reduced to a state of serfdom by the Spartans.

hetaira. A female companion. A term used for courtesans in Classical Athens.

hippeis. Knights; the second wealthiest class in the Solonian census.

Homonoia. Unity and Concord.

hoplite. A heavily armed foot soldier.

imperium. Sovereign civil and military power for the Romans; under the republic it was held by dictators, consuls, and praetors. Under the empire, only the emperor could hold it; he could also delegate it.

Latin League. The confederation of the cities in Latium, existing in Italy in the earliest historical times and continuing until 338 B.C. when the Latin towns were finally incorporated in the dominion of Rome following the Great Latin War (340–338 B.C.).

Lyceum. The school founded by Aristotle in Athens.

magister equitum. Commander in chief of the cavalry.

magister peditum. Commander in chief of the infantry.

magister utriusque militiae. Commander in chief of both cavalry and infantry.

metics. Resident aliens in a Greek city-state who had acquired a status distinguishing them from other foreigners.

optimates. Roman political group, though not an organized party. Aristocratic and conservative members of the Senate, they opposed the populares.

ostracism. In Athens in the fifth century B.C. a method of banishing for ten years a prominent citizen who had become unpopular. If the assembly voted in favor of holding an ostracism, it was held in the Agora, and the voter wrote on a potsherd the name of the man he wished to be banished.

patrician. Originally a member of the *de facto* Roman nobility providing senators (*patres*), then a member of the nobility by birth for whom access to certain priesthoods and the consulate was reserved. The republican patriciate was defined and formed in the fifth century B.C.

patron. Important personage with whom, by a bilateral commitment, individuals (*clientes*) or public collectives (cities, peoples, provinces) were linked. The patron ensured the daily security and legal defense of his clients, who in return owed him respect, help, and their votes. He acted as an intermediary between the state and the public collectives to whom he was patron.

Peloponnesian League. The modern name for an organization led by Sparta and dated to some time in the sixth century B.C. It consisted of Sparta and less powerful allied states who swore to have the same friends and enemies as the Spartans.

pentakosiomedimnoi. The wealthiest class in the Solonian census, consisting of persons whose estates annually produced 500 measures of produce or whose annual income in drachmas was of approximately the same value.

phalanx. The heavy-armed infantry in order of battle, close-formed and up to eight ranks deep, relying on the concerted weight of their charge.

phratry. An association (brotherhood) originally of close kinsmen; in early Athens, birth into a phratry was necessary for citizenship.

plebs, plebeians. Political grouping that appeared in 494–493 B.C. of all those in Rome, of any class, who opposed the patrician organization of the state. Composed of rich and poor, patrons and clients, native Romans and foreigners who had come into the city. At first their sole point in common was their opposition to the patricians. Subsequently plebeian *gentes* were formed, in opposition to the patrician *gentes*. At the end of the republic, the word defined common people.

polemarch. One of the nine Athenian archons appointed annually. Originally the commander of the army, he lost his military importance when, in the early fifth century B.C., the command passed to the board of generals. His later duties were primarily judicial, especially concerned with metics and foreigners.

polis. The Greek city-state.

pontiffs (*pontifices*). Roman college of six, later nine, and then sixteen priests with the duty of administering sacred and family law, religious jurisdiction, and keeping the *Annales*. They set the calendar, and their books were liturgical manuals. At their head was the great pontiff (*pontifex maximus*), who also had authority over all the other priests, whom he appointed and inaugurated. Under the Empire, the emperor was the *pontifex maximus*.

populares. A Roman political group, though not an organized party, that worked through and supposedly on behalf of the people, challenging the optimates of the Senate.

potestas. Civil (executive) powers of a Roman magistrate, inferior to imperium.

praetor. Senior magistrate especially responsible for justice. He performed some of the functions of the consuls in their absence.

Praetorian Guard. A body of troops originally formed by the emperor Augustus to protect his person and power and maintained by successive Roman emperors.

praetorian prefect. The commander of the Praetorian Guard.

princeps. First man, prince, emperor; leading personage within the governing class.

proconsul. An acting consul or an official having consular rank.

procurator. Inspector, tax collector, financial agent; governor of a minor province.

prytany. One of the ten committees of the Athenian boule, each consisting of fifty councilors (*prytaneis*) and presiding for a tenth of the year.

quaestor. Minor Roman magistrate whose special task was finance.

satrapy. The province of a Persian governor (satrap).

Second Athenian Confederation. A voluntary organization led by Athens that many Greek states joined, some at its inception in 377 B.C. and others later. It was finally dissolved when the Corinthian League was established in 338.

Second Sophistic. The revival of sophism in the Roman world c. 60–230.

senatus consulatum. Decision of the Senate that, under the empire, had the force of a law. In the event of major danger, under the republic, the *senatus consultum ultimum*, or ultimate senatorial decree, gave full powers to the consuls.

sophists. Teachers of rhetoric and the art of disputation. By the time of Plato, the term took on a derogatory sense and came to mean a man who merely feigned knowledge.

strategos. General. In the Greek city–states, this office was usually political as well as military. In Athens, after 487, the ten *strategoi* were the only elected high officials (the others were selected by lot); thus most of the powerful politicians of fifth-century Athens were *strategoi*.

suffette. Carthaginian magistrates. By the end of the fourth century B.C., two suffettes were appointed annually.

thetes. The fourth and lowest class in the Solonian census.

tribunes of the plebs (*tribuni plebis*/trib. pleb.). Roman college of ten magistrates whose task was the protection of the plebs; they were inviolable (*sacri*) and had the right of intercession over decisions of the magistrates, with the exception of dictators. Starting with Augustus, the emperor held the power of the tribunes (*tribunicia potestas*).

tribunician power. The power vested in a tribune.

triumph. The procession of a victorious Roman general to the temple of Jupiter Capitolinus.

zeugitai. The solid middle class at Athens, being the third class of the Solonian census.

Bibliography

Ackrill, J.L. *Aristotle the Philosopher*. Oxford: Oxford University Press, 1981.

Adcock, F.E. *Marcus Crassus, Millionaire*. Cambridge: Heffer, 1966.

Africa, T.W. *Phylarchus and the Spartan Revolution*. Berkeley: University of California Press, 1961.

Ahl, F.M. *Lucan: An Introduction*. Ithaca, NY: Cornell University Press, 1976.

Albenda, P. *The Palace of Sargon, King of Assyria*. Paris: Recherches sur les civilisations, 1986.

Alföldi, A. *Early Rome and the Latins*. Ann Arbor: University of Michigan Press, 1965.

Allen, R.E. *The Attalid Kingdom: A Constitutional History*. Oxford: Clarendon Press, 1983.

Alonso-Núñez, J.M. *The Ages of Rome*. Amsterdam: J.C. Gieben, 1982.

Ameling, W. *Herodes Atticus*. Hildesheim: Georg Olms, 1983.

Anderson, G. *Philostratus: Biography and Belles Lettres in the Second Century AD*. London: Croom Helm, 1986.

Anderson, J.K. *Xenophon*. London: Duckworth, 1974.

Andrewes, A. *The Greek Tyrants*. London: Hutchinson, 1956.

Armstrong, A.H. "The Peripatos." In *Cambridge History of Later Greek and Early Medieval Philosophy*, ed. A.H. Armstrong, 107–123. Cambridge: Cambridge University Press, 1967.

———. "Plotinus and the Religion and Superstition of His Time." In *Cambridge History of Late Greek and Early Medieval Philosophy*, ed. A.H. Armstrong, 195–210. Cambridge: Cambridge University Press, 1967.

Armstrong, D. *Horace*. New Haven, CT: Yale University Press, 1989.

Arnold, E.V. *Roman Stoicism*. Cambridge: Cambridge University Press, 1911.

Arnott, W.G., ed. *Menander*. 3 vols. Cambridge, MA: Harvard University Press, 1979–2000.

Ashe, G. *The Discovery of King Arthur*. Garden City, NJ: Anchor Press/Doubleday, 1985.

Ashmole, B. *Architect and Sculptor in Classical Greece*. London: Phaidon, 1972.

Asmis, E. "Philodemus' Epicureanism." *Aufstieg und Niedergang der römischen Welt* 2 (1990): 2369–2406.

Astin, A.E. *Cato the Censor.* New York: Clarendon Press, 1978.

———. *Scipio Aemilianus.* Oxford: Clarendon Press, 1967.

Austin, C., and Kassel, R., eds. *Poetae Comici Graeci.* 8 vols. Berlin: W. de Gruyter, 1983–1998.

Badian, E. *Lucius Sulla: The Deadly Reformer.* Sydney: Sydney University Press, 1970.

———. "Tiberius Gracchus and the Beginning of the Roman Revolution." *Aufstieg und Niedergang der römischen Welt* 1 (1972): 668–731.

Baharal, D. "The Portraits of Julia Domna from the Years 193–211 C.E. and the Dynastic Propaganda of L. Septimius Severus." *Latomus* 51 (1992): 110–118.

Balsdon, J.P.V.D. *The Emperor Gaius.* Oxford: Clarendon Press, 1934.

Baltussen, H. *Theophrastus against the Presocratics and Plato: Peripatic Dialectic in Desensibus.* Leiden: E.J. Brill, 2000.

Barber, G.L. *The Historian Ephorus.* Cambridge: Cambridge University Press, 1935.

Barker, A., ed. *Greek Musical Writings.* Cambridge: Cambridge University Press, 1984–.

Bar-Kochiva, B. *Judas Maccabeus. The Jewish Struggle against the Seleucids.* Cambridge: Cambridge University Press, 1989.

Barnes, J. *The Presocratic Philosophers.* London: Routledge and Kegan Paul, 1982.

Barnes, J.; Schofield, M.; and Sorabji, R., eds. *Articles on Aristotle.* 4 vols. London: Duckworth, 1975–1979.

Barnes, T.D. *Athanasius and Constantius: Theology and Politics in the Constantinian Empire.* Cambridge, MA: Harvard University Press, 1993.

———. *Constantine and Eusebius.* Cambridge, MA: Harvard University Press, 1981.

———. *The New Empire of Diocletian and Constantine.* Cambridge, MA: Harvard University Press, 1982.

———. *Tertullian: A Historical and Literary Study.* Oxford: Clarendon Press, 1971.

Barrett, A. *Agrippina. Sex, Power, and Politics in the Early Roman Empire.* New Haven, CT: Yale University Press, 1996.

Bartman, E. *Portraits of Livia: Imaging the Imperial Woman in Augustan Rome.* Cambridge: Cambridge University Press, 1999.

Bauman, R.A. *Women and Politics in Ancient Rome.* London: Routledge, 1992.

Beagon, M. *Roman Nature: The Thought of Pliny the Elder.* Oxford: Oxford University Press, 1992.

Benario, H. "Julia Domna Mater Senatus et Patriae," *Phoenix* 12 (1958): 67–70.

Beness, J.L. "The Urban Unpopularity of Lucius Appuleius Saturninus." *Antichthon* 25 (1991): 33–62.

Bennett, H. *Cinna and His Times.* Menasha, WI: G. Banta Publishing Company, 1923.

Ben-Sasson, H.H., ed. *A History of the Jewish People.* Cambridge, MA: Harvard University Press, 1976.

Benson, E.F. *The Life of Alcibiades.* London: Ernest Benn Limited, 1928.

Bernstein, A.H. *Tiberius Sempronius Gracchus. Tradition and Apostasy.* Ithaca, NY: Cornell University Press, 1978.

Beye, C. *Ancient Epic Poetry. Homer, Apollonius, Virgil.* Ithaca, NY: Cornell University Press, 1993.

Bigwood, J.M. "Ctesias as Historian of the Persian Wars." *Phoenix* 32 (1978): 19–41.

Billows, R.A. *Antigonus the One-Eyed and the Creation of the Hellenistic State.* Berkeley: University of California Press, 1990.

Birley, A.R. *The African Emperor: Septimius Severus.* Rev. ed. London: Batsford, 1998.

———. *Hadrian: The Restless Emperor.* London: Routledge, 1997.

———. *Marcus Aurelius*. 2nd ed. New Haven, CT: Yale University Press, 1987.

Boardman, J. *Athenian Black Figure Vases*. London: Thames and Hudson, 1974.

———. *Athenian Red Figure Vases: The Archaic Period*. London: Thames and Hudson, 1975.

———. *Greek Sculpture: The Classical Period*. London: Thames and Hudson, 1985.

Borza, E.L. *In the Shadow of Olympus: The Emergence of Macedon*. Princeton, NJ: Princeton University Press, 1990.

Bosworth, A.B. *Conquest and Empire. The Reign of Alexander the Great*. Cambridge: Cambridge University Press, 1989.

———. *From Arrian to Alexander: Studies in Historical Interpretation*. Oxford: Clarendon Press, 1988.

———. *A Historical Commentary on Arrian's History of Alexander*. Oxford: Clarendon Press, 1980–.

Bowersock, G.W. *Augustus and the Greek World*. Oxford: Clarendon Press, 1965.

———. *Julian the Apostate*. London: Duckworth, 1978.

Bowra, C.M. *Pindar*. Oxford: Clarendon Press, 1964.

Boyce, M. *A History of Zoroastrianism*. 2 vols. Leiden: E.J. Brill, 1975–1982.

———. *Zoroastrianism: Its Antiquity and Constant Vigour*. Costa Mesa, CA: Mazda Publishers, 1992.

Boyle, A.J., ed. *Roman Epic*. London: Routledge, 1993.

Bradford, E. *The Year of Thermopylae*. London: Macmillan, 1980.

Bradley, K. *Slavery and Rebellion in the Roman World 140 B.C.–70 B.C.* London: Batsford, 1989.

Branham, R.B., and Goulet-Cazé, M.-O., eds. *The Cynics: The Cynic Movement in Antiquity and Its Legacy*. Berkeley: University of California Press, 1996.

Braund, S.H. *Roman Verse Satire*. Greece and Rome: New Surveys in the Classics No. 23. Oxford: Classical Association, 1992.

Bremmer, J.N. "Romulus, Remus and the Foundation of Rome." In *Roman Myth and Mythography*, ed. J.N. Bremmer and N.M. Horsfall, 25–48. London: Institute of Classical Studies, 1987.

Bremmer, J.N., and Horsfall, N.M., eds. *Roman Myth and Mythography*. London: Institute of Classical Studies, 1987.

Brent, A. *Hippolytus and the Roman Church in the Third Century*. Leiden: E.J. Brill, 1995.

Briant, P. *From Cyrus to Alexander: A History of the Persian Empire*. Trans. P. Daniels. 2 vols. Winona Lake, IN: Eisenbrauns, 1997.

Brown, P. *Augustine of Hippo*. Berkeley: University of California Press, 1967.

———. *Religion and Society in the Age of St. Augustine*. London: Faber and Faber, 1972.

Brown, R.E. *An Introduction to the New Testament*. New York: Doubleday, 1997.

Brown, R.E.; Donfried, K.P.; and Reumann, J., eds. *Peter in the New Testament*. Minneapolis, MN: Augsburg Publishing House, 1973.

Bruno, V.J. *Form and Colour in Greek Painting*. London: Thames and Hudson, 1977.

Brunt, P.A. *The Fall of the Roman Republic and Related Essays*. Oxford: Clarendon Press, 1988.

Buckler, J. *The Theban Hegemony, 371–362 B.C.* Cambridge, MA: Harvard University Press, 1980.

Buitron-Oliver, D. *Douris: A Master-Painter of Athenian Red-Figure Vases*. Mainz am Rhein: Philipp von Zabern, 1995.

Bum, A.R. *Persia and the Greeks: The Defense of the West, 546–478 B.C.* 2nd ed. Stanford, CA: Stanford University Press, 1984.

Burnet, J. *Greek Philosophy, Thales to Plato*. London: Macmillan, 1914.

Burnett, A.P. *The Art of Bacchylides*. Cambridge, MA: Harvard University Press, 1985.

———. *Three Archaic Poets*. Cambridge, MA: Harvard University Press, 1983.

Burnyeat, M., and Frede, M., eds. *The Original Sceptics. A Controversy*. Indianapolis, IN: Hackett, 1997.

Bury, J.B. "Dionysius of Syracuse." In *The Cambridge Ancient History*, ed. J.B Bury, S.A. Cook, and F.E. Adcock, VI:108–136. Cambridge: Cambridge University Press, 1987.

———. *History of the Later Roman Empire from the Death of Theodosius I to the Death of Justinian*. 2 vols. London: Macmillan, 1923.

Cahill, T. *How the Irish Saved Civilization: The Untold Story of Ireland's Heroic Role from the Fall of Rome to the Rise of Medieval Europe*. New York: Doubleday, 1995.

Cairns, F. *Tibullus: A Hellenistic Poet at Rome*. Cambridge: Cambridge University Press, 1979.

Cameron, A. *Claudian: Poetry and Propaganda at the Court of Honorius*. Oxford: Clarendon Press, 1970.

———. *The Later Roman Empire A.D. 284–430*. Cambridge, MA: Harvard University Press, 1993.

Campbell, D.A., trans. *Greek Lyric*. 5 vols. Cambridge, MA: Harvard University Press, 1982–1993.

Carney, T.F. *A Biography of C. Marius*. 2nd ed. Chicago: Argonaut, 1970.

Cartledge, P.A. *Sparta and Lakonia: A Regional History 1300–362 B.C.* London: Routledge and Kegan Paul, 1979.

Cary, C., ed. *Lysias: Selected Speeches*. Cambridge: Cambridge University Press, 1989.

Castagnoli, F. *Orthogonal Town Planning in Antiquity*. Trans. V. Caliandro. Cambridge, MA: MIT Press, 1971.

Castriota, D. *Myth, Ethos, and Actuality. Official Art in Fifth-Century Athens*. Madison: University of Wisconsin Press, 1992.

Caven, B. *Dionysius I: War-Lord of Sicily*. New Haven, CT: Yale University Press, 1990.

Cawkwell, G.L. "Epaminondas and Thebes." *Classical Quarterly* 22 (1972): 254–278.

———. *Thucydides and the Peloponnesian War*. London: Routledge, 1997.

Chadwick, H. *Augustine*. Oxford: Oxford University Press, 1986.

———. "Justin Martyr's Defense of Christianity." In *The Early Church and Greco-Roman Thought*, ed. E. Ferguson, 23–45. *Studies in Early Christianity* 8. New York: Garland, 1993.

Champlin, E. *Fronto and Antonine Rome*. Cambridge, MA: Harvard University Press, 1980.

Charleston, R.J. *Roman Pottery*. London: Faber and Faber, 1955.

Chilton, B., and Evans, C.A., eds. *Studying the Historical Jesus: Evaluations of the State of Current Research*. Leiden: E.J. Brill, 1994.

Christie-Murray, D. *A History of Heresy*. Oxford: Oxford University Press, 1989.

Clarke, G.W. *The Octavius of Marcus Minucius Felix*. New York: Newman Press, 1974.

————, int. and trans. *The Letters of St. Cyprian of Carthage*. 4 vols. New York: Newman Press, 1984–1989.

Clarke, M.L. *The Noblest Roman. Marcus Brutus and His Reputation*. Ithaca, NY: Cornell University Press, 1981.

Clay, D. *Lucretius and Epicurus*. Ithaca, NY: Cornell University Press, 1983.

Colledge, M. *The Parthians*. New York: Praeger, 1967.

Connor, W.R. *The New Politicians of Fifth-Century Athens*. Princeton, NJ: Princeton University Press, 1971.

————. *Thucydides*. Princeton, NJ: Princeton University Press, 1984.

Connors, C. *Petronius the Poet: Verse and Literary Tradition in the Satyricon*. Cambridge: Cambridge University Press, 1998.

Conte, G.B. *Latin Literature: A History*. Baltimore: Johns Hopkins University Press, 1994.

Cook, J.M. *The Persian Empire*. New York: Schocken Books, 1983.

Cook, R.M. *Greek Painted Pottery*. 2nd ed. London: Methuen, 1972.

Corcoran, S. *Empire of the Tetrarchs*. Oxford: Clarendon Press, 1996.

Cornell, T.J. *The Beginnings of Rome: Italy and Rome from the Bronze Age to the Punic Wars (c. 1000–264 B.C.)*. London: Routledge, 1995.

Crook, J.A. *Life and Law of Rome*. London: Thames and Hudson, 1967.

Crouzel, H. *Origen*. Trans. A.S. Warrall. San Francisco: Harper and Row, 1989.

Cunneen, S. *In Search of Mary*. New York: Ballantine Books, 1996.

Cunningham, I., ed. *Herodas, Herodae Mimiamboi*. Leipzig: Teubner, 1987.

Cupaiuolo, G. *Bibliografia Terenziana 1470–1983*. Naples: Società editrice napoletana, 1984.

————. "Supplementum Terentianum." *Bollettino di Studi Latini* 21 (1992): 32–57.

Dandamaev, M. *A Political History of the Achaemenid Empire*. Trans. W. Vogelsang. Leiden: E. J. Brill, 1989.

Darwall-Smith, R.H. *Emperors and Architecture: A Study of Flavian Rome*. Bruxelles: Latomus, 1996.

Dietler, M. " 'Our Ancestors the Gauls': Archaeology, Ethnic Nationalism, and the Manipulation of Celtic Identity in Modern Europe." *American Anthropologist* 963 (1994): 584–605.

Digeser, E.D. *The Making of a Christian Empire: Lactantius and Rome*. Ithaca, NY: Cornell University Press, 1999.

Dihle, A. *Greek and Latin Literature of the Roman Empire: From Augustus to Justinian*. London: Routledge, 1989.

Dijksterhuis, E.J. *Archimedes*. Trans. C. Dikshoorn. Princeton, NJ: Princeton University Press, 1987.

Dixon, S. *The Roman Mother*. London: Croom Helm, 1988.

Donaldson, I. *The Rapes of Lucretia: A Myth and Its Transformations*. Oxford: Clarendon Press, 1982.

Dorey, T.A. *Latin Historians*. London: Routledge and Kegan Paul, 1966.

Dorey, T.A., and Dudley, D.R. *Rome against Carthage*. London: Secker and Warburg, 1971.

Drijvers, H.J.W. *Helena Augusta: The Mother of Constantine the Great and the Legend of Her Finding of the True Cross*. Leiden: E.J. Brill, 1992.

————. "Strabo on Parthia and the Parthians." In *Das Partherreich und seine Zeugnisse*, ed. J. Wiesehöfer, 279–293. Stuttgart: F. Steiner, 1998.

Driver, S.D. "The Development of Jerome's Views on the Ascetic Life." *Recherches de théologie ancienne et médiévale* 62 (1995): 44–70.

Duckworth, G.E. *The Nature of Roman Comedy*. 2nd ed. Princeton, NJ: Princeton University Press, 1994.

Dyer, R.R. "Where Did Parthenius Teach Vergil?" *Vergilius* 42 (1996): 19–24.

Dzielska, M. *Hypatia of Alexandria*. Trans. F. Lyra. Cambridge, MA: Harvard University Press, 1995.

Edelstein, L., and Kidd, I.G., eds. *Posidonius*. 3 vols. Cambridge: Cambridge University Press, 1972–1999.

Edwards, M.W. *Homer: Poet of the Iliad*. Baltimore: Johns Hopkins University Press, 1987.

Ellis, W.M. *Alcibiades*. London: Routledge, 1989.

———. *Ptolemy of Egypt*. London: Routledge, 1994.

Erim, K.T. *Aphrodisias*. London: Muller, Blond, and White, 1986.

Errington, R.M. *Philopoemen*. Oxford: Clarendon Press, 1969.

Evans, J.A.S. *Herodotus*. Boston: Twayne, 1982.

Evans, R.J. *Gaius Marius. A Political Biography*. Pretoria: University of South Africa, 1994.

Fairweather, J. *Seneca the Elder*. Cambridge: Cambridge University Press, 1981.

Ferguson, J. *Pelagius: A Historical and Theological Study*. Cambridge: W. Heffer, 1956.

Ferrill, A. *Caligula: Emperor of Rome*. London: Thames and Hudson, 1991.

Finley, M.I. *Ancient Sicily to the Arab Conquest*. 2nd ed. Totowa, NJ: Rowman and Littlefield, 1987.

Flower, M.A. *Theopompus of Chios: History and Rhetoric in the Fourth Century B.C.* Oxford: Clarendon Press, 1994.

Fornara, C.W. *The Nature of History in Ancient Greece and Rome*. Berkeley: University of California Press, 1983.

Fornara, C.W., and Samons, L.J. *Athens from Cleisthenes to Pericles*. Berkeley: University of California Press, 1991.

Forrest, W.G. *A History of Sparta 950–192 B.C.* 2nd ed. London: Duckworth, 1980.

Fortenbaugh, W.W.; Huby, P.M.; and Long, A.A., eds. *Theophrastus of Eresus: On His Life and Work*. New Brunswick, NJ: Transaction Books, 1985.

Fortenbaugh, W.W., and Schühtrumpf E., eds. *Demetrius of Phalerum*. New Brunswick, NJ: Rutgers University Press, 1999.

Fortenbaugh, W.W., et al., eds. *Theophrastus of Eresus: Sources for His Life, Writings, Thought, and Influence*. 2 vols. Leiden: E.J. Brill, 1991.

Fox, R.L. *Pagans and Christians*. New York: Alfred A. Knopf, 1987.

Fraenkel, E. *Horace*. Oxford: Clarendon Press, 1957.

Fränkel, H. *Early Greek Poetry and Philosophy*. Oxford: Blackwell, 1973.

Frend, W.H.C. "Augustine and Orosius on the Fall of the Roman Empire in the West." *Augustinian Studies* 20 (1989): 1–38.

———. *The Donatist Church. A Movement of Protest in Roman North Africa*. 3rd ed. Oxford: Clarendon Press, 1985.

———. *The Rise of the Monophysite Movement. Chapters in the History of the Church in the Fifth and Sixth Century*. Cambridge: Cambridge University Press, 1972.

Friedländer, P. *Plato*. Trans. H. Meyerhoff. 2nd ed. 2 vols. Princeton, NJ: Princeton University Press, 1973.

Furhmann, M. *Cicero and the Roman Republic*. Oxford: Blackwell, 1992.

Furley, D.J. *The Greek Cosmologists*. Cambridge: Cambridge University Press, 1987.

———. *Two Studies in the Greek Atomists*. 2 vols. Princeton, NJ: Princeton University Press, 1967.

Gabba, E. *Dionysius and the History of Archaic Rome*. Berkeley: University of California Press, 1991.

Gabbert, J.J. *Antigonus II Gonatas: A Political Biography*. London: Routledge, 1997.

Gagarin, M. *Drakon and Early Athenian Homicide Law*. New Haven, CT: Yale University Press, 1981.

Gagarin, M., and MacDowell, D.M., trans. *Antiphon & Andocides*. Austin: University of Texas Press, 1998.

Galinsky, K. *Augustan Culture: An Interpretative Introduction*. Princeton, NJ: Princeton University Press, 1996.

Garzetti, A. *From Tiberius to the Antonines*. London: Methuen, 1974.

Geiger, J. *Cornelius Nepos and Ancient Political Biography*. Stuttgart: Franz Steiner, 1983.

Gerber, D.E., ed. *Greek Elegiac Poetry from the Seventh to the Fifth Centuries B.C.* Cambridge, MA: Harvard University Press, 1999.

Gerber, D.E., trans. *Greek Iambic Poetry from the Seventh to the Fifth Centuries B.C.* Cambridge, MA: Harvard University Press, 1999.

Gillett, A. "The Accession of Euric." *Francia* 26.1 (1999): 1–40.

Gingras, G., int. and trans. *Egeria: Diary of a Pilgrimage*. New York: Newman Press, 1970.

Giuliani, L., et al., eds. *Euphronios: Pittore ad Atene nel VI secolo a. C.* Milano: Fabbri, 1991.

Gleason, M.W. *Making Men: Sophists and Self-Presentation in Ancient Rome*. Princeton, NJ: Princeton University Press, 1995.

Gottschalk, H.B. "Aristotelian Philosophy in the Roman World from the Time of Cicero to the End of the Second Century A.D." *Aufstieg und Niedergang der römischen Welt* 2 (1987): 1079–1139.

———. *Heraclides of Pontus*. Oxford: Clarendon Press, 1980.

Gould, J.B. *Herodotus*. London: Weidenfeld and Nelson, 1989.

———. *The Philosophy of Chrysippus*. Albany: State University of New York Press, 1970.

Gow, A.S.F., and Scholfield, A.F., eds. *Nicander: The Poems and Poetical Fragments*. Cambridge: Cambridge University Press, 1953.

Gowing, A.M. *The Triumviral Narratives of Appian and Cassius Dio*. Ann Arbor: University of Michigan Press, 1992.

Grant, M. *The Antonines: The Roman Empire in Transition*. London: Routledge, 1994.

———. *The Classical Greeks*. New York: Charles Scribner's Sons. 1989.

———. *Cleopatra*. London: Weidenfeld and Nicholson, 1972.

———. *From Alexander to Cleopatra: The Hellenistic World*. London: Weidenfeld and Nicholson, 1982.

———. *Greek and Latin Authors, 800 B.C.–A.D. 1000*. New York: H.W. Wilson Co., 1980.

———. *Greek and Roman Historians: Information and Misinformation*. London: Routledge, 1995.

———. *History of Rome*: 2nd ed. London: Weidenfeld and Nicholson, 1979.

———. *The Roman Empire: A Biographical Guide to the Rulers of Imperial Rome 31 B.C.–A.D. 476*. London: Weidenfeld and Nicolson, 1985.

———. *The Severans: The Changed Roman Empire*. London: Routledge, 1996.

Gray, G.B., and Cary, M. "The Reign of Darius." In *The Cambridge Ancient History*, ed. J.B. Bury, S.A. Cook, and F.E. Adcock, IV:173–227. Cambridge: Cambridge University Press, 1977.

Green, P. *Alexander to Actium: The Historical Evolution of the Hellenistic Age*. Berkeley: University of California Press, 1990.

———. *The Greco-Persian Wars*. Berkeley: University of California Press, 1996.

Greenhalgh, P. *Pompey: The Republican Prince*. London: Weidenfeld and Nicolson, 1981.

———. *Pompey: The Roman Alexander*. London: Weidenfeld and Nicolson, 1980.

Griffin, A. *Sicyon*. Oxford: Clarendon Press, 1982.

Griffin, M.T. *Nero. The End of a Dynasty*. London: Batsford, 1984.

———. *Seneca: A Philosopher in Politics*. Oxford: Clarendon Press, 1991.

Gruen, E.S. *The Hellenistic World and the Coming of Rome*. Berkeley: University of California Press, 1984.

———. *The Last Generation of the Roman Republic*. Berkeley: University of California Press, 1974.

Gulick, C.B., int. and trans. *Athenaeus, The Deipnosophists*. Cambridge, MA: Harvard University Press, 1961.

Guthrie, D. *New Testament Introduction*. 3rd ed. London: Tyndale Press, 1970.

Guthrie, W.K.C. *A History of Greek Philosophy*. 6 vols. Cambridge: Cambridge University Press, 1962–1981.

———. *The Sophists*. London: Cambridge University Press, 1971.

Gutzwill, K.J. *Poetic Garlands: Hellenistic Epigrams in Context*. Berkeley: University of California Press, 1998.

Habicht, C. *Pausanias' Guide to Ancient Greece*. Berkeley: University of California Press, 1985.

Hackforth, R. "Sicily." In *The Cambridge Ancient History*, ed. J.B. Bury, S.A. Cook, and F.E. Adcock, V:145–164. Cambridge: Cambridge University Press, 1983.

Hadas, M. *Sextus Pompey*. New York: Columbia University Press, 1930.

Haight, E.H. *Apuleius and His Influence*. New York: Cooper Square Publishers, 1963.

Halperin, D.M. *Before Pastoral. Theocritus and the Tradition of Bucolic Poetry*. New Haven, CT: Yale University Press, 1983.

Hamilton, C.D. *Agesilaus and the Failure of Spartan Hegemony*. Ithaca, NY: Cornell University Press, 1991.

Hammond, N.G.L. *Alexander the Great: King, Commander, and Statesman*. 2nd ed. Bristol: Bristol Classical Press, 1989.

———. *The Genius of Alexander the Great*. Chapel Hill: University of North Carolina Press, 1998.

———. *The Macedonian State*. Oxford: Clarendon Press, 1989.

———. *Philip of Macedon*. London: Duckworth, 1994.

Hammond, N.G.L., and Griffith, G.T. *A History of Macedonia*. Vol. 2, 550–336 B.C. Oxford: Clarendon Press, 1979.

Hammond, N.G.L., and Walbank, F.W. *A History of Macedonia*. Vol. 3, 336–167 B.C. Oxford: Clarendon Press, 1988.

Hanfmann, G.M.A. *Sardis from Prehistoric to Roman Times*. Cambridge, MA: Harvard University Press, 1983.

Hankinson, R.J. *The Sceptics*. New York: Routledge, 1998.

Hansen, E.V. *The Attalids of Pergamon*. 2nd ed. Ithaca, NY: Cornell University Press, 1971.

Hansen, M.H. *The Athenian Democracy in the Age of Demosthenes*. Oxford: Blackwell, 1987.

Hanson, W.S. *Agricola and the Conquest of the North*. New ed. London: B.T. Batsford, 1991.

Harries, J. *Sidonius Apollinaris and the Fall of Rome, A.D. 407–485*. Oxford: Clarendon Press, 1994.

Harrington, K.P. *Catullus and His Influence*. New York: Cooper Square Publishers, Inc., 1963.

Harris, E.M. *Aeschines and Athenian Politics*. Oxford: Oxford University Press, 1995.

Harvey, S.A. "The Sense of a Stylite: Perspectives on Simeon the Elder." *Vigillae Christianae* 42 (1988): 376–394.

Haspels, C.H.E. *The Highlands of Phrygia*. 2 vols. Princeton, NJ: Princeton University Press, 1971.

Hauer, C.E., and Young, W.A. *An Introduction to the Bible: A Journey into Three Worlds*. 4th ed. Englewood Cliffs, NJ: Prentice-Hall, 1998.

Havelock, C.M. *The Aphrodite of Knidos and Her Successors: A Historical Review of the Female Nude in Greek Art*. Ann Arbor: University of Michigan Press, 1995.

Havelock, E.A. *The Liberal Temper in Greek Politics*. New Haven, CT: Yale University Press, 1964.

Hawkes, C.F.C. *Pytheas: Europe and the Greek Explorers*. Oxford: Blackwell, 1977.

Hazzard, R.A. *Imagination of a Monarchy: Studies in Ptolemaic Propaganda*. Toronto: University of Toronto Press, 2000.

Heath, T.L. *Diophantus of Alexandria: A Study in the History of Greek Algebra*. 2nd ed. New York: Dover, 1964.

———. *A History of Greek Mathematics*. Oxford: Clarendon Press, 1921.

———. *The Thirteen Books of Euclid's Elements*. 2nd ed. New York: Dover, 1956.

Heather, P. *Goths and Romans 332–489*. Oxford: Clarendon, 1991.

Heather, P., and Matthews, J. *The Goths in the Fourth Century*. Liverpool: Liverpool University Press, 1991.

Heckel, W. *The Marshals of Alexander's Empire*. New York: Routledge, 1992.

Holford-Strevens, L. *Aulus Gellius*. London: Duckworth, 1988.

Holzberg, N. *The Ancient Novel: An Introduction*. Trans. Christine Jackson-Holzberg. London: Routledge. 1986.

Honoré, A.M. *Gaius*. Oxford: Clarendon Press, 1962.

———. *Ulpian*. Oxford: Clarendon Press, 1982.

Hornblower, J. *Hieronymus of Cardia*. Oxford: Oxford University Press, 1981.

Hughes-Hallett, L. *Cleopatra: Histories, Dreams and Distortions*. New York: Harper and Row, 1990.

Hutchinson, G.O. *Hellenistic Poetry*. Oxford: Clarendon Press, 1988.

Hutchinson, L. *The Conspiracy of Catiline*. London: Blond, 1967.

Huzar, E.G. *Mark Antony: A Biography*. Minneapolis: University of Minnesota Press, 1978.

Jaeger, W. *Two Rediscovered Works of Ancient Christian Literature: Gregory of Nyssa and Macarius*. Leiden: E.J. Brill, 1954.

Jedin, H., and Dolan, J., eds. *History of the Church*. 10 vols. New York: Crossroad, 1981–1982.

Jeffery, L.H. *Archaic Greece: The City–States c. 700–500 B.C.* London: Ernest Benn, 1976.

Jefford, C.; Harder, K.J.; and Amezaga, L.D. *Reading the Apostolic Fathers*. Peabody, MA: Hendrickson Publishers, 1996.

Jolowicz, H.F., and Nicholas, B. *Historical Introduction to the Study of Roman Law*. 3rd ed. Cambridge: Cambridge University Press, 1972.

Joplin, P.K. "Ritual Work on Human Flesh: Livy's Lucretia and the Rape of the Body Politic." *Helios* 17.1 (1990): 51–70.

Jones, A.H.M. *Augustus*. London: Chatto and Windus, 1970.

———. *The Later Roman Empire 284–602*. 2 vols. Oxford: Blackwell, 1964.

———. *Sparta*. Oxford: Clarendon Press, 1967.

Jones, B.W. *Domitian and the Senatorial Order*. Philadelphia: American Philosophical Society, 1979.

———. *The Emperor Titus*. London: Croom Helm, 1984.

Jones, C.P. *Culture and Society in Lucian*. Cambridge, MA: Harvard University Press, 1986.

———. *Plutarch and Rome*. Oxford: Clarendon Press, 1971.

———. *The Roman World of Dio Chrysostom*. Cambridge, MA: Harvard University Press, 1978.

Jouanna, J. *Hippocrates*. Trans. M.B. DeBevoise. Baltimore: Johns Hopkins University Press, 1999.

Kagan, D. *The Fall of the Athenian Empire*. Ithaca, NY: Cornell University Press, 1987.

———. *Pericles of Athens and the Birth of Democracy*. New York: Free Press, 1991.

Kazmierski, C. *John the Baptist: Prophet and Evangelist*. Collegeville, MN: Liturgical Press, 1996.

Keaveney, A. *Lucullus*. London: Routledge, 1992.

———. *Sulla, the Last Republican*. London: Croom Helm, 1982.

———. "What Happened in 88?" *Eirene* 20 (1983): 53–86.

Kelly, J.N.D. *Golden Mouth: The Story of John Chrysostom, Ascetic, Preacher, Bishop*. Ithaca, NY: Cornell University Press, 1995.

———. *Jerome: His Life, Writings and Controversies*. London: Duckworth, 1975.

Kennedy, G.A. *The Art of Persuasion in Greece*. Princeton, NJ: Princeton University Press, 1963.

———. *The Art of Rhetoric in the Roman World*. Princeton, NJ: Princeton University Press, 1972.

Kenney, E.J., and Clausen, W.V., eds. *Latin Literature. Cambridge History of Classical Literature*. Vol. 2. Cambridge: Cambridge University Press, 1982.

Kerferd, G.B. "Gorgias on Nature or That Which Is Not." *Phronesis* 1 (1955): 3–25.

———. *The Sophistic Movement*. Cambridge: Cambridge University Press, 1981.

Kidd, D., int. and trans. *Aratus Phaenomena*. Cambridge: Cambridge University Press, 1997.

Kingsley, P. *Ancient Philosophy, Mystery, and Magic. Empedocles and Pythagorean Tradition*. Oxford: Clarendon Press, 1995.

Kirk, G.S.; Raven, J.E.; and Schofield, M. *The Presocratic Philosophers*. 2nd ed. Cambridge: Cambridge University Press, 1983.

Kokkinos, N. *The Herodian Dynasty: Origins, Role in Society and Eclipse*. Sheffield, England: Sheffield Academic Press, 1998.

Kraus, C.S., and Woodman, A.J. *Latin Historians*. Greece & Rome New Surveys in the Classics 27. Oxford: Oxford University Press, 1997.

Kurke, L. *Coins, Bodies, Games, and Gold: The Politics of Meaning in Archaic Greece*. Princeton, NJ: Princeton University Press, 1999.

Lancel, S. *Carthage*. Trans. A. Nevill. Oxford: Blackwell, 1995.

————. *Hannibal*. Oxford: Blackwell, 1998.

Last, H., and Gardner, R. "Sulla." In *The Cambridge Ancient History*, ed. S.A. Cook, F.E. Adcock, and M.P. Charlesworth, IX:261–310. Cambridge: Cambridge University Press, 1985.

Lavelle, B.M. *The Sorrow and the Pity. A Prolegomenon to a History of Athens under the Peisistratids c. 560–510*. Stuttgart: F. Steiner, 1993.

Lawrence, A.W. *Greek Architecture*. 5th ed. New Haven, CT: Yale University Press, 1996.

Lawson, J. *The Biblical Theology of St. Irenaeus*. London: Ipworth, 1948.

Lazenby, J.F. *Hannibal's War: A Military History of the Second Punic War*. Warminster, UK: Aris & Philips, 1978.

Leadbetter, B. " 'Patrimonium Indivisum'? The Empire of Diocletian and Maximian, 285–289." *Chiron* 28 (1998): 213–228.

Lebel-Hadas, M. *Flavius Josephus: Eyewitness to Rome's First Century Conquest of Judea*. New York: Macmillan, 1993.

Lee, G., ed. *The Poems of Catullus*. Oxford: Oxford University Press, 1991.

Lee, G., trans., and Barr, W., int. *The Satires of Persius*. Liverpool: Francis Cairns, 1987.

Lefkowitz, M.R. *The Lives of the Greek Poets*. Baltimore, MD: Johns Hopkins University Press, 1981.

Lesher, J.H., int. and trans. *Xenophones of Colophon: Fragments. A Text and Translation with a Commentary*. Toronto: University of Toronto Press, 1992.

Lesky, A. *A History of Greek Literature*. Trans. J. Willis and C. de Heer. London: Methuen, 1966.

Levick, B. *Claudius*. New Haven, CT: Yale University Press, 1990.

————. *Tiberius the Politician*. London: Thames and Hudson, 1976.

Lienhard, J.T. *Paulinus of Nola and Early Western Monasticism*. Cologne: Peter Hanstein, 1977.

Lieu, J. *Image and Reality. The Jews in the World of the Christians in the Second Century*. Edinburgh: T. and T. Clark, 1996

Lilla, S.R.C. *Clement of Alexandria: A Study in Christian Platonism and Gnosticism*. Oxford: Oxford University Press, 1971.

Lintott, A.W. *Violence, Civil Strife and Revolution in the Classical City*. London: Croom Helm, 1982.

Lloyd, A.C. "The Later Neoplatonists." In *The Cambridge History of Later Greek and Early Medieval Philosophy*, ed. A.H. Armstrong, 272–325. Cambridge: Cambridge University Press, 1967.

Lloyd, G.E.R. *Magic, Reason and Experience*. Cambridge: Cambridge University Press, 1979.

Lloyd-Jones, P.H.J., and Wilson, N.G. *Sophoclea: Studies on the Text of Sophocles.* Oxford: Clarendon Press, 1990.

Loenen, J.H.M.M. *Parmenides, Melissus, Gorgias: A Reinterpretation of Eleatic Philosophy.* Assen: Royal VanGorcum, 1959.

Lomas, K. *Rome and the Western Greeks 350 B.C.–A.D. 200: Conquest and Acculturation in Southern Italy.* New York: Routledge, 1993.

Lombardo, S., int. and trans. *Callimachus. Hymns, Epigrams, and Select Fragments.* Baltimore: Johns Hopkins University Press, 1988.

Long, A.A. *Hellenistic Philosophy.* London: Duckworth, 1974.

Long, A.A., and Sedley, D.N. *The Hellenistic Philosophers.* 2 vols. Cambridge: Cambridge University Press, 1987.

Longrigg, J. *Greek Rational Medicine: Philosophy and Medicine from Alcmaeon to the Alexandrians.* London: Routledge, 1993.

Luce, T.J., ed. *Ancient Writers: Greece and Rome.* 2 vols. New York: Charles Scribner's Sons, 1982.

Lulofs, H.J.D. *Nicolaus Damascenus on the Philosophy of Aristotle.* Leiden: E.J. Brill, 1965.

Lund, H. *Lysimachus: A Study in Early Hellenistic Kingship.* London: Routledge, 1992.

Luz, M. "Antisthenes' Prometheus Myth." *Cahiers de Philologie* 16 (1996): 89–103.

Ma, J. *Antiochos III and the Cities of Western Asia Minor.* Oxford: Oxford University Press, 1999.

Maier, P.L. *Pontius Pilate.* Garden City, NY: Doubleday, 1968.

Mallowan, M. "Cyrus the Great (558–529 B.C.)." In *Cambridge History of Iran*, ed. I. Gershevitch, 2:392–419. Cambridge: Cambridge University Press, 1985.

Marshall, I.H. *Luke: Historian and Theologian.* Exeter: Paternoster Press, 1989.

Masters, J. *Poetry and Civil War in Lucan's Bellum Civile.* Cambridge: Cambridge University Press, 1992.

Mastromarco, G. *The Public of Herondas.* Amsterdam: J.C. Gieben, 1984.

Matthews, J. *The Roman Empire of Ammianus Marcellinus.* London: Duckworth, 1995.

———. *Western Aristocracies and Imperial Court A.D. 364–425.* Oxford: Clarendon Press, 1990.

Mayer, W., and Allen, P. *John Chrysostom.* New York: Routledge, 2000.

McGing, B.C. *The Foreign Policy of Mithridates VI Eupator King of Pontus.* Leiden: E.J. Brill, 1986.

McGuckin, J.A. "The Christology of Nestorius of Constantinople." *The Patristic and Byzantine Review* 7.2–3 (1988): 93–129.

———. "The Influence of the Isis Cult on St. Cyril of Alexandria's Christology." *Studia Patristica* 24 (1992): 191–199.

———. *St. Cyril of Alexandria and the Christological Controversy: Its History, Theology, and Texts.* Leiden: E.J. Brill, 1994.

Meeks, W.A. "Simon Magus in Recent Research." *Religious Studies Review* 3 (1977): 137–142.

Meier, C. *Caesar.* New York: HarperCollins, 1995.

———. *The Political Art of Greek Tragedy.* Cambridge: Polity Press, 1993.

Meier, J.P. *A Marginal Jew: Rethinking the Historical Jesus.* New York: Doubleday, 1991.

Mejer, J. "Diogenes Laertius and Greek Philosophy." *Aufstieg Niedergang der römischen Welt* 2 (1992): 3556–3602.

Melchinger, S. *Euripides*. Trans. S. Risenbaum. New York: Ungar, 1973.

Mellor, R. *Tacitus*. New York: Routledge, 1993.

———, ed. *From Augustus to Nero: The First Dynasty of Imperial Rome*. East Lansing: Michigan State University Press, 1990.

Meyendorff, J. *Byzantine Theology, Historical Trends and Doctrinal Trends*. 2nd ed. New York: Fordham University Press, 1983.

Millar, F.G.B. *A Study of Cassius Dio*. Oxford: Clarendon Press, 1964.

Milner, N.P., int. and trans. *Vegetius, Epitome of Military Science*. 2nd ed. Liverpool: Liverpool University Press, 1996.

Minns, D. *Irenaeus*. Washington, DC: Georgetown University Press, 1994.

Mitchell, T.N. *Cicero the Senior Statesman*. New Haven, CT: Yale University Press, 1991.

Mookerji, R.K. *Chandragupta Maurya and His Times*. 4th ed. Delhi: Motilal Banarsidass, 1966.

Moorhead, J. *Ambrose: Church and Society in the Late Roman World*. New York: Longman, 1999.

Murphy-O'Connor, J. *Paul. A Critical Life*. Oxford: Clarendon Press, 1996.

Murray, O. *Early Greece*. 2nd ed. Cambridge, MA: Harvard University Press, 1993.

———. "Herodotus and Hellenistic Culture." *Classical Quarterly* 22 (1972): 200–213.

Myers, S.K. *Ovid's Causes: Cosmogony and Aetiology in the Metamorphoses*. Ann Arbor: University of Michigan Press, 1994.

Nagy, G. *Greek Mythology and Poetics*. Ithaca, NY: Cornell University Press, 1990.

Navia, L.E. *Classical Cynicism*. Westport, CT: Greenwood Press, 1996.

Neugebauer, O. *A History of Ancient Mathematical Astronomy*. Berlin: Springer-Verlag, 1975.

Newlands, G.M. *Hilary of Poitiers: A Study in Theological Method*. Berne: P. Lang, 1978.

Newton, R.R. *The Crime of Claudius Ptolemy*. Baltimore: Johns Hopkins University Press, 1977.

Nicholas, B. *An Introduction to Roman Law*. Oxford: Clarendon Press, 1962.

Nicholet, C. *The World of the Citizen in Republican Rome*. London: Batsford, 1980.

Nisbet, R.G.M., and Hubbard, M. *A Commentary on Horace, Odes Book I*. Oxford: Clarendon Press, 1978.

Noble, J.V. *The Techniques of Painted Attic Pottery*. 2nd ed. London: Thames and Hudson, 1988.

North, J.A. "The Development of Roman Imperialism." *Journal of Roman Studies* 71 (1981): 1–9.

Norwood, G. *Plautus and Terence*. New York: Cooper Square Publishers, 1932.

Ober, J. "The Athenian Revolution of 508/7 B.C.E. Violence, Authority, and the Origins of Democracy." In *Cultural Poetics in Archaic Greece: Cult, Performance, Politics*, ed. C. Dougherty and L. Kurke, 215–232. Cambridge: Cambridge University Press, 1993.

O'Flynn, J.M. *Generalissimos of the Western Roman Empire*. Edmonton, AB: University of Alberta Press, 1983.

Ogilvie, R.M. *A Commentary on Livy Books 1–5*. Oxford: Clarendon Press, 1965.

———. *The Library of Lactantius*. Oxford: Clarendon Press, 1978.

O'Laughlin, T. *St. Patrick: The Man and His Works*. London: Triangle, 1999.

Oost, S.I. *Galla Placidia Augusta*. Chicago: University of Chicago Press, 1968.

Osborne, R. *Demos: The Discovery of Classical Attika*. Cambridge: Cambridge University Press, 1985.

———. *Greece in the Making: 1200–479 B.C.* London: Routledge, 1996.

Ostrogorsky, G. *History of the Byzantine State*. Trans. J. Hussey. Oxford: Blackwell, 1980.

Ostwald, M. *From Popular Sovereignty to the Sovereignty of Law: Law, Society and Politics in Fifth-Century Athens*. Berkeley: University of California Press, 1986.

———. *Nomos and the Beginnings of the Athenian Democracy*. Oxford: Clarendon Press, 1969.

Paul, G.M. *A Historical Commentary on Sallust's Bellum Iugurthinum*. Liverpool: Francis Cairns, 1984.

Pearson, L. *Aristoxenus: Elementa Rhythmica. The Fragment of Book II and the Additional Evidence of Aristoxenean Rhythmic Theory*. Oxford: Clarendon Press, 1990.

———. *Early Ionian Historians*. Oxford: Clarendon Press, 1939.

———. *The Greek Historians of the West. Timaeus and His Predecessors*. Atlanta, GA: American Philological Association, 1987.

Pelikan, J. *The Spirit of Eastern Christendom (600–1700)*. Chicago: University of Chicago Press, 1974.

Perowne, S. *The Life and Times of Herod the Great*. London: Hodder and Stoughton, 1956.

Peters, F.F. *The Harvest of Hellenism. A History of the Near East from Alexander the Great to the Triumph of Christianity*. New York: Simon and Schuster, 1970.

Pfeiffer, R. *History of Classical Scholarship: From the Beginnings to the End of the Hellenistic Age*. Oxford: Clarendon Press, 1968.

Phillips, E.D. *Greek Medicine*. London: Thames and Hudson, 1973.

Pickard-Cambridge, A. *Dithrymb, Tragedy and Comedy*. 2nd ed. Oxford: Clarendon Press, 1962.

———. *The Dramatic Festivals of Athens*. Ed. J. Gould and D.M. Lewis. 2nd ed. Oxford: Clarendon Press, 1968.

Plautnauer, M. *The Life and Reign of the Emperor Lucius Septimius Severus*. Westport, CT: Greenwood Press, 1970.

Podlecki, A.J. *The Life of Themistocles: A Critical Survey of the Literary and Archaeological Evidence*. Montreal: McGill-Queen's University Press, 1975.

———. *Perikles and His Circle*. London: Routledge, 1998.

Pollitt, J.J. *The Art of Ancient Greece: Sources and Documents*. Cambridge: Cambridge University Press, 1990.

Prioreschi, P. *A History of Medicine*. 2 vols. Lewiston: Edwin Mellen Press, 1996.

Purcell, N. "Livia and the Womanhood of Rome." *Proceedings of the Cambridge Philological Society* 32 (1986): 78–105.

Quasten, J. *Patrology*. 4 vols. Westminster, MD: Newman Press, 1950–1986.

Raaflaub, K., and Toher, M., eds. *Between Republic and Empire: Interpretations of Augustus and His Principate*. Berkeley: University of California Press, 1990.

Raby, F.J.E. *A History of Christian Latin Poetry*. Oxford: Clarendon Press, 1997.

Race, W.H. *Pindar*. Boston: Twayne Publications, 1986.

Rankin, H.D. *Antisthenes Sockratikos*. Amsterdam: Hakkert, 1986.

Rawson, E. *Intellectual Life in the Late Roman Republic*. London: Duckworth, 1985.

———. *Roman Culture and Society: Collected Papers*. Oxford: Clarendon Press, 1991.

————. "Scipio, Laelius, Furius and the Ancestral Religion." *Journal of Roman Studies* 63 (1973): 161–174.

Reale, G. *A History of Ancient Philosophy: From the Origins to Socrates.* 2 vols. Albany: State University of New York, 1985.

————. *Towards a New Interpretation of Plato.* Washington, DC: Catholic University of America Press, 1997.

Rees, B.R. *Pelagius: A Reluctant Heretic.* Wolfeboro, NH: Boydell Press, 1988.

Reinhold, M. *Marcus Agrippa.* Rome: L'Erma di Bretschneider, 1965.

Richter, G.M.A. *Kouroi: Archaic Greek Youths.* 3rd ed. London: Phaidon, 1970.

————. *The Sculpture and Sculptors of the Greeks.* 4th ed. New Haven, CT: Yale University Press, 1970.

Riddle, J.M. *Dioscorides on Pharmacy and Medicine.* Austin: University of Texas Press, 1985.

Ridgway, B.S. *The Archaic Style in Greek Sculpture.* Princeton, NJ: Princeton University Press, 1978.

————. *Fifth-Century Styles in Greek Sculpture.* Princeton, NJ: Princeton University Press, 1981.

Robertson, A.S. *Roman Imperial Coins in the Hunter Coin Cabinet, University of Glasgow.* London: Oxford University Press, 1962–1982.

Robertson, M. *A History of Greek Art.* 2 vols. Cambridge: Cambridge University Press, 1975.

Robinson, O.F. *Ancient Rome.* London: Routledge, 1992.

Rosen, R.M. *Old Comedy and the Iambographic Tradition.* Atlanta, GA: Scholars Press, 1988.

Rosenmeyer, P.A. *The Poetics of Imitation: Anacreon and the Anacreontic Tradition.* Cambridge: Cambridge University Press, 1992.

Ross, D.D. *Backgrounds to Augustan Poetry: Gallus, Elegy and Rome.* Cambridge: Cambridge University Press, 1975.

————. *Style and Tradition in Catullus.* London: Oxford University Press, 1969.

Ross, W.D. *Aristotle.* 5th ed. London: Methuen, 1964.

Rousseau, P. *Ascetics, Authority and the Church in the Age of Jerome and Cassian.* Oxford: Oxford University Press, 1978.

————. *Basil of Caesarea.* Berkeley: University of California Press, 1994.

————. *Pachomius: The Making of a Community in Fourth-Century Egypt.* Berkeley: University of California Press, 1986.

Rowland, I.D., ed. *Vitruvius: Ten Books on Architecture.* Cambridge: Cambridge University Press, 1999.

Rubenson, S. *The Letters of St. Antony. Origenist Theology, Monastic Tradition and the Making of a Saint.* Lund: Lund University Press, 1990.

Russell, D.A. *Plutarch.* London: Duckworth, 1973.

————, ed. *Antonine Literature.* Oxford: Oxford University Press, 1990.

Russell, J.M. *Sennacherib's Palace without Rival at Nineveh.* Chicago: University of Chicago Press, 1991.

Sacks, K. *Diodorus Siculus and the First Century.* Princeton, NJ: Princeton University Press, 1990.

Salisbury, J.E. *Perpetua's Passion: The Death and Memory of a Young Roman Woman.* New York: Routledge, 1997.

Salmon, E.T. *The Making of Roman Italy.* London: Thames and Hudson, 1982.

Salway, P. *Roman Britain*. Oxford: Oxford University Press, 1981.

Sanders, E.P. *The Historical Figure of Jesus*. London: Allen Lane, 1993.

――――. *Jesus and Judaism*. Philadelphia, PA: Fortress Press, 1985.

――――. *Paul*. Oxford: Oxford University Press, 1991.

Sanders, L.J. *Dionysius I of Syracuse and Greek Tyranny*. London: Croom Helm, 1987.

Sandmel, S. *Philo of Alexandria: An Introduction*. Oxford: Oxford University Press, 1979.

Sandys, J.E. *A History of Classical Scholarship*. 3 vols. New York: Haffner, 1958.

Sansone, D. *Plutarch: The Lives of Aristeides and Cato*. Warminster: Aris and Phillips, 1989.

Sarton, G. *Galen of Pergamon*. Lawrence: University of Kansas Press, 1954.

Schibli, H.S. "Xenocrates' Daemons and the Irrational Soul." *Classical Quarterly* 43 (1993): 143–167.

Schoedel, W. *Ignatius of Antioch*. Philadelphia, PA: Fortress Press, 1985.

Schulz, F. *History of Roman Legal Science*. 2nd ed. Oxford: Clarendon Press, 1967.

Scott-Kilvert, I., int. and trans. *Plutarch, the Rise and Fall of Athens*. Harmondsworth: Penguin, 1960.

Scullard, H.H. *From the Gracchi to Nero: A History of Rome from 133 B.C. to 68 A.D.* 5th ed. London: Methuen, 1982.

――――. *A History of the Roman World, 753–146 B.C.* 4th ed. London: Methuen, 1980.

――――. *Roman Politics, 220–150 B.C.* 2nd ed. Oxford: Clarendon Press, 1973.

――――. *Scipio Africanus: Soldier and Politician*. London: Thames and Hudson, 1970.

Seaford, R., ed. *Euripides: Bacchae*. Warminster: Aris and Phillips, 1996.

Seager, R. *Pompey: A Political Biography*. Oxford: B. Blackwell, 1979.

Sealey, R. *Demosthenes and His Time*. New York: Oxford University Press, 1993.

――――. *A History of the Greek City-States, ca. 700–338 B.C.* Berkeley: University of California Press, 1976.

――――. *Women and Law in Classical Greece*. Chapel Hill, NC: University of North Carolina Press, 1990.

Shackleton-Bailey, D.R., ed. *Cicero, Letters to Atticus*. 4 vols. Cambridge: Cambridge University Press, 1999.

――――. *Martial: Epigrams*. 3 vols. Cambridge, MA: Harvard University Press, 1993.

Shahid, I. *Rome and the Arabs: A Prolegomenon to the Study of Byzantium and the Arabs*. Washington, DC: Dumbarton Oaks Research Library and Collection, 1984.

Sharples, R.W. "Alexander of Aphrodisias: Scholasticism and Innovation." *Aufstieg und Niedergang der römischen Welt* 2.36 (1988): 1176–1243.

Shaw, G. *Theurgy and the Soul: The Neoplatonism of Iamblichus*. University Park: Pennsylvania State University Press, 1995.

Sherwin-White, A.N. *The Letters of Pliny: A Historical and Social Commentary*. Oxford: Clarendon Press, 1966.

Sherwin-White, S., and Kuhrt, A. *From Samarkhand to Sardis*. London: Duckworth, 1993.

Shipley, G. *History of Samos 800–188 B.C.* Oxford: Clarendon Press, 1987.

Siorvanes, L. *Proclus: Neo-platonic Philosophy and Science*. Edinburgh: Edinburgh University Press, 1996.

Sivan, H. *Ausonius of Bordeaux: Genesis of a Gallic Aristocracy*. London: Routledge, 1993.

Skutsch, O., ed. *The Annals of Q. Ennius*. Oxford: Oxford University Press, 1985.

Skydsgaard, J.E. *Varro the Scholar: Studies in the First Book of Varro's "De Re Rustica."* Copenhagen: E. Munksgaard, 1968.

Slater, N.W. *Plautus in Performance.* Princeton, NJ: Princeton University Press, 1985.

Slavitt, D., ed. and trans. *Aeschylus: The Oresteia.* Philadelphia: University of Pennsylvania Press, 1998.

Slavitt, D., and Bovie, P., eds. *Aristophanes.* 3 vols. Philadelphia: University of Pennsylvania Press, 1998–1999.

Smith, P.J. *Scipio Africanus and Rome's Invasion of Africa. A Historical Commentary on Titus Livius, Book XXIX.* Amsterdam: J.C. Gieben, 1993.

Smith, R.R.R. *Hellenistic Ruler Portraits.* Oxford: Clarendon Press, 1988.

Smith, W.D. *The Hippocratic Tradition.* Ithaca, NY: Cornell University Press, 1979.

Snodgrass, A.M. *Archaic Greece: The Age of Experiment.* London: J.M. Dent and Sons, 1980.

Sparks, B.A. *Greek Pottery: An Introduction.* Manchester: Manchester University Press, 1991.

Spatz, L. *Aristophanes.* Boston: Twayne Publishers, 1978.

Stahl, W.H., int. and trans. *Commentary on the Dream of Scipio by Macrobius.* New York: Columbia University Press, 1952.

Stahl, W.H.; Johnson, R.; and Burge, E.L., trans. *Martianus Capella and the Seven Liberal Arts.* 2 vols. New York: Columbia University Press, 1971.

Stansbury-O'Donnell, M. "Polygnotos' *Iliupersis*. A New Reconstruction." *American Journal of Archaeology* 93 (1989): 203–215.

———. "Polygnotos' *Nekyia*: A Reconstruction and Analysis." *American Journal of Archaeology* 94 (1990): 213–235.

Staveley, E. *Greek and Roman Voting and Elections.* London: Thames and Hudson, 1972.

St. A. Woodside, M. "Vespasian's Patronage of Education and the Arts." *Transactions of the American Philological Association* 73 (1942): 123–129.

Stewart, A.F. *Greek Sculpture: An Exploration.* 2 vols. New Haven, CT: Yale University Press, 1990.

———. *Skopas of Paros.* Park Ridge, NJ: Noyes Press, 1977.

Stewart, C. *Cassian the Monk.* New York: Oxford University Press, 1998.

Stockton, D. *Cicero: A Political Biography.* Oxford: Clarendon Press, 1971.

———. *The Classical Athenian Democracy.* Oxford: Oxford University Press, 1990.

———. *The Gracchi.* Oxford: Clarendon Press, 1979.

Sullivan, J.P. *Martial: The Unexpected Classic: A Literary and Historical Study.* Cambridge: Cambridge University Press, 1991.

———. *Propertius: A Critical Introduction.* Cambridge: Cambridge University Press, 1976.

Sumruld, W. *Augustine and the Arians: The Bishop of Hippo's Encounter with Ulfilan Arianism.* Selinsgrove, PA: Susquehanna University Press, 1994.

Sussman, L.A. *The Elder Seneca.* Leiden: E.J. Brill, 1978.

Sutton, D.F. *Ancient Comedy: The War of the Generations.* New York: Twayne, 1993.

Syme, R. *The Roman Revolution.* London: Oxford University Press, 1960.

———. *Sallust.* Berkeley: University of California Press, 1964.

———. *Tacitus.* Oxford: Clarendon Press, 1958.

Tadmor, H. *The Inscriptions of Tiglath-Pileser III. King of Assyria.* Jerusalem: Israel Academy of Sciences and Humanities, 1994.

Talbert, R.J.A. *Timoleon and the Revival of Greek Sicily 344–317 B.C.* Cambridge: Cambridge University Press, 1974.

———, int. and trans. *Plutarch on Sparta.* Harmondsworth: Penguin, 1988.

Tarn, W.W. *Antigonos Gonatas.* Chicago: Argonaut, 1969.

Tatum, J. *The Patrician Tribune. Publius Clodius Pulcher.* Chapel Hill: University of North Carolina Press, 1999.

Taylor, A.E. *Socrates.* Garden City, NJ: Doubleday, 1953.

Taylor, D. *Declinatio: A Study of the Linguistic Theory of Marcus Terentius Varro.* Amsterdam: John Benjamins, 1974.

Taylor, J. "The Early Papacy at Work: Gelasius I (492–496)." *Journal of Religious History* 8.4 (1975): 317–332.

Taylor, L.R. "Forerunners of the Gracchi." *Journal of Roman Studies* 52 (1962): 19–27.

———. *Party Politics in the Age of Caesar.* Berkeley: University of California Press, 1949.

———. *Roman Voting Assemblies from the Hannibalic War to the Dictatorship of Caesar.* Ann Arbor: University of Michigan Press, 1966.

Tellegen-Couperus, O. *A Short History of Roman Law.* London: Routledge, 1993.

Temple, O., and Temple, R., trans. *Aesop, the Complete Fables.* Harmondsworth: Penguin, 1998.

Thompson, E.A. *The Huns.* Oxford: Blackwell, 1996.

———. *Who Was St. Patrick?* Woodbridge: Boydell, 1985.

Tillyard, H.J.W. *Agathocles.* Cambridge: Cambridge University Press, 1908.

Todd, M. *The Northern Barbarians 100 B.C.–A.D. 300.* London: Hutchinson, 1975.

Toll, K. "Making Roman-ness and the *Aeneid.*" *Classical Antiquity* 16 (1997): 34–56.

Too, Y. *Rhetoric of Identity in Isocrates.* Cambridge: Cambridge University Press, 1995.

Toynbee, A.J. *Hannibal's Legacy: The Hannibalic War's Effects on Roman Life.* 2 vols. London: Oxford University Press, 1965.

Trypanis, C.A. *Greek Poetry: From Homer to Seferis.* London: Faber and Faber, 1981.

van Groningen, B.A. *Euphorion.* Amsterdam: Hakkert, 1977.

Van Winden, J.C.M. *Calcidius on Matter. His Doctrine and Sources: A Chapter in the History of Platonism.* Leiden: E.J. Brill, 1965.

Vasaly, A. *Representations: Images of the World in Ciceronian Oratory.* Berkeley: University of California Press, 1993.

Verbrugghe, G. *Berossos and Manetho: Native Traditions in Ancient Mesopotamia and Egypt.* Ann Arbor: University of Michigan Press, 1996.

von Staden, H. *Herophilus: The Art of Medicine in Early Alexandria.* Cambridge: Cambridge University Press, 1989.

Walbank, F.W. *Aratos of Sicyon.* Cambridge: Cambridge University Press, 1933.

———. *The Hellenistic World.* Rev. ed. Cambridge, MA: Harvard University Press, 1993.

———. *Philip V of Macedon.* Cambridge: Cambridge University Press, 1940.

———. *Polybius.* Berkeley: University of California Press, 1972.

———. "The Scipionic Legend." *Proceedings of the Cambridge Philological Society* 13 (1967): 54–69.

Walbank, F.W.; Astin, A.E.; Frederiksen, M.W.; and Ogilvie, R.M., eds. *The Hellenistic World.* Vol. 7.1 of *The Cambridge Ancient History.* 2nd ed. Cambridge: Cambridge University Press, 1984.

Walker, P.W.L. *Holy City, Holy Places?: Christian Attitudes to Jerusalem and the Holy Land in the Fourth Century.* Oxford: Clarendon Press, 1990.

Wallace-Hadrill, A. *Suetonius: The Scholar and His Caesars.* London: Duckworth, 1983.

Ward, A.M. *Marcus Crassus and the Late Roman Republic.* Columbia: University of Missouri Press, 1977.

Webster, G.A. *Boudica: The British Revolt against Rome.* London: B.T. Batsford, 1978.

———. *The Roman Invasion of Britain.* London: Batsford Academic and Educational, 1980.

Webster, T.B.L. *Hellenistic Poetry and Art.* London: Methuen, 1964.

———. *Studies in Later Greek Comedy.* 2nd ed. Manchester: Manchester University Press, 1970.

Weigall, A. *Sappho of Lesbos: Her Life and Times.* London: T. Butterworth, 1932.

Weigel, R.E. *Lepidus: The Tarnished Triumvir.* London: Routledge, 1992.

West, M.L. *Studies in Greek Elegy and Iambic.* Berlin: De Gruyter, 1974.

———, trans. *Greek Lyric Poetry.* Oxford: Clarendon Press, 1993.

Wheeler, E. *Stratagem and the Vocabulary of Military Trickery.* Leiden: E.J. Brill, 1988.

Whigham, P., and Jay, P., trans. *The Poems of Meleager.* London: Anvil Press Poetry, 1975.

White, C., trans. *Gregory of Nazianzus, Autobiographical Poems.* Cambridge: Cambridge University Press, 1997.

Wilken, R. *Christians as the Romans Saw Them.* New Haven, CT: Yale University Press, 1984.

Wilkes, J.J. *The Illyrians.* Oxford: Blackwell, 1992.

Williams, S., and Friell, G. *Theodosius: The Empire at Bay.* London: B.T. Batsford, 1994.

Winnington-Ingram, R.P. *Sophocles: An Interpretation.* Cambridge: Cambridge University Press, 1980.

Wiseman, D.J. *Nebuchadnezzar and Babylon.* London: Oxford University Press, 1991.

Wiseman, T.P. *Catullus and His World: A Reappraisal.* Cambridge: Cambridge University Press, 1985.

———. "From the Conference of Luca to the Rubicon." In *The Cambridge Ancient History,* ed. J.A. Crook, F.E. Adcock, and M.P. Charlesworth, IX: 614–637. Cambridge: Cambridge University Press, 1985.

Wood, I. *The Merovingian Kingdoms.* New York: Longman, 1994.

Wood, N. *Cicero's Social and Political Thought.* Berkeley: University of California Press, 1988.

Wood, S. "Memoriae Agrippinae. Agrippina the Elder in Julio-Claudian Art and Propaganda." *American Journal of Archaeology* 92 (1988): 409–426.

Woodhead, A.G. *The Greeks in the West.* London: Thames and Hudson, 1962.

Wright, M.R. *Cosmology in Antiquity.* New York: Routledge, 1995.

Yardley, J., trans., and Heckel, W., int. *Quintus Curtius Rufus, the History of Alexander.* Harmondsworth: Penguin, 1984.

Yavetz, Z. *Julius Caesar and His Public Image.* London: Thames and Hudson, 1983.

Young, F. *From Nicaea to Chalcedon.* Philadelphia, PA: Fortress Press, 1983.

Zanker, P. *The Power of Images in the Age of Augustus.* Trans. A. Shapiro. Ann Arbor: University of Michigan Press, 1988.

Index

Boldface page numbers indicate location of main entries.

About the Contributors

CARL A. ANDERSON, Classical Studies, Michigan State University

MICHAEL ANDERSON, Department of Theology, University of Notre Dame

ROGER W. ANDERSON, Argonne National Laboratory/North Central College

LISA AUANGER, editor, *Bibliography of the History of Art*

JEFFREY A. BELL, Department of History and Political Science, Southeastern Louisiana University

LEA BENESS, Research Fellow, Macquarie University

SUSAN CALEF, Department of Theology, Creighton University

GORDON CAMPBELL, Jesus College, University of Oxford

MARK W. CHAVALAS, Department of History, University of Wisconsin at La Crosse

DAVID CHRISTIANSEN, Director of Interdisciplinary Studies, Truman State University

JAMES A. COOK III, Department of History and Political Science, Southeastern Louisiana University

CHRISTINE CORNELL, Department of English, St. Thomas University

KATRINA M. DICKSON, History of Art Department, Yale University

RICHARD DRAPER, Professor of Ancient Scripture, Brigham Young University

LISA D. MAUGANS DRIVER, Department of Theology, Valparaiso University

STEVEN D. DRIVER, Ecumenical Institute of Theology, St. Mary's Seminar and University

ROBERT DYER, Emeritus Professor of Classics, University of Massachusetts at Amherst

DEBORAH EATON, Librarian, St. Edmund Hall, University of Oxford

CONNIE EVANS, Department of History, Baldwin-Wallace College

JANICE J. GABBERT, Department of Classics, Wright State University

ANDREW GILLETT, Department of Ancient History, Macquarie University

MARK GUSTAFSON, Classics Department, Calvin College

ANTONINA HARBUS, Department of English, University of Sydney

RON HARRIS, Department of English, University of Wisconsin at Madison

REBECCA HARRISON, Department of English, Truman State University

CHRIS HAUER, Emeritus Professor of Religion and Archaeology, Westminster College

TOM HILLARD, Department of Ancient History, Macquarie University

JAMES HOLOKA, Department of Foreign Languages, Eastern Michigan University

WILLIAM HUTTON, Department of Classical Studies, College of William and Mary

JENNIFER L. KOOSED, Graduate Department of Religion, Vanderbilt University

KENT P. JACKSON, Professor of Ancient Scripture, Brigham Young University

MICHAEL LABRANCHE, Department of Mathematics, Xavier University of Louisiana

CYRIL M. LAGVANEC, Department of History and Political Science, Southeastern Louisiana University

KENNETH D.S. LAPATIN, Art History Department, Boston University

WILLIAM LEADBETTER, Department of History, Edith Cowan University

RICHARD LOUTH, Department of English, Southeastern Louisiana University

MENAHEM LUZ, Department of Philosophy, Haifa University

HERBERT MARBURY, Graduate Department of Religion, Vanderbilt University

C.W. MARSHALL, Department of Classics, Memorial University of Newfoundland

KAREN McGROARTY, Lecturer in Ancient Classics, National University of Ireland

JOHN A. McGUCKIN, Department of Church History, Union Theological Seminary

OLIVIA H. McINTYRE, Associate Professor of History, Eckerd College

PAUL MILLER, Department of History, Louisiana State University

LUIS MOLINA, Department of History, City University of New York

FERNANDO OREJA, Institut für Philosophie, Wissenschaftstheorie, Wissenschafts- und Technikgeschichte, Technische Universität Berlin

CHARLES S. PAINE III, Department of History and Political Science, Southeastern Louisiana University

SOPHIA PAPAIOANNOU, Department of Classical Studies and Anthropology, University of Akron

ROBERTO PLEVANO, School of Philosophy, Catholic University of America

JOHN QUINN, Department of Modern and Classical Languages, Hope College

KIMBERLY RIVERS, Department of History, University of Wisconsin at Oshkosh

WILLIAM B. ROBISON, Department of History and Political Science, Southeastern Louisiana University

JEFF RYDBERG-COX, Department of English and Classical Studies at the University of Missouri at Kansas City

CECILIA SAERENS, Department of Classics, Vrije Universiteit Brussel

LIONEL SANDERS, Department of Classics, Modern Languages and Linguistics, Concordia University

JANA K. SCHULMAN, Department of English, Southeastern Louisiana University

ANDREA SCHUTZ, Department of English, St. Thomas University

JUDITH SEBESTA, Department of History, University of South Dakota

RONALD A. SIMKINS, Center for the Study of Religion and Society, Creighton University

DANIEL SMITH-CHRISTOPHER, Department of Theological Studies, Loyola Marymount University

ANDREW G. TRAVER, Department of History and Political Science, South-eastern Louisiana University

KAREN WAGNER, Department of History, Pike's Peak Community College

BRANNON WHEELER, Near Eastern Languages and Civilization, University of Washington